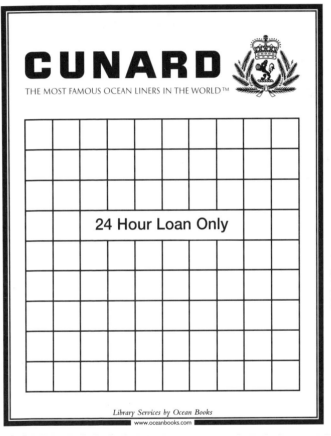
edition
3

www.bradtguides.com

Bradt Travel Guides Ltd, UK
The Globe Pequot Press Inc, USA

Explore bird-rich Braslav Lakes National Park on horseback *pages 251–2*

LATVIA

Braslav
Braslav
Lakes

Braslav Lakes National Park

Pay your respects at the National Memorial Complex at Khatyn, the village razed by the Nazis in 1943 *pages 176–8*

LITHUANIA

Amble through the boulevards and parks of Minsk, the Soviet Union's rebuilt 'Hero City' *pages 115–67*

VILNIUS ■

Smorgon

Molodechno

Lagoisk

Take a walk along Grodno's riverside and discover imposing Catholic architecture *pages 209–24*

Wander sumptuous palace rooms and relax in ornamental gardens in the 13th-century town of Njasvizh *pages 170–2*

Lida

MINSK ■

Nieman

Grodno

Shchuchin

Novogrudok

Njasvizh

Slutsk

POLAND

Nieman

Volkovoysk

Slonim

Baranovichy

Ruzhany

Byelovezhskaya Puscha State National Park & Biosphere Reserve

Tackle the steep Renaissance ramparts and towers of Mir Fortress *pages 168–9*

Luninyets

Pinsk

Pripyat

Brest

Pripet Marshe

Spot European bison, wild boar and elk in Byelovezhskaya Puscha National Park *pages 203–7*

Delve into Belarus' turbulent history at Brest Fortress *pages 195–8*

Explore Pinsk, the ancient capital of 'the land of woods, bogs and fogs' *pages 202–3*

Wander among historical buildings and golden-domed churches in Polotsk, the oldest town in Belarus
pages 243–50

Experience the Slavic Bazaar summer street party in Vitebsk
page 227

Stay in a snug wooden hut in the Berezinsky Biosphere Reserve
pages 252–3

Immerse yourself in rural life at the Dudutki Folk Museum
pages 174–5

Learn about the lives of Vetka's 'Old Believers'
page 288

RUSSIA

UKRAINE

Polotsk
Polotsk

Vitebsk

Berezinsky
Biosphere
Reserve

Orsha

Berezhina

Mogilev

Berezhina

Babrusk

Svetlogorsk

Vetka

Gomel

Rechitsa

Kalinkovichy

Mozyr

Khoiniki

Pripyatsky
National
Park

Polyessky
Radiation
& Ecology
Reserve

Sozh

Dnieper

Pripyat

0   50km
0   50 miles

KEY	
Capital city	■
Other city	●
Main town	○
Other town	○
Main road	
Other road	
Railway	
International boundary	
National Park/Reserve	

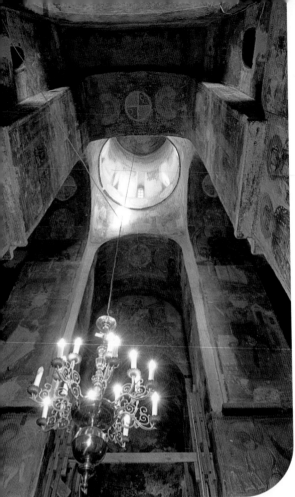

Belarus
Don't
miss...

Russian Orthodoxy
Polotsk, home to the Church of the Transfiguration, is considered by many to be the spiritual cradle of modern Belarus (VB/D)
pages 243–50

Soviet architecture
Stalinist architecture abounds in Belarus, including the imposing House of Government in Minsk (FS/S)
page 158

Memorials

Brest Fortress became famous for the bravery of its garrison during Operation Barbarossa in World War II, and was later made into a huge shrine (SN/S) pages 195–8

Forests and lakes

The River Sozh flows through the 'land of fogs and bogs' in southeastern Belarus, surrounded by forest and marshland (B/S) page 3

Minsk

The capital city's Holy Spirit Cathederal has a chequered history — it served as a Roman Catholic monastery, gymnasium, archive store and granary before its final incarnation as a Russian Orthodox church (S/D) page 165

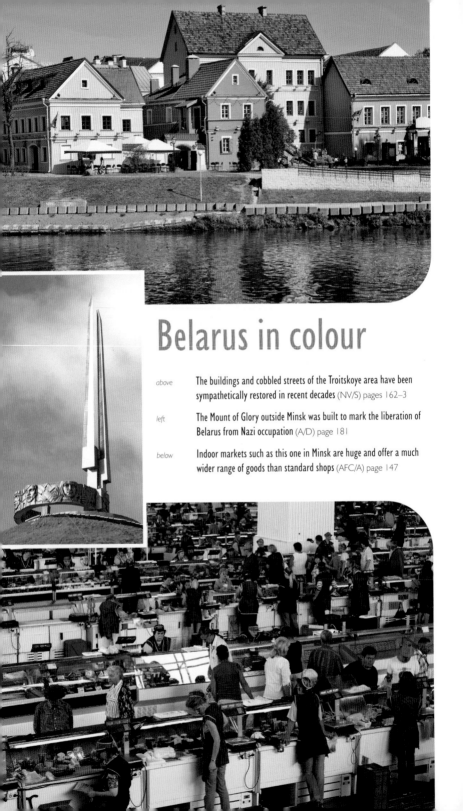

Belarus in colour

above   The buildings and cobbled streets of the Troitskoye area have been sympathetically restored in recent decades (NV/S) pages 162–3

left   The Mount of Glory outside Minsk was built to mark the liberation of Belarus from Nazi occupation (A/D) page 181

below   Indoor markets such as this one in Minsk are huge and offer a much wider range of goods than standard shops (AFC/A) page 147

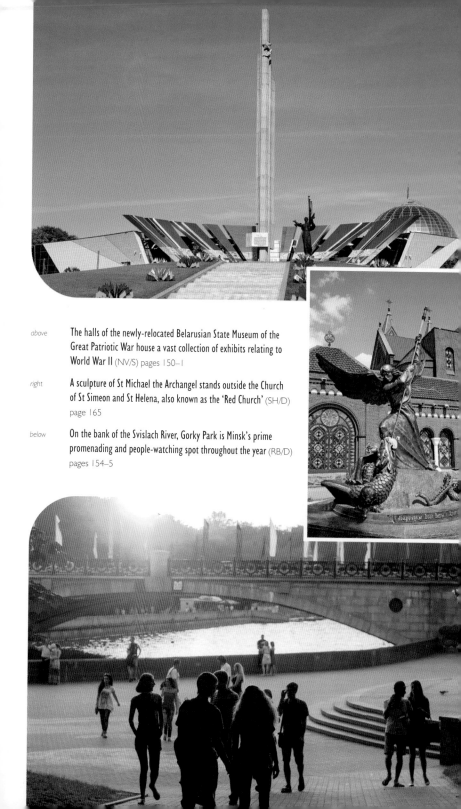

above The halls of the newly-relocated Belarusian State Museum of the Great Patriotic War house a vast collection of exhibits relating to World War II (NV/S) pages 150–1

right A sculpture of St Michael the Archangel stands outside the Church of St Simeon and St Helena, also known as the 'Red Church' (SH/D) page 165

below On the bank of the Svislach River, Gorky Park is Minsk's prime promenading and people-watching spot throughout the year (RB/D) pages 154–5

How did it all happen? George (my then husband) and I wrote the first Bradt guide – about hiking in Peru and Bolivia – on an Amazon river barge, and typed it up on a borrowed typewriter. We had no money for the next two books so George went to work for a printer and was paid in books rather than money.

Forty years on, Bradt publishes over 200 titles that sell all over the world. I still suffer from Imposter Syndrome – how did it all happen? I hadn't even worked in an office before! Well, I've been extraordinarily lucky with the people around me. George provided the belief to get us started (and the mother to run our US office). Then, in 1977, I recruited a helper, Janet Mears, who is still working for us. She and the many dedicated staff who followed have been the foundations on which the company is built. But the bricks and mortar have been our authors and readers. Without them there would be no Bradt Travel Guides. Thank you all for making it happen.

Hilary Bradt

Celebrate our anniversary and get a **40%** discount on all titles with the code BRADT40.

Available from www.bradtguides.com

AUTHOR

Nigel Roberts has been working on sustainable development projects with rural communities in Belarus blighted by the Chernobyl catastrophe for the past 14 years. By profession a lawyer, though he has now left that life behind, he is also a Russian speaker. His interest in the former Soviet Union was kindled as a boy and since then he has researched and travelled widely in the area. Since publication of the first two editions of this Bradt guide, he has written about his travels in Belarus for a number of periodicals, particularly concerning the close relationship he has developed with communities and families in the district of Vetka.

AUTHOR'S STORY

It was during my second visit to this much-misunderstood country that I convinced myself that here was a book just waiting to be written. It made no sense at all that I seemed to be the first to have this thought. And when I decided that I would be the one to write it, there was only one publisher to whom I was prepared to entrust the task of opening the door to the land and people that I had come to love. Bradt's enviable reputation not only for responsible travel writing, but also for being in the vanguard of blazing a trail to new destinations, ensured that in 2008 this was the very first book in the West to feature Belarus as a single subject. Once more, it's a real delight to be able to share my experiences with you in this third edition.

I'm writing this story as I ride the rails on the sleeper to St Petersburg. We're somewhere between Gomel and Mogilev (my destination), and I'm tired. Outside it's humid and gloomy and I'm sharing the compartment with an elderly lady. I'm hot and I need a break from speaking Russian, but my companion wants to chat. I'm soon glad that she does, because she is warm and friendly and particularly kind when I ask forgiveness for the limitations of my Russian. She's going all the way to St Petersburg, to see her sister. We exchange pleasantries and she settles into her book as I watch the countryside go by. Now I'm eating a tomato from the bag of food Tanya gave me as I left Vetka. My new friend looks up at me from her book, puts it down and begins to rummage around in her bag. She produces a tatty old medicine bottle, which she gives me with a smile. It's full of table salt. Next she offers me a knife. I give her one of my apples. She finds me a cucumber from the depths of her bag and hands me a napkin. 'Eat, eat, take salt,' she says. 'Thank you for the lovely apple'. On we rattle to St Petersburg. It's just a moment in time and after we part when the train reaches Mogilev, we shall never meet again. But it's a moment I shall cherish for always. I've been coming to Belarus for 14 years now and encounters like this happen wherever I go. Once again it's my very great pleasure to share with you many of the things I've seen and done in that time, and to open the window for you to peek inside at this beautiful country. I very much hope you visit one day, to discover for yourselves all there is to experience. My life has taken a new direction since I first came here. I can't promise that for you, but I shall be surprised if Belarus and its delightful people don't leave a lasting and positive impact for when you return home. Whatever your impressions, do write and tell me what you think.

PUBLISHER'S FOREWORD   *Adrian Phillips, Managing Director*

When we first announced that we'd commissioned a guide to Belarus, I received a phone call from a journalist with just one question: 'Why would anyone want to go there?' I suspect his was not an unusual reaction. While other former Soviet republics looked westward, Belarus remained entrenched in the past; for most outsiders, the country represents that bleak, utilitarian 'greyness' so frequently associated with communist states. However, as Nigel Roberts passionately demonstrates, such preconceptions are hugely unfair. And it seems many of you agree, since we're thrilled to be producing the third edition of this trailblazing book – which remains the only stand-alone guide to Belarus on the market.

Third edition published May 2015   First published May 2008
Bradt Travel Guides Ltd, IDC House, The Vale, Chalfont St Peter, Bucks SL9 9RZ, England
www.bradtguides.com
Print edition published in the USA by The Globe Pequot Press Inc, PO Box 480, Guilford,
Connecticut 06437–0480
Text copyright © 2015 Nigel Roberts
Boxed text on pages 31, 230–1, 240–1 and *By train* on pages 58–61 copyright © Nicky Gardner
Maps copyright © 2015 Bradt Travel Guides Ltd
Photographs copyright © 2015 Individual photographers (see below)
Project Manager: Maisie Fitzpatrick
Cover image research: Pepi Bluck

ISBN 13: 978 1 84162 909 4
e-ISBN: 978 1 78477 116 4 (e-pub)
e-ISBN: 978 1 78477 216 1 (mobi)

British Library Cataloguing in Publication Data
A catalogue record for this book is available from the British Library

Photographs Alamy: Agencja Fotograficzna Caro (AFC/A), ITAR-TASS (IT/A), Nina Lex (NL/A), Stephen
Street (SS/A); FLPA: Marko König/Imagebroker (MK/IB/FLPA), Duncan Usher/Minden Pictures (DU/
MP/FLPA), Konrad Wothe/Minden Pictures (KW/MP/FLPA); Dreamstime: Alexvalent (A/D), Maryia
Bahutskaya (MB/D), Ryhor Bruyeu (RB/D), Buslik (B/S), Ala Charnyshova (AC/D), Dtvphoto (D/D), Nataliya
Evmenenko (NE/D), Natallia Khlapushyna (NK/D), Nkarol (N/D), Olga355 (O/D), Natallia Reutava (NR/D),
Hanna Sarkisian (HS/D), Scanrail (S/D), Vital Sharepchankau (VS/D), Slowcentury (SC/D), Swisshippo
(SH/D), Yuri4u80 (Y/D); Shutterstock: Grisha Bruev (GB/S), Eillen (E/S), Aleksandr Hunta (AH/S), rsooll
(R/S), Fedor Selivanov (FS/S), Lena Serditova (LS/S), Nickolay Vinokurov (NV/S), Katsiuba Volha (KV/S);
Wikimedia Commons: John Oldale (JO/WC)
Front cover The *Thirst* sculpture at Brest Fortress (IT/A)
Back cover Njasvizh Palace (NK/D)
Title page Mount of Glory, Minsk (A/D); birch forest in summer (NR/D); Cathedral of the Holy Spirit, Minsk
(MB/D)

Maps David McCutcheon, FBCart.S

Typeset by Ian Spick, Bradt Travel Guides
Production managed by Jellyfish Print Solutions and manufactured in India
Digital conversion by www.dataworks.co.in

Acknowledgements

Without the love and support of Lizzie, Hattie and George at home, none of this would have been possible. You three are not only my sanctuary but also my inspiration and the reason I get out of bed in the mornings. I also want to acknowledge the hospitality of the family at 42 Karla Marksa Street, Vetka, who welcomed me with open arms on my first visit in November 2001 and have done so every visit I've made since. They never stop telling me that their home is my home, and my heart leaps each time I make it back to Belarus and stroll down Karla Marksa to wander into the shop for a beer with Valera and his mates. Tanya, Valera, Olya, Anton and Dima, thank you for all your kindness. I'm here for you always. It's because of you that I'm able to feel part of the landscape in Belarus, and I can't believe how lucky I am to feel that way about another country far from home. I have acknowledged the warmth and companionship of my many Belarusian friends and comrades in previous editions, and to that merry band I should now like to add Yury Prudnikovich in London and Sasha Lisnaya, my very dear English pupil in Vetka, whose English is already way better than my Russian will ever be.

For now, it is still rare to meet kindred spirits and road companions in Belarus, but it is my fervent wish that this new edition will continue the job begun by the first of introducing a new breed of traveller to its riches. I know for a fact that they do exist already, because many have taken the trouble to write to me with updates, and I've even had the pleasure of showing some of them around Vetka. So it is with very grateful thanks that I acknowledge the help and support of Katherine Bemben, Veronika Karsai, Jill Flanagan, Kevin and Jane O'Brien, Tim Baster, Isabelle Merminod, Andrew Cunningham, Ben Alltimes, Daniel Milbourn, Svetlana Marazevich, Zo Hoida, Brian Kaczynski, David Catherall, John Solovei, Annette Streicher, Peter Evans, Alexander Jacoby, Andrei Burdenkov, Ray Hayley-Barker, Robert Declerck, Casey Collins, Phil Wells and Neil Fox, all of whom have written to me from around the world not only to provide up-to-the-minute information for this third edition but also to share their own thoughts and experiences, and occasionally to put me right! And there's a special mention here for Phil the Flower Man. Furthermore, I am again indebted to Natalya Lisovskaya and her team at the Belarus Prime Tour agency in Minsk, who have made a wonderful job of collecting, assimilating and verifying a huge body of data for me. Enormous thanks are also due to Nikolai Dmitriev, the proprietor and publisher of *where Minsk* magazine, and to Nicky Gardner and Susanne Kries of *hidden europe* magazine in Berlin, whose delightful pieces within these pages add a touch of class and quality to my inane ramblings. This edition also sees much greater coverage of Jewish Belarus, and my grateful thanks go to Debra Brunner of Finchley Reform Synagogue in London and to Artur Livshyts in Minsk for invaluable guidance, help and support. As with previous editions, my very dear friend Jo Jones has given invaluable help as a sounding board for ideas, while there would be no third edition at all without the support of all at Bradt Travel Guides, particularly my editor and project manager Maisie Fitzpatrick, who can always see the wood for the trees when I manifestly never can...

DEDICATION

Mathew Ian Taylor
1983–2014

 At the last, this book is for you Mat and just for you, from your Uncle Ni with fondest love. You lit up every room you entered, and illuminated every life you touched with clear white light. All of us who had the good fortune to know you are immeasurably the richer for it. And if I can achieve in my life just a fraction of all you achieved, then I shall be very content with my lot. Until we meet again Mat, Keep Right On and Up the Blues.

BELARUS: A RAPIDLY CHANGING COUNTRY

When I asked readers for feedback on the first two editions of this guide, I expressed the view that the timing was then undoubtedly right for this delightful country to be 'discovered' some time very soon. But although there have been significant advances for the Belarusian tourism industry in the intervening period, with a consequent increase in visitor numbers, it remains largely undiscovered still. Yet each succeeding visit I make reveals more changes, some small and some not so small. In Minsk, the increasing amount of neon and designer product advertising is there for all to see; more and more Western-style boutiques and shops are opening all the time; and the range of different fast-food emporia is depressingly broad. Already, the reference in the first edition to the fact that, in 2006, I 'noted with resignation and a heavy heart that [Minsk] now boasts the country's first drive-thru fast-food emporium' seems rather quaint and some way out of date! The pace of change since then has not matched my original forecast, but I remain convinced that one day sooner rather than later it will accelerate significantly, a development that will continue to bring new challenges in maintaining up-to-date information. A good example of this concerns the World Ice Hockey Championships, which came to Minsk in May 2014. In a very short space of time around 15 new hotels opened up, along with significant numbers of cafés and restaurants. Keeping on top of all this was a significant challenge as I set about researching this new edition.

Please bear this process of change and development in mind as you embark upon your preparation for your first visit. As before, I have personally established and checked the accuracy of the information provided in this edition, or else corroborated data from a number of different sources, including an army of very willing and accommodating researchers on the ground. Yet notwithstanding the enormous effort we've all made between us, there remains the risk of anomaly; for example, in June 2014 I again came across that same restaurant in Brest still advertising different opening hours on two of its windows that I first saw in 2007! The primary difficulty is that the availability of consumer-based data for the edification of travellers, tourists and users of leisure facilities is still at a rudimentary stage of evolution, especially in comparison with the mind-boggling array of information that is available in the West. I very much hope that nothing herein is so utterly 'off the wall' as to be unreliable, but if you have the chance to check for updates or amendments as you go, I advise you to avail yourselves of the opportunity so to do. To help you with this, updates, changes and new developments will be regularly posted on the Bradt website. Don't be spooked, though; it's all part of the great adventure! And if you are participating in an organised trip, then everything will be arranged for you and all facilities included in the specification will be open, whatever the 'official' opening times!

The tales that I tell in these pages are taken from my own experiences and travels, but one of the chief pleasures that I derive from sharing them is the hope that those who will find new experiences on their own travels may in turn be motivated to share their stories, as many have done already. I very much hope that this third edition won't be the last, in which case your further feedback, comments and criticism will be most gratefully received and acknowledged (see box, *Feedback request and updates website*, page ix).

Contents

LIST OF MAPS

Introduction

When my dream to visit the old Soviet Union was first realised in the late 1980s, Belarus existed not as a sovereign state, but as Byelorossia ('White Russia'), one of the constituent republics of the USSR. Other than to those with more than a passing interest in the politics of the area, it was simply part of the vast swathe of red that formed the eastern half of the Cold War map of the world. With the fall of the Berlin Wall and the consequent disintegration of the USSR, a national identity for Belarus began to emerge. But as the other former Soviet republics turned their gaze westward to embrace political and economic reform through evolution or revolution, Belarus remained (and remains still) fiercely embedded in the past. Its neighbours to the west and north (Poland, Lithuania and Latvia) are now member states of the EU, while those to the east and south (the Russian Federation and Ukraine) move ever closer to embracing Western commercialism and the economics of the free market. But Belarus, the most westerly republic of the old USSR, clings steadfastly to the past. It prides itself on being situated in the heart of Europe, at the crossroads of ancient trade routes from west to east and from north to south. The first-time visitor might be forgiven for expecting things to be little different from the rest of eastern Europe but, even before leaving home, there are clues aplenty to suggest that this will not be so. Before this one, no guidebooks devoted to Belarus alone could be found on the shelves of Western bookshops. Maps could only be purchased in specialist travel stores or online. Information anywhere, paper or electronic, was conspicuous by its absence and needed to be searched for actively (and in part, this is still the case). It is an unknown land; yet it is much more than this. It is an undiscovered box of gems, with a history rich in heroism, tragedy and despair, natural wonders of great beauty and a people who have endured endless privations over the centuries, but whose hospitality is open and unconditional, notwithstanding all that has transpired on their lands.

I first visited the country in November 2001, arriving at Minsk in the dark of night. First impressions were intimidating, with an edge of danger. Back then, the process of entry via customs and immigration was interminable. Stern-faced officials in khaki uniforms were less than welcoming. Emerging into the night, I was led hurriedly to the waiting transport for a six-hour journey down to the southeastern corner of the country, on unlit roads through mile after mile of silver birch forest, stretching away into impenetrable blackness. Stopping briefly to stretch our legs in the middle of nowhere, the raw cold took my breath away as I gazed up into a dazzling panoply of stars, unpolluted by unnatural reflected light from below. As the first snows of winter began to fall, we arrived in Vetka and, over dirt tracks, we came to the old part of town, where wooden houses stood sentinel against the biting cold, windows rattling in ill-fitting frames as flurries of snow danced among the eaves. The front door to the house of my hosts opened with a dazzling burst of light and heat as I was ushered into warmth and safety. My life has never been the same since that day and every time I return, it is to the same family, and it always feels like coming home.

It's a cliché, I know, but a visit to this delightful country really is one of those life-defining experiences. It is still relatively free of the trappings of modern tourism and

Western materialism, such that it's very easy to feel a sense of having slipped into another time and dimension. In many ways, the country is a living museum of Soviet communism, but to treat it as such would be a gross disservice to the resilience of its people. Decades after the catastrophic nuclear accident at Chernobyl, Belarusians still feel like the forgotten people of Europe, overlooked and shunned by an international community that denies effective aid and assistance in the absence of political reform.

Sometime soon, I hope, I'm going to board a train at St Pancras Station in London and journey to Minsk via Lille, Brussels, Cologne, Warsaw and Brest. One January, I made it as far as the Polish border during the course of a trip from London via Berlin. I love traversing Europe by train and, on this occasion, I went on 28 trains in five days, which is presently my record. One of the favourite pastimes, particularly on dark winter nights, is to take down from my bookshelves the re-launched *European Rail Timetable* (*www.europeanrailtimetable.eu*), uncork an Irish malt whiskey and put together a pan-European journey; and with time on my side, I reckon London–Minsk–London would be a breeze to organise. One day…

So it is with the greatest of pleasure that I share with you everything that I have come to love about Belarus: the natural splendour of primeval green forests, clear rivers and blue lakes; rare flora and fauna; cities that rose from the flames of Nazi barbarism as monuments to post-war Soviet urban planning; stunning museums crammed with rare artefacts; rich culture and tradition; historical sites dating from the Middle Ages to modern times; beautiful churches and the mysteries of Russian Orthodoxy; and most of all, a people whose warmth, honesty and hospitality must be experienced to be believed. Yet whisper all this softly, for we must be careful to guard and not spoil these riches.

FEEDBACK REQUEST AND UPDATES WEBSITE

At Bradt Travel Guides we're aware that guidebooks start to go out of date on the day they're published – and that you, our readers, are out there in the field doing research of your own. You'll find out before us when a fine new family-run hotel opens or a favourite restaurant changes hands and goes downhill. So why not write and tell us about your experiences? Contact us on ☏ 01753 893444 or e info@bradtguides.com. We will forward emails to the author who may post updates on the Bradt website at www.bradtupdates.com/belarus. Alternatively you can add a review of the book to www.bradtguides.com or Amazon.

FOLLOW BRADT

For the latest news, special offers and competitions, subscribe to the Bradt newsletter via the website www.bradtguides.com and follow Bradt on:

- 🅕 www.facebook.com/BradtTravelGuides
- 🐦 @BradtGuides
- 📷 @bradtguides
- 📌 www.pinterest.com/bradtguides

HOW TO USE THIS GUIDE

MAPS

Keys and symbols Maps include alphabetical keys covering the locations of those places to stay, eat or drink that are featured in the book. Note that regional maps may not show all hotels and restaurants in the area: other establishments may be located in towns shown on the map.

Grids and grid references Several maps use gridlines to allow easy location of sites. Map grid references are listed in square brackets after the name of the place or sight of interest in the text, with page number followed by grid number, eg: [137 C3].

BELARUSIAN AND RUSSIAN PLACE NAMES Names of major places within this book are followed by their Belarusian and Russian names in Cyrillic. This editorial preference is intended solely as a means of assistance to English-speaking travellers and does not in any way intend to promote a particular cultural preference or political ideal.

EXCHANGE RATES AND PRICES As we went to press, the volatility of the political issues involving Russia and Ukraine was inevitably producing knock-on effects in this part of Europe, including a degree of economic instability for the nation states involved. The mid- to long-term impact on the Belarusian economy has yet to play out, but do bear in mind that currency exchange rates may well display significant swings, maybe even at short notice. Best advice is to regularly check a conversion site such as www.xe.com before you travel.

SEND US YOUR SNAPS!

We'd love to follow your adventures using our *Belarus* guide – why not send us your photos and stories via Twitter (@BradtGuides) and Instagram (@bradtguides) using the hashtag #belarus. Alternatively, you can upload your photos directly to the gallery on the Belarus destination page via our website (*www.bradtguides.com*).

BELARUS ONLINE

For additional online content, articles, photos and more on Belarus, why not visit www.bradtguides.com/belarus.

Part One

GENERAL INFORMATION

BELARUS AT A GLANCE

Location Eastern Europe

Neighbouring countries Borders Russian Federation, Ukraine, Poland, Latvia and Lithuania. The country is completely landlocked.

Size Total state border length 2,969km; area 207,600km²; maximum width west to east 650km; length 560km north to south

Geography Lowland terrain, with a mean elevation above sea level of only 160m, the highest point being 345m. Natural vegetation over around 70% of area, of which 38% is forest. Also 20,000 rivers and streams and 11,000 lakes, with significant areas of marsh territory.

Climate Moderately continental, with cold winters and warm summers. Average temperature January –6.7°C, July 17.8°C. Annual rainfall 550–750mm.

Status Republic

Population 9,345,000 (density 45/km²) (2014)

Life expectancy Male 66 years, female 77 years (2011 estimates)

Administrative divisions Six regions (*oblasts*), comprising 118 administrative districts

Capital city Minsk (population 1,921,000) (2014)

Other major cities Brest, Grodno, Vitebsk, Mogilev and Gomel

Economy Largely unchanged since Soviet times and currently around 80% state controlled

GDP US$63.3 billion in total, US$6,795 per capita (2012 estimates)

People Ethnic Belarusians (81%), Russians (11%), Poles (4%), Ukrainians (2%) and the remaining 2% comprising Jews, Lithuanians, Tatars, Azerbaijanis, Armenians, Latvians, Koreans, Germans, Georgians, Ossets, Moldavians and travelling people

Languages Belarusian and Russian have equal status as state languages

Religion Russian Orthodox, Roman Catholicism and Judaism

Currency Belarusian rouble (BYR)

Exchange rate £1 = BYR23,584, US$1 = BYR15,422, €1 = BYR17,612 (February 2015)

National airline/airport Belavia/Minsk-2 National

International dialling code +375

Time GMT +2

Electrical voltage 220–240 volts

Weights and measures Metric

Flag Two broad horizontal stripes of red and green, red being double the area of green, with traditional patterning of red on a white border down the left-hand side

National anthem '*Mbl, Senapycbl*' ('We Belarusians')

National flower Flax

National bird/animal Black stork/European bison

National sport Ice hockey

Public holidays 1 January (New Year's Day), 7 January (Orthodox Christmas), 8 March (Women's Day), Orthodox Easter, Catholic Easter, Radaunista (Ancestors' Remembrance Day) on the ninth day after Orthodox Easter, 1 May (Labour Day), 9 May (Victory Day, a glorious celebration of the end of the 'Great Patriotic War'), 3 July (Independence Day), 7 November (October Revolution Day), 25 December (Catholic Christmas)

1

Background Information

GEOGRAPHY

Whether you fly over the country or drive across it, the impression you get is always the same; it's very flat and there are lots of trees. The country has no sea borders and it sits in the heart of the mid-European plain between the Baltic Sea to the north and the Black Sea to the south. It borders Poland to the west, Lithuania to the northwest, Latvia to the north, Russia to the northeast and east and, finally, Ukraine to the south. The capital of the republic is Minsk and the distances to the capitals of its neighbours are as follows:

Capital city	Warsaw	Vilnius	Riga	Moscow	Kiev
Distance (km)	550	215	470	700	580

The country covers a surface area of 207,600km^2. The maximum distance from west to east is 650km and from north to south, 560km. The total length of its borders is 2,969km. Belarus ranks 13th of all European countries (excluding Russia) in area size. In all, it is slightly smaller than the United Kingdom, more than twice the size of Portugal and Hungary and no fewer than five times bigger than Holland and Switzerland. But if you look at the map, you will see that it is dwarfed by its gigantic neighbour Russia to the east, a rich metaphor if ever there was one. The plain upon which the country is located extends some way beyond the country's borders and in times of war this has been a distinct disadvantage, rendering it all too easy in geographical terms to invade and subjugate. In times of peace, however, this has meant that transport links, whether by road, river or rail, have been easy to establish and the trade routes that have passed in the direction of the four compass points have at times brought prosperity and multi-culturalism to these lands.

Those hills that exist here are barely hills at all, more rolling countryside; the mean elevation above sea level is only 160m, with the highest point being Mount Dzherzhinskaya in Minsk *oblast* at just 345m, although it is sufficiently elevated for there to be a modest winter sports resort there, including a ski jump. The lowest is the valley of the Nieman River in Grodno *oblast* at just over 80m.

Lakes (11,000 of them) and rivers (totalling 91,000km in length) are the major features, with significant areas of marshland in-between. The area of the Polyesye, the largest of the marsh territories, runs along the southern boundary of the country and is one of the biggest in Europe. In the north is the country's lakeland area. Five major rivers run through the territory of Belarus: the Nieman, the Dnieper, the Berazhina, the Sozh and the Pripyat, the last of which flows adjacent to the site of the former nuclear complex at Chernobyl in Ukraine, scene of the world's worst commercial nuclear catastrophe in April 1986. Approximately one-fifth of the territory of Belarus, mostly in the southeast, continues to be affected by radioactive fallout.

Over a third of the total landscape (38%) is covered by forest, much of it forming part of the vast primeval wood that once stretched across the whole of central Europe. Not only is it a valuable source of timber, it also performs other ecological functions, such as water conservation and soil protection, as well as being home to a rich variety of wildlife and also shelter for copious supplies of plants harvested for medicinal and food purposes (particularly mushrooms and berries). Other natural resources include peat fields (much depleted by intensive extraction) and small reserves of oil and natural gas, although production is insignificant. There are also 63 separate sources of mineral water supplying a significant number of sanatoria and spas throughout the country.

CLIMATE

The climate is moderately continental, ranging from unforgiving winters, when the mean January temperature is −6.7°C, to warm summers, when the mean in July is +17.8°C. The annual level of precipitation is 550–650mm in the low country and 650–750mm at higher elevations. The average vegetation period is 184–208 days. Generally, the climate is favourable for growing cereal crops, vegetables, potatoes and fruit.

NATURAL HISTORY AND CONSERVATION

VEGETATION Natural vegetation covers around 70% of the area of Belarus, 38% of which is forest. Farmland takes up 43.9% of the land mass, which includes arable land extending to 26.8% of the total. The best way to truly understand the extent of the Belarusian forest is to fly over the country, when the clear impression gained is that mile after mile of territory is covered by a green blanket that is only occasionally broken by concentrated areas of farmland connected by ribbon-like roads. True, there are subtle variances: in the north, the area of lakes, water is a contrasting feature, while in the south, the Pripyat River is cloaked in the Polyesye marshland. But still the overriding feature is the tree. In the north, pines and other conifers predominate, while in the south, forestry is primarily deciduous (most notably oak). Birch knows no geographical boundaries and can be found all over the country. Indeed, in those areas where active forestation has been undertaken, particularly of pine, you will see that every stand of pine trees is surrounded by a protective ring, square or rectangle of silver birch. This is because birch grows faster and, as it matures, it shelters the more delicate pine from the excesses of the weather, including the sun. Centuries ago, these areas of forestation together formed part of the great European primeval forest, most of which no longer exists, but here, such that remains is preserved as a natural treasure. Indeed, as well as having significance as a natural timber resource, it also forms an undisturbed habitat for a rich variety of wildlife and, increasingly, it is a resource for leisure and ecological tourism.

NATIONAL PARKS Belarus is particularly proud of its national parks. In 1992, 340km southwest of Minsk, the **Byelovezhskaya Puscha National Park** was included in the list of World Heritage Sites by UNESCO and, one year later, UNESCO granted it the status of Biosphere Reserve. This means that it is one of the sites monitored by ecologists to assess environmental changes taking place around the globe. Then, at the end of 1997, the Council of Europe recognised the park as one of the most conservation-conscious reserves on the continent. The characteristics and profile of the locality were first mentioned in chronicles in AD983, while the first attempts at establishing a formal reserve on this site were made early in the 15th century. The total area exceeds 90,000ha. The largest population of European bison roam free here; once to be found in abundance throughout the forests of Europe, the species is now extremely rare and the very fact of their existence in Belarus is something of a success story for the country's conservation policies. Also to be found in this reserve are red deer, wild boar, roe deer and elk. Natural predators include wolf, fox, lynx, badger, marten and otter. Birdlife is equally diverse and includes the greater spotted eagle and the aquatic warbler. Experts have estimated that around a thousand of the oaks in the park are between 300 and 700 years old, with some of the ash being 450 years old, certain of the pines being 220 and a number of junipers as old as 150. There are also white firs, spruce and pine.

In the south of the country is a wide lowland area consisting of hollows, plains, forests and marshes, pierced by many rivers and creeks flowing to the Pripyat River, a tributary of the Dnieper, which itself flows into the Black Sea. In the area lying between the Pripyat, Stivha and Ubort rivers is the significant marsh wetland known as the Polyesye that is home to around 265 species of bird, including heron, the rare black stork (and the more common white), grey crane, eagle owl, serpent eagle and marsh owl. Indeed, both white and black storks can be seen extensively in and around the villages in the south of the country and the first sighting of one of these birds on the wing is a great experience. Within the region of the Polyesye, the total area of the **Pripyatsky National Park** (established in 1996) covers 82,529ha and its territory extends for 64km east to west. Of particular interest are the areas around the banks of the river. The spring melt causes it to rise by 10–15cm each year and the floodplains have their own unique vegetation, with oak and ash further from the river being replaced by black alder and willow adjacent to it. Some 826 species of plant are to be found here, including an astonishing 200 different mosses.

In the northeast of the country, the **Berezinsky Biosphere Reserve** was created in 1925 to preserve the natural primeval landscape as well as game and other wild animals, such as the river beaver. Today, many animals and birds that are extremely rare or even extinct elsewhere live here, such as the brown bear. Much of this reserve (extending over 85,000ha) is covered by forest, most of it pine and spruce, the remainder being largely marshland interspersed with wooded islands. The main river that flows through the reserve (for 110km) is the Berazhina.

Narach National Park boasts one of the largest (shoreline 41km) and deepest (maximum 30m) lakes in the country, bearing the same name. The country's renowned Blue Lakes are also situated here. The largest concentration of ecological resorts and recreation complexes in the whole country is situated within the wider Narach area, including a total of 18 sanatoria and recuperation centres. There are also several natural springs and the area is famed for its mineral waters. The park itself was only established in 1999. It covers 94,000ha, 37,900 of which are forest, including the country's largest concentration of pine. Its 42 lakes have a total area of 18,300ha. This is a beautiful and romantic area, steeped in mystery and legend. The lakes are said to have been the creation of a tragic loss when Nara, the daughter of a forester, saw the death of her sweetheart in a magic mirror, which she then dropped in terror, the shards scattering all around. These fragments became the lakes that can be seen today. And Nara? She was turned into a white gull, and she can still be seen wheeling and turning across the water, calling for her lost love…

Completing the list is **Braslav Lakes Park,** where large numbers of lakes are surrounded by picturesque hilly landscapes. Brooks, rivers and channels, most of them navigable, form a water-bound labyrinth through which the visitor can cast off the trappings of modern life and meander undisturbed. Signs of life from ancient times, such as burial mounds, places of worship and evidence of settlements, complement the natural wonders of the area. Located in the northwest, the park was created in 1995 and its territory covers around 70,000ha. The lakes themselves extend over an area of 183km^2, the deepest of them, South Volos, extending to 40.4m. Lake Struso is particularly beautiful: at the centre is the Isle of Chaichyn, which has its own small inner lake. The water ecosystems here are particularly interesting and 20 of the 800 species of plant are on the endangered list (and consequently subject to special protection measures). Of 28 species of fish, eel are the most common and are extensively farmed. Badger, lynx, brown bear, squirrel, elk, wild boar and roe deer all live in the park.

ECOLOGY Overall, ecological tourism is a significant growth sector of the economy, although much remains to be done in terms of establishing a viable infrastructure if it is to be commercially competitive (see box on pages 90–1). As mentioned several times in a number of contexts throughout this book, the people of the country have an extremely close relationship and affinity with the land and the seasons. This theme dominates life in the rural areas and it only serves to highlight the tragedy of the Chernobyl catastrophe in 1986 and its significantly adverse consequences, which will endure for generations to come.

It would be impossible to make even a cursory and passing reference to ecological matters in Belarus without discussing Chernobyl (see pages 15–17). Prevailing weather conditions immediately after the explosion blew the deadly radioactive cloud over mainland Europe in a predominantly northwesterly direction. The region of Gomel in Belarus was directly in its path. Contamination was spread on an irregular basis as dictated by the weather. For example, there remain particularly radioactive hotspots today where rain fell at the time. Indeed, stories persist to this day that the authorities deliberately and actively dropped chemicals into cloud formations to make it rain (a process known as 'seeding') in an attempt to control the location of deposited radiation away from the largest centres of population, although this has been neither proved nor acknowledged. I know of a number of people in and around the area of Gomel *oblast* who to this day remember standing outside in something they describe as 'odd rain'. Whatever may or may not have happened, it is generally acknowledged that Belarus received about 60% of the fallout sustained by the Soviet Union.

Anyone interested in travelling to Belarus will be concerned to know just how safe it is in terms of radiation exposure. In the past, reliable information has not been easy to find, but it is now widely accepted as scientific fact that the risk of prejudice to health is minimal. In fact, it is even possible today to join a tour to Pripyat (in Ukraine) that will take participants to within 100m of the nuclear plant. In 2006, an Australian film crew went inside the reactor buildings to film, although for a few minutes only and even then wearing fully protective clothing. As the years have passed, more and more filming has been done in and around the plant, particularly by ecologists monitoring the impact of the disaster on the natural environment. Today you can still stand 100m away with a Geiger counter and the reading when it is pointed into the atmosphere is steady, but if you then point it at the reactor, it goes off the scale.

In Belarus it remains forbidden to visit any of the hotspot areas without official permission from the government and, even then, only if accompanied by 'officials'. Whole villages stand abandoned to the elements. Most of them have their own cemeteries, but only once a year are the bereaved permitted to return to tend the graves of their loved ones. With the passage of time, however, the extent to which the regulation of activity within these areas remains strictly monitored is becoming open to question.

The perceived wisdom is that a day in Pripyat will lead to radiation exposure that is actually less than is experienced on an eight-hour plane journey. It has also been said that if you stay there for seven consecutive days, your body will absorb no more radiation than it would if you were exposed to a single medical X-ray procedure at home. Given that current levels of radiation diminish incrementally as the distance from the plant increases, the danger for the short-term visitor to Belarus is negligible. Indeed, it is an unavoidable fact of modern life that radiation is all around us, whether from the sun, mobile phones, natural levels of radon gas or many other sources. The internet is now a mine of information on the impact of Chernobyl radiation and authoritative materials that seek to give reassurance to the short-term visitor are easily found. Be cautious and don't be foolhardy by venturing where you are not permitted to go, but look upon the consequences of the accident as a unique educational opportunity concerning some of the biggest issues facing society today and the future of the planet, in an environment that until the 2011 Fukushima disaster in Japan was literally like no other on earth.

HISTORY

No student of modern-day Belarus can hope to gain an insight into the mystery and enigma that characterise the national psyche without first engaging in at least a rudimentary study of all that has gone before. But there is very little to be found specifically about the country in Western books, although there is much to read on the subject of Holy Mother Russia and the former Soviet Union, both of which subsumed it at various times as an integral element of their empires.

There is one theme in particular that spans the centuries: that of suffering and privation. Whether subjugated to the yoke of Lithuanian, Pole, Tsar, Frenchman, Bolshevik, Communist, Nazi, Communist again or latterly oligarch, heroism and tragedy can be found on most of the pages of the country's history, as drama and melodrama unfold in the never-ending struggle to resist pain, anguish, grief and suffering. For generation after generation, there seems to have been no sanctuary from constant oppression, with the identity of the oppressor being largely irrelevant. Further, the media of oppression are many and varied: fear, dogma, hunger, poverty, lack of education, geography, climate and, in recent times, Chernobyl. Each succeeding generation has developed defences to resist every challenge that comes along, such that the people of today are characterised by an impressively stoical resilience.

ANCIENT TIMES Indications are that early civilisations began to populate the territory that is now Belarus from the middle Palaeolithic period, or 100,000–40,000 years BC, while available evidence suggests that the first significant settlements emerged 24,000–27,000 years ago.

EARLY CIVILISATIONS The area was then settled by the Dryhavichy, Krivichi and Radzimichy peoples between the 7th and 9th centuries AD, when the first Slavic alliances were formed. This was followed by the first state formations in the principalities of Polotsk, Turov and Smolensk. The town of Polotsk itself, founded by the Krivichi at the confluence of the Polota and Western Dvina rivers, is known to have existed since AD862 and it is still regarded as the first capital of the lands now recognised as Belarus. It is also still regarded as the spiritual cradle of the country. Its first chronicled prince, who ruled in the late 10th century, was Rogvolod. In the following century, the principality reached the zenith of its power and influence under Prince Vyseslav Bryachislavich, who is believed to have ruled for an incredible 72 years from 1029 to 1101. He was known as 'the magician' not only for his remarkable talents as military leader and statesman, but also because he was believed to be a literal shape-shifter, endowed with magical powers. At that time, the extent of Polotskian influence stretched from the Baltic Sea in the west and north to Smolensk in the east. This geographical location held the key to the non-aligned lands between the opulent extravagance of the Byzantine Empire in the east and the warlike Norse tribes of Scandinavia (known to the Slavic peoples as Varangians) and allowed Polotsk to gain many benefits from trade with Byzantium, the Baltic countries and Scandinavia. At the same time, Byzantine Christianity began to spread across these territories, doubtless as a result of trade links, so stimulating the development of culture through the arts and literature, along with the emergence of stone-based architecture.

A golden age of creativity had begun. The Turovsky Gospels were written in the 11th century and then, between 1050 and 1070, the first major architectural structure, the imposing Cathedral of St Sophia, was built in Polotsk. It quickly became the very manifestation of the state's might and significance, for at times foreign ambassadors were officially received here, both war and peace were declared here and it was also treated as the place of safe keeping for the public purse and sacred relics. Sister (later St) Ephrosinia, the heavenly 'mediatress' of Belya Rus whose selfless labour has long since passed into legend, was born at the beginning of the 12th century, around the time when master craftsmen were known to be working at the cathedral, such as the architect Johannes and the jeweller Lazar Bogsha. In 1161, Bogsha created the 'Cross for the Enlightener St Ephrosinia of Polotsk', a unique masterpiece of eastern Slavonic applied art. And among many contemporary Christian preachers and writers of note, Kirill Turovsky was particularly well known.

THE GRAND DUCHY OF LITHUANIA The 13th century marked a key phase in the history of modern Belarus. In its first half, the foundations of the Belarusian language began to form. This coincided with the establishment of the Grand Duchy of Lithuania, which brought together a number of Belarusian lands and principalities, primarily to meet the threat of invasion from crusading Teutonic knights to the west, Turks from the south and the Golden Horde of Mongol Tartars from the east. Many famous victories were won. The core lands of the duchy at this time were the territories around Kernave, Trakai and Samogitia, together with the city of Vilnius.

The coronation of the ruler Mindaug took place in 1253 and at the same time Novogorodok (now known as Novogrudok) became the capital of the Lithuanian duchy. In 1323, this status was transferred to Wilno (now Vilnius). Under the rule of Vitautis, the duchy reached the peak of its power and influence, expanding its frontiers and gaining international prestige. On 2 February 1386, Grand Duke Jogaila was crowned King of Poland and a personal union under one single monarch was established. Then at the famous Battle of Grunwald in 1410, the joint forces of Poland and Lithuania inflicted a crushing defeat on the Teutonic Order, an event of critical importance to the consolidation of the new state, whose power now extended all the way from the Baltic Sea in the north to the Black Sea in the south. The next significant stage of the state's development was the formation (by formal union) in 1569 of the Polish-Lithuanian Commonwealth and consequent creation of a new federative state known as Rzeczpospolita. It was ruled by the Grand Duke and Rada Polish landowners jointly, with the state being divided into provinces and administrative districts known as *povets*. The representative body of the feudal lords of the Polish gentry was known as the Sejm, with its deputies being elected at the regional councils of the *povet*, although simultaneously the former Lithuanian grand duchy maintained its own government, financial system, army and emblem.

The competing struggle for influence in the eastern Baltic region had instigated the Livonian War in 1558 against the state of Muscovy. This war lasted until 1583. The formal settlement of the 1569 union eventually enabled the new state to win the Livonian War, thereby returning areas of land that had been lost and, most importantly, consolidating and securing power and influence in the eastern Baltic.

From the early 16th century, massive agrarian reform (*volochnaya pomera*) had been taking place against a background of almost constant warfare, culminating in the embodiment of the concept of serfdom in a 1588 statute, one of three during the century that codified the fundamental elements of the grand duchy's status, the other two having been passed in 1529 and 1566. At the same time, those towns that had assumed self-government under Magdeburg Law since the end of the 14th century were now developing at an intense rate, with the establishment of urban crafts and consequent guild protection. This was an exciting time for those engaged in commercial interests.

THE CHURCH During the 16th century, the lands that now form Belarus saw the establishment of Lutheranism, Calvinism and other Protestant doctrines under the influence of the Reformation. This was a period of considerable religious tolerance and stability, but by the end of the century the Counter-Reformation had begun. Orthodoxy and Catholicism reached a compromise that resulted in the Brest Church Union of 1596, under which the Orthodox Church of the Grand Duchy of Lithuania recognised the supremacy of Rome, while maintaining its own rites, doctrines and customs. Inevitably, there was reluctance on the part of Orthodox believers to accept religious subjugation under the Union and this, along with inevitable economic pressures on the peasantry and the urban lower classes, resulted in considerable internal strife and opposition to feudalism.

THE RISE AND INFLUENCE OF RUSSIA Neighbouring Russia gleefully seized the opportunity to capitalise on these domestic difficulties within the state of Rzeczpospolita and launched a new war on its territory, which endured from 1654 to 1667. A large portion of modern-day Belarus was occupied and severe economic and demographic crises ensued. The population was reduced by half, whole towns fell into decay and there were many adverse consequences for all levels of society, but most notably the gentry and urban dwellers.

From 1700 to 1721, these lands formed the battleground in the North War waged by the Swedes on Russia and Rzeczpospolita. This war brought about decades of economic ruin, which only began to be overcome by the middle of the century with the revival of commerce and business in the form of a rudimentary market economy. Of more serious consequence even than warfare was the protracted political crisis that was wrought by consequent anarchy in the country and the growing power and influence of neighbouring nation states. The last single King of Poland and Grand Duke of Lithuania, Stanislas Augustus Poniatowski (1764– 95), tried in vain to consolidate central power, but he was confronted by an active opposition that sought aid and support from abroad. The situation was ripe for exploitation, and the neighbouring states of Russia, Prussia and Austria capitalised on these circumstances by taking advantage of the inequality of Orthodox and Protestant believers in relation to Catholics within Rzeczpospolita. All of this led to the first division of the country in 1772, following which the land that is now eastern Belarus was annexed and incorporated into the Russian Empire. A second division was effected in 1793, as a result of which central Belarus was also annexed. There was a limited degree of patriotic resistance, leading to the uprising led by Kostyushko, but in 1795 the third and final division of the country took place, with Russia subsuming the western lands of Belarus. Rzeczpospolita was never to exist again as a sovereign state and the administrative divisions, taxes and duties of the Russian Empire were finally imposed across all of its lands.

There followed a long period of Russian domination. During the Napoleonic invasion of Russia in 1812 the territory was the major theatre of war, resulting in huge losses and a significant diminution in the population. After the war, in the vacuum created by social and administrative disintegration, democratic ideas began to flourish, leading to the development of the first national liberation movement. As a consequence there was an uprising in 1830–31 to re-establish the state of Rzeczpospolita and restore the national boundaries that existed in 1772, the date of its first division. Inevitably, the uprising was suppressed, but the position of the gentry and of Catholicism had been weakened. Roman Catholic churches and monasteries were closed, while the lands, estates and possessions of the rebels were confiscated by the state. Other contextual events included the closure of the University of Vilno and the annulment of the statute of 1588, which had codified the autonomous Grand Duchy of Lithuania's governance arrangements. To all intents and purposes, the lands of modern Belarus now existed only as the northwestern region of the Russian Empire.

In the 19th century, broader issues within the empire began to take effect and, as the Tsars sought to cling on to power and perpetuate the subjugation of the people (in the face of increasing challenges through assertion of democracy and enfranchisement), Russian influences from the establishment grew incrementally stronger. By way of example, the compromise reached under the Brest Church Union of 1596 was reversed and the Uniate Church ceased to exist, allowing traditional Russian Orthodoxy to once more reign supreme. And while the peasants tended the fields, the landed gentry, the privileged classes and the re-established Church saw to it that any attempts to assert a specific identity for the Belarusian people were systematically suppressed, often with brutality. One of the many ways in which this suppression manifested itself was the proscription of the use of the Belarusian language in written form. Despite (and probably because of) this official denial of an independent Belarusian identity, nationalist ideas continued to flourish underground. The promotion of Belarusian literature, art, folklore and language began to take hold in the minds and consciousness of the people, notwithstanding the perpetuation of the prejudice and lack of opportunity suffered by native Belarusians in terms of access to significant administrative and governance positions of influence within the Russian Empire, as had earlier been the case for centuries across ceaseless periods of Lithuanian and Polish dominance.

Hand in hand with cultural development came increasing economic well-being, most notably in respect of the industrialisation of the country's richest natural resource (timber), although progress was only gradual and there remained painfully little change in the high rate of rural deprivation, which for the most part was worse than anywhere else in the empire. The majority of the population by far was still to be found on the land, maintained in a position of unrepresented subservience through poverty, ignorance, effective disenfranchisement and the power of privilege. Then in 1861, peasant reform abolished serfdom. The first underground newspaper, *Peasant's Truth*, was established between 1862 and 1863, then later that year and into 1864 the national liberation movement in the empire rose up against tsarism in the lands that are now Poland, Lithuania and Belarus, although brutal suppression once more ensued and a codified legal regime was enforced that was to endure into the 20th century.

In the 1880s, however, the revolutionary organisation Gomon was established by Belarusian students who had trained at the higher-education establishments of St Petersburg. This name became synonymous with the ideals and rights of an emerging Belarusian nation, while a fledgling national identity was again assumed through the media of language, culture and literature. An upsurge in democratic and national liberation ideas and thinking was now creating real conditions for the establishment of Belarusian statehood. This century also saw an important demographic development that was to have very significant and tragic consequences for future generations and society in general. Belarusian lands were included in the Pale of Settlement, the territorial area into which Jews from all over the empire were forced to relocate their homes and communities, such that by the time of the German invasion in 1941, the population of some of the towns that fell under Nazi oppression and tyranny were up to 70% Jewish.

THE 20TH CENTURY The first national political party (the Belarusian socialist Gromada Party) was created in 1903, with the objectives of overthrowing autocracy and bringing about a Russian federation of democratic republics. Each of these republics was to be a separate nation with statehood, cultural and national autonomy and the inalienable right to independent self-determination. After the

LATVIA

POLAND

Polotsk

Vitebsk

RUSSIAN SSR

MINSK

Mogilev

BELARUS SSR

Babrusk

Gomel

POLAND

Mozyr

UKRAINIAN SSR

BELARUS AND THE OTHER SSRs (1926)

abolition of serfdom in the wider Russian Empire in 1861, there had been slow but effective reform of the means of land allocation, but this did not prevent the mass displacement of the peasant classes from the lands of modern-day Belarus to Siberia. Approximately 335,000 people took this option between 1907 and 1914, while many more from the privileged classes dispersed further afield into western Europe and beyond to America.

As had been the case on countless occasions in the past, Belarusian territory was again a battleground when hostilities broke out in 1914, with bloody and brutal clashes between opposing armies of the German and Russian empires. After Russia's entry into the war, martial law was declared in Belarus. As with other conflicts across the centuries, there was widespread destruction and mass occupation, this time by troops under the German flag. Then in November 1917, the armed uprising in Petrograd (formerly St Petersburg) and the homecoming to Russian territories of the Bolshevik leader Vladimir Ilyich Ulyanov (the revolutionary Lenin) hastened the end of tsarism in the empire. Political activity in Belarus intensified and the first independent Belarusian democratic republic was established on 25 March 1918, despite the continuing German occupation. The influence of the Bolshevik Revolution was acquiring significant momentum and the German occupation came to an end, but the declaration of the new republic's status could not prevent the proclamation of Soviet power in Minsk. As a result, the Belarusian Soviet Socialist Republic (BSSR) came into existence in Smolensk on 1 January 1919.

The Russians subsequently occupied much of Lithuania and as a result in February 1919 the new state became the Lithuanian-Belarusian Soviet Socialist Republic, the capital of which was Vilnius. War between Poland and the emerging Soviet Union ensued, during which the territory of much of the nascent country was under Polish occupation (including Minsk). Then on 31 July 1920, the BSSR was proclaimed for a second time after the expulsion of Polish troops. Unfortunately for the new state, however, the 1921 Treaty of Riga resulted in the annexation by Poland of the western territories and the flickering flame of the emerging Belarusian identity was extinguished. Elsewhere, the rump of the BSSR, under Bolshevik control, continued to exist in the form of six administrative districts of the province of Minsk, with a total population of 1.5 million people. It joined the Union of Soviet Socialist Republics (USSR) on 30 December 1922 and its territories were expanded first in 1924, then again in 1926, when 17 western districts of the Russian SSR were added, the people of which were predominantly Belarusian. These districts remain part of modern-day Belarus.

In the years that followed (leading up to the outbreak of war once more in Europe in 1939), Soviet social policy made a dramatic volte-face. In a very short space of time, the USSR emerged as a massive world power, bringing together diverse cultures, races and former nation states across an enormous geographical area (and several time zones). At first, the concept of ethnicity was encouraged throughout the Union, with active promotion of disparate cultures and traditions, as if to show the world that 'the Revolution' truly was an international movement that could transcend barriers of class, language and background. The Party also saw this as the best form of protection against so-called pernicious Western influences. Against that background, traditionalism and the concept of a specific identity were allowed to flourish in the Belarusian SSR. Things proved to be very different in the 1930s. The Georgian Iosif Dzhugashvili (Stalin) had incrementally (and by design) inherited stewardship of the Revolution from Lenin as the 1920s drew to a close and a dark period in the history of these lands ensued, as the fear of internal opposition and the paranoia of the Soviet leader took hold. Millions were incarcerated, tortured and murdered across the USSR in Stalin's infamous purges. This was a time of neighbour informing on neighbour, the dreaded knock on the door in the middle of the night, worthless confessions obtained under torture and staged show trials in the full glare of publicity. As many times before in history, Belarusian nationalists were cruelly suppressed. The features and horrors of this dark period of world history are widely documented elsewhere, but the terrible contradiction of the huge advances proclaimed by the Soviet Union at the time in terms of astonishing economic growth against a background of mass murder and social re-engineering on a scale previously unimagined in the modern world is a grim one indeed. The new dawn of hope for Belarusian culture that had been so joyously celebrated in the 1920s proved to have been a very false one as the 1930s drew to a close.

Following the notorious and shameful 1939 pact of mutual non-aggression, German and Soviet tanks rolled simultaneously across Poland from the west and the east respectively. The state boundary that had existed immediately prior to the 1921 Treaty of Riga was quickly restored as the western territories and their communities were forcibly snatched back from Polish control and sovereignty. When the Nazis dissolved the pact in spectacular fashion by invading the Soviet Union in 1941 under Operation Barbarossa, which was designed to deliver Hitler's avowed intention to wipe the USSR from the face of the earth, the Soviet Union responded by entering the global fray. The 'Great Patriotic War' had begun. As the most westerly of the SSRs, Belarus was quickly overrun by the Nazis, in just two months. The occupation that followed was cruel and brutal. It was resisted by a mass movement of guerrilla and partisan activity throughout the republic involving many thousands of active volunteers, backed by many thousands more in reserve. The occupying forces were actively and ruthlessly opposed, but in turn this led to yet more atrocities on the part of the invaders. Almost 25% of the population were brutally murdered in hundreds of punitive operations that brought about the deaths of men, women and children through the systematic burning and destruction of thousands of villages and hamlets under the pretext of fighting guerrillas. Today, this tragic loss of life and brutal destruction of whole communities is commemorated at the memorial complex of Khatyn in Minsk province, the site of one such village burnt with its residents, a haunting and deeply moving memorial that is described elsewhere in this book.

In July 1944, amid scenes of unparalleled patriotic fervour and wild abandon, Marshal Zhukov's Red Army completed the liberation of the country following a major offensive. The cost was enormous, both economically and in terms of loss of life. The capital Minsk had been almost completely destroyed and today very few pre-war buildings are still standing. And of the two million Belarusian people who lost their lives in the war, many died in the concentration camps of the Third Reich across occupied Europe. In addition, almost 380,000 had been removed to Germany for the purpose of enforced labour. Incredibly, it was not until 1971 that the country's population again reached its pre-war level, although the Jewish community had been all but wiped out. Today, however, there are real signs at last that Jewish life in Belarus is returning, as communities begin to establish their identity once more. A significant number of small but active Jewish communities now exist in many parts of Belarus. Some are listed and described in these pages. Anyone interested in learning about these communities and the history of Judaism in the country can access more information in the United Kingdom from British sustainable development charity The Together Plan or in Belarus from local NGO Dialog. Full contact details can be found on page 35.

In August 1945, under the Soviet-Polish Treaty, 17 districts of Byelostock and three of Brest (but not the city itself) were formally transferred to Poland, although the majority of western Belarus was retained by the Soviet Union. Also in 1945, the Belarusian SSR was one of the 51 signatories to the founding of the United Nations Organisation. It says much about the national psyche that within the republic itself, as with others in the USSR, this act was regarded as an acknowledgement on the part of the international community of the contribution made by the USSR to the crushing defeat of Hitler's Nazi Germany. It is difficult to argue with this standpoint. Between 1941 and 1945, conservative estimates place the war dead of the USSR at an incredible 24 million people. Some place the actual figure at 30 million. This astonishing statistic is topped only by the fact that even the lower of these two figures exceeds the *total* of war dead of every other country in the world, on both sides of the conflict.

The damage and destruction of the war years was reversed in spectacular fashion and at an incredible pace by means of a rigidly enforced series of plans of regeneration through industrialisation and collective farming, all on a massive scale. A new Minsk, rising from the ashes of the old, was at the very heart of this process of rebirth and renewal. The BSSR established itself as a major centre of manufacturing within the USSR and the consequent creation of jobs brought in a huge immigrant population from the Russian Federation SSR, including into positions of influence within the government of the republic. As in earlier times, this process of mass immigration was said to be a form of 'protection'; as the most westerly of the Soviet republics, the BSSR was Stalin's first line of defence (militarily, culturally and ideologically) against the perceived moral bankruptcy of the West. But as had been the case in the 1930s, one consequence of this process of social engineering was that traditional Belarusian culture came under threat once more.

THE CHERNOBYL DISASTER The consequences of the accident that occurred in the early hours of 26 April 1986 at the Chernobyl nuclear power plant, then in the Soviet Union and now within the territory of Ukraine, have proved to be nothing short of a catastrophe for Belarus and, in terms of the economic, ecological and social impacts, it is universally regarded as the worst incident in the history of commercial nuclear power, although the full impact of the disaster at Fukushima in Japan in 2011 will only emerge with the passage of time. Certainly, there is much for the Japanese authorities to learn from the Chernobyl experience.

CHERNOBYL CAESIUM-137 CONTAMINATION (2001)

KEY

Caesium–137 contamination (curies per km²)

1–5   5–15   15–40   40+

Vitebsk

MINSK

Grodno

Mogilev

Babrusk

Vetka

Brest

Pinsk

Gomel

Mozyr

Chernobyl

0 ▬▬▬ 50km
0 ▬▬▬ 50 miles

During the course of tests to determine the ability of the fourth reactor to power safety systems if the external electricity supply was lost, a steam explosion occurred, triggering a fire, a further series of explosions and then a nuclear meltdown, in which the core of the reactor was destroyed. As the roof of the reactor was blown into the sky, the consequent inrush of oxygen reacted with the extremely high temperature of the reactor fuel to produce a graphite fire, which then hastened the spread of radioactive material. The fallout exceeded that generated by the explosion over Hiroshima in 1945 and was 16 million times greater than the release in the accident at Three Mile Island in Pennsylvania in 1978. As local people watched from the balconies of their flats in the nearby city of Pripyat, just 2km away, the explosion and the deadly cloud that billowed out in its wake (which is said to have been actively glowing) hurled nuclear fuel, intensely radioactive (but short-lived) isotopes, primarily iodine-131, and other long-lived isotopes such as caesium-137, strontium-90, americium-241 and plutonium-238, 239, 240 and 241, high into the sky and the atmosphere. It must have been quite a sight. And how chilling it is to reflect now that the onlookers can have had no understanding at all of the mortal danger in which the fates had placed them.

In 1986, Pripyat, Chernobyl and Belarus were all part of the USSR. Pripyat and Chernobyl are now in Ukraine. The city was once home to over 50,000 people, but today it is a ghost town, a snapshot in time, left exactly as it was when residents were evacuated later that day, with the remains of everyday life still to be seen all around.

Emergency measures that were immediately put into place succeeded in extinguishing the fires on the roof of the reactor, but the fire crews who rushed to the scene were not told of the extreme radioactivity of the smoke and debris. All of the firefighters received fatal doses, while the fire inside the reactor was not finally extinguished until helicopter crews had dropped large amounts of sand, lead, clay and boron on to it. By the end of the year, a concrete sarcophagus had been erected over the reactor, but it was always intended to be an interim measure only. It stands there still and lately cracks have begun to appear. The international community has come together to design a much more sophisticated tomb to encase the plant more effectively at an eventual cost of around US$1.5 billion, and although work adjacent to the site has been ongoing for some time, the conclusion of the project has been delayed a number of times. It's an ambitious venture. When completed some time in 2017, an enormous arch of stainless steel construction will be painstakingly wheeled into place over the remains of the reactor. The ends will then be sealed to ensure that there is no risk of any lingering radioactive material escaping into the atmosphere. This does leave outstanding, however, the question of whether or not any risk will remain of material leaching underground into the water supply. Meantime, the new structure is planned to endure for at least a hundred years, and probably more. Time will doubtless tell.

In the immediate aftermath of the catastrophe, the first response of the Soviet authorities was to say and do nothing, either by way of the release of information locally and internationally, or in terms of aid for people in the immediate area (other than enforced evacuation). This proved to be a catastrophic abrogation of social responsibility. For example, informed opinion suggests that had the authorities made supplies of non-radioactive iodine quickly available to the population, the absorption of radioactive iodine into the thyroid gland of many, with its consequent long-term deleterious health effects, would have been avoided.

In the days that followed, the evacuation of residents in the locality of the plant was stepped up, but people were not told why they were being moved. The international community began to hear rumours of a nuclear disaster, but every story was categorically denied by the authorities. Meanwhile, soldiers and workers known as 'liquidators' were sent in to mount a huge clean-up campaign. This began with the removal of debris in the vicinity of the plant, then spread to the large-scale sluicing down of buildings in an ever-increasing radius. All that this achieved, of course, was to ensure the spread of radioactive material into the ground.

Initially, several hundred people (mostly workers and liquidators) were hospitalised, of whom 31 died (28 from acute radiation exposure). Around 135,000 people were evacuated from the area and between 300,000 and 600,000 liquidators were involved in the decontamination of the 30km evacuation zone around the plant. Subsequently, hundreds of thousands more people were evacuated as the authorities began to comprehend the scale of the disaster and the area of land that had been affected.

The initial risk to health came from the concentration of radioactive iodine, which has a half-life of eight days. Iodine is readily absorbed into the thyroid gland. This happened both directly and also longer term as, for example, children drank supplies of contaminated milk. As a result, the incidence of thyroid cancer (and lesser conditions) has risen sharply over the years. Over 500,000 people in Belarus alone are thought to have thyroid pathology. Of greater impact on the infrastructure of society was the effect of contamination of the soil with caesium-137 (half-life 30 years) and strontium-90 (half-life 28 years). Indeed, 21% of the total area of Belarus is thought to have been contaminated with caesium-137. Where it is present in the soil, it is absorbed by plants, insects, grazing animals and crops, and by these means enters the local food supply.

THE CHERNOBYL LEGACY The long-term effects of the catastrophe have been subject to much speculation and conflicting hypotheses. It is true that relatively few people died directly as a result of the explosion itself. It is also true that the number of cancers and birth defects directly attributable to radiation has been very difficult to measure. Indeed, a report of the Chernobyl Forum (comprising a number of UN organisations, the World Health Organization, the International Atomic Energy Agency, the Belarusian government and others) sought to minimise the consequences of the accident. This report met with heavy criticism, particularly from those organisations working directly with communities in the affected areas. A subsequent report (TORCH), commissioned by a German MEP, predicted far greater consequences. Then in 2006, Greenpeace issued its own report to coincide with the 20th anniversary of the disaster, predicting yet more significant effects not simply from increased rates of cancer, but also from intestinal, heart, circulatory and respiratory problems, as well as damage to the immune system.

It is also widely accepted that in addition to specific health problems of this nature, those exposed to the radiation (and indeed, many who were not) continue to exhibit many of the symptoms that commonly manifest themselves in the aftermath of trauma, such as fear, stress, anxiety, depression, physical symptoms that are hard to explain and a feeling of hopelessness.

The state has sought to address all of these issues (at very significant cost to the economy) and is particularly concerned with the health and well-being of children living in contaminated areas. Many sanatoria and rehabilitation centres in so-called 'clean' areas exist to facilitate this. Charities and non-governmental organisations have been established in many of the countries in western and northern Europe to offer recuperation holidays to children. Working in partnership with local administrations in Belarus, these organisations have been able to offer hundreds of thousands of children the opportunity to leave their irradiated homeland for varying lengths of time. It is widely accepted that these breaks have a very positive effect on health.

Today, however, the reality of life in Belarus is that almost two million people continue to inhabit areas that were (and still are) subject to radioactive contamination to some degree.

THE CULTURAL CHERNOBYL Later in 1986, the policies of sweeping and institutional reform instigated by the Soviet President Mikhail Gorbachev (the conventional English spelling has been used throughout this guide, although a more accurate phonetic translation would be Gorbachov) afforded the Belarusian people an opportunity to reassert their national identity and rail back against the so-called Russification policy that had been followed since the early days of the Cold War. Formal representations were made, including by way of petition, to expose and highlight the long-term suppression of Belarusian culture and heritage. In the climate of the times, social commentators dubbed this turn of events the 'cultural Chernobyl'. By now, the seeds of unrest and revolution were beginning to be dispersed on the winds all across the lands of the Warsaw Pact. In June 1988, the bodies of as many as 300,000 of Stalin's victims were discovered in mass graves, although claims as to numbers, responsibility and even as to whether or not these murders ever occurred at all have been the subject of denial and counter-denial ever since the discovery of the site. Whatever the truth of the situation, the proponents of Belarusian nationalism used it as proof that the Soviet state did indeed engage in a deliberate policy of cultural and ethnic suppression. The socio-economic consequences of these events were such that political opposition began to achieve momentum that was ultimately irresistible during the last years and the eventual breakup of the USSR, even though Belarus was (and still is) considered to be one of the most traditionalist of the Union's republics. As the USSR lurched towards disintegration and nationalist voices began to be heard once more, the BSSR steadily began to assert its sovereignty.

The last throw of the dice for the ailing USSR was the bungled coup to remove Gorbachev (Yeltsin's finest hour!) in 1991. It failed within days and soon after, on 25 August, Belarus declared full independence. On 19 September the BSSR was officially renamed the Republic of Belarus, when the heads of the governments of the Russian, Ukrainian and Belarusian SSRs signed the Act on Denunciation of the Union Treaty of 1922. From that day, the USSR ceased to exist and a newly independent sovereign state of Belarusian peoples was born within the nascent Commonwealth of Independent States, in which it was joined by the Russian Federation and Ukraine.

On 15 March 1994 the Supreme Council of the Republic of Belarus adopted a new constitution, under which the country was proclaimed a unitary democratic legal state. On 10 July that year, Alexander Grigoryevich Lukashenko was elected the first president of the new republic. A firm opponent of the Gorbachev reforms, his background was state farm administration and he was swept to power on a ticket to restore stability. Against a background of mass insecurity and fear for the future, he promised a return to the safety of a regime whose loss was already being mourned. He captured the mood of the times perfectly. He holds the position of president to this day, following sweeping victories with very large majorities in the presidential elections of 2001, 2006 and 2010. The next election is due towards the end of 2015. In the run-up, observers within and outside the country will be interested to follow the course of the campaign in the context of the political circumstances that currently prevail (see *Today's political climate*, pages 21–4).

GOVERNMENT, POLITICS AND ADMINISTRATION

THE STRUCTURE OF THE POLITICAL SYSTEM First, the official facts as authorised by the authorities within Belarus: the head of state is the president, who is directly elected by the people for a five-year term of office, although initially this period was effectively extended to seven years as a consequence of a presidential referendum during the first term of the present incumbent in 1996, such that the next presidential election did not take place until 2001. The office holder is also the guarantor of certain inalienable rights and institutions, including the constitution and the rights and freedoms of individual citizens. In addition, the position carries with it a wide-ranging portfolio of rights, including to call national referendums, dissolve parliament, determine the structure of government, dismiss the heads of judicial and other bodies, conduct negotiations on and execute international treaties, declare states of emergency, impose martial law and abolish governmental acts. The president can also issue decrees and instructions of lawful and binding force throughout the country. The parliament is the National Assembly, which consists of two chambers: a lower house (the House of Representatives, with 110 members) and an upper house (the Council of Ministers of the Republic of Belarus, with 64 members). The council is the core organ of state administration, exercising executive power on behalf of the people. In so doing, the council is responsible and accountable to both the president and the parliament. It consists of the prime minister, deputies of that office, ministers and chairs of the various state committees. All of them are presidential appointees and there is no requirement that they be members of the legislature. The powers of the House of Representatives include to appoint the prime minister, propose constitutional amendments, call for a vote of confidence in the prime minister and make suggestions on domestic and foreign policy. The Council of the Republic has the power to select various government officials, conduct an impeachment trial of the president and to accept or reject bills passed from the House of Representatives. Each chamber may veto any law passed by local officials if contrary to the country's constitution. The judiciary consists of the Supreme Court and various other specialised courts, such as the Constitutional Court (comprising 12 judges 'elected' for an 11-year term of office), to deal with specialist issues relating to the constitution. The president himself appoints judges to this court, with appointments being confirmed by the Council of the Republic.

THE GENESIS OF THE CURRENT STRUCTURE In the USSR, the political system was a single-party one: the Communist Party of the Soviet Union. When the system began to unravel as an unintended consequence of Mikhail Gorbachev's sweeping reform by way of **openness (glasnost) and restructuring (perestroika)**, the plurality of the political landscape had already begun to emerge as, one by one, the former constituent republics declared independence. So it was that by the second half of 1993, the Ministry of Justice in Belarus had registered 12 political parties and seven non-governmental and political movements, including (among others), the Belarusian People's Front For Revival (1989), the United Democratic Party of Belarus (1990), the Belarusian Peasants' Party (1991), the Belarusian Social and Democratic Party Gromada (1991), the Party of Communists of Belarus (1991), the Belarusian Christian and Democratic Union (1991), the Slavic Assembly Belaya Rus (1992) and the Green Party of Belarus (1992). Generally, all of them had few members, pursued different political objectives and goals, followed different ways of attaining them and were organised along different lines. Many did not stand the test of time due to lack of popular support, while others joined forces. But the general characteristic of the 'opposition' as being a disparate array of disjointed and poorly organised groups was as true then as it is today.

The office of president was first established in 1994, following the adoption of a new constitution in March of that year. Six contenders for the presidency were presented to the people in June and **Alexander Lukashenko** secured 45.1% of

1

the popular vote, the highest of the six. In a second ballot run-off in July between Lukashenko and the second-placed candidate, former Prime Minister Kyebich, a self-styled 'traditionalist', Lukashenko secured more than four times as many votes as his opponent. Less than a year later, the first of a number of referendums was held, in which 83.3% of those who voted (64.8% of the electorate) agreed to the Russian language being granted official status of equality with Belarusian. A similar number agreed with the president's avowed policy of pursuing economic integration with Russia, while a lesser number (but still an overwhelming majority) agreed to adopt a new flag and to grant the president power to discontinue the Supreme Council.

The next referendum was held in November 1996, when 70% of those who voted agreed to new constitutional arrangements enabling the incumbent president's term of office to be extended to seven years and permitting the dissolution of parliament through the office of president. Western governments questioned the legitimacy of this referendum, but allegations of electoral impropriety have always been robustly denied by the Belarusian government.

Parliamentary elections were held in 2000 and 2004, with Lukashenko securing a second term of office following the intervening presidential election in 2001. The third national referendum was also held in October 2004, continuing the theme of increasing consolidation of presidential power. Almost 80% of voters are said to have agreed with the removal of the constitutional restriction on the number of terms for which an elected president could serve. All of these ballots attracted allegations of unfair practices and widespread fraud on the part of international observers, claims that were hotly denied by the Belarusian government.

Further elections took place on 19 March 2006, including for president. The candidates were the incumbent Alexander Lukashenko, who was able to stand again following the constitutional reforms legitimised by the 2004 referendum; Alexander Milinkevich, the head of a loose federation of opposition parties; and Alexander Kazulin, a Social Democrat. Several aspects of the administration of the election and of the campaign itself led to concern among Western governments and independent election monitoring bodies that there had been systemic failures in the process of democracy. There were allegations of intimidation and police brutality following several clashes between demonstrators and the authorities, including the forcible removal during the hours of darkness of a tented camp in central Minsk. On the other side, observers sent by the Commonwealth of Independent States declared themselves satisfied that all was in order and that the interests of transparency, lawfulness and democracy had been fully met. Senior Belarusian government sources hotly disputed claims of irregularity, entertainingly rebuffing the allegations in robust fashion by countering with claims of a similar nature in respect of the re-election of George W Bush to the White House. Whatever the reality, a landslide victory was declared for the incumbent president, with over 80% of the popular vote. Milinkevich polled just 6%. There were further parliamentary elections in 2008 and 2012, split by a presidential election in 2010. Lukashenko secured over five million votes, almost 80% of those who turned out to exercise their franchise. There were nine other candidates, the most popular of whom secured only 150,000 votes. All of these elections inevitably met with Western allegations of fraud, corruption, illegitimacy and intimidation, while CIS observers declared their validity and unconditional compliance in full with international standards. The next presidential election is due to be held in 2015.

The Council of Europe, which monitors democracy and human rights, has barred the country from membership since 1997. At various times the European Union has also imposed travel bans on the president and other senior members of the government, along with punitive economic sanctions. Observers and international human rights groups have also persistently criticised the Belarusian government for institutional suppression of free speech and human rights in its dealings with opposition politicians and their supporters, the independent mass media and other organisations that are not state controlled. To this day, the comment made in formal testimony by former United States Secretary of State Condoleezza Rice in 2005 that Belarus had been identified by the US government as one of a number of 'outposts of tyranny' around the world continues to be quoted. Routinely in the West, politicians, journalists, human rights activists and commentators label Belarus a dictatorship and continue to roll out the sound bite of the former Bush administration that Lukashenko is 'Europe's last dictator'. As might be expected, all of the claims of administrative, constitutional, democratic and human rights irregularities have always been vehemently denied by the Belarusian government, which seeks to draw on what it sees as the hypocrisy of the international community in its response to conflict within nation states elsewhere and its interference in areas such as the Middle East and Afghanistan. Meanwhile, the political rhetoric around the globe continues apace, while for ordinary people, life in the workplace and at home goes on as before.

TODAY'S POLITICAL CLIMATE As for present opposition to the government within the country, there is very little evidence of any impact today. This has been increasingly the case since the very first presidential election. A number of disparate groups have always existed, loosely headed at one point by Alexander Milinkevich, but they have been unable to agree on a united platform. While opposition rallies are periodically held in Minsk, no group has succeeded in calling on popular support; or at least, enough popular support to produce a groundswell of action to challenge the status quo. New potential opposition leaders emerge from time to time, but they do not remain on the scene indefinitely, merging into the background when activism is followed by political emasculation following a period of imprisonment for tax evasion or some other irregularity; or perhaps flight from the country when the personal risks of continued opposition to the state outweigh the benefits. The independent news analysis agency Belarus Digest has some interesting things to say on the subject of the difficulties faced by ordinary people in sourcing information concerning opposition movements, not least in its reporting of studies on the part of a number of socio-economic and strategic institutes. In October 2013 it was noted that political opposition in the form of parties and movements certainly still existed and was functioning in various forms, notwithstanding persistent suppression, but that its presence in the mass media between April and June 2013 failed to deliver any significant level of public support, even for the most publicly known individuals. Low levels of public trust in opposition politicians and relatively high levels of mistrust were also noted. Almost all opposition personalities functioned exclusively in Minsk, with presence outside the capital in decline. Individual opposition politicians were ranked in terms of their media presence, as were parties and movements but, by the time of the next study in April 2014, new personalities and groups were emerging while others seemed to have disappeared from the scene. Further, most opposition media pronouncements appeared to be reactive in nature, rather than proactively promoting alternative policies. However, greater media presence was noted in the period from July to September 2013, which may herald an attempt to deliver a higher public profile in the run-up to the 2015 presidential election. By August 2014, a number of key potential opposition leaders had declared possible interest in running for president this time around, including former candidate Alexander Milinkevich, though one of the most prominent personalities in the opposition fold, Mikalai Statkievich, also a former presidential candidate, will be unable to stand under current constitutional rules due to a recent period of incarceration. All of this renders it hugely difficult for ordinary people to identify with any individual or party of electoral credibility. In every respect, there is nothing to suggest there will be much change in the run-up to the election in 2015.

In terms of political and social unrest, demonstrations are not uncommon at certain times, most notably significant historical anniversaries and around elections. Oktyabrskaya Square in particular has seen a number of peaceful demonstrations with violent consequences. If there is any suggestion of such an event during your visit to Minsk, avoid venturing out on to the streets at all costs. Violence leading to brutal repression almost always ensues. The 2010 presidential election campaign saw significant instances of violence in clashes between opposition supporters and the police. Indeed, hundreds were arrested (including, it is said, seven of the ten candidates) when thousands took to the streets to protest against perceived irregularities on the occasion of the election itself. Two other specific events have particular significance. In July 2008, a concert in Minsk to mark the annual independence celebrations was rocked by the detonation of an explosive device that injured around 50 people. It is said that President Lukashenko was present at the event at the time of the explosion, although it appears that he was in no danger. The authorities described the bomb blast as an act of 'hooliganism', the term that is usually applied to any show of political opposition. Forensic examinations at the scene suggested that the device was crude and homemade. No individual or organisation claimed responsibility and, in spite of the fact that the state vowed to swiftly bring the perpetrators to justice, no-one stood trial in the aftermath. The fact that this event happened at all was a matter of the greatest surprise to observers of life in Belarus; incidents of this type were at that time almost unprecedented, the only other recorded events being two bomb blasts in Vitebsk in 2005 (also resulting in injuries but no deaths), which the government blamed on criminal elements within society. There was certainly nothing to suggest a political motive. Affairs took on a new dimension with the bombing of the Minsk metro in April 2011, when an explosive device packed with ball-bearings and nails was detonated (apparently by remote control) at Oktyabrskaya station, right in the heart of the city and close to the organs of state. There were 15 fatalities and injuries to hundreds more, with horror and outrage not only inside the country, but also among the international community. At the time, the situation within Belarus was increasingly tense, with an economic crisis of huge proportions gripping the nation. Coincidentally I had a meeting with a government official the very next day after the explosion. I was assured that the event, although a terrible tragedy, was no cause for alarm concerning social stability, because the government knew who was responsible and arrests were imminent. Two individuals were duly taken into custody the following day. Rhetoric at the time was suggestive of allegations of foreign involvement, but this was never developed or proved. When confessions were obtained, a link was established between this and the earlier detonations in 2005 and 2008. No political or terrorist motive was established and although there were suggestions of mental instability on the part of one of the perpetrators (taking the form of an apparent lust for blood), the perpetrators were declared sane. Guilty verdicts followed the suspects' trial and sentences of death were imposed. They were duly carried out with a bullet to the back of the head. Allegations persist to this day in Western media that the process of investigation was a sham, with confessions being obtained under duress and torture. It is even alleged in some quarters that the state's own internal security services were responsible for the outrage.

A COUNTRY AT A CROSSROADS The reality of life in today's Belarus is that prevailing circumstances there do not encourage the development of a properly organised and credible opposition that can offer a real alternative to the present government. Indeed, ordinary people sometimes regard the opposition groups that exist as little more than agitators. Many people are distrustful of their motives and think that no change will come, no matter who is in charge. This may go some way towards explaining why there appears to be so much inertia among the population when it comes to political activism. I try very hard not to discuss politics when I'm in Belarus, whether it's in my official dealings with government departments or around the kitchen table with friends and a bottle of vodka. But I listen to what people say among themselves. The reality is that ordinary people have no time for any individual seeking a political platform. 'They're all the same' is the epithet that most sums up the common view. Despite the crackdowns on opposition media, non-government newspapers can be seen on sale in kiosks and shops, in towns and villages all over the country. And when people read them, they scoff just as much as they do when they read the official word of the state on the pages of government newspapers. And all the while, the president continues to nurture popular support from the 'old guard' with agricultural subsidies and the prompt payment of pensions and salaries (and even percentage increases) to the militia and the armed forces. To this day, there remains an almost romantic affection for what are seen as the good old days of the USSR. While statues of leaders were torn down throughout the former Soviet Union as the Berlin Wall was reduced to rubble, Lenin still stands sentinel on a plinth of granite in every Belarusian town, city and village. Indeed, the government policy remains firmly to bring about ever closer relations with the Russian Federation, if not formal union with the state that many regard fondly as Mother Russia, whose President Putin continues to juggle many balls (if not flaming clubs) all at once in his pursuit of greater power and influence for Russia on the world stage, at the same time as he seeks closer integration within the alliances of Western democracies, or at least, greater access to the global markets that seem to wield more power than the democratically elected governments of nation states.

Today Belarus finds itself with an interesting conundrum. Historically, culturally and economically, there are strong ties with Russia, the neighbour that dwarfs it in every way. The rose-tinted spectacles of those who hark back to the Soviet Union and would welcome the idea of integration or strong federation at the least are a real feature of life here. And the markets of Russia, especially oil and gas, are hugely important to the economy of Belarus. Yet the pull of the West's own huge markets is also strong. For its part, Russia needs a strong ally on its western border, but it also needs to regularly show that ally who is boss. Meanwhile, the European Union and NATO would doubtless welcome the opportunity to push the borders of their sphere of influence ever closer to Russia, but will offer few inducements to Belarus until such time as there is movement in accommodating the need they perceive for significant political and human rights reform. President Lukashenko finds himself right in the middle of two giant markets run by opposing principles of governance, both of which are prepared to offer significant inducements, but only in return for favours.

In recent times, political and social unrest within Ukraine and other of the former Soviet states has led to increased tensions in this part of Europe, adding to the complexity of the dynamics of the relationships, most notably the short-lived hostilities in 2008 between Russia and Georgia, and latterly the terrible events within neighbouring Ukraine, as tensions between the elected government in Kiev

1

and separatists in the east backed by the Kremlin spilled into open hostility and bloodshed. International condemnation followed first the annexation of the Crimea on the part of Russia in March 2014 and secondly the outrage of the Malaysian airliner apparently shot out of the sky just four months later by a ground-to-air missile launched in eastern Ukraine. In this part of Europe, the struggle to establish national and ethnic identities proceeds unabated in the aftermath of the Cold War. Some say that the new line of the Cold War is in the process of being drawn somewhere across the fracture that is presently to be seen within the Ukrainian state. For observers of international relations, diplomacy, society and culture, these are interesting times indeed, while for those living in the disputed areas (and beyond in the case of the families around the world who lost loved ones when the Malaysian airliner was downed), the reality of life is bloodshed, humanitarian crime, loss of life and bereavement. The cycle of human tragedy in this corner of Europe that has endured across the centuries continues to revolve.

Within Belarus, ordinary people go about their daily business with a concerned eye on events further east, and although the strength and stability of the organs of the state lead most to feel reasonably secure (howsoever that stability has been established), still many of my friends there talk about the uncertainty of the consequences for 'when war comes' to Ukraine, as they put it. These are indeed nervous times. Meantime, President Lukashenko continues to hone his political game-playing skills on the international stage, against the backdrop of the strategic and geographical significance of modern Belarus between the European Union and NATO on one side of the country and Russia on the other. Sometimes there is overt criticism of the West, and sometimes there appears to be a thaw in the form of a gesture to appease and mend fences, such as the release from jail of noted human rights campaigner Ales Bialiatski in June 2014. Not much changes in this part of the world.

Two recent examples within days of each other highlight the complexity of the situation. In the run-up to Independence Day on 3 July 2014, Radio Free Europe reported that the president took observers by surprise when, during the entirety of a public speech, he addressed the nation in the Belarusian language for the first time in 20 years. Some saw this as an attempt to distance himself from Russia in the aftermath of that country's annexation of the Crimea. And yet the very next day, Independence Day itself, Bielsat TV noted that Presidents Lukashenko and Putin stood side-by-side at celebrations in Minsk to commemorate the 70th anniversary of the end of the Nazi occupation. The state-run news agency BelTA quoted the Belarusian leader as proclaiming, '[this] symbolises our unity. It says that we were together and we always will be.' He added, says the agency, 'as I said once when I was criticised by some people: do not worry. If need arises, we will stand shoulder to shoulder and will defend ourselves – we will fight back together as we once did.' Then later that day at the opening of the newly relocated Belarusian State Museum of the Great Patriotic War, Bielsat TV reported a message for the West: 'one would assume that western nations should appreciate the contribution of our nations to the Great Victory, however, instead of gratitude we get high-handed dictate and sanctions.' The purpose and intent of the rhetoric can be argued in many different ways, but one thing is certain: ambiguity is everywhere to be seen.

ADMINISTRATIVE AREAS In administrative terms, the country is divided into six provinces, known as *oblasts*, each of which is named after the city serving as its administrative centre, with the *city* of Minsk, which is situated in the *province* of Minsk, having its own unique status. This form of administrative division is a clear inheritance from the days of the Soviet Union. The *oblasts* are further subdivided into *raions*, commonly translated as districts. Local legislative authorities are elected by the residents of each district, while local executive committees are appointed by higher executive authorities. The same applies to each *oblast*, with the leader of the executive authority being appointed by the president himself. The seven administrative provinces are Minsk city, Brest, Gomel, Grodno, Minsk, Mogilev and Vitebsk.

ECONOMY

FROM INDEPENDENCE TO THE PRESENT DAY The period since independence has not been an easy time for Belarus in economic terms but, in spite of difficulties that endure to this day, there are indicators to suggest stability and even a modicum of growth over the entirety of the period, although a major economic crisis in 2011 caused a huge wobble throughout society. This apart, relative stability has been achieved against a background where the Belarusian economy is still believed to be significantly state controlled, and in some ways continues to display characteristics of the economy of the old Soviet Union. The reality of state control is manifested in two ways; first, in the form of business that is directly state owned, state run and therefore entirely state controlled, but also indirectly in the form of a massive edifice of regulations, rules, bureaucracy and red tape that faces any business in private ownership. For both sides of the economy, state and private, there is thus little de facto difference. This means that official statistics showing a steady and incremental rise in private enterprise tell only part of the story. Further, considerable reliance is still placed on the supply of raw materials from the country's gigantic neighbour Russia, while every now and again President Putin flexes Russian muscles and reminds Alexander Lukashenko who is in charge by turning off the tap on the supply of oil and natural gas. Over a third of goods produced in the country are exported to Russia, while almost two-thirds of goods imported come from that source. On its own, therefore, Belarus simply does not have the clout, the money, the influence or even the nous to muscle into the marketplace except under the benevolence of its avuncular neighbour.

Most of the industrial and agricultural enterprises in Belarus remain in state hands, certainly the larger ones. At various points since independence, particularly in the early days, there were experiments with more market-based ventures on an ad hoc and ill-conceived basis, but for the most part the results were spectacularly underwhelming. This was not least because the old-style Soviet mentality of the bosses and the workforce was ill-equipped to survive, let alone flourish, in global markets that were becoming ever more competitive and cut-throat. This remains largely the case.

Today in Belarus, as before, collective state farming dominates agriculture, which is based on cattle and pig breeding, the cultivation of potato, beet, grain and vegetables, milk production and also the processing of timber from the vast areas of forestation in the country. Light and heavy industry features the production of plant, machinery and mechanical vehicles, chemical processing, textiles (particularly linen) and white goods for domestic use. During the 1960s, heavy industry and mechanical engineering, most notably the manufacture of tractors (for which the country is still well known) made a significant contribution not only to the country's own economic stability, but also to the economy of the USSR. In those terms, it was punching well above its weight, for notwithstanding its modest size, the Belarusian SSR was one of the most industrially advanced of the Soviet republics. All of that ended with the fall of the USSR. And of course, the consequential political and social upheaval came at a time when the western republics of the Soviet Union were already struggling with the crippling economic and social impact of the Chernobyl disaster.

In the post-Soviet era of the early 1990s, rudimentary market structures with non-existent governance arrangements in this part of Europe meant there was a free-for-all in state trading between the component former republics. It was all just a little like the Wild West for a while, as could be seen in Russia with the outrageous sale of huge state assets for next to nothing and the subsequent establishment of a powerful oligarchy. One of President Lukashenko's early moves in his first term was the introduction of a hybrid market economy run on socialist lines. The intention was clear; take the best of both worlds to deliver not only stability but also steady growth in safe circumstances. The reality, however, was the tendency for the worst of both to come to the fore. The imposition of stifling bureaucratic and legal controls over market trading, costs and currency exchange, in a culture where the taking of responsibility and the exercise of initiative on the part of business strategists and managers simply did not exist, was never going to work effectively. As can be seen the world over, unregulated markets produce disastrous results in terms of governance and even adherence to the law, while overregulation in abundance cripples initiative and enterprise. And the world over, the search for the happy medium goes on.

Against all the odds, the traditional industries managed to deliver modest but incremental growth in the early years. At first, fledgling private enterprise was crippled by the extent to which the state could directly interfere in the running of a business. Over time this burden has been relaxed to an extent, in the hope that foreign investment might be encouraged. There has been partial success. It is certainly the case that, latterly, money has flowed in from abroad to deliver significant construction projects, both in the residential sector and in the leisure and tourism industry. However, not all negotiations between the government and international backers have been successful. There are reports that a number of high-profile projects have stalled and even been abandoned when foreign corporations simply would not accept the terms the government was seeking to impose. Further, the West's perception of a need for major political reform and a greater commitment to the observance of human rights means that it is not easy for foreign investment to be attracted. It's just as well, then, that even though the tap is periodically turned off, the trade in oil and natural gas with Russia delivers a valuable commodity to Belarus at a knock-down and heavily discounted price, which it then sells on the open market at considerable profit. And goodwill visits to Moscow often see President Lukashenko returning to Minsk with loans of a billion US dollars or more in his pocket.

GOVERNMENTAL STRATEGY Certainly the government sees the importance of competing on the world stage and significant attempts continue to be made to adapt to the ever-changing demands of international trade; but the reality for business in Belarus today is still that elements of the old monopolistic approach on the part of the state are underpinned by rules that appear to manifest as a toweringly bureaucratic monolith of decree, regulation and statutory obligation, such that not only businesses of every size and profile, but also charitable non-governmental organisations, are subject to a rigorous and often debilitating regime of interference on the part of the state. In the past this took the form of random changes to the law, some of which retrospectively applied fresh requirements, all glued together by a burdensome process of complex inspection and monitoring. I even know of one business in the charitable sector that claims it must comply with two sets of directly applicable regulations that are entirely contradictory, such that complying with one set means infringing the other. Whether this says more about the reality of business life in Belarus today, or that element of the national psyche that sees the glass half empty and will find a million ways why something cannot happen (but not a single means of achieving it), is open to debate. I don't know the answer, but I suspect it lies somewhere along the line of a broad and complex spectrum. Official statistics point to a buoyant economy where enterprise, hard work, initiative, lateral thinking and imaginative business practices are rewarded. My informal discussions with ordinary people in cities, towns, villages and homes tell a different story. It's just another example of the ambiguity you find everywhere in this fascinating country.

In late 2008, I attended an international business symposium in London organised by the Belarusian government to extol the virtues of the country's economy. At the time, free markets all over the world appeared on the brink of meltdown following the global crisis that threatened to bring down the economies of nation states and democratically elected governments, in circumstances where the larger global corporations appeared to be able to exercise greater power and influence than those states and their governments themselves. At the time this particular drama still had many acts to unfold; and in the years since, further rumblings have suggested that the crisis certainly wasn't a one-off. The message from the symposium was that the prudence of the Belarusian government's benevolent stewardship of the state's economy was delivering stability, while elsewhere all was chaos and despair. It was said that Belarus was entirely protected from the world crisis. The constant theme of the conference was that these recent events proved without equivocation that the Belarus model represented the right course both to deliver growth and to provide effective protection from the worst excesses of the market. Yet by early 2011, this model was on the brink of collapse. First came rumours of currency devaluation, followed by the inevitable panic among ordinary people to ditch the rouble in exchange for US dollars (and to a lesser extent the euro). Official devaluation by a third preceded one of my visits that spring. Everywhere I went, I saw fear that society was about to implode. People were telling me that the price of ordinary household items such as bread and milk was doubling overnight. Salaries were halved, inflation exceeded 100% and punitive rates of interest rendered borrowing impossible. Everyone was offering me increasingly extravagant rates of black market currency exchange. Signs were appearing in banks that no supplies of dollars were being held there. I particularly recall standing in line at a bank in Vetka, with people whispering to each other. 'Does he have any dollars?' was the urgent refrain. In all my visits over the years, the tension at this time was most palpable. I never once feared for the security of my position or the safety of my money, but I could taste the desperation among everyone I met. The independence from the vagaries of the market that was being so lauded at the London symposium had turned into isolation, with no access to support from Europe and beyond. In spite of it all, both the country and the president survived. Today, there is stability once more. In 2000, GDP stood at 5.8%, but after peaking at over 11% in 2004, it had fallen to 0.9% by 2013. Notwithstanding the claims made at the conference I attended in London, in the aftermath of the global crisis of 2007–08 it stood at a paltry 0.2% in 2009. For 2014, the government itself was predicting modest growth of 3.3%, against its forecast of 8.5% for 2013. Once more there are fears of currency devaluation on the streets of towns and villages, but Russia's own position in the world at present can only impact adversely on its ability to carry its neighbour through any new difficulties. There may be choppy waters ahead.

THE FUTURE In terms of support from the international development community, the most cursory examination of any international funding stream or source of aid, particularly those of the European Union, the World Bank and the International Monetary Fund, shows that compared with other countries in the region, it has been treated extremely partially. At the same time, the call by those in control of the purse-strings for political and human rights reform is a constant backdrop. For years now European Union resolutions have imposed a series of sanctions, including the freezing of the assets of the president and a number of government colleagues. Travel and visa bans to EU countries have also been imposed. These sanctions were a direct consequence of the EU's belief that successive elections have been unlawfully conducted, fraudulent and improper, against a background of human rights abuse, suppression of free speech and the stifling of political opposition. Yet there is nothing to suggest that sanctions and limitations on aid have any effect other than to place the people of the country themselves at the sharp end of hardship.

It is little wonder, then, that from top to bottom, all the way from the president himself to the man and woman walking village streets, there is collective belief still that the very best interests of the country and its people lie in ever closer alignment with the systems and structures of the Russian Federation. From the very beginning of his presidency, Alexander Lukashenko made clear his avowed intention to deliver integration and he embarked on developing policies to achieve this outcome. One of his proposals was to introduce a single currency for a united Russia and Belarus. This has never happened. At the opening ceremony of the first Belarusian-Russian economic forum in Minsk on 6 September 2005, Alexander Lukashenko addressed participants using these words: 'Without losing either country's sovereignty, we aim to develop a unified legal, economic and administrative system to become the foundation for our union state.' While the message of today's rhetoric is less direct, there is nothing to suggest that this aspiration will suffer a volte-face anytime soon. Only time and the government of the Russian Federation will determine the accuracy of its predictive foresight.

PEOPLE

Official figures show that on 1 January 2014, the population of the country was 9,345,000. The earlier census taken in June 2009 revealed the figure then to be 9,663,500, with the count in December 2005 showing 9,750,500. In February 1999 it was 10,045,237. The figures speak for themselves in consistently establishing negative growth rate. News that the population is continuing to fall will come as no surprise to those who know the country, for the leading ambition of many Belarusians, particularly the young, is to find a 'better life' elsewhere, usually in the West.

Government figures suggest that over 130 nationalities call Belarus their home, with by far the largest demographic group being that comprising native Belarusians, who make up 81% of the total population. Russians come next, with 11%, then Poles and Ukrainians, accounting for 4% and 2% respectively. Roughly 80% of the people are classed as belonging to the Russian Orthodox Church and around 10% are believed to be Roman Catholic, with the remaining 10% being Protestant, Jewish or Muslim.

Estimates also show that the diaspora consists of 3–3.5 million native Belarusians residing outside the country's borders, most of them in the United States, Russia, Ukraine and Poland.

The population density is around 45 per km^2 and over 70% of people live in urban areas. Not surprisingly, the most densely populated area is Minsk *oblast*, with 81 people per km^2, while the most sparsely inhabited area is in the north of Vitebsk *oblast*, where the figure is fewer than ten. Approximately 25% of the urban population, 1,921,000 people, live in the capital city, Minsk. Then come Gomel (506,000), Vitebsk (361,000), Mogilev (360,000), Brest (293,000) and Grodno (277,000).

Some 15.7% of the population is aged 14 years and under, with 69.7% being between 15 and 64. Those aged 65 and over account for the remaining 14.6%. The median age is currently 37.2 years. The birth rate is 11.16 births per 1,000 people and the death rate is 14.02 deaths per 1,000 people. The infant mortality rate is 12 deaths per 1,000 live births (as compared with 18.9 in 1994), with the life expectancy at birth being 69.08 years (66 for males and 77 for females). The size of the average family is 3.2 people (2 parents and 1.2 children). In 2003, there were 88 males for every 100 females living in the country. Interestingly, there has been a significant drop in fertility rates from 1.88 children per female in 1994 to 1.43 in 2007.

But all of these statistics (collectively and individually) are just numbers on a page. However commentators choose to interpret them, they say nothing about the national characteristics of the Belarusian people, and only by spending time in the community, getting to know individuals and by earning their trust and respect

FOOLISH BRAVADO AND DESERVED HUMILIATION

One day, hopefully soon, I shall sit down to write a travelogue by way of homage to the many delightful people I have met in 14 years of getting to know this country. It may or may not include the aged *babooshka* whom I was foolish enough, in a moment of utter madness and entirely baseless bravado, to challenge to a drinking contest on one of my first visits. In my head, at least, that's what I was doing. It would not even have occurred to her that this foolish foreigner could be so disrespectful. I cringe inwardly now to think of the naivety and foolhardiness I must have displayed during this and my other early encounters in Belarus. After an evening of sumptuous but simple provender with a group of friends in a rural homestead close to the Russian border, we sat down to exchange traditional songs, tell stories and debate big issues. Almost everyone you meet has an enviable grasp of significant international affairs. The level of intellectual debate on matters of relevance to the future of the planet and to society puts us to shame in the West. One toast followed another as each topic of conversation came to a head, then we reached the point at which only she and I had yet to refuse the inevitable invitation for our glasses to be filled to the brim. Each round, my exhortations that she should drain hers met with a nonchalant look of utter indifference. Her timing was never short of perfect; only when she was ready did she proceed to raise the glass to her lips, then slowly but steadily, drink to the bottom before returning it to the table with precision and a further look of indifference bordering on contempt. I should have seen the signs and backed away in shame. But I persisted. And as my foolish bravado drove me on, she maintained her steady hand, inscrutable visage and a clear resolve to see me off. Through my vodka spectacles I couldn't see the fool I was making of myself. At least my humiliation was decent spectator sport for everyone else there. I didn't admit defeat and back down for at least four toasts after the first dawning look of realisation came into my eyes. And the *babooshka*? The only indication of any slight effect of the vodka was that she sang louder and louder, but no less melodiously. That apart, not a single word passed between us.

can this be revealed. There are many features. Resilience, self-respect, pride, self-discipline, stoicism, hospitality, warmth, generosity, humour and the ability to sing and drink the night away are only some of them. A visit to this fascinating country leaves many indelible imprints on the memory from things that are experienced and seen, but the ones that last the longest are memories of ordinary encounters with everyday people.

Belarusians who are able to do so live close to the earth, and their relationship with nature and the seasons is intense. Spring, summer and autumn are spent tending the land and in preparation for the long, dark winter. Those who live in the town will spend as much time as they can at a modest wooden cottage (*dacha*) owned by someone in their family, while rural dwellers will have their own extensive plot of land at home. The stockpile of produce from the year's labours will then be shared within the community. Indeed, the concept of the extended family is alive and well in Belarus. Whenever I sit down to eat at the table of my Belarusian family, the man of the house will reach for a slice of bread, close his eyes, bring the bread to his nose, inhale deeply, then look solemnly into my eyes and nod his head with a smile of understanding. The sense of a real fondness for and dependence upon the land is a palpable one.

LANGUAGE

Russian and Belarusian have equal status as formally adopted national languages. Belarusian is one of three historic eastern Slavonic languages, all of which have some basis in Cyrillic script. Common elements of grammar and vocabulary can be recognised readily in each of them. And as might be expected, the cycle of development and suppression of the Belarusian language has followed the course of political and social changes across the centuries. In the 1920s, for example, the huge changes in this part of the world following significant armed conflict saw an upsurge in the promotion of Belarusian culture, language and literature. Then in the 1930s, as the people of the Soviet Union were subjugated by Stalin's terrifying political and cultural clampdowns, this blossoming was brutally suppressed. For example, the primary intended outcome of the state's grand 'Reform of Belarusian Grammar' in 1933 was to ethnically cleanse the language of unwelcome historical contamination on the part of neighbouring cultures to the north and west (primarily Baltic and Polish) as well as to remove the perceived archaic colloquialisms romantically in use among Belarusian nationalists (who were seen as a counter-revolutionary threat to the solidarity of the Soviet Union), thereby paving the way for greater integration between the Russian and Belarusian languages. Indeed, the latter was very much seen as the language of the peasantry, a prejudice that endures to this day among some. There was further reform in 1959 and this revision holds good today (with only modest periodic amendment since). During perestroika ('restructuring') in the final days of the Soviet Union, Belarusian and other historical languages among the constituent republics met with a significant revival as new nation states began to emerge. Indeed, in 1990 it was envisaged that the language of all administrative and official documentation of the then Belarusian SSR would change from Russian to Belarusian by the year 2000. Interestingly, this was halted after the election of Alexander Lukashenko as president in 1994, even though he addressed the nation in the Belarusian language on Independence Day that year, an event that was not to be repeated for another 20 years. Following a referendum in 1995 that was not without controversy in some quarters, the Russian language was afforded equal status. At times, following independence, there have been suggestions of further grammatical

Nicky Gardner

The Belarusian language is something of an enigma. In the first year or two after the breakup of the Soviet Union, the language had a huge boost with the media and state institutions promoting the use of Belarusian in the affairs of newly independent Belarus. Unsurprisingly, this generated a degree of angst among those elements of the population who spoke or wrote Belarusian only falteringly. In May 1995, a referendum in Belarus restored the status of Russian as an official language – nominally on a par with Belarusian, but in practice Russian is overwhelmingly dominant, and language activists have highlighted their fears for the future of Belarusian which has now been relegated to second place. A much-reported comment by the country's president, Alexander Lukashenko, allegedly deriding Belarusian as being ill-suited to great thoughts, has done nothing to promote the language.

Yet Belarusian happens to have a rather intriguing history, being one of the few languages with a literary tradition in Arabic, Latin and Cyrillic scripts. Some of the first printed books in central Europe were in Old Belarusian, thanks to the pioneering efforts of Francisk Skoryna from Polotsk (near Vitebsk) who opened a publishing house in Prague in 1517. Skoryna's books used the Cyrillic script. But around the same time, manuscripts were being produced aplenty in the Belarusian lands between Vilnius and Polotsk, and these volumes were rendered in the Arabic script. These early manuscripts were known as *kitabs* (from the Arabic word for book). Many of the scholars who wrote these texts were of Tatar descent, and the tales they recounted in the *kitabs* often had an oriental flavour. Curiously, there were even a few early Polish texts written in the Arabic script. At the same time as some scholars were producing *kitabs*, others were writing Old Belarusian in the Latin script.

By the second half of the 19th century, Belarusian was rendered almost exclusively in the Latin alphabet, although growing contact with a vibrant Russian literary tradition meant that Cyrillic was becoming ever more common. But the story of Belarusian deserves to be better known and the *kitabs* in particular are a remarkable part of the country's cultural heritage.

Nicky Gardner is co-editor of hidden europe *magazine. Find out more about her work at wwww.hiddeneurope.co.uk*

review and reform of the Belarusian language, but there is currently no official word on this. Furthermore, some commentators claim that there has been a de facto reduction in the significance of the Belarusian language over that period, marked by diminishing numbers of specific language schools, books and periodicals. My experience suggests the contrary. Increasingly, public displays in Belarusian are to be seen all over the country, whether in the form of official pronouncements, signs marking public and state buildings, tourist sites or street names. The situation is further complicated by the perception in some quarters that the Belarusian language has been adopted by opposition groups and those sympathising with their cause, as well as by nationalists and intellectual thinkers seeking to establish an independent and romanticised history and culture for the concept of a separate Belarusian identity. I know of one proud Belarusian who refuses to be addressed by me in anything other than his own language, which presents me with something of a challenge. As with so much in this interesting country, the language debate contains elements of myth, cliché, revisionism and romanticism, with truth and reality lying somewhere within the vortex of contradiction and complexity.

On the streets and in homes, the untutored Western eye and ear would discern very little difference between written or spoken Belarusian and Russian. And for observers of eastern European politics and society, it will be fascinating to see which influence prevails; will there be greater linguistic convergence if circumstances force Belarus and Russia closer together socially, politically and economically, or will a tide of Belarusian nationalism see the emergence of an increasingly separate linguistic identity? This is such an interesting part of the world.

RELIGION

Across history, Belarusian lands have been at the crossroads of culture and ideology, where two worlds have often collided, with tragic consequences. Both the West and the East have influenced social, political and ideological development and this applies to **religious beliefs** as much as to anything else. For most of history, there has been peace between the two major Christian churches in Belarus (Orthodoxy and Catholicism), with relations between the two being characterised by at best tolerance and peaceful coexistence and at worst a tacit acceptance on the part of both of the presence of the other. This has certainly been so since compromise resulted in the Brest Church Union of 1596, under which the Orthodox Church of the Grand Duchy of Lithuania ceded the spiritual high ground by recognising the supremacy of Rome, the price of this self-imposed subjugation being permission to maintain its own rites, doctrines and customs. Initially (and inevitably), though, there was still reluctance on the part of Orthodox believers to accept a higher authority in this way. Before the Union, the Orthodox population was very much in the majority, in contrast not only to Catholic believers, but also Jews, Muslims and Protestants. But from the 17th to the 19th centuries, most followers of the Orthodox Church were gradually converted to the Uniate, which maintained many Orthodox traditions and rites. By the end of the 18th century, in fact, Uniate believers made up almost 70% of the population, although today only a small community remains. The balance of 30% comprised 15% Roman Catholics, 7% Jews, 6% Orthodox believers and 2% Protestants and others. The Union eventually came to an end in 1839 when the Uniate Church merged with the Russian Orthodox Church, after which the Orthodox population again predominated, comprising over 60% of the population by the early 20th century.

As traditional Belarusian culture acquired a new prominence towards the end of the 20th century with the seismic changes in politics and dogma of the time, so the **Orthodox Church** came to be regarded both by people and state as a medium for the spiritual foundation of the community. Old eparchies were revived and new ones founded under the administration of a synod headed by the Minsk and Slutsk Metropolitan Filaret, the patriarchal exarch of all Belarus. And by early 2009, the doors of 1,274 Orthodox churches were open for worship, with another 152 under construction. In January 2002, there were 1,119 priests, compared with 399 in 1988.

And yet today a significant section of the Orthodox community still consists of Староверы ('Old Believers'), who first appeared on Belarusian territory in the late 17th century. They adhere to the Orthodox canons that existed in Russia prior to the major reforms of the time. Under Catherine the Great of Russia, they were widely persecuted for their beliefs. Today most live in the Gomel region, with a particularly large community in the district of Vetka. I have good friends in that community, and I look forward to the day when they honour their promise to tell me all about the issues and the persecutions their beliefs have faced across the generations.

The most revered of Orthodox symbols are the saints of the Church, with nearly every place of worship claiming the body or a physical remnant of at least one, as well as prominently displaying significant numbers of icons and other holy relics. Different saints are identified as being associated with different needs or specialisms. At any hour on any day, local people will visit specific icons of particular saints in their local church, praying, incessantly crossing themselves and lighting beeswax candles before them as a sign of faith and by way of an offering. Every church will have at least one corner in which *babooshkas* take charge of stalls selling a huge range of relics, from candles of varying length and girth, to icons of every size and form, for the home, office and even the car.

Indeed, icons are ubiquitous and every home will have a corner of a living room opposite the door as a shrine, in which the most revered and favoured family saint is portrayed in iconic form at the highest point of the room, as close to the ceiling as possible, reverently gazing down from on high to bless the family and its home. At their most ornate, they are painted on wood and covered with gold and silver plate. Other family items of significance such as photographs of elders and of the departed are displayed next to the icon. Icons are not only revered but also treated with great deference, believers vesting them with mysterious and mystical powers. Today, most motorists (devout believers or not) will embark on their journeys with a simple icon on the dashboard or hanging from the rear-view mirror.

Orthodox churches were traditionally built in the shape of a Greek cross and even newly constructed ones bear the hallmark of the familiar onion dome embossed with gold colouring, topped by the familiar Greek cross. Originally built of wood, no nails were ever used in the construction, the whole being held together by the intricacies of the design. Inside, the iconostasis, a sacred wall covered in icons, holy murals and other pictures of saints, closes off the public area from the section to which only priests are permitted access.

On most days of the week, churches are a hive of activity. Participating in an Orthodox service is a stirring and emotionally charged experience. Priests in flowing robes and with the deepest of baritone voices chant prayers and intonations while vigorously swinging incense holders, often with an unseen choir making rousing interventions by means of soaring responses. All the time, believers stand in rapt concentration (there are no chairs), constantly crossing themselves and joining in with the responses. This is absolutely not to be missed, but visitors must be sure to treat the occasion with the utmost respect. Without fail, men should remove hats and women cover their heads. Taking photographs is not a good idea, while purchasing and lighting a candle before an icon will always be regarded favourably.

One of the most moving sights is to witness a less formal ritual involving a junior priest and perhaps one or two *babooshkas*. This is a particularly common event. The priest will recite certain prayers and the ladies will respond with light, beautiful and haunting harmonies. Even sceptical hearts will miss a beat.

Given the history of **Catholicism** in the area and with Polish Catholics on the western border of the country, it is no surprise to find a significant community still in Belarus. Around 10% of the population is Roman Catholic, roughly half of whom are ethnic Poles. Not unexpectedly, the biggest enclave of Catholicism is to be found in Grodno, bordering Poland in western Belarus. In 2009, there were 467 such communities, 161 of which could be found in the Grodno region. In all, there were 451 Roman Catholic churches throughout the country, with another 35 then under construction.

Protestantism (in the form of Lutheranism, Calvinism and Evangelical Christianity) is slowly but incrementally expanding from west to east, although it remains a small community consisting mostly of ethnic Germans.

Judaism in Belarus can be traced back as far as the 9th century, with a number of sizeable communities in existence along the line of the current western border of the country by the end of the 1300s. Only a century later, the upper strata of the Grand Duchy of Lithuania's administrative functions featured Jews in prominent positions. During the 16th century, migrants from countries further west established new communities deeper into Belarusian territory.

Over the course of the next 200 years, successive Russian emperors sought to convert the empire's Jews to the Orthodox faith, on pain of expulsion if they refused. Then in 1791 Catherine the Great established the principle of the Pale of Settlement, the geographical area within which Jews were allowed to make permanent homes. Its borders were susceptible to change until the end of the Romanov dynasty in 1917, when the Pale formally ceased to exist, though the broad thrust over time was an increase in the size of the area. During its existence, one consequence of wars and diplomatic settlements with Russia's neighbours was that the location of lands available for Jews to live on was in a state of flux. At times, new areas came into the Pale, while old ones were removed. All of modern-day Belarus was included, as was a significant portion of European Russia. Beyond the Pale (presumably the derivation of the colloquial saying), a permanent home was broadly denied, though at various times a limited number of categories of Jewish citizenship were exempt from this prohibition under the terms of a formal state dispensation, the criteria for the granting of which were arbitrary and subject to reversal. Enforced removal from certain of the bigger cities encouraged the rise of rural communities known as *shtetls*. At the time of its greatest significance, more than five million Jews lived in the Pale, then the biggest concentration of Jewish settlements anywhere in the world.

The influence of Judaism within the lands now known as Belarus was most significant early in the 20th century, when the Jewish population was in the majority (sometimes up to 90%) in many small towns throughout the country and some of the larger cities. It was common to hear Yiddish spoken all over these towns and cities. Literally meaning 'Jewish', Yiddish is a High Germanic language developed as a fusion of dialects and written in the Hebrew alphabet. Today it is written and spoken in Orthodox Jewish communities wherever they are to be found in the world.

By the end of the Great Patriotic War, the entirety of the Jewish community in Belarus had been all but wiped out as part of the Nazis' 'final solution'. Today, however, there is a new revival as small Jewish communities begin to establish themselves in towns and cities all over the country, notably in Minsk, Grodno, Brest, Vitebsk, Polotsk, Slutsk and Babrusk, as well as in other places. Once more Yiddish is beginning to be spoken and heard among elderly members of these communities, freely and without the need to hide, as new roots are laid down, Judaism is reclaimed and connections are re-established with their Jewish heritage and identity. There are small but fascinating museums of Jewish heritage in Minsk and Brest, together with Jewish memorials and old cemeteries in many locations. Much of historical Jewish Belarus has yet to be rediscovered, with new finds being made all the time. There are many international organisations supporting Jewish community development that can provide in-depth information, broker meetings with members of Belarusian Jewish communities and arrange tours of culture and heritage sites (including to former cemeteries and the small number of synagogues still in existence), as well as being in a position to offer help and support in establishing and finding Jewish roots and heritage, together with assistance in obtaining invitations and visas. There are two with which I personally work. In London, contact British sustainable development charity **The Together Plan** (see page 107 for contact details), while the Belarusian NGO **Dialog** (☏ +375 (29) 627 34 00; e *dialogorganisation@gmail.com*) is based in Minsk. Faultless English is spoken and I commend both of these organisations to anyone with an interest in Belarusian Judaism, past and present.

There was a thriving **Islamic** population at the time of the Golden Horde in the Middle Ages, but in modern times only modest numbers of Tatars still live in the country, although small numbers of new mosques have opened in recent times.

EDUCATION

The system of **education** in Belarus is state administered and funded directly from the budgets of local tiers of government, to which schools report. The structure consists of first kindergarten education, then school education and training, vocational and technical education, secondary special education, higher education, training of scientific and scientific pedagogical personnel and the retraining and self-development of adults. In 2012, almost 71% of preschool children were in full-time education in nurseries and kindergartens, although attendance there is not compulsory. Most children start school at the age of six, and by law all are required to follow the prescribed curriculum up to the age of 15. Nearly all stay on until they finish their high-school education at 18, before entering university. Indeed, Belarus has one of the highest student-to-population ratios in Europe. Most university courses run for five years. The two state languages of Belarusian and Russian are used equally for teaching and training. The whole process is overseen by the state Ministry of Education, which has developed a curriculum that consists of compulsory and optional disciplines. The compulsory modules are society and humanitarianism, nature and science, culture and the arts and physical and sports development. Within this overarching structure, there is a surprising degree of autonomy for schools locally to design their own media for teaching, based on capacity, resources and the wishes of parents. Much of the learning is done by rote. The commitment of teaching staff to the education of the state's children is admirable and beyond question, but it is clear that, in terms of strategic educational planning, there is much progress to be made.

CULTURE

Across the centuries, the maintenance of 'traditional' Belarusian culture (whatever that may mean) has been problematic. Indeed, the first difficulty is to establish the characteristics of that culture, so diverse were the founding influences, the subsequent means of suppression under various regimes and the romantic ideals that have been brought to bear in the search for a separate Belarusian identity and culture.

DRESS The origins of traditional Belarusian dress are as difficult to establish as any area of culture, and at different points in history various sources have been claimed to suit particular political expediency. Some claim that today's perceptions of the foundations owe much to incursions south by the Viking princes in the 9th century, but not surprisingly, dress also displays the influence of the neighbouring countries (Poland, Lithuania, Latvia and Russia) to which at various times throughout history Belarus has been closely linked in terms of statehood, governance, culture and society. Primarily made from wool and hand-produced linen, its key features are straight lines and red and white colouring, often with intricate patterns at the edges (as with the national flag), dependent upon the place of origin. There are many subtle variances of design from region to region and even from district to district. Historically, variances from village to village were not uncommon. The rules of society used to dictate which garments were to be worn on which occasions. For example, it was considered indecent for a man to go outdoors without wearing a particular form of jacket over his shirt. It was also prohibited for married women to go out unless wearing a headdress and apron. For both, it was also considered a minimum standard of decency for the neck, elbows and knees to be covered. Special attention was paid to female clothing at festival times, reflecting the status of women in Belarusian culture as mothers and home-keepers. Today, examples of national dress are displayed in museums up and down the country. It is most frequently worn at festivals and special occasions such as weddings, or at events promoted for the edification of foreign tourists. It remains the most prominent embodiment of traditional culture and can most often be seen at public commemorations of special events in history, in tableaux presented on national days or in state processions.

CRAFTS Traditional crafts include pottery, wood engraving and plait work with straw, willow, root and bark. Again, examples are displayed in museums in even the smallest of towns. The most notable and uniquely attributable example of Belarusian folk art is the *rushnik*, or ceremonial towel. Flaxen threads are woven together, usually on looms of historic design, to form delicate silvery white and grey geometric patterns, with ancient symbols featuring in the woven or embroidered decoration of symbolic red colouration at the edges. Each village will have its own specific design. When news of the Nazi invasion was broadcast in 1941, it is said that *babooshkas* in villages all over the country set about weaving *rushniki* in order to protect their homes from the rampaging hordes. These sacred items have a very significant place in the hearts and lives of Belarusians. Not only have they long been used for practical and decorative purposes, but they also have an important role in the performance of certain rites, such as those at family meals on national holidays, weddings, christenings, funerals and for welcoming guests to the home with bread and salt. *Rushniki* are commonly to be found draped over icons, both in church and at home. The village of Nyeglubka, in Vetka district of Gomel *oblast* down in the southeast, has a traditional weaving school (see page 288) where students learn the old ways of crafting this most iconic of Belarusian symbols.

CUISINE Traditional cuisine displays the same diversity of influence as dress and crafts, although the common perception is that it largely resembles that of Lithuania. Travellers who have been to other parts of eastern Europe will encounter much that they have seen before and little that they will not have seen. Great significance has always been attached to bread, both as a staple foodstuff and as an important symbol in many rituals. The potato forms the basis for many meals (historically referred to as 'second bread') and the plentiful supply of mushrooms in the forests that extensively cover the land ensures their prominence in many recipes. The best-known traditional dish is *draniki* (potato pancakes), usually served with a rich pork stew in pots, the meal liberally lubricated with the ubiquitous elixir of life, vodka. Only moderate seasoning is used in cooking.

LITERATURE Many of the chronicles written in the 12th and 13th centuries endure today both as historical records and as works of great literature in their own right. The only earlier examples of literature that are known to have existed are religious works from the 11th century. The ancient Belarusian language was granted state legitimacy when Belarusian lands were subsumed within the Grand Duchy of Lithuania, a significant event that made a real contribution to the development of literature in the 14th to the 16th centuries. The earliest literary figure of repute was the humanist and scientist Francisk Skoryna, who was a well-known writer and translator in the ancient city of Polotsk. Between 1517 and 1519 he translated much of the Bible into the ancient Belarusian written language for the first time, before publishing his work in Prague and Vilnius. This was one of the first acts of mass printing in book form in Europe. In 1562 the philosopher Simon Budny, a renowned figure of the European Reformation as a publicist and translator, published the first printed book in ancient Belarusian on the territory of modern Belarus.

In the 1600s the Belarusian-Russian poet, playwright and enlightener Simeon of Polotsk was a prolific figure. He introduced the grand Baroque style of writing which was followed up to the first half of the 19th century, when new trends of Romanticism began to reflect the living language and folklore of the population in a sentimental homage to the perceived idyll of self-styled 'traditional' bucolic life. The most prominent figure of this movement was the great Polish-Belarusian poet Adam Mitskevich. He was born in the district of Novogrudok and dedicated his great epic poetic work *Pan Tadeush* to his homeland. At the same time, Vincent Dunin-Martinkevich, who is considered by many to be the father of modern Belarusian literature, began to consolidate his reputation with the publication of notable collections of verses. Another prominent figure at the end of the 19th century was Frantishek Bogushevich, a poet who is credited as being the first national writer of folklore. The first nationalist newspapers to be granted lawful status, *Nasha Dolya* ('Our Lot') and *Nasha Niva* ('Our Cornfield'), served as a useful public platform to promote the works of such eminent writers as Yanka Kupala, Yakub Kolas, Eloisa Paskevich, Maxim Bogdanovich, Maxim Goretsky and others, in the form of plays, prose and dramatic poetry imbued with the Romantic and patriotic ideal of independent nation statehood.

After the October Revolution in Russia in 1917, national and revivalist themes dominated Belarusian literature as part of the movement to encourage Belarusians to adopt greater self-awareness and identification of their heritage. As with the Belarusian language itself, this was dealt a severe blow by the ideological repressions of the 1930s but, as is often the case, suppression and persecution begat creativity in the form of a number of magnificent works of poetry and drama by artists such as Vladislav Golubok, Mikhas Charot, Vladimir Dubovka, Kondrat Krapiva and Pavlyuk Trus. During the Great Patriotic War, art and satire were particularly powerful tools, as well as poetry and heroic novels. The theme of the war, especially in the context of suffering and misery, dominated the Belarusian and Soviet literary landscape for a long time, notable examples in prose form being *Deep Flow* and *Troubled Happiness* (Ivan Shamyakin), *Unforgettable Days* (Mikhas Lynkov), *Khatyn Story* (Ales Adamovich) and *Neidorf* (Ivan Ptashnikov). Classic epic poems included *Blockade* by Rygor Borodulin and *It Doesn't Pain the Dead* by Vasil Bykov. As the destruction of wartime was replaced by regeneration and rebuilding in the peace that followed, the perceived idyll of rural life began to be promoted again, generally with an abundance of over-sentimentality, this time in the works of Melezh, Adamchik, Streltsov and others, while historical themes and heroic traditions again found a voice as well, the most famous proponent being the brilliant Vladimir Korotkevich.

The 1950s through to the 1970s saw the emergence of many notable poets, novelists and dramatists, such as Sergei Zakonnikov, Viktor Kozko and Nikolai Matukovsky. After 1986, the Chernobyl catastrophe began to feature as a dark and sombre theme, most notably in the works of Shamyakin, Alexyevich, Karamazov and Buravkin.

MUSIC Musically, Belarus boasts a mixture of artists and styles. Folk music derived from the culture of the east Slavic tribes, the Krivichi, Dryhavichy and Radzimichy, is particularly prominent; consistent themes through the ages have included the adventures of dynastic families and also a celebration of farming through the seasons. As with so much of the tradition and culture of the Belarusian people, the historical realities of suppression and of life inextricably linked to the land have been the inspiration for many an epic song chronicling the lives of farm labourers, peasants, workers and revolutionaries. A new form of musical expression, that of the stirring melody and heroic lyric, was born out of the escapades and heroism of the partisans and guerrillas in the Great Patriotic War. Today, a number of higher-education establishments in the country are devoted to the promotion and study of the theory, history and practice of musical folklore. *Skomorokhs* (travelling minstrels) were the first to perform secular music in the early Middle Ages, but they were also prominent in promoting ritualistic songs and chants (such as canticles and psalms), which formed part of religious ceremonies.

The tide of Belarusian musical culture was to ebb and flow over the course of the 20th century according to the prevailing political circumstances of the times. In more recent years, new groups have formed, such as Pesnyary, Syabry, Palats, Krama and Troitsa, all of whom inject a more modern rock feel to traditional songs, but without losing sight of their heritage. The number of festivals devoted to ethnic music has also increased, attracting significant popular support not only through attendance at the events themselves, but also through high-profile television networking. A number of the more prominent Belarusian performers are showcased regularly in Poland and Lithuania, where substantial Belarusian communities still exist as a result of the many changes in national boundaries in this part of Europe over the centuries. Rock music is hugely popular among the youth of the country, the most famous Belarusian band being Lyapis Trubyetskoi. Until they announced an intention to split in August 2014 after 25 years together, the guys had been on the scene since the early 1990s, their popularity never waning during a highly successful career. Of more dubious worth culturally is Belarus's enthusiastic participation in the pan-European 'Eurovision Song Contest' since 2004, the country finishing one place above the United Kingdom in 2010. The UK came last.

THEATRE AND BALLET Traditional theatre was based on folk rituals and games, relying originally upon the work of strolling minstrels to spread its influence. This is not unique to Belarus, of course; far from it. Puppet theatres were particularly popular in the 16th century, a tradition that continues to this day, with most towns boasting their own. Popularity with children here is still very high indeed. Theatre schools gained widespread support in the 16th to 18th centuries, and in the latter half of the 18th century performances were regularly given by theatre companies that were established and sponsored by rich magnates and estate owners, under whose patronage many of them flourished. Some of these companies consequently acquired professional status. The National Academic Theatre was established in 1920 under Zhdanovich, followed by the second Belarusian State Theatre in 1926, in the town of Vitebsk. The 1930s saw steady progress in the staging of plays devoted to historical events, but during the Great Patriotic War most troupes suspended their theatre-based activities, preferring instead to take their shows on the road wherever possible to visit active army units at the front and to maintain focus on keeping the morale and spirits of troops and civilians alike as high as possible. Today, festivals promoting the dramatic arts are regularly held all over the country, featuring artists from home and abroad.

The history of professional ballet dates back to the middle of the 18th century, and in modern times the **National Academic Bolshoi Theatre of Ballet of the Republic of Belarus** has gained an enviable reputation, notwithstanding the higher profile of its equivalent in Moscow. Today, every town of significant size will have its own flourishing opera and ballet theatre. Any opportunity to attend a performance of Belarusian ballet in Minsk should be eagerly taken; the standard is high, the price of admission ridiculously cheap by Western standards and there is a degree of informality about proceedings that lends itself to a most enjoyable experience. The audience is always full of children and families, with the dress code being relaxed in the extreme. No-one stands on ceremony, but unfortunately this has a downside. It is particularly unnerving, for example, to hear the occasional ringing of a mobile phone during a performance, and then hugely irritating when the call is actually answered.

In the West, take every opportunity you can to see performances of the **Belarus Free Theatre** company (66 *The Cut, London SE1 8LZ;* \ *0207 922 2998;* e *info@ belarusfreetheatre.com; www.belarusfreetheatre.com*). Established in 2005 in Belarus, part of the company still performs underground in Minsk at risk of being raided, though the founding members left to escape persecution in 2011 (finding political asylum in London). The very informative website will tell you all you need to know.

FINE ARTS The history of fine art as a synthesis of cultures from the East and West can be traced back to the second half of the 14th century. The development of icon painting and the production of book miniatures were greatly influenced by the art and folklore traditions of Byzantium, including a high level of manuscript illumination art. After the October Revolution in 1917, the town of Vitebsk, still renowned for its links with the arts, became the centre of the revolutionary avant-garde movement, enabling brilliant and talented artists to forge their reputations. Perhaps the most famous of them all was Marc Chagall. Born in Vitebsk in 1887,

Chagall gained his primary artistic education in the studio of the well-known painter Jehuda Pen, before studying in France. Upon his return to Vitebsk, he founded, lived and worked at an arts school that attracted all of the best talent of the day from around the country. Today, the house where Chagall spent his youth is a popular visitor destination. For more on Chagall and his significant influence on Belarusian culture, see pages 237–8. When the ideological oppression of the Soviet Union was lifted in the early 1990s, artistic life became more dynamic and much more diverse. Design, photography and computer graphics became new media for expression, while the avant-garde movement of the Vitebsk art school also found new life.

Today the art scene continues to thrive as a form of expression not only for mainstream ideas, but also as a voice for contemporary underground movements. Minsk has a number of excellent galleries where works of historical significance rub shoulders with constantly changing exhibitions showcasing the work of modern artists. It's the same in all of the major cities. Indeed, the work of artists old and

THE BATHHOUSE CULTURE

The *banya* (bathhouse) is a distinct feature of rural Belarusian life, and you should gleefully accept any invitation to partake of its riches. Traditionally made of wood, it stands in the garden of a dwelling house, perhaps close to the river or stream in the rural hinterlands, though there are also communal public bathhouses within centres of population. Inside is a wood-heated stove containing stones. The stove is fuelled up ready for use over the course of the day and when the operating temperature is reached the door to the stove is opened and water is thrown on to the stones to create intense amounts of steam. Participants throw water and sometimes beer on to the hot stove to create a fragrant, steam-filled atmosphere. To enhance the whole experience, they slap each other with a sheaf of oak or birch twigs and leaves tied together in a bundle. This is done firmly and enthusiastically in order to exfoliate the skin. Usually, the sheaf has been soaked for a few days prior to use in natural oils. This intense aroma, when added to the steam, makes for a very heady atmosphere.

Three separate activities make up a complete cycle. First, participants sit in the bathhouse, on wooden slatted benches, to begin the process of perspiration. This initial phase normally lasts for ten to 15 minutes before everyone takes a breather by sitting in the small anteroom (which is not much bigger than a large cupboard, but considerably cooler than the steam room) and having a beer. To maintain hydration, naturally. In the second phase, guests are invited to lie across a bench, first on their front and then on their back, while the host whacks them with the sheaf. Guests then return the compliment. At this point everyone repairs to the anteroom for another gulp or two of beer. Then it's back in for the final time, to thoroughly wash and rinse your tingling body with soap and water heated by the stove and decanted into a large metal bowl. Cold water will also be at hand and you can expect your hosts to be playful with it. Afterwards, everyone relaxes together in the anteroom with more beer and occasionally vodka, in which case the sensation of intoxication, after all that perspiring, is almost instantaneous. At this point, if you are deep in the country, expect to be invited to jump in the river or lake. If you are really lucky, it will be winter and you will be encouraged to roll in the snow.

new is commendably accessible throughout the country. One of my personal contemporary favourites is Vladimir Shappo, whose studio is to be found in Minsk (*www.shappo.org*).

UPDATES WEBSITE

You can post your comments and recommendations, and read the latest feedback and updates from other readers, online at www.bradtupdates.com/belarus.

2

Practical Information

WHEN TO VISIT

The likely assumption for the uninitiated is that since Belarus used to be part of the Soviet Union, the weather will always be grey, featureless and, in winter, bitingly cold. This is only partly correct. Each of the four seasons is distinct and boasts its own features. Winter is indeed bitingly cold for the most part, with the first snows tending to fall in late November, but the temperature does not plummet until the turn of the year. December is often wet and slushy. Come January, the thermometer can free-fall to the minus 30s, with long periods of snow accompanied by bitter winds. The scenery can be dramatic: clear blue skies, a watery sun, heavy frosts and thick, immovable, impenetrable ice. But these conditions tend to be the exception rather than the rule, and for the most part the temperature averages around –7°C with consistent and regular snowfall. It is a time when most people remain indoors unless necessity drives them outside to work or study.

Spring is a time of intense activity in the fields. This is also the time to see storks on the wing and nesting atop the high poles that are erected in villages for this very purpose. The temperature is generally warm and welcoming. Summers can be extremely hot with temperatures into the 30s, while biting insects are voracious in forests and near to water. Be sure to wear long trousers and clothing buttoned to the neck and wrists, accompanied by some form of insect repellent, particularly at dusk. But don't be discouraged: this is a time of long days, balmy evenings, glorious sunrises and sunsets, a verdant landscape and fresh produce in the markets and by the roadside. As if to store up reserves of fresh air and sunshine for those long winter nights, people spend as much time outdoors as they possibly can. In rural areas, this means tending the fields, while in the town, the promenade remains a favoured pastime.

Autumn is a glorious time to be in Belarus. Summers tend to last well into September, but come harvest time in October, the colours of the fields and forests simply take your breath away. There is no real diversity of colour but, almost everywhere as far as the eye can see, a golden scene stretches into the distance. One Sunday predawn morning in October, I left Mozyr in the south by car in pitch darkness to catch a lunchtime flight from Minsk. As the first rays of the sun began to illuminate the landscape with a deep and warm glow, followed by brilliant bursts of gold, the song 'Fields of Gold' was playing on the radio. I know that's a really twee story to tell, but it was a lovely moment and one that I am very pleased not to have missed.

The intensity of the Belarusian people's relationship with the land (and by association, with the seasons) means that holidays and festivals are imbued with heavy symbolism and significance. Orthodox Christmas is celebrated on 7 January, when Grandfather Frost (the eastern Slavic equivalent of Santa Claus) brings traditional presents and sweets for children. Anyone who is horrified by the nightmarishly cynical commercialism of Christmas in the West is encouraged to spend this time of year in Belarus, just to restore a little faith. In recent times, fireworks have

EASTER, VODKA STYLE

On Easter Day in small rural communities, everybody greets everyone else, stranger or friend, with a shake of the hand and a hearty 'Christ is risen!' The response is always the same: 'He is risen indeed!' I remember my first Easter Day in Belarus with much affection. The church procession and service late on the Saturday night had been an intense experience, as is always the case with religious festivals. Breakfast the following morning was a bounteous affair of home-produced foods, with the family patriarch Valeri and I exchanging toasts of locally distilled vodka. He and his wife Tanya then invited me out for the day on a forest picnic. We walked deep into the forest for several hours, pausing regularly for them to show me wild flowers and insects and to explain about the natural order of things here, before resting on the bank of the river, with a mountain of home-prepared provender and, inevitably, another half bottle of vodka. We walked (a little unsteadily) back in the direction of the town and then made for the home of Valeri's mother. She had been waiting patiently for some hours with food on the table. Unfortunately food wasn't all that was on the table. In honour of our visit on this holiest of holy days, the *babooshka* had decreed that only a drink of a rare and exquisite vintage could match the solemnity of the occasion. And so it was, after a day's serious drinking and as the sun slipped slowly away from a sky of astonishing crimson, that Valeri and I were to be found deep in animated conversation on international and political affairs, drinking to the very bottom of a bottle of home-distilled vodka and then holding each other up as we staggered home in an extravagant zigzag from one side of the road to the other, Tanya giggling as she brought up the rear, poised to pick us up when we fell over. The rest of the evening passed in a blur.

become a widespread feature on the evening of 6 January, though safety precautions leave a little to be desired. I once spent an interesting 6 January night in Vetka's Red Square, with people letting them off all over the place. This holiday used to be followed on the night of 13 January by observance of the symbolic passing of the old year, or *Kaladya*, with young people parading in fancy dress, often as animals, singing traditional Kaladya songs as they walked from one house to another, with homeowners treating them to edible delicacies as they passed through. Today, this is more of an image from a romanticised version of life in Belarus, though the tradition is certainly still observed on the part of some over the Christmas/New Year period. Historically, Kaladya represented a ritualistic celebration of the coming and passing of the winter solstice.

By tradition, late February or early March used to see the symbolic observance of the passing of winter (*Maslenitsa*) in the run-up to Orthodox Easter. Again, observance is much less widespread today than it used to be and, like Kaladya, it speaks more of homespun cliché than of reality. In rural parts of the country you are more likely to see the tradition upheld. In times gone by, people would bake pancakes, the shape and colour of which symbolised the growing strength of the sun with the coming of spring.

Orthodox Easter is the biggest festival in the religious calendar. In rural communities especially, the woman of the house will spend all day on Easter Saturday preparing food to be blessed by the local priest, before taking it by hand (and generally on foot) to church. At midnight, families congregate at their local church and parade three times around the outside of its perimeter in solemn procession behind the priest, carrying beeswax candles and thinking positive thoughts for good fortune. After returning home in the early hours, everyone except the matriarch (who has much still to prepare and cook) will go to bed, then wake to a sumptuous feast that has by then received the solemn blessing.

The first day of May (Labour Day), 9 May (Victory Day) and 3 July (Independence Day) are celebrated exuberantly with all the pomp and ceremony that used to be associated with the Soviet Union (especially Victory and Independence days). Town and village centres are taken over by parades of young people, war veterans, local dignitaries, the emergency services, the army and every conceivable representative body of civic society. Traditional costumes, singing and dancing are everywhere to be seen. The long days of summer then form the backdrop to many outdoor festivals celebrating the folklore and traditions that are the bedrock of modern Belarus (or at least, its own vision of its past). *Kupalye*, celebrated over the night of 6–7 July, is the most mysterious of them all. It represents an acknowledgement of the significance of the summer solstice in the same way that Kaladya observes its winter cousin. There are clear parallels with the observance of pagan festivals and rituals on the longest day the world over. Legend has it that at midnight on this date and no other, the flower of a particular variety of fern unfolds and that the one who finds it will be blessed with eternal youth, happiness and the gift of foresight. In rural areas, young men still set off into the forests hoping that this is the year when a miracle will occur and they will find the mythical flower. Meanwhile, girls pick field flowers, bind them into wreaths and float them down streams for single young men to collect them, thereby enabling the girls to discover their destiny and learn of the one whom they will marry. It's all about fertility, you see; and although it all sounds incredibly kitsch, the reality is that some young people in villages and small communities really do engage with this festival.

HIGHLIGHTS

Belarus offers much more to experience and to see than a single visit will allow, but a week would make for a fascinating, if intense, first trip. It is not possible to see all of the key centres of interest in that time, so be selective. The best advice is to visit Minsk and probably at least one other of the big towns, plus as much of the rural hinterland in-between as can be accommodated in the time available. Below are some of the top sights, in no particular order.

MINSK The capital city and living monument to the grandeur of post-war Soviet urban planning, where expansive boulevards, stretches of water and vast green areas guard the last piece of the Old Town that the Nazis could not destroy. It's also home to 17 museums, 12 theatres and 38 palaces and centres of culture. See pages 115–67.

NATIONAL MEMORIAL COMPLEX AT KHATYN Just 54km from the capital, this complex commemorates the hundreds of villages the Nazis razed to the ground in the Great Patriotic War. See pages 176–80.

BELARUSIAN STATE MUSEUM OF FOLK ARCHITECTURE AND RURAL LIFE Near the village of Strotchitsa, 12km from Minsk. See pages 175–6.

MUSEUM TOWNS Make time to visit the museums and sites of the historical towns of **Mir**, **Njasvizh** (both UNESCO World Heritage Sites), **Novogrudok**, **Pinsk** and **Polotsk**. See pages 168–70, 170–2, 172–4, 202–3 and 243–50.

BREST This frontier town in the southwest of Belarus, home to the hero-fortress, is where religious history was made in the 16th century (see pages 195–8) and where eastern and western Europe meet, at the symbolic gateway to the old Soviet Union. See pages 183–202.

GRODNO Located near the Polish border, on the banks of the Nieman River, Grodno has beautiful architecture (including the stunning Polish cathedral) and historic Lithuanian connections. See pages 209–24.

KOMOROVO This village community, close to the Lithuanian border, has its own microeconomy and the administration is run strictly along sustainable development lines, based on traditional crafts and cottage industries. See page 95.

VITEBSK The birthplace of the painter Marc Chagall, with many summer arts festivals and rich artistic traditions. See pages 227–42.

MOGILEV With its historical centre and the beautifully restored Leninskaya Street, this is the city where the last tsar of Russia, Nikolai II, had his final residence. See pages 255–66.

GOMEL The country's second-largest city, which is home to the impressive park, palace and cathedral complex founded by Prince Rumyantsev in the 18th century. See pages 267–85.

VETKA This town and district, home to 'Old Believers', has a world-class museum of iconography, the traditional weaving school at Nyeglubka, historic churches and locations of considerable ecological interest. See pages 285–7.

NATIONAL PARKS Be sure to visit **Byelovezhskaya Puscha** (the third UNESCO World Heritage Site in Belarus), **Braslav Lakes**, **Berezinsky**, **Narach** and **Pripyatsky** national parks, where the wilderness and biological diversity of the country can be enjoyed in a glorious celebration of the natural world and where ecological tourism is steadily beginning to take hold. See pages 5, 203–7, 251–2, 252–3 and 288–9.

SUGGESTED ITINERARIES

Although the main tourist sites (identified in the previous section) form a good basis for the structure of a visit, the best way to get to the heart of the country and its greatest treasure, its people, is to strike out alone. The task should not be underestimated, for to do so is not in the least easy. One of the hang-ups from the days of the old Soviet Union is a complete lack of understanding of the concept of the independent traveller. It also says much for the hospitality of the Belarusians that they are keen to share their country's riches by offering personal guides to everything that there is to experience. This means that guided tours will certainly show you a great deal, although the level of control over the structure and pace of arranged itineraries will not suit the traveller with an urge for personal discovery. Overall, in the context of discovering and experiencing as much as possible, the arguments in favour of either independent or guided travel are very finely balanced, but perhaps the safest option, certainly if you are on a first visit and don't have contacts in Belarus, is to stick to the main travel agencies. A major advantage of this option is that the process of obtaining an entry visa will be considerably simplified (see *Red tape*, pages 50–5). Then, after your first experience of spending time here, you will have gained the confidence to head out solo on subsequent visits. Here are some options for that first trip but be warned; there's a huge amount packed into each, with little or no downtime to catch your breath!

FIVE DAYS
- Cities, history, the arts and folklore: Minsk–Khatyn–Dudutki–Strotchitsa–Vitebsk–Polotsk–Minsk
- Cities and history: Minsk–Grodno–Brest–Minsk
- Cities, ecology and sustainable development: Minsk–Berazhina and Narach national parks–Komorovo–Minsk
- Cities and museum towns: Minsk–Mir–Njasvizh–Novogrudok–Minsk

ONE WEEK
- Western Belarus: Minsk–Grodno–Byelovezhskaya Puscha National Park–Brest–Pinsk–Minsk
- Eastern Belarus: Minsk–Polotsk–Vitebsk–Mogilev–Gomel–Minsk

Both of these week-long trips would include visits between cities to ecological and historical sites of interest.

TWO WEEKS The following will deliver the full experience of city and nature, arts and culture, history and society, but you might just need a holiday to get over it!

- Three nights: Minsk (with day trips to Khatyn, Dudutki and Strotchitsa)
- Two nights: Grodno via Mir, Njasvizh and Novogrudok
- Two nights: Brest via Byelovezhskaya Puscha National Park
- One night: Mozyr via Pinsk and Pripyatsky National Park
- Two nights: Gomel (with day trips to Vetka and locations affected by Chernobyl)
- One night: Mogilev
- Two nights: Vitebsk (with a day trip to Polotsk)
- One night: Minsk (with a final round-up of activities, including a performance of the State Ballet Company) via Berazhina National Park

TOUR OPERATORS AND TOURIST INFORMATION

OUTSIDE BELARUS There are few tour operators in the UK offering programmes for visits to Belarus. If you point your computer's search engine at 'Belarus tour operators in the UK', you will find links to a number of information websites hosted by travel experts providing basic data on possible trips, with links to partner organisations who will take care of the detail of the arrangements, in terms of booking flights, accommodation, transport, etc. To arrange a bespoke tour via a one-stop agency with ATOL protection, try **Regent Holidays** (*see ad, 2nd colour section; 6th Floor, Colston Tower, Colston Street, Bristol BS1 4XE;* ✆ *020 7666 1244;* e *regent@ regentholidays.co.uk; www.regent-holidays.co.uk*), which offers a 'Best of Western Belarus' tour from £940 for eight nights. Alternatively, **Explore Worldwide Limited** (*Nelson House, 55–59 Victoria Road, Farnborough GU14 7PA;* ✆ *0843 634 5157;* e *sales@explore.co.uk; www.explore.co.uk*) offers small group tours ('Belarus Explorer' and 'Russia, Belarus and the Baltics') from £950 for 10 days without flights.

For those with a specific interest in wildlife and particularly birdwatching, a number of organisations in the UK are promoting bespoke tours, including

The Travelling Naturalist Wildlife Holidays (*PO Box 3141, Dorchester, Dorset DT1 2XD;* \ *+44 1305 267994;* e *info@naturalist.co.uk; www.naturalist.co.uk*). The company's 'Fabled Marshes and Primeval Forests' eight-day tour is priced at £1,945 and the maximum size of the group is 14.

The paucity of general agency support outside Belarus itself will present no obstacle to the intrepid traveller, however, as the internet is now a mine of information on anything you might need to know in tourism terms. Just point your favourite browser at 'Belarus' and settle back for a good read. Recommended websites are www.belarus. by (the country's own official website), www.belarustourism.by (the state's national agency), www.belarusguide.com (an independent virtual guide to the country), www.belarus.net (a vast information and data network), www.belarusdigest.com (an extremely interesting independent source of objective information aimed at the English-speaking world), www.belarustoday.info (for news, current affairs and culture), www.belarus-online.com (a listings site of internet resources on all matters Belarusian) and www.belarus-misc.org (as you might expect from the title, a miscellany of information with a particular emphasis on politics). For region-specific information go to the sites of the *oblast* executive committees, all of which have English pages, as follows: www.minsk-region.gov.by, www.brest-region.gov.by, www.grodno-region.gov.by, www.vitebsk-region.gov.by, www.mogilev-region.gov.by and www.gomel-region.by. Additionally, the executive committees of the six cities all have their own English sites; in each case, type the name of the city into your browser followed by the suffix '.gov.by'. Many Belarusian tour operators have their own informative websites in English, with operators speaking good English at the other end of a phone line or computer terminal to take care of your needs directly.

Additionally, the Belarusian embassies in the UK and the USA both have information on Belarusian tour operators as well as stocks of brochures, leaflets and business cards (see *Embassies*, pages 55–6).

IN BELARUS In Belarus itself are a large number of tour operators, many acting under the umbrella of the **National Tourist Agency of the Republic of Belarus**, its main outlet being the excellent and enormously helpful web-based resource at www. belarustourism.by, which also signposts visitors to many other related resources. The Agency was established by the State Ministry of Sport and Tourism in December 2001 to promote and co-ordinate overall support for the tourism market. It aims to develop the tourism potential of Belarus, certify hotels and tourist services, and train tourism professionals. It has made good progress in the last couple of years with its PR strategy, and an increasing number of written materials are available in English. The marketplace for independent tourist agencies that are not part of the state system is beginning to flourish and there are now hundreds of stand-alone organisations, with new ones opening up for business all the time. However, do take care to check credentials and bonding arrangements before making any financial or contractual commitments. The following is a selection of the largest and most oft-used companies in operation, both state and independent. They are well known, have been prominent in the sphere for a number of years and have established reputations for decent service. For my part, I always use **Belarus Prime Tour** and have done since 2009 for all of my travel requirements within Belarus.

AlatanTour 33B Internatsionalnaya St, Minsk 220030; \ +375 17 227 74 17; e incoming@ alatantour.com; www.welcomebelarus.com. Operating since 1993, this private company continues to maintain its reputation as one of the country's leading tour operators, offering a full range of services for private & business travel, including agro- & ecotourism, as well as Jewish heritage tours.

Association of Agro- and Ecotourism 'Country Escape' 6 Dunina-Marshinkyevicha St, Minsk; +375 17 205 01 74/04 65; e info@ruralbelarus. by; www.ruralbelarus.by. Active in the market for over 10 years, this is a key co-ordinating body for the development of ecological tourism. The Association maintains a database of properties that are available for rent and can help with bookings, though most Belarusian tourist agencies will also have access to the same information & will be able to assist with making the necessary arrangements. This is a fast-developing market that in truth still has some way to go in terms of its strategic development. One of the significant players in ecological tourism in the country is Eduard Voitekhovich, a forward-thinking visionary who has helped many small enterprises throughout Belarus to develop microeconomies in rural tourism. Eduard is the director of the LLC Development Centre of Rural Entrepreneurship at Komorovo in the north of the country, a splendid facility where traditional crafts & ways of living are encouraged to flourish (*14 Zelenaya St, Komorovo, Myadel district, Minsk region;* +375 17 973 73 94/73 04 or 29 627 27 89; e center@komarovo.com) (see box, *Living the good life*, pages 90–1).

Belarus Prime Tour (See ad, page 112) 40A Orlovskaya St, Minsk; +375 17 334 02 27/29 162 62 70; e incoming@belarusprimetour.com; www. belarusprimetour.com. This is my own partner of choice in all matters concerning Belarus tourism. I have worked with the company (an independent operation) for a number of years and have recommended their services to many travellers,

all of whom have been well served. I commend the company to you. The full range of services that all other agencies offer are available here, but the company will always go the extra mile in delivering beyond industry standards, including specialist activities, cultural events & individually tailored tours.

Belarus Tour Service (See ad, 2nd colour section) 89-20A Rosa Luxemburg St, Minsk 220036; +375 17 200 56 75; e service@welcome.by; www.belarustravel.by. Another company with a track record of long-standing service in visa support, hotel bookings, local excursions & bespoke guides.

Belintourist 19 Pobediteley Av, Minsk 220004; +375 17 226 91 00; e incoming@belintourist. com; www.belintourist.com. In business for over 55 years, Belintourist is the long-established national tour operator, specialising in visa support, hotel accommodation, transport & transfers & booking a diverse range of specialist tours & excursions.

Top-Tour 22 Chkalova St, Minsk 220092; +375 17 228 02 05; e incoming@toptour.by; www. toptour.by. Active in the market since 1992, the company offers visa support & a comprehensive package of services within the country, including in relation to accommodation, tour programmes, day excursions & leisure/entertainment.

Vokrug Sveta 10 Internatsionalnaya St, Minsk 220050; +375 17 226 83 92; e incoming@ vokrugsveta.by; www.bel.vokrugsveta.by. This company has grown steadily since its foundation in 1994 & now claims a substantial percentage of all incoming tourism to Belarus in both the private & corporate sectors. All services can be accessed here.

TOURIST INFORMATION A brief word now about the availability of tourist information. In the first two editions of this guide I cautioned travellers not to expect to find anything like as much as would be found elsewhere in the developed world in the way of leaflets and brochures. However, under the auspices of the Ministry of Sport and Tourism, the fledgling tourist industry has now begun to sharpen up its act in terms of marketing and public relations. The product has branding at long last and, in my meetings with senior officials in Minsk, I now discern that some imaginative and strategic thinking is guiding the future development of the travel industry within the country. The National Tourist Agency has been using the adopted logo for its range of publications in many languages for some time now, and there is a considerable portfolio of brochures and leaflets to cover a broad range of activities and services of interest to visitors, although the use of English is occasionally rather quaint! So as well as finding leaflets relating to accommodation and some eateries, mostly in hotel lobbies, you will also be well served with brochures about museums, cultural events and visitor attractions. The excellent (and free) monthly listings magazine *where Minsk* is widely available at locations throughout the city. And the concept of the 'tourist information centre' that has been adopted in the rest of Europe for so long is at last catching on in Belarus. Full listing details are to be found in the chapters for each of the six cities. There is still a little way to go, however, in terms of the service ethic. In every city, staff at the TICs are enormously helpful and will go the extra mile when offering help and assistance. In many of them, some English is spoken and varying amounts of written materials in English are dispensed. But they still close for lunch and most are shut at the weekend. Although I still say it cautiously, things are definitely continuing to change for the better and real progress is being made. Yet the most frustrating thing of all remains the fact that there is a rare and precious commodity to market in this country in terms of tourism, which I maintain is likely to be of the greatest interest to a significant constituency of travellers from the West, who will be able to find much that no longer exists in other parts of Europe, all of it less than three hours from London by plane, but the construction of the bridge between the two has progressed little beyond its foundations. The good news with all of this remains that now *really* is such a good time to find out for yourself what this delightful country has to offer before everybody else wakes up and catches on (see box, *Living the good life*, pages 90–1).

RED TAPE

When it comes to bureaucracy, Belarus is a world leader. Inevitably, this is a relic of the old Soviet days. The level of detail, process and checking involved in the most simple of procedures is mind-boggling. Of crucial importance throughout, however, is the ability to smile and to show the utmost patience and civility when coming up against process and procedure. Anger and intolerance are viewed with disdain and will always be greeted with a wry smile, a shrug of the shoulders and a process at least twice as long as the original would have been. Don't be flustered; admire the view and take some time out to relax. And a few words of Belarusian or Russian never go amiss. An attempt to speak the language, however feeble, will generally melt even the coldest of bureaucratic hearts.

The monolithic wall of red tape is of course at its very best when it comes to regulating the entry arrangements for visitors from abroad. A number of key players within the tourism industry outside Belarus tell me that this remains a huge obstacle to the development of incoming tourism and that until such time as

A DUMMY RUN

Belarusian customs may be tighter than just about anywhere, but one thing that you can bring into the country is a very large lawnmower. I know, because I've done it. My Russian is none too shabby when it needs to be but it was sorely tested on that occasion, although not as much as when I took 24 full-size dummy heads through. They were resuscitation aids to help with an injury minimisation programme we were running for children in schools and kindergartens. The customs official may have spotted a golden opportunity to supplement his income, because he persisted in telling me that there was duty to be paid. One of my Belarusian NGO colleagues came through from the arrivals lounge to assist with the bartering process, but to no avail. That is, until the official got bored and just shrugged his shoulders, before walking away. To look for more sport elsewhere, I guess.

the entry requirements are completely overhauled, simplified and indeed relaxed, visitors from other countries simply will not come. Sadly, it's very hard to mount a plausible and persuasive argument to the contrary. The reality is that all visitors to Belarus from the UK will require a visa, no matter the purpose of the visit or length of stay. For UK applicants to obtain a Belarusian visa from the London embassy, the following documents should be submitted to the consular and visa section. These can either be delivered personally by the applicant or on his/her behalf by a visa services company, or sent by Royal Mail or by courier.

- A valid original passport with at least two blank pages available for visas. The passport must be valid not less than 90 days beyond the date of planned departure from Belarus.
- A completed visa application, which can be downloaded in standard form via the UK embassy website (*www.uk.belembassy.org/uk*) or from the Ministry of Foreign Affairs (*www.mfa.gov.by/visa*).
- 'Visa support documents' depending on the purpose of travel, such as an original invitation or application from a Belarusian legal entity on headed notepaper in the case of a business trip, or written confirmation of a hotel booking if the visit is for tourism.
- A recent passport-sized colour photograph meeting international requirements.

A visa application fee must also be paid (full details of which can be found on the embassy's website), the size of the fee being dependent upon the citizenship of the applicant and the type of visa requested. There are three types: transit (valid for two days), short-term (valid for up to 90 days) and long-term (valid for up to one year for any number of visits cumulatively totalling no more than 90 days). Additionally, visas may stipulate that they are single, double or multi-entry in nature. In each case, the amount of time permitted in the country will be for the period specified in the visa within the time of stated duration and cannot cumulatively exceed 90 days in any single year. The consular officer with responsibility for granting visas will normally make his decision within five working days (two in the case of urgent applications) and may impose such conditions as are deemed appropriate. The decision of the officer is final and there is no obligation to indicate the reasons for any refusal, in which case the application fee will not be returned. For my part I have never encountered a single issue when applying for a visa for dozens of visits over a period of 14 years or more, but I have spoken to one eminent journalist who was told not to apply during the course of a telephone conversation, because the application would be refused. I'm also aware of one other individual whose long-term visa was cancelled without notice or explanation at Minsk airport as he flew out of the country for a short visit home.

Visas can be issued on an individual or group basis. Full details of the specific additional documentary evidence in the form of 'visa support documents' that will be required to be produced for different categories of visa (covering trips for business, participation in sports or cultural events, study, religious purposes, tourism, journalism, implementation of humanitarian programmes and private purposes) can be found on the website of the Ministry of Foreign Affairs at www.mfa.gov.by/en/visa/. There are four pages of closely typed script going into the minutest detail, but a period of attentive study will tell you all you need to know. And of course, one advantage of booking your trip through an accredited tourist agency is that the intense headache of applying will be taken care of for you by somebody else. Me, I've always enjoyed the challenge…

I should mention at the start of this tale that it is now seven years old and that nothing like it has happened to me since the particular events I hereinafter recite. This means I share it not as a representation of what you can expect today, but purely for its entertainment value, a purpose for which I'd like to think it still retains a degree of validity. You can be the judge of that claim. Anyway, I knew we were in for trouble the moment the two militia officers strode out of the airport terminal. They headed for us with far too much purpose and intent for comfort. We had just paid the cab driver and were about to check in for the flight home to London. 'Good day. Passports please.' While one stood sentinel, the other leafed through the pages, one by one. When he came to my immigration document and turned it over to find a blank page, without a stamp, I'm sure that a flicker of a smile played at the edges of his mouth. 'There is no registration stamp. Why not? This is a very big problem.' All of my visits to that point had been on invitation from one of the regional executive committees and not once in the past had it proved necessary for us to register locally. We were always in the country on official business. But it seemed that the rules had changed and I instantly had a feeling that I knew where this was all leading. We were instructed to pick up our bags and follow the officer into the terminal, where he again looked at my immigration document. Again, 'This is a very big problem.' He took out his mobile, spoke quietly into it and 30 seconds later, another militia officer appeared, this time with a bigger hat. He too looked at the document, shook his head and said to me with grave solemnity that this was 'a very big problem'. The two of them turned their backs and whispered to each other, before our new-found friend motioned for Richard and me to go with him and to bring our bags with us. It's a very long walk from one end of the departure terminal to the other, particularly when your mind is racing from one scenario to another, as you try to think of a way out of a fast-developing situation. He was actually quite chatty and as we walked past the departure gates, he cheerily pointed out which of them was ours. By now, Richard had turned very pale.

As we reached the end of the terminal and passed through a small door, the turn of events that I had started to expect did indeed come to pass. 'Do you have money?' he asked. I replied that I had some roubles, but this clearly wasn't the right answer. 'No. Dollars.' Now that the likely endgame was becoming more apparent, I was able to start thinking a little more clearly about an exit strategy and I could give Richard the reassurance that he clearly needed, even though I wasn't entirely sure myself how this was going to turn out. My big worry had been that we would be detained until our flight had gone, which meant that we would have to stay another night, by which time our visas would have expired. Then we would have been in real trouble. We were instructed to follow the officer into a very small and very hot lift, with barely enough room for two nervous travellers, two large bags and a militia man with a large hat who held every card in the deck.

Within five working days of arrival in Belarus, visitors should report details of their temporary address and duration of stay to the local Citizenship and Migration Office. Before passing through immigration, you will be required to complete a migration form in duplicate for presentation at your point of entry. One part is retained when you enter, while the other part is returned for you to obtain the required registration stamp. Guard it as you would your passport, at all times. It will be stamped at the Citizenship and Migration Office for you to hand in when you

We descended all the way to the bottom and he motioned us to step out of the lift and into a vast, gloomy and deserted area. He stood looking at me, expectant and confident of his position. I took a deep breath, apologised for the oversight, stressed that it was entirely unintended and asked what we could do to address the difficulty. 'This is a very big problem for you. The court will impose a very heavy fine. But I can fix it. If you give me a hundred dollars.' The endgame at last. I thought for a few seconds and then nodded. He smiled and indicated that we should join him in the lift again. Just after it began to ascend, he leaned across me, pressed the 'stop' button and with a judder and a bump, we came to a halt. The defining moment had come. Richard had turned grey by this time. It was now very hot and the silence roared in my ears. If I didn't pay up, then it was clear that we weren't getting on our flight. But what if I did offer him money, only for him to announce that now, we were in serious trouble? Breach of immigration laws was one thing, but attempting to bribe an officer of the state was a different matter entirely. In reality, I'm sure that it took only a few seconds to make the decision, but it felt like hours. I reasoned that US$100 in the officer's back pocket was going to be much more important to him than ensuring observance of the laws of the land. Not entirely with conviction, I reached into my wallet, counted out the last hundred that I had left (a lucky break) and handed over the wad. He smiled, folded it away (it really did go into his back pocket), leaned across me once more and pressed the 'start' button. I thought Richard was going to faint. But as we left the lift and walked back into the departure lounge, the tension had palpably relaxed. Except that we still had two major obstacles to overcome. There were two official procedures to be observed in terms of checking our documents before we could leave and I was starting to envisage two more 'fees' of a hundred dollars each. And I had no more dollars. I mentioned this to my militia friend, but with a smile and a reassuring arm on mine, he told me that everything would be OK.

Bless him, he was clearly a man of honour. After a cursory word with a colleague, who went over to have a word with somebody else, we were ushered through at speed. The final check of the papers, before a stern officer in uniform, can often take five minutes and more. He/she will scrutinise every single page of the passport, scan the photograph, occasionally pick up the phone and sometimes summon a colleague to recheck everything, all of the time looking quizzical and glancing up to look into your face. This time? Ten seconds at most. He took my passport, turned straight to the right visa, stamped it with a flourish and handed it back. We were through and out. But Richard didn't relax until our plane had landed at Milan for our connection and he was well inside the terminal on terra firma. The moral of the tale is a statement of the blindingly obvious. Never, ever play fast and loose with bureaucracy and red tape in this country. And always have a few dollars spare, just in case you need an upgrade in services.

leave the country. If staying in a hotel, the stamping process will be discharged by the hotel's administration services. Do not, *under any circumstances*, fail to register within the required five-day period. Checking on departure used to be arbitrary but is now rigidly enforced. Just be sure to avoid the need for 'the Platinum Emigration Service' (see box above). I haven't repeated the oversight I made then and so don't know the consequences of a similar failure to register today, but it's just not worth the risk.

IMMIGRATION AND CUSTOMS Procedures can be tortuous in the extreme. It's no longer necessary to complete the former customs declaration form on arrival and departure, when it used to be a requirement that visitors state the amount and origin of currency in their possession, together with details of credit cards and the like, although you will still be required to fill out a migration document as above. And technically, it is still not permitted to take Belarusian currency out of the country at the end of a trip, although I've never been challenged on this. Whatever the detail of the paperwork, your first experience of Belarusian officialdom will be to stand in a long and interminable line, waiting for a uniformed immigration official to scrutinise every last detail of your passport, visa and migration form, apparently with the deepest suspicion, before allowing you entry.

In common with other nation states the world over, there are some things that cannot be brought into or out of the country by visitors. The list for Belarus includes, not surprisingly, drugs (narcotic and psychotropic), weapons, ammunition, military equipment or clothing, explosives, poisonous, virulent or radioactive materials but interestingly, it also includes 'printed and audio-visual materials or other information media that could do harm to the political and economic interests of the Republic of Belarus, to its national security and to the health and morale of the population'.

The maximum that a single person can import into Belarus without duty is 50kg of luggage and contents for personal use, the value of which may not exceed €1,500 (or €10,000 if your arrival is by plane). Excess baggage is liable to duty at a rate of 30% of its value, but not less than €4 per excess kg. I rarely see the baggage of travellers weighed on entry and I've never seen a charge for excess baggage imposed, but don't take the risk. Within the limits stated, specific items that can be taken into the country duty-free by persons aged 18 and over include one litre of spirits, three litres of beer, 200 cigarettes, 50 cigars or 250g of tobacco, subject to a total weight limit of 250g for all tobacco-related products.

Medical insurance is required for all foreign citizens travelling to Belarus and, to be eligible for emergency medical care, visitors should possess a medical insurance agreement with a Belarusian insurance company, or with an authorised foreign insurance company (as will be the case for most travellers). The visa application form calls for full details of your policy and it's essential to have a copy of the policy and schedule with you for the duration of your stay. These papers will be needed to access medical care and you may also be asked to produce them if making a personal application to the local Citizenship and Migration Office to register your stay within the required period of five working days. The risks covered by your policy must meet the requirements of the laws of the state and be valid on Belarusian territory. The minimum liability limit is US$5,000, though most standard policies on the market will meet this requirement many times over. Should you (unwisely) be travelling without the benefit of insurance, representatives of Belarusian insurance companies will provide the necessary insurance agreements and certificates at any border-crossing point, with premiums for foreign citizens ranging from €2 for a stay of up to four days, to €85 for a stay of one year. However, medical insurance is not required for tourists with transit visas crossing Belarus, diplomats and official delegations, crew members of air and rail vehicles, citizens of the CIS states or holders of travel documents issued to stateless persons and refugees.

For up-to-the-minute information on the rules relating to immigration, customs, visas, duty and insurance, see the official website of the Belarusian national state tourism agency (*www.belarustourism.by*) or the site of the Ministry of Foreign

Affairs (*www.mfa.gov.by*). And for a fascinating read, go to the site of the State Customs Committee of the Republic of Belarus (*www.gtk.gov.by*).

EMBASSIES

BELARUS EMBASSIES ABROAD

Argentina Cazadores 2166, CP 1428, Buenos Aires; +54 11 478 893 94; e argentina@mfa.gov.by

Armenia 375009 Yerevan, Abovyan St, Apt 23; +374 10 22 02 69; e armenia@belembassy.org

Austria A-1140 Huttelbergstrasse, 6, Vienna; +43 1 419 96 30 21; e mail@byembassy.at

Azerbaijan Genclik, Kral Huseyn kucesi, 64, Baku AZ 1069; +994 12 436 46 38; e azerbaijan@mfa.gov.by

Belgium Av Moliere 192, 1050 Brussels; +32 2 340 02 70; e belgium@mfa.gov.by

Brazil Rua Lauro Muller 116, Sala 603, Botafogo, Rio de Janeiro 22290-160; +55 21 25 41 22 15; e consuladodebelarus@terra.com.br

Bulgaria Bvd Reduta, Nikola Karadz St, 1505 Sofia; +359 2 971 95 28; e bulgaria@belembassy.org

Canada Suite 600, 130 Albert St, Ottawa, Ontario K1P 5G4; +1 1613 233 9994; e canada@mfa.gov.by

China 1702F, 2299 Yanaan Rd W, Shanghai 200336; +86 10 65 32 16 91; e china@belembassy.org

Cuba Av 5ta No 6405 e/64 y 66, Miramar, Playa la Havana; +53 7 204 73 30; e cuba@mfa.gov.by

Czech Republic 626 Sadky St, 17100, Prague 7; +420 233 540 899; e czech@mfa.gov.by

Egypt 26 Gaber Ebn Hayan St, Dokki-Giza, Cairo; +20 2 33 38 95 45; e egypt@mfa.gov.by

Estonia Magdaleena 3, Sektsion B, 11312 Tallinn; +372 651 55 00; e estonia@mfa.gov.by

Finland 18 Unioninkatu, 00130 Helsinki; +358 94 247 2056; e finland@mfa.gov.by

France 38 Bd Suchet, 75016 Paris; +33 1 44 14 69 79; e france@mfa.gov.by

Germany Am Treptower Park, 32, 12435 Berlin; +49 30 536 3590; +49 30 536 23359; e germany@mfa.gov.by

Hungary 3B Agardi St, 1126 Budapest; +36 1 214 05 53; e hungary@belembassy.org

India 163 Jor Bagh, New Delhi 110003; +91 11 24 69 45 18; e india@belembassy.org

Iran 1 Azar Alley, Shahid Taheri St, Fallahi St, Zafaraniyeh, Tehran 19887; +98 2 1 22 75 22 29, +98 21 22 75 13 82; e iran@mfa.gov.by; http://iran.mfa.gov.by/en/

Iraq Babil, Arassat Al-Hindiyah 929/5/47, Baghdad; +964 719 55 65; e iraq@belembassy.org

Israel 3 Reines St, Tel Aviv 64381 POB 11129; +972 3 523 1259; e israel@belembassy.org

Italy Via Delle Alpi Apuane, 16, 00141 Rome; +39 06 820 81 430; e italy@mfa.gov.by

Japan 4-14-12 Shirogane, Shirogane K Hse, Minato-ku, Tokyo 108-0072; +81 3 34 48 16 23; e japan@belembassy.org

Kazakhstan 35 Kenesary St, 010000 Astana; +31 72 32 48 29; e kazakhstan@mfa.gov.by

Korea (South) 432-1636 Shindang-dong, Choong-gu, Seoul 100-835; +82 2 223 78 171; e korea@mfa.gov.by

Kyrgyzstan 210 Moskovskaya St, Bishkek 720040; +996 312 35 28 33; e kyrgyzstan@mfa.gov.by

Latvia 12 Jezusbaznicas iela 12, Riga LV 1050; +371 67 22 25 60; e latvia@belembassy.org

Libya PO Box 1530, Tripoli; +218 21 361 25 55; e libya@belembassy.org

Lithuania 13 Mindaugo St, 03225 Vilnius; +370 5 266 22 00; e lithuania.emb@mfa.gov.by

Moldova 83/1 Maciejevich St D, 2009 Kishinev; +373 22 60 29 80; e moldova@belembassy.org

Netherlands Groot Hertoginnelaan 26, 2517 EG The Hague; +31 (70) 302 80 30; e netherlands@mfa.gov.by

Poland 58 Drilling St, 02-952 Warsaw; +48 22 742 09 90, +48 22 742 09 80; e poland@belembassy.org

Romania 6 Tuberozelor St, Sector 1, 011 411 Bucharest; +40 21 223 17 76; e romania@mfa.gov.by

Russia 101990 Moscow, Maroseika St 17/6; +7 495 628 78 13; e mail@embassybel.ru

Serbia 11000 Belgrade, ul Deligradska 13; +381 11 36 16 938; e sam@belembassy.org

Slovakia 811 02 Bratislava, ul Yanchova, 5; +421 2 622 50 152; e slovakia@belembassy.org

South Africa 327 Hill St, Arcadia, Pretoria 0083, PO Box 4107, Pretoria 0001; +271 2 430 77 09; e rsa@mfa.gov.by

Sweden Herserudsvagen 5, 4th Floor, 181 34 Lidingo, Stockholm; +46 8 731 57 45; e belarusembassy@telia.com

Switzerland Quartierweg 6, 3074 Muri bei, Bern; +41 31 952 79 14; e switzerland@mfa. gov.by

Syria Mezzah East Villas, 13 Quartaja St, PO Box 16239, Damascus; + 963 11 611 80 97; e syria@belembassy.org

Turkey Abidin Daver Sokak 17, 06550 Cankaya, Ankara; + 90 312 441 67 69; e turkey@belembassy.org

Turkmenistan Ashgabat, ul Maxim Gorky (2056) 51; +993 12 97 11 83; e turkmenistan@mfa.gov.by

Ukraine 3 Kotsyubinsky St, 01901 Kiev; +380 44 537 52 00; e ukraine@mfa.gov.by

United Arab Emirates Villa 434, 26th St, Al Rouada Area, PO Box 30337, Abu Dhabi; +971 2 4453 399; e uae@mfa.gov.by

United Kingdom 6 Kensington Court, London W8 5DL; +44 207 937 3288; e uk@belembassy.org

USA 1619 New Hampshire Av NW, Washington DC 20009; +1 202 986 1604; e usa@belarusembassy.org, usa@mfa.gov.by; also 20th Floor, 708 Third Av, New York, NY 10017; +1 212 682 5392; e gcny@belembassy.org

Uzbekistan 75 Gulyamova St, 700047 Tashkent; +998 71 120 75 11; e uzbekistan@mfa.gov.by

Venezuela Quinta Campanera, Tercera transversal, Municipio Sucre, Caracas 1071; + 58 212 239 27 60; e venezuela@belembassy.org

Vietnam 66 To Ngoc Van Rd, Tay Ho district, Hanoi; +84 4 37 19 29 74; e vietnam@belembassy.org

FOREIGN EMBASSIES IN BELARUS

UK 37 Karla Marksa St, Minsk 220030; +375 17 229 82 00; e ukin.belarus@fconet.fco.gov.uk; www.ukinbelarus.fco.gov.uk

USA 46 Starovilyenskaya St, Minsk 220002; +375 17 210 12 83/29 676 01 34 (after-hours emergencies); e webmaster@usembassy.minsk. by; www.minsk.usembassy.gov

GETTING THERE AND AWAY

BY AIR All international flights and most of those from the other CIS countries go to **Minsk International Airport,** otherwise known as **'Minsk-2'**. Of the regional airports, only Gomel is presently in limited use and then only for a handful of flights to destinations in Russia. The national airport is situated approximately 40km east of the city on an extension of the M2 motorway. Charmless but functional, and a glorious monument to brutalist Soviet architecture, it was extensively modernised in 2005, then further significant structural works were undertaken in time for the World Ice Hockey Championships held in Minsk in the spring of 2014. Additional works are still in the course of being completed and indeed, there has been something going on somewhere in the airport complex by way of building activity every time I've passed through since my first visit in 2001. The terminal building is divided into two wings, with the left-hand side serving flights in and around the CIS countries and the right-hand side for international flights. Arriving passengers emerge from the tiny and cramped baggage 'hall' (room) on the ground floor, with all departure gates located on the third floor.

Services within the terminal are few and far between. When I was last there in the spring of 2014, all was bright and shiny inside following the building works, but the service units had yet to be filled. At least the terminal now boasts its first escalators. Much of the building is still a vast network of stairs, doors and unlit areas with nothing going on in the spaces between. It remains to be seen if the next phase of development changes this. For now, most of the services are collected in and around the departure gates themselves. You should be able to find currency-exchange and banking facilities, car hire, small retail outlets selling souvenirs, newspapers, magazines and limited refreshments, general enquiry desks/windows and, of course, toilets. The offices of all airline companies operating to and from Belarus are on the first floor, but they are usually closed. Indeed, opening times for all the service outlets are very hit-and-miss. Frankly the best advice is to think ahead and not to rely on needing to access anything at the airport except the toilets. The only exception is in respect of the duty-free facilities after you check through for your flight out. The units are small but well stocked, and always open. There is also a small and very busy café here with long queues.

Overall, the scale of the refurbishment works suggests that facilities are about to receive a major upgrade. Not before time, I say. For **access to and from the city** centre, a one-way ride by taxi costs around US$50. The journey takes approximately 30 minutes in normal conditions and more in rush-hour traffic. Buses run from outside the terminal building to the city's central train and bus stations (with limited stops *en route*) approximately hourly between 06.00 and 23.00. The journey time is around one hour. The Ministry of Sport and Tourism tells me that 2015 will see the opening of a brand new express train service to and from the city centre. I hope it happens: it will certainly transform access arrangements. For now, further details of the airport's facilities can be found on its rudimentary website (*www.airport.by*).

The other airport, '**Minsk-1**', is located well within the city's boundaries (only 3km from the centre) and right in the midst of high-rise residential housing. It mostly caters for local CIS flights, but the daily service to and from the country's second city, Gomel, no longer operates, the carrier Gomelavia having gone out of business. It is a functional building with very few facilities, none of which I've ever actually seen open (with the exception of the toilets), although its architecture is a prime example of post-war Stalinist design. Access between the airport and the city centre is straightforward, with a number of trolleybus and bus services to choose from. The taxi fare should be around US$20. Flights out of Minsk-1 are something of an experience. The former daily departure for Gomel was by twin-propeller Antonov. As it left the runway, the proximity of the nearby blocks of flats was more than a little unnerving, as was the cruising altitude, which was surprisingly low. The pilot simply followed the main road all the way to Gomel. Whenever I mentioned to anyone locally that I was flying out of Minsk-1 on an internal flight, the response was universally the same: 'don't do it, under any circumstances'. I was always advised that safety records for internal flights were appalling. The same is said for all internal flights within the countries of the former Soviet Union. There is a rumour that the state airline, Belavia, is planning to open up internal routes, but this remains to be seen. For now, I'm glad to be able to say that I experienced internal air travel here (and lived to tell the tale), but it's not something I would be keen to repeat. The website www.airportminsk1. by is well worth a look. It's in Russian only, but it gives you a really good feel for the place.

Only a limited number of carriers fly into the country and, as a result, tickets are expensive. The national airline is **Belavia** (*www.belavia.by*), with daily flights around the world, mostly via connections. The Russian airline, Aeroflot, also has numerous options. From Europe, the main carriers are Austrian Airlines, Lufthansa (Germany), Lot (Poland), Czech Airlines, Air Baltic (a cheap option from Riga) and Turkish Airlines. El Al has flights to and from Israel, while Etihad operate between Abu Dhabi and Minsk. The only direct London flight, taking just under three hours, is to and from Gatwick on a Wednesday and Sunday via Belavia, increasing to three flights a week (to include Fridays) over the summer. And since summer 2010, a weekly service to and from Manchester has appeared in the airline's schedules. Belavia has representative offices as follows:

Head Office   14 Nemiga St, Minsk 220004; \+375 17 220 25 55; e support@belavia.by; ⏰ 09.00–20.00 Mon–Sat, 09.00–18.00 Sun

UK   5 Lower Grosvenor Pl, London SW1 0EJ; \020 7233 8559; e england@belavia.by
USA (ECVO Tours)   Suite 909, 45 W 34th St, New York, NY 10001; \212 563 6394; e ecvo@ecvotours.com

I have also flown from the UK with Lot Airlines (via Warsaw), Lufthansa (via Frankfurt) and Alitalia (via Milan). There is more choice of flights by doing it this way, but the travel time is considerably longer and there is little to choose between them in terms of cost. An alternative worth considering is to fly to **Vilnius** in Lithuania, and this is currently my route of choice. A number of budget airlines include this destination in their schedules, my preferred operator being Wizz Air (*www.wizzair. com*). The airline flies to Vilnius out of Glasgow, Liverpool, Doncaster/Sheffield and London Luton in the UK. I use the London/Luton option. There are currently two flights a day each way and, with a degree of forward planning, this is a very cheap way of getting close to the Belarusian border. There is easy access into Vilnius itself from the airport and then several fast and comfortable routes by modern train and bus every day to Minsk, with journey times between 2½ hours and 3 hours for the train, and around 4 hours for the bus. This includes time spent crossing the border. Minsk is only 90 minutes from the Lithuanian border by road. The only downside is that the times of trains and buses to and from Minsk are not that well co-ordinated with flight arrival and departure times. Entry at budget cost via Lithuania is also possible by flying Ryanair to **Kaunas** and then taking the express bus from outside the passenger terminal to Minsk. The schedule is co-ordinated to meet the times of every incoming and outgoing Ryanair flight, but do check ahead to ensure this is the case when you want to travel. It is possible to hire a car in Lithuania for entry into Belarus by road, but it's expensive to do so.

Another option is to fly to **Kiev** in Ukraine. Many international airlines fly there, including British Airways. You can then hire a car and enter Belarus from the southeast, again with cost implications. The drive to the border from Kiev takes around two hours, with the drive to Gomel on the other side taking no more than 45 minutes. However, whether you enter Belarus from the northwest via Vilnius, or from the southeast via Kiev, in each case there is the unknown factor of waiting times (plus bureaucratic inconvenience) at the land border crossing. It all depends on how adventurous you are feeling.

Crossing by land is an experience all of its own (see boxes, *On the border*, pages 62–3 and *Through the back of the wardrobe*, page 65). Some will see this as an enhancement to the travelling experience. I certainly do. But you will be wise to allow at least three hours to pass through the interminable checkpoints and, when you add this element to the time actually spent travelling, it's not a speedy way to get from A to B. And if there is a problem with your papers, or the guards are in a particularly playful mood (as they can be with nationals of another country), no man's land can be a rather lonely place, especially if you don't speak the language. With a degree of hesitancy, therefore, my advice is to save the border-crossing adventure until you are comfortable with the language, or have a Belarusian travelling companion with you to assist in times of difficulty, in which case it's an intensely interesting experience that is not to be missed. Sadly, however, as we went to print news was emerging that the crossing point from Lithuania at Kamyeny Log has been closed to travellers on foot.

BY TRAIN   *by Nicky Gardner, Editor of* hidden europe *magazine* (www.hiddeneurope.co.uk) The one thing you will certainly discover on any visit to Belarus is that it reshapes your view of Europe. That different perception of the continent will be all the more vivid if you take time to travel overland to Belarus. Western Europeans heading east by train to Belarus discover that our home continent is much larger than they ever imagined. If you are starting in London or anywhere else in western Europe, try to make time to travel by train to Belarus. Do it just once, and you may well be seduced by the entire experience.

Direct trains to Belarus Belarus is well connected by train to the rest of Europe. Indeed, Minsk has direct trains from more than a dozen different countries. You can travel in style in Russian Railways' (RZD) comfortable sleeping cars from cities across western and central Europe direct to Minsk and other Belarusian cities. The trains will be bound for Moscow (or, less frequently, St Petersburg), but it is perfectly possible to book just to cities in Belarus.

The information in this section reflects the pattern of rail services in early 2015. Yet it is always worth checking details before travel. For example, some sources still refer to daily direct trains to Belarus from the Netherlands, Switzerland and Germany's Rhine-Ruhr region (Cologne and Dortmund), but these were all axed in 2013.

Our table (below) shows direct trains from principal cities in the European Union to Minsk.

Direct trains from major cities in the EU to Minsk

From	Frequency per week		Travel Time to	Other stations served
	Winter	Summer	Minsk (hours)	in Belarus
Berlin*	3	5	16	Brest, Orsha
Budapest	1	1	21	Brest, Orsha
Frankfurt (Main)	3	5	23	Brest, Orsha
Milan	1	1	33	Brest, Orsha
Nice	1	1	39	Brest, Orsha
Paris	3	5	30	Brest, Orsha
Prague	3	3	20	Brest, Orsha, Vitebsk
Riga	2	7	9	Polotsk, Maladzechna
Strasbourg	3	5	26	Brest, Orsha
Vienna	4	4	20	Brest, Orsha, Vitebsk
Vilnius	27	35	3	Maladzechna, Orsha
Warsaw	17	19	10	Brest, Orsha

* Much improved rail services between Berlin and Minsk will run from 2016, when Russian Railways (RZD) introduces its sleek new *Talgo* trains on the Berlin–Warsaw–Minsk–Moscow route. There will be daily departures. The travel time from Berlin (and also from Warsaw) will be about three hours shorter than at present.

Our list gives just a selection. There are also year-round direct trains to Minsk from Genoa, Hanover, Innsbruck, Katowice, Linz, Mannheim, Poznań and Verona. In addition there are direct trains to Minsk from major cities in the Russian Federation and Ukraine.

Links from Russia If you are travelling by train to Belarus from the east, you'll find excellent connections. Up to a dozen trains daily leave Moscow for Minsk, generally taking nine hours for the journey. Services from St Petersburg are less frequent and slower, although if you are bound for Vitebsk and the northeast corner of Belarus,

2

DISTANCES (KM) FROM MINSK TO EUROPEAN CAPITALS

Amsterdam	1,739	Paris	2,129
Berlin	1,120	Prague	1,141
Budapest	1,110	Rome	2,268
Helsinki	1,148	Sofia	1,753
Kiev	580	Warsaw	550
London	2,180	Vienna	1,164
Moscow	700	Vilnius	215

then the train from St Petersburg is a useful option. The journey from St Petersburg to Vitebsk takes nine hours, while to Minsk it is 13 hours. The main railway station in Minsk is certainly a place to fire the traveller's imagination: trains departing to Siberia, the Russian Arctic and to Black Sea ports are an invitation to adventure.

The Trans-European Express The classic route to Belarus from the west is from Paris, where the *Trans-European Express* departs at least thrice weekly for Minsk and Moscow. Despite its name, this train is hardly an express. It dawdles, and is all the better for that.

The *Trans-European Express* sticks to traditional rail lines through France and Germany rather than the new high-speed routes that defy the warp and weft of the landscape. So on the morning journey out from Paris you'll cruise gently up the Marne Valley, passing celebrated Champagne vineyards. By early afternoon, you'll be crossing the River Rhine near Strasbourg, where arrival in Germany is marked by the magnificent mosque on the east bank of the river at Kehl. In the evening, your Russian train will be skirting lakes and forests on its approach to Berlin. The train slips through Poland by night, and you'll be awoken about 06.30 in the morning as the train approaches Poland's eastern border. All frontier formalities are conducted on board, with Polish officials coming through the train at Terespol, the last station in Poland.

The train then crosses the valley of the River Bug, which in soft morning light can be extraordinarily beautiful. The very fact that the valley was for so long the western edge of the Soviet Union and still today marks the outer edge of the EU (and Fortress Europe) has given it protected status. The wetlands, reed-beds and backwaters of the Bug Valley have been out of bounds to mere mortals for decades, allowing the preservation of a natural wilderness.

Bridging the Bug The train crosses the valley on a long bridge. On the eastern side of the river, passengers are greeted by the rich red battlements of the fortress at Brest and by a huge sign in Cyrillic welcoming them to Belarus – a reminder that the Bug is a fault line in writing conventions as well as in politics. After Belarusian officials have completed their frontier checks, the train is shunted into a shed where the bogies are adjusted to suit the wider gauge tracks that are the norm in Belarus and the Russian Federation. You can stay on board the train while this takes place.

This is train travel as it should be: all passengers are accommodated in comfortable sleeping cars and a restaurant car is there for passengers who want to munch their way across Europe. The Polish restaurant car which is attached to the train from Paris to Warsaw serves good international dishes at reasonable prices, but the wines are pricey. A Russian restaurant car, which is hooked up to the train at Brest, serves good-value Russian fare.

Connections from London For travellers from Britain, the disadvantage of the route via Paris is that it requires an overnight stay in Paris, as the *Trans-European Express* leaves the Gare de l'Est around 08.00. To avoid this extra night *en route*, you can instead leave London later, taking Eurostar to Brussels and then travelling on via Cologne to Berlin. A crack-of-dawn departure from London will have you in Berlin by late afternoon, leaving time for some sightseeing and supper before joining the *Trans-European Express* when it stops in the German capital just after 21.00. By this route, if you book well in advance, it is possible to travel from London to Minsk for about €200 one-way.

Local trains to Brest All major trains to Belarus via Poland use the Terespol to Brest border crossing. These services are strictly limited to those with advance reservations. For those who wish to retain a little spontaneity in their travel, and are thus unwilling to commit in advance, there are useful thrice-daily local trains that shuttle over the Bug Valley from Terespol to Brest. You can therefore make your way by regular domestic Polish services (which are very cheap) to Terespol and then, provided you have the requisite Belarusian visa, just hop on to one of the local cross-border services.

Belarus's back door from Poland The only other similar cross-border rail service from the EU into Belarus that can be used without prior reservation is the local link from Białystok (in northeast Poland) to Grodno in Belarus. This one-time main line, once used by the grand expresses from Berlin to St Petersburg, is now reduced to the status of a minor railway with local trains running over the border twice or thrice daily (depending on season). It is a route much favoured by traders from Grodno looking to make a fast buck in the markets of northeast Poland – a region where there is a substantial Belarusian minority. Dedicated smugglers from Grodno play cat and mouse with Polish customs officials, which makes for some fine theatre on the train. In a recent move, high fences have been erected beside the railway on the Polish side of the border to thwart the efforts of smugglers arriving from Belarus who are inclined to throw parcels from the train to local middlemen waiting by the tracks.

The scenery on this 'back-door' route into Belarus is very fine, with the train traversing beautiful open heath and birch woods on the run from Białystok towards the border. The Polish border checks are made at Kuźnica Białostocka (which is the last halt before the train leaves the EU). On the Belarusian side, the train pauses at an improbably remote spot in the forest just after crossing the border, where customs and immigration officials climb on board. The main immigration procedures are handled upon arrival at Grodno station. This unusual route into Belarus has much to commend it. Grodno is one of the most amiable of Belarusian cities – a great place to get a first taste of the country.

Arriving at Minsk Station *by Nigel Roberts*

The relatively new railway station is situated right in the heart of Minsk and all international trains arrive and depart from this location. As a major crossing point for services throughout the continent, it's loud, full of travellers wheeling cases, jostling and pushing, always hot and a fantastic people-watching opportunity. Exits from platforms are down the ramps into the basement, with toilet facilities, the left-luggage office, a few small shops, a café and a maze of walkways leading to the metro station and under the station square to emerge on the other side close to the lofty towers known as the City Gates. From the basement, stairs lead up to the ground floor, where you will find a currency exchange, small retail outlets, general enquiry

ON THE BORDER

It is 19.40 on a dark, wet and windy September night. We have been on the road north from Kiev for the last two hours, with only a vast panoply of stars for illumination. But we are approaching the border area and it has begun to rain heavily. We are crossing into Belarus from the Ukrainian side by car and a line of long, low buildings has just appeared out of the blackness on the treeline. Tatyana confirms they are the administration and living quarters of the border guards. Beyond them lies deep, impenetrable darkness, with mile upon mile of forest. I am immediately reminded of a black-and-white spy drama from the 1960s. The rain beats down on the roof of the car as the gloom intensifies. 'Sometimes,' says Tatyana with a deep sigh, 'people wait here for three days. The queues can be very long.'

Little by little, we inch towards the first obstacle: Ukrainian emigration. Shadowy figures drift in and out of the darkness. We reach the head of the queue and an official in uniform peers through the car window at our passports. Then we move painfully slowly to the next checkpoint, a large, purpose-built, multi-storey monument to officialdom. As we wait, I ask Tatyana about security along the length of the border. 'It's a big stretch to police,' I say. 'How is it patrolled?' She and Yura exchange views in Russian, before agreeing that most of the roads are impassable, save for the official crossing points, other than on foot. And right now, the other official crossings are closed, so that this is the only means of access by road between Ukraine and Belarus.

Plain-clothes officials mingle with uniformed soldiers and militia, all under blazing arc lights. We reach the front of the queue, where two soldiers (one sporting a very large peaked hat) sit impassively at a small table, surrounded by pens, paper, ancient computer hardware and a scanning device. Out jumps Yura to hand over sheaves of passports and stamped paperwork. Another huge hat joins the first at the flimsy table. One of them scrutinises every single page of our passports and scans in the photographs, before purposefully (but with one finger) pressing keys on his keyboard, occasionally glancing up at his screen as he types. We notice with some amusement that his table, the extent of his domain, is only partly protected from the elements by the overhead canopy, so that the many wires coming out of the back of his kit are now being liberally rained upon. As we pass by, he stares wistfully at us from under his enormous peaked hat, perhaps longing to be a passenger in a car that takes him away somewhere, anywhere.

And so into no man's land. No lights, just darkness stretching into the night. Unexpectedly, ghostly figures emerge from the gloom. All are women, pushing bicycles with one hand, sporting umbrellas in the other and peering through every car window as they pass by, offering coffee and food from their panniers. One by one, engines are switched off and lights extinguished. After 20 minutes, all is dark and silent. The rain stops as suddenly as it began, and overhead the vista is once more a stunning display of stars. I fall in and out of fitful sleep. 'We should be through… in the next 24 hours,' offers Tatyana and it is not easy to spot if this is irony or a cheap shot at humour. As I ponder this, the driver of the lorry next to us in the parallel queue fiddles irritably with the aerial of his ten-inch portable television, as the screen changes from images of lurid colour to grainy black and white. Every ten minutes or so, we start to inch forward, just one car's length at a time. Now more shadowy figures criss-cross the lines of traffic, sometimes

windows and ticket booking offices, while postal, mobile phone and banking services are located on the first floor. The second floor has a café, bar, waiting rooms, currency exchange and more shops. A restaurant and a bar, as well as administration offices, standing in small groups, their faces eerily lit by a combination of cigarette ends and vehicle tail lights.

Our progress is mind-numbingly slow. To our right, a bicycle vendor strikes it lucky, as a lorry driver beckons her over and gestures for her to pour coffee into a plastic cup from her flask. Then much to our surprise, our progress quickens and the next booths appear closer and closer, grotesquely back-lit by huge overhead arc lights. The guards seem to have decided that the lorries are going nowhere that night, for their queue has ground to a complete halt. Another very large hat appears at the driver's window and Yura tells the official he has three 'foreigners' on board, from England. Three immigration forms appear through the open window from an unseen hand. There is much more activity here; more people, more uniforms, more women on bicycles, more noise, more light. There is only one queue now and we finally reach the front. Our guard is a striking blonde woman; her friendly manner is most unexpected, but deceptive. She peers alternately at our passports and through the open door, softly speaking our names in anticipation of some recognition on our part. She motions our vehicle forward and invites us to park up, still on the exit lane, but kind of out of the way, in an 'in the way' sort of way. Yura accompanies her into the office while she scans our passports.

Ten minutes later, Yura returns and opens the door. 'She wants to see your insurance papers.' He scurries off with them. Then two more very big hats walk out with Yura, deep in conversation. Tatyana too is summoned to join the gathering, before she returns to open the car door to enquire sweetly of Richard as to whether or not he has any more photo ID, as the computer is unable to scan his passport photograph. He gazes imploringly into my eyes and I know at once that he has been transported back to our little adventure at Minsk Airport, when it cost me US$100 to get us out of the country (see box, pages 52–3). 'Don't worry, this won't be a problem,' I say, as I begin to feel the first flutterings of irritation. Here we go again…

But it's all a game. Yura returns to move the car 2m forward and perhaps 10cm closer to the kerb, presumably as instructed, before returning back inside. The merry-go-round spins on. Yura keeps pacing to and fro and the hats keep scrutinising our papers. A large hat appears and points the way forward for us, towards the nirvana of customs (and the final control point) 100m in the distance. Our hearts lift, but the dawn is a false one. Yura does indeed drive towards the customs zone, but when we are tantalisingly close, he turns through 180° (as instructed by the hat) and parks up near to the office. He turns off the engine, climbs out and disappears. He is gone maybe 15 minutes and we begin to wonder if we are ever going to escape this scene. Then a figure appears from the inky blackness, striding purposefully forward, head down and hand clutching a wad of documents. It is Yura. He flings open the door, climbs in with purpose and we drive around a corner… and into a queue. Yura is quizzed by a large hat, but this one has the inclination neither for confrontation nor for sport and we are flamboyantly gestured forward into another queue, where another booth and another hat await. We are waved on and before we know what is happening, Yura is gunning the car into the Belarusian night, while an astonishing display of stars shine in the firmament overhead. The whole experience took two hours 45 minutes from start to finish and I wouldn't have missed it for the world.

are located on the third (top) floor. The whole of the station's frontage is glass, so the higher you go, the better the views of the world outside and through the City Gates, as well as down into the station below. For those in need of a bed on arrival, the Hotel

Express is located right next to the station. It is then a relatively straightforward task to reach any part of the city by metro, bus, trolleybus or taxi from the railway station square. The website for the state railway system (*www.rw.by*) is very informative and now has English pages with excellent graphics telling you all you need to know about timetables, services and the country's top 20 stations.

BY COACH There are three bus stations in Minsk (Central, Vostochny and Moskovskaya), all of which serve international routes. The two-floor building of the central station is located next door to the railway station, with only the Hotel Express between the two. It has few facilities of its own, but those of the railway station are only metres away.

Central terminal 6 Bobruskaya St; ☎ 227 04 73   **Vostochny (Eastern) terminal** 34 Vaneyeva St;
Moskovskaya terminal 59 Filimonov St; ☎ 219   ☎ 248 06 28
36 22

The main carrier in Europe is **Eurolines**. Full details of all services and costs can be found on the company's website (*www.goeuro.co.uk*). Operating with partner coach companies, international services to Minsk are generally run by **Ecolines** (*www. ecolines.net*). There is a twice-weekly service from London at 08.30 on Mondays and Saturdays, the total journey time being around 35 hours. It's the cheapest way to cover the miles, but it's certainly the longest and the most tiring.

BY CAR The main pan-European route across Belarus for road transport is the E30 motorway from Paris to Moscow, via Berlin, Warsaw, Brest and Minsk. Within Belarusian borders it is delineated the M1 motorway, and it crosses the country diagonally in a northeasterly direction from Brest in the southwest to a point south of Vitebsk in the northeast, *en route* to Smolensk in Russia and beyond. There are many border crossings into Belarus for vehicles and passengers, both private and freight, from its neighbours Poland, Latvia, Lithuania, Russia and Ukraine. If you're driving your own car, do be sure to check first that your chosen point of entry is open to private vehicles. Not all of them are. From **Poland**, the major crossing points are at Terespol, Koroszczyn, Slawatycze, Kuźnica Białostocka, Połowce and Bobrownik, the most-used being Białostocka and Terespol (the point at which the E30 European highway enters the country, with the city of Brest but a handful of kilometres across the Warsaw Bridge). All of the crossings from **Latvia** are into Vitebsk *oblast* and include Urbany, Gavrilino and Lipovka. Major crossings from **Lithuania** include Privalki (for Grodno) and Kamyeny Log, the main road from Vilnius to Minsk, and the point at which I crossed the border on foot in the spring of 2014 (see box, *Through the back of the wardrobe*, opposite). There is a line of crossings from **Ukraine** across the length of the southern border of Belarus, including Tomashovka, Mokrany, Vyerchny Terebyezhov, Novaya Rudnaya and Novaya Guta (where I once crossed by car as described in *On the border*, pages 62–3). Travelling from **Russia**, customs checkpoints have been removed and unrestricted access on all routes crossing the border is permitted unhindered, although sporadic checks and controls are occasionally enforced.

As might be expected, clichéd and stereotypical encounters with border guards are commonplace, particularly as a significant amount of freight carried by road haulage is still being imported as humanitarian aid for those affected by the Chernobyl catastrophe. Long waits are all too common, with officials taking hour after hour

'All the arrangements are made,' said Artur. 'When you land at Vilnius, walk out of the terminal and look for a Mercedes Vito. The driver will take you to the border for 20 lita.' But when I walked into the car park, there was no Vito to be seen. 'Relax, he'll be there in ten minutes.' He actually arrived in seven, cruising slowly up and down before finding a space to park. It was dusk. I wandered over and asked if he was going to the border. With a nod and a gesture towards the passenger door he started the engine, and within seconds we were on our way. It's no more than 20 minutes to the border crossing at Kamyeny Log, but you know you're getting close around a mile and a half away, when you reach the end of the line of parked-up wagons at the side of the road. I counted well over a hundred.

The driver dropped me off at a petrol station and café 200m from a cluster of low buildings, with overhead gantries above the carriageway. I walked towards them, past a line of private cars, and up to the mirrored window of Lithuanian emigration control. A small section at the bottom opened for me to hand over my passport. It was returned after a rustle of paper and the tapping of a few computer keys. On I walked into no man's land, a broad area comprising lanes of tarmac, markings in the road, clusters of vehicles, single buildings and gantries, but very few people. Out of a hut appeared a Belarusian border guard in uniform, looking about 15 years old. He checked my passport and wrote my name in Cyrillic on a scruffy piece of official paper, handed it to me, and on I walked. There were wagons parked up everywhere, with an occasional short line of cars, none of them moving, each one occupied by a driver and passengers. I felt a strong sense of Europe in transit, but suspended in limbo. After another few hundred metres I reached Belarus passport control and immigration. This time the scrutiny of my passport was something more than peremptory.

On I walked. A small café appeared, followed by a tatty prefabricated duty-free shop, which was my cue to find the small piece of paper on which I had written Artur's list of requests. Purchases made, I walked on. Another uniformed border guard, who also looked no more than 15 years old, ticked off the last formality. He glanced at my passport, took the scruffy piece of paper given to me by his colleague and waved me through. And that was it. I was in. Artur's BMW was parked 100m away in the car park. The entire experience from Vito to BMW took no more than 45 minutes. And the wagons? They will have waited for hours and hours, maybe days. The queues leaving Belarus were even longer. The drive to Minsk in the darkness and torrential rain presented the ideal opportunity to reflect on the experience and, just as I did when I crossed the border from Ukraine by car a few years earlier, I felt I'd been a bit-part character in a black and white 1960s Cold War tale, a Len Deighton or a John le Carré. The image that came to mind when I completed the walk in reverse ten days later was an entirely different one, after an eventful visit of big experiences every day, some of them positive and some of them less so. On the short drive back to Vilnius airport with the same mustachioed driver, I reflected on all that I'd done and seen. The fact of literally *walking* into and then back out of a country where the experience is so very different from anything else that happens in my life brought Narnia to mind. I'd walked through the back of the wardrobe into a different world. I can't articulate the feeling any better, and I can't find the words to explain the way it made me feel actually to walk from one world to another. But I can't wait to do it again.

(and sometimes days) to authorise official papers. Travellers in groups, particularly on tours where bookings have been made through state tourist agencies such as Belintourist, will find that their party will be waved through much quicker, effectively by jumping the queue. The same applies if you cross on foot. At certain crossings you won't be alone in doing this, and the beauty of a pedestrian crossing is that you walk straight past the never-ending line of vehicles and directly up to the various points at which papers are checked. When I last crossed on foot into Lithuania at Kamyeny Log, the walk out of Belarus, across no man's land and into Lithuania took no more than 25 minutes, including four separate stops at specific checkpoints.

For drivers of private vehicles, a customs declaration form is required, which must also provide certain information relating to the vehicle itself. You must also be able to produce original ownership documents at customs offices at border crossings. Note that only originals of these documents are accepted. British driving-licence holders must additionally possess a valid International Driving Permit to drive legally in Belarus (available from most but not all main post offices in the UK, or via the major motoring organisations, for a fixed 12-month period). When driving anywhere abroad, it used to be the case that British motorists would need to be able to produce evidence of relevant insurance cover in the form of the mythical Green Card. With the development of EU cross-border arrangements over the course of the last 20 years or so, this is no longer a requirement for most European countries, but guess what: Belarus is one of the few that still requires it. If you have a Green Card with you, this ought to be the end of it, but don't be surprised if you are told at the border that you still need to purchase specific Belarusian cover there and then. If you don't have a Green Card you will definitely be required to buy cover. Every border-crossing checkpoint at which domestic vehicles are permitted to cross has its own insurance bureau and, in theory, according to official sources, it takes less than ten minutes to obtain the necessary cover. In reality it often takes considerably longer. The cost of the premium depends on the length of stay in Belarus, ranging from €5 for 15 days to €53 for one year. And do please note that in accordance with Belarusian law, your own driving licence and International Driving Permit will only permit you to drive in Belarus for three months. If you want to drive for longer, you need first to obtain a Belarusian driving licence; and to get one of those, you must first attend a Belarus driving school for three months and pass the necessary knowledge and skills tests. Really, you do…

HEALTH *with Dr Felicity Nicholson*

IMMUNISATIONS No specific vaccinations are required for Belarus, although it is recommended that travellers should be up to date with the following to remove the risk of contracting contagious diseases: tetanus, diphtheria and polio, which can be given as the all-in-one vaccine Revaxis, and hepatitis A. Hepatitis B, which can be spread through blood and other body fluids, may also be recommended, as would a three-dose course of rabies vaccine as Belarus is considered to be a high-risk country for this disease.

Hepatitis A vaccine (Havrix Monodose or Avaxim) comprises two injections given about a year apart. The course costs about £100, but may be available on the NHS; it protects for 25 years and can be administered close to the time of departure. **Hepatitis B** vaccination should be considered for longer trips (two months or more) or for those working with children or in situations where contact with blood is likely, eg: playing contact sports. Three injections are needed for the best protection and can be given over a three-week period, if time is short, for those aged 16 or over. Longer schedules give more sustained protection and are therefore preferable if time allows. Hepatitis A vaccine can also be given as a combination with hepatitis B as 'Twinrix', though two doses are needed at least seven days apart to be effective for the hepatitis A component, and three doses are needed for the hepatitis B part.

Three doses of **rabies** vaccine are needed over a minimum of 21 days as a full pre-exposure course. This then changes the postexposure treatment, making it simpler and more readily available. While rabies vaccine is not the cheapest (typically around £55 per dose), it does last for life unless you are working as a vet abroad when yearly boosts or blood tests are advised (see *Rabies*, pages 68–9).

Tick-borne encephalitis can be encountered outdoors in Belarus and particularly in heavily forested areas, where the undergrowth is dense. It is caused by a virus and is usually spread by bites from ticks that are infected with the virus. The disease can be serious with a 10–15% chance of lasting neurological problems. The mortality varies depending on the type of virus but ranges from 1% to 20%.

Anyone liable to go walking in late spring or summer when the ticks are most active should seek protection. Tick-borne encephalitis vaccine (Ticovac) is available in the UK in an adult and paediatric form. Two doses given at least 14 days apart, though ideally a month, give about 90% protection. If sustained cover is needed then a third dose should be taken 5–12 months later. Whether or not you have the vaccine, preventative measures are also very important. When walking in grassy and forested areas, ensure that you wear a hat, tuck your trousers into socks and boots, have long-sleeved tops and use tick repellents containing DEET. It is important to check for ticks each time you have been for a long walk. This is more easily done by someone else. Don't forget to check your head and in particular behind the ears of children. Ticks should ideally be removed as soon as possible as leaving ticks on the body increases the chance of infection. They should be removed with special tick tweezers that can be bought in good travel shops. Failing that you can use your fingernails by grasping the tick as close to your body as possible and pulling steadily and firmly away at right angles to your skin. The tick will then come away complete as long as you do not jerk or twist. If possible douse the wound with alcohol (any spirit will do) or iodine. Irritants (eg: Olbas oil) or lit cigarettes are to be discouraged since they can cause the ticks to regurgitate and therefore increase the risk of disease.

Go as soon as possible to a doctor as tick immunoglobulin should be available for treatment if you have not had the vaccine. Any redness around the bite should also stimulate a visit to the doctor.

As some vaccine courses take time to be given, ensure that you visit your doctor or travel clinic well in advance of your trip.

HEALTH INFORMATION AND TRAVEL CLINICS The International Society of Travel Medicine is one of a number of organisations worldwide that has a plentiful supply of excellent information and advice relating to health for travellers (*www. istm.org*). Other informative websites include www.travmed.com, www.cdc.gov, www.aafp.org and www.thetraveldoctor.com. The UK government's Foreign and Commonwealth Office (*www.fco.gov.uk*) and its Department of Health (*www. dh.gov.uk*) also provide sensible, if generalised advice.

In the United Kingdom, www.travelhealth.co.uk is an independent website offering comprehensive advice to travellers, with links to a great many other internet resources. Another good source of practical advice, including details of clinics nationwide in the UK and links to other resources, is the website www. traveldoctor.co.uk.

A full list of current travel clinic websites worldwide is available from the International Society of Travel Medicine on www.istm.org. For other journey preparation information, consult www.tripprep.com. Information about various medications may be found on www.emedicine.com.

IN BELARUS Travellers to new destinations anywhere in the world inevitably encounter scare stories about risks to health.

Radiation
Radiation is still present in Belarus following Chernobyl, but with sensible precautions, such as not drinking local water or eating dairy produce, mushrooms and fruits in and around the clearly marked exclusion areas most affected by the fallout, the risk of radiation-related health problems is extremely slight.

HIV/AIDS
HIV and AIDS have seen exponential growth throughout eastern Europe in recent years and Belarus is no exception. HIV is a sexually transmitted virus and AIDS is the life-threatening immune failure that occurs late in the progression of HIV. Very early stages of HIV just after infection resemble flu or other viral infections. There then follows a latent stage, often years long, with various symptoms, many of them nonspecific and easy to misdiagnose. AIDS becomes much more characteristic in the latter stages of the disease where immune failure becomes almost total. The profile of the social group that is most at risk tends to include people who actively engage in sexual activity (not only through prostitution) or abuse drugs. The very clear advice for travellers to Belarus is no different from that which applies to travellers the world over. Don't have unprotected sex (and the best advice is to buy condoms or femidoms before you leave home to guarantee quality), avoid multiple sexual partners and don't share needles. If you notice any genital ulcers or discharge, get treatment promptly since these increase the risk of acquiring HIV. If you do have unprotected sex, visit a clinic as soon as possible; this should be within 24 hours, or no later than 72 hours, for postexposure prophylaxis.

Rabies
Animals should always be approached with the utmost caution, even in urban areas, where dogs live a very outdoor life and strays often roam the streets in packs, scavenging for food. They are prone to carry disease, rabies being the most obvious risk, and you can never guarantee that they won't attack. The number of cases of rabies has been steadily increasing in Belarus from 27 in 1996 to 1,628 in 2006. Most cases have been reported in foxes but numbers are also increasing in racoons. There were two human fatalities from rabies in 2006.

Rabies can be contracted by a bite, scratch or lick over an open wound from any infected mammal (bats, dogs, racoons, etc). The animals may look perfectly well so it is not possible to tell whether they are infected or not. First scrub the wound with soap and running water for around ten to 15 minutes then apply an antiseptic or alcohol if you don't have any. Seek medical treatment as soon as possible. If you have not had the pre-exposure course of rabies vaccine then you need to have five doses of vaccine over about 28–30 days and at the beginning of treatment you will need a dose of rabies immunoglobulin (RIG). RIG is in worldwide shortage, very expensive and is very unlikely to be available in Belarus, meaning you would have to evacuate as soon as possible. If you have had all three doses of the pre-exposure course then you don't need RIG at all and only two further doses of vaccine are needed to be given within three days of each other. The rabies vaccine may be available in Belarus, but even if it is not then it will be far easier to obtain than RIG so it is still worth doing before you go.

The bottom line here is not a pleasant one; if untreated, rabies is almost 100% fatal and also a terrible way to die.

Biting insects You can probably expect to contract some form of minor illness or condition at some point in your stay. During visits to rural areas from late spring to late autumn, flying insects of various types can give you a very nasty bite, particularly at dusk. Take the obvious precaution of covering ankles, wrists, legs, arms and your neck, with the added protection of using insect repellent, ideally with DEET (50–55% strength is best).

Drinking water The best advice is never to drink water directly from the tap, although boiled tap water will present no risk. Bottled water, both carbonated and still, is available in abundance wherever food and drink is sold, and will be widely in use in every home.

Diarrhoea On the law of averages, you are likely to pick up a dose of diarrhoea sometime, but obvious measures like thoroughly washing your hands with soap at every opportunity will help, or better still use an alcohol hand rub which then eliminates the risk of infection from contaminated water. If you do get it, be sure to take as much clear fluid as possible to facilitate the rehydration process. Rehydration sachets (such as Electrolade or Dioralyte) are also a good idea to rebalance any salts lost in the diarrhoea. Remedies such as Imodium should only be used as a last resort on their own, but can be used if you are also taking a short-term antibiotic treatment such as Rifaximin or ciprofloxacin. These two medicines are only available on prescription so you will need to consult with your GP or travel clinic expert. If you are unlucky enough to develop a fever with the diarrhoea or notice blood or slime in the stool then seek medical help as soon as possible as longer courses of antibiotics may well be needed.

LOCAL HEALTHCARE The standard of healthcare available in Belarus is generally below that which might be expected in the UK and the USA. The state endeavours, under significant economic limitations, to provide comprehensive medical support to its citizens. It is usually the case that medical staff, particularly doctors, display very high standards of professionalism and commitment. They are extremely well trained, but there is a chronic shortage of equipment, materials and medicines. I have visited many hospitals boasting gifts of equipment from other nation states in Europe, where instruction manuals, if available, are in a foreign language and where postdelivery support simply does not exist. Thus no training in the use of equipment is available, no spares are supplied and repairs cannot be undertaken. Drugs and medicines supplied by donor countries are often out of date.

There is no free medical treatment for foreign visitors, so it is essential to ensure that you travel with comprehensive health cover and that you take all sensible precautions against exposure to risk. It used to be a requirement that all visitors take out a Belarusian health insurance policy on arrival, either at the airport or at a border crossing, at a cost of around US$5, although this was relaxed some years ago and is no longer necessary. If you are normally on any medication, then ensure that you take adequate supplies with you to cover your trip. Be sure also to take a **first-aid and medical kit** with you, which at the very least should include the following:

- first-aid primary care guide
- antiseptic cleansing wipes

- scissors
- safety pins of different sizes
- tick tweezers
- basic hypodermic needles and syringes
- wound closure strips
- assorted plasters of various sizes
- zinc oxide tape
- assorted bandages, dressings and fabric adhesive strips
- disposable latex gloves
- paracetamol/ibuprofen/aspirin tablets (both as painkillers and also as anti-inflammatories), insect repellent, antiseptic cream, antihistamine cream and oral rehydration sachets
- antibiotics such as Rifaximin or ciprofloxacin for travellers' diarrhoea

A number of ready-made kits are available on the market and one of the best ranges I've seen is produced by Lifesystems (*www.lifesystems.co.uk*).

TRAVEL CLINICS AND HEALTH INFORMATION A full list of current travel clinic websites worldwide is available on www.istm.org. For other journey preparation information, consult www.nathnac.org/ds/map_world.aspx (UK) or http://wwwnc. cdc.gov/travel/ (US). Information about various medications may be found on www.netdoctor.co.uk/travel. All advice found online should be used in conjunction with expert advice received prior to or during travel.

SAFETY

As a result of the highly visible militia – or police – presence on the streets there is very little crime in Belarus, and even less that is likely to have an impact on visitors from abroad. The country is governed by a strong presidential system, with security forces that are extremely loyal to it. Historically, the authorities have shown little tolerance for opposition politicians, activists and supporters. Where events organised by opposition groups take place, there is generally heavy-handed use of the security forces to disperse and intimidate. As such, you should studiously avoid all demonstrations and rallies. At all other times, just exercise common sense and vigilance, respect people that you encounter on your way, and be alert to the possibility of mugging, pickpocketing and theft from vehicles and hotel rooms, without the need to exercise any greater care than you would at home. Don't be ostentatious with your money or place yourself in a position of vulnerability in higher-risk areas like train or bus stations and marketplaces. It is also a good idea to be on guard when drinking with people you have just met. On the streets, however, you are very unlikely to see evidence of petty crime or even antisocial behaviour, such as alcohol-fuelled violence, the scourge of town centres at home. Taxis are safe, even in the suburbs and rural areas, but you should never pay up front. To put things in perspective, I have never encountered a single crime incident during all of my time in Belarus. I have never heard of anyone else, visitor or local, who has been the victim of crime. I have been out walking at night on my own and taken solo taxi rides by dark, both in well-known areas and those that are less so. Indeed, I have no hesitation in saying that you are much more likely to be treated with kindness, courtesy and unconditional hospitality than as a target for crime. If you ask for directions in the street, the likelihood is that the person you approach will go out of their way to take you where you want to go. In

Most of your encounters with local people are likely to be positive ones, because of the genuine sense of unconditional hospitality that runs through the whole of Belarusian society. I once attended the consecration of a new church in the small town of Vetka, close to the Russian border. The Metropolitan Filaret of all Belarus was there to perform the ceremony and the church was packed with local people. There was a huge surge as he entered and I was separated from my rucksack, which contained not only all of my personal belongings (passport, wallet, credit cards, cash and the like), but also a very substantial sum of US dollars. There is much poverty in and around Vetka, and the contents of my rucksack represented a fortune by local standards. I was separated from my bag for almost an hour and I am ashamed to say that I feared the worst. But I only had to report the loss to my colleagues in the local administration for things to swing into action. The chief executive of the local authority spoke to the chief of police and there was an immediate flurry of activity. Within minutes my bag and I had been reunited. It was instantly apparent that it had not been opened. It was handed to me by a militia man with the broadest grin I have ever seen, who told me with a mischievous wink that the only matter of concern was whether or not I was a terrorist with a bomb, intent on harming the Metropolitan Filaret. It was handed in by one of the locals as soon as he spotted it, and other local people had joined in the search as soon as word got around that my bag was missing.

14 years of visiting this country I have never felt vulnerable, at risk or insecure. So just be sensible, but don't allow feelings of insecurity to deny you the opportunity of interacting with local people.

There is much apocryphal talk and rumour about Mafia-style organised crime, which probably owes much to tales that originate in neighbouring Russia and Ukraine, but even if true, mobsters will have little or no interest in foreign travellers who stay well away from their 'business'. In the unlikely event that you become a victim of crime, always pause briefly before acting and think things through. If you are travelling with a tourist agency or staying in a hotel, report the crime to the agency and the hotel first. If your passport is stolen, contact your embassy immediately. Only then should you file a police report. Experiences with the local militia can be mixed and it pays to remember that, as a foreigner, you will be treated with just as much suspicion as likely miscreants, if not more.

Scams and swindles are on the increase, although again, you are unlikely to encounter any of them. But take great care every time you use a debit or credit card and never let it out of your sight. ATMs at banks are safe but, as people living in the West already know, increasingly sophisticated means of reading and decoding cards are in operation in Europe and Russia, so Belarus may be next. And you should never, under any circumstances, agree to change money other than through a bank, currency-exchange bureau or reputable hotel. By Western standards, most people in Belarus have pitifully small financial resources at their disposal and travellers from Europe and the USA are seen as fabulously wealthy. In relative terms, they are. Bear this in mind at all times and be studiously discreet with your money, to avoid placing temptation before locals who can only dream of having the amounts routinely found in your wallet. If anything, the greatest risk of all will be encountered before you even arrive, through access to services requiring payment over the internet. Be very cautious of entrusting your personal details, financial or otherwise, to local sites that profess to be secure. Try to make all your arrangements through reputable agencies with appropriate bonding and insurance.

ROAD SAFETY The quality of driving in Belarus is erratic and motorists will find extravagant ways of avoiding obstacles and delays, including mounting the pavement if necessary. Taxi drivers are no exception. You will need to be particularly alert at night in the towns and cities, where many (but not all) junctions with traffic lights have flashing amber for all roads into the junction during the hours of darkness. The mindset of local drivers (without exception) is that, come what may, they will keep going. The concept of 'giving way' is not even an afterthought. Local drivers are beginning to wear seat belts as a matter of course, but not everyone does. It goes without saying that you should always use yours, even though you may be encouraged not to and even though some drivers will view it as an adverse comment upon their driving skills and a personal slight. I recall one journey across the country when I was a front-seat passenger, being driven by an eminent physician who began the journey by describing a recent road traffic accident in which a mutual friend had lost his life, in vivid and gory detail. As I reached for my seat belt, he told me, 'That's OK, you don't need to; I'm a good driver.'

But having said all of this, I have criss-crossed the country at the wheel countless times and always without (significant) incident. If you use your common sense and stay fully alert, I wouldn't expect you to encounter any difficulty. If anything, the experience puts me in mind of motoring 30 years or so ago, when the number of vehicles on British roads was a fraction of the horde that clogs up the highways and byways most days of the week now. The 'motorways' here are in name only when compared with British ones, other than the Minsk orbital road and the new sections of dual carriageway you will find within a radius of 50km or so of the cities, and at various other apparently random locations on main roads throughout the country. As we go to press, though, the state's road-building programme is increasing at dizzying pace, not least in relation to the new culture of tolls (see pages 85–6). When complete, road travel all over Belarus will be much transformed for the better. For now, the significant number of roadwork sites presents its own challenge for drivers. You won't find hazard signs and mile after mile of coned-off highway with workers nowhere to be seen. Instead, don't be surprised if the highway just seems to disappear into a pile of sand, with little warning. It will probably be unlit at night. That said, driving speeds are considerably slower than you will be used to at home, so there is little risk. Just stay alert at full times and expect the unexpected. Indeed, driving on single carriageways, even on major routes, is a largely relaxed experience, because of the low number of vehicles on the road. There are few bends, other than long ones, and, for the most part, roads are flat and unendingly straight. This means that you have a good clear view of what lies ahead and can plan overtaking manoeuvres with a good degree of preparation. The busiest roads are those to and from Minsk, especially the M1, M5 and M6 between the capital and Brest, Gomel and Grodno respectively, all of which have a high proportion of long-haul freight passing through the country into and out of Russia and Poland for all points in the European Union. This means that, on certain days of the week and at certain times of the day, journeys on these roads can be of the 'white knuckle' variety...

One other thing: whatever the time of year, even if the sun is beating down from a cloudless blue sky, drivers will have the heater on full, with the blower set to maximum. Be warned.

Belarus 'A-class' highways are in average to good condition. The condition of 'B-class' roads varies considerably and some are impassable for periods in winter. Drivers should also note that cavernous pot-holes can be found anywhere. Pony and cart combinations are often encountered outside city limits, presenting a specific hazard for drivers in unlit rural areas.

You should observe the **speed limit** at all times. The standard speed limit is 40km/h (25mph) through villages and intensely built-up areas, 60km/h (37mph) on the fringes, 90km/h (55mph) outside built-up areas, 100km/h (62mph) on main routes and 120km/h (75mph) on upgraded motorways. These limits are rigidly and ruthlessly enforced by mobile electronic checking, especially in rural areas, where spot fines significantly swell the coffers of the local militia. But this is a country travelled by knights of the road, where the code of chivalry is routinely observed. This means that whenever any driver passes through a militia speed check, he or she will routinely flash every oncoming driver, without exception, for the next 3km or so. Just make sure you return the compliment!

As well as observing speed limits at all times, do not be tempted to drive after drinking alcohol, however minimal your intake may be. There is zero tolerance of any trace of alcohol. Just don't do it. You should also drive with your lights on at all times between November and March. There are frequent police checkpoints on routes throughout the country. Drivers should stop at these when instructed and have all necessary vehicle papers immediately to hand, as otherwise there is a substantial risk of a fine and consequent delay. Finally, motorists entering Belarus should ensure that they do not overstay the temporary import consent for their vehicles. Violation of the exit deadline may result in confiscation of your vehicle at the Belarusian border or at a police checkpoint within the country.

WOMEN TRAVELLERS

Notwithstanding the (slowly) developing tourism market, any foreign traveller continues to be viewed with considerable curiosity in Belarus, not least because of their relative rarity. This is even more true of women travellers (alone and in numbers), who are rarer still. But women travelling together should not expect to encounter harassment, as two or more local women without male company is a not uncommon sight in bars and restaurants in the big cities.

Single women should exercise caution, however. On your own you might find that you are approached for 'business' by potential 'clients'. Hotel lobbies are notorious for this, where members of staff and prostitutes who are their associates work closely together to ensure that all available 'business' comes their way. Any woman who is not known in these establishments is viewed with the greatest suspicion and even hostility. This actually happened to a Belarusian charity colleague of mine a number of years ago. We were in Minsk with a tourist group, both of us staying at the same hotel as the group. On returning to the hotel alone, my colleague was first of all told in no uncertain terms to leave on the basis that the lobby was the preserve of other working girls; then later she was again refused entry to the hotel proper, because hotel staff were convinced she was clearly touting for business!

As with everything else in a new destination, female travellers should exercise obvious caution and take the same precautions they would in their own country. It's all a matter of common sense. Avoid being on the street alone late at night, particularly in badly lit or secluded areas. Try not to take cab rides alone in the dark with small taxi firms, but instead always look for signs and phone numbers on taxis, together with formal identification papers for the driver before you step inside. Be

2

alert in subways. Don't go out at night without being sure of where you are going to sleep and how you are going to get there. It's always best to ensure that someone knows where you are and when you expect to be back. In any situation, try to act with confidence but not aggression. A show of helplessness might be viewed as vulnerability. Be careful about accepting drinks from strangers that you have only just met. And it is never a good idea to accept the invitation of a lift or a coffee.

Be wary of travelling alone on overnight trains, as you will have no choice as to your companions in your allotted sleeping compartment (even in first class, you will not have the luxury of sleeping alone). But again, Belarusian hospitality is likely to come to the fore. You will most likely encounter interesting and sociable companions (male and female), without there being any question of an uncomfortable, claustrophobic or threatening atmosphere. And there are clear rules of etiquette that are universally followed. For example, women can expect absolute privacy to change clothing and prepare for bed. In addition, you will always be offered the lower berth for sleeping.

Young Belarusians are extremely fashion-conscious. Both sexes have a clichéd role in society and are keen to emphasise their sexuality. For men, this translates into the promotion of a very 'macho' image, while young women tend to accentuate their physical attributes with a dress code that is likely to be viewed as more overt than elsewhere in western Europe. Very short skirts and low-cut tops are *de rigueur*, but since this is accepted behaviour in Belarus, everyone is generally treated with commendable respect (there being no trace of a 'lad and ladette' culture yet, thankfully), and women are not harassed because of their dress.

TRAVELLERS WITH DISABILITIES

Wheelchair users will find that Minsk is not the most accessible of cities, and other cities and towns are less so. Things are slowly changing for the better, but staff in the tourism trade are generally not used to taking care of visitors with specific needs. You will find that increasing numbers of hotels, restaurants and museums have disabled access and facilities, but you should not assume that this will be so. Always check ahead and don't expect people to proactively anticipate the support you might require. Sadly, disability awareness still has some way to go and staff are likely to be caught unawares without prior knowledge of a visitor's specific needs. But if you are travelling with one of the major tourist agencies and they are advised of your requirements in advance, you can expect to have your needs accommodated.

A word on travel insurance: these days, consumers have a huge variety of **insurance providers** from which to choose, most of whom offer a broad range of cover to anticipate most situations that might arise (subject of course to exceptions and caveats). All of us have insurers of choice, which probably means that we have existing policies to cover our individual needs. It always pays to shop around of course, and in addition to the obvious big players there are also a number of bespoke providers specialising in the provision of insurance for disabled and older travellers or to cover pre-existing medical conditions. In the UK they include All Clear Options (*www.allcleartravel.co.uk*), Atlas Direct (*www.atlasdirect.co.uk*), Direct Travel Insurance (*www.direct-travel.co.uk*), En Route Insurance (*www.enrouteinsurance.co.uk*), Free Spirit Travel Insurance (*www.freespirittravelinsurance.com*) and Freedom Insurance Services Ltd (*www. freedominsure.co.uk*). In the USA, have a look at Travelex Insurance Services (*www.travelexinsurance.com*).

ETHNIC MINORITY TRAVELLERS

Belarusian society likes to think that it is tolerant and embracing of multi-culturalism, but the reality is somewhat different. Sadly, incidences of racism are not uncommon. Given that poverty and deprivation are widespread, this may be linked to inequalities of wealth rather than prejudice based purely on skin colour and appearance. Minority ethnic travellers are likely to be stared at and viewed with great curiosity, but this should not be seen as overt racism. Rather, it reflects inquisitiveness on the part of local people towards anyone who is viewed as a foreigner.

GAY AND LESBIAN TRAVELLERS

Notwithstanding its own view of itself as a tolerant culture, intolerance and homophobia remain present in Belarusian society and, in a survey undertaken in April 2002, 47% of people questioned thought that gays should be imprisoned. Since March 1994, the law has acknowledged same-sex relationships between consenting partners, but there is no support for gay initiatives or organisations, so gay life is still largely underground. But youth culture, which is trying to break free from the shackles of state oppression, is increasingly tolerant of homosexuality. It remains to be seen whether this becomes a truly broad and unconditional acceptance of diversity, or just a passing fashion. Meanwhile the powerful Russian Orthodox Church, which claims that 80% of the population are active followers, considers homosexual relationships as among the 'gravest of sins'.

The Belarusian League for the Freedom of Sexual Minorities (LAMBDA) actively campaigns for gay rights. Part of the International Lesbian and Gay Association, it chronicles specific instances of discrimination on the part of state authorities and organisations and publishes its own magazine. A successful gay pride festival took place in 1999, but subsequent events have been cancelled.

TRAVELLING WITH KIDS

As there is universal acceptance in Belarusian culture that heterosexuality is 'the norm', as are distinct stereotypical gender identities for men and women, it is no surprise to find that a husband, wife and children travelling together will be broadly welcome wherever they go. There are no specific obstacles for families and no inconveniences that cannot be encountered elsewhere in the world. In practical terms, essential items for infants such as nappies, formula milk, general toiletries and medicines for paediatric pain relief are widely available in towns and cities. Don't expect to find imaginative concessions to the challenges of getting around with pushchairs (eg: on public transport), but with a spirit of adventure, patience and a sense of humour, few places will be out of bounds.

A few years ago I helped a British family with two young children to arrange a holiday in Belarus. All went smoothly and the feedback I subsequently received was extremely positive: 'We are so glad we went. We found the people friendly and accepting of us. Our children enjoyed the trip too. We found plenty to entertain them and the food is easy enough for them to adapt to, which helped. We found quite a few things to do with the children. We found there to be a surprising safety culture, eg: strapping children on to the horse of a carousel at a funfair, which would probably go against most people's stereotypes.' I'm delighted all went well!

In the big cities, it is increasingly common to find consumer goods that will be familiar to those brought up on Western culture. This means that it is no longer necessary to pack for a trip to Belarus as though you're preparing to enter another dimension. When travelling in the old Soviet Union, it was always the case that you would need your own bath plug in every hotel, no matter how swish. This is not necessary today. The issue of availability of goods seems to relate more to quality. This means that you can buy cosmetics, sanitary products, clothes, gadgets (such as torches, radios and corkscrews) and all the trappings of modern living, but don't expect them to be of anything other than average quality or to last very long. That said, things *are* changing, and it is now possible to purchase a broader range of higher-quality essentials, in Minsk at least. Before you go though, do make a list of all essentials you may want to buy or replace, as well as specific items that will need to be of decent quality. One thing that's very useful to have with you is a large packet of antiseptic wipes, which are very versatile and serve a number of purposes. Given that photography is an important medium for capturing your experiences, be sure to take more batteries and memory cards than you think you will need. You will encounter many more things that you will want to record than you expect.

Most importantly of all, find room in your luggage and day baggage for two rolls of toilet paper. Hotel rooms will have adequate supplies, but elsewhere you should not rely on expecting to find anything at all, including in restaurants, bars and other public places. Things are definitely improving in the major tourist areas, particularly in Minsk, but do be warned that toilets elsewhere in Belarus can be smelly, require you to squat instead of sit and have a wastepaper basket for used paper, which is deposited rather than flushed. That's one use for those antiseptic wipes. Conveniences in public spaces such as parks and at railway stations are quite an experience. There is always an attendant on hand to charge a fee, usually around BYR500, and although facilities are often basic, you will always find a vase of flowers (sometimes plastic) and pictures on the walls. Finally, don't forget to take a first-aid kit (see pages 69–70 for details of what it should include), plus a sewing kit for emergency repairs.

CLOTHES Belarusians are very conscious of status. They take great pride in their appearance and will take every opportunity to wear their most fashionable items of clothing whenever they can. The best advice is to take things in which you will feel comfortable, but have with you at least one smart outfit. For men, this need be no more than pressed trousers, smart shoes, a laundered shirt and a tie. Don't worry about a jacket unless you feel underdressed without one. It's all a case of personal preference. For women, a dress or skirt and formal blouse are a good idea. Attendance at a formal event is always on the cards and first impressions go a long way towards establishing cordial relationships with your hosts. But ostentatious gear with exclusive designer labels and accompanying 'bling' will have the opposite effect. For outdoor wear, bring practical clothing with several pockets and a pair of sturdy shoes.

Summers can be very hot. Shirts, trousers and long flowing skirts made of baggy cotton will help you to be more comfortable. Button-down sleeves and button-up collars minimise the risk of overexposure to the sun. But do remember that Belarusians dress to emphasise their sexuality, so you can expect to see both sexes scantily clad when the temperature rises. In rural areas men will often appear topless but, as a foreigner, you will still be expected to display appropriate decorum and restraint.

By contrast, winters can be freezing. Anyone visiting Belarus from November through to March will need lots of warm clothing. Being outdoors in winter is a wonderful experience if you're prepared for it, but it can be extremely uncomfortable if you're not. It's better to wear a large number of thin layers, which allow you to adjust your body temperature more easily. In all probability, you will be going in and out of transport and buildings on a regular basis. It is here that the importance of being able to shed layers comes to the fore, because cars, buses, trains and buildings are like furnaces in wintertime. Whenever you enter a public building, you will be expected to check in your overcoat, hat and any baggage you have with you at the cloakroom. Winter means snow, so strong, warm, waterproof footwear is a must. Take the thickest overcoat that you possess for extra warmth, but also a waterproof jacket for when it rains. An insulated hat, scarf and gloves can also be considered essential.

BOOKS AND MAPS   Authoritative and up-to-date guides and maps for Belarus are still few and far between. Those that exist are stocked in specialist travel bookshops, such as Stanfords (*www.stanfords.co.uk*), Daunt Books (*www.dauntbooks.co.uk*) and the Map Shop (*www.themapshop.co.uk*), or are available online from the usual outlets. Books play a huge role in Belarusian culture and when you get there you will find that, even in small stores, there are lots of glossy paperbacks and hardbacks on the history, culture and ecology of the country. English-language books are increasingly available.

A decent number of maps covering the whole of Belarus are now available for purchase in the UK, while in Belarus itself, the government produces its own 1:800,000 map via its agency Belkarta. It is easy to read, has English translations of place names and sites, contains key pieces of information and, best of all, it incorporates plans of the six major cities on the reverse side. One of the best and largest scale maps available in Europe appears to be the 1:600,000 version sold by the Canadian company International Travel Maps and Books (*www.itmb.com*). Inevitably, the most detailed maps are only available for purchase in Cyrillic script in Belarus itself. The tourist industry there still has far to go, but it has begun to sharpen up its public relations strategy of late, so that decent-quality hand maps and pocket guides are now starting to be distributed free in some hotels and transport hubs. Just don't count on it, because you might very well find the dispenser empty when you need it most. The very best advice is be prepared for any eventuality by taking your own with you.

SPEAKING THE LANGUAGE   You will be surprised at how many metaphorical doors are opened for you if you try a few words of Russian, especially with children and young people, so as a basic 'must do', take a pocket phrasebook with you. It's worth trying to learn the Cyrillic alphabet in advance, because it makes no end of difference if you can sound out letters and thereby read place names. For those without even a rudimentary knowledge of the alphabet or how to pronounce the letters, it can be a very intimidating language. But trust me on this: when you can sound out letters, then you can sound out words as well and you will be surprised, first at how easy it can then be to sound out quite long words and secondly, by how many of them you can actually take a good guess at translating.

There are many **phrasebooks** on the market: my two favourites are those published by Rough Guides and Lonely Planet. Both have basic but useful dictionaries within the text, along with practical sections designed to help you get by in the most common everyday situations. There is nothing to choose between them in terms of quality and it's all a matter of personal preference. Either will enable you to deal with most situations you encounter.

When it comes to **basic language courses for self-study**, the market is saturated and you will be spoilt for choice, particularly in respect of online resources. And if you have a smartphone, the number of apps available for downloading seems to grow by the week. Those (like me) who love books are still well served. I find the *Teach Yourself* series (Hodder and Stoughton Publishers; *www.teachyourself.co.uk*) particularly useful, because they publish an extensive range of materials to enable the student to prepare through different learning disciplines. Passing no comment on the choice of descriptive term in the title, *Russian for Dummies* (Wiley Publishing; *www. dummies.com*), in audio and book form, is an excellent way to prepare for practical experiences. The layout is imaginative and the style of teaching effective. I also like the *New Penguin Russian Course* (Penguin Books; *www.penguin.co.uk*), which packs a lot of learning into one portable volume. Nowadays, there are a number of books and CDs on the market that profess to be more effective because they use so-called 'new ways of learning'. My own view is that there is no substitute for learning the basics of the alphabet, pronunciation and grammar in the traditional way, if you want things to stick in your mind. This isn't everyone's view and it may very well be that new and different ways of learning suit you best, in which case, just go with whatever meets your preferred style of learning.

A word about **online language courses**. One of the best I have seen is *Master Russian* (*www.masterrussian.com*). The resources available on this site are very comprehensive, including a number of online multiple-choice tests for you to take and submit, with instant feedback on your results. This isn't the only site, of course, and time spent web-browsing to find one that suits your own tastes best will never be wasted.

When you are ready to take your study to the next stage, you will need to acquire a more technically based **grammar book**. My personal preference is the series produced by Barron's Educational Series in the United States (*www.barronseduc. com/foreign-languages-russian*). The company's books on verbs, grammar, idiom, vocabulary and pronunciation are especially good. And for a single volume to slip into your pocket that is compact but full of essential learning, take *Oxford Russian Grammar and Verbs* (Oxford University Press; *www.oup.co.uk*).

Finally on books, my view is that you cannot do without a **dictionary** once you have moved beyond the elementary stage of study. If you're serious about your learning, then a weighty tome to keep at home or in the office (or wherever you study) is indispensable, in which case the *Oxford Russian Dictionary* (Oxford University Press; *www.oup.co.uk*) is difficult to beat. I also recommend that you acquire a smaller, pocket dictionary to take with you on your travels. My own preferred choice to slip into a pocket is the *Langenscheidt Pocket Russian Dictionary* (Langenscheidt; *www.langenscheidt.com*), although equally good are the *Oxford Colour Russian Dictionary* and the *Berlitz Russian Phrase Book and Dictionary* (*www.berlitz.co.uk*).

If you are only able to acquire one learning tool both for home study and to take with you, then buy the *Oxford Beginner's Russian Dictionary*. The dictionary section itself is more than comprehensive, but in the same tome you also have a 'learning and lifestyle kit', which includes a great deal of useful tips, as well as some essential background information on lifestyle, etiquette and culture.

My own view is that the very best way to learn any language is to attend a **language school**. If you ensure that your teacher is a native speaker (usually the case, but not always), you will have the opportunity not only to hear the language as it is truly spoken, but also (and just as important) to learn with others in an interactive manner. Many of the course providers will give you the opportunity to enjoy at least a week's learning at a school in Russia, but naturally this comes at a cost. Language Courses and Language Services UK (*www.listenandlearn.org*) offer individual and group courses at many locations throughout the United Kingdom. And if you make enquiries of your local school or college, you will probably be surprised at how easy it is to find a course close to where you live. In my experience, the best course provider is the Brasshouse Language Centre (*50 Sheepcote St, Birmingham B16 8AJ;* \ *0121 303 0114;* e *brasshouse@birmingham.gov.uk; www. brasshouse.birmingham.gov.uk*). Part of Birmingham City Council, it is the largest adult education centre in the country specialising in languages. Thirty languages can be studied here and course fees are extremely competitive. It is possible to start your studies at beginner's level and go all the way to postgraduate standard. I know this place is good, because I studied here for two years in evening classes and I highly commend it to you.

If you have a burning desire to maintain your interest in this country and its people after you return home from your first visit, then I seriously recommend that you embark upon some study of the language. It will call for a degree of commitment, certainly in terms of your time, but the task is one that will give you great satisfaction as your learning develops. And you can do it in the comfort of your own home if you wish! Just don't set your sights too high to begin with.

ELECTRICITY

As in Russia, electricity in Belarus is 220–240v, 50Hz (alternating current). All plugs are symmetrical two-pin, typical of those used in western Europe. It's a good idea to take at least two international adaptor sets with you. For safety, always unplug appliances that are not in use, as random power cuts and subsequent reconnections causing surges are not uncommon.

MONEY

The national currency is the Belarusian rouble (BYR), which is divided into kopeks, with 100 kopeks to the rouble. For practical purposes, however, this is a worthless denomination, because there is no coinage in circulation and the smallest note is worth BYR50. The other denominations are 100, 500, 1,000, 5,000, 10,000, 20,000, 50,000, 100,000 and 200,000. As at August 2014, US$1 was worth BYR10,390, while £1 equated to BYR17,462 and €1 would buy BYR13,915.

EXCHANGING MONEY Foreign currency should only be exchanged at banks or official currency-exchange bureaux, which includes the currency desks at hotels. In the cities and towns, even smaller ones, you will have no difficulty in finding them. It is best to change money from US dollars, euros, UK pounds sterling or Russian roubles, as travellers may encounter difficulties with other currencies. If you have booked on a tour through Belintourist or another recognised tour operator, then accommodation, transport and meals will already have been paid for, so large amounts of spending money are not necessary. The US dollar is still the most desired currency, with euros and UK pounds sterling next. You may have difficulty exchanging your money if your notes are not new and crisp. Unfortunately, the same cannot be said for the Belarusian currency that you will receive in return.

CREDIT CARDS Major credit cards are widely accepted in hotels, shops and restaurants. Visa and MasterCard are most widely recognised. Plastic fraud has not yet taken a hold but doubtless will one day soon, so try not to let your card out of your sight when you pay. Always check your receipt and keep it until you have been able to compare it with your next statement when you return home.

ATMS ATMs can be found all over Minsk and in the other cities, and in increasing numbers in towns big and small. Most of them in the major areas of population will dispense US dollars as well as Belarusian roubles. I've occasionally encountered random problems with my cards not being recognised by machines, though not often or to a significant degree. You won't need to have a wide selection of cards with you, but one alternative to your main card of preference will be a good idea. Just bear in mind that your bank is likely to charge a fee (and perhaps more than one) for the use of your card abroad.

PREPAID CASH CARDS A number of these are now available on the market, and in security terms they represent a much safer alternative than cash. And they can of course be topped up from home by those you leave behind! With recognised backing for your cash card of choice (eg: from Visa and MasterCard) you should not have any difficulty in withdrawing cash from an ATM. Just check before you buy that the one you choose will be valid in Belarus.

TRAVELLERS' CHEQUES American Express travellers' cheques are no longer valid for encashment and payment in Belarus. For a number of years they were treated with suspicion and cash was always much easier to exchange. Even bank staff in Belarus didn't really understand the concept of travellers' cheques and in times past I accompanied a number of English visitors on hugely frustrating bank visits that ultimately ended in successful encashment, but only after repeated explanations and a mass of bureaucracy. Just don't bring them.

CASH Exercise common sense with your money and you won't go far wrong. It's best to take a supply of crisp US dollar bills or euros, a debit card to access the local currency from an ATM and one credit card to use in hotels, shops and restaurants, perhaps with one additional card to use in the unlikely event that you encounter any technical difficulty with the others. Keeping each of them in a separate pocket decreases the risk of total wipe-out by theft. Flourishing a large wad of cash is never a good idea, even in roubles. The pocket money that you have with you is likely to be more than the average Belarusian earns in a month. And to avoid accumulating scores of tatty rouble notes in a Monopoly-style wad of enormous proportions, take a little time to count out the smallest that you have when making a purchase, otherwise you will very quickly build up a large stash of extremely grimy and smelly notes.

BUDGETING

The question of how much currency to take with you depends on your tastes and how much you plan to spend. If you are travelling with a party booked through an agency such as Belintourist, most of your payments will be made up front before you travel. If you are going solo, it will still be easy to comfortably get by spending only a little if you are so minded. You can eat and drink very cheaply by avoiding the flashy joints, as you would in any capital city, and getting around by car, bus or train is astonishingly inexpensive by European standards. Entrance fees to museums and theatres are also amazingly good value, particularly given the wealth of treasures to be experienced.

If you are travelling independently and solo, it will be possible to stay in a comfortable (but not luxury) hotel, eat well (but not lavishly), take in a museum or two and cover your transport costs, all for US$175–200 per day. This may not be so for much longer, however. As soon as the local economy begins to realise that the number of foreign visitors is on the increase (as will inevitably be the case), prices will start to rise. The largest item of additional expense is likely to be the purchase of transport and accompanying guides on specific excursions. If you don't understand the language, then self-guided tours will be of little use, as facilities for English-speaking visitors are few and far between at museums and historical sites.

The import and export of local currency is prohibited and all remaining banknotes must be reconverted at the point of departure. That said, I have never encountered any difficulty in taking out any cash left over at the end of a trip for use on the next one. The import of foreign currency is unlimited, subject to declaration, while the export of foreign currency is limited to the amount declared on arrival.

As for tipping, most restaurants will include an element for the service charge in the bill (generally 10–15%), although it always goes down well if you leave something extra, but always in roubles. To leave US dollars on the table after your meal would be viewed as the height of arrogance.

Here are three tentative budgets for a week (seven days and seven nights), at the luxury end of the scale, living comfortably (but not extravagantly!) and as economically as possible. There is one huge caveat to all of this: prices are changing virtually by the day and although this information is current at the time of writing, things may well be different when you come to travel. Just do your research before you go! You will see that these tables *exclude* air fares, as well as internal travel from city to city. And if your trip is arranged with a tour operator, then much of the expenditure will be included in the basic tour price. So for the purposes of this exercise, my assumptions have been that you are travelling independently and staying in one city, probably Minsk. Prices are given in US dollars per person:

Expenditure (type)	Luxury	Comfortable	Economical
Hotel (including breakfast)	2,500	1,000	400
Lunch and dinner	525	210	140
Urban travel	150	60	25
Museums, sights and excursions out of town	425	175	40
Theatre and culture	125	50	25
Souvenirs and gifts	300	100	25
Total	**4,025**	**1,595**	**655**

GETTING AROUND

Travellers planning a first trip to Belarus must ask themselves: do I go it alone, or should I book through an agency as part of a group? Each experience will be different and each has its pros and cons. As a former Soviet republic, the country still finds it difficult to cater for independent travellers (other than in respect of main train and bus routes between the six major cities), because in the old days the state would need to know exactly what locals and tourist groups were doing at any given time. As was the case then, heavy state control remains an aspect of everyday life. If you are part of a group hosted by one of the state travel operators, the clear instruction given to your guide will be to chaperone you every moment of your stay. Virtually the only time you will be alone will be in your hotel room.

On the up side, the time you spend waiting around at immigration, customs, restaurants, hotel check-ins, theatres and museums will be considerably less. You will also have the services of an English-speaking guide. But essentially, you will only see what the authorities want you to see. Nowadays this probably has as much to do with Belarusian hospitality as it does state control: people want to show tourists everything of which they are proud. They want you to have a good time and they want you to be impressed. Independent travel has the advantage of allowing you to do what you want, when you want. And you have greater control over your budget. But if you can't speak the language, you will be at quite a disadvantage. The Cyrillic alphabet bears very little resemblance to that of Western languages and without a rudimentary understanding, communication (especially written) will be impossible. Some of the people that you are likely to encounter as you travel around (and with whom you will need to communicate) are going to speak at least rudimentary English, but this is not something to be expected as a matter of course. Young people generally have enviable language skills, but staff in train and bus

ON THE ROAD

Olya was fed up with her lot. She had finished university early in the summer, had just started her first teaching job at the school where she herself had studied and she was working extremely hard. Life was just a little tough. So when I told her that I wanted to visit the west of the country, along the Polish border, she jumped at the chance to join me. We borrowed a car from the brother of a very good friend of a very good friend of mine (that's how things are done here) and set off on a beautiful autumn morning.

The road from Gomel to Brest is a delight. It runs east to west in a virtually straight line for 538km, through the low-lying marshland of the Poleysye. It carries very little traffic, so the drive is actually very relaxing. The road stretches to the horizon without bend or hump and overtaking is a joy. The only slight inconvenience is that you have to stop periodically to clean the windscreen of ex-mosquitoes, in their hundreds. And even though it is a thriving border town of some 300,000 residents, driving through the city of Brest itself is also a delight. The signs are good (if you can read Cyrillic), the layout of the roads is easy to fathom and your co-motorists are generally courteous. Driving techniques are occasionally quirky, but there is very little aggression or competition and certainly not the vaguest hint of 'road rage'. You just need to be careful to avoid the pot-holes around town, which can be alarmingly deep.

I also love the back roads from Brest to Grodno, where there are usually very few cars for company. But, however hard I try, I can never find the right road out of Volkavuysk. The signs are less than helpful and I always seem to be heading in the direction of the opposite point of the compass to the one I intend. It's clearly a Belarusian version of the Bermuda Triangle.

My first night behind the wheel on the streets of Grodno was a bit of a challenge. We had been on the road all day and arrived to find no hotel rooms available. We secured an apartment for the night in one of the suburbs, but try as we might to find it, we couldn't hit the right street, let alone the right block. In exasperation, we phoned the landlord and he agreed to come out to meet us. He was a very young man with a very fast car. As dusk approached, he took off into the gloom like a bat out of Hades, leaving me to pursue him as best I could, all the while watching the stations, hotels, restaurants and shops do not. Very few museums have information available in English. The same applies to menus in restaurants.

BY AIR Although a number of regional airports remain open, their business is almost universally freight and business. There are currently no internal passenger flights, although there is talk that the state airline Belavia is planning to open up routes within the country. This remains to be seen.

BY RAIL I should make my position abundantly clear from the outset. I *adore* travelling by train in this country. Actually, I adore train travel anywhere. I've ridden the rails all over Belarus by night and by day. I've met so many interesting people and I've watched the landscape roll by for countless hours. It was always a cliché that under Soviet dictators the one thing upon which absolute reliance could be placed was that the trains always ran on time. In its day, the Soviet rail system was the largest in the world, crossing 12 time zones. In common with its neighbour Ukraine, Belarus inherited its share of the network when the Soviet Union collapsed. Nowadays, as then, trains between major cities are frequent and

road (Grodno drivers are more excitable than their counterparts in Brest), reading the map and checking the signs. In Cyrillic text.

The only dodgy moments of the trip came on the following day. I was clearly tired. Driving around town, I couldn't understand why the car was a little sluggish. And why there was a smell of burning. Then my hand slipped to the handbrake. It was, of course, fully engaged. Please don't tell my mate's mate's brother. The second episode was more scary. It's interesting the way the thought process works when you're tired and when the evidence of your own eyes doesn't seem to compute in your head. On the road to Minsk we hit another long, straight stretch and I counted a line of nine huge wagons heading in our direction for Poland, maybe a kilometre ahead. Then all of a sudden, I couldn't see the path of our side of the carriageway ahead. This confused me, because only a second ago, everything had been perfectly clear. I was even more confused when it seemed that one of the wagons was side-by-side with another. Then it dawned on me. He was overtaking. I felt like an extra in the Circus Maximus, standing in the path of the onrushing chariot race in *Ben Hur*. By this point in the journey we were on single carriageway. With a yank to the right on the steering wheel, we were into the dirt by the side of the road, great clouds of dust billowing behind us as we bounced along. The wagon made it back in, just in time, but it wasn't a risk I was prepared to take. Olya wasn't in the least bit concerned. She slept through it all.

Overtaking can be challenging if the road is busy and there is a long line of cars, wagons, bicycles, tractors and horse-drawn carts on each side of the road, because everyone seems to be pulling out at the same time and trying to overtake the car in front, which has already started its own overtaking manoeuvre. And when I pulled out from behind a truck on the road to Gomel to take a quick look myself to see if it was safe to overtake, I'm not sure who was more surprised, me or the driver of the oncoming militia car.

For the most part, though, it's stress-free motoring. You can relax, enjoy the scenery and wait for the exotic Beamers and Mercs with blacked-out windows to glide effortlessly by and away into the distance. Ah, the joys of the open road.

relatively cheap, but slow. If you have the time to spare, this is no problem at all; gazing out of a train as it lazily meanders across the country is an excellent way to get a feel for the terrain and the environment. And taking the overnight sleeper from Minsk to Gomel, especially in the dead of winter, is an experience not to be missed. This said, booking train tickets can sometimes be problematic, as it is not uncommon to find that timetable information doesn't match what you are told at the booking office.

Although some parts of the rail network have been modernised, many of the trains are fairly old, particularly those running on local services. These older trains have a distinct charm, with wooden frames and white curtains around the windows. Carriages are heated in the winter, though they can be draughty. Overnight trains usually have traditionally designed compartments with closing doors, with a bench seat on each side and fold-down berths above. If you get to choose, always go for the lower-level berth, as the top berths slope inwards (away from the wall) and there's a good chance you'll fall out in the middle of the night. I did once, somewhere between Minsk and Gomel, and it hurt. Bedlinen is available for hire at a ridiculously cheap price. The carriage attendant will even offer bedding on long daytime journeys. A restaurant car will be available, and your attendant will also periodically come round taking orders for coffee and tea. There will be a menu on the window table in each compartment. You will not be allowed to board without first showing your ticket, and as the attendant will be providing your bedding and refreshments, and the nights can be very long, it's best to greet him/her with a smile and a few words of basic but welcoming Russian. If you strike up an early rapport, the journey will be much more pleasant.

There is a certain code of etiquette relating to travel by **overnight sleeper**. Unless you are travelling in a group of four, you will be sharing your compartment with strangers. When you enter your allotted compartment, be sure to introduce yourself. If you have your own food and drink with you, share it around. And if you have beer or better still, vodka, you'll find your new companions won't be strangers for very long. Just don't expect to get much sleep. If you are male, remember to offer the lower bunks to female companions and don't forget to excuse yourself from the compartment to permit them the privacy of changing their clothes for bed.

Carriages on **day trains** consist of either old-style compartments with doors or the usual open-plan arrangement with rows of seats. It is normally possible to order tea, coffee and snacks. Local vendors with fresh produce may also be waiting as each train pulls into the platform for scheduled stops. Toilets are located at the end of each carriage, but they may be closed while the train passes through urban areas or as it crosses a national border. And don't forget to take your own roll of paper, just in case.

To access more rural areas, shorter local lines run through small stations that are little more than a platform, seemingly in the middle of nowhere. These trains are often packed in the early mornings and evenings (mostly with country dwellers travelling to sell their own produce in local markets) and just a little uncomfortable, with people crammed on to bench seats of only rudimentary comfort.

Buying train tickets is tricky if you don't have the language. Ticket windows are not difficult to identify, but don't expect to be greeted with an overabundance of patience on the part of either ticketing staff or those in the queue. **Left-luggage facilities** are available at the stations serving the six major cities and many of those in smaller towns. They will either be automatic, in which case you will need to buy a token from the nearby booth, or a room with shelves attended by a member of staff, most likely a *babooshka*. These are quite secure, but don't lose the scrappy piece of paper that the attendant gives you, because 'jobsworths' are everywhere to be found in officialdom in this country. No ticket, no luggage!

For all relevant information, the website of the state railway (*www.rw.by*) is useful and practical, with lots of photographs and a significant number of English pages.

BY BUS Generally travel by bus is a little cheaper and quicker than by train, although you may be compromising on comfort. For longer journeys, your coach might be relatively plush, but if you're unlucky it could be old and rather rickety (and almost certainly will be for local travel, especially in rural areas). Crammed and claustrophobic minibuses also operate on local routes. The timetable is always fairly flexible – again, more so in rural areas. Try not to rely on too much forward planning and if you can, just turn up at the bus station and see what time the next one leaves. When on board, don't be surprised if your bus stops wherever it is flagged down. This makes it a true community facility, but it also makes overcrowding much worse. According to official statistics, 4.3 million passengers travel by bus each day along 4,290 routes – so you'll be pretty unlucky not to find a bus to take you where you want to go. Just don't be surprised if it feels like all 4.3 million are travelling on the same bus as you.

BY CAR The supposed difficulties and risks associated with driving in Belarus are frequently exaggerated. Various travel websites will tell you that you'll have to contend with bad roads, on-the-spot fines from traffic police and speeding maniacs in blacked-out BMWs, not to mention that all signs are in Russian or Belarusian. You will read that every other road user drives excessively fast and recklessly, that they ignore pedestrians and traffic lights, that the roads, even the main arterial ones, are full of cavernous holes and that snow, ice and fog in the winter are a major hazard. The last two points have far more truth to them than the first two, but you're unlikely to have any trouble if you keep your wits about you, exercise common sense, observe the rules of the road and act with courtesy at all times. True, I've witnessed some extravagant (and dangerous) overtaking manoeuvres on most of the motorways, which are generally single carriageway except for the sections extending 80km out of Minsk and less for the other cities, but you are unlikely to run any risks if you stay alert, although you might want to bear in mind the experiences recited in the box, *On the road*, on pages 82–3.

The state is currently funding a massive road improvement programme. When complete, the network will have been substantially upgraded and motoring will be all the better for it. For now, however, expect to come upon substantial roadwork sites anywhere with little notice in advance. Hand in hand with a newly modernised road system comes the advent of a state-of-the-art electronic system for the collection of tolls ('BelToll'). Introduced on 1 July 2013 and initially in operation on the main national M1 motorway (the pan-European E30 route) and a number of specific sections elsewhere, including the M2 spur to the airport, it replaced the old system of tollgates that used to operate on certain of the main routes. Phase 1 of the roll-out covering around 815km of national roads is now complete. Phase 2 is in the course of being introduced and, by the summer of 2014, a total of 1,200km of road were subject to toll payment, including sections of the M3, M4, M5, M6 and M7 motorways. Drivers are required to register on the system's website (*www.beltoll.by*) and, having paid the necessary deposit, they receive the dashboard unit applicable to their grade of vehicle, which then transmits data to digital receivers at toll stations positioned at various points on the network. Automatic collection of the relevant toll from the registered account then ensues. On-board units can also be acquired at BelToll Customer Service Points at selected border crossings and other locations throughout the country. Up to 16 specially equipped vehicles will also be patrolling the network checking for non-compliance. At the time of writing, domestic vehicles less than 3.5 tonnes from countries of the Customs Union (Belarus, Russia and Kazakhstan) were exempt from payment. Other exemptions include motorcycles, emergency vehicles and buses. For all other vehicles the tariff depends on weight and ranges from €0.04 to €0.12 per km. For further information see the extensive English pages of the system's helpful website (see page 85).

The good news is that because of the low population density, traffic queues in Belarus are few and far between, even in the big cities (although you might want to avoid being downtown in any of the six big cities, especially Minsk, in the traditional rush hours), and out of town there is a real feeling of liberation and a sense of being back on the open road. In the country, you can drive for miles without passing another vehicle. The final piece of good news is that fuel is much cheaper than elsewhere in continental Europe (approximately half the price payable in the UK). And Belarus is at last catching on to the concept of service stations, with new ones opening all across the network. Only a handful of them are open 24 hours, but the rest will be open for business early in the morning and late into the night.

Car hire The concept of commercial car hire has become considerably more accessible over the course of the last few years and facilities are now easy to find, predominantly at Minsk International Airport and at all the major hotels in Minsk (particularly the new ones), or other central locations. Rates vary considerably and different conditions apply. Big international companies ply their trade side-by-side with the Belarusian outfits. You can afford to be choosy, so undertake your research before you arrive, but do book ahead. This is even more important if you will be arriving over the course of a weekend, because the offices of most hire firms are only open between 09.00 and 18.00 Monday to Friday. Many advertise the option of extended hours, including at weekends for collection and drop-off, but this cannot be guaranteed. Don't take the risk. Anyway, once you get there, you are a captive market and the price is susceptible to adjustment upwards, sometimes outrageously. But if you do the deal before you leave home, pay up front and are content with a modest vehicle, such as a Skoda Fabia, Toyota Yaris or Peugeot 208, expect to pay anything from £200 to £400 for a week's hire. Daily rates are also available, and some companies offer unlimited mileage. Always check the insurance arrangements in advance and don't forget to bring your international driving permit. On arrival at Minsk International Airport, most of the hire companies ply their trade at gates 3, 4, 5 and 6.

One word of caution: although car crime is not endemic, the company details on the vehicle will mark you out as a wealthy foreigner. Park in public places and not in secluded locations. Exercise common sense and take the obvious precautionary measures with valuables and possessions.

The following listings are a selection only of the biggest international hire firms and others are available, particularly Belarusian outfits; exercise your own judgement on the merits of each.

Avis Minsk Int Airport; ☎+375 17 234 79 90; also Bldg 2, Office 329, 11 Nyezalyezhnastsi Av (rear of Hotel Minsk), Minsk; www.avis.com

Europcar Gates 3–4, Minsk International Airport; ☎+375 17 279 22 41; also at Bldg 2, Office 319, 11 Nyezalyezhnastsi Av (rear of Hotel Minsk), Minsk; ☎+375 17 209 90 09; www.europcar.com

Hertz Hotel Minsk, 11–13 Nyezalyezhnastsi Av, Minsk; ☎+375 17 209 90 91; www.hertz.com

Rhino Car Hire Gates 5–6, Minsk International Airport, Minsk; ☏ in advance from the UK 0845 508 9845 and from the USA +1 888 882 2019; www.rhinocarhire.com

Sixt Gates 5–6, Minsk International Airport, Minsk; ☏ +375 29 251 75 17; www.sixt.com; also at Crowne Plaza Hotel, 13 Kirova St, Minsk

HITCHHIKING Although hitchhiking – the culture of 'on the road' adventures where the traveller sets out to discover as much about him/herself as the land through which the journey takes place – is not common, because there is no concept of a free ride from strangers just for the sake of travelling around, you might still find that, as a driver, you are flagged down in urban streets and on main highways by people looking for a lift as an entirely practical and expedient means of getting from point A to point B. Your would-be travelling companion will expect to pay, but the best advice is not to take any risks at all by picking up strangers. Interestingly, you will rarely see a car that is not full to bursting with passengers. This is not just because the strong sense of community means that friends and relatives will be offered lifts by a car owner, the driver timing his own arrangements to fit in with those of his passengers, but also because motorists will look to supplement their income by giving lifts to those in need, particularly around transport hubs such as coach and rail stations (and even bus stops). I cannot recommend Belarus as a destination for hitchhikers, but if you need to get from A to B and know where you're going, if you're feeling adventurous and you want a real alternative to bus or train travel, this is a great way to interact with local people. They will be fascinated to learn that you are a foreigner and will treat you with respect and affection if you try out a few words of Russian on them. The driver will probably take whatever you offer by way of payment, so be generous, but not flash. He might even refuse to accept anything

---

HOTEL LADIES OF THE NIGHT

Each hotel will have its own regular group of working girls (I wonder what the most appropriate collective noun would be?). They meander around the lobby in heels and short skirts, gently smouldering and oozing availability. Every man who passes, whether or not accompanied by colleagues, family, spouse or partner, receives the sultry look and 'come hither' stare. Sometimes the bait is taken, the line is reeled in and the parties repair to the bar to close the deal. Occasionally the deal is struck much more quickly, in hushed and whispered tones. Then with a nod to the lobby staff, the players stroll arm in arm to the lifts. The security guards also receive their cut of the takings. It is their job to ensure that no interlopers are allowed to muscle in. And so it is that every female who enters the lobby, no matter how respectable and whatever the company she keeps, is given the once over. Some nights, business is slow and the girls are underemployed. So when you take your key from reception staff and it is obvious that you are going to bed, your room number is passed to one of the girls, who will then give you a respectable time to get into bed before she comes to call on you. The knock is generally a soft one and she will not persist, although your phone will always ring ten minutes later if you don't answer the knock. If you then answer the phone, you will be offered 'company', but a polite refusal on your part will be an end to the matter. You won't be harassed. But to avoid any embarrassment, just don't answer the phone. Then the following night and every night after that, the merry-go-round in the lobby will spin all night long.

when he knows you are a visitor from abroad, but persist inventively without being overbearing. Suggest that he uses the money to buy something for his wife, children or mother. You may even be offered the hospitality of his home for a meal and a bed. Just be fully aware of the potential danger of climbing into a car without knowing anything about your travelling companion. Or companions.

ACCOMMODATION

Your accommodation costs will easily be the biggest expense on your visit and at the higher end they can be substantial. A star system ranging from one to five is in operation in the country, but it bears little resemblance to anything that you will have seen before. The exception to this is the growing number of new private enterprise hotels, where standards match those found elsewhere in Europe. The older Soviet-style hotels have a bewildering variety of rooms of different class and status, with prices to match. You can expect to be offered, for example, a room that is economy, standard, business, semi-suite or deluxe, with daily rates starting at US$60 and going all the way up to US$900 and beyond. You will be encouraged to indulge yourself at the top end of the range, but if all you want is somewhere to rest your head, then rooms at the bottom end will be more than adequate. And if you have the time and confidence to shop around a little, you can usually find a reasonable deal on a decent room. In recent times, a number of new breed hostels have opened for business in Minsk and elsewhere in the large cities. Well appointed and with high standards of service, they represent excellent value for money.

In part, however, tourist accommodation is no exception to the general rule that, everywhere you look, you will still see relics and reminders of the days of the Soviet Union. In the 1960s and 1970s, when the first intrepid European tourists pioneered holidays there through the only medium that was available, the state tourist agency Intourist, they all returned home with tales of having stayed in soulless, monolithic concrete buildings, where the awfulness of the food was matched only by the surliness of the staff, there was no hot water, every fitting was hanging off, there was never a plug for the bath, the windows didn't fit their frames and guests were kept awake all night by the cockroaches. Today, things are different: the food is pretty good, the staff try to smile (some of them, sometimes), you don't need to bring your own bath plug and perhaps most important of all, the cockroaches seem to have gone. But the soulless monolithic buildings are still there, as is the concrete, both more crumbly and neglected than they were back then.

ACCOMMODATION PRICE CODES

Accommodation listings are laid out in decreasing price order, under the following categories: Luxury, Upmarket, Mid-range, Budget and Shoestring. The following key (also on the inside front cover) gives an indication of prices. Prices are based on a double room per night in high season, including any taxes. See box, page x for a note on exchange rates and prices.

Luxury	$$$$$	BYR1,752,000 +
Upmarket	$$$$	BYR1,300,000–1,752,000
Mid-range	$$$	BYR884,500–1,300,000
Budget	$$	BYR347,000–884,500
Shoestring	$	<BYR347,000

Wherever you stay, other than in extreme circumstances of misfortune you are going to have a fairly comfortable bed, unlimited hot water, clean sanitation, central heating, a television and a lockable door for your room. You'll also have the services of a concierge on your floor (although these services are usually limited to the shrugging of shoulders when you complain that something in your room is either missing or not working), at least one bar and one restaurant, a newspaper stand, currency-exchange facilities and staff with a smattering of basic English. And free entertainment in the hotel lobby during the hours of darkness (see box, *Hotel ladies of the night*, page 87).

When you **check in**, you will be asked to present your passport and immigration form, which will be kept for the duration of your stay unless you ask for it back. Don't be alarmed. State regulations require that every visitor is formally registered and hotel staff will perform this function by stamping your immigration form, which you then hand in when you leave the country. Perhaps someone somewhere in some organ of the state cross-checks your visa details, your passport, the duration of your stay and your itinerary against information supplied or held elsewhere. Whatever the reality, your passport will be perfectly safe and will be returned to you when you leave the hotel at the end of your stay. Behind the desk will be secure safe-deposit facilities, although each room in the more upmarket hotels will have its own safe. Don't be too paranoid. Things left in your room will almost always be safe. Just be sensible, lock valuables away or keep them with you, and don't put temptation in anyone's way.

If your hotel booking has been made through one of the country's tourist agencies, they will usually act as the middle man and take payment from you in advance, so you won't need to pay the hotel other than for items purchased during your stay and charged to your room account. Just be sure to check in advance what is included in the stated price (eg: breakfast). If you have to settle an account when you leave, check it scrupulously. Nearly all hotels (even those at the bottom end) have facilities to take payment by credit or debit card. There will usually be an ATM in the lobby if you prefer to pay by cash, but you will only be able to do so in Belarusian roubles.

Of course, not everyone wants to stay in a hotel. **Private apartments** are available for rent in all of the big cities and many of the towns, with the advantage that you can self-cater. Rates are usually very competitive. In times gone by, I have arrived in both Brest and Grodno in the early evening without booking accommodation in advance, to find there was not a single hotel room to be had in either town. It's a good job I was travelling with Olya. For the cost of a local newspaper and a few calls, we rented an excellent apartment in Brest (five minutes from the city centre) for US$30 a night and another in Grodno, equally well located but to a higher specification, for US$70 a night. Bedlinen, towels, cutlery and crockery are always provided. And you have the advantage of feeling right at home when you return after a day or evening out. In some parts of the country, health sanatoria have opened their doors to tourists, offering bespoke programmes lasting from one to ten days.

Since 2004, following a presidential decree, there has been a real move to promote **ecological and agro-tourism** in rural areas, where visitors have the opportunity to stay 'down on the farm' or in private homesteads, where they can live the good life and engage in various ecological activities. Resourceful homeowners outside of the towns are beginning to see that here is an opportunity to supplement their income, particularly as the decree from the president conferred certain tax advantages. One of the key co-ordinating bodies in Belarus is the Association of Agro- and Ecotourism (see page 49 for more details). Accommodation is also available in lodges and tents for those interested in

In 2007 I was keen to try out agro-tourism for myself and, with the help of Tatyana, Saturday afternoon saw our arrival at the home of Sergei Staska in the picturesque village of Parichi, north of the town of Svetlagorsk on the banks of the delightful Berazhina River. His home is large, with quaint outbuildings in the extensive garden, in one of which is to be found the bathhouse. In fairness, there is much to be done at the property in terms of preparedness for visitors and travellers, but if there is any justice in this world, then Sergei will get the help he so richly deserves. He is one of the kindest, most gentle men I have ever met. Nothing was too much trouble for him during our stay. In a country where hospitality is to be found wherever one travels, Sergei still manages to stand out from the rest. A father of three children, life hasn't always been easy. Years of devoted service in the naval forces must surely have contributed to the breakup of three marriages and now he and his aged mother strive to make a life that will be better than hitherto. We were encouraged to treat his home as our own in every way. Food and drink were in plentiful supply at every meal, where the two of them were in constant and vigilant attendance.

One of the purposes of my visit here was to meet with Eduard Voitekhovich, one of the country's leading lights in ecotourism. He was attending meetings in the area and I was anxious to hear from him about tourism generally. Other colleagues from Belarusian NGOs with an interest in community development joined us for the discussion, together with another mother and son from a nearby homestead who offer dinner, bed and breakfast at their home. And Sergei was to receive some advice, particularly with regard to funding. Things can be really infuriating in this country. I have been trying for some little while to convince the authorities that the time is right for the tourism industry to take greater steps towards meeting the market that already exists. I have been encouraging the production of leaflets and brochures in English. But if you search for information in the major cities, it can still be difficult to find. Absolutely the key issue is that the tourism 'product' massively exists already in Belarus, the market is ready and waiting elsewhere, but there is no bridge between the two!

I made this point to Eduard, as we all sat around Sergei's table, a large pile of roasted pumpkin seeds before us. I didn't even notice that Sergei had gone, until I saw him return bearing a huge pile of leaflets and brochures, which he presented to me with a broad grin and a flourish. I leafed through the pile open-mouthed. Here, in a rural idyll far from the city, in the home of a splendid Belarusian host who didn't speak a word of English, was the bridge for which we had been searching. Information, photographs, descriptions and key facts for visitors. In English. I read page after page of brochures that were nowhere to be found in Minsk or elsewhere at the time. The most infuriating thing of all was the directory of agro-tourism, detailing names and addresses (with photographs) of participants in the scheme, with information as to the facilities on offer. I was given a copy for each of the last three years. The earliest was in English, but when I asked how many copies had been printed and where they had been distributed, Eduard could only shrug his shoulders. At best, there had been 500 copies. I had never seen one before. And the latest two were only in Russian. Poor Sergei. What chance does he

activity holidays in the national parks. And down in the southeast of the country, NGOs from the UK and Belarus are working in partnership with local executive authorities in developing a homestay programme, where excursions and visits are have? We later learned that the government has turned down his application for funding under the rural tourism scheme, because Parichi is deemed to be a town and not a village. It looks like a village to me. But Sergei won't give up. And in the light of all the difficulties that face him, the nightly rate of US$15 for dinner, bed and breakfast is but a drop in the ocean. I really, really hope he gets there.

The second day of our visit took us to another eco-project. In a clearing in the forest, half a mile along a bumpy track, stands the country's only original, working windmill. At least it will function, when the works of reconstruction are finished. It was originally built in 1924 and, soon after, the Soviet government ordered the owner to gift it to the state. Three times he refused and three times he was imprisoned. He was eventually shot in 1938 in one of Stalin's loathsome gulags. His daughter eventually gave it to our host Volodya in 2004 and it is clear that he is determined to honour the memory and the courage of the original owner. Just before the gift, the government again asked the daughter to donate the windmill to the nation. But having seen her father spend 14 years of his life in jail before being murdered by the state, she wasn't about to defile this testament to the memory of one man's lone gesture of defiance in the face of the brutality of the Party machine.

Sergei and Vladimir are working on this project also. When complete, there will be a complex of ten self-catering wooden chalets. The first is well on the way to being finished. Even though some structural work has still to be done, such as adding staircases, the bedrooms already contain beds that have been laid with fresh linen. We sat outdoors to discuss the future, with cheese, peppers, oranges, peaches, vodka and the refreshing juice of the birch tree. Volodya has invested much of his own money in the project. After initial opposition from the local state authorities, the national decree in 2004 that first encouraged ecotourism came at just the right time. As a result, the bank has been much more benevolent than before the decree and the local authority no longer places obstacles in Volodya's path. He is someone else who deserves to succeed.

Since those two early visits I've stayed in a number of similar facilities, all privately owned, where the owners have dreams and hopes but very little money. The last time was during a visit to Polotsk in the early summer of 2014. We drove out to a rural hamlet and thence down a bumpy track to a building site. We had a basic meal in a cold and unwelcoming shed and, while everyone else drank tea, the owner showed me around. He was convinced everything would be ready for a grand opening in September. With great pride and in hushed tones, his eyes full of enthusiasm, he pointed out that here would be the kitchen with a beautiful range, here would be the cosy lounge, here would be the luxurious bedrooms, and here would be the bathhouse. It was just a shell without a roof. His world is a fantasy one. Yet with the help of the state elsewhere, other complexes (some small and some quite large) are being built and seem to be flourishing. Like everything else here, I guess it's a question of who you know. I haven't heard whether or not the dream was ever realised. My aim is to visit again in 2015 and nothing would please me more than to see the operation flying. Sadly I'm not hopeful…

designed locally and travellers stay in the homes of local people. This initiative is very much in its early stages, but already it affords the opportunity for visitors to get right to the heart of local communities.

EATING AND DRINKING

DRINK It will come as no surprise that this section begins with a few words about **vodka**. Virtually all of the countries in this part of the world lay claim to being the first to distil this spirit of mythical status, each claim probably having as much validity as the others. Whatever the truth, it's an inescapable fact that vodka distillation is big business. Every supermarket and shop has row upon row of vodka bottles of all shapes and sizes, with a wide variance in quality and price. It's usually colourless and free of flavourings, although there is a huge market around the world for spirits flavoured with so-called complementary additives such as pepper, honey, grasses and fruit (eg: lemon, raspberry or cranberry). Most people in Belarus drink it straight and unflavoured, as do I. There is an active market in home-distilled vodka and people out in the country are particularly inventive when it comes to making use of organic material for this purpose, usually potatoes. It often tastes surprisingly smooth but can be astonishingly high in alcohol content, so if offered, by all means give it a try but do treat it with extreme caution and absolute respect. I've experienced a few terrible hangovers after a night of *domashnaya* ('home') vodka. And I have never drunk it without knowing its source or being able to trust the founder of the feast.

It's very important to understand how and why people here drink vodka. They don't do so for recreational purposes, sipping from a tumbler at home or in a bar as they socialise with friends and family. Vodka has a much more important role than that in the culture of Belarusian society. Every holiday, birthday, wedding, christening and funeral is celebrated with traditional toasts. Family events and social gatherings, particularly to welcome new friends and visitors, would be unthinkable without the presence of a half-litre bottle on the table, with plenty more in reserve should (when!) the need arises. To give an indication of the ubiquity of the vodka toast in Belarusian culture, I have drunk it with the Metropolitan Filaret of All Belarus, with a state lawyer at 09.30 (in his office) to celebrate his birthday, with a headmaster in his office during the school day, at breakfast with the father of my host family, and by night on a farm next to a roaring fire with rural elders gathered around, singing songs and exchanging stories, all accompanied by toast after toast after toast. And although it's a cliché to say that vodka is a reflection of the fire and passion of the Russian soul, as well as an enduring image of 'Holy Mother Russia', there is nonetheless a degree of familiarity to this statement that those who know Belarus will recognise.

All of that said, however, there is also a dark and dangerous story to be told. The tragic reality is that vodka has destroyed many lives and, to this day, its effect on family and community life is as pernicious as it has always been. In the rural communities that I know so well, I am acquainted with a number of individuals who pass each day in a state of abject intoxication. For them, it is the only antidote to 'life'. I know families deprived of a father through alcoholism; and I have visited many state institutions for children abused by parents of both sexes because of drink. Capable of being a sociable companion, it can also be a cruel master.

Beer (пиво) is popular as a staple alcoholic drink for recreational consumption. Much of it is bottled or cask-conditioned, but there is a growing trend for local microbreweries to produce their own diverse beers of high quality. If you're an aficionado, you will have no difficulty in sourcing an increasing number of excellent examples. In bars and restaurants, mass-produced, conditioned beer from the Baltika brewery is most in evidence. Established in 1990 in St Petersburg, it is probably still the market leader, but it has many competitors. It brews nine varieties (unimaginatively numbered from one to nine, each being known by its number rather than by an individual name), ranging from a light ale with an alcohol content of 4.7%, up to a strong lager of 8%, with pale, classic, original, gold, porter, export and wheat beers in-between. Baltika 7 is Olya's favourite, and probably mine too if I'm drinking Baltika, although my preference is to search out the product of a small local microbrewery.

No **wine** is produced in Belarus, but decent Georgian and Moldovan reds are widely sold and are popular. Also available cheaply is 'Soviet champagne', a sickly, sweet, gaseous and hideous drink that bears no resemblance to the French original.

As an alternative to vodka (not that one is needed), **cognac** from Armenia is very popular. It is also very competitively priced and of a high standard.

In terms of non-alcoholic beverages, *kvas* makes for a great alternative to the usual soft drinks that can be bought here as easily as in the rest of the world. Made by fermenting bread baked with wheat, rye or barley, it is sometimes flavoured with herbs, fruit or berries. Many homes produce their own but it is also made commercially and widely distributed in shops and supermarkets in bottled form. It has a malty taste and is very refreshing when served chilled on a hot day. In the summer months, vendors are ubiquitous in the city and, even in a plastic cup, it's an especially satisfying (and cheap) thirst-quencher in the heat and the dust.

People also bottle *kompote*, a rich essence of home-grown fruit (usually red berries), sugar and boiled water. It's absolutely delicious. A full range of fruit juices is available in shops, restaurants and bars, but most are made from concentrate. The usual international varieties of bottled mineral water are commonplace. Also served is a Belarusian variety that is highly carbonated and tastes salty and mineral-rich. It's definitely an acquired taste, but I think it's delicious.

Coffee (кофе) and **tea (чай)** are drunk throughout the country. Tea is normally taken with lemon and sugar (or even jam or honey), so you can expect a quizzical look if you ask for milk.

FOOD The cuisine of Belarus derives from the same historical and cultural sources as those of its neighbours and is an articulation of the people's relationship with the land. So if you've travelled in Russia, Ukraine, Poland and the Baltic states, you will recognise dishes and recipes that are common to each. For generations, local people have grown their own produce, particularly potatoes, root vegetables and fruits. This is no surprise, for to do so reflects some of the key historical features of life here across the centuries: long and unrelenting winters, short but intense growing seasons, political and social tyranny, the intensely physical and demanding workload of the peasantry and periodic famine. The resilience needed to combat all of these privations has to be fuelled by hot, nourishing and restorative food. For generations it was a simple question of survival.

As has been discussed elsewhere in this book, one of the consequences of the political and societal changes over the last 125 years in this part of Europe as first the Russian Empire crumbled, then the Soviet Union, leading to the emergence of an independent Belarusian state, has been a cyclical process of first denial then rediscovery (and even reinvention) of traditional Belarusian heritage. This has related as much to cuisine as to anything else. Today, the fond remembrance (or perhaps rewriting?) of that heritage has its metaphorical roots firmly in the land and in the seasons. The post-independence phase has seen acceleration of the 'rediscovery' of lost traditions. But if you ask a sample of the people themselves where their preference for cuisine lies or if they are even bothered about their culinary heritage, a significant proportion will probably say that they are more interested in sampling and getting to know international dishes. This will certainly be so for those living in the big city. For the people of provincial towns and villages, however, the connection to the land will be more direct. This is certainly so in Vetka homes, where for 14 years I have been treated to the wonderful home cooking of simple but delicious dishes of high nourishment and intense natural flavour. But on my last road trip with Olya around the country (it was only a flying visit of three days' duration) our evening meals were curry, pizza and pizza, in that order! In fact, the closest reference that I have been able to find on my travels in Belarus to anything approaching acceptance of an ethnic *Belarusian* foodstuff (as opposed to Russian) is that, quaintly, when people refer to the potato, they tend not to use the Russian word (картофель), but instead, a term that is unique to Belarus: 'bulba' (бульба). Whenever I use the word at table, I am always slapped roundly on the back and treated to broad grins, accompanied by enthusiastic nodding of the head on the part of my fellow diners. It's clearly more a term of fond affection than a simple noun!

The staple diet of those in rural communities was always related to the **potato** and other root vegetables because, for those living close to the land, this type of dish made good use of produce that was grown locally. Historically, the timing of meals for those working the fields always depended upon the beginning and end of their working day. A big breakfast, around dawn, based on boiled potatoes and baked pancakes, was followed by the main meal of the day around noon. Often served in the fields, the first course would consist of *borsch* (beetroot soup) laden with vegetables, potatoes, mushrooms and occasionally meat. In fact, to call this dish 'soup' does it something of an injustice, for it is a meal all of its own. The second course would be a dish based on cereals and more potatoes, washed down with *kvas*, *kompote* or sour milk. When the sun was at its height, it was a nourishing, filling meal, packed with energy-fuelling nutrients to keep the workers going until dusk. Supper at home after dusk would inevitably be more potatoes, this time with some form of stock. There was always a plentiful supply of bread, cereals and meat in the autumn and winter. Spring was the hungriest season of all, simply because last year's store of produce would have been consumed during the harsh winter.

Like Ukrainians, Russians and Poles, Belarusians are still fond of borsch with a very large dollop of sour cream (*smyetana*) and it is particularly warming and nourishing in the depths of winter. A thinner chilled version in the summer is hugely refreshing. Borsch is still omnipresent today on every menu, whether in a restaurant or at home. And given the historical context for modern life, it is no surprise that wherever 'Belarusian cookery' is found, whether homage to the past or invented cliché, it is based on traditions which have steadfastly survived turbulent political times. Whoever is in power, the land must be worked and mouths must be fed, whatever the privations of the people. For this reason, many dishes still are based on the potato. One particular and popular favourite is *draniki*, pancakes prepared from shredded potatoes, often fried with mushrooms and served with sour cream. It's absolutely delicious.

Historically, **meat** was often in short supply and was only really eaten on the occasion of significant Christian festivals. These days, you will find few beef dishes on a menu of Belarusian cuisine (it has never been highly regarded here), but pork has always been a favourite, along with salted pork fat, which is regarded still as a great delicacy. One of the most popular pork dishes is *machanka*, a personal favourite of mine. It is said to date from the 18th century and consists of chunks of meat in a rich and thick gravy, served in a stoneware pot with fried pancakes.

You can expect to find it on every restaurant menu. On my last visit, my family introduced me to the concept of eating (wait for it) *frozen* pork. Smoked, placed in the freezer and then eaten straight from it, your senses will tell you that everything is wrong about this curiosity, but when it (literally) melts in your mouth as you chew it, the experience is unexpectedly tasty. If it's ever offered, do give it a try.

As for **fish**, modern Belarus has no sea borders and even historically, there is no tradition of seafaring and farming of the oceans from the days when the country was included with other lands bordering the Baltic and Black seas. Much more common are lake and river fish, notably perch and carp. They are particularly tasty when served stuffed with vegetables and mushrooms. At home, river fish (locally caught, naturally) are often baked or boiled without seasoning and occasionally fried. Fish is also served in thick chunks in soup. Eels, smoked or stuffed, are the speciality of the northern lakeland territories. I have eaten eel with Eduard Voitekhovich at Komorovo, close to the border with Lithuania, freshly caught (and still alive when we got there), heavily salted and barbecued at dusk. And absolutely delicious.

The intense relationship that people in rural hinterlands still have with the land is reflected in an almost spiritual fondness for **mushrooms and berries**. Harvesting them is one of the great activities of late summer and autumn. Many dishes include fresh, salted and pickled mushrooms, together with berries of many varieties, some of which will be unfamiliar to Western visitors. Mushrooms are also often used in stuffings, sauces or fillings. Most households preserve and pickle fruits and vegetables for the winter months when there is a shortage of fresh seasonal produce.

Eating out If you eat in a restaurant outside Minsk at lunchtime you may well be the only customer and, even in the evenings, your fellow diners will most likely be the local nouveaux riches, foreign diplomatic staff (in Minsk) and businessmen. At weekends, however, it's different, with families celebrating birthdays, anniversaries and other special occasions. If a particular restaurant takes your fancy, do book in advance to avoid disappointment. For example, the most popular restaurants may well be closed to paying guests because of wedding parties.

Restaurants are increasingly offering international cuisine and traditional dishes on the same menu (the latter mainly for tourists on group tours). There are also more and more fast-food restaurants all over Minsk. In plentiful supply is the Soviet-style eatery with synthetic disco music and décor to match, with dubious cabaret entertainment. Menus are largely in Russian and Belarusian only, although restaurants are increasingly attempting English translations (often with hilarious results). They are frequently the thickness of a magazine – not because of the range of dishes on offer, but because each part of a meal is priced separately by weight. And don't be surprised to be told that several alternatives of your choices are not available! It's all part of the fun, I say.

Café culture is considerably more egalitarian in its patronage than are restaurants. Coffee bars are plentiful in the larger towns and cities, where students and young people meet to hang out and look disdainfully superior.

A cheaper but less pleasant alternative to the cafés are the shacks with outdoor seating where loud disco music is played, young waitresses wearing far too much make-up and little else lean on the counter looking very bored and the fare on offer is gassy tasteless beer and tired open sandwiches.

PUBLIC HOLIDAYS

1 January	New Year's Day
7 January	Orthodox Christmas
8 March	Women's Day
(movable)	Orthodox Easter
(movable)	Catholic Easter
9th day after Orthodox Easter	Radaunista (Ancestors' Remembrance Day)
1 May	Labour Day
9 May	Victory Day, a glorious celebration of the end of the 'Great Patriotic War'
3 July	Independence Day
7 November	October Revolution Day
25 December	Catholic Christmas

SHOPPING

In the 1970s, it was always said that in the Soviet Union shop windows were full of tempting things to buy, but that when you went inside, there was nothing on the shelves. For the most part, this was true. No self-respecting Russian would be seen out on the street without an old and tatty plastic bag, whatever the hour of day or night, just in case they came across something to buy somewhere, whether or not they actually needed or wanted it. But now, especially on the streets of Minsk, there are new designer stores selling exclusive Western labels and pharmacies selling top-range cosmetics, all with flashy billboards to match. By night, the glare of neon is beginning to light up the sky on street corners and at major road intersections. Shopping malls with piped mindless muzak and supermarkets (including 24-hour hypermarkets) are springing up all over the suburbs of major cities and on the streets of towns big and small. This even includes provincial Vetka, which will soon have its own national chain hypermarket.

For a more intriguing shopping experience that will take you back to the days of the Soviet Union, try the GUM department store in Minsk. It's a fascinating slice of post-war Soviet social history. Typical goods that make decent souvenirs include lacquered inlay caskets and trinket boxes, laminated wooden spoons, framed straw animals, ceramic plates, decorative amber incorporated into pictures of rural scenes, wooden carvings, religious artefacts, decorated wooden eggs, cheap metal badges with grand Soviet slogans under a portrait of Lenin, traditionally embroidered blouses, linen tableware, original samovars and the ubiquitous wooden *matryoshka* doll (many of which have the face of modern politicians instead of the traditional peasant woman). It's also fascinating to browse the departments of homeware, white goods, shoes, clothing, music and toys to see what's available for locals to buy.

Elsewhere on the streets, particularly in suburban neighbourhoods, you will find small metal kiosks selling newspapers, magazines, sweets, chewing gum and beer. The vendor will hardly be visible through a tiny hatch opening, while the walls and glass frontage are literally plastered with the goods that are available for purchase.

Shops are open seven days a week but some will still close on Sundays, or at least operate at reduced hours. Opening times for most shops are generally from 09.00 (occasionally from 08.00) until 18.00 and sometimes later. With the advent of more and more shopping malls and supermarkets comes a steady pushing back of opening hours, such that late-night shopping is on the increase. You will even find new hypermarkets that are open 24 hours. Indoor markets are huge, inexpensive and offer more choice than the shops. Wherever you find yourself, do try to look out the nearest one. And if you can, it's worth visiting an open-air market, particularly in the smaller towns and villages. Locals will often ride to market in a horse and cart, with the man of the house (usually elderly) up front with a large stick and a *babooshka* at the back, precariously perched among piles of turnips, potatoes and beetroots. Dress down as much as possible, try to be inconspicuous and be prepared for some lively bartering. In both types of market, be aware that 'designer' items and CDs/DVDs sold at very cheap prices will be fakes, and that pickpockets may be about, so keep one eye on your wallet and valuables at all times.

ARTS AND ENTERTAINMENT

In all the countries of the former Soviet Union, the fine arts (whether classical or avant-garde) play an important role in everyday life. On Saturday nights, concert halls and theatres across Belarus are filled with the elderly, families and young people, there to celebrate the best of Russian and Belarusian culture. Even the smallest community will have its own theatrical troupe and modest concert hall.

The price that local people pay for tickets is very low (even for the best seats at a performance given by one of the state companies in Minsk), though as a tourist you will have to pay considerably more. Don't be put off, as the price is still far less than you would pay at home. Audience knowledge of the arts is impressive and, more often than not, the quality of the performance will be very high. It's a special moment to be sitting in a theatre in Minsk as the orchestra strikes up the overture to a Tchaikovsky **ballet**, then to witness the colour and splendour of the set and the athleticism of the dancers. At the end, members of the audience will vie to be the loudest to shout bravo as awestruck little girls in their finest dress clothes nervously hand bouquets to the principal dancers.

Among the best performances are those of the National Academic Bolshoi Opera and Ballet Theatre Company, and the Belarusian State Philharmonic. Do try to take in a performance given by one of these companies. If you are travelling with one of the main tourist agencies, this will probably be included as a matter of course, but even if not and you have to book yourself, ticket availability should not be a problem (see pages 166–7 for details).

Puppet theatres and **circuses** are still very popular with children of all ages (even grown-up ones). The state circus regularly draws large crowds, but although the tumblers, jugglers and clowns are highly polished entertainers, for me the whole experience is marred by degrading animal acts such as 'flying bears', which may make you feel pretty uncomfortable. I've only been once and it's not something I'd care to repeat, much though the acrobats impress me.

In the larger towns, **live music** can be enjoyed most nights of the week, ranging from ethnic folk and jazz ensembles playing in intimate, smoke-filled venues to the latest Belarusian group hammering out stadium rock. Many restaurants have live acts, especially at weekends, the style of music reflecting the restaurant's image. Trendy places will put on a cabaret show, 1970s style, while the 'traditional' venues aiming at the tourist market will showcase folk acts, usually solo performers or duets, strumming guitars and singing of unrequited love, historical melodrama, the glory of the peasant lifestyle or the celebration of the potato harvest (and often all of them at once).

Every town will have at least one **cinema** and in Minsk there are dozens, including an open-air drive-in, together with several cinemas with surround sound, state-of-the-art digital projection and air conditioning. The latest releases are regularly shown, although they may be dubbed (badly).

Even in the smallest towns, **museums** display impressive collections of historical artefacts that tell the story of the locality through the ages. There will be exhibits focusing on the earliest settlements, the evolution of agricultural and industrial practices, folk art and ecology. These can be fairly dry, especially for children. Museum staff will be readily available to chaperone visitor groups and to offer detailed commentaries on the displays. *Babooshkas* are often on hand to collect your admission fee and to jealously guard endless rooms of exhibits.

The post-Soviet era has also led to the growth of some less family-oriented distractions. The shadier *biznizmyeni* in all six cities (and especially Minsk) have bankrolled numerous casinos, nightclubs, strip joints and lap-dancing clubs, usually adjacent to or incorporated within the larger hotels. The prostitution industry, always lucrative in the past, is still booming.

PHOTOGRAPHY

Always have with you more digital memory space than you think you are going to need. You will be able to find cards in shops in the cities and larger towns, but they won't be cheap and shops won't supply much of a variety of specialist equipment. It's also worth bringing spare camera batteries.

People you meet will usually allow you to take photographs, though you should always ask permission first. Even if they readily accept, people will often pose in very stiff and formal ways, with very serious facial expressions. Elderly people in particular will stare fiercely into the lens. If you can, make arrangements to send on a printed copy and be true to your word. The photo will take pride of place in a modest home and will be a conversation piece for guests. It's also a good idea to take photos with you of your family and children, as people will take great interest in them.

Don't be tempted to take pictures of military facilities, soldiers, militiamen, policemen, offices of the KGB (still omnipresent) or government buildings. The first sight of a camera will be greeted by a shrill blast on a whistle from a member of the militia whom you did not even know was there, and your film or camera may be confiscated.

MEDIA Ever since the date in 1991 when Belarus came into existence as an independent nation state on the disintegration of the Soviet Union, there have been claims that state control of all forms of media communication (newspapers, journals, periodicals, internet websites, email, mobile telecommunications, radio and television) has been all-encompassing, just as it was in the days of the USSR. Ironically, this followed a period of relative freedom in the final years of the Soviet Union, when President Gorbachev essayed in vain to bring about real reform of the system through glasnost ('openness') and perestroika ('restructuring'). But since that time, there has been sustained criticism on the part of human rights and 'media watch' organisations that freedom of speech has been universally suppressed in Belarus and that the state-controlled media outlets have enjoyed privileges that have been denied to independent ones. Against all the odds, some independent publications appear to have survived, but life is not easy for them. Increasing regulation of their activities makes it all too easy for them to run the risk of non-compliance, with closure being an ever-present threat. Meantime, everywhere you look, on television or in newspapers, the state's view of things is omnipresent. Suppression of freedom of speech is firmly denied by the government. The universal mandate given to the president in successive elections is cited as authority for the claim that the people are happy with things as they are. Doubtless, the small and poorly organised opposition see things differently. The context to all of this is that the United States of America and the European Union continue to cry 'foul' and to impose economic sanctions on Belarus both directly and indirectly. By way of example, the European Parliament passed a resolution under reference C157/465 in July 2005 in which it 'strongly condemns the Belarus regime's indiscriminate attacks on the media, journalists, members of the opposition, human rights activists and any person who attempts freely to voice criticism of the President and the regime'. This and all other criticism has met with robust and withering rebuttals on the part of the Belarusian government, along with suggestions that Western democracies might care to reflect on their own policies and human rights records, domestic and foreign. All the while, the Russian Federation sits impassively in the ambivalence of its own relationship with Belarus and the West. It's as though the Cold War had never ended. Inevitably, the truth lies somewhere along the great divide. Certainly, there are many pertinent questions to be asked and answered, but the same can be said for many political regimes around the world, including some very close to home. Perhaps the best indicator is the view of the human rights and 'media watch' charities that have critically reviewed the substantial body of evidence of state control and suppression of freedom of speech that is said to exist in abundance. You must make up your own mind from all that you read and see. The official website of the Republic of Belarus is www.belarus.by. The President's own website is www.president.gov.by. For an alternative view, you might continue your research on the website of Charter 97 (*www.charter97.org*), an independent organisation campaigning for human rights and democracy in Belarus. The websites of NGO Human Rights Watch (*www.hrw.org*) and not-for-profit organisation Reporters Without Frontiers (*www.rsf.org*) are also an interesting read.

An information portal that I follow by email subscription and on Twitter is the excellent Belarus Digest (*www.belarusdigest.com*). Launched in 2008, its team of contributors is headed by Yarik Kryvoi. As an online provider of non-aligned analysis on all matters pertaining to Belarus specifically aimed at an English-speaking audience, articles are extremely readable and accessible. The website's homepage commendably states its position thus: 'the conduct and poor reputation of the Belarus regime provides fertile ground for all kinds of myth and speculation. Belarus Digest tries to demystify Belarus and write about what is actually going on in the country.' On this very point, one of the most interesting pieces of journalism that I have ever read from within Belarus concerning this much-misunderstood country appeared on the *Belarus Digest* website on 19 February 2014. Entitled 'Is Belarus a European North Korea? – Top Three Myths about Belarus in Western Media', it was written by Artyom Shraibman, an analyst and political observer working for an independent news agency in Minsk. It should still be available to read in the archive section of the website (see above) and I do commend it to anyone interested in looking beyond sound bites and strap headlines. Generally, the internet is of course a treasure trove of information and a few hours spent on detailed research through the medium of your favourite search engine before you visit will be time extremely well spent.

Press The country's largest state-controlled news agency is BelTA (*www.belta. by*). It claims that on 1 January 2014, 712 newspapers and 793 magazines were in publication in the country, more than two-thirds of them apparently privately owned and run. In terms of print media, the English-language paper *Belarus Today* (*www.belarustoday.info*) is published weekly. The principal dailies are *Narodnaya Gazyeta* (*www.ng.sb.by*), *Sovyetskaya Byelarusiya* (*www.sb.by*) and *Respublika* (*www.respublika.sb.by*), all of them official state newspapers. Printed in Belarusian only is the daily *Zvyazda* (*www.zviazda.by*); PDF versions can be downloaded from the website. *Belaruskaya Dyelovaya Gazeta* (*www.bdg.by*), which temporarily closed in 2003 and again in 2006, has since resumed publication and is the main private daily paper. *Belaruskaya Gazeta* (*www.belgazeta.by*) is a weekly private publication. Also look for *Argumyenty I Fakty* (*www.aif.by*): sadly not available in English, it's a source of comment on the stories behind news and current affairs. Regional newspapers published in each of the major cities are available in each *oblast*. Most towns will have their own district newspaper, which will often be a single folded sheet containing local news of a parochial nature.

Television The state says that on 1 January 2014, 93 television stations were broadcasting daily. The state-controlled Belarusian National State Television and Radio Company, Belteleradio (*www.tvr.by*), broadcasts five channels within the country, as well as the internationally available 24-hour satellite channel Belarus 24. Its portfolio of channels within the country consists of Belarus 1 (primarily news), Belarus 2 (entertainment, culture and sports), Belarus 3 (covering, as it says itself, 'the state informational policy in the field of culture'), NTV Belarus (linked to the Russian broadcaster NTV) and Belarus 5 (exclusively sports). It's also easy to pick up a large number of stations broadcasting from Russia, and the usual international stations are available via cable and satellite. Currently 94% of television broadcasts are digitally based, with the switch from analogue to digital expected to be completed sometime in 2015.

Radio The state also says that on 1 January 2014, 169 radio stations were on air daily. The state-run company Belteleradio broadcasts five stations: 1st Channel (the flagship station for news, information and culture, the largest in the country), Radio Belarus (*www.radiobelarus.tvr.by*), which broadcasts in Belarusian, Russian, German, Polish, French, Spanish, Chinese and English; Culture, promoting national and international culture; Stolitsa, the first FM station in the country broadcasting in the Belarusian language only; and Radius FM (*www.radiusfm.by*), which delivers news and popular music 24/7. Belteleradio also broadcasts regional stations from the five major cities outside Minsk, as do a range of other service providers. Many other state-controlled stations broadcast special interest programmes. Non-state broadcasters include the popular 24/7 Euroradio FM (*www.euroradio.by*), which is aimed at the 15–35 market and broadcasts in the west of the country. Stations broadcasting from outside Belarus can also be received of course, some of them specifically targeting Belarusian listeners, such as Radio Svaboda (*www.svaboda. org*), with links to Charter 97 and Radio Free Europe (*www.rferl.org*).

Internet All of the media organisations listed above have their own websites packed with informative pages of news, comment and data. In each case, just bear in mind the identity of whoever is running the site. And do please note that those I list represent only a selection. Your browser will take you to a whole world of alternatives. As mentioned above, I follow the work and output of Belarus Digest (*www.belarusdigest.com*). You might also want to see what the organisation Charter 97 has to say (*www.charter97.org*)

POST The state post (*www.belpost.by*) offers the usual full range of postal services. Just bear in mind that mail that's not in Cyrillic script, either posted in Belarus for destinations outside the country or posted outside for delivery within Belarus, may very well not reach its destination. If you are sending mail home to the UK or US, then at the very least write ВЕЛИКОБРИТАНИЯ ('Great Britain') or СОЕДИНЕННЫЕ ШТАТЫ АМЕРИКИ ('USA') at the end of each address; that should at least guarantee that your correspondence gets to the UK or USA at some point in time, though not necessarily until after you return home. The English pages of the company's website are a mine of information and will tell you all you need to know before you travel. Branches and kiosks are everywhere throughout the country in cities, towns and villages. When you're in Minsk be sure to visit the splendid building of the central post office and don't forget to look out for the Soviet-style clock above the entrance.

TELEPHONE SERVICES The state-controlled National Telecommunications Operator of the Republic of Belarus, Beltelecom (*www.beltelecom.by*), provides a full and varied range of modern telephony services to domestic and business users. It is widely believed within the country that telephony services are routinely monitored by the state. No different from the rest of us, then…

The country code for calls from outside Belarus is 375 and the relevant code for each of the six cities and regions of the country is as follows:

Minsk	+375 17	Brest	+375 162	Mogilev	+375 222
Grodno	+375 152	Vitebsk	+375 212	Gomel	+375 232

To make an **international call to Belarus**, dial 00 (or +) 375, followed by the city/region code, and the subscriber's number, though any leading zero should be omitted.

To make an **international call from Belarus**, dial 8, wait for the continuous dialling tone, dial 10, the country code, the city code (minus the first zero), followed by the subscriber's number.

To make a **landline to landline call within Belarus,** dial 8, wait for the continuous dialling tone, then dial the city/region code followed by the subscriber's number. If making a **landline to mobile call within Belarus**, substitute the relevant mobile code (either 25, 29, 33 or 44) for the city/region code.

2

To make a **landline call within the same town in Belarus,** dial 2, then the subscriber's number only.

Cellular (mobile phone) services are supplied by Velcom (*www.velcom.by*), MTS (*www.mts.by*) and Life (*www.life.com.by*), all of which provide international roaming services. Like everywhere else in the world, mobile telephony is a hugely expanding market in Belarus and, by Western standards, it's an extremely cheap means of communication within the country's national borders. If you are going to make significant numbers of calls to local numbers within Belarus from your own mobile, you will save pots of money by purchasing a local SIM card when you arrive. Available at any retail outlet of the three mobile operators, you will need to show your passport and pay a modest registration fee. You can also obtain credit there and then. It's very easy to subsequently top up your balance online, by calling an automated number, or at a bank or mobile phone outlet. It's also a very cheap way of staying in touch with mobiles in the UK by way of SMS (text) messaging. A single message costs no more than a handful of pence, but it's not a cheap way to make voice calls. Your credit will disappear before your very eyes at a rate of knots.

For **international calls to subscribers of Belarusian mobile networks**, dial +375 then the relevant mobile code (as above) followed by the subscriber's number.

Emergency telephone numbers within Belarus
Fire brigade ✆101   **Ambulance** ✆103
Police ✆102

INTERNET As with telephony, the state-controlled National Telecommunications Operator of the Republic of Belarus, Beltelecom (*www.beltelecom.by*), oversees and runs the country's servers, a role that includes managing every connection to and from the outside world. The control of the state is, therefore, all-encompassing. In Minsk connections are fast, and secure Wi-Fi is widely available. Outside the capital, connection to the internet is largely by dial-up and is very slow. Many hotels and other public spaces throughout the country advertise the availability of secure wireless facilities. Do ensure, however, that your antivirus and security software is the best it can be. Internet cafés exist in all of the major cities and in many of the towns, big and small.

BUSINESS

Usual **business hours** for offices are 09.00–18.00 Monday–Friday; for banks 09.00–17.00 Monday–Friday; for general stores 09.00–21.00 Monday–Saturday, 09.00–18.00 Sunday; and for food shops 09.00–20.00 daily (with some of the newer supermarkets and hypermarkets open 24 hours in the city suburbs and malls). That said, a growing commitment to the adoption of standards of business services you might recognise in the West means that opening hours generally are being extended, although these hours will be more unpredictable and unreliable outside the big cities, and closure for lunch everywhere between 13.00 and 14.00 is fairly common.

If you are in Belarus on business, remember that **bureaucracy and red tape** is a frustrating and omnipresent obstacle to speed, efficiency and flexibility with any transaction, so do plan ahead as much as you can. And do try very hard not to show frustration at legal or administrative requirements and bureaucracy in general. If you do, then things will always be slowed down and another obstacle placed in your way. There's nothing wrong with persisting if you think you're being fobbed off, but this can be done with courtesy, respect and a smile. If you are unsure of your ground it's preferable not to try to blunder on unaided in the search for a way forward. You will always be able to engage the services of a local lawyer or other business consultant to help smooth the way. Belarusians are used to functioning in an impenetrable miasma of contradictory rules and regulations, which means they will generally reserve judgement on an issue or question until they are sure of themselves in any situation.

At first meeting, you can probably expect a brief but very firm handshake and a curt nod of the head by way of introduction. Don't expect effusive enthusiasm and open doors at the outset of negotiations. It's then a question of deporting yourself with all the usual niceties and common courtesies of civilised **business behaviour**. Listen closely, never interrupt or patronise anyone, always acknowledge the other person's point of view, then put your own arguments quietly, respectfully and without histrionics. A touch of dry humour usually goes down very well. Don't try to suggest that your position is in any way stronger than anyone else's or seek to impose your point of view with conduct that might be viewed as bullying. If you do, the shutters will come up and there will be no progress. Bureaucracy and red tape here is difficult enough without you making it easy for someone to shrug their shoulders and tell you that something cannot happen because 'it is not permitted' (a phrase oft used). If you stay calm throughout with a smile on your face, then you can expect to be listened to respectfully, especially if you are also prepared to make concessions in an effort to move things along. And it helps to show that you regard your counterparts as being of equal status to you in every way.

If and when a decision is made on an issue that is acceptable to all sides, the matter does not end there. Decisions are made in stages, upwards through a hierarchy, so even if you manage to gain agreement at one level of an organisation, it does not automatically follow that superiors will agree. Generally speaking, the higher up you go, the easier it is to get a 'yes', but it is not uncommon for matters to proceed a very long way (and right to the point of conclusion), only for everything to be called off without explanation. So always have an alternative plan ready. And as with negotiations the world over, in business or life in general, if you can make the other side think that it was all their idea in the first place, so much the better.

Overall, there are continuing signs that, in economic terms, the country is beginning to open up internally and to look outside its borders in terms of trade, business and commerce. The obvious caveat here is the all-encompassing nature of state control. The economy continues to be run on a rigidly planned basis, and even though a growing number of entrepreneurs are looking to imaginatively transact business across national borders, all private operations are subject to registration, detailed scrutiny, regulation and bureaucracy. Whether private or state, the control of every enterprise is absolute. The government is ever more keen to encourage foreign investment into the country, and there are many examples of significant joint enterprise ventures to be seen, although it's usually on the basis that strategic and practical decisions on the way all monies are spent remain fully in Belarusian hands. This has led to a number of high profile deals running into the sand.

It remains to be seen how much further the country will extend its hand towards the economic markets of Europe and beyond. It's not an agenda Belarus can control unilaterally, however. At one level, neither the European Union nor the United States of America believe that conditions are favourable for businesses in their countries to trade here. Even before this point can be reached, de facto sanctions operate extensively in the absence of the significant political reform and evidence of a commitment to free speech and the unconditional observance of human rights that the West deems both necessary and appropriate. Meantime, President Lukashenko shows no sign of embracing political reform or abandoning the state's commitment to a planned and controlled economy in favour of more free-market principles. Yet the language of every public statement is about opening up trade with the rest of Europe and beyond. There are many agendas at work here. Belarus continues to push for greater co-operation and ultimately perhaps even formal union with the Russian Federation. But President Putin is walking a very thin line. He wants to see Russia playing a full part on the world economic and political stage, but he knows full well that those with the biggest clout, most notably the USA, view Belarus as a market and administration in need of major governmental reform. In 2014, relations between Russia and the West steadily worsened as the crisis in Ukraine sank to the edge of the abyss. It is very difficult to forecast how things will go from here.

BUYING PROPERTY

Type 'buying property in Belarus' into a search engine and you will immediately gain access to several websites telling you how easy it is to become a property owner in Belarus. Don't be fooled. Although the voracious market in land and property deals is focusing increasingly on the countries of the former Eastern bloc as the latest source of cheap investment, Belarus is firmly closed for business in this market. There is no real concept of proprietorial land ownership as there is in the West. Many people rent their homes from the state. In the country, there is no zeal for being ostentatiously seen as lord and master of the land, as evidenced by a distinctly laissez-faire attitude to the delineation of property boundaries. People here just aren't in the least bothered about being seen as land and property owners. They have far more important things to occupy their time and thoughts.

CULTURAL ETIQUETTE

The characteristics of the Belarusian people are hard to generalise, and in any event it's hugely difficult to give a view without sounding monumentally patronising. The general adage that 'you can only speak as you find' is as true with this as with anything else. The comments that follow, therefore, are an articulation of the impressions I have gained from interacting closely with a range of people over a period of 14 years, including senior government officials, journalists, business people, teachers, academics, public officers and, perhaps most importantly of all, a multitude of everyday folk in their homes and communities. If I have to generalise, I would say that a calm demeanour, tolerance and a wicked sense of dry humour have often manifested themselves in my time in Belarus. And people here can get very passionate when debating the big issues of the day, which often happens around the kitchen table. You will be expected to play your part in the debate and will be asked a great many questions about life where you come from. Be honest, but be very careful about how you comment on Belarusian society. Derogatory statements will not go down well. Never be critical of the government or of the president, as you never know who might be listening. When it comes to how you behave, it's a cliché, but Soviet trains really did run with absolute punctuality, so never be late for events or meetings.

Despite the legacy of the Soviet era, the outward face of Belarus is youthful, energetic and optimistic. Young people are encouraged to pursue every sport going, including track and field athletics, gymnastics, cross-country skiing, ice hockey, volleyball, tennis and handball. For a small country it has performed consistently well at successive summer and winter Olympic games for years, with the haul of six gold medals at the Sochi winter games in 2014 being the high point of achievement. In Max Mirnyi, the country had one of the top men's doubles tennis players in the world a few years ago, while in the same sport Victoria Azarenka is a former world number one and singles grand slam winner. Track cycling and ice hockey world championships have both been held in Belarus in recent years. President Lukashenko, a major ice-hockey fan, has decreed that every town is to have its own sports palace, offering a full range of sporting opportunities to the country's youth.

The *banya*, or Belarusian sauna, can be a great way to bond with hosts and friends (see box, *The bathhouse culture*, page 40). There are communal *banya* in many towns with nominal entrance fees. The format is largely the same as private *banya*, but the anteroom will be much larger and will contain communal shower facilities, while cold water will be available in a plunging pool outside the steam room. You will inevitably be in the company of strangers here, so the bonding experience of the more intimate private *banya* shared with friends will probably be supplanted by macho posturing.

TRAVELLING POSITIVELY

When I talk to people about how unspoilt and uncommercialised Belarus is and about how that makes it a destination of rare interest for the visitor, the response is always the same: that nobody will go until budget flights are available.

That is a very depressing supposition. Put bluntly, there is a very persuasive argument that the footprint we leave as we depart a country has considerably greater importance than the intentions and aspirations we have for our visit when we arrive. Budget flights anywhere do not necessarily encourage such an altruistic aim, and the very opposite can sometimes be an unfortunate consequence.

Since the Chernobyl catastrophe, much of the aid that has been targeted at Belarus and its people has been by way of humanitarian assistance. Yet for a number of years, sustainable development programmes have been on the increase, with the purpose of transferring skills and experience to help build an infrastructure for local people to develop local solutions to their own problems.

Your presence in Belarus and the interest you show in the people you meet and all that you see will be a very good start. To give you a few ideas about continued involvement on your return home, you might want to have a look at the websites listed on page 107. They will give you a broad feel for the types of project that are being supported by the international community. I shall be very surprised if you do not return from your first visit with a burning resolve to put something back into this wonderful country and its people. Plenty of options exist, certainly in the UK and Ireland. The best thing of all is that you can get involved quickly in your own locality and pretty soon you will have the chance to take a direct and active part. My own view is that while humanitarian assistance can certainly help to alleviate some of the hardship that exists in this country, it does little to stimulate growth and development within the regions in sustainable terms. And it is only by this means that communities and individuals will be able to build confidence and self-respect in the search for ownership and control of their own destiny. The development work that I have had the opportunity to undertake with Belarusian communities over the last 14 years is *absolutely* the most rewarding and fulfilling thing that I have ever done. At the outset, I had no specialist skills in the field, but by learning with people in the communities themselves (as they progressed their own learning and experience), I have been fortunate indeed to feel that it really is possible to make a difference to (and have a positive impact on) the lives of real people. The work

One of the early projects that WOVA chose to support in its infancy was the establishment of a goose-farming co-operative in the village of Svetilovichy, right in the heart of the contaminated zone in southeastern Belarus. A beautiful (but very hot) summer's day saw me standing by a dusty roadside on the edge of the village, waiting to chaperone a flock of goslings to their new homes. After an hour or so, a battered and beaten saloon pulled up. Out clambered the driver, extremely hot and bothered. When he opened up the back I could scarcely believe my eyes, for crammed in from floor to ceiling was tray after tray of two-day old goslings, 750 of them. They had travelled all the way from Minsk, a seven-hour journey, without water or fresh air. Miraculously, all survived. After a cursory examination of the precious cargo, we led the saloon through the village to a small farmstead, where local villagers had been waiting patiently for over two hours in the heat of the midday sun. They formed an orderly queue to the rear of the saloon and each family or individual took charge of 20 inquisitive and noisy birds, some of the villagers stuffing them into wicker baskets for transportation home. Many of the aged *babooshkas* had tears of gratitude in their eyes and flowing down their cheeks as they headed slowly home with their new charges. Witnessing this scene of real community engagement, it was impossible not to be moved and deeply humbled. The local co-ordinator Anna wept uncontrollably as we stood side-by-side and hand in hand to watch the distribution process. I drive through this village regularly on my travels. On one such occasion, our car pulled to the side of the road and there stood Anna, overjoyed to see me again and tearful as ever, to give extravagant hugs and kisses and to press a plastic carrier bag of gifts into my hand for my wife and children, before pushing me gently (but with purpose) back into the car. The whole encounter took no more than 30 seconds, but she had heard that I was in the locality and had waited by the roadside for my car to pass through, to give me presents for my family. As for the fate of the geese and the co-operative? Ah, that's another story for another book…

isn't easy and is sometimes very frustrating, yet in terms not only of the outcomes delivered in Belarus, but also my own personal development, I wouldn't change a single moment of it. My colleagues and I have made plenty of mistakes, but I'd like to think we have learned from all of them and have tried to put the experience of that shared learning into positive outcomes in our subsequent project work.

In 2009, I was taken to see the grimly named 'Children's Correction Centre' in Vetka. It supports children and their families across a full spectrum of special needs, from slow learning and speech therapy at one end, all the way to profound physical and mental disability at the other. That first visit made it very clear that the centre itself had many needs, and when I went back in 2010 to spend the week there, I could see this was the project that the charity I helped to found back in 2001 (West Oxfordshire Vetka Association, see opposite) had been waiting to find. For starters, half of the centre's buildings were derelict and in need of major works of structural repair. We developed a detailed project plan and a strategy for sourcing offers of expertise, funding and support to deliver the facilities that the children, their families and the devoted staff so richly deserve. Full details, including copies of the project documents themselves, are available from the WOVA website. It was a difficult and frustrating journey. Although now a patron, I'm no longer directly involved with WOVA's day-to-day activities, but I'm very happy to report that before I moved on, the good news in the spring of 2014 was that the vast majority of the necessary works had been completed. I and my co-trustee David Tee were invited to attend the grand opening that was due to take place in September 2014, but we politely declined. It was more than enough for us to know that local children and families supported there would have the centre they needed. We didn't embark on the project for public acknowledgement and a high-profile media presence. We'll leave all that to the ex-politicians now playing a public role in the higher strata of international organisations who fly into areas of need by helicopter and fly out a few hours later after being photographed with local dignitaries and posting self-publicising material on their Twitter and Facebook accounts. This has happened many times in the areas where we have worked, but I'll save the articulation of my frustrations on this for my blog and other publications beyond the remit of this guide. For now, read more about some of the remarkable children I have met and a little of my encounters involving the centre in the boxes, *So who is correcting whom here? (Parts I, II and III)*, on pages 108–9, 110–11 and 282–3 respectively.

All of the projects I have worked on, even those with less success than others, have enriched my life beyond measure. And to feel that I have been taken into the hearts of people in a very different community from my own is truly humbling. Every time my plane touches down at Minsk or I cross the border, it feels like coming home. Getting involved couldn't be easier. Over to you now to play your part.

Chernobyl Children's Project www.chernobyl-children.org.uk. An umbrella charity with regional groups in England, Scotland & Wales working with children, families & young people in the aftermath of the nuclear disaster. Support is given to children's cancer treatment, hospices, orphanages & holiday camps within Belarus, while every year recuperative holidays in the UK are offered to groups of children living in the areas blighted by radiation.

Chernobyl Children International www.chernobyl-international.com. Based in Ireland, this organisation has undertaken an astonishing amount of work over the last 20 years or so, raising around €96.5 million of direct aid to regions affected by the catastrophe & arranging recuperation breaks in Ireland for approximately 24,500 children.

United National Development Programme www.un.by/en/undp. This website is dedicated to the United Nations Development Programme in Belarus. The entirety of the programme has a global application in the field of sustainable development. There are many initiatives presently under way in Belarus.

West Oxfordshire Vetka Association www.wova.org.uk. I make no apology for including this small charity in the directory, even though for many years I was one of the founding trustees. I do hope that readers will forgive this rather shameful piece of opportunistic advertising for a cause that remains close to my heart even though I am no longer directly involved in its work. The aim of the organisation is to promote & deliver sustainable development projects jointly with local representative bodies & NGOs in communities affected by Chernobyl in the Vetka region of Gomel *oblast*.

The Together Plan ✆+44 208 445 5057; m +44 7887 687501; e thetogetherplan@gmail.com. A UK charity based in London and working closely with partner organisation Dialog in Minsk, its aim is to help & support a number of Jewish communities in Belarus to develop & realise their potential, including the Minsk Jewish Ghetto Survivors Association (see box, *Frieda's Story*, page 164).

A brief word now about local charities and NGOs operating in Belarus that are not related to the alleviation of Chernobyl consequences. They certainly do exist and indeed, I have many Belarusian friends and colleagues undertaking splendid work in the field of community development and the promotion of family health and well-being, but if you type 'charities in Belarus' into your internet search engine, page after page will appear with a Chernobyl theme. I know of many small individual NGOs operating in the regions and indeed, I have worked closely with a number of them on locally focused projects designed to benefit particular communities, or parts of them. State rules and regulations applicable to NGOs in this country are extremely comprehensive (that's a euphemism) and life can be difficult for them. The best way to gain access to their areas of activity is via the United Nations and its constituent bodies, such as UNDP or UNICEF. An hour or two spent on the relevant websites will enable you to locate projects of specific application, including details of local partner NGOs and charities in Belarus itself.

Alternatively, all of the charities whose objects are related to the alleviation of problems and consequences for Chernobyl children and their families have

SO WHO IS CORRECTING WHOM HERE? (PART I)

David and I are spending the day at the Children's Correction Centre in Vetka. We walk into a small room, where soothing music is softly playing. It has simple, basic furniture and ordinary décor. At a table in the middle of the room sits Zhenya. He is 14 years old. When he first starting coming to the centre, all he could do was walk and lie down, but not sit. As he rocks slowly backwards and forwards, his head on his chest, the face of teacher Galina glows with pride as she tells of the great progress he is making, and how it is a wonderful achievement for him to be able to sit unaided. Sometimes he lifts his head, mutters indistinct sounds and smiles. He is the eldest child of four in his family, and lives in a village 30km away, where there are still hotspots of radiation following the Chernobyl catastrophe 28 years ago.

Zhenya is doubly incontinent, and sometimes his family has no nappies for him. With love and devotion, Galina works with him every day to develop his basic motor functions. She begins each session by gently massaging his hands. He is unable to hold a pencil, and wouldn't know what to do with it anyway, but with Galina's guiding hand, he becomes an artist. She paints his own hand with bright red paint and then gently places it on a sheet of paper for him to make his handprint. Today he has a cold. He sneezes and snuffles, and sits and rocks.

In a corner of the same room, held on a rudimentary couch of cushions by a single harness attached by velcro, lies Nina, who is also 14 years old. Her mother sits quietly in another corner, hands in lap, patiently watching all that transpires in this room of calm, loving care. Nina has profound and very significant needs, the most pressing of which are caused by acute hydrocephalus. Mum says that inside her head, which teacher Tatyana gently strokes, 20% is brain and 80% is water. In the UK, the condition can be treated by the application of a routine procedure to drain the fluid. Here in Belarus, it seems that no such procedure is available.

Nina can see and hear and she smiles a great deal, especially when she is spoken to and when you hold her hand. She has the most beautifully radiant smile, which lights up the room and makes everyone's heart sing. She adores music and she loves to be touched and stroked. When David and I sit by her side and hold her hand, in slow and deliberate motion she turns her head towards us, and she beams that dazzling smile. Tatyana and Mum release the harness and together they lift her into a semi-upright sitting position, which is no easy task; she has little or no motor function. But when you hold her hand, she hangs on for dear life. For many moments, this girl is the centre of the universe for us all.

Mum tells us that she is able to sound out simple words – 'mum', 'dad', 'give' – and that she has very discerning taste. At every meal, Mum chews Nina's food and locally based activities and functions throughout the UK, Ireland and many other countries in western Europe. Offers of help and assistance, particularly with regard to hosting Belarusian children on recuperative holidays, are always gratefully received. Wherever you live, a local branch is unlikely to be far away. I have met many families who have offered their homes to children in this way and entirely without exception, the experience has always been described to me as a life-affirming one. Irrespective of this being a wonderful opportunity for you to 'give something back', it will also greatly enhance your own personal development and that of your family members, particularly children. Kids are rarely burdened with the baggage that only comes with adulthood and to see deep friendships flourish between youngsters, notwithstanding language barriers, is an experience not to be

then transfers it into her mouth. If she doesn't like it, she spits it out. We hear that she particularly likes chocolate. Not for the first time today, I think of my own kids.

It is at this point that Galina whispers to our translator Oxana that she would like to ask her a personal question outside. When they come back into the room, Oxana quietly says that Galina is worried we might be upset by today's experience, that we might find it 'distasteful'. They aren't used to people (anyone) even coming to the centre to show the slightest passing interest, let alone sitting with the children, touching them, talking to them.

Nina is yawning now and we leave her to rest for a while. In his corner, Zhenya snoozes fitfully, his hands behind his head. Over a cup of tea, the centre's Director, Elena, tells us more about the two children, and also about Vanya. His hydrocephalus is severe and specialists attend him at home, because he cannot be transported to the centre. He is blind and has only limited hearing. November will see his 16th birthday. Support to his family includes a significant psychological element for his mother. She cries a great deal.

Today is our third consecutive visit. Each time, around lunchtime, we have taken tea with Elena. And on each occasion, as we look out of the window, the centre's bus draws up outside the window. Galina and Tatyana hold a hand each to walk Zhenya out for the ride home. Cradling her precious child carefully in her arms, Nina's mum carries her to the bus and climbs aboard to sit with her on her lap. There is no harness and no seat belt. Today I see them to the bus and wave as the door is closed. Nina smiles and she is gone. Every day, the driver covers 360km of Vetka's roads, some of them dirt tracks, to collect the children and then return them home again.

Later, as we emerge into the spring sunshine for a walk, we ask if Elena and Oxana will do us the honour of allowing us to buy them lunch. Our offer is politely declined. Then with the trace of a smile, first Elena tells us that she likes red roses, then Oxana tells us her preference is for black. Later, as we walk back through town, Elena announces that she has changed her mind. It would please her greatly if we could buy nappies. Zhenya has no need for red roses.

The next day, David and I go to the market. We buy nappies, washing powder and food for Nina, Zhenya, the others and their families. We spend less than £20. A measly 20 quid. A fast-food meal for four at home. A third of a tank of fuel for a family car. Three packets of cigarettes. So who or what really needs correcting here?

For Part II see pages 110–11; for Part III see pages 282–3.

2

missed. And this can be the door that leads you to other community-based activities for the benefit of families and individuals in Belarus. There are opportunities to support any number of projects that are designed to build capacity and well-being, from investment, funding and monetary donations on the one hand, all the way to more direct contributions on the other, including for example, offering skills and expertise for building projects, driving vehicles bearing humanitarian aid or

SO WHO IS CORRECTING WHOM HERE? (PART II)

For Part I see pages 108–9; for Part III see pages 282–3.
There is an inevitably depressing reality about every block of flats in Belarus, and in every former Eastern bloc state that I've been to for that matter; the concrete is archetypically Soviet and almost always crumbling, the condensation on the windows is impenetrable, there's usually an overweight topless bloke leaning over a balcony somewhere smoking a cigarette, and the common areas are unremittingly grim. And as we mount the stairs to the top floor of this particular block on Sverdlova Street in the town of Vetka, deep in the heart of the Chernobyl radiation zone, I feel nervous. Elena asked us to think very carefully before we agreed to meet Vanya. His mother cries a lot. We might be upset, or offended, she says.

We reach the top floor and knock on the last door. We are welcomed inside and we enter a world of calm, peaceful order. The weather is really hot this week and inside the flat, it's rather airless and oppressive (or is that just our nervousness?). I feel clumsy as introductions are made, and in my haste to remove my shoes I tread on the phone and send it flying. But Vanya's mother Natasha greets us warmly. She is anxious that we meet her son.

He lies on a covering on a rubber sheet on a short bed in a small room, where Belarusian folk music gently plays on a small music system. Vanya likes music, you see, and he especially likes Belarusian folk. The first thing I notice is the size of his head. His face is turned in our direction and his eyes are open, but I know at once that he doesn't see us. Those sightless, unfocused eyes roll in their sockets as we gather round him. His breathing is steady. A blanket covers him from the neck down (it's the mosquito season), but we can tell at once that his small body is motionless and locked in the foetal position.

Natasha talks to him and we can see that he knows her voice. His carer Anna says that he likes to be touched (just like Nina). She delicately taps the side of the wardrobe above Vanya's head, and his mouth opens into an enormous smile. Even though he cannot see and can only slightly distinguish between dark and light, his hearing is good and he adores that knocking sound.

As I hold Vanya's hand, which is grotesquely locked in an unnaturally awkward position, Anna gently unfurls two of his fingers, which are long, and slim, and quite beautiful. The fingers of a musician, we all agree. Later, after we have gone, Anna will dab paint on his finger, just as Galina and Natasha do with Zhenya and Nina at the centre, then she will gently press it to the paper on which is drawn a beautiful tree in springtime, with long branches and nascent greenery; for it is Vanya's job to add the finishing touch of blossom. That beautiful picture will be framed when we get home, and prominently displayed.

David and I want people to know about Vanya.

It is time to let him rest, and Natasha ushers us into the living room. She has 'English tea' for us, as well as freshly baked buns. With something of a flourish, she reaches into the sideboard behind her, produces a bottle of vodka, and presents it collecting plant and equipment in your own country for transportation to Belarus. Among other things, I have taken through customs a computer modem, medical equipment, toys, books, writing equipment, resuscitation dummies, clothes and a coffee jug. Oh and the lawnmower, of course (see box, page 50). Opportunities to make a contribution really are boundless and you won't regret a single moment or a single penny.

to me to take home. While I'm saying thank you, she reaches for another bottle. This time it is Russian champagne. We raise our glasses and drink to Vanya. Natasha tells us all about him. Everything about his birth was normal and for the first few weeks of his life, there were no indications that anything was amiss. Then one morning, as she stood over his crib, he woke. She watched as his eyes first opened, and then slowly rolled to the top of their sockets. Natasha's own eyes are now watery as she tells us that with each day that passed, his head began to grow; how he would cry every day, and that he was inconsolable. They didn't know what to do. No-one could help. It has been a long, steady process of decline and degeneration since then. Natasha tells us how lucky she is that Vanya's father, Kolya, is so devoted to him. Every day, he carries Vanya to the bath, climbs in first with the boy in his arms, and lowers him slowly into the water as he sits down beneath him, a feat of formidable endurance and strength. The dignity and strength and love and endurance of this family leave all of us in awe, and the living room is very quiet now.

Natasha turns to the sideboard again, rummages in a box of papers, and pulls out two documents. Vanya has not only a civilian passport issued by the government, just like everybody else, but he also has an army one. We hear of Natasha's pride, and also of her anguish, the day the military came to tell the family they wanted Vanya to play his part in the defence of the Motherland. He would never be able to, of course, but the bestowing of such revered status was nonetheless a source of great honour. This boy has the authority of the state and of the military to go anywhere in the world, but his condition is so severe that he cannot leave his home, not even to go to the centre; his world is his bedroom, the bathroom and the living room of this top-floor flat. He has no motor function, must be carried everywhere, and his whole body, especially his head, must be fully supported at all times.

Natasha's tears flow again as I squeeze her hand.

Later in the week, David and I would meet the local Director of Education, and give our pledge not to abandon Zhenya and Nina and Vanya and the others. As I hold Natasha's hand now, I look into her eyes and give the same pledge. She is grateful that we have come, and that we have listened. Some visitors from elsewhere in Europe came last year, she tells us; they took photographs and tea, and smiled and laughed, then left. She hasn't seen or heard from them since.

Footnote: Over the next two years, David and I got to know Kolya, Natasha and Vanya really well. We spent many hours in their company. Then one Friday night in March I was at a football match in Doncaster with my son George when I received an unexpected and very distressed phone call from Natasha. Vanya was unwell, she told me, and was in hospital. The doctors said there was nothing they could do. After a short illness, Vanya Agophonov died on 30 March 2012. He was 17 years old. Our dear Vanya was laid to rest the very next day.

Part Two

THE GUIDE

3

Minsk City and *Oblast*
Мінск / Минск

Telephone code 17

Minsk (Belarusian Мінск and Russian Минск) is the capital and largest city in Belarus, with a population of 1,921,000 in 2014. As the national capital, it has special administrative status in the country and it is also the administrative centre of Minsk *oblast*. Perhaps surprisingly, given the geographical size and metaphorical significance of its giant neighbour the Russian Federation, Minsk is also the headquarters of the Commonwealth of Independent States (CIS), which was formed on the breakup of the Soviet Union. In truth, however, the significance of this status is minimal. The CIS was always a fluid federation, honoured more in concept than reality, and the extent to which it even actually still exists is very much open to question.

First reference to a settlement here appeared in the *Primary Chronicle* of 1067 (acknowledged as an authoritative work of written Kievan Rus history). Situated on one of the most significant trade routes connecting the Baltic and Black seas, today this reconstructed city of expansive boulevards, wide streets, modern and Classical architecture, huge shaded parks, fountains and monuments to heroism on the banks of the Svislach River has an appeal all of its own that it will take you some while to articulate, even though you feel it as soon as you set foot here. It has long been regarded as one of the most impressive cities in all of the republics of the former Soviet Union. Almost completely destroyed by the Nazis in World War II (still referred to in the former Soviet republics as the 'Great Patriotic War'), Stalin ordered it to be rebuilt after the conflict ended in a manner that would stand as a testament to the rest of the world of the might, resilience and ingenuity of Soviet communism. As such, it remains the best example of post-war Soviet urban planning on a grand scale (and the only one of the western Soviet republics' capital cities largely untainted, for now, by Western commercialism, though the balance is tipping ever more quickly). Herein lies its appeal and idiosyncrasy, for after a short while here you begin to realise that it is unlike any other capital city that you have visited before.

Minsk is the sort of place where you can feel relaxed and at ease without even knowing it. Most capitals of the world are characterised by a high level of ambient noise and a jumble of activity wherever you look. Not so Minsk. For a city of nearly two million people, the atmosphere is universally calm. Outside rush hour, when there is gridlock at major junctions and drivers are impatiently leaning on car horns, ten-lane boulevards are often devoid of traffic. In many cities of the world, there is a feeling of claustrophobia as buildings close in on top of each other. But in Minsk, the skies are huge and there is a real sense of open space. Everywhere you go, there are vast and sweeping panoramas to take in, all with a host of different sights. At times, you can seemingly stroll for ages in areas of parkland and not see another soul, but without feeling nervous in the process. The streets are spotlessly clean and free from crime. Access to all areas of interest to the visitor by public transport is simple and uncomplicated, not to say impressively efficient. Many of the sights can be reached on foot and in so doing, you will rediscover an activity that is largely lost in the West: that of promenading. This is because walking is seen as so much more than simply a mechanical act of propulsion from A to B. Rather, it is an art form to be savoured, with every footstep to be relished. Everywhere you look, even in the depths of winter and no matter what the time of day or night, you will see people strolling, apparently aimlessly, but locked in conversation and arm in arm. Here in Minsk (and indeed, everywhere in Belarus), teenagers mingle with families, young children, older people and young women on their own or in twos, just taking the air, enjoying the sights, chatting and relishing the fact that they have, for a short while, stepped off the merry-go-round of life.

My favourite time to be in Minsk is on a Sunday, before breakfast. I always set the alarm early and get out on the street as soon as I can lever myself out of bed, just to walk and walk. The grandiose buildings and particularly the monuments to the heroism of the city and its people during the privations of war are all the more impressive if you can enjoy them in solitude and in silence. Inner peace, serenity, a feeling of security and a rare connection with the soul, all on the streets of a major capital city? Count on it!

GEOGRAPHY AND CLIMATE

As your plane gradually descends on its approach into Minsk, you may be surprised to find relatively dense forest not that far from the airport. It's true that Minsk-2 National is a little way out of town, but a drive through the suburbs of the city also reveals pockets of dense woodland either side of the main routes. They have been ingeniously incorporated into areas of parkland, but the whole effect is to give a very clear impression of the great swathe of primeval forest that once covered the entirety of the central European plain.

The hills across which the city has spread over the centuries and through which the Svislach River gently meanders can hardly be called hills at all, for the mean altitude above sea level struggles to reach 200m. And whether you approach Minsk by land or by air, from any direction, the impression gained is always the same: it's pretty flat.

A cursory glance at the map of Europe shows that Belarus is situated right in the middle of the continental land mass, with the capital city itself at the heart of the country.

All of these factors combine to produce a moderate continental temperate climate. Prevailing winds are westerly, northwesterly and southwesterly, a consequence of which is the relatively frequent incidence of moist air masses from the Atlantic. So it is that average temperatures for each season and the annual level of precipitation, as both rain and snow, sit in the middle of the average for the whole country.

HISTORY

It does not overstate the issue to say that the entire history of Minsk (and indeed, of greater Belarus) is characterised by conflict, invasion and subjugation. It is a quirk of fate or the whim of the gods that it just happens to have been in absolutely the wrong place on so many occasions, caught between the envious gaze of warring and expansionist neighbours on all sides. This is reflected in the history of the city. First mentioned in chronicles as Menesk in 1067, it was founded on the banks of the Svislach and Nyamia rivers, when the population of an older settlement 16km away on the Menka River (from which Minsk derives its name) moved to a more favourable location, the site of the present city. Today, the village of Gorodische is located on that original site. The first settlement was no more than a fortified wooden fortress incorporating the homes of the townspeople, the whole being surrounded by earthen ramparts. It came under the protection of the state of Polotsk, widely regarded as the first ever independent Belarusian state. The first structures of stone had appeared by the middle of the 12th century, by which time the significance of the town was incrementally rising as a consequence of the separation of Polotsk into a smaller number of independent jurisdictions, each under the control of its own prince. Before the split, the territory of the town and the entirety of the area had been scarred by the violence of warfare as opposing princes sought supremacy. Its geographical location at the heart of the European continent, situated on important trade routes by road and by river, ensured its significance as a conquest to be prized.

THE 13TH TO 18TH CENTURIES When the Grand Duchy of Lithuania acquired it in 1242, key members of the local elite quickly began to enjoy privileged rank and status in the state's hierarchy and in society. As a consequence, the town soon became one of the largest and most significant in the whole of the duchy. Prince Vasily is mentioned as being ruler in 1325 and then in 1387 Prince Yagyela gifted the town and its surrounding settlements to his brother Skyrgal, who passed them to Prince Vitovt only five years later. Around this time, Minsk was added to the Wilno (now Vilnius) province of the grand duchy, before gaining greater significance as the centre of its own administrative area later that century. The emerging status of the city was recognised further in 1499, when the great Lithuanian prince Alexander bestowed Magdeburg rights of self-determination upon it. By this time, the population was around 4,000. Warfare and conflict returned again in 1505 when the town was burned and looted by the Mongol Golden Horde, although the fortified castle held out. Two years later, it came under siege again, this time by troops under the command of the Moscow prince Mikhail Glinsky. But in 1569, it became the capital of its own province upon the formation of the mighty Rzeczpospolita state (when the Treaty of Lublin united the Grand Duchy with the Kingdom of Poland). It quickly became the largest city at that time in the territory of modern Belarus, incorporating 60 other towns and villages. The Union brought about the first significant societal development of the city for some while, as a significant Polish community settled there and quickly began to influence its culture and administration.

The struggle for supremacy over this important settlement proceeded unabated. Surrounded by the three mighty states of Poland, Lithuania (which by then had joined into one) and Russia, this is hardly surprising. The Livonian War with Russia under Ivan the Terrible (which had begun in 1558) did not end until 1583, although the city's position as a powerful seat of government was further recognised in 1580 when the Grand Duchy's Supreme Court of Appeal was relocated there, alternating every two years with Wilno and Novogrudok. All the while, the cultural, commercial and spiritual development of the city was proceeding apace, despite the constant threat of warfare. As significant architectural features began to spring up all over town, its civic status was recognised when it was granted its own coat of arms (in 1591). Again, armed conflict exacted its price and significant structural damage was suffered in the war between Russia and Rzeczpospolita that began in 1654. Russian forces occupied the city in 1655, but very few houses survived and the population had been halved (to around 2,000) by the time they were expelled. In fact, the city was under Russian administration until 1667. More was to follow. The extensive works of restoration and rebuilding that were put in train thereafter were then wiped out during the Northern Wars between Russia and Sweden, first under the occupation of Swedish forces in 1707, then again when the city was retaken by Russian troops under Peter the Great.

A period of relative stability followed throughout the remainder of the 18th century, but the long period of destruction had left its mark and Minsk was by now little more than an insignificant provincial settlement of some 7,000 people. But the days of the once-mighty state of Rzeczpospolita were numbered and upon the occasion of its Second Partition in 1793, Minsk became part of another mighty state, this time the Russian Empire. It quickly acquired the status of capital of a Russian province (in 1796) and, under the patronage of its powerful new rulers, it began to grow and develop exponentially. The original blueprint for the modern city is still recognisable from this time; for example, the line of the main Zakharyevskaya thoroughfare remains as originally laid out. It subsequently became known as Francyska Skoryny Avenue, then Nyezhavizhimosty (Russian for 'Independence') and today is known as Nyezalyezhnastsi (Belarusian for 'Independence'). At this time, the city's buildings were still predominantly of wooden structure, but three major fires in the period up to 1835 had enabled the pace of redevelopment to quicken. By this time (and inevitably) civic and architectural progress had again been interrupted by warfare, when the 1812 invasion by French troops under Emperor Napoleon decimated the city's population (from 11,200 to just under 3,500). During the war, Minsk was used by the French army as a major base for munitions and weapons, as the front line moved eastward towards Moscow.

It is quite a thought to muse on the contradiction that is inherent in a city trying to grow and develop across the centuries against a backdrop of almost ceaseless destruction and bloodshed. As discussed elsewhere in this book, this contradiction and its consequential privations have gone a long way towards shaping the national psyche of the country and its people.

19TH CENTURY PROGRESS As the decades of the 18th century passed, the march of progress proved irresistible. Minsk was rebuilt as a network of streets and boulevards was established. The first library was opened in the 1830s, and the city's first fire brigade was commissioned. This was followed by the establishment of the first theatre company. Broadsheet newspapers began to appear. The population grew to around 30,000 by the middle of the century, as trade, commerce and civic administration helped to bind and strengthen the community. Not even armed insurrection on the part of nationalists in 1830 and then again in 1863 was able to halt this progress. The significance of the ancient trade routes through the city was emphasised with the construction of major road and rail links, from east to west linking Warsaw and western Europe beyond to Moscow, and from north to south linking the Baltic and Black seas. Developments to the commercial infrastructure quickly followed, as supplies of water, telephone, electricity and urban transport were established, along with new factories. In turn, this led to greater community and societal development, as churches, schools and places of entertainment sprang up all over town. As the 20th century approached, the population of the city climbed steadily towards the 100,000 mark.

WORLD WAR I AND ITS AFTERMATH Then, just as the people were getting used to stability and relative affluence, the spark of revolution grew stronger and stronger throughout the Russian Empire, as social and political emancipation gathered pace. In Minsk, major industrial development saw the rise of worker militancy, while the nationalism evidenced by the armed risings of 1830 and 1863 continued to smoulder. Then the flames of destruction burned again as the continent was ravaged by battle and bloodshed during World War I. During 1915, Minsk once again found itself a battle-scarred city right on the front line (Germany's Eastern Front) in a major theatre of warfare, as it had so many times in its history. Minsk was chosen as the location for the headquarters of the Imperial Russian Army (although the tsar and the chiefs of staff were away to the east in Mogilev), with large infrastructure facilities (such as munitions bases and military hospitals) close by. As before, the city suffered structural damage and a significant diminution in the population as citizens became refugees on the long road east in search of safety in the arms of the Motherland. The revolutionary movement sought to exploit these difficulties and a massive campaign to undermine the morale of the troops proved to be successful. As the Bolsheviks promised bread and peace to soldiers, workers and families alike in the internationalist fight against the global oppression of the ruling classes, matters came to a head when Lenin swept into government following the November Revolution of 1917. A Soviet of Workers was immediately established in the city as the army simply imploded, with disillusioned soldiers deserting in their tens of thousands and trudging home eastward. At the end of December, the National Belarusian Congress made a formal declaration of the birth of the Belarusian People's Republic, an independent nation state. As a result of the negotiated Treaty of Brest-Litovsk (a staggering piece of exploitative and politically expedient diplomacy on the part of Lenin), which delivered Russia's withdrawal from the war, Minsk fell under the occupation of German troops in February 1918. Then on 25 March, the declaration of independence made in December was formally adopted and the city was pronounced capital of the nascent state. Independence lasted less than 12 months, and in December 1918 the Red Army marched into town. Its status as a capital city was reaffirmed in January 1919, but this time of the brand new Belarusian Soviet Socialist Republic (BSSR). A new order had begun, although further destruction and loss of life followed in the war between the emerging USSR and Poland, as Lenin sought to unite many territories under the red flag. The war was not formally ended until the Treaty of Riga, when (once and for all) Minsk became capital of the BSSR (one of the founding republics of the newly proclaimed USSR), a position that the city held until the breakup of the Soviet Union in 1991, when it became the capital of the newly independent Republic of Belarus.

Throughout the remainder of the 1920s and the 1930s, Minsk (in keeping with the rest of the Soviet Union) benefited from exponential development on a startling scale. An ambitious programme of industrialisation and reconstruction began as soon as hostilities ended and, within a short space of time, it had gained pace and momentum never before seen in the Western world. In a few short years, huge new industrial complexes were in full production to deliver the state-controlled objectives of succeeding Five Year Plans, while the workers and citizens themselves began to benefit from ambitiously established social welfare and community facilities in the form of new schools, hospitals and places of entertainment. But nothing was as it seemed, of course. It was only decades later that details of the backdrop of ideological, social and artistic persecution perpetrated by Stalin's brutality in the name of protecting 'the Revolution' began to emerge.

THE GREAT PATRIOTIC WAR The cyclical view of history is generally found to be correct, and it was again the city's destiny that one yoke of oppression was replaced by another. The rise of Nazi barbarism in Germany throughout this time was a cause of great anxiety, both East and West. Prior to the outbreak of hostilities in September 1939 the population of the city was around 300,000, but after Germany unexpectedly tore up the notorious Molotov–Ribbentrop Pact of Non-Aggression by launching Operation Barbarossa and invading the Soviet Union on 22 June 1941, Minsk again found itself right on the front line of battle as it had so many times before in its history. The city suffered the horror of aerial bombardment by Blitzkrieg on the very first day of the invasion as Hitler sought to subjugate the population through terror and it was no surprise when it fell to the invading German army just six days later. The occupation was to endure for 1,100 days. Stalin's policy had been to buy some time by falling back immediately in the defence of Moscow and, as a result, a great deal of plant and machinery from the majority of the factories in the city, along with tens of thousands of people from the civilian population (with the most precious of museum and gallery artefacts), had already been shipped eastward deeper into the Motherland, for protection, security and to be preserved for future use.

The Nazis immediately declared Minsk the centre of a new Eastern Reichskommissariat and local people were treated with merciless and abject brutality. The context for this was Hitler's absolute belief that the Slavs were a 'subhuman' race that was to be eradicated from the face of the earth. So it was that communists, so-called 'sympathisers', partisans and ordinary men, women and children were imprisoned, tortured and murdered. Public parks became the site of mass hangings. Many more from the local population were pressed into slave labour, both within Belarus and also following transportation to all corners of the Reich. Food became scarce in the extreme as supplies were requisitioned to feed the occupying forces and thousands of civilians starved to death. The worst of the barbarism was inflicted on the Jewish community (see *Frieda's Story*, page 164 and *Jewish Minsk*, pages 161–2). It is not widely known that the city became one of the largest of the Nazi ghettos throughout Europe in the war, with up to 100,000 Jews imprisoned there. But by early 1942, the city and its people had begun to fight back, as Minsk became the focal point and pivotal administrative centre of the entire Soviet partisan resistance movement throughout the struggle against oppression in Stalin's Great Patriotic War.

LIBERATION AND THE SOVIET UNION Minsk was eventually liberated by Soviet troops amid scenes of unbounded joy on 3 July 1944 (now celebrated as the Republic of Belarus National Independence Day, a national holiday), but the German army had clung on tenaciously throughout the first six months of the year and the destruction was almost total. Most of the houses, factories and administrative buildings had been flattened, while much of the road, rail and bridge infrastructure had been bombed out of use. When the Red Army re-entered the city, it was to find that its population had been decimated from 300,000 at the start of the war in 1939 to little over 50,000 at the cessation of hostilities. Over 70,000 of Minsk's residents had been murdered. When those who lost their lives in the surrounding districts are taken into consideration, the total rises to more than 400,000 people.

At first, serious consideration was given to leaving the ruins of the city untouched, abandoning it and moving the national capital to Mogilev but, with the final defeat of the Nazis in 1945, the process of rebuilding began. As far as was possible, this did not mean reconstruction, and every effort was made to restore as much of the city as could be saved. Sadly, precious little was left and today only a small part of the Classical architecture remains, concentrated mostly in Old Town (Старый Город), close to the city centre. Even there, much could not be saved. Throughout the late 1940s and 1950s, a new city centre rose from the rubble and ashes of the old one, as imposing new buildings in the grand design that became synonymous with Stalin appeared alongside expansive boulevards and within huge squares. Once more, the city grew and began to flourish, as a result of a process of massive and unprecedented industrialisation, which exceeded even that seen in the 1920s and 1930s. Hand in hand with the re-establishment of the social and administrative infrastructure was exponential population growth, as young people moved to the 'big city' from the rural hinterland. There was also a rigidly planned and controlled state policy to migrate skilled workers into the region from other parts of the Soviet Union to finally deliver regeneration. To meet the consequent housing need, Minsk spread outwards beyond its former city boundaries and upwards in the form of archetypical, high-density and high-rise concrete apartment housing.

But in spite of this fundamental transformation, a grateful nation never forgot the sacrifices made by the people of the city, and with others elsewhere in the USSR, Minsk was bestowed the honour of being officially recognised as 'Hero City (Город Герой) of the Soviet Union' in 1974.

THE POST-SOVIET REPUBLIC After the fall of the Soviet Union in the early 1990s, the city's evolution continued, but in a different direction. As the new state sought to establish its credentials on the European and global stage, Minsk began to assume the status and the adornments of an international capital city. Embassies and consulates were opened in abundance as governments worldwide sought to present their credentials and establish their interests, while the administrative buildings that formerly supported the Soviet machine now became centres of national republican government. But as the new republic struggled to find its feet in the wake of the consequences of the Chernobyl catastrophe and the large-scale collapse of the institutions of the former USSR, economic instability was everywhere to be seen. Yet since the turn of the century, things have begun to change for the better. The drive into the city from out of town used to be categorised by the sight of half-built and long-abandoned building projects, but today there is a marked change. Just inside the orbital motorway on the outskirts of Minsk, many new mini-suburbs (some of them extremely affluent) have sprung up and metro lines have been extended. Today there is huge redevelopment within the city centre itself, and more metro stations have been opened. There is talk that the motorway ring road (which today marks the furthest boundaries of the city) will become an inner orbital, with a new outer ring road to be constructed further afield. The occasion of the World Ice Hockey Championships in the city in May 2014 saw new hotels and infrastructural development appearing all over town. Even before the current proposals, the road system (including the existing Minsk orbital motorway and inner ring road) had been improved dramatically. Much of the city is under government-financed development, but money from sources all over the world is also pouring in, a sure sign of growing economic confidence both within and outside the country. And the march of Western commercialism threatens to alter the landscape irretrievably, with more and more neon on every street corner and increasing numbers of drive-through fast food emporia and new designer stores. Some might say the barbarians are at the gates again.

HIGHLIGHTS

There is a strong commitment throughout Belarusian society to promoting culture and the arts, not only in terms of governmental public and social policy, but also for ordinary people in their leisure time. Allied to this is a national enthusiasm (if not passion) for sport and outdoor pursuits. It's no surprise, then, to find that history, fine art and sport are well represented in terms of public facilities, with something to please every taste. The best of the attractions for the first-time visitor include the following:

MUSEUMS AND GALLERIES State Museum of the Great Patriotic War, Museum of Ancient Belarusian Culture, National History and Culture Museum, Museum of Nature and Ecology, Museum of Minsk History, State History Museum of Theatre and Music Culture, National Art Museum, Museum of Modern Fine Art, History of Belarusian Cinema Museum, Historical Museum of Belarusian Literature, Maxim Bogdanovich Literary Museum, Yakub Kolas Literary Museum, Yanka Kupala Literary Memorial Museum, Museum of Olympic Glory, Azgur Memorial Museum, Museum of the History of the National Academy of Sciences and Museum of Contemporary Belarusian Statehood.

PARKS, OPEN SPACES AND RECREATIONAL AREAS Gorky Park, Alexandrovsky Public Garden, Yanka Kupala Park, Central Botanical Gardens, Chelyuskintsev Culture and Leisure Park and Pobyedy (Victory) Park.

SQUARES, MONUMENTS AND SIGNIFICANT ARCHITECTURAL FEATURES Privakh-Salnaya Square, Nyezalyezhnastsi (Independence) Square, Oktyabrskaya Square, Pobyedy (Victory) Square, Island of Tears, Jewish Minsk, Upper Town, Troitskoye (Trinity) suburb, the National Library and the buildings of Nyezalyezhnastsi Avenue.

CATHEDRALS AND CHURCHES Church of Sts Simeon and Helena, Holy Spirit Cathedral, Mary Magdalene Church, Maryinsky Cathedral of the Holy Virgin Mary, St Alexander Nevsky Church and Cathedral of Sts Peter and Paul.

THEATRES AND CONCERT HALLS National Academic Bolshoi Opera and Ballet Theatre, Yanka Kupala National Academic Theatre and the Belarusian State Puppet Theatre.

Further information on all of these attractions can be found later in this chapter.

GETTING THERE AND AWAY

As you might expect, Minsk is the geographical focal point for all means of transportation into and out of the country. It is the main (and for the most part only) entry and exit point for air travel to Belarus. Major European road and rail links converge on the city from all points of the compass. Details of air routes, carriers and airport facilities can be found on pages 56–66, together with key information on rail travel, access by coach, roads, border-crossing points and a few tips on independent travel by car.

AIRLINE OFFICES

In Minsk City

✈ **Aeroflot** Office 101, 25 Yanka Kupala St; ☎279 12 70; e msqtosu@aeroflot.ru; www.aeroflot.ru; ⏰ 09.00–17.00 Mon–Fri

✈ **airBaltic** Room 6, 19 Pobediteley Av (Hotel Yubilyeynya); ☎226 90 43; e minsk@airbaltic.com; www.airbaltic.com; ⏰ 09.00–18.00 Mon–Fri

✈ **Austrian Airlines/Swissair** 38 Nyezalyezhnastsi Av; ☎288 25 35; e office.minsk@austrian.com; www.austrian.com; ⏰ 09.00–17.00 Mon–Fri

✈ **Belavia** 14 Nemiga St; ☎220 28 38; e info@belavia.by; www.belavia.by; ⏰ 09.00–19.00 Mon–Fri, 09.00–17.00 Sat–Sun (also sells tickets for its partner companies Aeroflot, Austrian Airlines, LOT Polish Airlines, CSA Czech Airlines & airBaltic)

✈ **CSA Czech Airlines** Office 313, 1B Platanova St; ☎284 91 01; www.csa.cz; ⏰ 09.00–17.00 Mon–Fri

✈ **El Al Israeli Airlines** Office 515, 6A Partizansky Av; ☎211 26 06; e airtickets@32l.by; www.elal.com; ⏰ 09.00–18.00 Mon–Fri

✈ **Etihad Airways (United Arab Emirates)** 33B Internatsionalnaya St; ☎328 49 11; www.etihadairways.com; ⏰ 09.00–17.30 Mon–Fri

✈ **LOT Polish Airlines** 7 Pobediteley Av; ☎226 67 53; www.lot.com; ⏰ 10.00–17.00 Mon–Fri

✈ **Lufthansa** 56 Nyezalyezhnastsi Av; ☎292 89 99; e msqgutem@dlh.de; www.lufthansa.com; ⏰ 09.00–17.30 Mon–Fri, 09.00–13.00 Sat

✈ **Turkish Airlines** Office 111, 25 Yanka Kupala St; ☎328 68 98; e thy.minsk.sales@gmail.com; www.turkishairlines.com; ⏰ 09.00–18.00 Mon–Fri, 09.00–13.00 Sat

Minsk-2 National Airport

✈ **Austrian Airlines/Swissair** ☎279 15 39; www.austrian.com; ⏰ 09.00–17.00 Mon–Fri

✈ **Belavia** ☎279 10 32; e info@belavia.by; www.belavia.by; ⏰ 09.00–19.00 Mon–Fri, 09.00–17.00 Sat–Sun

✈ **LOT Polish Airlines** www.lot.com; ⏰ during take-offs & landings only

✈ **Lufthansa** ☎279 17 45; www.lufthansa.com; ⏰ 09.00–17.30 Mon–Fri, 09.00–13.00 Sat

✈ **Turkish Airlines** ☎279 18 83; www.turkishairlines.com; ⏰ Mon/Thu pm only, when flights depart for Istanbul

BY METRO, BUS, TRAM AND TROLLEYBUS Public transport in Minsk is extremely cheap and unfailingly reliable, but somewhat overcrowded. If you want to feel like a local, however, then you must give it a try. Other than walking (and most of what you will want to see is accessible on foot), you have considerable freedom of choice, given that any of the options (metro, bus, tram and trolleybus) are all user-friendly. Each journey costs just BYR3,700, or BYR4,000 if your ticket is purchased from the driver in the case of bus, tram and trolleybus journeys. **Tickets** can be purchased from kiosks, post offices and stores all over town and, in the case of **metro tokens**, at every station; and if your stay is for a few days or more, tickets are available for periods of three, five, ten, 15, 20 and 30 days, or for five, ten, 20, 30, 40, 50 or 60 specific journeys. Public transport is exceptionally cheap, and these multiple tickets represent even better value. For ease of use and greater convenience, it is also now possible to purchase **contactless smart cards** that are time- or trip-limited, and which can be reloaded as many times as needed. A modest deposit is payable at the point of purchase, but this deposit is refunded if the card is returned undamaged and capable of resale.

With just two intersecting lines, the **metro system** is very easy to work out. During the day, the service runs every 2½ minutes, then every ten after 23.00 hours until the system closes for the night at 01.00, before opening for business once more at 05.30, Monday to Sunday. To access the network, buy your tokens (or 'jetons') from a window near the barriers (or in advance as above), insert one into the slot adjoining the barrier and walk through when the green arrow is lit. Alternatively, touch in with your smart card. Don't forget your *jeton* or card and don't try to ride the system for free: if you attempt to walk through without inserting a token or touching in with your card, then the seemingly open barrier will slam shut with a vengeance, attempting to cut you in two. I've seen it happen; I can't speak for the poor miscreant, but it made *my* eyes water and I was only a spectator. (See map opposite for details of the two lines and all stations.)

Buses run between 05.30 and 00.30, while **tram and trolleybus** services, like the metro, finish 30 minutes later. And if travelling by bus, tram or trolleybus, don't forget to punch your ticket at the machine on board to validate it. All the information you could ever need relating to the city's public transport system can be found at the extremely helpful website www.minsktrans.by.

BY TAXI Taxis in Minsk are fairly cheap and reasonably reliable but, as in any city in the world, as a foreigner you are at risk of being ripped off by unscrupulous operators, and perhaps more so in Minsk on account of the language difficulty. Only ever use officially licensed cabs. You will recognise one when you see it. Look for a yellow car, some with a light on top of the roof and/or decals of black-and-white patterned squares, but all with a number prominently displayed. Some of the more common are 135, 252 and 7788. This is also the local number for you to ring.

This is the right point in the narrative to remind readers of the caveat in the *Feedback request* on page v, relating to the shortage of information on opening hours, telephone numbers and prices for restaurants, bars, clubs, museums and the like, at least when compared with other world locations. And don't forget that in some instances, conflicting information can be provided by different sources. That

MINSK METRO

KEY
- Avtozavodskaya line
- Moskovskaya line
- Under construction
- Planned
- Cross-over point

N

Bradt

Stations:
Uruchye, Borisovsky Trakt, Vostok, Moskovskaya, Park Chyelyuskintsyev, Akademya Nayuk, Ploshchad Yakuba Kolasa, Ploshchad Pobedy, Oktyabrskaya, Kupalovskaya, Nyemiga, Frunzyenskaya, Molodyezhnaya, Pushkinskaya, Sportivnaya, Kuntsyevschina, Kamyenaya Gorka, Yubileynaya Ploshchad, Ploshchad Frantiska Bogushevicha, Vokzalnaya, Ploshchad Lenina, Institut Kultury, Gruschyevka, Mikhalovo, Petrovschina, Malinovka, Pervomaiskaya, Proletarskaya, Traktorny Zavod, Partizanskaya, Avtozavodskaya, Mogilevskaya, Kovalskaya Sloboda, Aerodromnaya, Nemorshanskiy Sad, Slutskiy Gostinets

said, every effort has been made to personally establish and corroborate every last detail. The fact that things are still developing so rapidly in this country is another challenge for the visitor. I do remain convinced, however, that all of this *will* change for the better. Every year I meet with senior officials at the Ministry of Sport and Tourism, and each time I encounter infectious enthusiasm and a willingness to learn new and better ways to present this country's tourism product. In any event, there should be real comfort for you in the knowledge that if you are on an organised visit, then you are bound to find that places on the tour *will* be open! And for my part, I always find that a modest degree of ambiguity (and even contradiction!) adds to the value of the adventure and of the experience. There are always times, of course, when you need to be able to rely on the accuracy of data, and new listings websites are appearing in increasing numbers all the time, so let your search engine do the work for you. In other words, come to this town prepared and bring your own downloaded information with you.

When you do find yourself in Minsk, two **tourist information centres** (TICs) are at your disposal. A little out of the city centre is the one next to Hotel Yubilyeynya run by the state tourism agency Belintourist (see page 49), but the second is more centrally located at 13 Revolutsionaya St (\ *203 39 95; e tic-minsk@ mail.ru; www.minsktourism.by;* ⊕ *08.45–13.00, 14.00–18.00 Mon–Thu, 08.45– 13.00 & 14.00–16.45 Fri*). Quaint it may be, but it shows that the tourist industry here still has work to do when the city's prime information hub for visitors closes for lunch, finishes early on Fridays and is closed at the weekend. That said, when it *is* open, the staff are helpful and accommodating, English is spoken, and all of the usual bookings can be made for you, including hotels, theatres, restaurants, day trips, and trips of longer duration. Brochures, leaflets, maps and guides in English are also available.

Additionally, more and more English guidebooks and maps are now finding their way on to the shelves of bookstores, hotel lobby shops and newspaper kiosks. In particular, look out for the excellent panoramic city map of Minsk showing each building drawn in 3D (price BYR15,000), which provides an exceptionally useful pictorial representation of the city and is thus a most useful aid to navigation, as well as the very good local guidebook *Minsk in One Day* (text by Chrystaphor Khilkevich, photographs by Sergei Plytkevich, published by Riftour). It contains more pictures than text, but it still has a great deal of interesting information as well as its own excellent panoramic map. For general up-to-the-minute listings information, the best publication by far is *where Minsk* magazine. Produced monthly with a circulation of 25,000, it is distributed free of charge in hotels, restaurants, the TICs and public places generally, and you will have no difficulty in sourcing a copy all over town. Most of it is in Russian, of course, but the English pages are very informative and there are useful maps at the back. The magazine's website (*www. whereminsk.by*) is also an excellent source of listings data and, although it is only in Russian at present, an English version is in the course of development.

 # WHERE TO STAY *Map, pages 128–9, unless otherwise noted.*

The biggest percentage of your budget is going to be blown on accommodation costs, so it pays to be choosy. It used to be the case that most hotels were very much of a muchness, the industry standard featuring a monolithic tower block that incorporated varying amounts of crumbling concrete, 1970s décor, a smart (if sterile and soulless) lobby and functional facilities. This has changed in the last couple of years, with a significant number of new hotels being built to meet perceived demand from the business community and foreign tourism. The same old atmosphere of sterility often still pervades, but there has been a big effort with the new build to accommodate the demands of the market. Whatever the issues, as a visitor from the West your perceived wealth will be very much in demand. It used to be the case that foreigners could expect to pay a considerably higher rate than was on offer to locals and people of other CIS countries, although by 2010 Belarusian tourist agencies were claiming that this differential no longer existed in most hotels. Finally this now seems to be the case and in any event you will be paying less than in other major European cities – in some cases, much less. In recent years, increasing numbers of private enterprises have emerged to threaten the state's monopoly, including some multi-nationals. This has encouraged the upgrading of many of the old state hotels, a process which now seems to be more or less constant. You can play safe and book through a Belarus tourist agency as the low-risk option, or you can strike out alone and make your own arrangements. Most of the hotels (and all of the new ones) have facilities to book directly and online. And if you still relish the idea of an old-fashioned Soviet experience, it's there to be found!

For ease of comparison with other hotels in the rest of Europe and beyond, the price code in this guide covers the cost of a standard double room in high season and includes buffet breakfast. All luxury and upmarket hotels (and most of the others) will accept payment by credit or debit card, but payment by cash will need to be in Belarusian roubles only, *not* US dollars, euros or any other currency. And do remember: these are not the only hotels in the city, just a selection. They are, however, ones that have been personally tested, or reviewed by local friends and colleagues whose judgement and objectivity I trust, in circumstances where there is also a wealth of descriptive information available on the growing number of tourism websites to help you make your choice. Like everything else in this country, your hotel will be something of a first-time adventure, so if you adopt that mindset, you won't go far wrong!

LUXURY

In this category, you can expect to find something a little out of the ordinary &, unusually for this country, each hotel is independently appointed & designed. You will pay for the privilege, of course, but this is the best of the bunch in town.

🏠 **Europe** [Map, page 137] 67 rooms: 18 sgls, 37 dbls, 11 suites – 5 executive suites, 4 business suites, 1 junior suite, 1 presidential suite – & 1 apt) 28 Internatsionalnaya St; 📞229 83 33; e reservation@hoteleurope.by; www.hoteleurope. by. Right in the heart of the city, on the corner of Lenina & Internatsionalnaya Sts & close to a number of key sights, this imposing 7-storey hotel opened in Sep 2007 on the spot where a hotel has existed since 1841, although the original was completely destroyed in the Great Patriotic War. The country's 1st genuine 5-star establishment until the President Hotel opened in 2013, it was considered before then to have overtaken the Minsk as the swankiest hotel in town, a privilege in status for which visitors

should still expect to pay, & in no uncertain terms. The best rooms enjoy impressive panoramic views over Old Town. All are extremely well appointed & those at the top of the range are the very latest in luxury. Some of the rooms are non-smoking & (unusually for Belarus) there are also facilities for the less able. The shiny lobby oozes money, although every time I've been there it's been close to empty. Even if you're not in residence, wander in off the street & take a look at the lovely central atrium. Don't forget to look up. In addition to an exclusive restaurant with 125 covers, 5 opulent bars & a nightclub, there is a business centre, conference & meeting rooms, library, secure underground parking, car-hire facilities, a laundry service, beauty parlour, gift shop, currency exchange, fitness centre, gym, sauna & pool. **$$$$$**

🏠 **Minsk** [Map, page 137] (252 rooms, 35 of which are classed 'luxury suites') 11 Nyezalyezhnastsi (Independence) Av; 📞209 90 62/75/78; e hotelminsk@pmrb.gov.by; www. hotelminsk.by. Until the arrival of the Europe &

A
B **15**
ORLOVSKAYA STREET
C
D

1

NOTE
For key to accommodation
and eating and drinking,
see page 130

SURGANOVA

CHYERVAKOVA STREET

13

Museum of Jewish
History & Culture

BOGDANOVICHA STREET

Komarovsky
rinok

☆ Reaktor

Museum of
Olympic
Glory **30**

2
Victoria Olimp, Sport Time,
Zamok shopping centre,
Korona shopping centre,
Minsk Arena sports hall

Mary Magdalene
✝ Church

Byelaya
☆ Vyezha **22**

MASHEROVA AVE

Ploschad Yakuba
Kolasa **26**

NYEZALYEZHNASTSI

Victoria
☆ **8**

Victory
Park

Belarusian State Museum
of the Great Patriotic War
3

MAXIMA

KISYELEVA STREET

29

20 **28**

Museum
of Moder
Fine Art

Matchbol café

POBEDITELEY

STAROVILYENSKAYA ST

Svisloch

12

M

Ploschad
Pobedy

3
Madison Royal &
Africa nightclubs

5 ☆ Vkus Nochi

National Academic
Bolshoi Ballet &
Great Opera Theatre
of Republic of Belarus
33

AVENUE

Tykehas ☆ **9**

Island
of Tears **36**

OLD TOWN
(TROITSKOYE)

YANKA KUPALA ST

Yanka
Kupala Park

Victory
Square

14

7

Zaslavskaya
Jewish Memorial

16

Bonhotel, Hotel Orbita,
Laguna nightclub,
Gubernia restaurant
29

Gorky Park

PYERVOMAISKAYA ST

1

4
Yubileynaya Ploshchad/
M Frunzyenskaya

NEMIGA STREET

Svobody
Sq

INTERNATSIONALNAYA ST

Oktyabrskaya
Sq

Alexandrovsky
Public Garden

Erivan restaurant

32

RAKOVSKAYA

KOMSOMOLSKAYA ST

LENINA

ENGELSA ST

Azgur
Memorial
Museum

Holocaust Museum
& Research Studio

19

GORODSKOI
VAL ST

KARLA MARKSA ST

KIROVA

KRASNARMEISKAYA STREET

Svisloch

5

17

18

SOVYETSKAYA ST

✝

✉

ST

Pervomaiskaya
M

see page 137

2

6

MYASNIKOVA ST

M
Independence
Square

Ploshchad Lenina/
Vokzalnaya

☆ Shangri La
Casino

27

ULYANOVSKAYA ST

SVYERDLOVA ST

OKTYABRSKAYA STREET

M
Pryvaksalnaya
Square

6
Hotel Zvezda,
Internationale Bildungs-
und Begegnungsstätte &
Westphalia restaurant,
Titan Nightclub

Underground
shopping mall

Main Railway
Station

4

Aparthotel Comfort
Hotel Sputnik

A
B
✈ Viva Hostel
C
✈ Dejavu
D

latterly the President, this was the only truly 4-star
hotel in the whole country & it's a fairly opulent
base for your stay in town. Located downtown
on the main drag & on the edge of the imposing
Nyezalyezhnastsi Sq, within easy walking distance
of many of the sights, this former Soviet hotel
was given a major face-lift in 2002 with a marble

lobby, state-of-the-art conference facilities for
50 ppl, business services, fitness centre, sauna,
casino, ATM, currency exchange, tourist agency,
secure car parking, car-hire facilities, shops &
'vitamin bar'. All rooms are elegantly furnished
& have the usual mod cons you would expect
to find in a hotel of this quality. It also boasts 2

E   Varadero restaurant   F   Bastion café   G   H   National Library

NYEZALYEZHNASTSI AVENUE

M Moskovskaya — Beltransgaz Hotel — **1**

STREET

NLO ☆ **29**

YAKUBA KOLASA STREET

35 21

Akademya Nayuk

Max Show ☆ **M**

34

M Park Chelyuskintsev

Natvris Khe

Chelyuskintsev Culture and Leisure Park

Museum of the History of the National Academy of Sciences of Belarus

Yakub Kolas Literary Museum & National Academy of Sciences

2

FILIMONOV STREET

SURGANOVA ST

Palace of Water Sports

AVENUE

25 ☆ Dozari ☆ XO casino

11 23 24

SUM (Department store)

Museum of Ancient Belarusian Culture

Central Botanical Gardens

3

PLATONOV ST

Belarusian State Philharmonic

St Alexander ✝ Nevsky

KOSLOVA STREET

STOLETOV STREET

31

Christians of ✝ Seventh-day Adventists

4

DOLGOBRODSKAYA STREET

Postoyalets Hostel

N

Bradt

5

0 —————— 1000m
0 —————— 1000yds

M Proletarskaya

Palace of Culture of the Tractor Works

M Traktorny Zavod **M**

6

East Time, Hotel Turist, Hotel accommodation at Eastern Bus Station

MINSK *Overview*

3

restaurants (inc 'Seventh Heaven' on the 7th floor with fine panoramic views of the city), 2 bars, a nightclub & a banqueting hall. Some of the rooms are classed as 'non-smoking' & there are limited facilities for the less able. Europcar & Avis have desks in the lobby, though often unmanned. If so, walk through the back of the lobby, left across the

car park & into the hotel's business centre. On the ground floor here is a bank, further ATMs, another travel agency, small café & access to the adjoining supermarket. Take the elevator to the 4th floor for car hire. **$$$$$**

⌂ **President** [Map, page 137] (154 rooms: dbls, dbls premium, twins, studios, suites, apts,

apts superior & presidential suite) 18 Kirova St; 📞 229 70 00; e info@president-hotel.by; www. president-hotel.by. Newly constructed on the site of the old Oktyabrskaya Hotel, this is intended to be the jewel in the crown of Minsk's hotels. It's certainly the 1st choice of the business community & all is very glitzy & shiny, with staff going the extra mile to provide high-quality service. The conference hall itself seats 600 & already this hotel is fast becoming the city's premier conference facility, with state-of-the-art equipment & services. After a few teething issues, everything here is now 1st rate. There are 3 very good restaurants, a 'wellness centre', spa, gym, 25m swimming pool, sauna & shops. There's even a VIP presidential suite with its own pool, sauna & elevator. Every room comes with AC & disabled facilities are good. There's parking underground too. Well located for all the sights, the real excitement value here comes from its position right next to the Office of the President of the Republic, so security is high & the atmosphere extremely businesslike. Whatever you do, don't be tempted to take the opportunity to photograph the office building. Instead, confine yourself to watching out for the president's heavily guarded motorcade leaving at high speed. **$$$$$**

UPMARKET

In this category, all of the hotels are very well appointed, comfortable & with excellent facilities (plus prices to match of course), but they lack that certain special quality to elevate them into the luxury bracket. You won't be disappointed with these, but you won't be wowed either. The exception is the delightful Garni Hotel (see opposite), which has the 'it' factor but not the prices to match.

🏠 **Beijing** (183 rooms) 36 Krasnoarmeiskaya St; 📞 329 77 77; e beijinghotel@ beijinghotelminsk.com; www.beijinghotelminsk. com. Located close to the Svislach River, facilities inc. the Seasons Chinese restaurant, Style slavic restaurant, Oasis café, Orchid banqueting hall, fitness health & beauty centre, currency exchange, shopping arcade, casino, business centre, on-site parking & airport transfers. **$$$$**

🏠 **Crowne Plaza** [Map, page 137] (115 standard, superior, club & designer rooms, plus 11 suites, 2 of which are 'Presidential') 13 Kirova St; 📞 218 34 00 (call centre), 200 93 53 (reservations); e info@cpminsk.com, reservation@cpminsk.com; www.cpminsk.com. Situated directly opposite the Dynamo Minsk national football stadium (currently a vast building site) & with most of the city's sights easily accessible on foot, this significant chain hotel, part of the Princess Group International, opened for business in May 2008. Self-assessed as 'a 5-star international hotel' & aimed at the business market, the facilities are comprehensive & doubtless match those to be found in every other of the 200 Crowne Plaza venues across the world, but the real plus here is the quality of the staff, who are consistently praised for the highest standards of service. The rooms are well appointed, with all the mod cons you would expect, & the hotel's facilities inc. full business services, 6 conference rooms, fitness centre, gym, jacuzzi, swimming pool, Diamond casino, Next nightclub, 2 restaurants (Dolce Vita & Empire), Star café/bar, shops, car hire, dry cleaning & a laundry. Some of the facilities are accessible to those with disabilities. **$$$$**

🏠 **Garni** [Map, page 137] (50 rooms: sgls, dbls, family & deluxe suite) 11 Internatsionalnaya St; ☎229 76 00; e info@hotel-garni.by; www. hotel-garni.by. Well located in the centre of town in an attractive 19th-century building, this small but charming hotel opened for business in Sep 2012. It's part of the Minotel group that also inc. the Belarus & Sputnik hotels in town. The design is classy & the décor is of the highest standard, with each of the rooms comfortable & very well appointed. All now have AC. Staff are very professional & English is spoken. Facilities inc. a fine restaurant, together with conference & full business services. There are lots of really nice little touches about the service you will receive, & many ppl have contacted me to let me know how good this place is (both friends in Belarus & visitors from abroad). Highly recommended. **$$$$**

🏠 **Renaissance Marriott** (267 rooms, inc 30 suites) 1 Dzherzhinsky Av; ☎309 90 90; www. marriott.co.uk. Part of the worldwide Marriott chain, facilities inc. the Arborea restaurant, lobby bar, fitness centre, spa, swimming pool, health & beauty centre, currency exchange, gifts/newspaper desk, business facilities, 10 meeting rooms & on-site parking. **$$$$**

🏠 **Victoria** (168 rooms: 115 sgls, some of which are adapted for wheelchair users, 45 dbls, 8 luxury suites, plus 1 'Presidential Suite') 59 Pobediteley Av; ☎239 77 77/204 88 44 (24hr information line 204 88 55); e reservation@ hotel-victoria.by, info@hotel-victoria.by; www. hotel-victoria.by. This top-of-the-range 4-star hotel, aimed clearly at the business market, welcomed its first guests on 1 Jul 2007. Shortly thereafter, the president himself paid a visit, an event that signified the importance that the state places on the success of the venture. Indeed, the vast new presidential palace is right across the road on the edge of Pobyedy Park. Situated on the banks of the Svislach River not far from the city centre & with lovely views over the park's Komsomolskoye Lake (but not as close to the city centre as the blurb would have you believe!), this hotel seeks to combine state-of-the-art business facilities with luxury accommodation. It still looks sparkly & is very 'new money'. In the spring of 2014 the complex was in the process of being massively expanded to inc. the new Victoria Olimp Hotel further up the road. Two other brand new Minsk hotels, the Zamkovy & the Monastyrsky, are also inc. in the Victoria portfolio. The business centre itself boasts multimedia projection equipment, high-speed Wi-Fi, simultaneous translation facilities, seminar rooms & a 300-seat conference hall, all supported by secretarial & administrative services. All bedrooms are fully AC, with LCD interactive satellite TV, internet access & minibar. Facilities also inc. nightclub, casino, swish restaurant, vitamin bar, lobby bar, 24hr on-site underground car parking, beauty centre (with spa), solarium, massage facility, sauna, hairdresser, laundry, currency exchange, ATM & souvenir/ newspaper stand. If the PR hype is to be believed (some ppl in town think so), then this place is something special, but for the traveller without business interests its appeal is likely to be limited. **$$$$**

🏠 **Victoria Olimp** (238 rooms; 12 categories of comfort from sgls to apts, inc 6 rooms adapted for travellers with disabilities) 103 Pobediteley Av; 📞308 75 55; e reservation@olimphotel.by; www.olimphotel.by. Included in the Victoria chain & part of the massive Victoria redevelopment on Pobediteley Av, facilities inc. the Olympia restaurant, café-pizzeria, lobby bar, banqueting hall, gym, spa, sauna, health & beauty centre & state-of-the-art business services, inc. 260-seat conference theatre, 70-seat hall & meeting rooms. **$$$$**

🏠 **Zhuravinka** [Map, page 137] (17 rooms: 13 sgls, 4 dbls, plus 1 'Presidential Suite') 25 Yanka Kupala St; 📞328 69 00. Modern in design (it was built in 2001), comfortable, compact & handily located on the banks of the Svislach River near to Old Town, this one is something of an oddity. For starters it's difficult to find, sited as it is in a building that looks like any other office. When you find your way inside, there is no lobby, just a desk in front of a lift. The PR blurb describes an entertainment complex (inc. 10-pin bowling), a casino & 2 restaurants, but they are in a separate building, around the back & across the car park. Within the hotel itself, facilities inc. massage room, solarium, fitness centre & bars. All of the bedrooms

are on 1 floor, where the carpet is plush & there's an air of faux exclusivity, but it's not to my taste. The outrageous Presidential Suite boasts 2 jacuzzis, 2 enormous beds, a TV the size of a cinema screen & its own swimming pool. All in all it's very 'new money' & I reckon there's a better Minsk experience waiting for you elsewhere. **$$$$**

MID-RANGE
Here, all of the hotels are very much alike: 1970s-style Soviet design with only limited aesthetic appeal. But all are well appointed & comfortable, if wholly interchangeable. Many are in the process of refurbishment. Prices are very competitive by Western standards, although each hotel has its own complex pricing structure with countless numbers of categories at differing rates.

🏠 **Belarus** (520 rooms) 15 Storazhevskaya St; 📞209 71 00/06; e secretary@minotel-belarus.com; www.hotel-belarus.com. An imposing 22-floor concrete high-rise, this hotel dominates the skyline around Pobyedy Park & its Komsomolskoye Lake, towers over the Minsk Hero City monument & the recently relocated Museum of the Great Patriotic War & has spectacular views across parkland & the Svislach River towards Old Town & the Island of Tears, particularly by night. Subject to complete renovation & only opened again in the spring of 2014 as part of the Minotel group of hotels, the view from the high-quality top-floor Panorama restaurant is stunning. Many of the rooms have their own balcony & all of them are now reasonably well appointed. There are several bars & eateries, a conference hall, business centre, sauna & shops. There is a choice of sgls, dbls & suites of various sizes. **$$$**

🏠 **Bonhotel** (127 rooms) 2 Pritytskava St; 📞389 73 89; e info@bonhotel.by; www.bonhotel. by. Not far from Pushkinskaya metro station, facilities inc. the Bonbistro restaurant, lobby bar, tourist booking services, ATM, car rental, conference services (inc. 40-seater conference room & meeting room), parking & airport transfers.

🏠 **Internationale Bildungs-und-Begegnungsstätte** (37 rooms) 11 Gazety Pravda Av; 📞270 39 94; e hotel@ibb.by; www.ibb. by/hotel. This slick business facility, incorporating state-of-the-art conference facilities in 5 seminar rooms & a function hall seating 350, was constructed in 1994 in partnership with a German venture. Not quite as swish as it once was, & it's in danger of being overtaken by the new kids on the block who are taking conference & business facilities to a new level in this town. That said, it still feels classy & has a relaxed & calm ambience, not least because it is around 10km from the general brouhaha of the city centre, in a suburb to the southwest. Facilities inc. sauna, bar & the excellent Westphalia restaurant. All rooms are well appointed: 3 have been adapted for wheelchair use. **$$$**.

🏠 **Orbita** (248 sgl/dbl rooms, plus 28 suites) 39 Pushkina Av; ✆ 206 77 81; e reservation@ orbita-hotel.com; www.orbita-hotel.com. Opened in 1991, this is a 14-storey high-rise. There is a restaurant, pizzeria & a banqueting hall, together with several bars, conference facilities, sauna, casino, nightclub & parking. **$$$**

🏠 **Planyeta** (310 rooms) 31 Pobediteley Av; ✆ 226 78 53; e booking@hotelplaneta.by; www. hotelplaneta.by. Extensive renovation has placed this hotel on a slightly higher-quality threshold than the others in this category, although the wall-to-wall pseudo-marble in reception is a little gaudy. Located within a few mins' walk of the Belarus & Yubilyeynya hotels, rooms range from sgls to VIP apts, all of them clean & comfortable. Facilities inc. business centre, currency exchange, Hertz car-hire office, shops, meeting/conference rooms, restaurants, bars, sauna & a casino. **$$$**

🏠 **Sputnik** (162 rooms) 2 Brilyevskaya St; ✆ 220 36 19; e info@sputnik-hotel.com; www. sputnik-hotel.com. Now part of the Minotel group, the location is not great. Directly validated information is scarce & difficult to find, but the website is helpful & this hotel is always busy. All of the usual facilities are available. **$$$**

🏠 **Turist** (215 rooms) 81 Partizansky Av; ✆ 295 40 31; e office@hotel-tourist.by; www. hotel-tourist.by. Located close to large-scale shopping facilities, this is a functional but comfortable 15-storey high-rise. Amenities inc. restaurant with 180 covers, banqueting hall, bar, summer pavement café, casino, gambling centre, conference hall, currency exchange, ATM, hairdresser, hotel transfers & paid parking. The staff are friendly & a stay here represents good value for money. If you want basic facilities &

rudimentary comfort without the frills, this is the place for you, although the location is not that convenient for visitor attractions or restaurants. Rooms comprise sgls, dbls, trpls & even quadruples, all in either economy or business class. **$$$**

🏠 **Yubileiny** (239 rooms) 19 Pobediteley Av; ✆ 226 90 24; e info@yhotel.by; www.yhotel.by. Overlooking the Svislach River & built on the site of a former mosque close to Pobyedy Park, this is a very busy hotel, full of hustle & bustle. The rooms at the lower end of those available are a little shabby, while the higher-grade ones have recently been decorated. But for sheer value for money, this hotel takes some beating. Maybe it's just familiarity, but if I need a hotel in town it's the one that I always use. It's nothing special, but all is dependable at this cosy old sweater of a hotel. Facilities inc. business centre, 250-seat conference hall, restaurants, bars, sauna, shops, ATM, bowling & casino. **$$$**

BUDGET

🏠 **40 Let Pobyedi (or '40th Anniversary of Victory Day')** (132 rooms, but only 50 available to tourists) 3 Azgura St; ✆ 294 79 63; e 40hotel@ tut.by; www.40hotel.by. Situated behind Gorky Park & within walking distance of most sights, you get what you pay for in this 12-storey Soviet-style apt block, which is not a criticism. It's cheap, functional & the staff are friendly. The hotel belongs to the Ministry of Defence, & only part of it is available for tourists. There is also a small café/ coffee shop. Ask for one of the refurbished rooms when booking. **$$**

🏠 **Beltransgaz** (30 rooms: 11 sgls, 16 dbls, 3 trpls) 4 Francisk Skoryny St; ✆ 219 19 50; e hotel.mag@btg.by; www.btg.by/hotel. Built in 2003, facilities inc. banquet hall, café, bar & shop. Established primarily for travelling executives of the state gas company, a stay here will give you a different experience, but the location is some way off the main drag. That said, the rooms are big & well appointed. There is a general air of freshness about the place, & it's different! Pay extra for b/fast in the café. **$$**

🏠 **East Time** (134 rooms) 5 Velosypedny Lane; ✆ 630 24 00; e info@easttime-hotel.by; www. easttime-hotel.by. Close to Vostochny bus station, services inc. café, lobby bar & car hire. Has 2 rooms for disabled use. **$$**

Sport Time (134 rooms) 2 Myastrovskaya St; 279 39 60; e info@sporttime-hotel.by; www.sporttime-hotel.by. In the same ownership as the East Time Hotel & 10mins from the Minsk Arena sports, concert & shopping complex, services match those at East Time & inc. café, lobby bar & car hire. There are 2 rooms adapted for disabled use. **$$**

U Fontana (18 rooms) 4 Amuratorskaya St; 203 09 58; e u-fontana@bk.ru; www.ufontana.com. This small hotel is a decent walk from the sights, but it's comfortable enough if your budget is tight. The facilities are modest but perfectly acceptable, & there is free parking. The restaurant has a sports theme, with trophies on display & signed shirts & other memorabilia on the walls. Interestingly, the menu boasts 'exclusive recipes from Belarusian & Russian sports stars'! During the summer months, there is a pleasant dining area outside, where shashlik on the barbecue (a version of shish kebab ubiquitous in this part of the world) & a cold beer come recommended. There is also a sauna, (very) small pool & games room. **$$**

Zvezda (93 rooms) 47 Gazyety Zvezda Av; 270 74 85; e admin@hotelzvezda.by; www.hotelzvezda.by. Built in 1982, this establishment (a joint Belarusian-American venture) is a good bet if you are travelling independently & with your own transport. Located in a southwestern suburb of the city, it is 15min drive from the cultural & business centres. There is an Italian café, sauna, hairdresser & small meeting room. This hotel does not appear to be widely used by visitors from abroad, though a selling point that will be familiar to Westerners is the availability of guest packs, inc. toothbrush, toothpaste, soap & shampoo, with complimentary bottled mineral water on a daily basis. Just bear in mind the relative remoteness of the location, although it's well placed for public transport. **$$**

SHOESTRING

Eastern Bus Station 34 Vanyeyeva St; 247 63 74. There is rumoured to be a hostel on the top floor of this bus station, which is meant to be for bus drivers in need of somewhere to lay their head between one job & the next, but authentic travellers have also been known to be allowed to stay here. No information is available, so realistically, this is an emergency option of last resort. **$**

Express (56 rooms) 4 Privakhsalnaya Sq; 225 64 63; e hotel-express@tut.by. Adjacent to the main railway station on the right as you exit the main hall, this is the place for the budget traveller on a shoestring arriving tired by train with nothing booked. Just keep your expectations low & don't expect to be able to book in advance. There are sgl, dbl & trpl rooms, but you should expect to share. There are no English speakers among the staff. **$**

Postoyalets (5 dbls & 4 dorms sleeping 6 & 8 persons) 147 Patisansky Av; 543 49 81; e book@hotel-ru.com; www.hotel-ru.com. An economy hostel located 500m from Mogilevskaya metro station. One of the new breed of decent & reliable hostels that fit the bill, it's cheap, friendly, cheerful & comfortable, with a range of good facilities to enhance the value of your stay. If you're on a tight budget it's great value for money. **$**

Revolucion Hostel [Map, page 137] (1 sgl, 1 family room & 8 dorms sleeping 4, 6, 8 & 10 persons) 16 Revolutsionaya St; 614 66 65; e booking@revolucion.by; www.revolucion.by. Only open since 2013, the location of this hostel is handy, 400m from Nemiga metro station, next to a cinema & in the heart of the historic area, with many of the sights only a short distance away, as well as cafés, bars, nightlife & shopping. Inside the décor pays homage to the heroes of the Revolution. Like Postoyalets (see above), it's one of the new breed & is a decent option. **$**

Viva (4 dorms sleeping 4, 6 & 10 persons) 4 Zhukovskova St; 627 11 33; e hostelviva.by@gmail.com; www.hostelviva.by. Open since 2012 & a 7min walk from Centralnaya bus station & the railway station, with metro station Institut Kultury close by. Like Postoyalets & Revolucion (see above) it's another good hostel option for accessing great budget accommodation with a range of decent facilities & services on site. **$**

RENTING APARTMENTS This is becoming an increasingly viable and attractive option, particularly if you are looking to stay for a week or more (although rental by the night is also possible if you need it). In those circumstances, there is simply no comparison on cost and this is much the best way to do it if you want to live like a local for the duration of your stay. You also have the opportunity to very much please yourself as to your comings and goings. As a resident of the city, albeit a temporary one, you're going to feel much more part of the landscape than as a hotel tourist. Just exercise common sense with your enquiries and negotiations: this market is developing rapidly and there does not appear to be much of a safety net (if any at all) to regulate the activities of agents who may charge a significant fee, just to put you in direct contact with unknown property owners. It is to the owners that the actual rental will then be payable. So be careful out there: constantly check costs and look diligently for hidden charges. Make sure you know what you are getting for your investment, and do please satisfy yourself as to how you're going to register your passport with the authorities, as required by national immigration laws. Actually, some agencies offer a registration service as part of the deal, as well as transfers to and from the airport. As with so many markets and services, word of mouth is the best medium for securing a good deal on a rental. There's no substitute for acting on personal recommendation and if you can make your arrangements with the help and advice of someone who's been there, done it and bought the T-shirt, so much the better. Ask around and find someone who knows where to go for the most reliable deals. For my part, I'm fortunate to be able to stay with friends these days when I'm in Minsk, but for a number of years I had no hesitation in renting apartments both in Minsk and in other Belarusian cities. I'd have no hesitation in doing so again. I've never encountered a single problem. There's no substitute for feeling like a local, so get out there and find yourself a deal.

As well as local agencies within Belarus, a number of American and European companies operate international rental agencies; some of them claim to have access to their own apartments in Minsk, but a lot of these companies seem to be little more than clearing houses to facilitate contact with the real owners. With that in mind, point your internet search engine at 'apartment rental in Minsk' and browse away to your heart's content! If you can speak the language with confidence and don't mind being in town without having anywhere booked, the best way to avoid the attentions of agents is to buy a local newspaper when you get there and browse the listings. Dozens and dozens of apartments will be listed and the phone number provided will almost always be the landlord in person. I have done this before, and I've never had any difficulty in finding an apartment, even for one night. Just don't forget to register your passport within the necessary period as the law requires.

To dip your toe in the water and as a compromise between a hotel stay at one end of the scale and going solo with renting an apartment at the other, a decent option you might want to try is **Aparthotel Comfort** (*64 one-room studios, 64 two-room apts & 6 three-room apts; 1 Schorsa St;* \ *328 15 87;* e *info@comforthotel.by, reservation@comforthotel.by; www.comforthotel.by*). Open since 2012, this mixed development of apartments over nine floors is 3.5km out of the city centre, but near to Institut Kultury metro station. The quality of décor and facilities is decent. Short, medium and long-term lets are available. Guests can have a buffet breakfast in the café on site.

✖ WHERE TO EAT AND DRINK *Map, pages 128–9, unless otherwise noted.*

The restaurant trade is another of the rapidly expanding markets in this fast-developing country, with new eateries opening up all the time. Many of the places listed here are some kind of throwback to the 1970s, particularly in terms of gaudy Soviet-style décor, but the range of cuisine available is diverse and quality is often high. Overall, prices are lower than in other European cities, but Minsk is catching up fast. With so much choice available, you can afford to experiment and be adventurous. Most of them will have menus in English, but not very informative ones. All of these restaurants should take major credit cards, but do check first. The price code covers the average price of a main course, but do remember that things are changing very rapidly. Do your research in advance if you can.

RESTAURANTS
Traditional Belarusian

✕ **Berezka** 40 Nyezalyezhnastsi Av; ☎288 18 47; www.berezka.by; ⏱ 11.00–23.00 Sun–Thu, 11.00–midnight Fri & Sat. Located on Pobyedy Sq, good-quality Belarusian & international cuisine is served in pleasing surroundings by competent & attentive staff. $$$$

✕ **Gostyny Dvor** [Map, opposite] 17 Sovyetskaya St; ☎328 64 27; www.gostinydvor.by; ⏱ noon–midnight daily. Centrally located close to the Red Church, 'Old Russian' cuisine is served here. There is an open fire & live music to complete the experience, along with suits of armour & medieval drapes on the walls. Think Middle Ages & castles, but it's all done with style, service is excellent (if a little slow) & the food is very good. You might even have it all to yourself; on my last visit with a small group of friends midweek we were the only ones there. $$$$

✕ **Grunwald** [Map, opposite] 19 Karla Marksa St; ☎210 42 55; ⏱ 08.00–midnight Mon–Fri, 10.00–midnight Sat & Sun. Belarusian, Polish & Lithuanian cuisine in a relaxed & friendly atmosphere. It's intimate, classy & reminiscent of Old Europe, but don't expect speedy service. Come prepared to stay for the whole evening & just people-watch while you eat. I first came here in 2002 & it's still one of my favourite haunts in town to while away a few hrs enjoying good food. $$$$

✕ **Gubernia** 28 Odoyevskaya St; ☎207 67 66; ⏱ noon–midnight daily. Slavonic cuisine, with the emphasis on Belarusian & Lithuanian. Located quite some way to the west of the city centre, it's OK if you happen to be in the vicinity, but lacks charm & the food is no better than can be found elsewhere. It now has karaoke… $$$$

✕ **Kamyanitsa** [Map, opposite] 18 Pyervamaiskaya St; ☎294 51 24; e cafcam@tut.by; www.kamyanitsa.by; ⏱ noon–23.00 daily. The proprietor is keen to stress that the food here is prepared to recipes from the days of the Grand Duchy of Lithuania & of the mighty Rzeczpospolita state. It might be hype, but everything is done with style here; the medieval setting is classy, staff are helpful &

well presented & the food is good, complemented by live roots music in the evening. $$$$

✕ **Korchma Starovilyenskaya** [Map, opposite] 2 Starovilyenskaya St; ☎335 45 02; ⏱ 09.00–midnight daily. Located in a prime position on the banks of the Svislach on the edge of Old Town, the décor represents a worthy attempt at recreating a historical setting, if a little twee. The view over the river is quite splendid though. Belarusian & Italian cuisine. The food is good &, in the summer, the atmosphere is relaxed. $$$$

✕ **Kuchmistr** [Map, opposite] 40 Karla Marksa St; ☎327 48 48; ⏱ noon–23.00 daily. Well placed in the heart of town, there's nothing flash about this place but it has a good reputation for traditional food served with a touch of panache, yet without fuss or pretension. There's an easy charm about the service and the ambience is relaxed. Good English is spoken, & a group of Geordies & Scousers have written to me to confirm they had no difficulty in being understood! Also served here is a variety of home-distilled spirits, inc. a fiery horseradish concoction. Everything about this venue is classy & understated, which puts it high on my own list. $$$$

✕ **Mirsky Zamok** [Map, opposite] 9 Gorodskoi Val St; ☎328 69 38; ⏱ noon–23.00 Sun–Thu, noon–02.00 Fri & Sat. This is a really good try at establishing an authentic taste of Old Belarus (whatever that might be). The décor is heavily medieval & reminiscent of the citadel at Mir from which it takes its name. The food is excellent & the service very efficient, but expect to pay for it. It's easy to stay here all day long. $$$$

✕ **Pechki Lavochki** [Map, opposite] 22 Nyezalyezhnastsi Av; ☎327 78 79; ⏱ noon–23.00 daily. Another village-style interior serving passable Belarusian, Russian and Ukrainian dishes. Its reputation was once excellent, though I've heard it said that standards have slipped somewhat. It's right in the heart of the city though. $$$$

✕ **Rakovsky Brovar** [Map, opposite] 10 Vityebskaya St; ☎328 64 04; www.eng.brovar.by; ⏱ noon–midnight daily. This is a classy restaurant with its own microbrewery. It's located in the

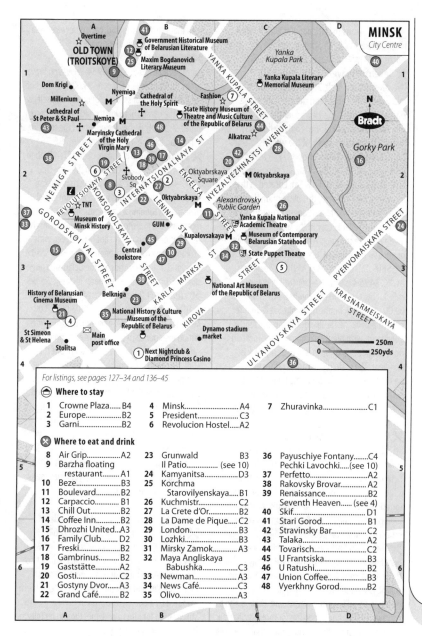

OLD TOWN (TROITSKOYE)

Overtime ☆

41 Government Historical Museum of Belarusian Literature
12
25 Maxim Bogdanovich Literary Museum
9

Yanka Kupala Park

40

Yanka Kupala Literary Memorial Museum

Dom Krigi

Millenium ☆

Nyemiga

Cathedral of St Peter & St Paul

Nemiga

43

M Nemiga

Cathedral of the Holy Spirit

Fashion ☆ 7

48

14

State History Museum of Theatre and Music Culture of the Republic of Belarus

Alkatraz ☆ 44

28

Maryinsky Cathedral of the Holy Virgin Mary

46
13
19 39 17
38
6 18
8 22
Svobody Sq
27 Oktyabrskaya

42
20
Oktyabrskaya Square

M Oktyabrskaya

26
Alexandrovsky Public Garden

Yanka Kupala National Academic Theatre

Museum of Contemporary Belarusian Statehood

24

Yanka Kupala Park

Yanka Kupala Park

Gorky Park

N

16

37
33

Museum of Minsk History

TNT ☆

GUM

11

Kupalovsakaya

29
10
47

45

Central Bookstore

32
34

State Puppet Theatre

5

15

31

30

Belkniga

History of Belarusian Cinema Museum

21
4

35

23

National History & Culture Museum of the Republic of Belarus

National Art Museum of the Republic of Belarus

St Simeon & St Helena

Stolitsa

Main post office

Dynamo stadium market

1 Next Nightclub & Diamond Princess Casino

36

0 ————— 250m
0 ————— 250yds

For listings, see pages 127–34 and 136–45

🛏 Where to stay

1	Crowne Plaza	B4	4	Minsk	A4	7 Zhuravinka......C1
2	Europe	B2	5	President	C3	
3	Garni	B2	6	Revolucion Hostel	A2	

✕ Where to eat and drink

8	Air Grip	A2	23 Grunwald	B3	36 Payuschiye Fontany......C4
9	Barzha floating restaurant	A1	Il Patio (see 10)		Pechki Lavochki.....(see 10)
10	Beze	B3	24 Kamyanitsa	D3	37 Perfetto......A2
11	Boulevard	B2	25 Korchma Starovilyenskaya	B1	38 Rakovsky Brovar......A2
12	Carpaccio	B1	26 Kuchmistr	C2	39 Renaissance......B2
13	Chill Out	B2	27 La Crete d'Or	B2	Seventh Heaven......(see 4)
14	Coffee Inn	B2	28 La Dame de Pique	C2	40 Skif......D1
15	Dhrozhi United	A3	29 London	B3	41 Stari Gorod......B1
16	Family Club	D2	30 Lozhki	B3	42 Stravinsky Bar......C2
17	Freski	B2	31 Mirsky Zamok	A3	43 Talaka......A2
18	Gambrinus	A2	32 Maya Angliskaya Babushka	C3	44 Tovarisch......C2
19	Gaststätte	A2	33 Newman	A3	45 U Frantsiska......B3
20	Gosti	C2	34 News Café	C3	46 U Ratushi......B2
21	Gostyny Dvor	A3	35 Olivo	A3	47 Union Coffee......B3
22	Grand Café	B2			48 Vyerkhny Gorod......B2

historical part of the city & the décor is a cross between a Belarusian hunting lodge & 19th-century Scandinavia. Think wood panelling, plus drapes & tapestries in abundance. On entry, you will be greeted by a huge sturgeon in a tank, but don't be put off. Behind is a sports bar with big screens backing on to the brewery itself. Alfresco

dining is well served by a cosy patio downstairs & a terrace on the top floor. The beer is excellent & the food superb, with service to match. One other venue bears the same name in town (& is in the same ownership), but it's a café-bar & not a restaurant. Do give this one a try, but be sure to book or at least get there early, as its high reputation means that it's popular with locals & tourists alike. I've been coming here for years & it's still one of my favourites in the city. $$$$

✕ Seventh Heaven [Map, page 137] 11 Nyezalyezhnastsi Av; ☎209 90 87; ⊕ noon–midnight daily. Located on the top floor of the classy Minsk Hotel, the views over the city are splendid, while the cuisine is only a short way behind. There is live music at the w/ends. $$$$

✕ Stari Gorod [Map, page 137] 19 Maxima Bogdanovicha St; ☎286 05 08; ⊕ noon–midnight Sun–Thu, noon–02.00 Fri & Sat. Located in the reconstructed Old Town, this place might be aimed at the tourist market but it doesn't cut corners on quality. The cellar is cosy in the winter & the terrace inviting in the summer, while the food is always good & well presented. Give this one a try. $$$$

✕ Skif [Map, page 137] 34 Nyezalyezhnastsi Av; ☎284 75 41; e cafe_skif@tut.by; www.cafeskif.by; ⊕ 09.00–midnight Mon–Thu, 09.00–02.00 Fri, noon–midnight Sat & Sun. Yet more medieval castle-like décor, but the food is good here (with plenty of choice) & the location right outside one of the gates to Gorky Park is excellent. The main restaurant is rather heavy on the historical accoutrements for my liking & I much prefer the ambience in the covered veranda. Service could be a little slicker too, but it's worth a visit. $$$$

✕ Talaka [Map, page 137] 18 Rakovskaya St; ☎203 27 94; ⊕ 10.00–06.00 daily. Another establishment where the theme is clichéd Belarusian village home, but there's something a little out of the ordinary here & it's all been put together with thought & some quirky touches. The food is consistently good & it's a popular venue, especially with local people. $$$$

✕ Traktir Na Parkovoi 11 Pobediteley Av; ☎203 69 91; ⊕ noon–midnight daily. Only a stone's throw from Hotel Yubileiny, Belarusian & Slavonic cuisine is served here in a setting that is modelled on a traditional Belarusian farmstead. There is also a courtyard with a huge open fire for cooking. Shashlik is a particular speciality. Romany music is played by a fiddler or accordionist wandering from table to table & it's impossible not to be seduced by the romance of it all, even though you know it's tacky & clichéd. The only downside is that tourists love it & they all seem to know about it. Just to say you've been once though, give in to it & indulge yourself. I still go periodically & I haven't been disappointed yet. To keep that warm glow going, each diner receives a complimentary liqueur upon leaving. $$$$

✕ U Frantsiska [Map, page 137] 19 Nyezalyezhnastsi Av; ☎664 09 34; www.eng.brovar.by/eng/u-francziska; ⊕ noon–23.00 daily. Part of the Rakovsky Brovar stable (a good sign in itself) & right in the middle of town, the olde worlde décor is done reasonably well & the quality of the traditional Belarusian food on offer here is decent. $$$$

✕ Vyerkhny Gorod [Map, page 137] 4 Svobody Sq; ☎321 20 89; ⊕ 10.00–midnight Sun–Thu, 10.00–02.00 Fri & Sat. An indicator that you can expect good things at this fine restaurant is that close friends running a travel business not only recommend it to visitors, they dine here themselves. The location in this lovely square is perfect, with excellent views of the Cathedral of the Holy Spirit & beyond. The best dishes are the Belarusian ones, service is professional & the décor is classy. $$$$

✕ Lido 49/1 Nyezalyezhnastsi Av; ☎302 59 59; e info@lido.by; www.lido.by; ⊕ 08.00–23.00 Mon–Fri, 11.00–23.00 Sat & Sun. Less of a fine dining experience (it's self-service) & more a safe option for families with children, but the staff are cheerful in this chain emporium & the cuisine is better than you might expect. There's an imaginative children's menu & themed events for little ones. Trouble is, once you've seen the interior of 1 medieval recreation, you tend to be less impressed by the others. Maybe one to avoid unless you have your children with you (in which case they will love it), it's also a little out of the centre just off Yakuba Kolasa Sq, yet it has many fans. Make up your own mind. $$$

Eastern European and ex-USSR

✕ Astara 37 Pulikhova St; ☎299 97 61; ⊕ 10.00–23.00 daily. A big experience in every way awaits in this corner of Azerbaijan. Don't go if you're looking for understatement & a quiet night, but I'm told that the food is excellent. Much favoured by a good friend who lives close by, I'm still waiting for him to take me, though he tells me it's worth the wait. $$$$

✕ Chumatsky Shlyakh 34 Myasnikova St; ☎190 77 77; ⊕ 10.00–23.00 daily. Traditional Ukrainian recipes served in a rustic interior by staff in national dress. Live music is played at w/ends & a delivery service is available. Sample Belarusian cooking elsewhere first, then come here to compare notes. $$$$

✖ Dejavu 6 Volodka St; 124 24 90; www.
dejavu.by; noon–23.00 Mon–Thu, noon–03.00
Fri & Sat. So you've sampled the cuisine of the
constituent republics & now it's time for the glory
of the CCCP. Back in the USSR indeed. The food is
decent, the décor is unashamedly retro-Soviet with
some splendid accoutrements & there's a nice touch
of irony to the service. There's even a bust of Lenin in
the corner. Loud & lively, especially at the w/end, so
only come if you're in the mood. $$$$

✖ Erivan 3 Pyervy Zagorodny St; 170 08 08;
www.erivan.by; noon–midnight Sun–Thu,
noon–02.00 Fri & Sat. To complete your culinary
tour of the Caucasus, try this lively Armenian
restaurant. It's another big night out & the floor
show is extravagant. $$$$

✖ Gabrovo 81 Nyezalyezhnastsi Av; 287 30 53;
10.00–midnight Mon–Fri, 11.00–midnight Sat
& Sun. Authentic Bulgarian cuisine in a traditional
setting, with seating available outside all year round,
serviced by large burners for heating. $$$$

✖ Natvris Khe 4 Svyazistov St; 385 02 55;
noon–midnight Tue–Sun. A truly authentic
Georgian experience can be had here, all to the
accompaniment of live roots folk music. The setting
is beautiful & the food is good, but it's a long way
out in the suburbs. $$$$

✖ Tiflis 3 Tolbukhin St; 385 64 74;
11.00–23.00 daily. It's another Georgian
experience & one that's worth the trek out of
the centre, especially as the location close to
Chelyuskintsev Park & the Botanical Gardens
makes this a decent shout for lunch on a day of
meandering among the greenery. The food is
excellent here. $$$$

✖ Tovarisch [Map, page 137] 21 Yanka Kupala
St; 327 34 35; www.tovarisch.by; noon–
midnight Sun–Thu, noon–01.00 Fri & Sat. There's
another full-on Soviet Union experience to be had
here. As with Dejavu, the retro décor is impressive
& it's particularly lively at the w/end. Both food &
service are good. $$$$

✖ Verba 51 Kropotkina St; 334 69 95;
11.00–23.00 daily. A fine venue specialising
in Caucasian food. It is very much a local
neighbourhood restaurant, so free of the trappings
associated with those frequented by tourists.
The soup piti with lamb, potatoes & hummus is
a delight, as are the lyula kebab & pork shashlik.
There's a main dining room, which has a touch
of the 'Soviet' about its style & ambience, a bar

& several discreet, well-appointed private rooms
seating up to 6 ppl. I like this one, as do others, inc.
a number of my correspondents. It's unpretentious
& knows that it's a hip venue, so it doesn't have to
try. $$$$

European haute cuisine

✖ Falcone 9 Korolya St; 377 77 76; e info@
falcone.by; www.falcone.by;
noon–02.00 daily. Without doubt, this fine
Italian restaurant is the real deal. Michelin-
starred head chef Domenico Acampora brings
a singularly impressive CV to Minsk & it's no
wonder that this is the haunt of the city's elite.
All is elegant here, from the décor to the service,
& the menu is a culinary delight. There's even
a children's playroom to keep the little ones
entertained so you can relish every pampered
moment of the dining experience. Don't miss
out, but expect to pay for the privilege. $$$$$

✖ Grand Café [Map, page 137] 2 Lenina St;
703 11 11; noon–midnight daily. Fine dining
at its best, this is the favourite restaurant of many
in Minsk, inc. a number of my close friends. The
food is exquisite, the décor elegant & the service
highly professional. The location is central, across
from Hotel Europe on the opposite side of Lenina
St. It's not cheap, but you get what you pay for.
If you're a non-smoker, the only downside is that
the smoking and non-smoking areas are two
halves of the same room, but overall this is a very
classy establishment. Highly recommended if your
budget can take the hit. $$$$$

✖ La Crete d'Or [Map, page 137] 3 Lenina St;
105 05 03; e zolotoigrebeshok@tut.by; www.
grebeshok.by; 11.00–midnight daily. Classic
French cuisine is on offer here in a very elegant
setting, where the standard of service is second to
none. Most of my friends prefer Grand Cafe for fine
dining, but this classy restaurant is not far behind
in their estimation. I can't decide between the two,
which are almost opposite each other on Lenina St.
Either way there's an air of refinement here. Next
door is a coffee shop of the same name serving
decent coffee & snacks. Also next door is a branch
of Belarusbank with an ATM. You're going to need
it! $$$$$

**✖ La Dame de Pique (Pikovaya
Dama)** [Map, page 137] 17 Yanka Kupala St;
www.pikovayadama.by; 227 73 14; noon–
midnight daily. A Belarusian portrayal of French

elegance & style, where the décor is sumptuous & the food exquisite. Oozing high style in every way, you will pay for the privilege. $$$$$

X **Newman** 36 Nemiga St; ☎777 42 42; e info@tomat.by; www.newman-rest.by; ⊕ noon–midnight Mon–Thu, noon–02.00 Fri & Sat, noon–23.00 Sun. Steaks are a speciality here (& they are very good steaks), but there's also a broader menu of decent cuisine in the bar. Service is slick & fast without being obsequious. Overall it's not top of the list, but it is impressive. $$$$$

X **Renaissance** [Map, page 137] 23 Svobody Sq; ☎327 09 91; ⊕ noon–02.00 daily. This is another elegant venue in a splendid location serving excellent cuisine, where the décor is classy & the service understated & professional. On my 1 visit here everything was the epitome of laid-back refinement, with mellow live jazz. It was also empty… $$$$$

X **Panorama** 15 Storazhevskaya St; ☎198 16 85; ⊕ noon–02.00 Sun–Thu, noon–04.00 Fri & Sat. Located on the 22nd floor of the now fully refurbished Hotel Belarus (see page 132), the panoramic views of the city are unsurpassed (look out especially for the National Library, lit up by lasers like a Christmas tree), while the food, from an international menu, is of a consistently high standard. Having survived a long period of closure throughout the hotel's massive overhaul, this restaurant is now back to its best. I love it for the view alone. Service is helpful & professional. $$$$

X **Westphalia** 11 Gazyety Pravda Av; ☎270 57 27; www.westfalia.by; ⊕ 07.00–23.00 daily. Some way out of town in the joint Belarusian-German venture IBB hotel & conference complex, this restaurant is well worth a visit nevertheless. It's been open a long time & has thus stood the test of time, especially as it's off the main drag. The food is exquisite, the service slick & the wine list (inc. cocktails) comprehensive. There is live music Wed–Fri. Excellent value for money. $$$$

Italian

X **Bella Rosa** 3 Gikalo St; ☎284 53 03; www.bellarosa.by; ⊕ noon–02.00 daily. This is a classy Italian with food of high quality & prices to match. $$$$$

X **Bergamo** 37 Kulman St; ☎334 45 56; ⊕ 10.00–midnight Mon–Sat. Quality Italian

food in a decent setting & much frequented by the Italian community in town. Enough said? Expensive, though. $$$$$

X **Carpaccio** [Map, page 137] 4 Staravilyenskaya St; ☎334 97 21; ⊕ noon–midnight Sun–Thu, noon–01.00 Fri & Sat. Located in a beautiful spot on the edge of Old Town, this classy restaurant presents a fine & imaginative menu. Service is also very good. It's only small & very popular, so don't expect to turn up for a table without booking first. $$$$$

X **Payuschiye Fontany** [Map, page 137] 5 Oktyabrskaya St; ☎500 00 00; e font328@tut.by; www.jazzfontan.relax.by; ⊕ 08.00–midnight Mon–Fri, noon–midnight Sat & Sun. There's a lot going on here. It's a long, sprawling sgl-storey warren of rooms that seem to go on forever in a pleasant area of greenery close to the river. The award-winning Italian chef oversees b/fasts first thing, then business lunches, before serving high-quality evening meals to the accompaniment of delightful live jazz. This is a classy place with classy food, so you might want to dress in style. I've been several times for lunch & dinner & I've never been less than impressed. You won't be disappointed. $$$$

X **Teatro** 6 Maxima Bogdanovicha St; ☎334 13 52; ⊕ 10.00–23.00 daily. Classy & slick, there are 30 different pizzas available here. Just wear black to match the décor. It's close to the National Opera & Ballet Theatre, so combining the 2 is a decent option. There's also a delivery service. $$$$

X **Tempo** 78 Nyezalyezhnastsi Av; ☎278 56 80; www.tempo.by; ⊕ 08.00–23.00 daily. It's a chain restaurant with branches all over town, but if you're in a hurry for fast sustenance while you're ticking off the sights, give it a try for Italian standards cooked well. The website will tell you where the others are, as well as all you need to know about what's on offer. Always busy, always lively, service is slick & it does the job. A delivery service is also available. $$$$

X **Freski** [Map, page 137] 19 Internatsionalnaya St; ☎327 81 72; ⊕ 10.00–01.00 Sun–Wed, 10.00–05.00 Thu–Sat. Decent food, OK service, good location. $$$

X **Il Patio** [Map, page 137] 22 Nyezalyezhnastsi Av; ☎327 17 91; www.ilpatio.by; ⊕ 09.00–23.00 daily. Still a very popular venue among locals and visitors alike, the decent-quality food is served competently & without fuss. Not spectacular, but good value. $$$

Mediterranean

✗ Porto del Mare (formerly Porto Maltese)
3 Kozlova St; 288 11 53; www.portodelmare.com; noon–midnight. Specialising in seafood, it isn't cheap but service is very good & the quality of dishes ranges from medium to high. More often than not it's close to empty, which probably reflects the high prices, but those who go like it. It's worth a visit for the food, but try to get someone else to pick up the tab. $$$$$

✗ Casa Augustine Lopez
31 Zakharova St; 233 95 84; noon–01.00 Sun–Thu, noon–03.00 Fri & Sat. Less than 10 mins on foot from Ploschad Pobyedy metro station, Spanish dishes are a speciality here. The paella is tasty (if a little short on fish), & any of the beef & pork dishes are recommended. Do book in advance at w/ends, as this place is much favoured by wedding parties. A cosy setting, with suitably Iberian décor. $$$$

Oriental

✗ Jomalungma
7 Gikalo St; 280 53 88; www.jomalungma.by; 11.00–02.00 daily. Still 1 of my favourites after all these years. A 5min walk from Ploschad Yakuba Kolasa metro station & close to the Bella Rosa Italian restaurant, Indian, Tibetan, Nepalese, Japanese, Chinese & Thai cuisine are all on offer here, inc. limited hotel delivery service. I love this place. The décor is fabulous, the food is of a high standard & service is good, with the proprietor in constant attendance. He drives the staff incredibly hard & isn't fussy about closing the kitchen door before tearing them off a strip. The 1970s cabaret floor shows are more than a little incongruous! There is also a 'hookah' bar (noon–02.00 daily) & a tearoom here, but you might want to give the karaoke bar a miss. And the dining outlet at Minsk-2 National Airport is now a Jomalungma! $$$$

✗ Taj
26 Romanovskaya Sloboda St; 711 11 10; www.taj.by; noon–midnight daily. I have yet to try this one, but Minsk friends have been urging me to do so for some time. They tell me the excellence of the food is matched by the service & that everything here is impressive. Where Jomalungma has familiarity on its side, the reputation of the Taj is continuing to grow. $$$$

South and Central American

✗ Varadero
5 Myelezha St; 262 14 16; www.varadero.by; noon–midnight daily. The interior is in the style of Old Havana, with 5 dining areas & food served under the direction of an internationally renowned chef trained in the best Cuban restaurants). Live (& conversation-stoppingly loud) music in the bar (17.00–02.00 daily), Cuban rum & very large cigars complete the experience. $$$$

CAFÉS AND COFFEE BARS

⬛ Air Grip
[Map, page 137] 19 Komsomolskaya St; 328 37 93; e air_grip@anitex.by; 24hrs daily. Italian ices served alfresco in the garden. Relaxed & pleasing, it's a good place to recharge your batteries, not least because it's right in the middle of where you're likely to be doing most of your meandering.

⬛ Barzha floating restaurant
Riverbank mooring, Svislach River, Troitskoye suburb; 355 00 22. Easy to spot at its mooring at the bottom of this popular tourist area, it's never busy & the standard of food & service is always high. Given the location & the quality of the views across the water, it's well worth a visit for a coffee, drink or meal.

⬛ Bastion
35 Volgogradskaya St; 280 17 67; noon–23.00 daily. Cheap & cheerful ethnic Slav dishes in a traditionally styled environment. Pleasant but uninspiring.

⬛ Boulevard
[Map, page 137] 22 Nyezalyezhnastsi Av; 111 47 47; 11.00–23.00 daily. Situated on the corner of Engels St, this elegant café should be high on your list. The view from the terrace is lovely. Expect high-quality food & service.

⬛ Beze
[Map, page 137] 18 Nyezalyezhnastsi Av; 328 64 09; 10.00–midnight Sun–Thu, 10.00–01.00 Fri–Sat. Quaint & charmingly retro, the richest of desserts are served here, so this is the place if you have a sweet tooth. The apple & cherry strudels are delicious.

⬛ Chill Out
[Map, page 137] 4 Svobody Sq; 328 63 43; 11.00–midnight Sun–Thu, 11.00–04.00 Fri & Sat. Small & modern of design, this actually is something of a calm haven. The music is relaxing & as a medium for stepping off the pace for an hour or so it works, especially as it's handily situated behind Minsk City Hall.

⬛ Coffee Inn
[Map, page 137] 23 Internatsionalnaya St; 227 40 41; 08.00–01.00 Mon–Thu, 08.00–03.00 Fri, 10.00–03.00

Sat, 10.00–01.00 Sun. Cosy & popular, so often crowded, but worth the effort. Good location, near to the Palace of the Republic.

⌨ Family Club [Map, page 137] Gorky Park; ☎620 20 35; ⊕ 11.00–22.00 daily. As the name & location suggest, this is one for families. It's also one of my own favourites in town. Right in the middle of the park, it offers an oasis of calm to escape the hustle & bustle of the city. The food is good (especially the pizza) & service is always excellent. Rarely busy (though it's very popular for wedding parties), it comes recommended.

⌨ Fresh 42 Nyezalyezhnastsi Av; ☎284 54 04; ⊕ 10.00–01.00 daily. 'Fresh' indeed, if unremarkable, but handily placed for a break from your sightseeing. Also at 2 Khmelnitskova St (☎292 10 94; ⊕ 10.00–23.00 daily).

⌨ Golden Coffee 26 Maxima Bogdanovicha St; ☎756 21 17; www.goldencoffee.by; ⊕ claims to be open 24hrs, but seems to close 06.00–08.00 for a 'technical break'. One of a chain that features widely across Latvia, Lithuania & Ukraine, there's decent tea & coffee here. Very lively & good value, but lacking charm. The new roof bar is now open. Also in the Expobel shopping mall (☎237 93 90; ⊕ 10.00–23.00 daily).

⌨ London [Map, page 137] 18 Nyezalyezhnastsi Av; ☎289 15 29; ⊕ 10.00–midnight Sun–Thu, 10.00–02.00 Fri & Sat. A cosy venue offering a huge selection of teas & coffees, with cakes & sweets to match. You'll have to ignore the tacky London décor & paraphernalia, however.

⌨ Lozhki 34 Komsomolskaya St; ☎327 07 72; ⊕ 11.00–23.00 Sun–Wed, 11.00–midnight Thu–Sat. I have yet to sample the delights here, but my correspondent Jill Flanagan tells me there's a good range of decent beer, teas, coffee, milkshakes & pastries. Bizarrely the walls are decorated with spoons & the ceiling has a spoon chandelier.

⌨ Matchbol 40 Zhudra St; ☎312 18 53; ⊕ 11.00–23.00 daily. A Vietnamese café specialising in national dishes & snacks. It's a long way out of the city centre (& a 20-min walk from Sportivnaya metro station), which is a pity, because it has a simple charm all of its own.

⌨ Maya Angliskaya Babushka [Map, page 137] 36 Karla Marksa St; ☎327 22 24; ⊕ 09.00–23.00 daily. Its location just across the road from the British embassy might have something to do with its name, which translates as 'My English Granny'! It's tiny, but cosy & rather romantic, & also easy to miss,

as you need to descend steps from street level to enter. Assorted teas & delicious pastries are served to customers on comfortable sofas in a Victorian setting. Full meals (inc b/fast) are also available until 17.00. Recommended.

⌨ Netto 13 Krasnaya St; ☎668 13 13; ⊕ 24hrs daily. Located 5min walk from Ploshad Pobyedy metro station, this is a very popular establishment where the ambience is good, the food decent & the service top drawer. Those of my friends who like it all remark that it's a comfortable & relaxing venue.

⌨ News Café [Map, page 137] 34 Karla Marksa St; ☎103 11 11; ⊕ 08.00–midnight Mon–Fri, 11.00–midnight Sat & Sun. Close to Maya Angliskaya Babushka & the British embassy, its reputation has it as one of the most glamorous places in the city; indeed, luxury motors, bling & the glitterati are to be seen in abundance here. Not my scene, I'm afraid, but the coffee is good & service is first class, I'm told.

⌨ Olivo [Map, page 137] 13 Volodarskovo St; ☎327 81 47; ⊕ 11.00–23.00 Sun–Thu, 11.00–01.00 Fri & Sat. This is a decent place for a pit stop, with good coffee & lots of snacks on offer. Trendy, popular & relaxed, all at the same time. Do bear this place in mind if you're dashing around & need a quick break. Also at 46 Nyezalyezhnastsi Av (☎284 88 41; ⊕ 10.00–23.00 Mon–Thu, 10.00–01.00 Fri, noon–01.00 Sat, noon–23.00 Sun) and at 35 Yakuba Kolasa St (☎785 58 30; ⊕ 11.00–midnight Sun–Thu, 11.00–01.00 Fri & Sat).

⌨ Perfetto [Map, page 137] 1 Romanovskaya Sloboda St; ☎200 28 99; e info@perfetto.by; www.perfetto.by; ⊕ noon–midnight daily. Opposite McDonald's on the corner of Nemiga St, all is very shiny & very Italian here. If you want more than just coffee, the food is consistently good.

⌨ Salodki Falvarak 2 Maksima Tanka St; ☎306 34 11; www.eng.brovar.by/eng/salodki-falvarak; ⊕ 11.00–23.00 daily. These emporia are part of the Rakovsky Brovar stable & thus worth a visit for that reason alone. Modelled on a Parisian café, there's a good range of coffee & tea, but the pastries are strictly Belarusian. Only sample if you're in need of an intense sugar rush or are extremely hung-over, though locals love it here. Also at 37 Nyezalyezhnastsi Av (☎284 30 79; ⊕ 11.00–23.00 daily). Located near to Ploshad Pobyedy metro station, there's more of the same here, but in a larger venue with interesting Cubist décor. Now also at 41 Surganova St (✆ 555 51 12; ⏱ 10.00–23.00 daily).

💻**Shtolle** 53 Nyezalyezhnastsi Av; ✆ 331 77 77; www.stolle.by; ⏱ 10.00–23.00 daily. One of a chain, there are 7 of these in prime locations in the centre of the city. Think pies and pasties, both savoury & sweet, with a delivery service if you need. Otherwise it's a great way to access tasty food on the go. Consistently decent standards. My friend Olga thinks so too. She lives & works in Minsk & is a regular patron.

💻 **Union Coffee** [Map, page 137] 18 Nyezalyezhnastsi Av; ✆ 180 00 11; www. unioncoffee.by; ⏱ 08.00–02.00 daily. One of my personal favourites in town. The city centre location is perfect for a break from your meandering & the noise of the streets melts away when you walk through the door. The coffee is good, the food consistently tasty & the service understated but professional. You won't find haute cuisine here, but there's a wide choice of lightish bites that do the job. Last visit I had a bacon club sandwich with chips & cocktail sauce & a beer, which was just what I needed after 4hrs of furious scribbling on the streets with Moleskine notebook & pencil in hand! If you're hot & flustered from your time wandering the city, the splendidly appointed loo in the basement is a real bonus.

BARS

Although only a modest number of venues are listed here, many of the places described earlier as restaurants & cafés also double as bars, with most of them readily serving drinking clientele as well as diners. There are many others out there, with more and more opening all the time. Minsk is currently experiencing exponential growth with its leisure-time services and both locals and visitors are spoilt for choice right now. So, embark on a voyage of discovery and perhaps you can find somewhere new. If you do, be sure to tell me about it.

🍷**BierKeller** 12 Voiskovoi Lane; ✆ 286 00 39; ⏱ noon–midnight Sun–Wed, noon–02.00 Thu–Sat. Not surprisingly it's very German in every way (food, beer, décor, costumes). The food is decent & the pavement terrace ideal for people-watching in the summer. My good friend Artur who lives round the corner was keen for me to

sample the impressive range of beers & I wasn't disappointed. Close to Gorky Park if you're thirsty after a meander.

🍷**Bierstrasse** 40 Arlovskaya St; ✆ 721 33 33; www.bierstrasse.by; ⏱ noon–midnight Sun–Wed, noon–02.00 Thu–Sat. A little further out of the city centre than others, you can get the same experience elsewhere without having to go so far, but if you're in the locality give it a try for decent beer & food.

🍷**Dhrozhi United** [Map, page 137] 2 Sverdlova St; ✆ 200 54 56; ⏱ 09.00–02.00. Ahem. Even Minsk has its own Irish bars. This was the 1st in town and it's more than a little clichéd, but proper Guinness is served well & it's worth a visit for the craic. Guinness, football on the big screen & live music; my Irish roots may be colouring my judgement I suppose, but what is there not to like? Czech & German beers are also available.

🍷**Doo Dah King** 14 Bersona St; ✆ 103 10 00; www.doodahking.by; ⏱ 17.00–05.00 daily. A good night out is to be had here, with live music nightly.

🍷**Gambrinus** [Map, page 137] 2 Svobody Sq; ✆ 321 23 76; ⏱ 11.00–midnight. Splendidly located in a lovely central square, this could be listed as a restaurant given that the cuisine is decent, but all of my Minsk friends who come do so for the beer, which is excellent. Lively & popular, the ambience makes this one for your list. Expect it to be busy. It's the 1st choice of my Minsk friend Natalia.

🍷**Gaststätte** [Map, page 137] 16 Revolutsionaya St; ✆ 306 20 62; www.gaststatte. by; ⏱ noon–midnight Sun–Wed, noon–02.00 Thu–Sat. One of the new breed of 'beer restaurants' in town, the location in the heart of the city is excellent, as is the experience here. As you might expect, it's done out like a Bavarian bierkeller. There's a fine choice of quality beers & an extensive menu of GDR-themed sausages & salads (whatever that means) with all the trimmings. My warm beef salad was delicious when I came midweek & it was very busy. Many of my friends in town think this is the best of its kind. Live music most nights of the week from 21.00. Come for a few beers, a sausage or two & immerse yourself in the Latin rhythms of live flamenco guitar (it's kind of fusion, this place). A downside is that there is only one toilet each for boys and girls, so expect to queue.

♀**Gosti** [Map, page 137] 25 Nyezalyezhnastsi Av; ☎677 79 99; ⏰ noon–01.00 Sun–Thu, noon–02.00 Fri & Sat. Opinion is divided among my Minsk friends & views are either very positive or at the other end of the scale. I think it's OK, but standards of customer service do need an overhaul. Live (& very loud) music if that's what you need.

♀**Gvozd** 5 Gikalo St; ☎583 83 83; www.pubgvozd.by; ⏰ noon–midnight Sun–Wed, noon–02.00 Thu–Sat. Good food, great choice of beer, friendly staff, chilled ambience & decent live music at the w/end. It ticks all the right boxes & is popular with locals & visitors alike. My Minsk friend Olga says it's the best in town.

♀**Stravinsky Bar** [Map, page 137] 25B Nyezalyezhnastsi Av; ☎227 31 13; ⏰ 17.00–02.00 Sun–Thu, 17.00–06.00 Fri & Sat. Come here for cocktails & a classy night out rather than beer & in-your-face entertainment, but you won't be disappointed. I have yet to find somewhere in town that does the job better.

♀**U Ratushi** [Map, page 137] 1 Gertsyena St; ☎226 06 43; ⏰ noon–02.00 daily. Handily placed in Old Town, this venue has been open a long time, & it's still popular with its loyal following. I first came around 6 years ago & I think it's now looking a little tired, not least as to the food, but I'm one of those loyal followers & I'm willing it to pick up.

ENTERTAINMENT AND NIGHTLIFE

CASINOS AND CLUBS If you read the publicity blurb that is aimed at enticing would-be punters in search of hedonistic pleasure into these establishments, you would be led to believe that they are the only places in town for aspiring socialites, sophisticates and the well-to-do to be seen. True it is that the country's nouveaux riches *biznizmyeni* and their glamorous escorts are to be found at leisure here, often until dawn (it's the same the world over, after all), but some of these places are also the haunt of the seedy underside of society. In particular, prostitution is rife and ladies of the night can be seen plying their trade among the tables. But if you exercise some common sense, then the art of people-watching can richly be served here. Stay sober, keep a tight hold on your wallet, keep your wits about you and you won't go far wrong. You will need to pay an entrance fee just to cross the threshold of these emporia, ranging from US$20 to US$30 for standard club venues, all the way to US$50+ for a more sophisticated and chic experience in the 'classier' locations. At the weekend, the prices are hiked up significantly. If this is your bag, however, then for a broad overview of the night-time scene in Minsk go to www.minsknightlife.net and take your pick.

☆ **Africa** [128 A3] 9 Timiryazheva St; ☎219 00 10; ⏰ 22.00–06.00 daily; www.africaclub.by. Located very close to the Madison Royal Club & mainly aimed at the teenage market, all that you would expect to find in a nightclub is here. See if you can guess the theme…

☆ **Alkatraz** [137 C2] 25 Nyezalyezhnastsi Av; ☎226 06 45; ⏰ noon–06.00 daily. The usual fare is on offer here: booze, loud music & scantily clad young women cavorting on stage, all within the expected prison theme.

☆ **Byelaya Vyezha Casino** [128 C3] 17 Masherova Av; ☎284 69 22; ⏰ 24hrs daily. Once the most popular nightclub in the city with a state-of-the-art dance floor equipped with 9m-high video plasma screens, only the restaurant & casino on the ground floor remain, though it still attracts a large crowd of serious punters.

☆ **Casino Royal** [137 A4] 11 Nyezalyezhnastsi Av; ☎111 33 33; e info@royal.by; www.royal.by; ⏰ 24hrs daily. The casino at Hotel Minsk (see pages 127–9).

☆ **Diamond Princess Casino** [137 B4] 13 Kirova St; ☎226 14 96; www.worldofprincess.com; ⏰ 24hrs daily. Like Next nightclub, this gambling emporium is part of the Crowne Plaza Hotel complex (see pages 130–1). Princess Group International has a number of casinos in the city, so you have more than one chance to enrich the company's shareholders.

☆ **Dozari** [129 E2] 58 Nyezalyezhnastsi Av; ☎345 22 33; ⏰ 22.00–06.00 (closed Mon & Tue). Only a few years old, this appears to be the place to be seen for night-time activities. Hugely popular.

☆ **Fashion** [137 C1] 25 Yanka Kupala St; ✆ 539 11 11; www.fashion-club.by; ⏱ 22.00–06.00. Relatively new, there's little you can't find elsewhere, but it does appear to be popular & to enjoy a decent reputation for a good night out.

☆ **Madison Royal** [128 A3] 9 Timiryazheva St; ✆ 219 00 10; www.madisonclub.by; ⏱ 22.00–06.00 (closed Mon). Following a major process of refurbishment, which inc. adding the accolade 'Royal' to its title, this club is regarded by many as the premier night spot in town. It modestly claims to be the only luxury club in the city, but aficionados must judge for themselves. It's certainly one of the places to be seen & consequently, the admission fee is on the steep side. Expect the usual facilities & distractions.

☆ **Max Show** [129 E2] 73 Nyezalyezhnastsi Av; ✆ 292 00 38; www.maxshow.by; ⏱ 22.00–06.00 daily. More non-stop erotica with all the attachments.

☆ **Millenium** [137 A1] 7 Pobediteley Av; ✆ 577 00 77; ⏱ 24hrs daily. Casino & entertainment complex with a thousand ways to empty your wallet.

☆ **Next** [137 B4] 13 Kirova St; ✆ 718 77 77; www.nextclub.by; ⏱ 22.00–06.00 daily. Part of the Crowne Plaza Hotel complex, it's regarded as glamorous, although the majority of the clientele appear to be young Belarusian women escorted by more mature foreign businessmen. Enough said, I suspect.

☆ **NLO (the UFO)** [129 E1] 37 Yakuba Kolasa St; ✆ 290 20 80; www.nlo.by; ⏱ 18.00–05.00 Tue–Thu, 16.00–06.00 Fri, noon–06.00 Sat–Sun. This place reckons it has the best sound system in Minsk. Electronic music, live acts & original themed party nights make it popular with the young crowd.

☆ **Overtime** [137 A1] 4 Pobediteley Av; ✆ 203 02 24; ⏱ 18.00–06.00 daily. Very loud music & an enormous bar appear to be 2 of the attributes that render this club overcrowded much of the time. Close to Nemiga metro station, its location is very handy & by reputation it's the favourite of locals & visitors in Minsk. There's also a sports bar, & live broadcasts of major sporting events prove very popular.

☆ **Reaktor** [128 C2] 29 Very Khoruzhey; ✆ 288 61 60; www.reaktorclub.com; ⏱ 22.00–06.00 daily. Pulsating music aimed at the teenage market. Themed on the nuclear age, it also reckons to have its own reactor. Hmmmm. Now marketing special events, underground concerts & non-mainstream performances.

☆ **Shangri La Casino** [128 C5] 8/3 Kirova St; ✆ 321 20 22; www.shangrila.by; ⏱ 24hrs daily. Just up the road from Crowne Plaza Hotel.

☆ **Titan** [128 A6] 104 Dzerzhinskava Av; ✆ 709 10 10; ⏱ 23.00–06.00 daily. Reckoned to be the largest club and entertainment complex in the city, but it's a long way out, beyond IBB hotel.

☆ **TNT** [137 A2] 9 Revolutsionaya St; ✆ 655 55 55; ⏱ noon–02.00 Sun–Thu, noon–04.00 Fri & Sat. Relatively new and in a very central location, correspondent Jill Flanagan tells me this is a really friendly place, with live music, decent food & cocktails of quality. The critique of other friends is that rock fans will love it, particularly the more mature ones. Very loud & in-your-face, get yourself warmed up with German beer & sausage at Gaststätte beer restaurant just up the road (see pages 143–4), then come here for some serious head-banging. A frighteningly good night out, but keep the next day free.

☆ **Tyekhas** [128 B3] (attached to Hotel Yubilyeynya) 19 Pobediteley Av; ✆ 226 99 04; ⏱ 20.00–05.00 daily. A small & uninspiring venue offering adult entertainment.

☆ **Versus** [137 A4] 11 Nyezalyezhnastsi Av; ✆ 200 25 20; ⏱ 21.00–07.00 daily. Erotic shows & all the trappings at Hotel Minsk (see pages 127–9).

☆ **Victoria** [128 A2] 59 Pobediteley Av; ✆ 306 08 08; www.casino-victoria.by; ⏱ 24hrs daily. This casino at the rapidly expanding Victoria Hotel complex opposite Pobyedy Park is said to have the largest number of gambling tables in the city.

☆ **Vkus Nochi** [128 A3] (attached to Hotel Planyeta) 31 Pobediteley Av; ✆ 330 53 30; ⏱ 22.00–04.00 daily. Accessed through the night bar in Hotel Planyeta, this is strictly a venue for adult entertainment only.

☆ **XO Casino** [129 E2] 56 Nyezalyezhnastsi Av; ✆ 777 77 51; e info@casinoxo.by; www.casinoxo. by; ⏱ 24hrs daily. Another new addition to the city's nightlife, with every encouragement to part with your cash. Floor shows & live music are the backdrop.

DEPARTMENT STORES AND SHOPPING CENTRES There is a whole world of discovery by way of retail therapy just waiting for you. Should anything catch your eye in a shop window as you promenade along the boulevards, just step off the pavement and take a look. Shop browsing is a real art in this city and the best thing of all is that you won't be hassled by manic assistants eager to secure their commission on a sale. It's a stress-free experience and a great way to observe another interesting slice of Belarusian life.

Western designer goods are becoming increasingly available from new boutiques that are springing up all over the city, but why shop for things that you can get back home? The main drag for shopaholics is **Nyezalyezhnastsi Avenue** and, in particular, the section northeast of the Hotel Minsk. The two large state department stores can be found here: **GUM** [137 B3] (*21 Nyezalyezhnastsi Av;* \ *227 88 76;* e *09.00–21.00 Mon–Sat, 10.00–19.00 Sun; nearest metro: Oktyabrskaya/Kupalovskaya*); and **TSUM** [129 E3] (*54 Nyezalyezhnastsi Av;* \ *284 21 64;* ⊕ *09.00–21.00 Mon–Sat, 11.00–18.00 Sun; nearest metro: Yakuba Kolasa*). Shop here for all things Belarusian, including ethnic souvenirs and books. Just browsing is an experience in itself. GUM in particular is a must for those on the trail of Soviet-style memorabilia, especially cheap lapel badges which all seem to show Lenin's profile against a variety of backdrops. Part of the massively expansionist building programme at the end of the Great Patriotic War, the architecture and décor are classically Stalinist, even down to the trademark red stars in the glass of the windows and the grand statuettes in heroic poses on the staircases inside. With hammer and sickle motifs all around you, it's like a 1950s time warp. Many other specialist stores can be found on this avenue. Window-shopping is also a fine complement to the art of promenading, particularly when accompanied by an occasional diversion to a pavement café. **Nemiga department store**, with its ancillary outlets and food supermarket, is located at the junction of Lenina and Nemiga streets, close to the Nemiga/Frunzhyenskaya metro entrance (*Na Nemiga; 8 Nemiga;* \ *220 97 47;* ⊕ *09.00–21.00 Mon–Sat, 10.00–20.00 Sun*), but it's all rather tired and drab. It's still worth a browse. Further along the street is the ubiquitous McDonald's restaurant where Natalia and I took my daughter Harriet and her friend Daniel after a night at the ballet. They were in need of a slice of balancing Western culture, you see. In front of us in the drive-through queue were two teenagers on bicycles. The throng here is always massive and the enterprising youngsters had worked out that this was the route to speedier service!

New malls and hypermarkets are under construction and opening in many other locations. They include the **Zamok Shopping Centre** at 65 Pobediteley Avenue (\ *309 54 50;* ⊕ *10.00–22.00 daily*) and the gleaming and extremely busy **Korona Shopping Centre at Arena City** at 84 Pobediteley Avenue (\ *394 47 36;* ⊕ *10.00–22.00 daily*). Also here is the splendid **Minsk Arena Sports Hall**. With a capacity of 15,000, the European Track Cycling Championships were held here in 2009, and in May 2014 it was the main arena for the World Ice Hockey Championships. The whole country came to a standstill when the Belarus team was playing and many of my friends were lucky enough to get tickets. They all look at me in disbelief when I tell them the event merited not even a passing mention in the UK media. A major underground shopping centre, the **Stolitsa** [137 A4], opened beneath Nyezalyezhnastsi (formerly Lenin) Square a couple of years ago. After stumbling around the hazards of the largest building site I have ever seen for as long as I could remember, it was quite a surprise to see it open at last. As you enter the complex it looks just like any other soulless mall in the West, with piped muzak and shiny fittings. Most of the units are now filled, but it hasn't managed to attract Western designer-label outlets and, if you peek beneath the glossy veneer, the goods on offer are pretty second rate. But like Nemiga, it's worth an hour of your meandering time to experience life as the locals see and live it, especially as, whatever the time of day, it's pretty quiet. There's seating in the central atrium, with natural light from the cupola above to remind you of the real world outside retail land.

MARKETS The biggest market in town is **Komarovsky rinok** (*6 Very Koruzhey St;* \ *232 66 08;* ⊕ *08.00–19.00 daily; nearest metro: Yakuba Kolasa*). It's a vast covered hall where all manner of goods are available for purchase, including an astonishing array of fresh produce. This is a fantastic place to meander and people-watch, but do keep your wits about you and be on the lookout for pickpockets. Don't allow your carelessness to spoil a truly authentic slice of archetypical Belarusian life. The market at **Dynamo Stadium** [137 B4] (*8 Kirova St;* \ *227 26 11;* ⊕ *08.00–17.00 daily*) is currently closed during the significant refurbishment and rebuilding programme at the stadium.

BOOKS Probably the best bargains of all by way of souvenirs are books. Glossy pictorial guides are available very cheaply and although many of the tomes are in Russian, there is a significant (and growing) number of English works. But to my mind, Cyrillic printing is a work of art in itself. In any event, you can always look at the pictures and maps to remember your stay. There are many bookstores all over town and every one is well stocked, but my personal favourite is **Tsentralnaya Knigariya (Central Bookstore)** [137 B3] (*19 Nyezalyezhnastsi Av;* \ *227 49 18/226 10 52;* ⊕ *10.00–15.00 & 16.00–19.00 Mon–Fri, 10.00–15.00 & 16.00–18.00 Sat; nearest metro: Oktyabrskaya/Kupalovskaya*). This shop has the largest stock of books in the city, with an ever-growing selection of Belarus guides and maps (some in English) as well as a fine range of postcards and Soviet-style posters and calendars. Also along this section of the avenue on the opposite side (towards the main Post Office) is the **Belkniga bookstore** (⊕ *10.00–20.00 Mon–Fri, 10.00–18.00 Sat, 11.00–17.00 Sun*), where you will find a good selection of pictorial guides. On my last visit I asked if they had an English-Belarusian dictionary. 'That's a very good question' was the reply; 'no, but we have an English-Polish one…' Some 250m further along and directly opposite the KGB building is a smaller branch selling a wide selection of maps and atlases only. Another branch of the bookstore is situated on Karla Marksa Street next door to My English Granny café. I also like **Dom Knigi** [137 A1] 'House of Books') (*11 Pobediteley Av;* \ *203 34 96;* ⊕ *10.00–19.00 Mon–Fri, 10.00–18.00 Sat*). The favourite of my bookworm friend Roni Karsai from Budapest, it's not as big as the Central Bookstore, but the quality of its material is high and I've always found it less crowded, making browsing more relaxed. And as I often stay at the Yubilyeynya when I'm in Minsk, I always pass it on my way into or out of town. If you're searching for mementos of your visit or gifts for those back home, there are fridge magnets, flags and tacky souvenirs galore in these book emporia, but for something a little out of the ordinary, they also sell notebooks and other stationery with images of the country and of the Soviet Union that make really good presents and souvenirs at a fraction of the cost.

OTHER PRACTICALITIES

BANKS Banks and booths offering money-exchange facilities are in plentiful supply all over town, but particularly in the centre. Travellers report no exchange controls when leaving the country, and this is certainly my experience, although it is nonetheless worth holding on to your receipts, just in case. As well as banks, it is also often possible to exchange currency at any Velcom agency. The one on

Kubysheva Street across from the Parking shopping centre is open until 21.00 from Monday to Saturday. Money can also be changed in the Nemiga shopping complex (see page 146) on Sundays, when the banks are closed. With more and more outlets opening everywhere, you won't encounter any difficulty with currency exchange.

Here are the main head office addresses for a selection of major banks. Most of them also have a considerable number of branches scattered throughout the city offering the usual banking, currency and exchange services. Full contact details for branches can be found on the websites listed. Standard opening hours are 09.00–17.00 Monday–Friday, but opening and closing times may vary by 30 minutes to an hour either way, with some closing early on Friday. Nearly all will have at least one ATM. Machines are also to be found in increasing numbers at other locations, such as the lobbies of the larger hotels, or in shopping centres and the many hypermarkets that are now appearing all over the suburbs.

For all information concerning banking and finance generally, go to the English pages of the website of the **National Bank of the Republic of Belarus** (*20 Nyezalyezhnastsi Av;* ✆ *306 00 02; www.nbrb.by*).

$ **Absolutbank** 95 Nyezalyezhnastsi Av; ✆237 07 02; www.absolutbank.by

$ **Alfa-Bank** 70 Myasnikova St; ✆217 64 64; www.alfabank.by

$ **Belagroprombank** 3 Zhukov Av; ✆218 57 16; www.belapb.by

$ **Belarusbank** 18 Dhzerzhinskava Av; ✆218 84 31; www.belarusbank.by

$ **Belarusky Narodny Bank** 87A Nyezalyezhnastsi Av; ✆309 7 309; www.bnb.by

$ **Belgazprombank** 60/2 Pritytskava St; ✆229 16 16; www.belgazprombank.by

$ **Belinvestbank** 29 Masherova Av; ✆289 28 12; www.belinvestbank.by

$ **Belpromstroibank ('BPS')** 6 Mulyavin Bd; ✆289 46 06; www.bps-sberbank.by

$ **BelSwissBank** 23/3 Pobediteley Av; ✆306 20 40; www.bsb.by

$ **BTA Bank** 20 Very Khoruzhey St; ✆334 54 34; www.btabank.by

$ **Deltabank** 95 Rosa Luxemburg St; ✆279 02 79; www.deltabank.by

$ **Fransabank** 95A Nyezalyezhnastsi Av; ✆389 36 36; www.fransabank.by

$ **Home Credit Bank** 129 Odoyevskava St; ✆229 89 89; www.homecredit.by

$ **IdeaBank** 25 Karla Marksa St; ✆328 63 02; www.ideabank.by

$ **Moskva-Minsk Bank** 49 Kommunisticheskaya St; ✆237 97 97; www.mmbank.by

$ **MTBank** 6A Partizanskaya Av; ✆229 99 99; www.mtbank.by

$ **Priorbank** 31A Very Khoruzhey St; ✆289 90 90; www.priorbank.by

$ **Technobank** 44 Kropotkina St; ✆283 28 28; www.tb.by

$ **Trustbank** 11 Ignatenka St; ✆203 24 67; www.trustbank.by

$ **VTB Bank** 14 Moskovskaya St; ✆309 15 15; www.vtb-bank.by

COMMUNICATIONS
Telephone See pages 101–2.

Internet Internet facilities can be found in hotels and post offices in any district of the city, but this isn't a cheap way to access the web. There are also a very large number of busy internet cafés. The biggest in town is **Soyuz Online**, situated at 3 Krasnoarmeiskaya Street, where terminals are in plentiful supply and a good service is on offer. Two others are the **Café Virus**, which is a slightly disconcerting choice of name in an increasingly paranoid electronic age, situated at the intersection of Krasnaya Street and Masherova Avenue, with the entrance on Krasnaya; and the 24-hour café on the edge of Alexandrovsky Public Garden, near to Oktyabrskaya metro station. The building can be identified by the red Soviet star above the entrance, with the internet café itself being accessed via the staircase to the left, on the second floor. To help you find it, look for the Soviet-era tank monument to the right of the building. And not surprisingly, Wi-Fi hotspots are appearing all over town. Sometimes it's a free service, but not always.

Fax Fax services are available in all larger hotels.

Post and courier The main post office is situated at 10 Nyezalyezhnastsi Avenue (✆ 200 04 06; call centre ✆ 154; www.belpost.by; ⏰ 08.00–20.00 Mon–Fri, 10.00–17.00 Sat–Sun). Telephone, telegraph, fax, photocopying and internet services are available here. It's a delightful building inside and out, with hammer and sickle motifs everywhere to be seen. Look especially for the archetypical Soviet-design clock on the front façade. One of my correspondents tells me about a delightful experience here thus: 'I wandered into the post office for some stamps and the first (elderly) lady I approached behind the counter took me under her wing, marched me to the front of the queue and then personally stuck all of our stamps on our postcards with glue and a lovely big smile!' You can post mail from hotels or any post offices, and it is processed regularly.

Express delivery services are available from the following establishments:

✉ **DHL** 70 Myasnikova St; ✆ 200 11 55; www.dhl.com. The company also has a number of other offices & outlets throughout the city, inc. at the main post office.

✉ **EMS** 10 Nyezalyezhnastsi Av; ✆ 327 58 39; www.belpost.by. This is the state service located at the main post office.

✉ **FedEx** (via its nominated contractor M&M Militzer & Munch) Office 902, 1 Melyezha St; ✆ 268 41 11; e info@mum.by; www.mum.by; also at 19 Pobediteley Av; ✆ 226 99 09; e callcenterfx@mum.by

✉ **TNT** 10 Platanova St; ✆ 294 80 00; e tnt@tnt.by

✉ **UPS** 3 Muzikhalny St; ✆ 327 22 33; www.ups.com

HOSPITALS AND CLINICS

✚ **City Accident & Emergency Hospital** 58 Kizhevatova St; ✆ 212 76 21; bsmp.by

✚ **Dentko Dental Clinic** 58 Nyezalyezhnastsi Av; ✆ 284 45 11; www.dentko.by

✚ **Minsk City Clinic Number 1** 64 Nyezalyezhnastsi Av; ✆ 331 92 58; www.1gkb.by

✚ **Minsk City Clinic Number 2** 25 Engelsa St; ✆ 327 50 29; www.2gkb.by

✚ **Minsk City Clinic Number 3 (Klumov Ophthalmology)** 30 Lenina St; 178 58 11; www.3gkb.by

✚ **Minsk City Clinic Number 4** 110 Rosa Luxemburg St; ✆ 208 75 70; www.4gkb.by

✚ **Minsk City Clinic Number 5** 9 Filatova St; ✆ 296 49 63; www.5gkb.by

✚ **Minsk City Clinic Number 6** 5 Uralskaya St; ✆ 245 26 21; www.6gkb.by

✚ **Minsk City Clinic Number 8** (Gynaecology) Bldg 3, 53 Senniskaya St; ✆ 205 42 30; www.ggb.by

✚ **Minsk City Clinic Number 9** 8 Semashka St; ✆ 272 70 91; www.m9gkb.by

✚ **Minsk City Clinic Number 10** 73 Uborevicha St; ✆ 345 30 46; www.10gkb.by

✚ **Minsk City Clinic Number 11** 4 Korzhenevskova St; ✆ 278 58 15; www.11gkb.by

✚ **Minsk City Clinic Number 12** (Dental) 28 Kedyshka St; ✆ 268 84 71; www.12stom.by

PHARMACIES

✚ **Belfarm Centre** 12 Chkalova St; ✆ 224 04 82; ⏰ 24hrs daily; also at 43/1 Yakuba Kolasa St; ✆ 216 10 00; ⏰ 24hrs daily

✚ **Belfarm Pharmacy** 44 Nyezalyezhnastsi Av; ✆ 284 93 81; ⏰ 08.00–22.00 Mon–Fri, 09.00–20.00 Sat & Sun; also at 78

Nyezalyezhnastsi Av; ✆ 280 60 21; ⏰ 10.00–21.00 daily

✚ **Belfarmatseya Pharmacy Number 7** 62 Partizansky Av; ✆ 295 01 03; ⏰ 24hrs daily

✚ **Belfarmatseya Pharmacy Number 13** 16 Nyezalyezhnastsi Av; ✆ 227 08 54; ⏰ 24hrs daily

✚ **Belfarmatseya Pharmacy Number 32** 87
Nyezalyezhnastsi Av; ☎ 292 05 31; ⏲ 24hrs daily
✚ **Belfarmatseya Pharmacy Number 36** 11
Shevchenka Bd; ☎ 288 97 43; ⏲ 24hrs Mon–Sat
✚ **Belfarmatseya Pharmacy Number 58** 25
Korzanevskava St; ☎ 278 35 10; ⏲ 24hrs daily
✚ **Belfarmatseya Pharmacy Number 78** 78
Gazety Zvezda Av; ☎ 271 48 40; ⏲ 24hrs daily
✚ **Belmedinfarm Pharmacy Number 12**
153A Maxima Bogdanovicha St; ☎ 288 47 34;
⏲ 24hrs daily
✚ **Doctor Do Pharmacy Number 6** 30
Nemiga St; ☎ 211 06 75; ⏲ 24hrs daily; also at
118 Maxima Bogdanovicha St; ☎ 237 53 68;
⏲ 24hrs daily
✚ **Doctor Do Pharmacy Number 13** 20 Karla
Marksa St; ☎ 220 28 44; ⏲ 24hrs daily
✚ **EuroPharmacy Number 5** 1 Pobediteley Av;
☎ 306 26 98; ⏲ 08.00–22.00 daily
✚ **Panagiya Pharmacy** 8 Nemiga St; ☎ 327 54
00; ⏲ 09.00–21.00 Mon–Sat, 10.00–18.00 Sun

✚ **Pharmacy Number 1** 25 Maxima
Bogdanovicha St; ☎ 334 00 34; ⏲ 08.00–22.00
Mon–Sat, 09.00–21.00 Sun
✚ **Pharmacy Number 1 (Healthplanet)** 18
Nyezalyezhnastsi Av; ☎ 226 17 81; ⏲ 08.00–21.00
Mon–Fri, 09.00–21.00 Sat & Sun
✚ **Pharmacy Number 8 (Healthplanet)**
147 Maxima Bogdanovicha St; ☎ 335 24 77;
⏲ 09.00–22.00 Mon–Sat, 10.00–22.00 Sun
✚ **Pharmacy Number 14 (Healthplanet)**
2 Glebki St; ☎ 253 03 23; ⏲ 09.00–22.00 daily
✚ **Pharmacy Number 19** 2 Kirova St; ☎ 227
05 86; ⏲ 08.00–21.00 Mon–Fri, 10.00–18.00
Sat–Sun
✚ **Pharmacy Number 28** 48 Nyezalyezhnastsi
Av; ☎ 284 85 68; ⏲ 08.00–22.00 Mon–Sat,
10.00–18.00 Sun
✚ **Rosfarm Big Pharmacy** 58 Nyezalyezhnastsi
Av; ☎ 331 06 87; ⏲ 09.00–21.00 daily; also at 3
Kirova St; ☎ 328 47 05; ⏲ 08.00–22.00 daily

WHAT TO SEE AND DO

MUSEUMS
The Belarusian State Museum of the Great Patriotic War [128 A3]
(*8 Pobediteley Av;* ☎ *327 11 66;* e *museumww2@tut.by; www.warmuseum.by;*
⏲ *10.00–18.00 Tue, Thur, Fri & Sat (last entry 17.00), 11.00–19.00 Wed & Sun
(last entry 18.00)*) At the time of writing, the vast collection of exhibits forming
the basis of this magnificent museum was in the process of being relocated to its
new home here in Pobyedy Park from its former location in Oktyabrskaya Square,
such that the new museum had not yet been unveiled when I was last in town. In a
highly symbolic gesture of unity, it was expected to be opened jointly by presidents
Lukashenko and Putin on Independence Day in the summer of 2014 at a ceremony
to mark the 70th anniversary of the country's liberation from Nazi occupation.
Expect to find museum updates on the Bradt website to prepare you for your visit.
Quite rightly, the president and the country as a whole regard the events of the Great
Patriotic War as being of huge significance, to the extent that they dominate the
national psyche even today, 70 years on. The new museum is confidently expected
to be even more impressive than the old one, which was a truly sombre record
chronicling the terrible events of World War II from the perspective of the USSR
(and for many years, the only one of its kind in the whole of the Soviet Union). I
visited many times and it never failed to impress. Three floors and 32 halls of exhibits
contained displays of great detail, crammed with memorabilia. Documentary films
were constantly showing. Periodically, war veterans were present to recount their
experiences. There was a harrowing scale model of the concentration camp the
Nazis built at Maly Trostenyets just a few miles to the east of Minsk, plus photo after
photo of public executions by hanging in the city's parks. There was also an excellent
and extensive featured exhibition devoted to the famous and heroic Belarusian
partisan movement, which made such a significant contribution to halting the Nazi
invasion and undermining the occupation. The website is hugely informative, both

on the museum and on the broader context of the conflict, though the text is sadly only in Russian. There is every indication that the museum's reincarnation will be an experience not to be missed and I'm eagerly awaiting my first visit. Expect to be deeply moved by all that you are likely to find here.

Museum of Ancient Belarusian Culture
[129 F2] (*1 Surganova St;* ✎ *284 27 32;* ⏰ *09.00–16.00 Mon–Sat; nearest metro: Akademya Nayuk; admission free*) As might be expected from the title, the exhibits here are primarily archaeological, including the remains of a Palaeolithic boat excavated from the mud of the Sozh River in the southeast of the country (there is a very similar exhibit in the museum in Vetka; see page 287). There are also exhibits of traditional folk art, household items, clothes and religious artefacts (including icons) from areas affected by the Chernobyl disaster. Everything is presented in a very traditional, not to say old-fashioned manner, so this is probably one for the specialist. Hands-on and interactive it isn't.

National History and Culture Museum of the Republic of Belarus
[137 B4] (*12 Karla Marksa St;* ✎ *327 43 22;* e *histmuseum@tut.by; www.history.museum.by (for a brief overview in English), www.histmuseum.by (detailed, but in Belarusian and Russian only);* ⏰ *11.00–19.00 Tue–Sun; nearest metro: Oktyabrskaya/ Kupalovskaya; admission BYR15,000, plus additional charge for specific exhibitions, free to all last Wed of month*) Some regard this as the foremost historical museum in the whole country, but as with the Museum of Ancient Belarusian Culture (see above), everything is displayed in a rather dreary and unimaginative way. Still, if you're a traditionalist when it comes to museums, you won't be disappointed. The bare facts show that there are an incredible 338,000 exhibits grouped into 45 collections that include archaeology, religious relics, weapons, fine arts, icons, photographs, manuscripts, historic printing and much, much more. On the ground floor of the same building is the **Museum of Nature and Ecology**, where tens of thousands of exhibits are stored, including a rib and shoulder blade of a mammoth, a horn of an auroch, and a giant mushroom. There was once also a quaint display of potatoes (I kid you not), but correspondent Zo Hoida tells me the display is no more. Pity.

Museum of Minsk History
[137 A2] (*10 Revolutsionaya St;* ✎ *321 24 30;* e *muzejminska@gmail.com;* ⏰ *11.00–19.00 Wed–Sun; admission BYR20,000*) Relatively new and located in a lovely late 19th-century building in a central location, the architecture itself is as much a part of what's on show as the exhibits themselves, a good proportion of which are artefacts from archaeological digs in the vicinity of Old Town, where the original castle (now long gone) was built. Four of the ten rooms are used for temporary exhibitions, concerts and performances.

State History Museum of Theatre and Music Culture of the Republic of Belarus
[137 B1] (*5 Muzikalny Lane;* ✎ *220 26 67;* e *mhtmc@tut.by;* ⏰ *10.00–18.00 Mon–Sat*) Also located in a lovely 19th-century building, the so-called 'House of Masons' (where the masonic lodge 'Northern Torch' held its meetings), 14,000 exhibits are displayed here, including collections of costumes, music scores, gramophone records and posters, together with musical instruments, playbills, programmes, personal documents, sculptures, drawings and paintings. Events to commemorate significant anniversaries relating to notable personalities of theatre and music are also held here.

National Art Museum of the Republic of Belarus [137 B3] (20 *Lenina St;* ☏ *327 71 63;* e *nmmrb@bk.ru; www.artmuseum.by;* ☻ *11.00–19.00 daily, last entry 18.30, closed Tue; admission BYR50,000, plus additional charge for specific exhibitions*) Plundered by the Nazis during the Great Patriotic War, this is still the country's largest museum of Belarusian and foreign art, with over 25,000 works on display in 13 halls. It's a magnificent collection, but don't expect to find any of Chagall's works here. The fate of the vast majority of its original contents remains a mystery to this day but, little by little, its collections were painstakingly reassembled during the post-war years and now include Belarusian art, icons, manuscripts and books from the 12th to the 20th centuries, western European art from the 16th to the 20th centuries and oriental crafts from the 15th to the 20th centuries. The website's English pages are extremely informative and a visit here is recommended.

Museum of Modern Fine Art [128 D3] (47 *Nyezalyezhnastsi Av;* ☏ 284 86 21; e *artmodernmuseum@gmail.com; www.modernartmuseum.by:* ☻ *11.00– 19.00 Tue–Sat, last entry 18.30*) Located on the edge of Yakuba Kolasa Square, this is another splendid museum and gallery that is worthy of your attention. There are 4,500 exhibits comprising paintings, graphics, sculptures, decorative art and posters. It's a vibrant celebration of the creative arts and a visit here is highly recommended. The English pages of the website are full of interest; check before you visit for details of the latest exhibitions and events. There's a lot happening here.

History of Belarusian Cinema Museum [137 A3] (4 *Sverdlova St;* ☏ 327 10 75; e *cinema@museum.by; www.cinema.museum.by;* ☻ *10.00–18.00 Mon–Sat; admission BYR15,000*) Not easy to find, this small but quaint museum is located in a small yard between the Hotel Minsk and the Red Church (of which more on page 165). Ask for directions at the reception desk in the lobby of the hotel. The subject matter will of course primarily appeal to those with an existing interest in cinematography, but first-timers will also appreciate a glance at a specific aspect of the country's social history. There are displays of photographs, posters and sketches representing Belarusian cinema through the ages, as well as artefacts and exhibits featuring articles of cinematic equipment. Given that the location is central to many of the things you are likely to be visiting, don't overlook this one.

Government Historical Museum of Belarusian Literature [137 B1] (15 *Maxima Bogdanovicha St;* ☏ 334 56 21; e *bellitmuseum@tut.by; www.bellitmuseum. by;* ☻ *10.00–19.00 Tue–Sat, 10.00–18.00 Sun; admission BYR15,000*) Located on the edge of Old Town, this is one of the most significant literary museums in the country, with a unique collection of manuscripts, first editions, rare books, photographs, artwork and personal mementos of many of the most renowned Belarusian literary giants. In all, it contains over 50,000 items, some of them dating from the 11th century. There are also paintings, sculptures and exhibits of regional everyday life through the ages. And if you're in literary mode, it's a stone's throw from the Maxim Bogdanovich Literary Museum (see below). The website is most informative but is in Belarusian only.

Maxim Bogdanovich Literary Museum [137 B1] (7A *Maxima Bogdanovicha St;* ☏ 334 42 69; e *bagdanovich@tut.by; www.bogdanovich.by;* ☻ *10.00–18.00 Mon–Fri; admission BYR12,000*) Housed in a beautifully restored 19th-century building with ironwork and balconies, close to the Svislach River in Old Town, this collection is dedicated to the famous Belarusian poet and includes original manuscripts, books of collected verses printed during the poet's lifetime, photographs and personal belongings. There is also a recreation of some of the rooms of the house where he was born. Romance, drama and tragedy abound here. Both general and themed tours are available with the services of a guide, but not yet in English. Literary recitals and musical evenings are also held here. The web pages in English are most informative and really interesting.

Yakub Kolas Literary Museum [129 E2] (5 Akademicheskaya St; ☎ 284 17 02; e muzeykolas@yandex.ru; www.yakubkolas.by; ⊕ 10.00–17.30 Mon–Sat; admission BYR9,000, free to all last Sat of month)
Situated a short distance from Nyezalyezhnastsi Avenue in the grounds of the National Academy of Sciences, this attractive pale blue stucco building was the national poet's home from 1944 until his death in 1956. It's a charming museum that recreates his life in the form of the restored drawing room, dining room, office and bedroom as they were between 1947 and 1952, when the house was a focal meeting point for many of the intellectuals and artists of the time. Other rooms contain collections of additional exhibits, mementos and artefacts.

Yanka Kupala Literary Memorial Museum [137 C1] (4A Yanka Kupala St; ☎ 327 78 66; e kupalamuseum@mail.ru; www.kupala-museum.by; ⊕ 10.00–17.45 Mon–Sat; admission BYR10,000, free to all last Mon of month)
Situated in a beautiful location in Yanka Kupala Park, close to the Svislach River where once stood his home, this is another specialist but charming literary museum, this time telling the story of the life and work of the famous Belarusian poet, playwright, translator and author, through the medium of recreated rooms, exhibits, works and personal artefacts. Readings of the great man's works are regularly given here.

Museum of Olympic Glory [128 D3] (2 Yakuba Kolasa Sq; ☎ 288 14 63; www.olimpicglory.by; ⊕ 11.00–17.00 Mon–Fri; admission BYR5,000)
Belarusian athletes now feature significantly on the world stage in a number of different sports, and the medal haul at Olympic Games both summer and winter since those in Beijing in 2008 have been impressive. Look for the colonnaded building displaying the five Olympic rings, where this small museum is located on the fifth floor. Opened two years prior to Beijing, it contains photographs, equipment, trophies, medals and personal artefacts from every summer and winter Olympic Games in which Belarusians have participated, including those held during the Soviet era. You may be surprised that you've never heard before how successful many of the country's athletes have been.

Azgur Memorial Museum [128 D5] (8 Azgura St; ☎ 236 73 01; ⊕ 11.00–18.00 Wed–Sun; admission BYR20,000)
My Hungarian friend Roni Karsai describes this museum as 'simply magnificent'. It is certainly unique. Ten minutes' walk from Pobyedy Square, it is housed in the studio of the renowned Belarusian sculptor Zair Azgur (1908–95). A member of the USSR Academy of Arts, Azgur completed a portfolio of sculptures of soldiers, generals, partisans and civilians during the Great Patriotic War. A lifetime's work is displayed in the huge workshop here, where Roni experienced an uncanny sense of being watched. She describes the workshop as 'a huge portion of history crammed into a single space', with hundreds of familiar and unfamiliar faces, including politicians, waiting to greet you. A visit here is highly recommended.

Museum of the History of the National Academy of Sciences of Belarus [129 F2] (66 Nyezalyezhnastsi Av; ☎ 284 18 01; e nasb@presidium.bas-net. by; www.nasb.by; ⊕ 09.00–17.00 Mon–Fri; admission BYR15,500) This specialist museum, situated within the grand and imposing National Science Academy of Belarus, is dedicated to the academy's history and achievements throughout all aspects of Belarusian history, life and culture. The collection is certainly impressive and science academics will find much of interest here. I'm not a scientist, but even I was thoroughly engaged.

Museum of Contemporary Belarusian Statehood [137 C3] (entrance 4, 38 Karla Marksa St; ☎ 327 43 22; e msbg@tut.by; ⊕ 10.00–13.00, 14.00–17.00 Mon– Fri, 10.00–13.00 & 14.00–15.00 Sat; prearranged timed tickets only; admission BYR20,000, guide BYR35,000) This little-known museum, located in the presidential office building, has only been open since August 2012. The reason so few people know about it may well relate to the number of hoops to be jumped through just to get in here. Visitors are not permitted to turn up on the day as is usually the case with museums; first it is necessary to go to the National History and Culture Museum along the road at 12 Karla Marksa Street for passports to be copied, telephone numbers to be noted and a date for the visit to be given. My Budapest friend Roni Karsai turned up one afternoon with her passport and was given a date 19 days later! It seems that at least two weeks' notice is standard. Established on the instructions of the president himself, the museum seeks to represent the country's national identity, with the principal goal of creating an attractive image. It covers the period from the establishment of the republic in 1991 to the present day, showcasing images of many aspects of statehood and the country's achievements in various spheres, including industry, agriculture, education, science, sport and international relations. Over 22 hours of film are shown, and there are many photographs of the president on display. If you're interested and you can pass the endurance test for entry, it's quite something to be able to say you've been! Roni certainly recommends it.

PARKS, OPEN SPACES AND RECREATIONAL AREAS
Gorky Park [137 D2] (22 Nyezalyezhnastsi Av) Or to be more precise, 'Central Children's Gorky Park' to give it its full name. Here for over 200 years and originally the oldest of the governor's gardens in the city, this lovely park is situated on the banks of the Svislach River. The main entrance is through a large and imposing gate off Victory Square, next to Café Skiff. There are many attractions for children, together with an observatory and planetarium, a covered skating rink and a stage for summer concerts. Horseriding and boating are available and the big wheel has fine panoramic views of Minsk from its 56m high point. Installed in 2003, it has enclosed cabins, unlike its rather ramshackle predecessor. For those with a head for heights, it also has open seating, with nothing between your legs except a lot of fresh air. A ride in a closed cabin costs BYR15,000, while adventure seekers pay BYR12,000 to sit out in the open. One circuit takes nine minutes. I haven't ridden it though it looks reasonably high-tech and secure, unlike the one in Gorky Park that I did ride in 1990 in the last days of the USSR, but that's another story for another day.

The abundance of manmade entertainment features are clearly designed with children in mind (particularly those at the top of the park by the Ferris wheel where you will find rides, candy floss, ice cream and cheap toy stalls), but don't think that there's nothing for adults here, as its generally attractive and relaxed ambience has more to do with the natural environment. There are groves of lime and maple trees that have stood for a hundred years or more, along with rare cedars and pines. While you're here, look out for the statue of Maxim Gorky at leisure on a bench near to the central gate (erected in 1981). With three cafés within its boundaries (including Family Club, one of my personal favourites in town), this is the ideal location for promenading and people-watching, whatever the season. At the time of writing, however, the ambience was spoiled somewhat by the mammoth building site on the banks of the river where the new Kampinsky Hotel was in the course of construction. And there's more bad news: locals are up in arms about the fact that the size of this new hotel is going to completely overshadow the much-loved Minsk State Circus building. The joys of town planning…

Alexandrovsky Public Garden [137 C2] (*Nyezalyezhnastsi Av*) Originally laid out in 1872, this attractive green space closer to the city centre along Nyezalyezhnastsi Avenue (on the south side of Oktyabrskaya Square) is more an open public area and less of a formal park and garden these days (locals may even look at you blankly if you ask for directions!), but I always find it pleasing to walk here. It contains the city's oldest public fountain, *A Boy and a Swan*, together with a number of significant sculptures, both Classical and modern. Immediately following its opening, it became a favourite place of rest and relaxation for intellectuals and writers, which is why a theatre was built in its southwestern corner in 1890. It was never popular with local people, not least because plays in Belarusian, Polish and Hebrew were banned there until 1905. Today, it is the National Academic Theatre bearing the name of the famous poet Yanka Kupala. Before you move on, look for an enduring symbol of the Great Patriotic War: mounted on a plinth is one of the first T-34 tanks to enter the city when it was liberated by the Red Army in 1944.

Yanka Kupala Park [137 C1] (*Nyezalyezhnastsi Av*) Yanka Kupala, a politically active poet and writer, is a favourite son of the Belarusian nation. He and his contemporary Yakub Kolas are widely regarded as the most significant figures of modern Belarusian literature and language. Designed in 1962, 20 years after his death, and situated just across the avenue from Gorky Park, it is home to the Yanka Kupala monument and Museum, along with many other sculptures. Its broad central walkway slopes gently down to the Svislach River, which forms a boundary on two sides and is 120m wide on one of them, with fine views towards the lovely buildings on Kommunisticheskaya Street where Lee Harvey Oswald rented an apartment in 1960. Over 4,000 trees and many more shrubs were planted when this park was laid out, making it an oasis of green in the heart of the city (especially as there are few cafés within its boundaries other than summer ones by the river) and a splendid place for an afternoon's stroll. Less manufactured than Gorky Park and smaller, it actually feels bigger, with more room to breathe and to appreciate the greenery. With considerably fewer people around, it's possible to amble for ages and not feel that you're in a major capital city at all. The Yanka Kupala museum within the park stands at the location of the wooden house where once he lived. The house itself (containing much of his work) was flattened in the Great Patriotic War.

Central Botanical Gardens [129 F2] (*2 Surganova St; e office@cbg.org.by; www. cbg.org.by; ⊕ 1 May–31 Oct 10.00–18.00 daily; admission BYR10,000*) Founded in 1932 and now under the stewardship of the National Academy of Sciences, there are many varieties of plant life here, all in a setting that is most pleasing on the eye. The rose garden, alpine garden and landscape park are particularly attractive, and in spring the rhododendrons are a delight. It is a very popular place of relaxation for the city's residents and, because it's a little way out of the city centre, you should find that there are fewer tourists than elsewhere. The English pages of the website are a treasure trove of interesting and practical information. Opening times are rather ad hoc, dependent largely on the weather, so do ring in advance to avoid the risk of a wasted journey.

Chelyuskintsev Culture and Leisure Park [129 G2] Opened in May 1932 and adjacent to the Central Botanical Gardens, attractions include a children's amusement park and a delightful miniature railway. There's a large slice of Minsk life to be experienced here, with lots of places to sit and watch the world go by, along with summer cafés where the shashlik comes highly recommended. There is also a large area of urban forest, which gives a clue to the former ecology of the land on which the city now stands. As with the Botanical Gardens next door, the location a little way out of the city centre and closer to the suburbs means that it's frequented by many more locals than tourists, a huge point in its favour in my view. Nearly all of my Minsk friends with families agree. For my good friend Artur, there's no question about it: he always brings his family here for leisure time, even though Gorky Park is just minutes away from their apartment on foot.

Pobyedy (Victory) Park [128 A2–3] Founded in 1945, this enormous wooded area contains the huge Komsomolskoe Lake and is a very popular location for promenaders. It's certainly one of my favourite haunts for an early morning stroll on a Sunday. Significantly redeveloped in recent times and now benefiting from major enhancement, it is also now the home of the Belarusian State Museum of the Great Patriotic War. At the time of writing, the building works and the process of relocation were still ongoing, but as a glorious homage to the perceived golden days of yore and the heroism of the ultimate victory over the Nazis, the iconic hammer and sickle flag of the USSR was flying proudly from its cupola in the middle of the building site. The Minsk Hero City monument on Pobediteley Avenue marks the main entrance to the park and the new museum is immediately behind it. Walk through the main gate and uphill along the avenue to Victory Fountain at the top, where a delightful panorama across the lake and beyond awaits. This is a lovely spot. You are likely to share it with elderly folk holding hands, children rollerblading with their mothers and couples promenading. If you live in one of the many high-rise developments that surround the park, it's a wonderful garden to have right outside your building, all at your boundless disposal and free. Head on down to the side of the lake and track left towards Bird Island with its boardwalks and nature trails through the woods. From the edge of the island there are fine views across to the suburbs beyond the lake, with the BelExpo exhibition centre and the new-build of the president's huge and ornate office and residence in the foreground. Completed in the autumn of 2013, it was not in use at the time of writing. Retrace your steps off the island across the wooden bridge festooned with the padlocks of lovers and head lakeside to your right, where you will find seating galore and a summer café to enhance your appreciation of the view. At this point you will be alongside the massive redevelopment at Hotel Victoria. At the weekend, there are families at leisure as far as the eye can see here. And if you're in need, the sweetest public lavatories you will ever encounter can be found in the park, directly in front of the main BelExpo hall, complete with a lobby, ornaments, artificial flowers galore and two elderly attendants waiting to charge you the princely sum of BYR3,500 to avail yourself of the services there. As you walk on past the new presidential

complex, it just gets bigger and bigger until it fills your field of vision. Look out particularly for the design of the glass panels matching the edging on the country's national flag. You can then complete your circumnavigation of the lake and park, through picnic areas with sunshades and outdoor showers, beaches with delightful children's play areas complete with a mini-lighthouse and jetties, and a fitness trail, before you reach the grand entrance gate where your exploration began. At this juncture in your ambling I have one more thing for you to do. Walk out of the park at the main gate on the corner of Masherova Avenue, cross over the road and head uphill along Drozd Street for 200m, turn round, and take in the vista laid before you. To my mind, it says *everything* there is to say about this city, this country and the national psyche. The glory of the Victory monument, with the gleaming new Great Patriotic War Museum behind it, the hammer and sickle flag of the old USSR fluttering in the breeze; eight-lane boulevards carrying very little traffic, with hardly anyone walking the scene; block after block of Soviet-style concrete in a 360-degree panorama; wide open spaces and grand Utopian town planning on a massive scale; trees and concrete under huge open skies, where the eye is always drawn up and to the horizon. It's quite a view, and a rare treat for the senses…

SQUARES, MONUMENTS AND SIGNIFICANT ARCHITECTURAL FEATURES – A CITY WALKING TOUR

The following entries from Privakhsalnaya Square to Victory Square follow a more or less straight line bisecting the city in a northeasterly direction along Nyezalyezhnastsi Avenue. Here lies the heart of the city and a day's amble to take in the sights as listed comes highly recommended. *En route*, you will pass a host of bars and eateries to keep you fortified, as well as any number of diverse shops for a little retail therapy and souvenir hunting along the way.

Privakhsalnaya Square [128 B6] Originally home to the city's first railway station, constructed of intricate red brick in the 1870s, the impressive new station was built here in the 1990s. All around, the sense of space, air and grandeur is impressive and it's a very busy spot, full of hustle and bustle, noise and motion. Archetypical Stalinist granite buildings on a grandiose scale can also be found here, including the two lofty towers known colloquially as the 'City Gates'. Consisting of 11 storeys on three tiers in the style of a wedding cake and positioned at the corners of two five-storey blocks of flats, they form an impressive entrance to this open and sweeping public space, which itself forms an integral part of the post-war spatial planning of the city. Begun in 1948, the final brick was laid in 1956 under the watchful gaze of chief architect Rubyanenko from Leningrad (now St Petersburg). At the time of construction, these two dwelling units were something of an exception in social planning terms, for they were entirely self-contained, incorporating their own shops, restaurants, pharmacies, school and medical facilities. When originally built, the two towers were topped with spires, while sculptures stood on the corners of the first tier. Façades were decorated with ornate stucco. Sadly, all of the apocrypha concerning Soviet concrete are true and these adornments are long gone, their crumbling demise a portent of the collapse of the system that created them. All that remains is the country's biggest clock (diameter in excess of 3.5m and over a hundred years old), along with the country's former coat of arms. The new railway station faces you on the other side as you enter the square through the City Gates. The concept of imaginary twin gates replicates in fond homage the design of the original station, which itself featured double-tier pavilions either side of its entrance. But the new structure extends horizontally rather than vertically, with the onlooker's gaze drawn between the imaginary gates

3

to the soft and rounded lines of the central access, which is topped by a simple but impressive pyramidal roof skylight. The whole effect is set off beautifully by the reflection of the entire square in the mirror-like walls of the spacious foyer, giving the visitor the perception of a grand city entrance through triumphal portals. Walk out of the square through the City Gates, turn half left at the first junction along Sverdlova Street, and into Nyezalyezhnastsi Square.

Nyezalyezhnastsi (Independence, formerly Lenin) Square [128 B5] If the sense of space and air in Privakhsalnaya Square is impressive, here it is breathtaking. A great many pre-war Stalinist buildings survive and of course there is also yet another imposing statue of Lenin, master of all he surveys. The best panoramic view of the square can be seen through the arch in Leningradskaya Street, when the buildings on the north side, dominated by the House of Government (with Lenin in the foreground) and the red Catholic Church of St Simeon and St Helena (see page 165), stand open to the eye in all their glory. Government House is a monument to simplistic symmetry, with several buildings of different heights overlooking the central ten-storey structure, the whole being recessed from the square at a distance of 50m, just to add to its imposing and monumental appearance. Built between 1930 and 1934 as a manifestation of civic power and influence, the architectural design of this building was originally intended to be the blueprint for the whole of the city. The eastern side of the square where Nyezalyezhnastsi Avenue begins is flanked by the Neoclassical lines of the magnificent Hotel Minsk, built in 1957, and the impressive Central Post Office, built in 1953. The southern side consists of the Belarusian State University (1962), the Minsk City Executive Council buildings (1964) and the Metro Administration building (1984). In many ways, this magnificent square contains the beating heart of the country. It has survived military occupation by a cruel oppressor, has been the sight of countless processions to celebrate revolution and freedom, hosted demonstrations in the era of perestroika as the Soviet Union breathed its last and then, finally, was the location from which the birth of the newly independent republic was proclaimed on 19 September 1991. For many years latterly, the whole experience of standing in this symbolic and visually arresting place was ruined by the presence of a huge and cavernous building site right in the very middle of the square, as an underground shopping complex slowly took shape. Happily, all of the remedial work in the square has at last been completed. Do try to spend a little while in this impressive location and focus your attentions on the splendour of all that can be seen around you.

Nyezalyezhnastsi Avenue The city's main thoroughfare, which runs away from Independence Square down through Victory Square, is the axis around which the great works of reconstruction were designed after the war. In 1944, a documentary film was shot to give a bird's-eye panorama of the centre of Minsk. To view it now, especially with the benefit of a visit to the city as it currently stands, is a sobering and sombre experience. Of the 825 major buildings that stood at the outbreak of hostilities, only 60 of stone and 20 of wood survived. One cannot but marvel at the resilience, commitment and civic pride of a country and people who set about the task of regeneration with such gusto. This imposing avenue, which was built anew with geometric precision on the site of the former Sovyetskaya Street, is said by many to resemble the famous Nevsky Prospekt in St Petersburg, not only for its architectural prominence, but also for its human side, represented by a café-style culture. Promenaders stroll hand in hand in an ambience of relaxed sophistication. Join them! Amble at leisure and let the

charm of the environment seduce you. Release your senses and most of all, let your surroundings draw you in. The spell is not even broken when you reach an enormous building of pale yellow stucco and Neoclassical design, with a grandiose entrance flanked by enormous pillars on the left-hand (northwestern) side of the street, even though it's the home of the KGB. At the corner with Komsomolskaya Street look right down the hill. It's an attractive street leading to the building site of the Dynamo Stadium. Currently in the process of being massively overhauled, it was originally constructed in 1931 on the site of an old Jewish cemetery. The graves were bulldozed and the stones used for hardcore in road construction. This was not uncommon; the same fate befell the cemetery in Vetka in Gomel *oblast*. Along the centre of Komsomolskaya Street are pleasant gardens, at the top of which is the bust of the much-feared Felix Dzherzhinsky. Born in territory that is now part of Belarus and of Polish extraction, he was one of Lenin's closest acolytes and founder of the hated Cheka, the forerunner organisation to the KGB. Moving on towards first Oktyabrskaya and then Victory Square, you will first pass the National Bank building on the right of the street, which is directly opposite the GUM state department store. Built on the corner of Leninskaya Street in 1951, 'this shoppers' paradise' (as the official description has it) boasts exquisite décor that is best appreciated from the opposite side of the street. The junction of Nyezalyezhnastsi and Leninskaya is a major crossing point in the city. There's so much going on here! It's a good point to take in the sumptuous view. Be sure to take time to look all around you and especially to look up, then, when you're ready, cross through the underpass and on down Nyezalyezhnastsi.

Oktyabrskaya (formerly Central) Square [137 B2] This square probably suffered more architectural damage during the war than any other part of the city. There is yet more Stalinist architecture here, including the imposing Trade Unions Palace of Culture (built in 1954) and the more simply designed museum dedicated to the Great Patriotic War, now closed for relocation to Pobyedy Park. The square was made complete by the construction in 2001 of the dominating Palace of the Republic, which put the finishing touches to the original post-war plan of connecting the historical heart of the city with its new administrative centre, high on a plateau above the Svislach River. In recent years this square has been the site of a number of significant political demonstrations and sit-ins, including in 2010 when there were scenes of violence and bloodshed as the authorities broke up the camp established by demonstrators there. On the south side of the square is **Alexandrovsky Public Garden**, behind which is the imposing edifice of the pre-war Communist Party of Belarus Central Committee building, which today is the location of the Office of the President. Be very careful when taking photographs here. If spotted by the militia, you will have some explaining to do. Continuing along Nyezalyezhnastsi, you pass **Yanka Kupala Park** to the left and **Gorky Park** to the right, both bounded by the Svislach River (see pages 154–5 for further details). Just after the river on the left is one of the most picturesque thoroughfares in the entire city, Kommunisticheskaya Street, with grandly opulent buildings on one side and the landscaped riverbank opposite Yanka Kupala Park on the other. Building number 4 is where Lee Harvey Oswald lived.

Pobyedy (Victory) Square [137 D1] Situated further downtown on Nyezalyezhnastsi Avenue and downhill from Oktyabrskaya Square in the valley of the Svislach River, where this main route out of town in the direction of Minsk-2 National Airport meets a number of attractive thoroughfares, stands Victory

Square. It used to be round but is now elliptical, such that it alarmingly resembles the chariot scene from the movie *Ben Hur* in rush-hour traffic. I've driven it several times and it's not for the faint-hearted. That said, being a front-seat passenger in a car driven by a local is considerably worse, but that's another story. The whole is dominated by the imposing monument to commemorate the nation's losses in the Great Patriotic War. Many Minsk residents still refer to the square as the 'Circus', as it was formerly called before the great obelisk was erected in 1954. At 40m tall, it is topped with the 'Order of Victory', the trademark Soviet red star. On 3 July 1961, an eternal flame was lit at its base. Wedding bouquets are commonly to be seen here, for it is an accepted feature of wedding ritual in this country that the bride and groom (with their full entourage) will pay homage to those who have fallen in war at memorials such as this. It's a necessary and essential photo opportunity for them as part of the day's proceedings and indeed, you can expect to see a wedding party at any number of locations in the city, arriving at speed in a motorcade, windows down and horns blaring.

At the design stage for this imposing and solemn monument, many of the best-known Belarusian sculptors of the time were commissioned to contribute to the scenes shown in bas-relief on the four facets at the foot of the column. They are named *9 May 1945 Victory Day, Soviet Army During the Years of the Great Patriotic War, Belarusian Partisans* and *Glory to the Fallen Heroes*. If you look carefully here, you will find the site of a neat microcosm of Soviet revisionism. Stalin was already dead by the time these reliefs were sculpted and his profile, not surprisingly, was added to the fresco, originally appearing on the flag next to Lenin's portrait. But as the years passed and Stalin's legacy hastened his fall from grace, his profile was quietly and without ceremony transformed into Lenin's ear. The dominance of the column has its best perspective from a distance, but a closer view lends greater appreciation to the scenes depicted at the base.

At the same time, take a look around you. The classically constructed houses on the south side, each with beautiful entrances and neat towers, are connected by handsome rows of columns. There is also an underground hall containing a commemorative material that is well worth a visit. And if you have the energy for further exploration, you might carry on up Nyezalyezhnastsi to **Yakub Kolas Square** for one last slice of architectural splendour. One of a number of attractive sculptures in the central area of gardens is that of the national poet and writer himself, deep in thought and contemplation. Retrace your steps back to Privakhsalnaya Square on foot if you want to view all that you've seen again but from the other direction, or else jump on the metro and head for some sustenance at your favourite café or bar. You've earned it!

OTHER NOTABLE MONUMENTS AND ARCHITECTURAL FEATURES

Island of Tears [128 B4] Situated on the Svislach River directly opposite Old Town and inaugurated on 3 August 1996, this is a commemorative memorial to the fallen in the USSR's ill-fated and disastrous Afghanistan campaign (1979–88). The central feature is a chapel, upon the walls of which bleak and harrowing images of bereaved widows and mothers are sculpted, all waiting in vain for their loved ones to return. Inside are four altars bearing icons, together with small shrines dedicated to the fallen from each of the country's administrative *oblasts*, their names listed on the walls. In the centre, memory bells have been lowered into a sunken recess containing soil from a number of graves, along with a sealed capsule containing soil from the fields of battle in Afghanistan where some of the nation's sons fell. This is a highly symbolic and ritualistic gesture, often to be found at memorial locations in this country. Nearby is the statue of a doleful angel in mourning, weeping because he could not save the boys' lives. The Afghanistan fiasco matches the American misadventure in Vietnam for mind-numbing folly. For years after the war ended, veterans received no recognition either from an ungrateful state or from the Party machine. The authorities simply wanted to turn their collective back and pretend that the madness had never even happened. Access to the chapel is via a short footbridge from the Troitskoye suburb, or Old Town (see pages 162–3), but beware the street vendor waiting to accost you at the bottom of the footbridge with tacky souvenirs, including out-of-date calendars. He has an interesting collection of badges from the old Soviet Union though, most of them featuring Lenin's gaunt face atop a Party slogan exhorting the workers to ever greater achievements. The short written guide to the Island of Tears memorial is also worth buying for the photographs alone, as a reminder of your visit.

Jewish Minsk Perhaps the most widely known of the historic sites of Jewish Minsk is the **Zaslavskaya Memorial** [128 B4]. This moving, bleak and harrowing sculpture of a line of terrified men, women and children seen descending a steep slope marks the very spot where, on a single day in March 1942, 5,000 Jews from the Minsk ghetto were shot to death by the Nazis. This number included 200 children from the ghetto's orphanage. Around 500 of the bodies were dumped in the pit that was dug here. The bronze obelisk at the bottom is inscribed in Russian and Yiddish. This location marks the boundary of **Rakovskaya suburb**, the location of the ghetto (one of Europe's biggest) from 1941 to 1943. It is thought that only 13 individuals survived to the Soviet liberation out of the community of 100,000 and more who endured the Nazi occupation in the most barbaric and inhumane of circumstances within the confines of the ghetto. Nearby on the site of the old Jewish quarter is the **Holocaust Museum and Research Studio** [128 A5] (*25 Sukhaya St;* \ *200 76 26;* e *kozak@ibb.by; www.gwminsk.com;* ⊕ *09.00–17.00 Mon–Fri*). Located in a Jewish house over a hundred years old, directly opposite the site of a former Jewish cemetery, there is no external sign to acknowledge its significance. The entrance houses a memorial to the 33,000 Jews transported to the Minsk ghetto from all over occupied Europe. In the first pogrom, 10,000 Minsk Jews were murdered to make room for 10,000 more arriving by train from other locations. Each room of the museum houses a number of exhibits, the most moving of which are the display boards telling the story of individual families. Images of lives brutally snatched away can be seen all over the rooms here. There is also a German military map of Minsk marking the area of the ghetto and photographs of the Maly Trostenyets concentration camp on the eastern edge of the city. President Lukashenko acknowledges that the fate of the country's Jews is a national tragedy and has committed resources for the establishment of a memorial complex on the site of the former concentration camp, including research and educational facilities. The president also decreed in 2008 that this Holocaust Museum should receive the protection of the state, a number of attempts having been made to close it for new buildings to be constructed. At long last, the stories of the Jewish victims of Nazi oppression in this country are beginning to be translated into English (see *Frieda's story*, page 164), although sadly there are no English display boards at the museum. A visit here is nonetheless an essential part of your time in Minsk.

Across the road, the site of the old Jewish cemetery bears a number of memorials (including a symbolic broken table) with inscriptions in Russian, German and Yiddish. The only other evidence that this was once a cemetery consists of the broken gravestones scattered all around.

Minsk also has a **Museum of Jewish History and Culture** [128 C2] (*28 Very Khoruzhey St;* ☏ *286 79 33;* e *jewish_museum@mail.ru;* ⊕ *noon–17.00 Mon–Fri, 14.00–17.00 Sun, closed Sat*). Situated on the Minsk Jewish Campus (*www.meod.by*), more than 10,000 artefacts have been collected for display, including documents and photographs, to promote the history and culture of the Jewish community. Educational and research facilities are available here, and a number of specific exhibitions are also featured. For further information on anything concerning Jewish Minsk, to arrange access to memorial sites and to meet members of the current community, including Frieda Wulfovna, or to arrange museum visits or tours of Jewish Minsk with Russian- or English-speaking guides, contact British sustainable development charity **The Together Plan** (see page 107 for contact details) or Belarusian NGO *Dialog* (☏ *+375 (29) 627 34 00;* e *dialogorganisation@gmail.com*).

Upper Town Located in and around the delightful **Svobody Square** [137 B2], many of the lovely buildings here are reconstructions, including the impressive **City Hall** (completed as an exact copy in 2006), but it's a splendid spot for an amble nonetheless. A symbol of municipal government has existed on this spot since the 16th century and today's monument to civil governance, modelled on the last incarnation of City Hall before total destruction in the 19th century, is but the latest in a long line of them. Outside in the square, the sculpture of the governor's carriage presents a photo opportunity that many are unable to resist. It's another example of the delightful work of Vladimir Zhbanov, whose street statuary appears all over town and elsewhere in Belarus. The **Holy Spirit Cathedral** [137 B1] and the **Maryinsky Cathedral of the Holy Virgin Mary** [137 B2] are on the fringes of the square, while elsewhere you will find Hotel Europe (see page 127) and a number of high-quality restaurants and bars. The view down to the Troitskoye suburb, then over Komsomolskoye Lake and beyond, presents an irresistible vista by day and by night. Even though most of what you see in and around the square is a reconstruction, there is a charm to this place that to my mind somehow gives it a better feel than Old Town. This is an entirely subjective, of course. See what you think.

Troitskoye (Trinity) suburb (Траецкае / Троицкое) Famous for its bars and taverns since the 13th century, this attractive historic area down by the Svislach River is known as 'Old Town'. It's mostly a reconstruction, although there are those in this town who will tell you indignantly that what you see is wholly original. The truth is likely to lie somewhere between the two, so let's say that the original buildings here have been substantially and sympathetically renovated. Certainly, the works undertaken to the brightly coloured two- and three-storey buildings during the 1980s and subsequently have been sympathetically accomplished, enabling the visitor to experience the city as it existed a century or so ago. Then, the dwellings were of stone and the streets were cobbled. This was a non-aristocratic part of the city, housing factory workers, peasants, craftsmen, traders, civil servants of low rank, military personnel and the petty bourgeoisie. Today, their successors are the owners of the offices, shops, cafés, bars and restaurants that occupy the buildings here. To wander the cobbled streets at will is a pleasing diversion from the noise of the city. To orientate yourself, first walk down to the water's edge of the Svislach across Staravilyenskaya Street, and take in the view of the Island of Tears (see pages 160–1) and the lake beyond, then walk along Staravilyenskaya towards the Velcom building. Trinity suburb lies on your left now and you can dip in at will to find cobbles, corners and steps. It's not a large area and you won't get lost. In the centre you will find the **Maxim Bogdanovich Literary Museum**. Natalia tells me that his work is not popular among Belarusians, 'but I think his words are so beautiful', she tells me. Behind Korchma Staravilyenskaya restaurant is the **'Folk Gallery' store**. Focused exclusively on the tourist trade, it sells 'traditional' souvenirs and trinkets, all of them priced as you might expect. Right next door is the **'Vyanok' store** with an interesting and unusual selection of very reasonably priced antique books. Also look out for the **Barzha floating restaurant** (\ 355 00 22) moored on the riverbank in this locality. Overlooked by many as a probable tourist trap, it's never busy and whenever I've stopped off for lunch the food and service have always been consistently good. Even the staff seem surprised that someone actually wants to eat there. Then while you are in the vicinity, walk across to Nemiga metro station just across the river from Old Town, at the junction of Leninskaya and Nemiga streets. In May 1999 on the day of a local festival a terrible tragedy occurred here, when hordes of excitable youngsters ran into the adjoining pedestrian underpass to shelter from torrential rain: 53 of them were trampled to death. A plaque commemorates this awful event. All these years later, you will still find personal mementos and reminders left by family and friends. In a country where loss and tragedy are commemorated everywhere, this is a particularly poignant spot and all who pass by are given to pausing for quiet reflection.

The National Library [129 H1] (*116 Nyezalyezhnastsi Av;* \ *266 37 02;* e *inbox@nlb.by; www.nlb.by;* ⊕ *10.00–21.00 Mon–Fri, 10.00–18.00 Sat & Sun, with shorter opening during the summer schedule; tours by prior arrangement*)

Opened by the president himself on 16 June 2006, this most unusual building makes for a really eye-catching sight in all of its futuristic splendour. The correct term for its geometric shape is, apparently, a rhombicuboctahedron. Whatever the technicalities, it's quite a sight. Located on Nyezalyezhnastsi Avenue and a little out of town on the main thoroughfare into the city from Minsk-2 National Airport, it dominates the skyline for miles around, particularly at night, when it is illuminated in a dazzling display of colour, although the construction of new developments in the vicinity is beginning to encroach on it. For the geometrically uninitiated, the architects based the whole concept on the shape of a diamond; the problem is, at first glance it appears to be perched precariously at ground level on little more than one of its points and there is apocryphal rumour locally that it is dangerously unstable in its design. Some 14 million books have now been moved here. The English pages of the library's website are extremely informative, so do pay some attention to this quirky feature before you go, then stop off on your travels (it's a five-minute walk from the Moskovskaya metro station) for some great photo opportunities (while it's still standing). There is an indoor observation platform on the 22nd floor (⊕ *noon–23.00 daily, last entry 22.30*) and it's also possible to venture outside although, at 73m above the ground, you will need a head for heights. It's well worth it, because the views over Minsk by night and by day are unsurpassed. All in all this is a wonderful public service. Facilities include 20 reading rooms, a theatre, a 22nd-floor coffee bar, ground-floor restaurant, museum, art gallery, children's room, exhibition space, internet centre with free access at 20 terminals and even a fitness centre with sauna. Anyone presenting a passport is given a reader's ticket for 5 years (cost BYR30,400), including nationals of other countries. It's an impressive commitment to public education and enlightenment. Also here is an interesting **book museum** (\ *293 25 85;* ⊕ *10.30–19.00 Tue, Wed, Fri, 10.00–06.00 Thu, Sat & Sun, subject to changes, 1 Jul–31 Aug; admission BYR10,500*). Exhibits cover the history of book printing in Belarus, modern publishing internationally and the history of the library itself.

FRIEDA'S STORY

It's a cold grey Thursday morning in Minsk. I'm standing in the snow with five Jewish families from London, in an open area between apartment blocks close to the city centre. This is the site of the Minsk Ghetto, first established in 1941 during the Great Patriotic War. We're on the edge of an enormous hole in the ground, with steps descending to the bottom, along the line of which stands a doleful memorial to the dead of the ghetto. This is the pit into which the Nazis threw the bodies. We're here to listen to Frieda Wulfovna, a ghetto survivor. For years she couldn't talk about the things she had seen as a young girl. She didn't think people would believe her. Then one day, while visiting the Jewish Centre in Minsk that had been established to record all that happened here between 1941 and 1944, she opened a book written by a fellow survivor and began to read about all the terrible things she had witnessed for herself as a young child. Screams, executions, rivers of blood. From that moment she knew that people would believe her own story and she began to find the words to articulate her memories. This is an extract from that story, in her own words and transcribed as translated, recalled and told on the site of the former ghetto as the snow came down, on the edge of the pit of death. The full transcript of Frieda's story appears on the Bradt website.

I remember a terrible pogrom that lasted four days. People were desperate to find hiding places between buildings and behind false walls, ceilings and floors. I can recall hiding in one such place, between buildings, for all of those four days. Sixty of us were crammed into a tiny, confined space. I could barely move. A little girl of four years was there. Like all of us, she hadn't eaten for four days and she began to cry. To save the rest of us, that child's mother placed her hands around her neck and suffocated the life out of her.

Before the Ghetto, there used to be a Jewish market within the area. The Nazis used it as a place of execution. I remember being there one day when the Nazis took only young girls. I can recall a group of 20 to 25 of them, some barely 18, all with their eyes covered. The Germans chose this occasion to test out new experimental bullets that exploded on impact. It was raining that day. The streets ran red.

The Nazis didn't just murder people. They were cruel and perverted. They would take people as they walked through the streets near to their homes, so their families watching from their houses would see. People were shot indiscriminately. Lorry loads of drunken soldiers used to arrive by night and open the gates, randomly butchering entire households. There were three mobile gas chambers within the Ghetto. The local Nazi commander asked for more, so that more people could be killed faster. Himmler came to Minsk one day in 1942 to make a plan for getting rid of Jews more quickly. The screams I heard every single day in the Ghetto I still hear now, as I walk the streets where once it stood.

Frieda Wulfovna has travelled all over Germany with other survivors to recount the events that happened in the ghetto. Their story is beginning to be told at last.

There are 400 rare books and manuscripts from the 15th to the 20th centuries on display, the most precious of which is the Bible published by the first Belarusian printer, Francisk Skoryna, in 1517.

CATHEDRALS AND CHURCHES
Church of St Simeon and St Helena [137 A4] (*17 Sovyetskaya*) Erected and consecrated between 1908 and 1910, this imposing structure with its 50m-high belltower is known locally to residents simply as the 'Red Church'. See if you can guess why! One of the city's iconic landmarks and an ever-present feature of its publicity blurb, it is situated on the north side of the vast Independence Square. Lenin stands on his plinth just along the way. After the October Revolution it was used first as a theatre and then as a film studio. It even survived the massive development of the square in the 1960s, when the city's planners wanted it to be pulled down and replaced by a wide-screen cinema. I'm glad that it did. The impressive buildings all around are fine examples of post-war Soviet planning on the grandest of scales, but there's something special about the endurance of this single building. There are daily services at 09.00 and 19.00, plus 10.00 and noon on Saturdays and 11.00 and 13.00 on Sundays. Outside and within its curtilage, look first for the symbol of Good triumphing over Evil, the sculpture of the Archangel Michael, wings outstretched, 4.5m tall, slaying the dragon; then find the poignant Nagasaki memorial bell erected in September 2000, a powerful symbol uniting two communities ravaged by the elemental power of nuclear energy gone wrong.

Holy Spirit Cathedral [137 B1] (*3 Kirilla i Mefodya St; www.minskcath.anitex. by*) Another of the city's iconic landmarks, this splendid Eastern Orthodox Baroque cathedral on the edge of Svobody Square was originally constructed between 1642 and 1687 as a Roman Catholic monastery of the Bernadine Order. Part of the monastery complex remains. Ravaged by warfare and long in disuse through damage and disrepair, it was eventually passed to the Russian Orthodoxy and consecrated to Saints Cyril and Methodious in 1860. After the 1917 Revolution, it first became a gymnasium for the fire service, then a repository for documentary archives and later a grain store. It is also said that it was used as a political prison. During the entirety of its chequered history, it has benefited from many phases of renovation following damage and periods of closure. It is now one of the last surviving monuments of Old Minsk, and an enduring image of its history. It houses a number of impressive icons, including that of Our Lady of Minsk, which is said to have miraculously appeared on the bank of the Svislach River in 1500. It is an essential 'must-see', with a good souvenir shop. Evening services are held at 18.00 every day except Monday. Outside there are fine views to Pobyedy Park over the Svislach River and Komsomolskoye Lake, but expect to share it with vast numbers of tourists and pigeons; this is probably the city's most frequented go-to place for visitors.

Mary Magdalene Church [128 B3] (*42 Kisilyeva St*) This lovely church is my favourite in all the city, not least because it's just a little off the main tourist track so you're likely to have it all to yourself. Located above one of Minsk's main roads, the matte black of the cupola studded with golden stars and of the lovely belltower contrasts beautifully with the white stucco of the façade. It was built in 1847 to replace an earlier church here, while the delightful Starovezhskaya Gate on the edge of the grounds was added later. In recent times the entirety has been beautifully maintained. Inside is a dazzling array of icons and relics, the air heavy with the scent of incense. As I sat outside taking it all in on my last visit, I watched as a young mother wheeled her pram to the main door. She asked my companion to mind her baby while she went inside to fill three plastic bottles with holy water. At the same time, a family was standing outside with their tiny baby wrapped tightly in blankets, waiting for the time of the child's baptism. This is a beautiful place of living worship.

Maryinsky Cathedral of the Holy Virgin Mary [137 B2] (*3 Svobody Sq*)
Located across the street from the City Hall and sandwiched tightly between
buildings constructed later, what you see today is all that remains of the Jesuit
monastery built here in the 18th century. A Baroque masterpiece, it's a wonder that
anything at all remains. The two belltowers were rebuilt in recent times after the
Communists blew them up in 1951, the building having suffered extensive damage
during the Great Patriotic War. The interior is exquisite. Hemmed in by adjoining
development, it's easy to walk past and leave this delightful cathedral unnoticed,
but do find the time to pause and take a look. Just inside are display boards with
interesting photographs showing the history of this holy place. Evening services are
held at 19.00.

St Alexander Nevsky Church [129 E4] (*11 Kozlova St*) Worthy of a short
detour when you tick Pobyedy Square off your list, this small but imposing red-
brick construction with the archetypical domes of gold is most pleasing to the eye.
It has been opened and closed time and again during warfare and in peacetime,
according to whatever political circumstances have prevailed during its hundred-
year existence. Consecrated on 2 February 1898, it replaced the original wooden
church on this spot. During the Great Patriotic War it survived (perhaps with
divine intervention?) when a Nazi bomb crashed through the central dome from
on high to land near to the St Nicholas icon, but failed to explode. There is also a
military cemetery here. Evening services are held at 18.00 and 20.00.

Cathedral of St Peter and St Paul [137 A2] (*4 Rakovskaya St*) Located next
to the Nemiga department store and built between 1611 and 1613 with donations
from 52 nobles and inhabitants of the area, this lovely 'yellow church' (so named
colloquially because of the colour of its pale stucco façade) is said to be the oldest
of the city's functioning places of worship. It's had a chequered history, however; a
cycle of disrepair and neglect followed by renovation under the patronage of the
Russian nobility played out over three centuries, before Stalin closed it down in the
1930s, since when it has served variously as a fish store, residential dwellings and a
document archive, only being restored as a place of worship in the 1970s. Evening
services are held at 18.00.

THEATRES
**National Academic Bolshoi Opera and Ballet Theatre of the Republic of
Belarus** [128 C3] (*1 Paris Commune Sq;* \ *334 80 74;* e *ticket@belarusopera.by;*
*www.bolshoibelarus.by (an excellent website in Russian & English); nearest metro:
Nemiga or Oktyabrskaya/Kupalovskaya; buses: 24, 38, 57 & 91; trolleybuses: 12, 29,
37, 40, 46 & 53*) Built in 1938 and located at the bottom end of Yanka Kupala Park,
on the edge of Old Town, the theatre building itself recently underwent three years
of substantial and significant reconstruction. During that period, performances
of ballet were generally held in the Great Hall of the Palace of the Republic, 1
Oktyabrskaya Square. Now that the old theatre has been restored (and beautifully
so), all performances start at 19.00 and generally feature popular ballet classics such
as *Swan Lake*, *Sleeping Beauty*, *Giselle* and *Don Quixote*. Opera buffs will not be
disappointed either, with regular performances of well-known works such as *La
Traviata*, *Aida*, *Carmen*, *La Bohème* and *The Barber of Seville*. Throughout the year,
the theatre also presents a very broad repertoire of work by lesser-known composers.
Tickets can be purchased from the theatre box office at 1 Paris Commune Square
(⊕ *10.00–14.00, 15.00–20.00 daily*), or from the following locations: one of two

theatrical booking offices at 19 Nyezalyezhnastsi Avenue (near to the entrance of the flower shop) and the TSUM central department store (*54 Nyezalyezhnastsi Av*), on the third floor, next to the dry cleaners; the ticket office on the second floor of the GUM department store; and at the subway adjoining one of three metro stations: Yakuba Kolasa Square, Institut Kultury or Oktyabrskaya/Kupalovskaya. By Western standards, tickets are astonishingly cheap (BYR20,000–40,000), while the standard of performance is exceptionally high. This is an experience not to be missed, but do be sure to book ahead and as early as you can.

Even if a night of high culture fails to appeal, a visit to this lovely theatre and its gardens is highly recommended. Meander at leisure to inspect the charming statuary, including the monument to poet Maxim Bogdanovich, erected in 1981 to commemorate the 90th anniversary of his birth. Born just across the street from here, he was only 26 when he died. Stand by the fountains and admire the splendour of the theatre's entrance (ticket windows are to be found either side of the main doors), then walk up the steps, turn and pause to take in the view over the fountains towards the Cathedral of the Holy Spirit and former Bernadine Monastery in Upper Town. Allow your gaze to scan right of centre, past the ugly modern buildings in the foreground, to spot the pale pink stucco that marks the boundary of Troitskoye suburb. Further to your right is the impressive architecture of the Minsk Military Academy, named after Russian general Alexander Suvarov, who was prominent in the 18th-century invasion of the country. This is a fact that troubles my dear friend Natalia, who thinks the Academy should be named after a Belarusian hero, not someone leading an occupying force. Quite right too.

Yanka Kupala National Academic Theatre [137 C3] (*7 Engelsa St;* ☏ *327 60 81/42 02; www.kupala-theatre.by; nearest metro: Oktyabrskaya/Kupalovskaya*)
Situated on the corner of Alexandrovsky Public Garden and built in 1890, this theatre was used as a congress hall after the 1917 October Revolution. It was here that, in March 1918, the All-Belarusian Congress made the declaration of independence of the first (and short-lived) republic. Restored to use as a theatre in 1920, today performances are held daily (except Tuesday) at 11.30 and 19.00, in the Belarusian language only. Tickets can be purchased from the theatre box office or at the ticket booth in the subway adjoining Oktyabrskaya/Kupalovskaya metro station (⊕ *10.00–19.00 daily*).

Belarusian State Puppet Theatre [137 C3] (*20 Engels St;* ☏ *327 05 32; www. puppet-minsk.com; box office* ⊕ *10.00–17.00 Tue–Fri, 10.00–16.00 Sat & Sun and 13.00–20.00 on the days of evening performances; tickets BYR25,000–40,000; nearest metro: Oktyabrskaya/Kupalovskaya*) This delightful Belarusian institution, originally founded in Gomel 75 years ago before moving to Minsk in 1950, performs just down the road from the Yanka Kupala theatre. The troupe spends much of its time on tour and only a limited number of performances are held here. If you're lucky enough to be in town when there's a show on, don't miss it. Adults will be just as entranced as children.

OUTSIDE MINSK

The best way to visit any of the following places is likely to be by booking a local tour through one of Minsk's agencies (see *Tour operators*, pages 47–50, for further details). Many of the sites will benefit from a whole day each, while others can be combined if you have limited time at your disposal. For example, a day's visit to Mir

3

and Njasvizh together makes for a long but splendid excursion. Do shop around, because prices vary significantly. Some companies will offer a cheap flat rate that excludes everything when you get there (admission, meals, separate features, etc), but others will quote an 'all-in' price. For example, a flat-rate half day in Dudutki will cost around US$125 (plus everything else, ie: admission, meals, separate features, etc, to be paid when you get there) and for an all-in excursion, around US$250. Whichever of the following you choose, you won't be disappointed; all are listed because they are worthy of your time and attention, so take your pick.

Upon leaving Minsk, the terrain very quickly becomes much more reminiscent of western Europe, with rolling wooded hillsides of oak and beech replacing the silver birch that is omnipresent elsewhere in Belarus. Halfway to Mir on the right-hand side and adjoining the carriageway, look for the gleaming new **Westa Hotel** (✆ *165 44 86; www.westa.by*) with its lake, healthcare and sports facilities. I haven't stayed there, but it looks to be a decent bet if you're in need of out-of-town accommodation while on the road.

MIR (MIP / МИР) Around 90km southwest of Minsk and just 15 minutes off the main M1 motorway to Brest lies the small museum town of Mir and its beautiful 16th-century fortress.

The settlement of Mir was looted and burned by invading crusaders in 1395. By 1434, it had fallen into the ownership of the 'big baron' Radzivili family, whose patronage ensured a steady increase in the significance of the settlement, as it grew first into a township and then into the administrative centre of Mir county. In the late 16th and early 17th centuries, earthen walls were built around the township and it became a fortress. Four corner gates, the foundations of which have now been excavated, gave access from the four main roads that originally met here. In 1579, the township was granted rights of limited municipal self-determination and government, so that it very quickly attracted craftsmen and tradesmen of various nationalities, including Belarusians, Tartars, Jews and ethnic travelling people. Indeed, the extravagant duke Carol Stanislav Radzivili bestowed upon a certain Jan Martsynkyevich the grand title of 'King of the Gypsies' of the great principality of Lithuania in 1778, also declaring Mir to be their capital.

Naturally, the mixture of cultures and ethnicities had a defining influence on the community that was established here. It is for this reason that a Roman Catholic church, an Eastern Orthodox church, a synagogue and a mosque were built in close proximity. Very quickly, the township began to attract merchants and their goods from all corners of Belarus, Poland, the Baltic states and Russia.

Getting there and away By car, take the main M1 motorway (a toll road in part) from Minsk to Brest and take the turn north on to the P64 road signposted Mir for 8km. The town is situated on the bus route from Minsk (departing from the central bus station) to Novogrudok, the ride taking around two hours.

What to see and do
Mir Fortress (Мірскі Замак / Мирский Замок) (✆ *1596 28 2 70;* ⏲ *10.00–18.00 Wed–Sun, closed Tue; admission BYR60,000*) Shortly after turning off the motorway on the P64 road, the fairy-tale castle comes into view. Situated on the edge of the town in a delightful setting overlooking a serene lake and built largely of stone and red brick, it is not only a powerful monument to the influence of the princes who commissioned its construction, but also very pleasing on the eye. Since 2000, it has been designated a UNESCO World Heritage Site, one of four in the country.

The walls and towers of the castle (still known today as the 'medieval flower') first appeared in the 1520s, followed by the construction of the Renaissance palace itself between the late 16th and early 17th centuries. After a battering during the war with Russia in 1655 and the later Northern War, it gradually fell further into disrepair, before a revival in the 1730s when a portrait gallery and ornate banqueting hall were added, together with a beautiful Italianate garden containing citrus, fig, myrtle, cypress, box, mahogany and laurel trees. The scent on the breeze of summer evenings must have been extravagant and intoxicating. Latterly, the complex suffered extensive damage in the Great Patriotic War. A Cossack regiment was stationed here and a number of engagements took place in the vicinity. A very significant programme of restoration is now all but complete and this beautiful walled structure of five towers (after the first four, a fifth was added for security purposes in the centre of the west wall facing the road to Vilnius, as the only means of access by drawbridge and portcullis) and a courtyard accommodates a small hotel, conference hall and traditional restaurant in addition to the museum of exhibits housed in various rooms throughout the building. Caution is needed when negotiating the steep, narrow and winding staircases which permit access to those parts of the castle that are open to the public, with some of the steps being quite large. It is possible to climb to the very top of the southwestern tower, the best-preserved of the five, from which there are extensive panoramic views over the town and surrounding countryside. The five floors currently house works of fine art.

Around the castle wall by the lakeside used to be a host of souvenir stalls, some tacky, but some with attractive artefacts and books at reasonable prices, although all have now been moved to the adjoining small car park (where you will also find a café), such that the panorama as you walk towards the fortress, free of retail mania, is magnificent. My own preference is not to use this car park, but to use the much bigger one further up the hill. It's only a short walk to the fortress, but the view to it over the lake from this point is majestic. In the castle grounds stands a pretty chapel of Modernist style (built in 1904) that served as a burial vault. Across the lake are remains of the former estate buildings. The landscaped 16ha park around the lake was established at the same time as the chapel. There are many varieties of trees and a wooden bridge that accesses a small islet in the lake. This is an excellent spot to take photographs of the castle and is frequented by newlyweds as part of their 'grand tour' (see page 160).

From the top car park walk to the left of the castle to enter through the main gate. After purchasing your ticket, the self-guided tour begins when you mount the stairs in the left-hand corner of the reception area. Audio guides are available. The works of restoration are truly impressive. Pause to examine the exhibits and display boards (some in English) in the first rooms, then mount the steep stairs into the dining room. The ceiling here is exquisite. At this point you must also put slippers over your shoes from the supply in the corner and if you don't, you will be sternly told off! Then continue to follow the markers around the rooms on your self-guided tour. When you emerge from the exhibition, the small hotel is on the left-hand wall, while on the other side is a souvenir shop. Diagonally opposite is the start of the walk around the ramparts and towers, which in places is extremely steep and narrow. You should think twice before tackling this adventure if your knees and joints are not in the best of order but, if they are, it's a glorious adventure indeed. When you're ready, leave the fortress by the gate through which you entered and turn left around the castle to walk up to the family chapel. You will be asked to show your castle entry ticket here. There is a simple iconostasis with examples of icons from Russia and Mir itself.

Other sites in Mir To complete your visit, take a stroll into the small town. Retrace your steps towards the bottom car park, cross the river and walk along the road and up the slight incline. Ahead of you at left of centre is the 16th-century Renaissance Roman Catholic Church of St Nikolai, currently undergoing reconstruction, although it's still possible to take a look inside. The Castles Road café is located here. A little further along the road on the right-hand side is the town's modest square, with market stalls in the centre. Like the castle, much of the town was destroyed in the war, so these buildings are reconstructions rather than originals, albeit painstakingly and lovingly restored. A clockwise stroll will take you past Café Rageda (closed on my last visit for a refit), a small shop and then Mir Hotel, where there is an ATM. Look behind the hotel to spot the original architecture of the **Jewish quarter**. Dating from the early 19th century, here stood the *kahal* (the self-government building), two synagogues and the *yeshivah* (a rabbinic academy for the study of Holy Scriptures), though now only part of the late 19th-century synagogue remains, next to the new one presently in the course of construction. Near here is a small museum dedicated to the Jewish history of the town. One of my correspondents describes the collection here as 'rather ramshackle but charming'! The entrance fee is BYR5,000, while the opening hours are less than reliable. Phone before you go (✆ *1596 23 4 70*) to check that it's open. On the far side of the square is the attractive 16th-century St Trinity Church, then you complete your circuit by walking past a number of shops and banks (also with ATMs) sandwiching the tiny bus station. For a different (and equally beautiful) panorama of the castle, look for the track between the first bank on this side and the bus station, which takes you back down towards the river through rows of old residential homes. It's not difficult to find your way and I do like circular perambulations! If you have the time, located behind the trees some way to the north of the castle is the **monument** to Jewish victims of the Holocaust. There is also an old Jewish cemetery. A total of 1,600 Mir Jews were executed on 9 November 1941 and a further 850 were imprisoned in the ghetto that was later established in the castle, all of whom were murdered on 13 August 1942. Also a little way out of town beyond St Trinity Church is a Muslim cemetery, and there is an Orthodox one at the Church of St George. If you're going on to Njasvizh under your own steam, turn left out of the top car park and keep going for around 30km.

NJASVIZH (НЯСВІЖ / НЕСВИЖ) Situated 120km southwest of Minsk and only half an hour from Mir by road is the delightful historic settlement of Njasvizh, one of the oldest in the country. Thought to have first been established as a settlement in the 13th century, historians believe that the town itself was founded around 1446. Though the new town is without charm, many of the oldest buildings have been retained in the historical area, and the former home of the Radzivili family is widely regarded as the most attractive palace that the country has to offer. It is surrounded by a large park boasting a number of ornamental lakes and sumptuous gardens. The family's ownership of the town began in the middle of the 16th century and was to last for more than 400 years, during which time it gained great fame for its prosperity. In 1586, the town was granted the Magdeburg rights of self-government and determination, which was a catalyst for rapid economic development. Many trade guilds were established and it was no surprise that, at the end of the 16th century, it was almost completely rebuilt, the chaotic and haphazard layout of its medieval streets being replaced by the geometric design that remains to this day. The main street crosses the town from east to west. It was originally surrounded by earthen walls that were constructed to make the town a fortress. Some of them,

most notably in the southeast, can still be seen. Over the centuries, many severe trials (such as plunder, fire and war) took their toll on the town but, through it all, the mighty Radzivili dynasty survived. The line finally ended in 1939, but not until it had first seen off not only the Great Lithuanian Principality, but also the might of the Russian Empire.

Getting there and away By car, take the same M1 motorway from Minsk towards Brest as if bound for Mir, then take the turn on the P11 road to the south signposted Njasvizh just after the turn for Mir and continue for around 20km. The town is situated on a main bus route from Minsk (departing from the central bus station), the ride taking around three hours. As with Mir, you should set aside a full day for Njasvizh to see all there is to see at leisure, but both can be combined in one day if time is at a premium.

What to see and do In addition to the palace and only a short walk away from it are the stunning Corpus Christi Roman Catholic Church (designed in early Baroque style by the 16th-century Italian architect Bernardoni, who also designed the palace), the tower of the castle gates, the remains of the town gate (this is the only one of the original four still to be standing) and the Benedictine monastery. A further short distance away is the town square, where the trades hall and market houses are situated. All of these buildings date from the 16th century. Representations of and artefacts from the life of this historic town are collected in the compact but engaging museum on Leninskaya Street. The outstanding Belarusian Renaissance thinker and humanist Symon Budny is known to have worked in the former **printing house** here. In 1562, he published a number of significant works at this site. His nearby statue marks this key point in the history of Belarusian literature.

The first stone in the construction of the palace was laid in 1584. It was rebuilt many times and to this day displays features of the Renaissance, early and late Baroque, Rococo, Classicism, Neo-Gothic and Modernism. The complex once numbered around 170 rooms, with a series of underground passages connecting it to the town's monasteries. It was originally encircled by ramparts, ditches, four towers and a series of ponds. It also boasted valuable collections of fine art, weaponry, books and family archives. Today, the only resident is the ghost of the Black Dame, who is said to restlessly wander the corridors on moonless nights. In fact, legend and mystery continue to dominate both this palace and the fortress at Mir. The treasures of the Radzivili family have never been found, although many locations at the two castles have been searched. The dungeons are so large that parts of them are as yet unopened. One of the most intriguing legends is that a cavernous underground passage, 35km long, was constructed between the two, large enough for two coaches to pass side-by-side. Needless to say, it also has never been found. The beautiful park and garden around the palace, which include some delightful ornamental ponds, were not laid out until the late 19th century. The total area is around 100ha, with a number of different styles and appearances to be seen, including a Japanese garden and a Russian wood.

The road through the town from the direction of Mir follows a straight line and, as you breast a small rise, the old town is ahead and slightly below, affording a first teasing glimpse of the treasures that await. If there is space, park in the small square by the Symon Budny statue, where you will also find **Corpus Christi Church**. The exterior is attractive, but inside it's exquisite. Do go in for a look – the magnificent Baroque friezes are simply stunning.

On leaving Corpus Christi, turn right and walk through the palace car park, past the tacky souvenir stalls and along the path to reach the information and ticket building on the right, just before the start of the walkway to the **palace** itself (✆ *1770 55 1 81;* ⊕ *09.00–18.00 daily; admission BYR70,000*). The path is a tarmac one and is raised above the level of the lake, so the views all around are delightful. Just before you reach the end of the path, bear right to see the Great Patriotic War memorial and eternal flame. This is a good photo opportunity, with the palace itself in the background, while the view of the palace from the rear of the memorial is simply beautiful. Now walk through the entrance archway (pausing to admire the unusual waterspouts), show your ticket and head on into the impressive courtyard. The self-guided tour starts at door 15 in the right-hand corner. Proceed up the stairs, availing yourself of the café facilities if in need, then through the door on the right to begin.

The first room contains informative display boards in English, while all of the rooms beyond contain items of interest, the last of them being an exhibition room. Exit down the stairs then cross the courtyard to enter the door marked 'Palace Interiors'. Here you will find a sumptuous exhibition. First leave your bags in the cloakroom and take a peek in the shop, where the goods on sale are less tacky than outside. Don't forget to put on your over-slippers, then amble through room after room of sublime décor containing fascinating exhibits. Audio guides are also available. There is a most glorious fireplace in the dining room, while the small dining room beyond and the ballroom are equally lovely. The next floor has rooms displaying Slutsk woven belts, before you pass through the splendour of the Knights Golden Hall and the Hunting Hall. Not to everyone's taste, the trophies here will certainly grab your attention. Following the signs will take you back to the beginning of the tour, where you exit the turnstile at the main gate. There are yet more tacky souvenir stalls here and a number of basic but adequate cafés. If you have time, turn right to walk around the perimeter of the palace, where you gain a real perspective of its size and grandeur. Keep looking into the delightful gardens on your left as you amble and, if time permits, dip in for a promenade. The grounds and lakes are extensive and really beautiful. On my last visit in spring, the birdsong, the breeze through the trees and the carpet of new living green were irresistible. It's now a short stroll back across the walkway as you contemplate the delights of your day here.

All in all, this splendid site is one of the finest in the country and, although many of the historic buildings are still undergoing great works of restoration, it's well worth a day of your time to meander and to take in the beauty of all there is to see. For years, the historical significance of this place went unnoticed beyond the country's national borders, but it was finally recognised in 2005 with its inclusion on the UNESCO World Heritage List. If you can, try to visit during one of the medieval cultural festivals that are held here. The biggest is called 'Ancient Njasvizh'. It usually takes place in July, when the streets and parks are full of scenes from centuries long gone, including jousting tournaments, battle recreations, dancing, juggling and displays of ancient crafts. It can be crowded of course, but it's a small price to pay, while the advantage of a visit out of season is that you can have the place to yourself (my very favourite time of all). Make your own decision when to go, but make sure you go all the same.

NOVOGRUDOK (НАВАГРУДАК / НОВОГРУДОК) In the 13th century, Belarus was the nucleus of the great principality of Lithuania and, when Mindaug was crowned Grand Duke of All Lithuania here in 1253, Novogrudok was named the great duchy's capital. The town is dominated by a hill on which the ruins of a 14th-century **castle** stand. Little of its structure remains today but, at the height of its influence,

the seven imposing towers made it the largest and most significant fortress in the country, as befitted the town's status. At 323m above sea level, the castle hill is one of the highest points in the country and the views over the town and surrounding Nieman River, with a radius of 15–20km, are singularly impressive. At the height of its powers, the town enjoyed extensive trade links with the countries of central Europe, the Baltic, Scandinavia and Byzantium. It also made a huge contribution to the development of the ideas of the Reformation in Belarus. Inevitably, conflict and war gradually weakened its position, so that today only traces of its former greatness remain. From 1654 to 1667, the castle itself suffered very significant damage during the war between the armies of Russia and Rzeczpospolita, and then between 1700 and 1721 it was all but destroyed by the Swedish army during the Northern Wars. Just two ruined towers and a portion of the exterior wall remain atop the bluff, although the **Farny Transfiguration of the Lord Roman Catholic Church** remains towards the bottom of the hill. Originally founded as a place of worship by Grand Duke Vitautis in 1395, the current church was built in 1723. It is a fine example of the 'Sarmat' Baroque style, which is characterised by a fortress-like appearance.

The great Belarusian poet Adam Mitskevich was born in Novogrudok and was christened in this church. Other sites within the town relating to the poet include the nearby **Barrow of Immortality**, at the foot of which is a memorial stone, the **sculpture** close to the mound on the other side of castle hill and the location of the **house** where he was born in the square at 1 Leninskaya Street, on the original foundations of which now stand a **museum** (*1 Leninskaya St;* ☏ *15 97 2 43 40;* ⏱ *09.00–18.00 Tue–Sun*) dedicated to his life and work. In the grounds, certain outbuildings of the original house have been recreated. Just off the square is another **museum** (*2 Grodnenskaya St;* ☏ *15 97 2 23 95*) devoted to the history of the region, with excellent and moving exhibits relating to the fate of the Jewish community and the activities of the partisans led by the Bielski brothers who were so active in the forests around here resisting the Nazi oppression in the Great Patriotic War. The Jewish community in the town before the war was a very significant one. The Nazis murdered almost all and the small number who survived were deported for slave labour. Four other places of worship, two of them Eastern Orthodox (the 18th-century Cathedral of St Nicholas and the 16th-century Church of Sts Boris and Hleb), one Roman Catholic (the 18th-century Church of St Michael the Archangel) and one a 19th-century mosque, are also all worthy of a visit. During the months of summer, the bloody history of the region is regularly recreated for the tourist through battle re-enactments, which attract very large crowds.

There is a ring road around most of the town and, whatever the direction from which you approach, you will find yourself looking upwards. Approaching from the north gives a much better impression of the strategic importance of the town and the dominance enjoyed by the castle. I have only ever come from the direction of Mir from the southeast or from Baranovichy to the south, and in either case the castle isn't easy to find. As you enter the town, look for the water tower on the horizon and keep heading upwards until you can go no higher, then the castle is relatively easy to spot. Leave your vehicle in the car park just off Lenin Square. Walk towards the right as you leave the car park and head into the castle grounds, past the Mitskevich statue on the left. The earthworks are massive. The Barrow of Immortality is on the left, and you should climb to the top to admire the magnificent 360-degree panorama. Again, it's easy to appreciate the significance of the strategic location of the defences. The Farny Cathedral is below and to the left of the two ruined towers, some way down the hill. The town itself is in the other direction, with fine views of the Cathedral of St Nicholas and the Church of Sts Boris and Hleb. The castle site itself is presently closed and staff in the tourist information centre tell me it is not expected to be fully open again until the summer of 2015 following the extensive renovation work.

Retrace your steps back into Lenin Square, where once the old market stood. There's a **tourist information centre** (*4 Patchtovaya St;* \ *15 972 77 47;* e *novtic@tut.by; www.tourgrodno.by;* ⏰ *09.00–18.00 daily*) where a deal of helpful information and a good number of informative booklets are available, some of them with English pages. The staff are very pleased to see visitors, though no English is spoken here. The centre itself is tucked away and is not easy to find. Pachtovaya is a small street leading to the Church of Sts Boris and Hleb out of the back of the square. You first spot a green 'i' sign on the wall; go past it and turn right into the yard, through the door and up the stairs into the darkness. Turn left and knock on the door to the left. On the same side of the square pause for coffee at Bar Rhum (*9 Lenina Sq;* \ *15 972 09 70;* ⏰ *07.00–01.00 daily Mar–Nov, 07.00– midnight daily Dec–Feb*), located just to the right of the pale orange-stuccoed House of Culture. Hotel Panski Dom (*3 Grodnenskaya St;* \ *15 972 53 85*) is a little further down the road leading to the Cathedral of St Nicholas, with Café Stary Gorod (\ *15 972 47 78;* ⏰ *noon–midnight Mon–Thu, noon–01.00 Fri & Sun*) right next door. The Adam Mitskevich museum is across the square and on the other side of the arresting war memorial.

Getting there and away Situated around 40km northwest of Mir on the P11 road, one way to see Novogrudok is to pay the town a visit by way of a detour from your excursion to Mir although, as with a trip to Njasvizh, this will make for a long though fascinating day. A stop off on the M1 journey from Brest to Minsk is also a possibility. The M1 is a good road, as befits its status as a major pan-European highway, with pleasing views. And even though it's one of the most significant routes across the continent, I've rarely seen much traffic on it! Take the P5 at Baranovichy, signposted Novogrudok. Roads off the main routes in this country are almost always empty of cars and it is still possible to experience the joy of motoring here. This road to Novogrudok is a good example. Five kilometres after you turn off the M1, look for the imposing Catholic church in need of repair at Stalovichi, before you pass through the attractive rolling hills around Gorodishcha. Fifteen kilometres further on, beyond the village of Porechye, is lovely Lake Svityaz and its sanatorium. Another 6km further is the very attractive church at Valyevka. You will cross the ring road shortly after this point. Alternatively, and if time is not an issue, book separate excursions from Minsk for each of these three historical towns to ensure that you get the chance to enjoy their charms at a leisurely pace.

DUDUTKI FOLK MUSEUM (\ *133 07 47;* ⏰ *10.00–17.00 Tue & Wed, 10.00–18.00 Thu–Sun;* e *info@dudutki.by; www.dudutki.by; admission BYR130,000*) Located 35km south of Minsk, near to the village of Dudutki on the banks of the Ptich River, is this former country landowner's estate, where life as it was lived in the 18th and 19th centuries is affectionately recreated. Both an open-air museum and a working farm, there is an original working windmill and other functioning workshops (located in traditional buildings of wood) displaying carpentry, pottery, braiding and other handicrafts, together with a blacksmith, a bakery and a cheese-maker. The craftsmen will be very happy to show off their skills and you will be invited to have a try! Vintage cars are also on display and visitors can take advantage of the *banya*, as well as taking part in horseriding, sledging and horse-drawn cart rides. Additional charges apply. There is an outdoor animal enclosure in which wild boar roam (reasonably at leisure) and there is also an ostrich pen, plus runs for standard farm animals such as pigs and goats. For the children, there are horses and rabbits. The atmosphere is extremely relaxed, so you can wander around at will. The riverside paths and farmland tracks make for an inviting backdrop to your lazy meanderings. Various guided tours are also available lasting approximately three hours, the cost being dependent upon numbers.

After your exertions, you can visit one of two excellent **restaurants** (where you can sit outdoors in good weather) for a splendid meal of locally produced and traditionally cooked fare, accompanied (of course) by vodka that is legally distilled on the premises. Bread, cheeses, butter and many meats are all sourced on site. Expect to pay around BYR200,000 per person for your meal. There is also a small **hotel,** but there are only four double bedrooms and inevitably tour companies make bookings well in advance. To round off your visit, spend some time in the shop, where you can buy high-quality goods manufactured on the spot at eminently reasonable prices. 'Gypsy performances' and concerts of traditional music are regularly performed, but the best time to visit is during one of the traditional festivals to celebrate, for example, the winter solstice, the arrival of spring, or harvest time, when the whole place is alive with colour and activity. All in all you could easily spend a whole day here. A good friend who runs a successful tour agency in Minsk thinks it's all very twee and tourist-focused here, aimed at those looking for a rose-tinted view of rural life as once it was in this country. I tend to agree, but that's not to say that a visit is without worth. Just bear in mind that much of what you see may be as much a cliché as historical accuracy.

To view some excellent photographs and videos and for a full background briefing on the history of the site, as well as comprehensive details of the modern-day activities on offer there, see the very informative website (details opposite); also check out www.belarus.net/polyfact for an overview in English before you visit.

Getting there and away By car, take the P23 road from Minsk, then follow the signs east for 12km. The village is on the bus route from the capital to Ptich, but the nearest stop to the museum is some 2km away. If visiting on a local tour through an agency, most companies allow a half day here, but you will be pushed for time if you want to see and do everything.

RAUBICHY MUSEUM OF BELARUSIAN FOLK ART (507 44 68; www.artmuseum.by/eng/filial/raub/the-museum-of-belarusian-folk-art-in-raubichi; ⊕ 10.00–17.00 Wed–Sun) Located only 24km from Minsk, this ethnographical museum is situated in the former Krestogorskaya Church. It has numerous displays of folk art from all over the country, including costumes, fabrics, weaving, pottery, carved wood, earthenware and straw goods. Only 10km away is the idyllic **Minsk Lake**, dotted with numerous islets and surrounded by forests of dense pine. Also nearby is the **International Sports Complex**, incorporating ski jumps, shooting grounds, tennis courts, football pitches and an international biathlon course, together with two hotels and a number of eating establishments. Again, organised excursions from Minsk are available.

BELARUSIAN STATE MUSEUM OF FOLK ARCHITECTURE AND RURAL LIFE (507 69 37; e info@etna.of.by; www.etna.by; ⊕ 10.00–18.20 Wed–Sun 1 May–31 Oct, 10.00–17.20 Wed–Sun 1 Nov–30 Apr, last entry 1hr before closing; admission BYR30,000) In the style of Scandinavian Skansen museums devoted to the history of architecture, where buildings that have been carefully deconstructed and then removed from their original location are then painstakingly rebuilt brick by brick

on the exhibit site, this outdoor museum of century-old buildings from different regions of Belarus is located near to Strochitsa, 15km southwest of the capital and in a very picturesque spot at the confluence of the Ptich River and its tributary the Menka. Featuring around a hundred buildings, including peasant dwellings, taverns (one serving delicious traditional meals), mills, a country school and a church, many guided tours are available, together with demonstrations of traditional crafts, including bee-keeping, fishing and weaving. There are also thousands of exhibits including kitchenware, tools, earthenware and national costumes. Here visitors have the chance to learn about regional folk architecture, as well as the country's myths, legends and fairy tales. In the opinion of my good friend who thinks that the Dudutki experience is somewhat hackneyed, a visit here presents an altogether much more authentic recreation of village life. I think she's right. The informative website will tell you all you need to know about what to expect. Highly recommended.

STANKOVO ECOPARK (ЦЭНТР ЭКАЛАГІЧНАГА ТУРЫЗМУ СТАНЬКАВА / ЦЕНТР ЭКОЛОГИЧЕСКОГО ТУРИЗМА СТАНЬКОВО) (*Stankovo village, Dzerzhinskava region;* ✆ *599 34 88;* e *stankovo@inbox.ru; www.ecopark.by;* ⏰ *10.00–19.00 Wed–Sun*) This is a newly developed centre for ecological tourism located 1.5km from the village of Stankovo and around 50km southwest of Minsk. Neither I nor anyone I know in Minsk have been there yet, but I list it here for information purposes and updates will be posted on the Bradt website (*www.bradtupdates.com/belarus*) as and when available. The attractions include a recreation of a wartime partisans' camp, 'fortified Minsk' (displays of weaponry), shooting galleries (including archery), zoological garden, children's rides and play areas, horseriding and the house of Grandfather Frost, while facilities include chalet overnight accommodation, a restaurant, cafés and a bathhouse.

OUT-OF-TOWN MEMORIAL SITES
National Memorial Complex at Khatyn (*Logoysk region, Minsk oblast;* ✆ *745 50 60, 745 57 87 (to arrange guided tours, but in Russian only);* e *khatyn@mail.ru; www. khatyn.by/en; site* ⏰ *24hrs daily; guided tours & photography exhibition 10.00–16.30 Tue–Sun; admission to the site is free; there is a charge of BYR2,350 for admission to the museum*) If you take only one out-of-town trip while in Minsk, then do try to make it this one. Only 75km from the capital, this memorial complex bears witness to the horrors of Nazi barbarism during the Great Patriotic War. It was constructed on the site of the former village of Khatyn, which was razed to the ground in the spring of 1943 and its inhabitants brutally butchered. At the centre of the complex is a truly astonishing bronze sculpture, the 6m-high *The Unconquered Man*. Before you go, do visit the excellent English-language website for a full description of the terrible events in 1943 and for further details of the memorial complex that exists today. The tragedy of Khatyn was not just an isolated episode in this tumultuous war, for the experience was replicated many times over on the territory of the Soviet Union. It is said that the inhabitants of 618 Belarusian villages were burned alive during the occupation in SS punishment operations against partisan groups. Of these villages, 185 were never rebuilt and have simply vanished from the face of the earth. Overall, every fourth Belarusian perished during the war: a total of 2.2 million people. This figure included the 380,000 who were deported to Germany as slave labourers, never to return home. A staggering 209 cities and townships and 9,200 villages were destroyed. So catastrophic was the impact on the population that it did not recover to its pre-war total until 1971. Every visitor to Belarus is struck by the large number of war memorials that exist and the extent to which the conflict continues to dominate the national psyche. A visit to Khatyn helps to place all of this into the right context.

So it is to the memory of all of these communities that the vast complex at Khatyn is dedicated. Across a total area of 50ha, the memorial has 26 symbolic chimneys, each with a mournful, tolling bell, to mark the site of each of the 26 houses, the boundaries of which are delineated by low concrete walls with gates, all of them depicted as being open as a metaphor for the hospitality of Belarusian people. Also marked are the sites of the village wells. On the face of each chimney is a plaque bearing the names of each family member who lived there, from aged grandparents to babes only a few weeks old. In itself, this is a truly sombre metaphor, for only the brick chimneys were left standing when the Nazis were burning log houses in Belarusian villages.

As you approach the complex from the car park, the lie of the land slopes gently down to *The Unconquered Man*, who stands facing you. A broad concrete path leads right up to the base of the sculpture, with its centre line planted with flowers. It is only when you visit at flowering time that you appreciate the significance of this, for the pattern of planting was very deliberately designed to display a long, meandering line of vivid red blooms all the way to the statue: a river of blood.

On your right as you first set foot on this path are two enormous granite plates at an angle. This is the location of the barn in which the villagers were murdered and they represent its collapsed roof. Elsewhere is a mass grave containing the remains of the villagers. There is also a separate cemetery for the other villages that were burned to the ground and are now lost, the symbolic graves bearing an urn containing soil from each one. There is a 'Wall of Grief' to commemorate concentration camp victims, with niches containing memorial plaques detailing the loss of life at each camp. Then set among three silver birches symbolising life burns the eternal flame to keep alive the memory of all who lost their lives in the conflict.

In 2004, by decree of the president, further enhancements to the site were undertaken to mark the 60th anniversary of the country's liberation, including the establishment of a small museum and photo montage to document both the occupation as a whole, this specific atrocity and the history of the memorial complex.

The memory of my first visit here will stay with me forever. As we walked into the complex on a chilly early spring morning, a rifle shot cracked out in the distance. It was probably hunters in the nearby woods. But the effect on us all was both immediate and startling. I have visited a number of times since and I have never failed to be deeply moved. I have taken several Belarusian friends there for their first visit. All were moved to tears. The mournful monotone of the tolling bells in the silence that pervades all around acts as a summons, inviting you to look, learn and never forget.

There are two important contextual points to bear in mind in all of this. First, following the liberation of the Soviet Union, a rampant Red Army took terrible and brutal revenge on the civilian population of Germany as the Nazi forces were driven back over the Rhine; then secondly – and with huge irony – this memorial complex at Khatyn should not be mistaken for the Katyn Forest memorial, located east of here (and 20km outside Smolensk in Russia), where in 1943, German forces uncovered the mass graves of more than 22,000 Polish officers and civilians shot by the NKVD on Stalin's orders. Only after the disintegration of the Soviet Union was vicarious responsibility for this atrocity accepted by Russia.

Getting there and away By car, take the M3 motorway north out of Minsk in the direction of Vitebsk. After 70km, take the right turn signposted Хатынь. The complex is located 5km along that road. There is no reliable access by means of public transport, although I know of one small and enterprising group of visitors who travelled there by prebooked taxi from Minsk. The driver waited in the car park for two hours while the party explored the site at their leisure, before taking them back to Minsk. The total cost was US$100, which represents good value.

'Stalin Line' Historical and Cultural Site

(✆ 503 20 20; www.stalin-line.by; ⏰ 10.00–18.00 Tue–Sun; admission BYR70,000) As Europe stumbled towards conflict in the 1930s and paranoia gripped the national psyche of countries across the continent, most foreign policies became increasingly obsessed with defence and self-protection. The Soviet Union was no exception. All along the western border of the USSR, from the Baltic to the Black Sea, Stalin ordered a network of defensive military fortifications to be built. In all, 23 fortified zones were constructed, four of them within the territory of Belarus. At that time, the border was a mere 40km from

MASSACRE AT KHATYN

Khatyn was once a small but thriving community in a picturesque wooded area, but this hamlet no longer appears on even the most detailed map today, other than as a memorial. The atrocity took place on 22 March 1943, when troops of the occupying German army completely encircled the village. Earlier that day, a skirmish had occurred in the vicinity, when partisans attacked a motor convoy on the highway just 6km away. A German officer was killed in the engagement. Whether or not anyone in the village knew anything about this is a matter of conjecture, but what then happened is beyond understanding even to this day. All of the villagers, young and old, healthy and infirm, women, children and babes in arms were driven from their houses at gunpoint and herded into the barn. No mercy was shown. Among them were Joseph and Anna Baranovsky with their nine children. So too were Alexei and Alexandra Novitsky with their seven children, along with Kazimir and Elena Lotko with their seven children, the youngest of whom was only 12 months old. Vera Yaskevich was also driven into the barn with her seven-week-old son Tolik. Vera's other daughter, little Lena, first tried to hide in the family home, but then she decided to run for the woods. At first she was successful in evading the trailing bullets, but the soldier who ran after her and overtook her showed no mercy, callously gunning her down before the eyes of her helpless and horror-struck father. Among those who found themselves in the wrong place at the wrong time were two people from other villages who by chance were in Khatyn that day.

When everyone was inside the barn, the doors were barred, the roof covered with straw and the building doused in petrol. After setting it alight, soldiers positioned themselves on all sides of the conflagration to machine-gun any of the suffocating people who managed to break out. The village was then looted and the 26 homesteads burned to the ground.

The whole scene is unimaginable. Terror-struck parents hopelessly striving to save their wailing children, throwing them through windows into the murderous gunfire, or else just sheltering them in their arms and with their bodies, helpless and powerless, themselves crying and overcome by panic. People stumbling from the building, their hair and clothes ablaze, straight into a hail of bullets. Choking smoke everywhere, the smell of burning and the deafening screams of despair.

In total, 149 people, including 75 children, were burned alive. Only one of the adults of the village survived; his tale, detailed on page 180, could not be more harrowing. Only three children – Volodya Yaskevich, his sister Sonia and

Minsk. In concept and design, it matched the Maginot Line along France's eastern border and it was intended to serve the same purpose, although it was nowhere near as imposing. The Nazis outflanked the Maginot Line, of course, while Stalin's equivalent was breached with little difficulty.

This network became known as the 'Stalin Line' and, on 30 June 2005, a precise reconstruction of a section of the historical layout covering 40ha was ceremonially unveiled in the presence of the president himself, resplendent in full military uniform, near the town of Zaslavl, 30km from the capital. Incorporating authentic equipment from the time (complete with dents from shells and bullet holes), it is an open-air museum of military fortifications, including the defence line itself with trenches, antitank obstacles and ditches, anti-personnel obstacles and machine-gun pillboxes. Today, visitors can walk around some of those pillboxes and sit in a

another boy, Sasha Zhelobkovich – had been able to hide from the murderers and would escape death, and by a miracle, two girls from two different families – Maria Fedorovich and Yulia Klimovich – were also spared from death in the barn. Somehow, they managed to escape the fire and crawl to the nearby wood, where they were later found by the inhabitants of the neighbouring village of Khvorosteny, barely alive. But after having survived this horror, the village of Khvorosteny was itself also burned to the ground later in the war. This time, the two girls did not survive. It beggars belief that fate can be so cruel.

Two other children not only escaped from the barn, but also survived the war. They were seven-year-old Viktor Zhelobkovich and 12-year-old Anton Baranovsky. Viktor's mother Anna was holding him firmly by the hand as she staggered through the smoke and flames of the burning barn. Mortally wounded by gunfire, she covered her son's body as she fell. Viktor had been wounded in the arm. He lay on the ground under his mother's corpse until the Nazis finally left the smouldering ruins of the village. Anton Baranovsky was wounded in the leg and also lay still, so as not to be discovered.

As the inhabitants of the neighbouring villages and hamlets later picked their way through the ruins, they discovered the two stricken boys, wounded and badly burned. After tending to their wounds, they took them to the orphanage in the small town of Pleshinitsy, where they were raised after the war.

The only adult witness to the massacre at Khatyn was the 56-year-old village blacksmith Joseph Kaminsky. Wounded and severely burned, he did not regain consciousness until late at night, when the fascists were already long gone. As he meticulously searched through the ruins of his village and the bodies that lay there, he came across his injured son among the corpses. The poor boy had received bullet wounds to his abdomen and he was severely burned. Joseph tended to his wounds as best he could, but as his father cradled him, he died in his arms.

And so it is that the only human sculpture of the Khatyn memorial complex, *The Unconquered Man*, tells the tragic story of Joseph and his son. It is a doleful and harrowing metaphor for the suffering not only of the villagers of Khatyn, but also of all who were bowed under the yoke of oppression and tyranny. When you see this sculpture of bronze for the first time, particularly if you have some prior understanding of what took place here, the power and impact of the image is staggering in its effect.

THE KHATYN SURVIVORS

Of the five children and one adult who survived the Khatyn massacre, three are still alive.

The village blacksmith Joseph Kaminsky lived for many years in the nearby village of Kozyry after the war. He would often go back to Khatyn and was to be seen by visitors cutting the grass and tending the site of his former home. He died in 1973 and was buried in Logoysk.

Volodya Yaskevich, who had been born and raised in Khatyn, was subsequently brought up in the orphanage at Pleshinitsy. He studied at vocational school Number 9, before starting work as a turner at the Minsk automobile plant. He served in the Soviet army before returning to the factory in Minsk in 1952, where he progressed to shop foreman. He retired in 1993 and still lives in the village of Kozyry, which was the home of Joseph Kaminsky for so long. He has a daughter, a granddaughter, a grandson and a great-grandson.

Sonia Yaskevich was also born in Khatyn and she too lived at the children's home in Pleshinitsy after the atrocity. She studied at vocational school of communication Number 15 in Brest before spending her working life as a typist in a Minsk post office. A pensioner now, she still lives in Minsk. She has two sons and a granddaughter.

Like Volodya and Sonia, Viktor Zhelobkovich was born in Khatyn, then raised in the Pleshinitsy orphanage. After studying at vocational school, he worked as a moulder in a machine tools plant. As with Volodya, he returned there when his army service was over. He then studied at and graduated from university, where he took evening classes specialising in mechanical engineering. He has been working in the design office of a precision engineering company since 1976. He presently lives in Minsk and has a daughter and a granddaughter.

As with the others, Sasha Zhelobkovich was born in Khatyn, then raised at Pleshinitsy. He studied at military school and attended military academy. He served in the armed forces and, after retirement, he continued as a reservist lieutenant-colonel. He died in 1994.

After leaving the orphanage, Anton Baranovsky lived in Minsk, but died in tragic circumstances in 1969.

gun emplacement, stroll along the trench system (although much of what remains is rather overgrown) and clamber over a tank. There is also an exhibition of other military hardware, featuring tanks, helicopters and fixed-wing aircraft. Escorted tours are available from guides dressed in uniforms of the day. It goes without saying that this is an excursion for a dry day. The excellent website is sadly in Russian only (apart from one English page) but, even without the language, the photographs and maps are extremely interesting.

If you do not have your own car, the complex is best accessed by means of a local excursion from Minsk. The cost per person will be around US$100, with the option of a guide and translator for the group at a cost of US$150. A more expensive option (but much better value for money) will be to combine your visit with a trip to the memorial complex at Khatyn (see pages 176–8) and the Mount of Glory (see opposite) at the same time. Expect to pay around US$200 each for this, with the price of admission to the sites themselves and all extras on top.

'Mount of Glory' (745 57 87; ⊕ *site access 24hrs; admission BYR3,000*) To honour the glorious victory of the Red Army over the fascist invaders, this monument atop a manmade hill consisting of scorched earth and soil brought from the nine 'hero cities' of the USSR and battlegrounds of the Great Patriotic War is visible for miles around. Created to mark the 25th anniversary of the liberation of the country from the Nazi occupation, it is located 21km out of the city centre at the side of the main highway to Moscow (where it joins the road to Minsk-2 National Airport). It stands an imposing 70m off the ground at its zenith and is situated in the vicinity of the last battle in the war to take place on Belarusian soil. It consists of four titanium-covered bayonets pointing directly to the sky, representing the four fronts on which divisions of the Red Army, partisans and members of other underground organisations successfully completed the liberation of the country. At the base of the monument itself is a golden circle, upon which images of the faces of soldiers and partisans have been sculpted, along with heroic inscriptions to the glory of the Red Army.

A row of tanks and other assorted military hardware lines the car park at the base of the mound and there is also a café selling the usual refreshments (with an outdoor barbecue area for national holidays and special commemorations). A concrete path winds around the mount to give access on foot to the obelisk itself and the entirety of the memorial stands in 26ha of parkland, in which are displayed sculptures of wood depicting folk art.

above left The 16th-century Mir Fortress is now one of only four UNESCO World Heritage Sites in Belarus (D/D) pages 168–9

above right The Kholmsky Gate, pockmarked by bullet-holes and shell craters, is testament to the severity of the attack on Brest Fortress during World War II (R/S) page 198 *top*   On the banks of the Nieman River, Grodno is renowned for its lofty feel and unique architecture, including the Drama Theatre (E/S) pages 209–24

above   The landscaped Rumyantsev-Paskevich Park in Gomel has an 18th-century Classical palace at its centre (O/D) page 281

left   Polotsk is one of the oldest cities in eastern Europe, and its side streets lined with historical buildings are ideal for exploring on foot (VS/D) pages 243–50

above 18th- and 19th-century rural life is recreated at the Dudutki Folk Museum, which features workshops in traditional wooden buildings (O/D) pages 174–5

left National holidays often feature parades of children and young people, traditional costumes, singing and dancing (NV/S) page 45

below left The *rushnik*, or ceremonial towel, is the foremost example of Belarusian folk art, and each village has its own specific design (KV/S) page 36–7

below right Home-distilled vodka can be found all over Belarus, and is often smooth-tasting but remarkably high in alcohol (AC/D) page 92 *above*   Vetka's Folk Arts Museum showcases the historical and cultural features of the Gomel region (HS/D) page 287

below left   Orthodox Easter is the biggest festival in the religious calendar; at midnight, families congregate at their local church and light beeswax candles (RB/D) pages 44–5

below right   At the Belarusian State Museum of Folk Architecture and Rural Life, *Kaladya* customs mark the passing of the old year (NE/D) pages 175–6

bottom   Historical re-enactments often take place in the summer; here actors participate in the commemoration of the Battle of Grunwald (RB/D) page 211

The Pripyatsky National Park covers a vast tract of marshy lowland and was established in order to preserve the area's ecosystems (SS) pages 288–9

Traditional, single-storey wooden houses are one of the iconic images of Belarus and can still be seen all over the country (N/D)

above **Wild boar (*Sus scrofa*)** (DU/MP/FLPA) page 5

above right **European brown bear (*Ursus arctos*)** (MK/IB/FLPA) page 5

right **European wolf (*Canis lupus*)** (KW/MP/FLPA) page 5

below **European bison (*Bison bonatus*)** (AH/S) page 5

above left At the National Memorial Complex at Khatyn, *The Unconquered Man* depicts Joseph Kaminsky, the only adult to survive the massacre, carrying his dead son (JO/WC) pages 176–81

above right The Zaslavskaya Memorial marks the spot where 5,000 Jews from the Minsk Ghetto were killed by the Nazis during the course of a single operation in March 1942 (SC/D) page 161

4

Brest City and *Oblast*
Брэст / Брест

Telephone code 162

Located in the southwestern corner of Belarus, Brest region has borders with both Poland and Ukraine. The administrative and cultural capital of the *oblast* is the city of Brest itself, which has a population of around 293,000. Only a short distance from the Polish border at the confluence of the Western Bug and Mukhavyets rivers, Brest is actually significantly closer to Warsaw than to Minsk. Its geographical position on the main Berlin–Moscow railway line and on the major intercontinental highway from west to east, together with its historical location as the crossing point on which trading routes from all points of the compass converged, has afforded the development over time of a unique environment for different cultures to meet and evolve together. It is very much the case, though, that Western influences predominate here. There's a bounce in the step of the locals and a degree of self-confidence hinting at a more outward-facing view of life, with a greater affinity to the West than can be found further east in the country. Furthermore, the position of the city, right on the western extremity of first, the Russian Empire, then latterly the Soviet Union, has bestowed upon it enormous strategic importance in times of war and peace. Today, Brest is not only a principal border crossing, but also a bridge: in cultural terms, between eastern and western Europe and politically, between the European Union and the Commonwealth of Independent States. This manifests itself in a number of ways, the quaintest of which is that travellers by train are delayed for several hours here because of the change in gauge of the track. This means that passengers must watch while their bogies are adjusted so that they fit the wider track in use in the East! All in all, the city very much feels like a major border crossing with a great deal of energetic hustle and bustle, but at the same time there is also a calm and relaxed side that speaks of charm, grace and elegance. There are many delightful avenues that are just right for promenading in this splendid city, with cosmopolitan restaurants, bars and cafés where you can stop and watch the world go by. Just watch out for the gargantuan pot-holes in the roads all over the city, even on main streets. In keeping with the city's reputation for energy is a growing culture of sporting activity and fitness. A number of sports complexes have been constructed to international standards and increasing numbers of national and international events are held within the city. In July 2010, the World Under-23 Rowing Championships were held at the purpose-built site located just outside Brest, which a number of independent observers have described as one of the finest facilities for this sport in the world. I discovered to my cost just how significantly Brest features on the international sports scene when one of my visits coincided with the opening of the first Eurasian Games, such that there wasn't a single available hotel room to be found in the whole of the city. More fool me, you might say, for expecting to turn up without advance notice and find an abundance of choice…

The establishment of the free economic zone over 50 years ago has helped to create an environment in which trade can flourish with confidence. Poland's entry into the European Union in 2004 will also have helped support trade, but the city's greatest claim to fame is its fortress, sited on an island and made legendary by the great heroism and deeds of sacrifice of its defenders during the Great Patriotic War.

Although not on the grand scale of Minsk, there is much to interest the visitor in the architecture of the city. A number of examples of the imposing Neoclassical style so favoured in the last decades of the Russian Empire can be found here (especially in and around the central station square). Not surprisingly, there is also much that is reminiscent of Poland, particularly the Roman Catholic churches, while a number of Orthodox churches are particularly pleasing on the eye. Also worth an hour or two of your time is a slow stroll along the bank of the Mukhavyets River, a pastime much favoured by promenaders of all ages. Just beware of the mosquitoes, so be sure to button up. The river runs east–west and is parallel to Masherova Avenue, half a kilometre to the south of this main thoroughfare. There are pleasant gardens and walkways on the northern bank.

The whole southern part of this region has its own natural and cultural identity as the Belarusian Polyesye. The main waterway flowing through it from west to east (as far as Chernobyl in Ukraine and beyond) is the Pripyat River and its many tributaries. This is a unique natural environment and 12 reserves and 29 other protected areas have been set up here with the objective of affording it as much protection as possible. Pride of place goes to the world-renowned state national park and biosphere reserve of Byelovezhskaya Puscha, a unique medieval woodland area 65km to the north of the city (see pages 203–7).

The territory of Brest *oblast* is rich in culture. There are around 120 historical parks and estates, together with over 2,000 buildings and monuments of historical interest. Among the oldest of the sites is the settlement of Beryestye, which has buildings dating from the 11th and 12th centuries, while many churches are worthy of note, including the Roman Catholic church in the original 'Belarusian Gothic' style in the village of Ishkold (Baranovichy district), the Roman Catholic Renaissance church in the village of Chyernovchytsy (Brest district), the Monastery of the Cartesian Order in Beryezha and the church of St George in the village of Synkovichy (Lunynyets district). Also of interest are the part-ruined remains of the 17th–18th-century Sapyegazh Palace in Ruzhany, with its imposing façade of columns and elegant galleries. The village of Kossava also has a spectacular ruined castle, along with a museum dedicated to the life of Tadeusz Kościuszko, a Belarusian-Polish aristocrat born near here who fought with George Washington in the American War of Independence, and later became a citizen of the United States. Finally, the ancient museum town of Pinsk, situated 150km east of Brest, still retains its charm and beauty.

HISTORY

THE CITY'S EARLY ORIGINS The city of Brest has long been regarded as the traditional western gate of the country, a city with a glorious and valiant history across the centuries, complemented by a vibrant and hopeful present and future. It was first mentioned in the *Story of Temporal Years Chronicle* in 1019 as Beryestye, in the context of the struggle for the crown of Kievan Rus between Duke Svyatopolk of Turov and Duke Yaroslav the Wise of Novgorod. A number of theories exist as to the original derivation of its name. Some believe that it comes from one or two Slavic words meaning either 'birch bark' or 'elm', while others are of the opinion that it is Lithuanian in origin, from the word meaning 'ford'. The preponderance of forest and the confluence of two major rivers here mean that either is possible. Brest developed over time as a frontier town and trading centre on the western fringes of Kievan Rus, a wooden castle being built there in the 12th century on the site of the current fortress. The historical chapters of this book repeatedly show how, for many hundreds of years, the territories of Belarus have been the rope in a tug-of-war between powerful and aggressive states on its borders. The strategic location of Brest ensured that it was a regular target for subjugation and it featured heavily in a number of bloody engagements. Early in the 13th century it was part of the Grand Duchy of Lithuania, having formally been a Polish town, before being sacked by the Mongol Horde in 1241. Then in 1390, it became the first city on Belarusian territory to be granted self-determination and government under Magdeburg Law, only a short period after suffering significant structural damage at the hands of the Teutonic Order.

As its cultural and social influence grew, it became more and more the location for key events. Meetings of certain of the state's most significant *sejms*, or parliamentary bodies with limited powers of local self-determination, were held here; and in 1553, a Calvinist cathedral and printing house were established under Duke Nikolas Radzivili the Black where, in 1558, one of the best-known of all Renaissance books was printed, the Brest Bible. In 1569, it became part of the mighty Polish-Lithuanian Commonwealth. In 1596, it hosted the historic council that established the Eastern Catholic (or Uniate) Church to reconcile (or perhaps forge a compromise between) Roman Catholic and Eastern Orthodox believers. Conflict returned in the 17th century, when Brest was first invaded by Russia (in 1654) and then all but destroyed in a series of wars involving Sweden. It was eventually restored to Russian hands in 1795 and renamed Brest-Litovsk on the occasion of the further partition of the Polish-Lithuanian Commonwealth.

THE WORLD WARS AND THEIR AFTERMATH The mighty fortress was constructed between 1836 and 1842, not only as a citadel for the protection of this frontier town, but also as a major component in the defensive structure of the giant Russian Empire. Unfortunately, however, it wasn't enough to protect the city and when the flames of World War I engulfed much of Europe it fell to the Germans in 1915.

In March 1918, in a ceremony as heavy with symbolism as the fortress itself, Lenin's Bolshevik government concluded the Peace Treaty of Brest-Litovsk with Germany, bringing the war to an end on the Eastern Front. In this treaty, Lenin gave up vast swathes of territory (the lands of the Baltic, Poland and large chunks of modern Belarus and Ukraine), including, of course, Brest. This was a masterstroke of political compromise and expediency on the part of the newly installed Bolshevik government, which was struggling to impose authority back home. On the face of it, the deal appears to have been a major defeat, but Lenin had little choice: quite simply, the enormous and so-called 'invincible' army of the Russian Empire had collapsed in anarchy. In tens of thousands, ordinary soldiers had given up the fight and were trudging home. Mutiny was everywhere. Domestically, all was in chaos and disarray following the Revolution in November 1917. But crucially, the peace gave Lenin enough breathing space to establish and consolidate Bolshevik control over the organs of the state.

The victorious Western powers overturned the German-Russian treaty as part of the settlement that came out of the Versailles Conference in 1919. Under the Treaty of Versailles, the restored but fledgling Polish state took control of Brest that year from the Germans, although during the conflict that ensued between Poland and the Soviet Union, the fate of the city was for it to move from the control of one state to another several times. At the conclusion of the war, Brest became Polish and the 1921 Treaty of Riga formally ratified this position. It remained so until the outbreak of World War II.

The fortress suffered very heavy damage during World War I but still retained its strategic importance and, after the conclusion of the 1921 treaty, it housed a significant Polish military presence. The garrison was pressed into service during the Nazi invasion of Poland in the early days of September 1939, when only four battalions stood shoulder to shoulder to defend the city against the formidable and overwhelming motorised force of the 19th Panzer Corps commanded by highly respected general Heinz Guderian. An intense and bloody battle ensued over four days, before the Poles withdrew. For a while, the focus of attention was diverted from the city, but Brest was annexed by the Soviet Union later that year under the secret (and shameful) Molotov–Ribbentrop Pact. In this unholy alliance of diametrically opposed totalitarian dogma, the USSR and Nazi Germany callously carved up the sovereign Polish state for themselves, as the democracies of western Europe turned their backs and looked away in the climate of appeasement that prevailed at the time. But the inhabitants of Brest (and the peoples of the greater Belarusian territories) had no interest in political expediency. In the eyes of many, the single consequence of this act was to bring about the rightful reunification of a single Belarusian nation under the constituency of the Belarusian SSR. Sadly, though, the grim reality was that the Nazis were soon to turn up in force on the western bank of the River Bug, almost at the same time as Soviet forces began to mass on the eastern side.

So it was that the peace was short-lived and the city was first in the line of fire when Hitler unleashed Operation Barbarossa on an unsuspecting and wholly unprepared USSR on 22 June 1941. Word of massive German troop movements in the vicinity of the border reached an increasingly panic-stricken Kremlin in the days before the attack began but Stalin did nothing, refusing to believe that the Molotov–Ribbentrop Pact was about to be torn up. The city itself fell within a few hours, but this was the start of the most stirring period of history for the fortress. The unparalleled feats of heroism and courage of its defenders in the weeks that followed have passed into legend. Not without good reason did a grateful nation subsequently bestow the title of 'Hero-fortress' (the city also being granted the status of 'Hero City of the Soviet Union', one of 13 throughout the USSR to be honoured thus). Those soldiers who were first to feel the might and fury of the Nazi war machine somehow held out throughout the summer of 1941 in conditions of intense attrition. Their bravery and self-sacrifice in holding back the invasion for six long weeks (as supplies of food and drinking water dwindled to nothing) gave the rest of the Soviet Union just enough time to gather itself for the withering onslaught that was to follow. To see now the vivid red-brick walls of the fortress, pock-marked with shell damage and riddled with machine-gun fire, is to gain some understanding of the enormity of the unfolding events that summer. By the time the fortress finally fell, nearly all of the defending troops had been killed. With tragic poignancy and as an enduring mark of their ultimate sacrifice, one of the last of them had inscribed in large letters on the wall of one of the barracks, 'I am dying but not surrendering. Farewell, Motherland!' By this time, the fortress was deep behind enemy lines, almost all of Belarusian territory now under the yoke of Nazi oppression. The years of tyranny that followed were brutal in the extreme. Brest's Jewish population was all but wiped out during the course of 1942, as was the case throughout the whole country, before the Red Army liberated the city in July 1944. The latest chapter in the long history of this cosmopolitan city was begun in February 1945 at the peace conference conducted by the Western powers at Yalta, when it was formally restored to the sovereignty of the Belarusian SSR and the greater Soviet Union. Upon the disintegration of the USSR, Brest became part of the newly created independent nation state of Belarus.

BY AIR The local airport is 12km east of the city. Built in the 1970s, it used to operate weekly flights to the capital Minsk and to 15 cities in the old Soviet Union, including Moscow, Kiev and Novgorod. At the time of writing, however, it was closed for commercial flights and there were no plans to reopen it for this purpose. If air travel is your preferred option, take one of the scheduled routes either to Minsk, Vilnius or Warsaw, then complete your journey by train. See *Getting there and away*, pages 56–8, for details of the airlines flying to these destinations.

BY TRAIN There is easy access from the West and the city finds itself on two major trans-European routes: Brussels to Irkutsk and Vienna to St Petersburg. Furthermore, every single train from Berlin to Moscow stops here. Most travellers journey by means of the daily services that depart from the central railway station in Warsaw (including a sleeper service) for its equivalent in Brest. A one-way ticket costs approximately US$56. The journey time by day is around five hours. From Berlin, the sleeper is much more expensive. Alternatively, take a cheap local train from the Polish border town of Terespol. Within Belarus, up to 13 trains a day leave Minsk for Brest, with prices starting at around US$4 for a one-way ticket; the journey time is approximately four hours, with one daily overnight sleeper.

Unfortunately the **central railway station** [190 D1] in Brest isn't very central and you will need to take a short cab ride into the heart of the city, or hop on any of the buses that pass right in front of the station, a large, Neoclassical building of archetypically pre-Revolutionary grandeur. Originally built between 1833 and 1866, when it was then one of the largest railway stations in the whole of the Russian Empire, this fine building was reconstructed in the Stalinist style in 1956. It sits in the middle of a huge jumble of criss-crossing lines heading to all points of the compass (there are railway lines everywhere in this town) and is still one of the city's best-known buildings. It's an enduring image that features extensively on promotional material for the whole country. In its heyday, it was not only one of the biggest but also one of the most elegant and sumptuous railway stations throughout the Empire, before it metamorphosed to bear the mark of classic post-war Stalinist design. It is divided into northern and southern sections, for trains travelling westward and eastward respectively. A large and very long station hall divides the two. The usual facilities are on offer, including kiosks for the sale of cigarettes and light refreshments, a luggage store and a currency exchange. The standard of service here is excellent; I have heard of one visitor who didn't speak Russian being taken under the wing of an attendant with a fine commitment to customer care, who closed her ticket booth to escort the weary traveller to the currency exchange, where she helped him to buy currency for his trip. There is also a restaurant here with a surprisingly decent standard of cuisine. All of the facilities are billed as being available 'round the clock' but, in reality, it would be unwise to count on this much beyond nine in the evening. Red tape is a painful experience because of the proximity to the national border and every passenger must go through customs and immigration before proceeding on to the platform. When leaving the station, just be careful not to become disorientated, because this splendid building is actually 'about-face'; the imposing frontage with its iconic hammer and sickle fresco actually faces the railway tracks, with access to the city itself being via the taxi rank at the back, on the other side.

BY BUS Brest is situated on the main transcontinental coach route and there are buses to all points of the international compass but, although this is a cheap option, the journey times are long and uncomfortable. The **bus station** [191 E2]

(*35 Mitskevicha Street;* ✆ *23 81 42;* e *av@brest.by; www.av.brest.by*) is situated in the middle of the city, 500m to the southeast of the railway station. There are four buses a day from Minsk and a one-way ticket costs around US$13. At least two buses a day arrive from Warsaw, a one-way ticket starting at US$25.

BY CAR There *should* be easy access by car on the main highway that crosses the border here. The Brest crossing is located at the Warsaw Bridge just out of town on the major pan-European highway but it is a place of some notoriety, for no other reason than the seemingly capricious nature of the guards. Unexpectedly long delays can be experienced, entirely without warning and apparently at the whim of the border guards on duty. Some of the tales told by travellers are approaching legend and waits of up to 12, 24 and even 36 hours have been reported. The average wait appears to be between two and six hours. It is rumoured that the guards are not immune to the odd monetary inducement to hasten the process, but this is no more than gossip and, in any event, is singularly not advised. Just sit tight and admire the view of a line of stationary and immobile vehicles snaking into the distance.

GETTING AROUND

There is no underground system in Brest, but the city centre is compact and most of the sights and facilities are within easy reach of each other. Cabs, buses and trolleybuses are all cheap, efficient, plentiful and easy to use.

Orientation is relatively easy. Apart from the fortress, many of the pre-war buildings are inevitably no longer standing and streets in the city centre were laid out in the trademark chequer-board style so favoured by post-war urban planners. The square in front of the train station is expansive and the large thoroughfare that leads out of it in a straight (southerly) line is Lenin Street, halfway along which can be found Lenin Square, where the old revolutionary continues to stand guard on his plinth, just across the street from the square itself, which is actually in the shape of a crescent. It has been pedestrianised and is attractively laid in bricks of different hues. This is the administrative centre of the city: the House of the Soviet, the offices of the regional and city executive committees and the regional office of the National Bank of the Republic are all to be found here. There is also St Christopher's Church. The tourist area of the city, where many of the shops, bars and restaurants are to be found, begins with the pedestrianised end of Pushkinskaya Street, which runs directly opposite Lenin's statue on the other side of the square. Three blocks to the east is Sovyetskaya Street, which is in the heart of the main shopping area. There are also many bars and street cafés here. The long process of pedestrianising Sovyetskaya itself is happily now complete, to match sections of other streets in the area, and this part of town is now pleasing on the eye. The entire street scene has been transformed by the addition of attractive lighting, paved areas and furniture. Most sites of interest are located within the compact centre, but the notable exception is the one thing that really is a 'must-see', the hero-fortress, which is located 2.5km away at the bottom of Masherova Avenue.

TOURIST INFORMATION

As highlighted previously, it is not always possible to access comprehensive tourist information in Belarus. How refreshing it is in this town, then, to happen upon a state tourism office and information centre inside the Hotel Intourist, at 15 Masherova Avenue (✆ *20 10 71;* e *tur_intourist@mail.ru; www.brestintourist.by;* ◷ *09.00–19.00 Mon–Fri, 09.00–13.00 &13.30–17.30 Sat*). Turn immediately right as you enter the

4

lobby and take the stairs in the corner to the first floor. What a find it is! The staff are extremely accommodating and only too pleased to help with bookings for guided excursions around the town, *oblast* or anywhere in the country. Excellent English is spoken and there is a good stock of tourist literature (in English) on the city and region. English-speaking guides are also on hand to lead any excursions and visits that you might arrange. Any visit to the city really should start here.

There is also a Brest Trans-Frontier Information Centre (*46 Sovyetskaya St;* ☎ *21 00 58;* e *infocentrbrest@mail.ru; www.tric.info;* ☉ *08.30–17.30 Mon–Fri*). This trans-border initiative was originally part of a European Union TACIS programme to increase co-operation and infrastructure integration in the region straddled by the border here. Primarily dealing with economic issues under the strap line 'contacts

Planyeta Rok 1

Korona Shopping Centre,
St Resurrection
Orthodox Cathedral

2

PIONYERSKAYA STREET

MITSEKYEVITSA STREET

PUSHKINSKAYA

STREET

Central
Market

23
15
13

17

8

GOGOLYA STREET

16

14

7
10
21

9

Belarus
Cinema

City Club

Regional Museum
of Ethnography

SOVYETSKAYA

MASHEROVA AVENUE

20

22

SHEVCHENKO BLVD

2

3

St Simeon
Orthodox
Cathedral

5
11

Univermag
Shopping
Complex

SOVYETSKAYA STREET

9

4

Evraopt
Shopping
Centre
12

N

Bradt

5

0   500m
0   500yds

without borders', it is also a useful source of local information. The website is a good start before you arrive.

Additionally, a great many national and local tourist agencies have offices in the city, with new ones appearing all the time. They will all be able to book local excursions for you. Before you leave home, you might find it useful to browse the site www.brest.by. Some pages are in English and the link to information relating to the Byelovezhskaya Puscha National Park is especially helpful. Best of all are the pages relating to the heroic fortress siege. Extremely well written, they tell the story in great detail, with some excellent photographs. There is also a large 'photo album' of numerous scenes around the city. Great works of photographic creative art they most certainly are not, but they do give you some idea of what to expect when you arrive.

UPMARKET

Hermitage (55 rooms: 36 dbls/twins, 12 studios, 3 junior suites, 2 luxe, 2 apts, with 1 room adapted for disabled use) 7 Chkalova St; ☏27 60 00; e hotel@hermitagehotel.by; www. hermitagehotel.by. Widely regarded as the best hotel in town & close to City Park & many of the sights, there's a touch of class & a high level of customer service here. The elegantly decorated bedrooms are spacious & well appointed. Facilities inc. excellent restaurant, bar, terrace, banqueting hall, karaoke club, 70-seater conference hall, hairdresser, spa, gym, tourist booking services, station transfers, ATM & secure parking. Themed events are also held here. **$$$$**

MID-RANGE

Belarus (89 rooms: 40 sgls, 35 dbls/twins, 11 luxe, 2 studios, 1 apt) 6 Shevchenko Bd; ☏22 16 48; e bresttourist@tut.by. Situated in a picturesque location close to the Mukhavyets River (45mins' walk from the bus & railway stations) & convenient for the Warsaw Bridge frontier crossing by road, this is a Soviet-style functional hotel with the usual facilities & little aesthetic appeal. In the course of refurbishment, don't go for the cheap option where the decorators have not yet been. Facilities inc. supervised parking on site, shop, currency-exchange facilities, games room, conference 'hall' with seating for 18, restaurant, café & bar. A casino & bowling alley are located next door. All major credit cards are accepted. **$$$**

Intourist (139 rooms: 69 sgls, 63 twins, plus 5 2-room suites & 2 apts) 15 Masherova Av; ☏20 09 50; e int@brest.by. Located on one of the city's main thoroughfares leading to the fortress & then out of town, so like the Belarus convenient for the Warsaw Bridge border crossing, it's also 25mins' walk from the bus & railway stations. A prime example of post-war Soviet urban planning, it is a charmless, high-rise concrete monolith, but is nonetheless functional & all basic needs are adequately catered for. There has been a significant make-over here but, as with the Hotel Belarus, don't be tempted to go for the cheap non-refurbished rooms. There is a cavernous restaurant, 2 bars (*one of them open ⏱ 24hrs*), banqueting hall, casino, massage room, hairdresser, currency exchange & an ATM in the lobby. On the 1st floor

is the city's excellent tourist information centre & travel agency. There is an extra charge for parking nearby in a secure area. All major credit cards are accepted. English is spoken here. **$$$**

Vesta (58 rooms: 29 sgls, 17 dbls/twins, 1 trpl, plus 11 suites) 16 Krupskaya St; ☏20 75 33; e hotelvesta@tut.by; www.hotelvesta.by. Centrally located in a peaceful neighbourhood not far from City Park, the concrete box exterior is not promising, but don't let this put you off. Inside, all is rather quaint & cosy. Significantly refurbished, much of it is fresh, if a little unexciting. If you can, get one of the older rooms, with faux wood panelling & 1920s-style décor. Facilities here are somewhat limited, though: there is a sauna, hairdresser, café, small 'banquet room' & 24hr lobby bar. All major credit cards are accepted. **$$$**

BUDGET

5 Kolyets ('5 Rings'; 21 rooms: 7 sgls, 14 dbls/twins) 9 Gogolya St; ☏20 84 95. Located within the football stadium at the Brest *oblast* sports complex & handy for all the sights in town, this is my preferred option for cheap & cheerful budget accommodation in Brest. Follow the signs from the stadium precinct to find the reception desk on the third floor. Staff are very friendly & the cost of the room is paid up front in cash. All is new & clean, spick & span & very basic, but it's fantastic value for money. Rooms are small but well appointed. B/fast is served in the small café. Dynamo Brest play premier league football at the stadium & if you're lucky there will be a home fixture while you're in town. A schedule of forthcoming matches is on the display board outside the ticket office. **$$**

Bug (72 rooms: 33 sgls, 33 dbls/twins, 6 luxe) 2 Lenina St; ☏23 61 70/64 17. Only 3 mins from the railway station on foot, this imposing building (named after the river, one hopes!) matches the station itself for faux grandeur, but despite the significant refurbishment in recent times it's all rather dark & gloomy inside, with old-style Soviet service matching the old-style Soviet décor. The restaurant here is unspectacular & b/fast not inc. in the price of your stay. There is also a hairdresser & currency exchange. It's another budget option in town, but it's without charm & the proximity to the station is its only true redeeming factor. **$$**

Brest is a cosmopolitan city with a direct and very large window overlooking the West. The diversity of food emporia reflects this, with eateries in significant supply particularly in and around the pedestrianised area of Sovyetskaya Street. Most establishments are of a similar standard in terms of quality and cost, so do experiment. Head and shoulders above the rest is my very favourite restaurant in all Belarus, so do try to pay the Jules Verne a visit and show the guys there your copy of this book! Then to get the ball rolling for alternatives, look out for the following:

RESTAURANTS

✖ **Hermitage** 7 Chkalova St; ✆27 60 11; ⏰ 07.00–11.00 (b/fast), noon–23.00 (lunch & dinner), 07.00–03.00 (drinks) daily. The restaurant at the fine hotel of the same name, it's open to non-residents & is well worth a visit. Staff are helpful & friendly, the varied menu is of high quality & the overall experience here is a very positive one. Just bear in mind that it's popular for weddings & special events, so check first before you go. **$$$$**

✖ **Jules Verne** 29 Gogolya St (at the junction with Karla Marksa St); ✆23 67 17; ⏰ noon–midnight daily. My personal favourite in town & indeed, the whole country, this restaurant is a joy. As you might expect from the name, the décor is pure Victoriana, with dark wood panelling, mock oil lamps & sepia etchings on the walls. But it's all very tastefully done & the food is excellent. Self-billed as offering 'world cuisine', northern European (particularly German & Scandinavian) & Indian & Thai cuisine are on offer in a comfortable & relaxed setting. The menu is available in English & there is even a special menu for children. First-class service & very professional, smiley staff complement the experience. On my first visit with Olya in 2007 we chose Indian & my chicken massaman with vegetables & garlic chilli nan was outstanding. Seven years later in spring 2014 I chose mutton biryani & cauliflower gobi, which was exquisite. I had with me the bill & the notes I wrote from that first visit, which I shared with the staff to their great amusement! There's also a 30% discount from noon to 16.00. This place gets better with age & an evening here is highly recommended. **$$$$**

✖ **La Provence** 50 Sovyetskaya St; ⏰ 11.00–23.00 daily. A decent Belarusian attempt at French cuisine (others available) in a decent location. There's a 15% reduction in the bill from noon to 15.00. **$$$$**

✖ **U Ozero** On the shore of the Upper Lake, Brest City Park; ✆23 57 63; ⏰ noon–23.00 daily. In a lovely spot right by the side of the largest ornamental lake in City Park, the décor is faux Belarusian village but it's done well. This café nestles among the trees & in the summer you can sit on the terrace sipping chilled Baltika beer as you watch your shashlik cooking on the barbecue. There is a wood fire indoors for the winter, when all is cosy & inviting. The menu has a wide variety of cuisine, inc. traditional Russian dishes. The food & service are good. **$$$$**

✖ **Pizzeria** Pushkinskaya St (just beyond the junction with Sovyetskaya St); ⏰ 11.00–23.00 daily. Another favourite of mine is this basement hang-out. It's nothing special but the pizzas are good & unless you know it's there you probably wouldn't venture in, so it's a great place to escape tourists & the hustle & bustle of the city. Olya & I found it while researching for the 1st edition. I've returned a number of times since & I've never been disappointed. To find it, go to the Café Zyevs (see page 194). It's right next door. **$$$**

✖ **Zio Pepe** 4 Shevchenko; ✆20 50 52; ⏰ noon–05.00 daily. Standard pasta & pizza restaurant, but it's cheap & open all night, largely because it shares the premises with a nightclub & casino. There is also a bar. **$$$**

CAFÉS

To complement the project to pedestrianise much of the tourist part of the city centre, a number of pleasing cafés have opened in recent times. All of the following are well worth a visit for a coffee while you amble, but you can also get a decent meal in most of them too.

🖳 **Art** 53 Sovyetskaya St; ✆23 22 22; ⏰ 10.00–23.30 daily. Very popular with young people & in a good location close to the monument to the history of the city – a good spot to watch the world go by.

🍴**Golden Coffee**   34 Sovyetskaya St; ☎27 90 31; ℯ info@goldencoffee.by; www.brest. goldencoffee.by; ◷ 08.00–01.00 daily. It's a chain café but these outlets are always popular wherever they are, & it's in a great location.

🍴**Pizza Smile**   11 Warsaw Highway; ☎50 11 40 (395 59 55 for deliveries); ◷ 11.00–23.00 daily. If you're on the road & simply in need of calories & sustenance by way of a pit stop en route through Brest, then this is an OK bet for pizza & sushi, either to eat in or take away. It's located on the site of the Evraopt shopping centre.

🍴**Shokoladka**   22 Pushkinskaya St; ☎21 94 95; ◷ 09.00–23.00 daily. In the same spot on Pushkinskaya as Café Zyevs & my favourite pizzeria, this one is good for coffee & desserts.

🍴**Stary Gorod**   103 Kirova St; ☎21 53 32; ℯ oldcity@mail.ru; www.oldcitybrest.by; ◷ 11.00–23.00 daily. Good food, pleasant ambience & relaxed service in a cosy setting.

🍴**Times**   30 Sovyetskaya St; ☎20 71 76; ◷ 08.30–23.00 Mon–Fri, 11.00–23.00 Sat & Sun. In a prime location, the outside terrace is a great spot for people-watching. The food (European) & service are excellent here & it's popular with locals. Fluent English is spoken & prices are very reasonable. It opens early on w/days & I hear it's a good bet for b/fast. One of my correspondents describes it as 'a little slice of Soho'.

🍴**Venezia**   5 Internatsionalnaya St; ☎20 33 49; ℯ kafevenezia@mail.ru; www.italbrest.com; ◷ noon–midnight daily. One of the most popular of Brest's cafés; good Italian cuisine is served in a very pleasing setting. There are also play areas inside & out for children.

🍴**Verdi**   112 Sovyetskaya St; ☎22 11 70; ◷ 10.00–22.00 daily. I hear this is a decent Italian café. I have yet to go but it's reputed to serve the best desserts in the city. Let me know what you think.

🍴**Zyevs**   20 Pushkinskaya St; ☎61 98 98; ◷ 11.00–22.00 daily. Next to the Pizzeria (see page 193). Excellent coffee bar.

BARS

Brest has a wide choice of bars. The following is but a small selection, & there will be others I haven't yet tried out that are equally worthy of mention. And not only do the upmarket & mid-range hotels listed on page 192 also have bars available to non-residents, but most of the cafés listed have a bar area for drinking as well. All of the bars are open from late morning until midnight or beyond.

🍷**Pub House**   Gogolya St; ◷ 10.00–01.00 daily. Absolutely ideal for a relaxing drink after a sumptuous meal at the Restaurant Jules Verne opposite (see *Where to eat*, page 193), this is a cosy, quiet & comfortable bar. Used by locals rather than tourists & neither busy nor empty on any of my visits, it's a great place to relax & chat. My favourite in town.

🍷**Moskva**   17 Masherova Av; ☎20 43 23/10 93; ◷ 09.00–02.00 daily. Right next door to the Hotel Intourist, it looks classy on a cursory glance, but it has always been empty when I've been there. The menu is not unappealing, but it's all just a little tired & sad. Still, if you're staying at the Intourist & feeling weary or not particularly adventurous, it will serve a purpose.

🍷**Vizhavi**   50 Sovyetskaya St; ☎23 05 50/14 94; ◷ 11.00–23.00 daily. Located right in the heart of town, this is a good place to stop off for a drink in the middle of your sightseeing or shopping. It also does the job of kick-starting a night on the tiles.

ENTERTAINMENT AND NIGHTLIFE

Clubs do not open until around 20.00, but you can dance the night away until at least 04.00.

CLUBS

☆ **City Club**   [191 E3] 73 Sovyetskaya St; ☎94 29 42; ℯ info@cityclub.by; www.cityclub.by; ◷ 22.00–05.00 Wed–Sun. All of the usual club facilities are on offer here & it's very popular with the locals. Centrally located in the heart of the town, so it's a decent bet for a late night out.

☆ **Planyeta Rok**   [191 H1] 48 Pionyerskaya St; ☎46 64 83; ℯ info@planetrock.by; www.planetrock. by; ◷ 19.00–05.00 Wed–Sun. As befits the name, this is a loud, brassy venue with thumping music as a constant backdrop. Relaxing it isn't, but it's ideal if you're in the mood to burn off some calories on the dance floor with gassy beer for refreshment. There's also a café & games room. The location, on the northeastern fringe of the city centre, is not ideal. ☆ **Zio Pepe** [191 F3] 4 Shevchenko St; 📞 20 50 52; 🕐 20.00–04.00 Wed–Sun. The nightclub & casino arm of the Italian restaurant (see page 193) has little to complement your pizza there. Standard club fare.

SHOPPING

Look no further than the central area bounded by Lenina, Gogolya, Kyubisheva and Mitskevicha streets for most of your purchasing requirements. Sovyetskaya Street runs north–south through it. Most of the best of the city's stores and boutiques are here and the convenience of a single, easily navigable location is too good to miss. On Sovyetskaya itself (on the left heading south, just beyond the Church of St Nikolai) is a children's store selling clothes and toys. Elsewhere in this area are many outlets selling fine sweets, presents, souvenirs, fashionable clothes and beauty products. To recharge your batteries, there are many bars and cheap eateries where you can obtain fast but tasty food and refreshments.

If you're in need of everyday essentials and everything under one roof, there are hypermarkets run by the chain retailer **Evraopt** at 11 Warsaw Highway, 8 Komsomolskaya Street, 44 Laktyonova Street, 6A Yasyenevaya Street and 5 Gvardeiskaya Street. As an alternative, try the **Korona Shopping Centre** [191 H2] at 210 Moskovskaya Street. I also have it on good authority from two reliable sources, which include my friend Olya, that the **Univermag shopping complex** [191 E3] on Masherova Avenue, 200m east of the Hotel Intourist, is an excellent source of good-value shopping. Clothes, beauty products, traditional souvenirs and other 'present material' are all available here at very competitive prices, Olya tells me. There is also the excellent **Central Market** on Pushkinskaya Street, with a wide range of fresh produce and other goods.

OTHER PRACTICALITIES

Currency-exchange bureaux are easy to find in this border town and, as it is a free economic zone, foreign currency is in plentiful supply. A useful tip is to have not only Belarusian roubles and US dollars with you, but also small supplies of euros and Polish zloty. After all, Poland is only a short walk away! There are lots of **banks** and **ATMs** all over town. There is also an excellent **post office** [190 D2] at the top of Pushkinskaya Street (at the Lenin Street end), on the left-hand side as you enter Lenin Square.

WHAT TO SEE AND DO

BREST FORTRESS (БРЭСЦКАЯ КРЭПАСЦЬ / БРЕСТСКАЯ КРЕПОСТЬ) [190 A3]

(*Masherova Av;* 📞 *20 03 65/00 12;* 🕐 *08.00–midnight daily;* e *brest-fortress@yandex. ru; www.brest-fortress.by; site admission free*) The largest and most popular visitor attraction in the city, a visit here is one of the truly 'not to be missed' events during the whole of your stay in Belarus, let alone your limited time in Brest. To do it full justice, you will need to give yourself at least four hours to see everything there is to see. The walk here from the city centre will take around 45 minutes; alternatively, the local bus service stops at points along Masherova Avenue, the main road running straight and true past the Hotel Intourist.

The location was very well chosen by the planners, because the complex holds a strategically important position at the confluence of the Bug and Mukhavyets rivers. It occupies a huge site, its diameter being around 1km, although much of the outer defence line was obliterated in the terrible fighting that took place here in

1941. The stronghold within occupies a small island in the centre of the river, which is connected to the remainder of the structure by three small bridges.

Construction began in 1838 and took four years. There is one single piece of architecture still standing in its midst from pre-1838 Brest, when the town centre stood here, the beautiful **Byzantine Church of St Nikolai** (not to be mistaken for its namesake on Sovyetskaya Street). It was severely damaged during the 1941 siege and reduced almost to rubble. While the exterior has been mostly renovated, its golden dome being a particularly striking feature, much remains to be done to the interior, although services are regularly held here. For now, the walls are bare brick and plaster (there are neither friezes nor murals), but this throws into even sharper relief the beautiful icons that are mounted in many places. And right in the centre of the church is its most beautiful feature: a huge golden chandelier, delicately suspended from the ceiling almost to head height, adorned with icons and ceremonial *rushniki*. As you pass through the main door, turn immediately right to view the small but informative pictorial display in black and white that reveals the church at various stages of splendour and misery through its cyclical periods of construction and destruction. It is something of an oddity to find such a sanctuary of reverence and piety in this location, when all around speaks of conflict and bloodshed. Devotional objects such as small icons and candles are available for purchase inside in the right-hand corner immediately after you enter.

The fortress had an important defensive role to play in World War I, after which it was used mainly for housing soldiers in the 1920s and 1930s. In 1941, it came to the attention of the world during the first six weeks of Operation Barbarossa, when the Nazis threw everything they could at it to break the resistance of the defending forces. The Germans took the entire town in the first few hours of their attack. Around 90% of the city was destroyed in a furious and relentless barrage of withering artillery fire. The fortress suffered severe damage too, but those garrisoned inside held out. The Nazis turned the focus of their strategy from attack to attrition and so it was that the siege began. Elsewhere, the German advance eastward was gathering pace by the day. Six weeks later, they had almost taken Smolensk, deep into Russian territory, before the resistance of the defenders of the fortress was finally broken. Much of it was in ruins and only a handful of men had survived but, in the context of the wider conflict, an invaluable job had been done. Citizens all over the USSR had been inspired by the daily news bulletins they received from the front line, telling of the heroism of the small band of Soviet troops striving valiantly against their Nazi aggressors. Stalin had been given just enough time to plan his campaign, so that when he issued his rallying call to every citizen of the Union to defend the Motherland to the death, the vast empire at his command swung into action in a patriotic fervour of almost spiritual intensity. Little wonder, then, that the 1939–45 global conflict is still referred to throughout the countries of the former USSR as the Great Patriotic War. At the end of hostilities, the decision was taken not to rebuild the fortress, but instead to turn it into a huge shrine, a giant monument to commemorate what transpired here. Exactly the same thought process informed the concept and design of the deeply affecting state memorial at Khatyn (see pages 176–8).

A walk around the complex Bear all of the history in mind as you enter the complex. The approach along Masherova Avenue is long, straight and slightly downhill, with sculptures in the shape and colour of the Soviet flag lining the route, upon each of which is embossed an image of the head and shoulders of one of the defending troops. On the left is a memorial to the heroes of the siege. Also on this side and adding nothing to the scene is an ugly and incongruous factory with an enormous red-and-white striped chimney, while on the right is the city's railway museum. At various points along Masherova Avenue and particularly in the vicinity of this museum, enormous works of construction are under way, both residential and commercial. There have also been massive road improvements hereabouts, the main border crossing at Warsaw Bridge being not far away. At the bottom of the avenue there used to be a huge car park for the fortress complex with space for over a thousand vehicles. On my first visit in 2007 it contained six cars. That car park is now much reduced in size to accommodate the expansion of the highway. As you cross the new road and begin the long walk towards the fortress, your eye is drawn to the first iconic sight, over 100m in front of you, where an enormous concrete block, grey and sombre, rests on the remains of the outer wall, into which has been cut a gigantic star. This is the entrance. Just inside is a small booth, where explanatory information in English is now available, and at least one of the staff on duty speaks faultless English. As you walk through, tape recordings are playing of the wireless broadcast that first broke the news of the invasion, laid over stirring military music and the sounds of battle. Coming out of the tunnel and another 150m ahead, the eye is immediately drawn to a massive, glistening bayonet obelisk, 100m high, near to which is an astonishing concrete sculpture (entitled *Courage*), into the top of which has been carved the head of a grim-faced defender. It is almost 34m high and the reverse side has carvings depicting various scenes from the heroic defence. At the foot of the obelisk is the inevitable eternal flame, guarded round the clock by four teenagers from the Corps of Pioneers. The vaguely comical ceremony of the changing of the guard does little to enhance the sanctity of this hallowed place; and if, like me, you ever witnessed the same process at Lenin's mausoleum in Moscow during the days of the Soviet Union, you will understand what I mean here. Next to the flame are three rows of symbolic tombstones bearing the names of the fallen heroes.

All of this awaits in the middle distance. For now, take a slow stroll along the paved pathway, past a row of tanks on the left, all the while admiring the beauty and the many species of tree that line the walkway on the edges of the river beyond on both sides. The willows are particularly beautiful. As you reach the end of the path and enter the circle within, pause for a moment to look around. Immediately to your left is a grim but moving sculpture, starkly entitled *Thirst*. It depicts a soldier, near to exhaustion or even death, lying on his side and half crawling, his right hand holding a machine gun and his left imploringly holding out a helmet for water. Legend has it that this depicts the last soldier left in the garrison when it was finally taken. He (and the handful of his comrades who remained) had gone without food or water for 40 days, so the story goes, and when the Nazis finally broke the resistance of the last survivors, so moved were they by this man's endurance and heroism, that they let him go. This tale may have been embellished in the telling over the years but, like all such stories, much of it is likely to be true.

Behind and all the way around this inner section lies an incomplete circle of two-storey buildings, the former barracks, most of which are still intact. Those to the left house a number of galleries for art and literature (⊕ *10.00–18.00*). The work of individual artists and writers is frequently on display here. In front of these bullet-riddled buildings are displays of military equipment. The centre ground is taken by the sculpture *Courage*, with the eternal flame, obelisk and symbolic tombstones. If all of this were not enough to paint a bleak tableau, piped choral music, sombre and doleful, plays constantly at a number of locations. Behind is the Church of St Nikolai and to the right, the brick remains of the **White Palace** can be seen, with most of the building's exterior intact. Entrance into the shell is forbidden, however, presumably for reasons of safety. It was here that Lenin pulled off his masterstroke of political expediency in 1918, when he negotiated the Treaty of Brest-Litovsk with the invading Germans. Further to the right is the **Defence of Brest Fortress Museum** (✆ *20 03 65;* ⊕ *09.00–18.00 Tue–Sun; admission BYR25,000*), which is well worth a visit. Neatly arranged exhibits tell the story of the construction and history of the fortress, as well as graphically depicting the conditions of the siege. Sadly, explanatory information is provided in Russian only, but non-Russian speakers will still get a good impression of its history.

The White Palace represents one of the entrances to the central stronghold and a small bridge behind it leads to the final small island at the centre. When you get there, it is worth gazing around you; the view of the battle-scarred red-brick **Kholmsky Gate** is one of the iconic images that you may have seen in books.

You should now take time to retrace your steps back through the entrance, pausing *en route* to look at the many plaques positioned throughout the site, on which a date appears in large letters, followed by a brief description of the key events at each location (sadly in Russian only). And for refreshment and reflection, turn left immediately after you pass the museum and walk down a short but beautiful tree-lined avenue to the Café Citadel (⊕ *10.00–23.00 daily*), housed in a series of vault-like rooms in a low, red-brick building; soft drinks, alcoholic beverages and snacks are available cheaply. Expect to find more staff there than customers. Toilets are also available here.

Do remember that the grounds of the complex are open until midnight. A promenade here at dusk is particularly atmospheric. And to prepare you for your visit before you leave home, spend some time on the English pages of the excellent website (details on page 195). It's packed with contextual and historical detail.

MUSEUMS AND HISTORICAL SITES
Beryestye Archaeological Museum [190 B4] (✆ *20 55 54;* ⊕ *Nov–Feb 10.00–17.00 Wed–Sun, Mar–Oct 11.00–18.00 Wed–Sun, last entry 30min before closing; admission BYR12,000, with extra charge of BYR5,000 to take photographs*) Situated south across the river from the fortress and with access from inside it, this large modern building was constructed around an excavation site. Now open again after extensive renovations, the vast single-storey canopied hall is home to more than 40,000 artefacts in 14 galleried exhibit areas from the 11th to the 14th centuries, all relating to the original settlement here a thousand or so years ago. Most were discovered in the course of the extensive excavations that have been ongoing for 40 years and, in one or two locations near to the museum, current archaeological digs can still be seen. The exhibits line the walls of the hall, while the enormity of the floor space is taken up with a sunken reconstruction of the original town as it stood in the second half of the 13th century. In total, the remains of more than 30 buildings are available for viewing and there's also a scale model of how it would have looked when first constructed. All in all, this museum offers a welcome respite from the sombre experience of cruel and bloody modern warfare that has assaulted you thus far in this place. There's also a souvenir stall by the ticket desk near the entrance. But do tread carefully around here and do not stray on to any path other than to the museum. After all, you are literally on the border with NATO at this point! On my last visit I went for a modest wander and it didn't take me long to come up against barbed wire and high fences, with the remains of an old watchtower from the days of the Soviet Union close by. I backed off immediately when a police car appeared from nowhere.

Brest Railway Museum [190 C3] (✆ *26 37 64;* ⊕ *Nov–Apr 11.00–17.00 Tue–Sun, May–Oct 10.00–18.00 Tue–Sun; admission BYR7,800*) On the left-hand side of

Masherova Avenue as you leave the fortress, 200m beyond the car park and across the new road, is the open-air railway museum. Opened in 2002, 48 historical steam locomotives from the 1930s and 1940s are on display here, together with a staff carriage dating from 1915. All of them are in full working order and have been beautifully maintained. The iconic Soviet red star is everywhere to be seen and there are some splendid photo opportunities. Guided tours for up to 20 people can be arranged in advance for an extra charge. The grounds and exhibits are frequently used for shooting films and as the location for festivals.

Museum of Brest History [190 D2] (*3 Levanyevskaya St;* ✆ *23 16 25;* ⏰ *10.00–18.00 Wed–Sun; admission BYR10,000*) As might be expected, artefacts and exhibits tell the story of the city through the ages, providing useful background information for the student of local history. And it's in a quaint building in a pleasant location.

Regional Museum of Ethnography [191 E3] (*60 Karla Marksa St;* ✆ *23 91 16;* ⏰ *10.00–18.00 Tue–Sun; admission BYR12,000*) Linked to the History Museum and located in a charming historic building (a 19th-century former hotel and theatre), the focus here is more on society and culture. There are extensive collections of artefacts from the region, rare books and archival antiquities.

Museum of Confiscated Art [190 D3] (*39 Lenina St;* ✆ *20 41 95;* ⏰ *10.00–17.00 Tue–Sun; admission BYR12,000*) Known locally as the 'Museum of Salvaged Artistic Valuables', this quirky concept has on display rare pieces of fine art from around the world. The factor of added interest is that they were all confiscated from would-be art thieves by customs officials at the nearby border! Some really interesting items are displayed here.

CHURCHES AND CATHEDRALS
St Christopher's Church of Exaltation of the Holy Cross [190 D1] This church was constructed in 1856 from the bricks of Catholic churches and monasteries that previously existed in the Old City. Within is the renowned 17th-century icon *Our Lady of Berestye*, richly decorated in gilt and precious stones. Services are held in both Polish and Belarusian. The acoustics of the building are of the very finest quality. This archetypical example of Catholic architecture is located just off Lenin Square, where the man himself remains on duty, ever alert. A nice contrast of belief and ideology.

St Nikolai's Church [191 E2] Situated on the northeastern side of Sovyetskaya Street (close to the junction with Mitskevicha Street), this delightful church is one of the most beautiful in the whole of the city. Built between 1904 and 1906 in the pseudo-Russian style to commemorate the end of the Russo-Japanese war, it is a stunning example of Orthodox décor, both outside and in. The deep blue cupolas decorated with gold stars are particularly striking, especially in the sunshine. Closed during the time of the Soviet Union, it was only restored and returned to its parish in the 1990s.

St Simeon Orthodox Cathedral [191 E3] This lovely example of 16th-century Orthodox architecture is situated on the south side of Masherova Avenue, right next to the Hotel Intourist and on the way to the fortress; its exterior is lime green in hue. *Very* lime green. You may be reminded of a highly decorated cake at first glance. Much of the current construction dates from 1865 and this is the only place of worship in the city that has never once closed its doors, whatever the prevailing circumstances outside. Inside and right of centre as you walk in is a tomb that is said to contain some of the earthly remains of the city's Father Superior and martyr Aphanasye, who was tortured to death for his Orthodox beliefs in 1648. His statue was erected and sanctified just outside the grounds of the cathedral in 2005.

St Resurrection Orthodox Cathedral [191 H2] On the way out of the city in an easterly direction, at the junction of Partizansky Avenue and Moskovskaya Street, stands the imposing St Resurrection Orthodox Cathedral. Its silver domes are particularly eye-catching. Built only in 2003, its altar was sanctified by His Holiness Alexei the Second, Patriarch of Moscow and All Russia. Below ground level is a special vault to honour the renowned icon *Our Lady of Kazan*.

JEWISH BREST After the privations of World War I, the few who survived in the Jewish community found themselves living in terrible conditions. Many were homeless and took refuge in the city's synagogues for shelter. In 1921, a relief programme initiated by American philanthropist Felix Warburg financed the construction of a new Brest suburb to accommodate homeless Jewish war veterans, their families and the many orphans of the community. Close by was a large Jewish cemetery that had been established in the 1830s. During the Great Patriotic War the Jewish community suffered abject brutality. Before the 1941 invasion by the Nazis the population of Brest was 52,000, half of whom were Jews. After hostilities ended only 19 Jews remained. The cemetery was desecrated and vandalised by the Nazis, then after the war it was ransacked by the Communists, who stole the gravestones and used them in construction. Some of the stones were used by ordinary people of the city to pave gardens at their homes and their dachas. In recent times, news of the discovery of some of these stones began to reach the ears of the Jewish community. Now over 1,200 of them have been recovered and are presently stored under the arches of the hero-fortress.

There has also been another recent discovery that has created significant interest within the community: some of the original Warburg houses are still standing, though their future is an uncertain one. Already two have been bulldozed to make way for a new supermarket and only five remain on Pyervy Minsky Lane. During the works of demolition and the digging of the new foundations, many gravestones were unearthed, while the site of the old Jewish cemetery is now a disused sports field and running track. All that remains is a hidden plaque marking the burial site of the great Rabbi Josef Dov Soloveitchik, from the Rabbinic dynasty that gave rise to the Brisk Yeshiva that exists today in Jerusalem. There are plans within the Brest community to create a memorial at the cemetery, but there are issues about the need for permission from the authorities and also funding. The clock is ticking for this important slice of Jewish history in Brest. A model of the original Warburg colony is displayed at the city's tiny **Holocaust Museum** (*22 Gogolya St*). Small it may be, but it provides a very informative history of Jewish Brest. Among the exhibits are Nazi records revealing that, on one single day in 1941, almost 17,000 Jews were murdered. North of Gogolya Street on Kubysheva Street stands the **bust of Menachem Begin**, the sixth Prime Minister of Israel, who was born in Brest in 1913. On a wall nearby is a plaque acknowledging that the building here was once the school he attended as a boy. Indeed, within the city boundaries stand a number of **Jewish memorials** at key locations of historical significance. Further information is available from organisations The Together Plan and Dialog (see opposite and page 107 for contact details).

Perhaps the most poignant site of all is the location of the foundation stones of the **original synagogue** within the curtilage of the **Belarus cinema** (*62 Sovyetskaya*

St). From the outside it is still possible to see the shape of the original walls because incredibly, the cinema was built *around* the synagogue! And inside, the arch of the original building still forms part of the architecture of the new. Enter the cinema through the main entrance and go down the stairs as you would if going to use the conveniences. You may have to explain to the attendant that the usual fee is not appropriate in this case. Then down in the basement area you will find row upon row of the original foundation stones. There is no plaque to mark their significance.

For further information on anything concerning Jewish Brest, to arrange access to memorial sites, to meet members of the current community or to arrange a museum visit or local tours with Russian- or English-speaking guides, contact British sustainable development charity **The Together Plan** (see page 107 for contact details) or Belarusian NGO **Dialog** (☏ *+375 (29) 627 34 00;* e *dialogorganisation@gmail.com*).

PARKS AND RECREATION
Brest City Park [190 C2] Originally laid out by Russian soldiers who were stationed near here in 1906, the park is only ten minutes' walk from the railway station on the right-hand side of Lenin Avenue. The original area of 4ha has been redesigned and significantly expanded to some 50ha. It reopened to visitors on 1 May 2006 and, not unsurprisingly for a former Soviet republic, its official title is now 'First of May Culture and Entertainment Park'. It is the largest in the city and a beautiful place to walk and meander, with dozens of species of trees that are not normally to be found in this part of Europe. There are also two delightful ornamental ponds, called the Upper and Lower lakes, which are connected by a canal through which water lazily flows. Newly built bridges of decorative iron span the canal, with another bridge linking the island in the centre of the Upper Lake to the shore. Two fountains complement the overall ambience. There are also tennis courts and many attractions for children. To complete your self-restoration, visit the lovely café U Ozero ('By the Lake'). When refreshed and relaxed, try your luck in the amusement park, listen to a performance at the open-air concert stage, or perhaps visit the large disco club (or then again, perhaps not!). Many refreshment kiosks are also situated throughout the park.

Sovyetskaya Street and its environs When I first visited Brest in 2007, works of pedestrianisation along Sovyetskaya and the streets off it where in full swing. Subsequent visits always saw progress, and I'm happy to report that everything is now pretty much done. That's not to say, of course, that the city's planners won't have new ideas to enhance the environment further. It's an attractive sight and a fine place for meandering, with lots of appealing street furniture. At the same time though, there's a real sense that this is a frontier town. The ambience is decidedly Western, which I guess is purely a matter of geography. There are countless numbers of bars and flashy shops, with money, money, money everywhere to be seen. After all, the European Union is literally a short walk away. Everything on Sovyetskaya speaks of capital and the West. When I was last here I found myself a little morose at the extent to which Western commercialism is steadily subsuming much of the old. I turned on to Pushkina Street where I saw a little old lady, arms weighed down with tatty old carrier bags. She was sorting through the rubbish in the gleaming new bins. Something of a metaphor, I suspect. At the junction with Gogolya Street is a small square where you will find the attractive **millennium sculpture**, with tablets at the base displaying summaries of key events in the city's history. Just above these tablets are attractive friezes depicting those events. From here, look to spot the cinema built around the **old synagogue** (see opposite).

FESTIVALS If you find yourself in Brest at the end of July, look out for the **city's birthday celebrations.** The official date is the 28th, but festivities take place over a number of days, culminating in the main event on the final Sunday of the month. Activities include parades of revellers in fancy dress, particularly knights of old, street theatre, concerts and sports events. Visitors come from all over the country to watch and take part, as the whole city swings into party mood in a dazzling display of colour, light and sound.

Then in October, Sovyetskaya Street is the scene for the **Autumn Fair**, a celebration to give thanks for the bounties of the harvest. The thoroughfare overflows with an abundance of natural produce, in a symbolic display of the enduring relationship between the people and the land.

OUTSIDE BREST

PINSK (ПІНСК / ПИНСК) Pinsk is the ancient capital of Polyesye, with a history enveloped in mysteries and mists. Its appeal and significance over the centuries have been shaped by the geographical location of the town. Formerly surrounded by swampland, it's little wonder that it has always been called, a little disparagingly, 'the land of woods, bogs and fogs'. But its strategic position, traversed by the Pripyat River and at the confluence of the Pinya and Strumen, compensated for this and it quickly gained power and influence as a major stopping-off point along the ancient north–south and east–west trade routes. Nowadays, it is a town with a population of over 128,000 and its significance as a fertile centre of agriculture is assured. There is also a small but specialist industry here manufacturing boats that sail the local rivers.

History The historical settlement of Pinesk, named after the Pina River that flows through the modern town, was first established over 900 years ago. This makes it one of the oldest Slavic settlements in the country. In strategic terms, it held an uneasy position between warring principalities. Although declaredly neutral, its sympathies were with the Novogrudok princes, and not surprisingly it was taken under their patronage in 1320 and subsumed within the Grand Duchy of Lithuania. In 1569, after the creation of the mighty Polish-Lithuanian Commonwealth, its strategic importance was recognised when it became the administrative centre of the province of Brest. Then in 1581, this status was further enhanced when the town was granted rights of self-determination and government under Magdeburg Law. Its significance and influence continued to grow exponentially as it developed into a large residential settlement. Only the commonwealth's capital Wilno (now Vilnius) was a more important town.

But the period 1640–1706 was a time of abject misery for the townspeople. Successive invasions and sackings on the part of Cossacks, Poles, Ukrainians and Russians decimated the population, destroyed much of the town's architecture and wiped out the community's infrastructure. Miraculously and in spite of almost relentless conflict, the city not only survived as a settlement, but also managed to flourish. From 1793 until 1939, it came under the jurisdiction of first the Russian Empire, then Poland after the Polish-Soviet war and finally the Soviet Union. At the outbreak of World War II, the Jewish community comprised over 90% of the town's total population and, during the tyranny of the Nazi occupation from 1941 to 1944, all were interned in concentration camps, most of them never to return. Records are incomplete, but it is believed that as many as 30,000 Pinsk Jews perished during 'the final solution', including 10,000 in just one day. It was liberated by the Red Army and returned to Soviet ownership in 1944, before finally coming under the jurisdiction of the Republic of Belarus in 1991, upon the creation of the new state.

Where to stay and what to eat There are several hotels and restaurants in town. The largest is the **Pripyat Hotel, Restaurant and Café Complex** (*229 rooms: 107 sgls, 103 dbls, 19 trpls, plus 8 luxury suites, with 1 room adapted for disabled use; 31 Dnyeprovskaya Flotilla St;* \ *35 96 33;* e *pripyat_pinsk@tut.by;* **$$**). As might be expected, it's a large, multi-storey concrete edifice that is archetypically Soviet, though the location is lovely, with delightful views across the nearby park and the river. It is located on the bank of the Pina River, east of the St Francis Monastery. Facilities include a restaurant (⊕ *07.00–01.00 for b/fast, lunch & dinner;* **$$$**), bar, open-air café, disco, ATM, conference room, business services and unattended car parking. There is also a helpful tourist office, from where tours can be booked. The railway station is 3.5km away and the bus station 4km. For eating, I hear that **Taverna Kafe** (*14 Korzha St;* \ *32 29 50;* ⊕ *noon–23.00 daily;* **$$**) serves excellent shashlik. There's a pleasant outdoor terrace if the weather is good, while inside the décor is of rustic wooden design.

What to see The best way to make the most of a visit here will be on an organised tour from Minsk or Brest with one of the state tourist agencies. There is much to see. Two of the most interesting visitor attractions can be found within walking distance of each other, not far from the banks of the Pina River. The first of these is the **St Francis Monastery and the Assumption of the Blessed Virgin Roman Catholic Church**, constructed between 1712 and 1730. Founded in 1396, this was one of the oldest religious sites in the Grand Duchy of Lithuania. The original wooden church was looted and burned many times before the Baroque structure of stone that replaced it was completed in 1730. Inside are seven ornate altars, together with myriad sculptures and carvings, all the work of master craftsman Jan Schmitt. There are also several beautiful paintings and frescoes. In the grounds is a belfry constructed in 1817.

On the other side of the road bridge (but on the same bank) is the **Jesuit Collegium,** built between 1635 and 1648. It is an imposing three-storied building, with Baroque and Renaissance features, walls that are 2m thick and impressive vaulted ceilings. In its day, it was an educational institution for both religious and secular teaching. The crypt contains the relics of the Jesuit martyr Andrei Babolya, who was murdered by Cossacks in 1657 and canonised in 1853. The library was emptied of its valuable collection of works in 1940, in anticipation of war. They were taken to Leningrad and have never been returned. Today the building houses the **Belarus Polyesye Museum** (*22 Lenin Sq;* \ *35 84 02;* ⊕ *10.00–18.00 Tue–Sun; admission BYR8,500*).

There is also a more modern structure worthy of a visit at the junction of Gorky and Pervomayskaya streets, north of the river. It is the **Consistory and the Resurrection Slovuschy Orthodox Church.** A wooden church built in 1668 originally stood on this site, before the stone building that replaced it in 1778 was destroyed during the Great Patriotic War. After the war, a cinema was built here, but the ground was subsequently reconsecrated and a new church built in 1995. Its black domes are especially striking, particularly under snow.

BYELOVEZHSKAYA PUSCHA STATE NATIONAL PARK AND BIOSPHERE RESERVE (НАЦЫЯНАЛЬНЫ ПАРК БЕЛАВЕЖСКАЯ ПУШЧА / НАЦИОНАЛЬНЫЙ ПАРК БЕЛОВЕЖСКАЯ ПУЩА) (*Kamenyuky, Kamenets district, Brest region;* \ *+375 1631 56 6 56;* e *npbpby@rambler.ru; www.npbp.brest.by*) First established as a national park in 1939 (although a 'park' has existed here since the Middle Ages), it joined the list of UNESCO World Heritage Sites on 14 December 1992, then in 1993 it was granted the status of Biosphere Reserve, affording unique opportunities for specialist ecological study. There are conference and library facilities here, together with accommodation for up to a hundred visiting scientists.

Today, the park is an integral and important feature of around 1,700km² of ancient primeval forest within Belarusian borders, although the woodland stretches across the border into Poland, which jointly administers the park with Belarus. This is all that now remains of a vast canopy that once covered the whole of the huge northern European plain, the former home and playground of Polish princes and Russian tsars. In fact, the last private owners of the forest were the tsars of the Russian Empire, from 1888 to 1917. After the Revolution, it was nationalised and brought under the jurisdiction of the state. More than 900 plant species have been recorded, including 26 tree and 138 shrub species. Almost two-thirds of them are indigenous to the area. A number of the mighty oaks may be over 650 years old.

Today life here is calm and the reserve is home to around 212 species of bird, including corncrake, eagle owl, white stork and white-tailed eagle, along with 59 species of mammal, including wild boar, wild horses, roaming elk, beaver, lynx, fox, deer, wolf, otter, badger, mink, ermine, marten and, perhaps most famously, bison. By 1920, the European bison was almost extinct. Once to be seen roaming the great continental plain in their thousands, only a handful remained. But with careful management and controlled husbandry in the intervening years, numbers have increased to more than 2,500 in eastern Europe. Several hundred are known to inhabit the park and can readily be seen from the roads and paths.

In 2009, the park celebrated its 600th anniversary. To mark such an auspicious event, the celebrations included an upgrade for many of the facilities here. The Museum of Nature is well worth a visit, and there are four decent hotels with a range of restaurants, cafés and bars. Extensive tourist trails have also been established throughout the park for the walker, horserider and cyclist alike. And children of all ages can pay a visit to the 'real' Grandfather Frost in the 'real' wooden fairy-tale house that he calls home, where he lives with his granddaughter Snyegoruchka, the Snow Maiden. Interestingly, Grandfather Frost is to be found here in full regalia all year round. I met him in April! The reserve is also home to around 4,000 people in scattered communities across the park, most of whose livelihoods are agriculturally based.

Getting there and away The park is located around 70km north of Brest and 20km from the nearest town, Kamenyets. Several buses a day run from Brest to the park gates and back again, both direct and around the houses via Kamenyets and Kamenyuky. The direct service out of Brest and back again means that if time is at a premium, it's possible to head to the park from Brest for a day trip, though a longer stay is to be recommended. There is no transport within the park itself, other than that arranged by official tour operators. As there are small communities within the park it is technically possible (just) to drive your own car around, but the state guards this natural treasure very jealously indeed and there are many red-tape hoops to jump through before a permit is granted. Also, this is border country, so security is high. Every time I've been, lorry loads of frontier guards could regularly be seen driving around. Even the wild animals don't get to cross back and forth. It's far better to come here with your own vehicle, which you then leave at the car park immediately outside the gates, or else on an organised tour, which can be arranged through staff at the Hotel Intourist in Brest, or any other agency there. If you want to deal with the arrangements elsewhere in the country, perhaps in Minsk, most tourist agencies within Belarus market a number of very comprehensive tours to this and other sites. Someone else then takes care of the driving and the itinerary; you can just sit back, admire the view and take in the sights. Either way, a large sign marks the crossing of the park territory boundary as you pass through the village of Kamenyuky, before the gates to the park proper appear ahead and the road just stops. Cars park to the left of the barriered entry and coaches to the right, and there are souvenir and ticket kiosks here too.

Facilities on site This is a really lovely place, with nourishment and regeneration for the soul. All is beautifully calm and quiet, with constant birdsong near and far as the backdrop to your wanderings. But if you're travelling solo and without Russian, the process of getting installed in your hotel is challenging. Walk through the barriered gates (you won't be challenged), past the war memorial and towards the large building facing you. This is the restaurant with Hotel Number 3 above. Walk to the left and enter the reception of Hotel Number 4. This is the main reception area for all three of the hotels within the park itself. If you're booked into Hotel Number 3, retrace your steps to enter the door facing you, immediately under the sign for Hotel Number 3. Walk straight down the long corridor to the desk at the end, show the piece of paper you were given in the main reception area, and collect your key. It's as simple as that…

The park's three small hotels (numbered 1, 2 and 3) and the one outside the park gates but less than 1km away in the village of Kamenyuky (number 4) all date from the Soviet era and were more than a little tired and shabby until they were all upgraded as part of the 600th-anniversary celebrations, although their appearance is still a tad dated. My view is that this adds to the charm of the place. A visit here is all about getting back to nature, and I always find the standard of the facilities to be commensurate with that aim. All of the rooms are neat, clean and with en-suite facilities. For my last visit I had booked a twin room with my travelling companion, but we turned out to be the only guests and were given a room each at no extra charge.

Visitor facilities are collected together at this site just inside the park gates. They include a number of cafés and restaurants, a sauna, swimming pools, bicycle hire and sports courts/pitches for those so inclined. The **Museum of Nature** is also located here. The exhibits are displayed in four halls on the second floor of the building and it's a first-class museum. You might want to visit here first before venturing into the park itself for a general overview, not least because an English audio tour is available for only BYR35,000. There is a commendable level of detail in the displays and the audio guide enables the visitor to dip in and out as preferred. My favourite exhibit is the scale model of the hunting palace built by Alexander III, the fate of which graphically illustrates the ping-pong nature of conflict, statehood and ownership in this part of Europe over the centuries. On the ground floor a video is shown (only in Russian though) and you can also find here the library, teaching room, informative display boards and a small shop for souvenirs and books, some of them in English. The opening hours for the shop are advertised as 09.00–18.00, but it's all a little hit and miss and depends largely upon whether or not there's anyone around to open up. That said, every staff member is unfailingly helpful and will go the extra mile to offer help and assistance. On my last visit I was the only visitor there.

Head out of the museum and walk straight ahead to find the **Valeri animal enclosure**. I've documented elsewhere in this book my disquiet over animals being restricted in pens. The opportunity to see wild creatures up close simply does not justify the denial of their freedom, in my view. Others may see it differently. I've only taken the 4km circular walk around the cages once and I found it a very uncomfortable experience. There is a wide variety of wildlife to see. Bison, deer and wild boar have sizeable enclosures in which to roam, but others, notably wolf, lynx, racoon, fox and birds of prey have little room to move and all looked decidedly stressed and unhappy when I was there. The animals were pacing up and down, backwards and forwards, never at rest and perpetually anxious. The birds repeatedly battered their wings on the fences around their enclosure. Worst of all was the fate of the two brown bears, who sat morosely on old rubber tyres in their secure metal box, 10m x 5m. It was very sad to witness, and it's the only negative experience in this otherwise delightful place. All around is the sound of birdsong and a cacophony of woodpeckers at work. At the top of the circular walk is an area of swamp beyond the path, and visitors should take care to avoid stepping on the dozens of frogs that cross at this point. I had never seen blue frogs before, but I did here, in abundance.

Tickets for bus tours, the museum and the Valeri animal enclosure are bought at the kiosks just outside the park gates. Entrance to the museum costs BYR20,000, while admission to the Valeri enclosure is BYR30,000. **Bus tours** of differing duration are advertised at a range of prices, but on my last visit in the spring of 2014 only the Grandfather Frost tour was running, price BYR75,000. I was feeling suitably festive, so went along for the ride. The audio commentary on the bus is only available in Russian, unfortunately, as is the walking tour to meet Grandfather Frost, but even without speaking the language I reckon it would still be worth doing and I enjoyed every minute of it. The ride deep into the forest takes about 20 minutes, before the bus reaches a fenced enclosure where a costumed handmaiden is waiting to escort the party around. There are tacky souvenir chalets at the entrance, as well as a café, and then the tour proper begins. It's all rather drawn out, with endless scenes and carvings from Belarusian folklore for you to see while the handmaiden recounts fairy tales and myths, enthusiastically encouraging audience participation in legend-laden ritual at various points on the walk. But the man himself is there, and when those assembled shout loudly enough, out he comes for a chat and to present the opportunity to be photographed with him. On my tour, when he found out that two Englishmen were in the audience the opportunity for some fun was too good to miss. 'Arsenal!' he shouted, thumbs up, followed by 'Juventus', thumbs down. Finally, after peeking into Snyegoruchka's bedroom and being photographed on the great man's throne, there's a gift for everyone, but you will have to go yourself to find out what it is. The whole experience is a glimpse into the legend, myth, superstition and ritual of the country and, even if it's a manufactured and clichéd one, you somehow don't mind. Then on the ride back we saw not only bison and boar in the wild, but also a number of border guards in their natural environment. The tour lasts two hours from start to finish.

A number of **bicycle routes** ranging from 10km to 27km in length have been laid out, all clearly marked. Maps are available, as are the services of a guide to lead you around if required. There are also a number of **walking routes** of modest length, including to 'the Tsar's Glade' and 'Forest Mysteries'. A number of the ancient oaks have their own name, including the 'Emperor of the North' and the 'Tsar Oak'. Some of the signposting is in English to help you find them. One of my correspondents describes a pleasing circular walk of around 6km in length from the rear of the Valeri animal enclosure, through the edge of the forest itself and past three pretty ponds. Specialist photographic safaris can also be booked.

Restaurant and café facilities in the park are all decent. If staying in any of three hotels at the park gates, breakfast is taken in Café Sosni, the wooden chalet on the left as you walk from the hotel area. The main restaurant (⊕ *noon–midnight daily, closed first Mon of the month;* **$$$**) is the large building you see first as you enter through the gates. It's a cavernous place with an enormous central room on the ground floor and smaller rooms off and upstairs. Dark wood abounds and a constant companion to your dining is piped Russian music. There are 250 covers in total. On a March Tuesday evening when I was last here, my companion and I had the large room all to ourselves except for one other family. And we still had to wait an hour after ordering for our dinner to be served. The menu offers such dishes as 'forester's dream salad', 'hunter's sausages', 'royal meat with garnish' and 'stewed wild game with vegetables', though I settled for some variety of cutlet/burger with salad, fries and a delicious mushroom preparation, all of which was not only edible but tasty, perhaps the more so for the wait.

Increasingly, the state and its expanding tourism industry are coming to recognise the significance and value of this unique environment. Tour operators within and outside the country are tapping into the growing constituency of wildlife tourists, such that more and more people are getting to know and experience the bounteous riches that are waiting to be discovered here. One time passing through Minsk-2 National Airport, I met a group of around a dozen British travellers who return to the park year on year. They were wary of sharing their experiences too widely, lest the trickle of visitors grows to a deluge. It might just pay to get here sooner rather than later. I love it here and never tire of returning.

KAMENYETS (КАМЯНЕЦ / КАМЕНЕЦ) This town is located on the road from Brest to the national park and is only 20km or so from its southern boundary. Chronicles show that in 1276, Duke Vladimir Vasilkovich dispatched his architect Olexa to the area to find a suitable location to construct a fortress to defend his lands and to house a settlement within its defences. By 1289, its construction had been completed. It was built on the motte and bailey principle, though only the tower is now left, the famous **Byelaya Vyezha (White Tower)**, while the settlement grew over time to become the town of Kamenyets as it is today. Sitting atop a mound of earth surrounded by a ditch, this cylindrical tower, 30m high and over 13m in diameter, isn't actually white anymore, but notwithstanding the inaccuracy of the name (which endures to this day), it is a splendid architectural monument in outstanding condition. Visible from all directions as you approach the town and situated at its highest point, park at the top of Lenina Street outside the Bel-Maris shop and café (⊕ *10.00–19.00 daily*) if you're travelling under your own steam. Here you will see the statue of the duke's architect Olexa with attendant bison. The delightful Church of St Simeon behind and to the right is well worth a look. Next cross the road, pausing to view the war memorial, before proceeding into the paved square in front of you, at the head of which stands the tower. It is said that underground passages were built beneath it at the time of original construction leading to the nearby river, presumably as a means of escape in times of attack. Today the White Tower houses a really interesting **museum** (⊕ *09.15–17.15 Tue–Sun; admission fee BYR12,000, with an additional charge of BYR5,000 to take photographs*). The ticket kiosk is to the right as you enter the square, separate from the tower. The entrance to the museum is through a small door at the bottom of the steps at the base of the tower. The basement and four floors above it house enchanting displays of exhibits, pictures and information boards, including a model of the fortress as originally built. The renovations, both inside and out, have been done extremely well. As in so many museums and places of historical interest in this country, we were the only visitors when I was last here, and an attendant followed us the whole way round. A visit to this lovely museum is wholly recommended, either during your stay in the National Park or as an excursion from Brest.

STRUVE GEODETIC ARC (ГЕАДЭЗІЧНАЯ ДУГА СТРУВЭ / ГЕОДЕЗИЧЕСКАЯ ДУГА СТРУВЕ) For those with a penchant either for ticking items off a list or for

4

Fiennesian exploration (perhaps both), Brest *oblast* has evidence of this impressive 19th-century wonder of geometrical surveying in three locations. Between 1816 and 1855, scientist and mathematician Friedrich Georg Wilhelm Struve (originally of German extraction but based in Russia) conducted a series of surveys along the line of the present 26th meridian extending south to the Black Sea from Norway. Acting under the patronage of Tsar Alexander I of Russia and with the intention of determining as precisely as possible the size, shape and circumference of the planet, a chain of 258 triangulation points was laid out over a distance of 2,820km. Thirty-four of the original points were added to the UNESCO List of World Heritage Sites in 2005, five of which are to be found in Belarus. Spread over ten modern-day countries, the 34 listed points are marked by small monuments of differing design, size and shape, mostly in isolated rural areas, though in Belarus each monument is the same: an inscribed, black rectangular monolith topped with a sphere representing the globe. They are not easy to locate and even more difficult to access. Three of the five can be found in the Ivanova district of Brest *oblast*, the other two being sited in the districts of Oshmyany and Zelva in Grodno *oblast*. For further information, go to the informative website www.struve.by. It's in Russian only, unfortunately, but there are useful photographs as well as precise co-ordinates for the location of each point.

5

Grodno City and *Oblast*
Гродна / Гродно

Telephone code 152

The region of Grodno is situated in the northwest of Belarus and has borders with both Poland and Lithuania. The administrative and cultural centre of the region is the city of Grodno itself, with a population of 277,000. Situated 278km west of Minsk and just 294km east of Warsaw, it is only 20km from Poland and 40km from Lithuania. Records indicate that the city has been in existence for at least 900 years. Not surprisingly, given its location, it has a significant Polish and Lithuanian heritage.

The greatest wealth of the Grodno region consists of the leafy groves forming the magnificent tract of natural forestation that occupies more than one-third of its territory to the northeast and southeast of the city, either side of the historic town of Lida. Comprising both coniferous and mixed woodland, it is pleasing to see that pockets of the ancient virgin forests that once covered this whole continent have survived more or less intact here.

From within Belarus, you will approach the city from the south or east. My first visit was when I drove the back roads from Brest in the south, a delightful journey of 240km through ancient villages. Given that most of the country is extremely flat, I was surprised to find that, 100km or so before I reached Grodno, the terrain became much hillier, with extensive panoramic vistas opening up expectedly. So it is in the city itself. My last visit was also by road, this time from Minsk on the M6. As with the road from Brest, the topography is moderately hilly, with pleasing views across the rolling countryside on both sides. A number of new roadside cafés have opened in recent times, including a decent 24-hour one at the junction with the P5 road to Novogrudok, although I haven't tested its 24-hour credentials yet. On this route, road improvements have established a periodic hard shoulder at the edge of the highway, which means it's now a faster drive than hitherto. Just be alert: oncoming vehicles executing an overtaking manoeuvre will expect you to move into it to give way. At one point on my last drive I thought it was literally going to be my last, when 500m ahead appeared three wagons abreast coming towards me, one on the hard shoulder on the other side, one on the adjacent carriageway and one on my side of the road. It was just as well that my hard shoulder was unobstructed…

This is also a land rich in lakes, large and small, but all of them picturesque, with a reputation for crystal-clear waters. The renowned Avgustovski Canal also runs through the region for around 20km on its meandering way to Poland. Once a year, a festival of culture takes place around the Dombrovka sluice, featuring ethnic craftsmen, folk musicians and performing troupes from Belarus, Poland and Lithuania.

The history of the region, characterised first by conflict and then by the ensuing peaceful coexistence of Baltic and Slavonic peoples, has left its mark on the territory. The original fortress of Grodno, built on the banks of the Nieman River in the 11th century, has now evolved into an elegant, thriving, bustling, energetic

Grodno City and *Oblast*

5

209

LITHUANIA

N

VILNIUS

0 — 30km
0 — 30 miles

Polotsk

P45

P48

P95

Oshmyany

P63 Smorgon
P63
P106

P146 P48 P95 Krevo

M7 Minsk

Kaunas

P145

M11

P89 P135 P48 M6 Minsk

Lida

**Minsk
Oblast**

P42

P41

M6 P11 P5

Grodno

P145 P51

M6

Shchuchin P141

Novogrudok

P10

P11

**Mir
Fortress**

M6

P99 P44 P41

Nieman E85

P10 P5

Mir

Bialystok

M11 P108

P142

Ishkold

M1 P2

P44

P41

P91

Bialystok

P78

P99 Volkovoysk P99 Slonim **Baranovichy**

P4 P13

Slutsk

POLAND

P78

P99

*Byelovezhskaya
Puscha State
National Park &
Biosphere Reserve*

P47

P44 P85 M11 P43

**Brest
Oblast**

Ruzhany

Kosava

Brest Kobryn, Brest

and cosmopolitan modern city, where more examples of Classical architecture have been preserved than in any other city of Belarus. Indeed, the national state government has declared the historical centre of Grodno a special architectural zone under the protection and jurisdiction of the state itself. Of the country's major cities, it is perhaps Vitebsk and Grodno that best lend themselves to an appreciation of their charms, apparent if you meander through the streets at a leisurely pace, gazing at the richness of the buildings that surround you.

There are also many fine examples of unique architecture in the region, such as unusual military churches. During the 15th and 16th centuries, many of the Eastern Orthodox churches were required to serve the dual purposes of worship and as places of fortified refuge against the attacks of aggressors. Many of those that are still standing look more like towered castles. The best examples of these fortress-churches can be seen in the villages of Synkovichy (built 1407) and Murovanka (1524). In Smorgon, the 16th-century Calvinist cathedral is well worth a visit.

And for students of topography and geometrical surveying, two of the points of the Struve Geodetic Arc (see pages 207–8) included in the five within Belarus on the UNESCO World Heritage List are to be found within the *oblast*, in the districts of Oshmyany and Zelva.

In short, this is a land full of ancient towns and villages that repay the close attention of admiring visitors many times over. Unfortunately, options for independent travel are limited so, for now, the best option to experience all there is to see is by booking one of the many organised tours and excursions that are available through the state agencies. It's not as good as independent exploration, but it's certainly the next best thing.

HISTORY

The town of Grodno is believed to have been founded as an important strategic, military and trade centre on the northwestern border of Kievan Rus, although evidence of Palaeolithic settlements dating back over 10,000 years has been discovered in the vicinity of the modern town. Between 1000BC and AD1000, the territory is thought to have been inhabited by confederations of Baltic tribes, but by the middle of the 11th century, the Slavic Krivichi and Dryhavichy tribes had begun a policy of expansionist colonisation in the area. It gained its first mention in the *Primary Chronicle* in 1127 and it is clear that, by this time, the geographical location of this Slavic settlement at the crossroads of many trading routes had enabled it to attain the status of capital of an independent principality, possibly as long ago as the 10th century.

Economic and cultural development was swift, such that later in the 12th century the city had its own architectural school, as evidenced by the splendid Kolozhskaya Church of St Boris and St Hleb (see pages 219–20). By 1280, Grodno had been subsumed into the mighty Grand Duchy of Lithuania. Indeed, under the rule of Grand Duke Vitautis, from 1376 to 1392, the town acquired equal status with Vilnius as a second state capital. Conflict with knights of the Teutonic Order lasted into the 15th century and it was from here that Vitautis led the forces of the duchy to victory in the famous Battle of Grunwald. Even today, this battle is still regarded as a major feature in the development of modern Belarus. Then in 1496, charter rights of self-determination under Magdeburg Law were granted. The King of Poland and Grand Duke of Lithuania **Stefan Batory** established his main residence in Grodno during the 16th century for more than ten years. His influence can be widely seen today in much of the city's architecture. From the second half of the 17th century, in the time of the influential Polish-Lithuanian Commonwealth, meetings of *sejms* (a branch of government with delegated powers) were regularly held here, as a result of which the town's influence on regional and national politics grew. The last ever of the commonwealth's *sejms* took place in 1793, before the final Rzeczpospolitan monarch Stanislas Augustus Poniatowski resigned the crown in 1795, leading to the **Third Partition of Poland**. Thereafter, the city passed into Russian hands, in which it served a key municipal function as the seat of a local administration, one of the most advanced in the whole empire. In 1859, the **Warsaw to St Petersburg railway** was completed through Grodno, which thus became an important junction on the line.

The start of the 20th century saw much revolutionary activity at key locations throughout the empire, most notably the revolution of 1905. At the same time, Belarusian nationalism was developing. Grodno played its part, with the first Belarusian periodicals being printed here.

The city and its environs were once more a war zone during the 1914–18 conflict and German forces were in occupation from 1915. As a consequence of the outrageously callous political expediency practised by Lenin to end Russian involvement in the war, these territories were formally ceded to Germany by the Bolsheviks under the **Treaty of Brest-Litovsk** in 1918, following which the first Belarusian nation state was allowed to come into existence.

It did not endure for long. Between 1919 and 1921, the area changed hands many times. Units of the Red Army established Soviet power on two separate occasions, with claims to sovereignty also being made by the newly created Polish state and by Lithuania. Then finally, the **Riga Peace Treaty** of 1921 incorporated Grodno region into Poland. The city of Bialystok, 100km to the southwest, became the capital of the region and Grodno's economic significance fell into decline, although it had risen again by 1930 with the growth of the Jewish population. Military units stationed here were pressed into action when the Nazis invaded Poland in 1939, then when the country was shamefully carved up by Nazi Germany and the USSR under the terms of the notorious **Molotov–Ribbentrop Pact of Non-Aggression**, a significant engagement took place in and around the city between the Red Army and Polish troops, as the Russians marched inexorably westward to establish a buffer to protect the sovereignty of Soviet national borders. Fighting was brutal and bloody. To this very day, each side continues to deny the claims of the other in terms of actual losses, although one fact has now been established without ambiguity. As accepted at long last, thousands of Polish officers who had been taken prisoner were subsequently murdered by the NKVD acting under Stalin's direct orders and buried in mass graves, most notably those discovered in relatively modern times in the forests of Katyn. When Grodno passed into Soviet hands as part of the Belarusian Soviet Socialist Republic, much of the Polish population was dispersed elsewhere within the USSR, before the city once more fell to the Germans in 1941 after the start of Operation Barbarossa. Liberation by the Red Army in July 1944 came too late to save Grodno's Jews, the majority of whom died in Nazi concentration camps. At the end of the war, Soviet sovereignty was restored. This endured until the **breakup of the Soviet Union**, when Grodno became one of the key cities of the newly established nation state of Belarus.

Today, the grace and charm of the historical centre conceals a competitive commercialism in the wider area. The *oblast* is probably the best developed in the entire country in terms of industrialisation: components of buses, tractors, combine harvesters, cars, agricultural machinery, radios and television sets, plastics, fertilisers, manmade fibres and threads, furniture, textiles, shoes and tobacco goods are all produced here in significant quantity, while a favourable climate and fertile soil have helped to promote agriculture as a key component of the local economy.

All in all, this is a very classy city indeed. It's hip and sassy, but at the same time, relaxed and comfortable. Even the high-rise suburbs have a certain elegance. I have stayed in crumbling Soviet-style apartment blocks in four of the six major cities and the urban scene here is by far the most attractive. Certainly, the concrete is still crumbling, but the design and exterior of the blocks is a cut above, with wide swathes of tree-lined parkland in-between. I was with my Belarusian travelling companion on her very first visit to Grodno. We've covered much of the country together and she was very impressed indeed. And like everywhere else, impressing the locals is no mean task. And it is also a truly multi-cultural city. Renowned for its tradition of tolerance and inclusivity, refuge has been given to Tatars, Jews and Prussians (among others) in times gone by. Today, communities of over 80 different nationalities exist somewhere in the *oblast*. One-third of the population classes itself as being Polish or of Polish descent, while there are also significant Russian, Ukrainian and Lithuanian communities. It's no surprise to find, then, that the city is home to the biannual Festival of National Cultures in June, when the streets become one giant stage for the performing arts. Anyone lucky enough to be in the city when the festival is on has a treat in store. As well as performances, dishes of many national cuisines are in evidence, along with national crafts, dances and music in different languages. There are fireworks and ornamental water displays. The grand finale takes place in the town's central square and continues until dawn. It's a most impressive spectacle.

GETTING THERE AND AWAY

BY AIR The airport is situated 18km southeast of the city. It has all of the facilities necessary to operate national and international flights, but there have been no commercial passenger arrivals or departures for some time now, notwithstanding that the airport was regularly in use during the days of the USSR.

BY TRAIN The train station (*37 Budenyi St;* ✆ *74 45 56*) is situated 2km northeast of the city centre. Four trains a day arrive from and depart for Minsk (with a one-way ticket starting at US$4), the journey taking between five and eight hours. The service to Brest and Vitebsk is much less frequent and, generally, the city is now served by far fewer trains than hitherto. Cross-border routes have been closed, doubtless due to the geographical proximity of EU borders.

BY BUS The bus station (*7A Krasnoarmeiskaya St;* ✆ *72 02 30*) is located in the east of the city, due south of the railway station and about half an hour's walk from the centre. Cross over the railway line and head due west along the arrow-straight Karl Marx Street. Today, the cheapest and most convenient way to get around within Belarus is by means of the intercity bus routes: many services leave Grodno every day for destinations in Russia, Ukraine, Lithuania, the Czech Republic, Poland and Latvia, stopping off at the major centres of population within the country *en route*. At least one bus an hour leaves for Minsk, with a one-way ticket starting at US$13. The proximity of the Lithuanian border means that the daily morning bus departing Kaunas, where the airport there is served by budget airline Ryanair, is one option for cheap travel into Belarus. A one-way bus ticket costs around US$30.

GETTING AROUND

ON FOOT Unlike Brest, Grodno's attractions are more widely spread over a larger geographical area, although it is possible to cover a good proportion of the main sites in one walkable sector of the town (see box, *A historical walking tour*, page 223). Unusually for a Belarusian city, the urban scene is particularly hilly, especially in the centre. Elsewhere, only Vitebsk matches its topography. This gives it an airy, lofty feel, with big skies and surprisingly impressive panoramas when you least expect them, especially from the northern bank of the river. This does mean that walking has its dividends.

BY BUS AND TROLLEYBUS Buses and trolleybuses are rather old and generally very full, but they are a great way to see the city and you will feel like a local in the process. A trolleybus ride is one of those experiences that is so totally eastern

European, and very evocative. Best of all, they are incredibly cheap: a single ticket anywhere in the city will you set you back no more than BYR3,200, a handful of pence only. Tickets are available from the driver or at kiosks located at many stops. Just don't forget to punch your ticket when you get on. Checks are frequent from plain-clothes inspectors and fines for violations are rigidly enforced.

BY MARSHRUTKA Travel by *marshrutka* (scheduled minibus) is also an option. The price is a little higher but, at BYR6,000, still very cheap. Just expect to be crammed in and not to have the most comfortable of journeys. Either pay the driver when you get in, or else pass your handful of notes over the heads of your fellow passengers if it's really crowded. A tap on the shoulder is most likely to be the next passenger behind you doing the same thing. If you sit on the front seat, you will be expected to act as the conductor! The price is the same for adult and child alike, however long your journey.

BY TAXI As everywhere else, cabs are readily available for more bespoke journeys. Expect to pay around BYR50,000 for a 15-minute ride. On local networks dial 107, 122, 125, 127, 156, 157, 158, 161, 163, 181, 183 or 189 for service.

TOURIST INFORMATION

The city now has a **tourist information centre** (*38 Ozheshko St;* ✆ *77 36 06;* e *grodnortss@gmail.com; www.tourgrodno.by;* ⊕ *09.00–13.00, 14.00–18.00 Mon–Sat*). You will also be able to buy maps, postcards and some guides (mostly in Russian) from the kiosks present in each hotel, but hours of opening are whimsical and wholly unpredictable. The state tourist agency **Belintourist** has a branch office at 13 Lenina Street (✆ *75 04 01/77 33 99*). The helpful staff there will be ready to arrange excursions for you. There are several other agencies in town, including the national Top-Tour.

WHERE TO STAY *Map, opposite.*

Despite its charm and the beauty of the architecture, Grodno was not (until quite recently) a great city to find attractive hotels; then came the Semashko, the Kronon Park and the Slavia. If you have a yearning for it, you can still sample the clichéd experience of knowing what it was like to travel around the Soviet Union in its heyday at the Turist or the Belarus, but if you can afford to go upmarket, then your stay in this delightful city is going to be the better for it. And a stay at the Neman (see page 216) is a decent compromise between the two ends of the scale.

UPMARKET

Semashko (55 rooms: 4 sgls, 10 dbls, 30 twin, 1 trpl, 1 luxe, 4 junior suites, 5 superior) 10 Antonova St; ✆ 75 02 95/99; e sem-hotel@tut. by; www.hotel-semashko.ru. Located close to both bus & train stations & only 10–15min walk from the sights, this privately owned hotel (the first to be opened in the city) offers an altogether different experience. The décor is shiny, fresh & bright (if just a little on the gaudy side; check out the bridal suites!) & the service extremely slick.

Opened in 2003, the facilities are spread over 3 buildings, all of which are equipped to Western standards & are well appointed, following an extended building programme in 2008–09. Facilities inc. a very good restaurant (⊕ 07.00–02.00 daily, with b/fast served until 11.00), café, open-air terrace bar, 'VIP bar', swimming pool & sauna, on-site parking, business facilities & conference room. It's very popular with wedding parties, so check ahead as to what is going on

For listings, see pages 214–18

Where to stay

1 Belarus
2 Neman
3 Semashko
4 Slavia
5 Turist

Off map
Kronon Park

Where to eat and drink

6 Astra
7 Basta Pasta & Baza
   nightclub
   Bistro (see 6)
8 Cheburechnaya
9 Coffee Mania
10 Cuba
   Karchma (see 9)
11 Magnolia

11 Magnolia
12 Neman Beer
13   Restaurant (see 2)
   Pirozhnya Patisserie
14 Ratushni Café
15 Retro Pizza (see 9)
   Semaphor Bistro
   Stary Lyamus

Off map
Kronon Park Restaurant
Salodki Pachastunak
   Tea Room
Semashko Restaurant
Turan

*Map labels:*

Alpha Centauri
KALINOVSKOVA STREET
Maxim Bogdanovich House & Literary Museum
Railway station
Zhilibersky Central Park
Epolyet
Museum of Gorodnitsa History
Kronon Park hotel & restaurant
Lenin Square
OZHESHKO ST
Eastern Orthodox Pokrovsky Cathedral
Stari Zamak & part of History and Archaeology Museum
SOVYETSKAYA ST
LENINA STREET
Belintourist
Kolozhskaya Church of Sts Boris and Hleb
Pharmacy Museum
Church of St Christmas & the Blessed Virgin
Sovyetskaya Sq
Jesuit Farny Cathedral
KARLA MARKSA ST
Novi Zamak, library & rest of History and Archaeology Museum
Batoriya Trading House
Kolizeum
ANTONOVA ST
POPOVICHA STREET
Drama Theatre
Bernadino Church & Seminary
Ranitsa Bookstore
Central Market
FLOW
Nieman
Salodki Pachastunak Tea Room
YANKI KUPALA AVENUE
N
Bradt
0   500m
0   500yds
GRODNO City Centre
Turan

here before you arrive. The excellent service so in evidence at this hotel extends to the preparation of picnics for guests leaving very early in the morning on tours out of town. **$$$$**

🏠 **Slavia** (37 rooms: 4 sgls, 24 twin/dbls, 1 trpl, 6 junior suites, 2 luxe) 1 Molodyozhnaya St;

📞 77 35 35; www.hotel-slavia.by. The latest of the private hotels to be opened in town (in 2009), its real selling point is the excellent location, close to many of the city's facilities & historical sights, although everything on offer here also matches what's available at the Semashko (excluding pool

& sauna), inc. picnics for departing visitors. It's also popular with wedding parties. The restaurant has not been tested, however. **$$$$**

⌂ **Kronon Park Hotel** (15 rooms: 3 standard, 1 attic, 2 superior, 4 deluxe, 3 deluxe suites, 1 Kronon suite, 1 presidential suite) Pishki Park, Pishki district; ☎ 73 98 00; e info@kronon.by; www. kronon.by. Another private venture (open since summer 2008) & situated on the western fringes of the city in beautiful woodland, this 2-storey boutique hotel is a real charmer, its picturesque location easily compensating for the lack of proximity to the main sights in town. The exterior is pseudo-Baroque & inside, the décor is sumptuous & elegant. The bedrooms are well furnished & benefit from all mod cons. In terms of facilities, it gives the Semashko a good run for its money & there is also a transfer shuttle to the railway station. Like the Semashko, the restaurant is worthy of a visit on its own. Rated by many as one of the best hotels in the country, in every respect the standards to be found here are high. **$$$$**

MID-RANGE

⌂ **Belarus** (189 rooms: sgls, twin/dbls, 1 trpl, 1 apt) 1 Kalinovskova St; ☎ 74 07 80. The city's biggest hotel &, like so many in this country, another concrete block. Quite frankly it's a grim & dismal place. The lobby is awful: it's like the waiting area of a bus station, but with less charm. The higher-specification 'luxury' rooms on 2 of the floors are reasonably well appointed, but you will pay for the privilege & the paucity of services means that it's not even good value. The bus & railway stations are both around 2km away.

Facilities inc. currency exchange, hairdresser & newspaper stand, together with a café & snack bar, but no English is spoken. 7 years have passed between my visits, with few changes in the intervening period. It just got shabbier. **$$$**

⌂ **Neman** (77 rooms: sgls, dbls, twin, junior suites, luxe apts, some rooms adapted for disabled use) 8 Stefan Batory St; ☎ 79 17 00; e info@hotel-neman.by; www.hotel-neman.by. My favourite hotel in the city for its all-round ticking of boxes. It lacks the charm of the upmarket places, but the location is good (on the edge of Sovyetskaya Sq), the décor is bright & shiny (opened 2010), the staff are cheerful & friendly (many speak good English), the beer restaurant is decent & the beds are the most comfortable I've slept in on my travels in Belarus. Services inc. parking front & rear, sauna, spa, ticket agency, restaurant (where b/fast is served), separate beer restaurant, bar, business services & ATM. Excellent value for money. I reckon the hotel & beer restaurant combo make for a good choice. **$$$**

⌂ **Turist** (134 rooms; sgls, dbls/twin, luxe) 63 Yanki Kupala Av; ☎ 56 55 90. Located 3km southeast of the city centre (3km from the railway station & 1.5km from the bus station) in a suburb across the river, this is another drab & gloomy 1980s concrete box. A cab ride from the city centre will cost around US$15. All rooms are adequately appointed & clean, but tired. There is a currency exchange, travel & excursion bureau, hairdresser, dry cleaner, newspaper kiosk & solarium, along with a restaurant, café, snack bar & disco bars. There are also conference & business facilities of sorts. **$$$**

✕ **WHERE TO EAT AND DRINK** *Map, page 215.*

Now that the pedestrianisation of Sovyetskaya Street is complete, there's a decent choice of eateries in this town, while three of the hotels (Semashko, Kronon Park and Neman) have restaurants that are worth a visit.

The main drag on Sovyetskaya Street and the top end of Sovyetskaya Square feature many **bars and cafés**, with more opening all of the time. None of the ones there and elsewhere in town as featured on pages 217–18 particularly stands out from the rest, but all are decent places to hang out for a beer or two, or to watch the city go about its business over a coffee. Some I have tried for myself, while others came recommended when I asked among local people in town.

RESTAURANTS

✕ **Karchma** 31 Sovyetskaya St; ☎ 72 34 11; ⏰ 10.00–midnight Mon–Thu, 10.00–01.00 Fri &

Sat. Centrally located at the bottom of Sovyetskaya St, this is one of the best in town. Hip & crowded, the locals love it & it's a fine venue for a night out.

The rustic décor is tastefully done & the whole package, from appearance to ambience, is classy. Belarusian cuisine is served & the standard is good (with decent service to match), but do get there early or you won't get in. $$$$

✗ Kronon Park Pishki Park, Pishki District; `73 98 00; www.kronon.by; ☉ 07.00–10.30, 12.30–16.00 & 18.00–01.00 Mon–Fri, 07.00–01.00 Sat & Sun. The restaurant at the hotel of the same name is a delight. Excellent food & service are complemented by the gorgeous setting in forested parkland. If the weather is right, dine alfresco on the terrace. Everything here is sophisticated & understated. The only downside is the distance from the city centre, but the overall quality here more than compensates for the need to take a cab ride. Recommended. $$$$

✗ Semashko 10 Antonova St; `75 02 80; www.hotel-semashko.ru; ☉ 07.00–02.00 daily. The restaurant at the hotel of the same name, Belarusian & European cuisine is served here. All is slick, classy & stylish, but you will pay for the privilege. $$$$

✗ Stary Lyamus 1A Dzerzhinskava St; `77 09 65; e markiza_todo@mail.ru; www.markiza. by; ☉ noon–02.00 daily. Situated right on the edge of Zhilibersky Park & close to Lenin Sq, Belarusian & European dishes are on offer here, to the accompaniment of live music & floor shows. Standards (both cooking & service) are very good, while the interior (pseudo-rustic) is relatively well done & pleasing on the eye. It gets noisy after 22.00 when the nightclub crowd arrives & it's used by national tourist agencies (presumably to give their foreign clients a taste of 'Old Belarus'). This is a good endorsement in terms of quality, but might not be an attractive feature if you particularly want the company of locals. That said, the quality factor edges it for me, so give it a try. $$$$

✗ Basta Pasta 35 Pobyedy St; `310 03 10; ☉ noon–midnight Sun–Thu, noon–02.00 Fri & Sat. Acceptable décor, helpful staff, decent pizza, pasta & sushi. You can do better in town than this, but it does the job for calories & sustenance if you're clubbing at the adjoining Baza nightclub (see page 218). $$$

✗ Neman Beer Restaurant 8 Stefan Batory St; `79 17 73; www.hotel-neman.by; ☉ noon–midnight Sun–Thu, noon–02.00 Fri & Sat. The beer restaurant at the hotel of the same name, this is

another of my favourites. If staying at the hotel, turn right out of the front door & right again, then down the steps. Soft lighting, elevator music & rustic décor with a surfeit of dark wood panelling greet the visitor, but don't be put off, not even by the screens showing sport and cartoons. The staff are attentive, prices are good and all is relaxed here. After a long day on the streets the ambience is welcoming, the beer is cold & you can fold straight into one of the most comfortable beds in the country if this is your hotel. Last time I chose the pork steak in a cream, mushroom & garlic sauce with fries & sauerkraut. My travelling companion went for fillet steak. Neither of us were disappointed. There's another restaurant in the bottom left-hand corner of the hotel lobby as you enter from the street where b/fast is served. Clean, bright, sparkly & without charm, it's open ☉ noon–midnight Sun–Thu, noon–02.00 Sat & Sun. Go for the beer restaurant option. $$$

✗ Retro Pizza 31 Sovyetskaya St; `74 00 56; ☉ noon–01.00 Sun–Thu, noon–02.00 Fri & Sat. Right next door to the Karchma & sharing the same address, the fare is standard pizza-style, but tasty. It's a useful consolation prize if you intended to eat at the Karchma but got there too late for a table. Pizzas are made to order from a wide variety of toppings. I especially rate the 'Mexicana' here. A good range of salads, pasta & meat dishes is also available. The décor is relatively pleasing on the eye, although just a little too orange for my liking. The low ceiling gives it a vault-like appearance, so it can be noisy, but the tables are thoughtfully laid out. Service is understated & efficient. In value-for-money terms, it's still my favourite in town. $$$

✗ Turan 15A Klyetskava Av; `566 22 28; ☉ 18.00–23.00 Tue–Thu, 18.00–02.00 Fri, noon–02.00 Sat & Sun. Located in a southeastern suburb, this newish venue is an OK bet if you're staying in this part of town, but probably isn't worth a trip out if you're not. The pizzas are decent though. $$$

CAFES AND BARS

Other places I've spotted on Sovyetskaya St but never had time to try include **Ratushni Café** at the top end, close to the cab rank (☉ *09.00–21.00 Mon–Fri, 10.00–19.00 Sat & Sun*), **Pirozhnya Patisserie** a short way down (☉ *09.00–21.00 daily*) and **Semaphor Bistro**, a little further down still & on the same side (☉ *noon–midnight*

Sun–Thu, noon–01.00 Fri & Sat). Give them a try & let me know.

🛋 **Astra** Immediately adjacent to the Bistro Bar (see below) on Sovyetskaya St; ⏲ 11.00–02.00 daily. Discreet & infinitely more charming than its neighbour, with a good selection of coffees to go with the usual alcoholic beverages.

🍸 **Bistro** 5 Sovyetskaya St; 📞 72 21 57; ⏲ 10.00–15.30 & 16.00–23.00 daily. Compact, bijou & a little frayed around the edges, this tiny bar is one for locals & drinkers.

🛋 **Cheburechnaya** 1 Ozheshka St; 📞 77 13 48; ⏲ 10.00–22.00 Mon–Sat, noon–22.00 Sun. Just around the corner at the bottom of Sovyetskaya St, you'll find cheap fast food, snacks & coffee here.

🛋 **Coffee Mania** 31 Sovyetskaya St; 📞 72 34 11; ⏲ 09.00–21.00 Sun–Thu, 09.00–23.00 Fri &

Sat. Also sharing the same address as the Karchma restaurant & Retro pizzeria, it's sandwiched between the two.

🛋 **Cuba** 12 Kaluchinskaya St; 📞 77 33 00; ⏲ noon–23.00 daily. Located just off Sovyetskaya St, I feel I've missed out by not sampling the coffee & cocktails here, because whenever I ask for a recommendation in Grodno, this is always the first name I hear. Only opened in 2013, it's already very popular. Give it a try & tell me what I'm missing.

🍸 **Magnolia** 31 Mostovaya St; 📞 72 00 87; ⏲ noon–midnight Sun–Thu, noon–02.00 Fri & Sat. Situated on the edge of Sovyetskaya Sq and virtually opposite the Neman Hotel, expect alcohol, bright lights & dancing. Enough said, but the central location (it couldn't be more central!) makes getting there & back very easy, especially if you're staying at the Neman Hotel.

ENTERTAINMENT AND NIGHTLIFE

If you have your dancing shoes and fancy a late night:

☆ **Alpha Centauri** 1 Sanatornaya St; 📞 555 44 22; www.alphacentauri.by; ⏲ 22.00–06.00 Thu–Sun. Largely interchangeable with other venues of its type, but it's popular.

☆ **Baza** 35 Pobyedy St; 📞 333 13 33; www.clubbaza.by; ⏲ 22.00–06.00 Fri & Sat. I'm no judge, but people tell me it's the best club in town.

☆ **Epolyet** 30 Ozheshko St; 📞 44 83 42; ⏲ 22.00–06.00 Thu–Sun. It's brash & noisy, but also a fun night out, I hear.

☆ **Kolizeum** 2000 31 Karla Marksa St; 📞 75 34 88; www.kolizey2000.by; ⏲ noon–06.00 Mon–Fri, 18.00–06.00 Sat & Sun. Interchangeable with others in the genre, but still popular.

SHOPPING

Confine your shopping expeditions to Sovyetskaya Street (see pages 221–2) and you won't go far wrong, but if you can't find what you're looking for there, you could try these; just don't expect to find anything else that you didn't find on Sovyetskaya, though.

Batoriya Trading House 10 Stefan Batory St, in Sovyetskaya Sq, 150m down from Farny Cathedral; 📞 72 39 18; ⏲ 07.00–23.00 daily. The pavement outside is widely used as *the* place to meet friends before a night out, or to just hang around together, especially for young people.

Ranitsa Bookstore 33 Mostovaya St; 📞 72 17 65. It's the best bookshop in town but others run it close, particularly the one on Sovyetskaya St.

Central Market 6 Poligrafistov St; 📞 75 22 34. For the hustle & bustle of market trading Belarusian-style.

OTHER PRACTICALITIES

There are many **banks** and **currency-exchange bureaux** in the centre of town, with ATMs in increasing numbers all over the city. Two **chemists** (⏲ *until 20.00 Mon–Sat and 19.00 Sun*) can be found on either side of Sovyetskaya Street. The city's **post office** is at 29 Karla Marksa Street off Sovyetskaya Square.

Because the city is located so near to the border with Poland and Lithuania, it has one of the largest concentrations of Roman Catholic worshippers in the whole of Belarus. It is also a centre of Polish culture, with the majority of ethnic Poles in the country residing in the city and its surroundings.

CHURCHES ALONG THE NIEMAN It is hardly surprising that Catholicism dominates much of the architectural heritage. One of the iconic landmarks of the city is the 17th-century Roman Catholic **Jesuit Farny Cathedral** at the top of Sovyetskaya Square. The construction of this fine and imposing example of high Baroque architecture, over 50m in height, was begun in 1678 by Stefan Batory at the same time as he was redesigning the Old Castle 300m or so to the southwest. As if these activities were not enough to keep a man engaged, he was also busy leading the mighty Polish-Lithuanian Commonwealth in a series of continuous and uninterrupted military campaigns at the time. So it was that the cathedral was not actually consecrated until 27 years after work began, in the exalted presence of Peter the Great and Augustus the Strong. Further additions were made in the early part of the 18th century and its late-Baroque frescoes and magnificent altars were not finally completed until 1752. In all, there are 14 altars, the main one of which is unique: at 21m high, it was the tallest in all Rzeczpospolita. The interior is simply stunning. To appreciate the grandeur of the exterior, walk across the square in front of the cathedral all the way to the steps of the House of Culture, then look back. The effect is particularly impressive by night.

At the bottom of the square to the left is **Bernadino Church and Seminary**. This 16th-century Roman Catholic complex stands in its own extensive grounds, 200m to the south of the Farny Cathedral, on a hill on Parizhskoi Kamuny Street overlooking the Nieman River. Originally of Renaissance design, it was substantially altered in both 1680 and 1738. It is archetypical of the styles that flourished in the 17th century, from Gothic to Baroque. The interior is considered a masterpiece of so-called Wilno (Vilnius) Baroque. The church suffered some damage during the Great Patriotic War, but renovations were later sympathetically completed. Today, the oil paintings, lavish décor, alabaster statues and displays of relics and other artefacts might lack the splendour of those to be found in Farny Cathedral, but they have a beauty all of their own. The large grounds are host to a number of other monastic buildings, including cloisters, a charming wooden two-storey dormitory, a convent and a Dominican monastery. When you leave by the front door, walk to the end of the garden for an excellent view of the unusual drama theatre (see pages 221–2) directly across the road. If you get the chance, try to do so at sunset. The quality of the light at this time of day is particularly impressive for both back-lighting the theatre and also bathing the front of the church in a rich luminescence, especially when set against a deep blue, cloudless sky.

To the right of the theatre, on the other side of Gorodenskava Street, is the delightful Orthodox **Church of St Christmas and the Blessed Virgin**. Constructed between 1721 and 1750, its whitewashed walls beautifully showcase the deep blue roofs and magnificent domes of matte black adorned with shimmering golden stars. The courtyard is pretty and the interior of the church is well worth a look.

Half a mile along the riverbank beyond the Old and New Castles (see pages 220–1) as the crow flies but further by road given the topography of this part of town, atop a hill of its own on the edge of neat parkland in a delightful suburb of old wooden houses, stands the oldest remaining building in the city: the **Kolozhskaya Church of St Boris and St Hleb.** Do try very hard to visit this special place. Three-quarters of the original stone sections remain from the 12th century, the south wall having collapsed in the landslide of 1859. This is hardly surprising. The high hill on which it is precariously perched stands right above the Nieman River. First mentioned in chronicles in 1183, this church is the only surviving example of the ancient style of 'Black Ruthenian' architecture, which can be distinguished from the style employed in the design of other Eastern Orthodox churches by the use of stones of blue, green or red hue, arranged to form crosses and other images on the wall. Inside and outside it is stunningly beautiful. After enjoying the enchanting design of the crosses on the exterior, take a look inside. The original stone walls and pillars are whitewashed and without frieze or other embellishment, but everywhere to be seen, hanging from pillar and wall, or just propped up in alcoves and corners, are countless icons, incense burners and gilt candle holders. I was lucky enough to visit on one of the special holy days of the Orthodox calendar, when a service of commemoration was in full flow. It was spine-tingling. As the officiating priest recited the holy incantations, a dazzling shaft of sunlight arrowed from the high window, diagonally to the floor at his feet, while incense swirled and danced in the beam. All the time, the choir sang a cappella and the parishioners seemed held rapt by the majesty of the occasion, some standing, some kneeling to kiss the floor, all incessantly crossing themselves and bowing. It was impossible not to be moved. When you have finished exploring within, go back out of the door, turn to the left, walk to the rail at the edge and lean for a while to take in the view. Far to the left is Farny Cathedral, and from this perspective you have a true idea of just how enormous its façade really is.

CASTLES AND OTHER HISTORIC BUILDINGS   Sweep your gaze westward (to the right). Next can be seen the old **Fire Tower**, built in 1912 as a belated response to the great fires of 1885 that destroyed around 600 houses, half of all the city's buildings. Next can be seen the New and Old castles. You have a good perspective of the hill on which they are built from here. To complete the panorama, you have a fine view upriver to the forests beyond the city boundary. If you have time, take a stroll down to the riverside along the new ornamental pathways that have been laid out to the right of the church. The gradient of the steps is gentle. Turn left at the bottom, all the while gazing up at the church above or taking in the view up and downriver, then to complete a short circuit back up to the church, take the first path on your left. It's steep but there's a handrail. If you're in a mood to amble further afield, continue towards town along the dirt track by the side of the river. The first road on your left will take you up to the Fire Tower; alternatively, keep going to climb the ornamental steps to explore the Old and New castles, and the Drama Theatre. If you have transport at the church, take a short stroll into the park before you leave to inspect the impressive monument to the foundation of the city. If you're a Tolkien fan, images of Middle Earth will come to mind.

Now retrace your route and head back towards the Drama Theatre. Before you get there and just as you pass the Fire Tower, look right to find the **Stari Zamak** and the **Novi Zamak** (Old and New castles) perched side-by-side on the hillside overlooking the river. This lofty position enables them to dominate the southwestern quadrant of the city and they can be seen for some distance, particularly from south of the river. The Old Castle, which is located on the site of an earlier fortress, was built of stone in the 14th century to the orders of Grand Duke Vitautis. It was then thoroughly overhauled in the late 17th century in the Renaissance style by the Italian architect Scotto at the behest of Polish king Stefan Batory, who made the castle his principal residence. He died there seven years later and is interred in Grodno. Several modifications have been made since, but the attractive 17th-century stone arch bridge linking the castle with the city to the east still survives.

The main building, which dates from 1678, contains part of the city's **History and Archaeology Museum** (❜ 72 18 51; ⊕ 10.00–18.00 Tue–Sun, last entry 17.00; e grodno_museum@tut.by; www.museum-grodno.by; admission BYR23,300). The collection is extensive, and to do it justice you will need at least two hours here. When you leave, walk down the brick-paved path from the entrance and pause to look over the wall. To the left, you will see cut into the hillside to separate the Old from the New an elegant set of ornate steps going all the way down to the riverside. There are pleasant gardens and walkways to be found here, along with a small cafeteria built in the medieval style, with an attractive outdoor seating area. Along the river to the left lies the bustle of the commercial city and to the right in the distance, extensive forests. In-between are attractive old wooden houses set in extensive green parkland on the opposite bank. If you look over to the right of the bridge, you can see the **Fire Tower** again. Before you move on, go back through the archway, bear round to the right and, when you reach the building in front of you, walk behind it to find the remains of the old castle walls. If you have the right footwear and a head for modest heights, pick your way across the top for some splendid views up and down the river. Note to self: next time, don't leave reading glasses perched on top of head while scrambling. It's a long way down to retrieve them…

Now retrace your steps back through the archway and continue to the end of the paved path. Pass through the double wrought-iron gates to find the New Castle, built in the Rococo style by architect Karl Pepelman between 1737 and 1742 as a summer residence for King Augustus III, who had ascended the throne of Poland in 1734. It suffered major damage during the Great Patriotic War, but over time the extensive rebuilding programme has restored much of the original Baroque elegance. The exterior looks a tad shabby, although inside the works of restoration are most impressive. The lack of attention to detail outside is in strict contrast to the manner of reconstruction elsewhere throughout the western territories of the former Soviet Union in the post-war period. Today, the section facing the river houses a library, while at right angles to it is the remainder of the city's **History and Archaeology Museum** (❜ 74 33 60; ⊕ 10.00–18.00 Tue–Sun, last entry 17.30). As with the Old, the exhibits here are well worth a couple of hours of your time. Returning outside, you will see that the courtyard is neatly laid out and populated with trees of different species.

Before you leave this part of town, take a small detour back to the **Fire Tower** for a look at the magnificent mural at its base. Also nearby is the magnificent edifice of the **Great Choral Synagogue of Grodno**. Originally built in 1578 and once one of the most beautiful in all of Europe, the structure and façade in recent times were in need of significant restoration. Work to the exterior had restored the building to much of its former glory, before a catastrophic fire in November 2013 caused significant damage to the interior. Ambitious plans to re-establish this important centre for the local Jewish community are currently in the course of being developed and realised. For further information, go to www.jewishgrodno.com.

AROUND SOVYETSKAYA STREET Standing directly between the New Castle and Bernadino Church is the unusual and slightly unnerving design of the **Drama Theatre** building. Looking like something modelled on the coronet of a Middle Earth monarch (your second Tolkien image in this city!), it was clearly intended to speak of opulence and wealth but, when I first came here in 2007, it didn't pay to look too closely. The exterior was shabby and in need of a whole new coat of paint. The intended effect was further prejudiced by the proliferation of empty beer bottles littering the pavement around the outside. It was all really disappointing. But I'm happy to report that when I returned in the spring of 2014, the theatre's fascia had received a major face-lift and the walkways around it had been upgraded. There was not a single empty beer bottle to be seen. The eye-catching design of the theatre is now displayed in all its glory and it takes its place as one of the leading images of the city at last. The ticket kiosk is tucked away to the left of the main entrance. As with the castles next door, the view across the river from the walkway behind the theatre is magnificent. It is also worthy of mention at this point that the view from the south bank is equally splendid, although the perspective is reversed, of course. As you drive or walk on to the bridge crossing the river, look up to see all of these buildings towering above you.

The theatre stands on a major traffic junction at the bottom of a vast pedestrianised area bordered by Mostovaya and Stefan Batory streets with **Sovyetskaya Square** at the top. Stand with your back to the tank on its plinth and look uphill across the square. Immediately on your left is the **Ranitsa bookstore** (⏱ *10.00–18.00 Mon–Fri, 10.00–17.00 Sat & 10.00–15.00 Sun*), where you can find a good selection of English material. Walk on past it to find an ATM, with decent views of the Fire Tower beyond and to the left. Next is the city's **Palace of Culture**. The pedestrianised area here is a skateboarder's paradise (as are the environs of the Drama Theatre). Look across the square at this point to locate (from left to right) Farny Cathedral, Batoriya Trading House, Neman Hotel and Restaurant, Tsentralny Store and the Bernadino Church and Seminary.

Keep going through to the top of the square and into **Sovyetskaya Street**, which is regarded as the main thoroughfare and centre of activity. It's certainly the best place to do your shopping, and it's also a good place to stroll and to people-watch. The city authorities were in the process of also pedestrianising this thoroughfare on the occasion of my first visit in 2007, but I'm happy to report that all of the works are now complete. And a pretty good job they have made of it too. The shopping streets of Minsk are now starting to look like those that we recognise in the West, with vulgar neon and shouty billboards, but elsewhere in Belarus things remain a little calmer and more understated. In Grodno and particularly on Sovyetskaya Street, small specialist shops, bookstores, cafés and bars nestle unassumingly behind pastel façades. There are also Western designer stores here, but advertising is almost non-existent. There are buskers in abundance, with street stalls and souvenir kiosks seemingly taking up every available plot on the pavement. At the top end on the right is one of the city's main department stores, Magazin, selling all manner of things on two floors. Some of the items appear to be quite luxurious and will probably be some way beyond the means of the average local resident. You can also buy some reasonable souvenirs here, especially ceramics, textiles and straw-crafted goods. Passing down the street, there is also a cinema, halfway down on the right-hand side. Then a little further down on the left is the Neman department store. Relatively new, it is bigger and fresher than Magazin. There is also a delightful street café right outside bearing the same name, selling soft and alcoholic drinks and snacks to customers at tables on the pavement under umbrellas. At the bottom of the street turn right and walk past the *Oblast Executive Building* (see if you can spot the plaque commemorating the visit of Felix Dzherzhinsky and the founding of the Grodno revolutionary war committee in 1920) to enter Lenin Square, where the old revolutionary still stands guard.

EASTERN ORTHODOX POKROVSKY CATHEDRAL This cathedral should not be missed if you have the chance to see it. Located on the corner of Ozheshko and Lenina streets beyond Zhilibersky Central Park and only a few hundred metres from the railway station, this Russian revivalist extravaganza of pale pink stucco, red roofs and matte black onion domes is a gem. Dating from 1907, it was built to commemorate the city's army officers who lost their lives in the 1904–05 Russo-Japanese war.

To take in a good selection of the best sights in town, you might like to try this circular walk. If you include shopping time and also stops for refreshments, you could spend a whole day on it. Begin at the Old and New castles, including a walk around the two museums there. Visit the Church of St Christmas and head east past the Drama Theatre, before crossing the road to Bernadino Church. When you leave the church, turn right along Stefan Batory Street, one of the boundaries of Sovyetskaya Square. Pay a visit to Batoriya Trading House for some souvenirs, before continuing on to Farny Cathedral. Upon leaving there, walk across the square, through the pleasant ornamental gardens and turn right down Sovyetskaya Street to the end, browsing and people-watching as you go. At the bottom, turn right and proceed into Lenin Square to see the old fella keeping watch. If you're feeling energetic, cross over the street for a promenade around lovely Zhilibersky Central Park, before retracing your steps back to Sovyetskaya Street. Walk back up it on the other side and through the square, the attractive paved area of which is much favoured by promenaders and skateboarders. Turn right at the bottom when you reach the Drama Theatre, retracing your steps back to the New Castle. Stroll down to the riverside and rest on a bench in the gardens there. You will have deserved it!

GORODNITSA HISTORY MUSEUM (*37 Ozheshko St;* ✆ *72 16 69;* ⊕ *10.00–17.30 Tue–Sat; admission BYR10,500*) Themed on the activities of the city's former Gorodnitsa trading district but with displays and artefacts relating to the history of the city generally, this museum incorporates a small but very attractive wooden building that is well worth a visit for its own sake. Only 8m by 9m and one of a number of master craftsmen's houses built along this street in the 1760s as far as the site of the modern-day Lenin Square, this is the only one left and is of considerable historical significance.

PHARMACY MUSEUM (*4 Sovyetskaya Sq;* ✆ *74 00 81;* ⊕ *09.00–17.00 Tue–Sat; admission free*) Situated right next door to Farny Cathedral, the building in which this unusual museum is housed was constructed by Jesuits in 1709, specifically for pharmaceutical research. It served this purpose until 1950, before closing its doors until 1996, when it opened to visitors once more as the country's only charitable museum dedicated to the history of pharmaceutics.

MAXIM BOGDANOVICH HOUSE AND LITERARY MUSEUM (*10 Pyervaya Maya St;* ✆ *72 22 54; www.bogdanovich.grodno.by;* ⊕ *09.00–17.30 Tue–Sat, last entry 17.30; admission BYR12,000*) The famous Belarusian poet lived with his family in this house between 1892 and 1896. It opened its doors as a museum dedicated to the life of the poet in 1982 and exhibits include family photographs, personal belongings and collections of poetry. Some of the rooms recreate the interior of the house as it would have been when the family was in residence.

ZHILIBERSKY CENTRAL PARK Only a short walk from Pokrovsky Cathedral on one side and Lenin Square on the other, this park was once shabby but has received a major face-lift in recent years, such that it has been transformed into a really lovely oasis of green within the city. Today it is a place for quiet reflection and gentle promenading. There is a lake, an ornamental bridge and a lazy meandering stream, with attractive

'There's a canteen in the apartment block opposite; would you like to try it?' I wasn't sure if Olya was joking or not. We were in Lida, and had driven hard from Grodno that morning, without breakfast or even refreshment *en route*. It was now almost 14.00 and both of us were hot, thirsty and hungry. Looking around, we didn't seem to have an abundance of choice. We strolled over, entered by the small, tatty door and stepped into a whole new world. Turning right up the stairs, we followed a line of local people into a freezing, cavernous hall with monstrous, nightmarish décor straight from the Soviet Union of the 1960s and the cheapest furniture and furnishings imaginable. We joined a silent queue shuffling towards a doorway through which could be seen a line of serving dishes, with the kitchens beyond. I was reminded of the early industrial scenes in David Lean's majestic movie of Pasternak's epic novel *Doctor Zhivago*. The smell of overboiled vegetables was unmistakable. The parallel with school dinners was also impossible to miss. I chose pork and mashed potato, liberally smothered with a sauce of indistinct origin, accompanied by a side salad of beetroot and potato, with watery tomato juice to drink. Olya went for fish and the same additions as I chose. The bill came to BYR6,500; around US$3 for the lot. And it was surprisingly tasty. Around us, our fellow diners ate in silence. When we had finished, we took our empty plates on our cheap plastic trays and placed them on the rickety, noisy conveyor at the end of the room, where they were transported with a judder directly to the kitchens. We went to the take-away hatch to buy two half-litre bottles of fizzy soft drinks for the rest of our journey. We chose two well-known American brands, which were plonked unceremoniously on the hatch by a scowling waitress who had snatched the wad of tatty notes from my hand without even a glance, let alone a word or acknowledgement of our presence. These drinks cost more than our lunch. We left in silence, glad to be returning to the warmth of the sun from our foray back in time. When I returned seven years later, nothing had changed. Not even the décor. If you're ever in the vicinity, then don't miss out on a truly memorable experience.

statuary throughout, while the walkways are illuminated by night. Cross the road out of Lenin Square and enter by the steps on either side. If you cross the wooden bridge to the right and pass under the road overhead, you come to a quieter, more secluded part of the park. Less populated than the main area, it's a delightful backwater. Here you have a first view of the delightful Pokrovsky Cathedral. Climb out of the park on the right-hand side, past the buildings of Yanki Kupala University, cross the road and pay the cathedral a visit. Before retracing your steps, treat yourself to a coffee from the H20 café next door, though it was closed for refurbishment when I was last in town.

OUTSIDE GRODNO

There follows a selection of the picturesque towns and villages that can be found in the greater Grodno region. There are many others, equally as pretty and with similar attractions, which have not even made it into the list. As mentioned in this chapter's introductory remarks, access is going to be a problem, as there is little public transport to speak of that will be easy to use without a good working knowledge of the language. So if you don't have your own transport or a local friend who can drive you, the only option is to book yourself an excursion through one of the tourist agencies in town. You will at least get to see something of the natural beauty and architectural splendour of this lovely region.

LIDA (ЛІДА / ЛИДА)   Lida is the second-largest town in the *oblast*. Situated 160km due east of Grodno on the M11, it suffered greatly in the chequered history of warfare that dominated the area in the Middle Ages, then again in the Great Patriotic War, when it was extensively damaged. Once upon a time, the mighty structure of the **castle** (*Komsomolskaya Bd;* \ *15 613 22 94/15 612 13 91;* ⊕ *09.00–18.00 Tue–Sat, 11.00–15.00 Sun, though currently closed for renovation; admission BYR10,000, plus another BY5,000 if you want to take photographs*) must have completely dominated the town, but when I first visited in 2007 it was dwarfed by a hideous apartment block right next to it. It was then under massive works of renovation and reconstruction, and although those works were still ongoing seven years later in the spring of 2014, the castle was expected to be open again by August 2014 in time for the historical festival of pageantry that takes place every year, when the Middle Ages come to life once more with jousting tournaments and battle re-enactments. Then in September, a huge celebration takes over the entirety of the castle's grounds to mark the occasion of *Dozhinki* (harvest festival). Happily the renovation work has already restored the castle to much of its former glory, such that the dominance of the Soviet apartment block next door has been much reduced. This is one of the biggest castles in the whole country, measuring 80m by 80m. Made of stone and brick, the design and style are very similar to that employed in the building of Mir Castle (see pages 168 –9). Construction began in the middle of the 14th century, then in the centuries that followed it was sacked and plundered a number of times. In 1953, it was included in the state's List of Protected Monuments and in 1976, works of restoration began. They have been ongoing ever since. The repairs to the exterior of the two corner towers and the massive walls appear to be complete. There is also a high-level walkway inside. It's going to be a magnificent spectacle when all the work has been finished. If travelling by car, take the M11 road off the M6 from Minsk. About 2–3km after entering the town, look for the Great Patriotic War train with its iconic red star, mounted on a plinth on the right-hand side of the road. The castle soon appears. Go past it and turn immediately right to park on the road outside the huge iron doors of the entrance. If there is no room for your vehicle here, retrace your steps back to the large car park at the bottom of the boulevard. Across the road from the main entrance is the **tourist information centre** (*8 Zamkovaya St;* \ *52 06 24;* ⊕ *08.30–17.30 Mon–Fri*). No English is spoken here, but the staff are extremely helpful and the centre is well stocked with leaflets and guides, some of them with significant English text. Ask for the excellent map and mini-guide to the sites of interest in the town, which includes text in English. **The Exultation of the Holy Cross Roman Catholic Church** is another of the town's main symbols. Built between 1765 and 1770 in the Baroque style, the interior is exquisite. The town also has a **museum of local history and art** (*37A Pobyedy St;* \ *53 22 94;* e *lixmuseum@mail.ru; www.lixmuseum.by;* ⊕ *10.00–19.00 Tue–Sun*) and there are various monuments commemorating events in the Great Patriotic War, including the eternal flame complex with the tomb of the Unknown Soldier, a sculpture honouring the partisans and soldiers who liberated the city, and the memorial stone marking the mass grave of over 5,000 Jews murdered by the Nazis on a single day in May 1942. Other than these sites, the town has little to commend it, being a typically charmless post-war urban planning nightmare. But for a truly authentic Soviet-style experience, leave the castle by the main entrance, cross the boulevard to the hideous apartment block opposite and pay a visit to the canteen to be found on the ground floor in the right-hand corner, as described in the box *Long live the Workers' Culinary Revolution!* on page 224 (⏰ *10.00–17.00 Mon–Fri*).

🏠 **Where to stay**   According to staff in the TIC, the best place in town for an overnight stay is the **Hotel Kontinent** (*8 Kirova St;* ☎ *56 73 66;* **$$$**). Less well-appointed but next door to the castle is **Hotel Lida** (*1 Grunvaldskaya St;* ☎ *52 69 95;* **$$**).

OSHMYANY (АШМЯНЫ / ОШМЯНЫ)
Oshmyany, a small, 14th-century town that was once a fortress of the Grand Dukes of Lithuania, is situated northeast of Lida, just 20km from the border with Lithuania. It boasts the beautiful **St Mikhail Archangel Roman Catholic Church**. Originally constructed in the early 15th century, it was rebuilt between 1900 and 1906 in the renowned Vilnius Baroque style. Also here is the brick-built Orthodox Church of the Resurrection. Together, both buildings frame the historical town square. The well-known Belarusian painter Korchevsky (1806–33) was born in the town. He studied in Vilnius and St Petersburg, before leaving the country for Italy in 1829.

KREVO (КРЭВА / КРЕВО)
Along the M7 road in the direction of Minsk, 30km to the southeast, is Krevo, with its ruined remains of a 14th-century castle in the style of Lida, Mir and Novogrudok, all of which were part of the same defensive line that was constructed to repel Crusaders. As with many of the castles along this line of fortification, it suffered extensive damage during the Northern Wars (1700–21). Its final destruction was all but complete during a three-year period in World War I, when Krevo found itself on the front line between the opposing armies of Germany and Russia.

SMORGON (СМАРГОНЬ / СМОРГОНЬ)
Some 30km northeast on the P106 road, Smorgon is an ancient town standing close to the Viliya River, surrounded by scenic countryside. The powerful Radzivili dynasty that so influenced the historic towns of Mir and Njasvizh had many connections here. Napoleon's long retreat from the gates of Moscow in 1812 passed directly through the town and the emperor himself made a last stop before passing over command to Marshal Murat and escaping to Paris with only his personal guard. The 19th-century **Roman Catholic Church of St Mikhail** has an extremely unusual structure, comprising an eight-sided base alongside a multi-tiered belfry with a hipped roof and octagonal drum at the apex.

SHCHUCHIN (ШЧУЧЫН / ЩУЧИН)
Some 60km due east of Grodno on the road to Lida lies the town of Shchuchin, with its rare fortress-church that dates from the 16th century. Near to the town's enormous central square, 100m by 200m, stand the **Roman Catholic Church of St Theresa** (built in the Classical style in 1827), the **Orthodox Church of St Mikhail the Archangel** (constructed in the second half of the 19th century) and some traders' houses dating from the late 18th to early 19th centuries.

UPDATES WEBSITE

You can post your comments and recommendations, and read the latest feedback and updates from other readers, online at www.bradtupdates.com/belarus.

6

Vitebsk City and *Oblast*
Віцебск / Витебск

Telephone code 212

Bordering Lithuania, Latvia and Russia, the Vitebsk region is situated in the north and northeastern part of the country and occupies almost one-fifth of the country's total territory. The administrative centre of the *oblast* is the charming and elegant city of Vitebsk, birthplace and long the home of artist Marc Chagall, with a population of around 361,000. Situated on the Western Dvina River (where the Vitba and Luchosa rivers also converge) and famed for its rich cultural and scientific traditions, it's my favourite of the country's six cities.

This whole area is the country's lakeland, with 11 out of the 19 major lakes of Belarus being found here. It is a region of delightful natural beauty and charm, of deep blue lakes and stunning pine forests, famed way beyond the country's national boundaries. The most precious gem in the entire area is undoubtedly the collection of Braslav lakes, 50 of them in total, covering a surface area of 130km², all incorporated into a national park, with rare species of plant and wildlife preserved in their natural environment.

Situated in the southwest of the region is the stunning Berezinsky Biosphere Reserve, over 85% of which is primeval virgin forest.

The concept of sustainable ecotourism is one that the country has been striving to promote, with limited success to date insofar as visitors from outside its borders are concerned (see box, *Living the good life*, pages 90–1). Probably more so than in the other *oblasts*, there is real potential for truly developing this concept in a manner that complements the natural resources existing in abundance, while at the same time securing their protection into the future. Tourism generally is on the up here although, interestingly, the population of the city has remained static for the last 25 years.

The oldest town in all Belarus, Polotsk, is in the Vitebsk region. Founded in AD862, this Slavic settlement is known to have been the centre of Christianity during the time of Rus, the first Russian state. Do try very hard to visit this delightful town. You won't be disappointed.

Vitebsk is widely regarded as being second only to Minsk as the cultural capital of the country and then not by much. It is the location of the popular and much-loved Slavianski (Slavic) Bazaar, an international song and culture festival that takes place annually in the open air in late July and early August. Most of the musical programme is devoted to a celebration of ethnic Slavic music. The main participants are artists from Russia, Belarus and Ukraine, but there are also guests from a significant number of other countries, both Slavic and non-Slavic. For one glorious week in high summer, the entire city turns into a gigantic street party, with 5,000 artists performing at significant and fringe events, seemingly on every street. The English-language website www.festival.vitebsk.by/en is a mine of colourful facts and information on

the history of the festival and current practical arrangements. The main events take place at the purpose-built 6,500-seat domed amphitheatre on Frunze Avenue in the middle of town, just along from the junction with Lenin Street. Now 25 years old, it's a sizeable concrete bowl and an enduring image of the city. Over three million people have attended events since it was built. As well as the bazaar, the city also hosts 27 other annual festivals celebrating the performing arts, including modern dance and chamber music. At times, it seems that the entire city morphs into festival mode. And the original School of Arts founded in 1919 by Marc Chagall continues to thrive. Overall, there is little doubt that the reputation of Vitebsk as an international centre for the promotion of the performing arts and fine art is assured.

HISTORY

It nicely fits the character of the city of Vitebsk (as a place where artistic temperament can flourish) that its foundation is based on the romance of legend. It is said that while travelling through the region in the year AD974, Princess Olga of Kiev was so impressed by the beauty of the hill at the junction of the Western Dvina and Vitba rivers marking the site of an old Slavic settlement of the Krivichi tribe, that she ordered a city to be founded in that very spot. At best this tale is apocryphal and at worst a manufactured fiction. But so attractive is it that 974 is the official year of the foundation of the city! In reality, it is likely to have first been settled by the Vikings exploring south, during their migration from their Scandinavian homelands in search of trade with Greece.

Whatever the true story, the existence of Vitebsk as a fortified centre of trade and commerce is recorded in chronicles dating from the 11th century. At this time, trade links with the Russian cities Kiev and Novgorod, with Byzantium and western Europe were already in existence along the Dnieper and Dvina. Unfortunately (but not surprisingly), this marked the territory as being prime for invasion and subjugation on the part of warring princes and foreign armies. It became part of the Grand Lithuanian Duchy early in the 14th century and then, on 15 July 1410, significant numbers of Vitebsk citizens helped the combined armies of Lithuania, Poland and the Czech kingdom to defeat the Teutonic Order at the famous Battle of Grunwald. In 1597, limited rights of self-determination under Magdeburg Law were granted, only to be taken away when all of the town's Orthodox churches were closed in 1622 following the assassination of Uniate archbishop Kuntsevich during the course of a riot in the city. Then between 1700 and 1721, Vitebsk suffered considerable damage to both fabric and infrastructure in the Northern Wars that set Sweden against the Russian Empire. The town was almost completely destroyed by fire in 1708 and, over time, trade fell away as the population diminished.

Vitebsk was annexed by Russia in 1772, leading to limited revival of the city's wealth, but when Emperor Napoleon invaded the country on 24 June 1812, Vitebsk found itself directly in the line of the march to Moscow. Napoleon had bought the loyalty of the noblemen of Vitebsk by promising to restore the right of self-determination that had been the privilege of the city in its time as an administratively autonomous region of the former Polish-Lithuanian Commonwealth. However, the peasants of the region were mobilised en masse by the Russian imperial army; and we all know who won in the end. On 11 July, the Russian army was billeted here on the retreat from Polotsk and then, over a three-day period from 13 July, there was very heavy fighting involving tens of thousands of troops on the western fringes of the city. At the conclusion of the engagement, the Russians were forced to retreat eastward. On 16 July, Napoleon entered Vitebsk. He established his headquarters in the Governor's Palace, high on the bank of the Dvina, but his stay was only a short one. The emperor had more pressing business in Moscow but, as history tells, he didn't quite get there.

In the meantime, incessant war had taken its toll on the city. By 1825, the population was fewer than 17,000 and it was not until the emancipation of the serfs throughout the Russian Empire in 1861 that its fortunes began to revive, greatly assisted by the construction of two major rail links (Moscow–Riga and St Petersburg–Kiev) that crossed here. The census of 1897 shows that the population was then over 66,000.

In 1892, the famous Russian painter Ilya Repin took up residence in the city. This was the start of its golden age as a spiritual home for notable painters, including Chagall himself, Kazimir Malyevich, Mstislav Daburzhynsky and others. Further, many masters came to teach at Chagall's school. It must have been an exciting time to be around, with the streets being turned into one enormous art studio, where buildings and the sights of the city were brought to life on canvas. Much of the substantial body of work that was created then is still to be found in the city, a rich representation in tableau form of life here early in the 20th century.

Always a multi-faith city, over 50% of the population prior to World War I was Jewish, with Yiddish in wide use as a common means of communication. During the war, Vitebsk became a military garrison close to the front line and the

For a week each July, Vitebsk is consumed by culture high and low. Offering everything from poetry to pop, artists from more than two dozen nations present themselves to attentive crowds. Of course, the locals love anyone with a Belarusian connection. 'Literature is the conscience of the nation,' proclaimed Yevgeny Yevtushenko gravely at a reading at the 2009 Slavianski Bazaar, a thought that was politely noted by the poet's devoted admirers. What really won their hearts, though, was the revelation that the Siberian-born poet (remember *Zima Station?*) has a local connection. Yevtushenko's grandfather was born in Belarus. In 2010, Georgian singer Lasha Ramishvili won the hearts of the Vitebsk crowd by astutely choosing to sing a traditional Belarusian folk song.

The city so intimately associated with Marc Chagall sparkles at festival time. The sun usually shines, there are barbecues and beer tents aplenty, and a diligent army of orange-clad litter collectors keep the city impressively clean. In a city that is always intimate, it is easy to get close to the performers. I learnt a little about fandom too, as a group of starstruck girls pressed around the doors of a smart hotel, anxious to catch a glimpse of their favourite pop idols. Men muttering into their lapels kept the minimally skirted crowd at bay.

As I walked with friends through Vitebsk after the 2009 opening ceremony, we heard a symphony of police sirens behind us on the main road. Loudspeakers then proclaimed that the road must be cleared. We watched and waited and then a cavalcade of limousines slid by, heading out of town. Were I at home, I might have been tempted to take a quick pic or two. But then I remembered Belarusian etiquette. The president may only be shot when he is on stage.

Nicky Gardner is co-editor of hidden europe *magazine. Find out more about her work at www.hiddeneurope.co.uk.*

population was swelled by a significant refugee contingent. In the climate of unrest and dissatisfaction that prevailed, Bolshevik propaganda was widespread. The town's soviet was established only two days after Lenin took power in the country, but there was more misery in the civil war that ensued. Little by little, things began to improve and the revival continued apace during the intensive industrialisation of the Soviet Union under Stalin, although the population suffered just as much as the rest of the country by reason of the infamous and brutal ideological purges of the 1930s.

This latest phase of industrial prosperity came to an end with the Nazi invasion in 1941. Only days after it began, bloody engagements were taking place in the vicinity of the city. Thanks to heroic rearguard action on the part of the Red Army on the western bank of the Dvina River, a significant proportion of the population and most of the industry of the town was evacuated and moved far to the east. But it was only a matter of time before the town fell. The Germans established a huge garrison and those who remained in and around the city were brutally repressed, not least as punishment and reprisal for the large-scale underground and partisan activity that was established here. The Red Army returned to claim the city once more in June 1944, but only after the fiercest of battles, often involving hand-to-hand fighting in the suburbs. Only 15 of the city's more significant buildings and 186 civilians survived from a pre-war population of 170,000, 30,000 of whom had been Jews. Nearly a quarter of a million of the region's inhabitants had either been killed in action or murdered in Nazi concentration camps. It was not to be until the end of the 1960s that the city's population reached that of 1939. For over 500 years, no war in this part of Europe has passed the city by without plunder, looting and destruction, such is the strategic importance of its geographical location.

Today, the region is home to some of the country's largest industrial and scientific plants as befits the area's scientific heritage, while cultural life and the arts are also flourishing. The great traditions begun by Repin and Chagall continue to be upheld, such that this cosmopolitan city can indeed be said to represent a nexus of the old and the new.

GETTING THERE AND AWAY

BY TRAIN Vitebsk is located at the crossroads of major pan-European rail links north–south and east–west. The splendid station building is located in a square of pleasant gardens at the western end of Kirov Street. There are several 'express' trains a day to Minsk, the journey taking around five hours. One-way tickets start at around US$4. In fact, it's no faster but cheaper than travelling by bus. Internally within the country, there are also slower and less frequent services to Brest and Grodno. Several trains a day call at Polotsk. Leaving the station, it's a straight 15-minute walk east to the Kirov Bridge and the town centre, where you can take your bearings for all of the city's major sites.

BY BUS There are 12 buses a day to and from Minsk that take around 5½ hours to complete the journey. The price of a one-way ticket starts at US$10. The bus station is located ten minutes on foot to the northeast of the railway station. And a journey from Minsk by *marshrutka* will take around five hours on good roads with light traffic, for BYR45,000. Polotsk is two hours away and the service is a regular one. Tallinn in Estonia can also be reached by coach and this is an interesting way to enter the country, if rather long.

GETTING AROUND

The city certainly repays exploration **on foot,** although the sites of interest are spread over a large geographical area. It's a very hilly town and there are climbs between the key locations. Come suitably shod and be prepared for some leg work! A number are located on either bank of the Dvina River, in the vicinity of the Kirov Bridge. On a bright and sunny day late in autumn, a stroll along the river here, through the splendid wooded gardens, is a real delight. The other advantage of walking is that it affords an opportunity to enjoy the pre-war architecture at leisure, such as remains, though there is a rich diversity of attractive architecture generally. Look particularly for examples of the low red-brick buildings so prominent in the works of Marc Chagall. And the upside of the topography is that there are big, expansive views to be had all over, with big skies and a real feeling of loftiness. Unexpected ravines hide lovely parks that are perfect for promenading, especially by the Vitba River. The best vantage point (and one of the finest urban views in all six of the country's cities in my opinion) is from the edge of the square at the front of the stunning Ouspensky Cathedral at the end of Krilova Street (off Suvarova), high above the east bank of the river. So, if the weather is fine, don't give yourself too onerous a task by trying to cram in an extra museum or two; plan to tick less off your list and spend more time ambling. Many people will tell you that the best time to visit is when the Slavianski

Bazaar is on, and it's certainly true that the dazzling array of colour and activity is irresistible. I have a friend, a local writer and journalist, who always encourages me to come at festival time, when the bars are full. I'm not so sure: my favourite time to meander the lovely streets is out of season, in spring and autumn; if you're lucky with the weather, it's a wonderful opportunity to stroll unhindered and appreciate the elegance of the city with very few people around.

Otherwise, take advantage of the cheap, cheerful and plentiful (but overcrowded) supply of **buses**, **trams** and **trolleybuses**. Most rides, however long, should not cost more than US$1. The tram system is one of the oldest in this part of Europe, second only to Kiev. It was constructed to facilitate the carriage of goods, materials and supplies, on the basis that the city was too hilly for horses! **Private buses** also operate in the city and they won't be as crowded as the public ones, but you will have to pay more. There are plenty of **taxis** and no fare anywhere should be more than US$10. Be sure to agree the price in advance.

TOURIST INFORMATION

As in previous chapters, please allow me again to mention that every effort has been made to establish comprehensive and corroborated information on opening times of restaurants, museums, bars and clubs, but occasionally you may find that reality appears to fly in the face of ostensibly reliable published data available from a number of sources. Wherever you can, do check ahead. Increasing numbers of tourist agencies, both state and private, can now be found in the city, but be sure to check their credentials first. The safest option and the best source of information is the Tourist Information Centre for Vitebsk region (*10 Stroityely Av;* \ *21 95 13;* ☉ *08.00–13.00 & 14.00–17.00 Mon–Fri, closed Sat & Sun;* e *tour-vit@mail.ru; www. tourvitebsk.gov.by*). If arriving in the city on your own, however, a decent map with good graphics (although in Cyrillic) can be purchased for BYR9,950 at booksellers, stalls and retail outlets in the city, including at the railway station.

WHERE TO STAY   *Map, page 234.*

UPMARKET

🏠 **Eridan** (12 rooms: 9 sgls, 3 dbls, plus 13 suites) 17/21 Sovyetskaya St; \ 36 24 56; www. eridan-vitebsk.com. Rated the best in the city, this is a smart boutique hotel. Make sure you check first if you want to use a credit card to pay when checking out. **$$$$**

MID-RANGE

🏠 **Luchesa** (155 rooms: 110 sgls, 18 twins, 27 trpls) 1 Stroityely Av; \ 29 85 00; e reception@ luchesa.by; www.luchesa.by. This is a concrete Soviet-style monolith with décor to match, but it does have the advantage of being at the intersection of major routes, although some way to the south of the city centre. There is easy access to the sights by public transport, however. It is 3.5km to both the railway & the bus station from here. Has a good restaurant ('Continent') serving Russian & European cuisine,

as well as a bar, meeting facilities, a conference hall seating 100, a hairdresser, solarium, a currency exchange & a kiosk selling souvenirs & newspapers. As with the Eridan, check first before relying on being able to check out with your credit card. **$$$**

🏠 **Vetrazh** (155 rooms) 25/1 Chyernikovsky Av; \ 27 22 75. Built in 1989 & located not far from the Luchesa on the eastern bank of the Dvina River, to the south of the centre. The railway & bus stations are 3.5km away. With rooms on 8 floors, it's pretty standard, Soviet-style stuff, functional, modest, but relatively cheerful. An increase in prices has placed this hotel in the mid-range bracket, though sadly there has been no corresponding increase in quality, notwithstanding some modernisation. Services inc. currency exchange, laundry, beauty parlour, travel & excursion bureau, restaurant (recommended), bar, snack bar (where b/fast & lunch are both excellent value) & a very noisy disco! **$$$**

For listings, see pages 233–6

VITEBSK
City Centre

Roman Catholic
Cathedral of St Barbara

House of
Marc Chagall

Marc Chagall
Museum &
Art Centre

Russian Governor's
Palace

Teatralnaya café,
nightclub & Yakub Kolas
Academic Drama Theatre

Ouspensky
Cathedral of
the Assumption

City Hall &
Regional Museum

Railway
station

KIROV ST

ZAMKOVAYA

Art
Museum

Holy Resurrection Church

FRUNZE AVENUE

Blagovezhenskaya
Annunciation Church
& Alexander Nevsky
Orthodox Church

Univermag
department
store

ST
LENIN
ST

Intercession
Cathedral

Western Dvina

Victory
Park

Victory
Square

MOSKOVSKY PROSPEKT

SUVAROVA STREET

SOVETSKAYA
STREET

GAGARINA ST

GENERALA LYUDNIKOVA AVE

KRILOVA ST

CHYERNIKOVSKY AVENUE

CHKALOVA STREET

Eastern Orthodox St
Protection Kazan Cathedral

STROITYELY AVENUE

Bradt

N

0 — 500m
0 — 500yds

For listings, see pages 233–6

🛏 **Where to stay**
1 Dvina
2 Eridan
3 Luchesa
4 Vetrazh
5 Vitebsk
6 XO Hostel
7 Zolotoy Telenok

✖ **Where to eat and drink**
8 Arena Pizza
9 Da Vinci
10 Kofeynya
11 Lya Ratushi
12 Melodii
13 Momento 1
14 Momento 2
15 Planyeta Burger
16 Schwarzwald
17 Traktir
18 Uklima
19 Zolotoy Drakon
20 Zolotoy Vyek

BUDGET

🏠 **Dvina** (57 rooms) 41 Ilinskava St; \37
75 56. Located on the western bank of the Dvina
River close to the Kirov Bridge (& therefore very
central), this hostel-like hotel has the usual
choice of rooms, along with a restaurant, disco
& secure parking. Cheap & cheerful. Pets are also
welcome! **$$**

🏠 **Vitebsk** (219 rooms) 5/2A Zamkovaya St;
\35 92 80. In the city centre & 1.5km from the
railway & bus stations, the hotel is on 12 floors
with a range of rooms & suites, a restaurant, bar &
casino – & lots of concrete. Don't expect too much
here, but it will serve a functional purpose at a

competitive price, especially as it's well situated for
easy access to the city's sights. **$$**

🏠 **XO Hostel** (56 beds in 4 12-bed dorms & 4
twin rooms) 10/2 Suvarova St; \23 66 26; **m** 29
618 45 54; **e** hotel.vit@mail.ru; www.xostel.by.
For cost, location & value for money this clean &
cheerful hostel cannot be beaten, but it's difficult
to find. At the junction of Suvarova & Krilova
Sts, look for an arch with a modest 'Hostel' sign
above on the south side of Krilova. Pass through
it & you'll find a door with an even smaller &
more unassuming sign, round the corner on the
right. Run by a husband & wife team who are
both friendly & cheerful, expect no frills, but the

common areas for cooking & washing are perfectly acceptable & the sleeping arrangements do the job. Another selling point is the location, which is first class. Metres from Ouspensky Cathedral & a range of eateries, it's the perfect base for your stay in this delightful city. **$$**

🏠 **Zolotoy Telenok** (24 rooms) 6A Belaruskaya St; ☎ 36 27 91. This is a small hotel/hostel within easy walking distance of both coach & railway stations. Amenities also inc. billiards & bowling. **$$**

✕ WHERE TO EAT AND DRINK *Map, opposite.*

The city's reputation has more to do with culture and the arts than fine dining, but a few restaurants are worthy of note. The restaurant at **Eridan Hotel** (see page 233) enjoys a fine reputation for excellent food and service, but it is expensive. As an alternative dining experience if you are **self-catering**, the huge supermarket Omega (on the corner at the junction of Stroityely Avenue and Chkalova Street) has delicious ready-cooked meals that are good to go; or try the excellent **take-away menu** at the gastronome on the west side of Chkalova Street, between Moscovsky and Stroityely avenues. Additionally, most branches of the supermarket chain Vesta have a good selection of meals to go.

RESTAURANTS

✕ **Da Vinci** 5/2A Zamkovaya St; ☎ 35 84 05; ⏰ noon–02.00 daily. The décor is elegant, but it's very expensive, the quality of the food doesn't match the cost & the service is unexceptional. **$$$$**

✕ **Teatralnaya** 2 Zamkovaya St; ☎ 36 99 86; ⏰ 11.00–17.00 & 18.00–23.00 daily. This is a trendy venue with a large artsy clientele; not surprising, really, as it's located in the vaults below the Yakub Kolas Theatre. The ambience is excellent & the food is very good. Traditional Belarusian & European cuisine from a varied & imaginative menu. After the restaurant closes, the venue becomes a nightclub, well into the small hours. **$$$$**

✕ **Arena Pizza** 57/4 Lenin St; ☎ 36 66 01; also at 3/3 Stroityely Av; ☎ 21 99 49; www.arena-pizza.by; ⏰ 10.00–23.00 daily. These 2 related emporia serve standard but decent-quality pizza fare in a mock Italianate café setting. There's a particularly fine vegetable pizza on the menu & a delivery service is available until 22.00. Very good value. **$$$**

✕ **Traktir** 2 Suvarova St; ☎ 37 01 07; www.vtraktir.com; ⏰ noon–midnight daily. Formerly regarded as the best restaurant in town both for atmosphere & the quality of its menu, the halo seems to have slipped just a little, but many still rate it highly. Well located, close to the City Hall & in one of the older, more attractive streets in the whole city. Part of the menu is also in English. Give it a try. **$$$**

✕ **Uklima** 10 Frunze Av; ☎ 37 29 67; ⏰ noon–midnight daily. There are 2 dining rooms here; both are pub-style cosy & the food is good. **$$$**

✕ **Zolotoy Drakon** 8–10 Krilova St; ☎ 23 63 00; www.zolotoy-dracon.relax.by; ⏰ noon–midnight daily. Located near to the Ouspensky Cathedral, decent Chinese food is served here at reasonable prices. Recommended. **$$$**

✕ **Momento 1** 27 Chkalova St; ☎ 37 29 67; ⏰ 09.00–midnight daily; also Momento 2, 1 Frunze Av; ☎ 37 73 92; ⏰ 11.00–midnight daily. As a slightly cheaper alternative to Arena Pizza, both of these offer decent quality & are good value for money. Momento 2 is a tad more plush than 1, & thus slightly more expensive. **$$**

✕ **Zolotoy Vyek** 20/13 Suvarova St; ☎ 35 81 11; ⏰ noon–midnight daily. On the same street as Restaurant Traktir but further up the hill between Ouspensky Cathedral & the Marc Chagall Museum & Art Centre, near the entrance to the zoo, this is one for the summer months, when good shashlik can be enjoyed alfresco on the terrace, though inside is recommended too. Enjoys a high reputation generally among locals & tourists alike. Good value, & regular live music. **$$**

✕ **Planyeta Burger** 5 Suvarova St; ☎ 35 84 44; ⏰ noon–midnight daily. It's a burger joint, period. Go with low expectations & you won't be disappointed. But it's centrally located & if you need calories on the hoof while you're exploring, it does the job. I speak from experience, but don't tell anyone. **$**

CAFES

Kofeynya 2 Suvarova St; 29 137 07 30; 10.00–23.00 daily. Retro & homely inside, there's a decent terrace for the summer & the coffee is good.

Lya Ratushi 10 Krilova St; 37 38 23; 11.00–midnight daily. Good location, a relaxed ambience, decent food & pleasing décor.

Melodii 63 Lenin St; 35 81 36; 10.00–midnight daily. An intimate venue with live music. Good food, better coffee.

Schwarzwald 4 Tolstova St; 35 81 56; 10.00–midnight Sun–Tue, 10.00–02.00 Thu–Sat, closed Wed. This basement venue is well located & can be very popular at the w/end.

ENTERTAINMENT AND NIGHTLIFE

Vitebsk has a greater than usual number of higher-education establishments for a city of its size and has a substantial student population. Not surprisingly, then, youth culture is reasonably well catered for. This means that you might expect to find a wide choice of bars, and you won't be disappointed, especially at the lower end of Suvarova Street and its environs. None comes more highly recommended than any other, so this is a good opportunity for you to undertake some exploration of your own. All of the bars are open from late morning until 23.00 or midnight, while those that are also clubs will stay open until well into the small hours for you to dance the night away until at least 04.00.

SHOPPING

Vitebsk is famed more for its status as a centre of fine art rather than for the quality of the shopping experience it offers. Chagall-related paraphernalia is omnipresent, but that apart, there is nothing here that you cannot find elsewhere in the country. The **Univermag department store** on Zamkovaya Street has a reasonable array of traditional Belarusian handicrafts on offer (as does the railway station and the open market situated close by). The town's distillery produces some of the highest-quality vodka in the whole country and bottles aimed at the tourist market (in other words, just a little kitsch) are available in shops throughout the city.

OTHER PRACTICALITIES

There are **banks** and **currency-exchange bureaux** aplenty here, particularly on Lenin Street, although these do tend to close early. **ATMs** are now located all over the city. There are two **post offices** on Lenin Street (*32 and 52/16*) that are both open until 19.00 on weekdays, as well as other branches throughout the city. Credit cards are generally accepted (certainly in the bigger hotels and restaurants) but, as elsewhere in this country, travellers' cheques are viewed with suspicion and you may not be able to exchange them.

WHAT TO SEE AND DO

Of the six major cities in Belarus, Vitebsk has been fortunate to be able to retain a palpable and living sense of history (much more so than any of the other five), notwithstanding the widespread destruction wrought in the Great Patriotic War. To varying degrees, the prevailing influence and atmosphere in those five is certainly the more recent Soviet past, but not so here. Whatever the reason, there is a delicate sense of refinement in this elegant town.

MUSEUMS AND GALLERIES In terms of the arts, it will be no surprise that Marc Chagall's presence dominates the city:

Marc Chagall Museum and Art Centre   (*2 Putna St;* ✆ *36 03 87 (also for booking guided visits); e chagall@chagall.belpak.vitebsk.by; www.chagall.vitebsk.by;* ⊕ *Apr–Sep 11.00–19.00 Tue–Sun, last entry 18.30; admission BYR11,000*) Opened in 1992, this fine building is situated in an especially green part of town that is pleasing on the eye, where a major European collection of 300 original works of art consisting of dreamy lithographs, xylographs, etchings and aquatints is displayed on two floors. The collection also owns the series of illustrations to Nikolai Gogol's novel *Dead Souls.* Note that photography is not allowed, but each work has an identifying label in English. I especially like *La ville* from 1968, with its depiction of the single-storey wooden houses to be found all over town a hundred years ago. The ground floor is devoted to works of the artist, while the second floor is used as an exhibition space. Displays of works of different artists are on show from time to time.

House of Marc Chagall   (*11 Pokrovskaya St;* ✆ *36 34 68;* ⊕ *Apr–Sep 11.00–19.00 Tue–Sun, last entry 18.30; admission BYR5,000*) The artist's father built this house at the end of the 19th century and it's an archetypically eastern European red-brick Jewish home. Chagall spent his formative years here; indeed, his earliest scribblings as a child were committed to paper as he lay above the fireplace in the kitchen. He also painted the view from the lounge window many times, subsequently recalling this period of his life with great affection in his autobiography. Opened to visitors at the same time as the museum (see above), articles and relics of Jewish family life from the late 19th and 20th centuries have been gathered and stored for display, though only the medicine cabinet and spice grinder in the kitchen are Chagall family originals. There are also copies of archive documents, photographs and works of art on the walls detailing the life of the artist and his family in the city. Look for *The Street* (1920), showing this very house, and also *Small Shop in Vitebsk* (1914), an image of the front room, which was used as a workshop and stall for selling everyday essentials to supplement the family income. Chagall's uncle was a self-taught violinist, though not a particularly good one. His grandfather's favourite perch was on the very roof of the building, and Chagall combined both into the fiddler on the roof image in *Death* (1908), also to be found on the wall here. The house is very small (11 people lived here!), but it's well worth a visit. Many of the exhibits have labels in English and there's a small selection of souvenirs and books at the entrance desk. Outside in the back garden is an attractive statue of the artist. Walk out of the yard and turn left along Pokrovskaya Street. In a few hundred metres you will come to another **Chagall monument** at the point where a number of roads converge. This used to be the market square, and a number of red-brick buildings of the time survive. His father worked as a fishmonger here. The statue was erected in 1992 to commemorate the artist's 150th birthday and it depicts his wife Bella floating above Chagall himself, who sits holding his hand to his forehead. The image of someone floating is classic Chagall. The pose of the artist himself is something of an enigma, though people locally say that his demeanour thus results from his position directly in front of the large Socialist mural opposite. Decide for yourselves…

Art Museum   (*32 Lenin St;* ✆ *36 22 31;* ⊕ *10.00–18.00 Tue–Sun; admission BYR5,000*) Many of the artists featured here were natives of the region, including Ilya Repin, who is widely regarded as being the founder of the art movement in the city.

Vitebsk has many sons and daughters of repute whose fame is well known within the country, but perhaps the most internationally renowned of them all is the 'brilliant dreamer', the Surrealist painter Marc Chagall (1887–1985). Born into a family of Hassidic Jews and one of ten children, some of his best works display a charming nostalgia both for his devout upbringing and for the city of his birth. Life was difficult for the family, his father being a menial worker in the local fish factory, although it is clear from the artist's autobiography that his childhood was a happy one, in which he was allowed to endlessly roam the suburbs of the city and the surrounding countryside. But where Chagall was a dreamer, his father most certainly was not. In the absence of support from his parents to pursue his great passion for art, he left the city that he so loved in 1906 to study in St Petersburg. He moved to Paris in 1910 under the patronage of lawyer Max Vinaver. There he was befriended by Robert and Sonia Delauney, in whose circles he found the time, space and inspiration to assimilate and develop Cubist ideas. He returned to Vitebsk prior to the outbreak of war in 1914 and married his fiancée Bella, who was to be a major influence on his later work. After the 1917 Revolution, he was appointed Commissar of Art for Vitebsk, a role that did not come easily to him. He also founded, directed and taught at the School of Arts in the city, but he moved to Moscow in 1920, then back to Paris in 1922. His work was denounced by the Nazis and, at the outbreak of war, the family moved to the south of France and then to the USA. When Bella died in 1944, Chagall was overcome with grief at the loss of his muse. He stopped painting for quite some time, although his subsequent relationship with Virginia Haggard (they had a son together) saw a return to his creativity. Returning to France in 1947, he subsequently married Valentine Brodsky (in 1952). In the 1960s, he was commissioned to design stained-glass windows for the Hadassah University Medical Centre in Jerusalem, work that profoundly impacted upon his faith. Further commissions for murals and costume design followed in France and America. He died in 1985.

Influenced by Cubism and Surrealism but always an independent artist of unique style, Chagall referred to Vitebsk as 'my second Paris' (although some claim that he actually called Paris his 'second Vitebsk'), and cameo sketches of the city as it was in the early 20th century are reflected in many of the works of this great master. In January 1991, Vitebsk celebrated the first Marc Chagall Festival, then in June 1992 a monument to him was erected on his native Pokrovskaya Street, with a memorial inscription being placed on the wall of his home at the same time. The small wooden house is now open to the public and the city also has a first-class Chagall Museum (see page 237).

The Yakub Kolas Academic Drama Theatre (*2 Zamkovaya St;* \ *(box office) 36 07 83; theatre@vitebsk.by; www.theatre.vitebsk.by*) Also built in the Classical style and once adorned with the same pale orange stucco as the City Hall and Russian Governor's Palace (it's now yellow), this theatre is home to a company that enjoys an enviable international reputation. It is only one of two in the whole country (and presumably the world) that presents performances exclusively in the Belarusian language. This should not be seen as a bar for foreign visitors, however, because presentations are usually so vividly striking and avant-garde in nature that language is only one part of the experience. The theatre's website is a mine of useful information on both the history of the company and the current repertoire. Stand outside the front on the right-hand edge of the building (with your back to it) and walk towards Kirov Bridge to admire the view uphill and right of the Ouspensky Cathedral. On the left-hand edge a glorious vista of the city's architecture unfolds across the lower and upper parts of the city.

CHURCHES Most of the churches in the city (particularly those from the time of the Polish-Lithuanian Commonwealth) were destroyed, either in warfare or under the communists. At one point there were 60 churches and almost the same number of synagogues in this city of hills. Many of the churches have been restored or rebuilt with glorious attention to detail, but no synagogue remains. All that is left is the ruined frontage of the one where the Chagall family worshipped, close to the old market square. Lean on the balustrade at the edge of the square outside Ouspensky Cathedral (see below) and, from your lofty perch, gaze over the lower city and count how many churches you can see. A splendid array of style and design awaits. Many are within walking distance of this point. Plot your route and away you go. Here is but a selection to tempt you:

The Ouspensky Cathedral of the Assumption Situated on the end of Krilova Street, high above the Dvina River on the eastern bank, this is an absolute delight. Originally constructed in 1777, little of the original building survived Stalin's demolition in 1936. Full works of reconstruction were only completed in 2000. The interior is a vast open space, but the décor is most sumptuous. Not only is the cathedral extremely pleasing on the eye inside and out, it is also ideally located for a fine meander. From the balustrade on the edge of the square, the view to the Kirov Bridge and beyond across the lower city is delightful, although the beauty of the vista hides dark deeds. On the other side of the river to the right of the bridge is old **Jewish Vitebsk** and there was a large ghetto here during the Nazi occupation, one of several across the city. Twenty thousand Jews were murdered in 1941 alone, up to 800 a day. Many were put on boats and drowned in the river. Reflect for a moment on the obscene disparity between the charm of the view today and the horrors that occurred here only decades ago. When you're ready to move on, the landscaped walkways down to the river and back are definitely worth exploring in every direction. Climb back up to the square and it's now a stroll of only a few hundred metres north high above the river to the Russian Governor's Palace and the Marc Chagall Museum and Art Centre, with the **City Zoo** in-between. The zoo itself is nothing special, though the old red-brick entrance building is a fine example of the early style once found all over the city. At any point of your choosing when you've seen enough, head east away from the river until you reach Suvarova Street. It has been attractively paved and pedestrianised, with a wide choice of coffee bars, restaurants and cafés if you're in need of sustenance. Just along from the cathedral on Krilova Street is **Zolotoy Drakon**, while **Zolotoy Vyek** is next to the zoo's entrance building on the corner of Suvarova and Yanki Kupala Streets. When refreshed, head downhill along Suvarova Street and explore the sights along Tolstova and Pushkina Streets leading down to Zamkovaya Street, including City Hall, the Pushkin statue, Yakub Kolas Theatre and a number of beautiful churches.

The Holy Resurrection Church Situated at the bottom of the hill on Suvarova Street, this is probably my favourite of the city's churches. Built between 1772 and 1777 but substantially rebuilt in 2009 after virtual destruction in 1936, the exterior murals are justly famed. Also impressive are the twin belltowers.

The Intercession Cathedral Located on Shubina Street near the junction with Lenin Street and a short walk north from Victory Square, the murals on the exterior of this beautiful 19th-century cathedral are worthy of your attention.

The Alexander Nevsky Orthodox Church Situated on Zamkovaya Street, close to the Western Dvina River, and just across the road from the Yakub Kolas Academic Drama Theatre and within the grounds of the reconstructed Blagovezhenskaya Annunciation Church (described opposite), this is a tiny but strikingly beautiful reconstruction in wood of the 10th-century church that originally stood on this spot.

FREE AS A BIRD   *Nicky Gardner*

Si je n'étais pas juif je n'aurais pas été un artiste
(Were I not a Jew, I would not be an artist at all)

Marc Chagall, *Ma Vie* (1931)

Frayvia foygl. Free as a bird. That was Moyshe. Local boy. Nice kid. His pa was in the herring business. The man reeked of fish. And Moyshe's ma, well she ran a shop. Groceries, that sort of thing. They lived out near the railway line. Brick house on Pokrovskaya. Simple, nothing fancy. Like most folk round these parts, they were a hard-working family. Quiet, I'd say. Observed shabbat of course. The Torah and trade make good partners. *Toyre iz di beste skhoyre* – that's the way they saw it. And that's the way I see it.

Hey, look at that man sitting up there on that pointed gable. So high. He goes up there every morning, perches on the roof and eats *tzimmes*. Cannot be so comfy right up there.

Anyway, I was telling you about Moyshe. He stopped going to the synagogue after his Bar Mitzvah. Until then, he'd gone to *heder* with the other local lads. Moyshe had a fine teacher at the *heder*, a good man who taught the boys the prayer book and took them down to the steam bath (*banya*) on Fridays. The talk was that Moyshe's Hebrew wasn't up to much, but he really lapped up all those old Yiddish tales of how life once was in these parts. Of course, it's all changed now.

See all those wooden houses across the way? The little grey house. That's my place. Typical Vitebsk. You can see the domes of the cathedral beyond, over on the side of the river where the Russians live. Looks like that fella over there is carrying his house on his back. All our people are on the move. *Di shtot geyt.* The whole town is leaving. Leaving for ever. All except the fella up on the gable. Not sure about him. Not quite right in the head, I'd say. Or just a *luftmentsh*. Just like Moyshe himself. He grew up to be a bit of a *luftmentsh*.

Young Moyshe often went out to Liozna. The family hailed from there. A smallish spot on the road to Smolensk. You probably know it. Last of the Jewish *shtetls* in the Pale. The end of our world. Moyshe's Uncle Zusya still had a place out there. A barber, I think. They had a shop too. Moyshe was good at art. Sort of taught himself. He showed me a sketch once that he'd done on one of those trips out to Uncle Zusya's place.

When I was young, there were two parts to my world. There was my Vitebsk. Safe, Jewish. My dad used to take me round to the home of the *rebbe*. And then there was the Russian part of town. That was a different Vitebsk. It had churches and cathedrals, but I didn't know any Russians. They came and went. St Petersburg, Moscow. Always with the *ayznban*. The train made Vitebsk part of Russia. The train is Russia. Not my world.

The Blagovezhenskaya Annunciation Church A church has been standing on this site in Zamkovaya Street since the middle of the 12th century, but the original building, which had been extensively renovated in the 14th and 17th centuries, was reduced to rubble by the communists in 1961. Then in 1992 it was fully restored to its original appearance and magnificence (or at least, to how the architects imagined it to have been). The design technique, limestone blocks separated by two rows of brick, with the exterior being covered with a thin layer of stucco, is classically Byzantine and, with the exception of this church, there is evidence of only one other (at Novogrudok) north of the Black Sea. Sadly, the church at Novogrudok was never actually completed and now lies in ruins.

After Moyshe stopped going to the *shabbat* service, his ma took him out of *heder* and sent him to the Russian school. Odd really. That sort of thing never happened in my day. They must have slipped the teacher something to get the boy in. The Russian school didn't normally accept Jewish lads. Everyone called him Moysey then. I guess it sounded a bit more Russian. Anyway, he must have done well because he went on to art college in St Petersburg, then moved to Paris.

You know, I didn't hear much of him for years. Then there was the Revolution, and next thing I knew Moyshe was back in town and one of the bigwigs. Grand title. Commissar for Art in Vitebsk. He founded the People's Art College, the local museum and got involved with the theatre. All good party stuff. By then he had married Berta. Local girl. You know her family, of course. The Rosenfelds. They had a jewellery store near the town hall.

Did I tell you about the green violinist? The fiddler on the roof? No, not yet? But that's not a tale for now, as dusk is falling. Strange, strange... look up by the church. There's a man flying over there. He has a sack over his shoulder. *Kol Israel, eyn torbe*. All the children of Israel in one sack. There'll be none of us at all left in Vitebsk soon. Good that Moyshe drew us all before he and Berta moved to France for good. There's even a picture of me, they say. I dunno if it's true. But a friend told me that Moyshe gave me a red beard in his painting. The red Jew. Keep a lookout for me, won't you?

C'est de cet instant (1911) que la métaphore, avec lui seul, marque son entrée triomphale dans la peinture moderne.
(It was at that instant (1911) and through him alone, that metaphor made its triumphant entry into modern painting)

The French poet André Breton writing in 1941 about the work of Marc Chagall.

Marc Chagall, born Moyshe Shagal in Vitebsk in 1887, died in exile in France in 1985. He left Vitebsk in 1922. The artist never returned to his native city. But scenes from Chagall's early life in the Vitebsk region continued to feature in his art to the very end of his life. His images, which dramatically defy the laws of physics, poignantly record the lost Jewish life of Vitebsk. Only Chagall, the master of metaphor, could capture all the colourful children of Israel in one sack.

Nicky Gardner is co-editor of hidden europe *magazine. Find out more about her work at www.hiddeneurope.co.uk.*

Work on both of them was probably undertaken by the same team of Byzantine architects and builders.

The Eastern Orthodox St Protection Kazan Cathedral
Erected in 1760 with elements of Baroque and early Classical, the white plaster of the exterior and the matte black of the cupolas splendidly enhance the glittering gold domes and crosses above. It is to be found on Maxim Gorky Street on the western bank of the Dvina River, away to the southwest of the city centre.

The Roman Catholic Cathedral of St Barbara
Built between 1884 and 1885 on the site of an earlier church established in 1785, this cathedral on Leningradskaya Street in the northwest of the city centre was built in the Neo-Romanesque style of architecture. It's very red indeed and is perhaps best described as 'Gothic' with a capital G.

OTHER BUILDINGS
Other historical buildings worthy of your attention include:

The City Hall
Located just along Lenin Street from the Art Museum and built in 1775, it has been extensively renovated. The current building replaced the original from 1597, when Magdeburg rights were granted. The beautifully ornate Baroque clocktower is an especially entrancing feature. Incorporated within is the **Regional Museum** (*36 Lenin St;* ✆ *36 47 12; www.ratusha.by;* ◷ *10.00–18.00 Tue–Sun; admission BYR1,040*). On display are relics, artefacts and memorabilia detailing the history of the city and region, with a particularly impressive collection devoted to the city's privations during World War II.

The Russian Governor's Palace
Built in the early 1770s and located in the pretty square to the right of the Marc Chagall Museum and Art Centre, this was the place chosen by Napoleon in 1812 to celebrate his 43rd birthday, during the long Russia campaign. A contemporary building of the City Hall, the pale orange stucco and Classical style make both of them pleasing to the eye. Later, during the October Revolution in 1917, this palace was home to the Military Revolutionary Committee that declared Soviet power in the city and *oblast*. Outside in the square is the stone **obelisk** commemorating the centenary of the Russian victory over Napoleon's forces topped by the iconic double-headed eagle, interestingly gazing north and south instead of east and west as is usually the case! Look for the missing chunk of stone shot off the monument during the first military engagement in 1941. Close by is the monument to the liberating forces of the Red Army, constructed on the line of the front where fierce engagements took place over a nine-month period in 1943–44. The ravine of the Western Dvina River is especially precipitous here.

Victory Square and Victory Park
Said to be the biggest square in the whole of Belarus (I haven't paced it out but I'm not sure if this claim can be right), this is a vast block-paved area used for public events on a grand scale. You'll find the complex at the bottom of Lenin Street south of the Kirov Bridge. The park contains the three-bayonet monument built in 1974 to represent the three Red Army fronts that liberated the city from Nazi occupation in 1944. Also here is the eternal flame and four separate memorials symbolising each of the four years of occupation, the whole commemorating the Soviet heroes of the Great Patriotic War – military, civilian and partisan. This is a fine location for promenading and, if you amble north along the bank of the Western Dvina, you will come to the Blagovezhenskaya Annunciation and Alexander Nevsky Churches (see pages 240–2) at the top of the park.

POLOTSK (ПОЛАЦК / ПОЛОЦК) Excluding Vitebsk itself, this is the region's second-largest town (83,000 inhabitants) and one of the most attractive in all Belarus. On its doorstep is the urban sprawl of the larger and much less attractive town of Novopolotsk ('New Polotsk', population 122,000), constructed in 1958 as a base for the local oil industry. There's nothing for you to see there but happily, lovely Polotsk has riches to spare. Located 105km northwest of Vitebsk along the A215 road, this historic settlement (and one of the oldest cities in the whole of eastern Europe) has a beautiful riverside location on the Western Dvina, which also flows through Vitebsk. It is often referred to as 'the city of all Belarusian cities', with a rich literary heritage. Poet, translator and teacher Simeon of Polotsk was born here, as well as the great humanist and translator of the Bible, Francisk Skoryna. This is an especially pleasant town to meander and explore on foot, and many people regard it still as the spiritual cradle and first capital of modern Belarus. This includes my good friend Larissa Yatskevich, a tour guide and former university lecturer, who told me once, 'It all started here for Belarus!' Interestingly, it was only after the collapse of the Soviet Union that people began to learn of such things; until then it appears only post-1917 history was taught in schools.

History The name of the town is derived from the Polota River, which flows into the Western Dvina here, at the foot of the magnificent Cathedral of St Sophia (see page 246). In fact, Polotsk was one of the earliest of the major settlements of the Slavic tribes and is widely regarded as having been the first independent 'Belarusian' state. It was first referred to in the *Primary Chronicle* of AD862 and it featured significantly in Viking incursions from the north. Norse sagas describe the city as the most heavily fortified in all of Kievan Rus.

Between the 10th and 12th centuries, the greater principality of Polotsk emerged as the dominant centre of influence in all of the lands now recognised as Belarus. It continually asserted its sovereignty over other powerful settlements and administrations of Kievan Rus to become not only a political capital, but also the episcopal see and the controller of certain subservient western lands occupied by Baltic tribes. In fact, its influence stretched from the shores of the Baltic Sea in the west to the area of Smolensk in the east. Its most powerful ruler was Prince Vyseslav Bryachislavich ('The Sorcerer'), who was believed by the people to be a magical shape-shifter, with the ability to assume the form of any animal at will. To this day there remains a statue of him in the town wearing a wolf skin and with eagles on his back. You can find it outside the market on the road to the Convent of St Ephrosinia, on the left. He reigned from 1044 to 1101 and an inscription commissioned by his son Boris in the 12th century can still be seen today on the huge boulder placed near to the Cathedral of St Sophia, which was built between 1044 and 1066 as a symbol of the power and independence of the city.

The town became part of the Grand Duchy of Lithuania in 1307. It is believed that its geographical location and the extent of its influence and power made it the most significant trading centre in the whole of the duchy. It was granted self-determination and the right to govern under Magdeburg Law in 1498, but was sacked by Ivan the Terrible in 1563, before being returned to Lithuania in 1578. This signalled the start of a long period of settled affluence and it was granted the status of regional capital in the Polish-Lithuanian Commonwealth until partition in 1772. Cyclical warfare in the region eventually took its toll and the city slipped into a gradual process of steady decline. After partition, it was relegated to the status of

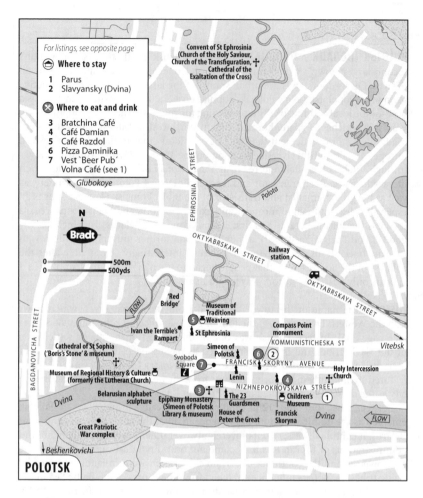

For listings, see opposite page

Where to stay

1 Parus
2 Slavyansky (Dvina)

Where to eat and drink

3 Bratchina Café
4 Café Damian
5 Café Razdol
6 Pizza Daminika
7 Vest `Beer Pub´
  Volna Café (see 1)

Glubokoye

N

Bradt

0 _____ 500m
0 _____ 500yds

Convent of St Ephrosinia
(Church of the Holy Saviour,
Church of the Transfiguration,
Cathedral of the
Exaltation of the Cross)

EPHROSINIA STREET

Polota

OKTYABRSKAYA STREET

Railway
station

OKTYABRSKAYA STREET

BAGDANOVICHA STREET

'Red
Bridge'

Museum of
Traditional
Weaving

Ivan the Terrible's
Rampart

St Ephrosinia

Compass Point
monument

KOMMUNISTICHESKA ST

Vitebsk

Cathedral of St Sophia
('Boris's Stone' & museum)

Simeon of
Polotsk

Svoboda
Square

FRANCISK SKORYNY AVENUE

Holy Intercession
Church

Museum of Regional History & Culture
(formerly the Lutheran Church)

Belarusian alphabet
sculpture

Epiphany Monastery
(Simeon of Polotsk
Library & museum)

Lenin

NIZHNEPOKROVSKAYA STREET

The 23
Guardsmen

House of
Peter the Great

Children's
Museum

Francisk
Skoryna

Dvina

Great Patriotic
War complex

Beshenkovichi

Dvina

FLOW

POLOTSK

a small provincial town of the Russian Empire, then during the invasion of Russia by the French in 1812 two decisive battles were fought here.

In 1897 the population of the town was 30,000, 12,000 of whom were Jews. But on 21 November 1941 the Nazis murdered every single surviving Jew (around 8,000) following the establishment of the first ghetto in the centre of town, the ghetto having been later relocated towards the Convent of St Ephrosinia (see page 249). In 1995, a monument to the dead was erected on the P20 highway on the edge of town in the vicinity of the site of the second ghetto. The monument is modest, but no less moving in its impact. It is believed that the murders took place in the woods across the other side of the highway. Since the war the Jewish community in the town has slowly begun to re-establish itself, but the wounds will never heal.

Getting there and away

There are several daily **trains** to Polotsk from Vitebsk and it's a two-hour journey (*one-way fare BYR9,000*). You can also get here direct from Minsk, but the journey is long (up to eight hours, although it can be quicker, dependent upon the service). The **bus** station is only 100m from the railway station, with several daily buses running to Vitebsk and Minsk. *Marshrutkas* depart from

Minsk Moskovskaya bus station several times a day, with the journey taking around 3½ hours (*one-way fare BYR30,000*). However, to get the best out of a visit here, arrange an excursion from Vitebsk (or even Minsk, which is 250km southwest on the M3 'motorway'), but do try to stop over at least one night in town as there's too much to cover in a single day's excursion.

Where to stay and eat *Map, opposite.*

🏠 **Slavyansky Hotel Complex** (also referred to as the **Hotel Dvina**) (110 rooms) 13 Francisk Skoryny Av; ⚟ 44 22 35. Located 1.5km east of St Sophia Cathedral, 1km from the railway station and 1.5km from the bus station, this is the largest hotel in town. Rooms consist of sgls, dbls & suites. The design of the building is repro-Classical, with a richly ornate & multi-pillared entrance. But inside, it's nothing special, if adequate as a place to rest your head for the night. In short, the hotel is acceptable & clean, the staff are reasonably friendly, but the bedrooms are showing their age. The Slavyansky restaurant (⚟ 46 07 97; ⊕ noon–22.00 Sun–Mon, noon–midnight Tue–Thu, noon–02.00 Fri–Sat; **$$$**) is part of the complex & is of a similar standard. **$$$**

🏠 **Hotel Parus** (50 rooms) 50A Nizhni-Pakrovskaya St; ⚟ 42 51 70; www.parus-polotsk. by. Built in 2011 on the Western Dvina at the eastern end of Nizhni-Pakrovskaya St, this is my own preference in Polotsk. It is part of a complex that also inc. a rowing club. There are no frills, all is cheap & cheerful, but it's clean and functional. **$$**

✕ **Pizza Daminika** Just west of the Slavyansky restaurant; ⊕ 10.00–23.00 daily. According to a reliable source, this is a pretty good pizzeria with a vegetable pizza on the menu sporting an unusual but tasty bean topping. **$$**

🍴 **Bratchina Café** 22 Nizhni-Pakrovskaya St; ⚟ 42 38 49; ⊕ noon–midnight daily. Down towards the river at the Simeon of Polotsk Library & Museum, the location is lovely. The café itself is pleasant enough & decent value for money.

🍴 **Café Damian** 41B Nizhni-Pakrovskaya St; ⚟ 42 87 66; www.vk.com/cafedamian; ⊕ noon–midnight daily. It's yet another tired recreation of a Middle Ages fortress, but the service is good and the food, though unspectacular, is wholesome & reasonably priced. The eating area is to the rear of the bar. There's enough here for me to keep returning.

🍴 **Café Razdol** 15 Tolstova St; ⚟ 42 04 33; ⊕ 10.00–22.00 daily. Located next to the Weaving Museum, it's adequate & cheap.

🍴 **Volna Café** Adjoining the Hotel Parus; ⚟ 45 81 73; www.volna.polotsk-portal.ru; ⊕ noon–midnight Sun–Wed, noon–02.00 Thu–Sat. Service is slick & courteous, the food is simple but tasty (I had very passable lemon chicken with blinis & sour cream), but the décor is hideous, and I do mean truly vile. It's a throwback to the old Eastern Bloc of the 1970s, perhaps 1972 Albania or 1974 Bulgaria. There are pink drapes, bright orange plastic lamp shades, tiny mirror balls with coloured lasers, and everything gleams like polished steel. Astonishingly loud cabaret to the accompaniment of electric keys & a boom box, followed by a disco, complete the scene. When last I was there, the final tune of the night was *Ra Ra Rasputin* by Boney M at alarmingly high volume. It's so awful that you simply *must* give it a go. I loved every second. The website's photo gallery will tell you all you need to know.

🍺 **Vest 'Beer Pub'** 14 Francisk Skoryny Ave; ⊕ 10.00–23.00 daily. It says outside in English that it's a 'beer pub', & that's what you get, although snacks & light meals (blini, pancakes, etc) are also served.

What to see and do

Two parallel roads, Francisk Skoryny (formerly Karl Marx) Avenue and Nizhni-Pakrovskaya (formerly Lenina) Street run east–west through town, and most of the things I describe in this section are to be found there. You will also find a number of other bars/cafés and shops and, on Francisk Skoryny, several banks with ATMs, including one immediately to the left of the Slavyansky Restaurant, where you will also find a display board of helpful tourist information in English. The area bounded by these two roads is very much the main drag and together they form the centrepiece of my suggested historical walking tour (see pages 246–50).

A historical walking tour With the exception of the complex at the Convent of St Ephrosinia (see page 249), all of the other sights in the town can be visited as part of an enchanting single circular tour on foot. And many of them have an information board outside with a short description in English. Further, the recently upgraded street furniture includes directional signs that are also in English, with larger information boards (again in English) at a number of strategic points along the way.

Along the riverbank My description begins at the magnificent **Cathedral of St Sophia**, which is situated in an elevated position just beyond the western end of Nizhni-Pakrovskaya Street, from which it dominates the town, but you can pitch into the walk at any point you choose. When first built, between 1044 and 1066, this glorious cathedral was a direct rival of those bearing the same name in Novgorod and Kiev. It bears a striking resemblance to the original Hagia Sophia in Constantinople, a symbol of the authority and prestige enjoyed by the city at the time. A rich library was maintained there which included the *Polotsk Chronicle*, but everything disappeared without a trace during the 16th-century Livonian Wars. On the orders of Tsar Peter the Great, it was blown up by retreating Russian forces in 1710, before being rebuilt by the Poles between 1738 and 1750 as a Baroque Roman Catholic cathedral. Today, only the eastern elevation and some of the basement walls are the originals, but when first built its seven towers must have been a particularly imposing sight. Further restored in 1985, it now houses a **museum** (*1 Zamkovaya St;* ✆ *42 53 40;* e *sophia.polotsk@museum.by; www.sophia. polotsk.museum.by;* ⊕ *10.00–17.00 Tue–Sun; admission BYR3,500*) dedicated to its history. There is also a concert hall seating over 300. Festivals of chamber music are held in April and November, with organ recitals every Sunday.

Just outside, between the cathedral and the river, is the huge boulder of **Boris's Stone,** upon which Vyseslav Bryachislavich's son Boris carved the inscription, 'Dear Lord, please help Boris, your slave' in the 12th century, along with a cross and other Christian symbols. There are splendid views up, down and across the river here. To the right, the Western Dvina is joined by the smaller Polota River. And on the south side of the river, directly opposite the cathedral, lies a complex dedicated to the Great Patriotic War, with a grassy pyramidal **memorial** (the 'Mound of Immortality') and a decent **museum** (*1 Tusnabolova-Marchenka St;* ✆ *43 44 21;* e *war.polotsk@museum.by; www.war.polotsk.museum.by;* ⊕ *10.00–17.00 Tue–Sun; admission BYR2,500*), with exhibits dedicated to the defence, occupation and liberation of the town, as well as stories relating to its inhabitants.

Take the steps down towards the river and you soon come to a tatty plastic pipe in a rather scruffy little area, with a trickle of water coming from it. This is actually a spring. The water has been tested and shown to be pure, such that the faith of local people in its recuperative powers is absolute. That being the case, it really needs something of a face-lift. If you carry on down to the riverside, looking east along Nizhni-Pakrovskaya on the left-hand side of the street is the former **Lutheran church**, a stone and red-brick Neo-Gothic building constructed at the beginning of the 20th century. No longer a church, it now houses the **Museum of Regional History and Culture** (*11 Nizhni-Pakrovskaya St;* ✆ *42 27 15;* e *local.polotsk@ museum.by; www.local.polotsk.museum.by;* ⊕ *10.00–17.00 Tue–Sun*). A short walk further along the street, on the right-hand side and with a lovely river frontage, is the beautiful **Epiphany Monastery**. Founded in 1582 and originally constructed of wood, it burned down in 1761 and was reconstructed in 1788 under the patronage of Catherine the Great. The primary centre of Orthodox worship and teaching in the town, it was closed after the October Revolution of 1917 and was not restored to full use until 1990, the extensive works taking nine years to complete. In 1994, part of the complex was opened as the **Simeon of Polotsk Library and Museum** (*22 Nizhni-Pakrovskaya St;* \ *42 63 39/42 57 25;* e *simeon.polotsk@museum.by; www. simeon.polotsk.museum.by;* ☉ *10.00–17.00 Tue–Sun*), the only museum devoted solely to book printing in the whole country. There is also a reading room with seating for ten. Simeon is an important literary figure in the history of this country. Poet, writer, playwright, translator and all-round enlightener, he is known to have lectured here in the second half of the seventeenth century.

If you look along the riverbank to the left from the rear of the museum, you will see the **Monument to the 23 Guardsmen**, erected in 1989 to commemorate the heroism of soldiers of the First Baltic Front who lost their lives when the Nazis blew up the only bridge across the river (a wooden one) at this location on 3 July 1944. Across the road from the printing museum and a little to the right is the **House of Peter the Great** (*33 Nizhni-Pakrovskaya St;* \ *42 28 41; www.wolk.polotsk.museum.by*). Built in 1692 as a small apartment building with elements of Baroque style, it was the residence of the tsar throughout the summer of 1705, during his time in command of the Russian imperial army during the Northern Wars that were raging at the time. It now houses a permanent exhibition ('A Walk Along Nizhni-Pakrovskaya Street'), access to which is available by contacting the museum direct in advance.

Around Svoboda Square Turning away from the river at the Epiphany Monastery and in towards the town, you very soon reach the central **Svoboda Square**. It's a vast, brick-paved open space with pale stucco buildings all around, with the exception of the brutalist Soviet apartment blocks immediately behind the war memorials, on the site of a former Catholic monastery blown up in 1963. An image of the monastery has been painted on the side of the Art School building directly opposite. The first war memorial is the Napoleonic War monument, built in 2010 as an exact copy of the original melted down in the Great Patriotic War for arms. Immediately behind is the monument commemorating the liberation of the town in 1944. To the left you will see the former Russian Governor's house (now a bank), with the town's administrative offices next left. Also here is the **tourist information centre** (*8 Francisk Skoryny Av;* \ *42 69 49;* e *tic_polotsk@belladvina.com; www.belladvina.com;* ☉ *08.00–17.00 Mon–Fri, closed for lunch 13.00–14.00, closed Sat & Sun*). Some information is available in English. On the opposite side of the square is a colonnaded yellow stucco building of some charm, which houses the *oblast* administrative offices. It's a copy of the original flattened by the Nazis. The oak tree outside the building to the left is colloquially regarded as a place of remembrance for those murdered during Stalin's purges.

Proceed out of the square to the right of the apartment blocks and past the bar dispensing fearsome beer brewed on the premises (I haven't sampled it but local friends advise extreme caution) and notice first the 18th-century Jesuit seminary on the left. Constructed during the days of the Grand Duchy of Lithuania, it became a military school during the subsequent Russian occupation. It was later a hospital and is now a university. If you can, visit between 08.00 and 14.00 to observe the chiming of the attractive clock built into the opposite wall as you enter the courtyard, immediately above the well (which is 29m deep). It's quite a performance. As the clock strikes the hour, piped music heralds a procession of figures from the town's history around the base, led by St Ephrosinia. If you've also visited Prague's clock there will be a strong resonance for you, though Polotsk people think theirs is better!

Retrace your steps out of the courtyard and immediately opposite are two sides of the ramparts built by Ivan the Terrible, 600m in length. Nothing remains of the former eight-tower fortress inside (it's now the site of a sports stadium), which was once a symbol of Ivan's brutal reign. He occupied the town for 16 years from 1563, during which time 3,000 Jews were murdered. If you head uphill to the left of the ramparts and then round to the left, you will be back at the stunning **Cathedral of St Sophia** (see page 246). I only mention it again here to help you get your bearings and because, as you walk towards it, a glance below to your left brings into view a fine example of a Russian red-brick building from the 19th century. Now retrace your steps back into Svoboda Square, with Ivan the Terrible's ramparts on your left this time.

A short detour along the road out of the northwestern corner of the square adjacent to a pretty landscaped area, downhill and under the ramparts, pausing briefly outside the *oblast* administrative offices to take a look at the **Monument to St Ephrosinia** on the right-hand side (the first woman to be canonised by the Orthodox Church and also the country's first saint), brings you to the grimly named **'Red Bridge'** over the Polota River. It was thus named to commemorate the bloody battles that took place near here in October 1812 during the Napoleonic campaign, when around 14,000 soldiers lost their lives, in equal numbers on both sides. The original bridge was a wooden one. On my last visit here, building works for a new three-star hotel had just begun immediately adjacent to the bridge. This road takes you to the **Convent of St Ephrosinia**, but other than for those with time to spare and a high level of fitness it's too far to walk, with little to see on the way other than the statue of Prince Vyseslav Bryachislavich described earlier.

Now return up the hill towards Svoboda Square. On the left before you get there, between the bridge and the statue of St Ephrosinia, stands the small **Museum of Traditional Weaving** (*1 Voikova St;* ☎ *42 30 41;* e *tkach.polotsk@museum.by; www. tkach.polotsk.museum.by;* ⊕ *10.00–17.00 Tue–Sun; admission BYR1,500*). Three rooms trace the history of this activity, so critically significant to the culture of the country, in relation to the Vitebsk region. Visitors receive explanations (Russian only, sadly) about the holy symbolism of images that feature in designs, along with the ancient myths that are encoded in ostensibly simple patterns. This museum is well worth a visit if you have a translator with you. Gaze around as you leave the museum. The landscape includes the faded glory of an imposing multi-colonnaded stucco building on one side (now in need of urgent and significant repair) and the might of Ivan the Terrible's ramparts on the other, with the road to the Red Bridge cutting through below. Suitably shod it's possible to pick your way up, over and along the ramparts. The views through the trees make it worth your while.

Along Francisk Skoryny Avenue Back in Svoboda Square, head diagonally across to the left and enter Francisk Skoryny Avenue. It is long, straight and almost 100m wide, with delightfully landscaped gardens, pathways and seating through the middle, which make it ideal for my favourite pastime in Belarus: promenading and watching the world pass by. Join the locals in a meandering amble. You first come to a literary symbol of some importance to the Belarusian language, the small **sculpture** placed here in 2003 to celebrate the 22nd letter of the Belarusian alphabet. The inscription reads 'from Ephrosinia, from Skoryna, from Polotsk has the world emanated'.

Walk on past shops and a bank with ATMs to reach the ubiquitous **Lenin statue**, then head left across the avenue to the **statue of Simeon of Polotsk** in a lovely little square. Also erected in 2003, it's another important symbol of the country's literary heritage. Continue down the avenue, past the **souvenir shop** at number 11 selling traditional gifts and **Pizza Daminika**, to reach the **compass point monument** sited at the *exact* centre of the continent of Europe. It must be, as Belarusian scientists have precisely calculated it to be so, though it is understood that other scientists of equal renown lay claim to the very same distinction in Ukraine. The information boards here are especially useful; the text is only in Russian, but the photographs will help you to orientate yourself. Walk on past the **Slavyansky Hotel and Restaurant** and into **Skoryny Square** to find the imposing **statue of Francisk Skoryna**, deep in thought.

Back down to the river Back on to the avenue, it's a short walk to the **brutalist Soviet monument** with its affecting images of Red Army soldiers, while down to the right, close to the road bridge over the Western Dvina, is the **Holy Intercession Church**, the history of which included conversion into a chocolate factory in the 1950s. It was standing outside this church that I experienced a David Lean moment on my last visit. The bridge road sits on a steep escarpment behind the church and, as I gazed up at it, with only a vast steel grey sky above and behind, I watched as a *babooshka* moved slowly, almost painfully, on the skyline. My eyes followed her all the way along the escarpment, my line of vision filled with a huge tableau of earth and sky, upon which a single point of solitary and almost imperceptible movement was the only other feature. Between the church and the river is a small children's amusement park, and to the right is the **Hotel Parus and Volna Café** (see page 245). Continue west past the hotel along Nizhni-Pakrovskaya Street to the **House of Peter the Great** (see page 247) and your historical circuit is complete. Shortly after the hotel on the left at number 48 is an archetypical red-brick building from the 19th century. There's another further along on the same side at number 26, just after the modest but attractive pink stucco apartment building of similar vintage at number 30. At this point look across the river to see the **19th-century Catholic monastery** and to its right, the delightful **Catholic church** with its blue roof and towers. *En route*, be sure not to overlook the quirky **Children's Museum** at number 46 (✎ *42 45 58;* e *children.polotsk@museum.by; www.children.polotsk.museum.by;* ⊕ *10.00–17.00 Tue–Sun*) with its 19th- and 20th-century artefacts for children to play with, such as old cameras, typewriters and sewing machines. The two **sculptures** (front and back) have idiosyncratic charms of their own. See also a little further on the **Monument to the 23 Guardsmen** (see page 247). And at any point along Nizhni-Pakrovskaya are opportunities to drop down for a riverside stroll.

The Convent of St Ephrosinia (*59 Ephrosyny Poltskoy St;* ✎ *46 14 29;* ⊕ *11.00–16.00 Tue–Sat; admission free*) This is the last of the sights in this lovely town, and one not to be missed. In the 12th century, Polotsk was the capital of a hugely significant principality (Minsk being no more than a small town in its shadow). St Ephrosinia was the daughter of Prince George and Princess Sophia of Polotsk. She shunned riches and refused all proposals of marriage, instead running away to become a nun against her parents' wishes. Legend has it that she was ordered in a vision to build a place of worship, and thus the **Church of the Holy Saviour** was established. It faces you within the complex as you pass under the belfry. Built and consecrated in 1161, it is one of the best-preserved examples of early church architecture in the whole country. On the outside, some of the original red brick from the 12th century has been left exposed. To the right are the graves of several nuns. Enter the church to see on the right a portrait of the saint bearing the sacred cross that she commissioned herself from skilled local craftsman Lazar Bogsha. This exquisite six-armed golden cross, decorated with enamels and precious stones, has seen many adventures. After being stolen for the first time it subsequently turned up in Smolensk, then disappeared again in mysterious circumstances in 1941, during the evacuation of the museum where it was stored. At the time, the cross is said to have incorporated a number of holy relics of enormous spiritual significance. It was never seen again and doubtless now sits in a private collection somewhere. A replica was made in 1992 and is displayed every Saturday and Sunday between the hours of 09.00 and noon. It remains a powerful and mystical symbol of the spirituality of true believers within the Orthodox community in Belarus. Continue on into the body of this small church, where a sight to take away your breath awaits. Every wall and pillar is adorned with 12th-century frescoes of exquisite beauty. Already long in the process of restoration since 1995, the repairs are not expected to be completed until 2015, but even as work in progress the impact is stunning. Every available space has its own fresco. In the 19th century, these beautiful images were covered in a layer of cement with oil paintings on top. No longer are they hidden from view. The original floor is also being restored. St Ephrosinia died in 1173 while on pilgrimage to Jerusalem. Her relics were later taken to Kiev before being returned to this lovely church by Tsar Nikolai II in 1910. Interestingly, they were exhibited in museums all over the Soviet Union after the Revolution, miraculously surviving the destruction of Vitebsk during the war. Now kept at the convent complex, they are currently in the process of restoration before being displayed once more in the church founded by the saint herself.

Outside to the left is the slightly larger **Church of the Transfiguration** (built in 1842). To the right stands the imposing, black-domed 1897 **Cathedral of the Exaltation of the Cross.** Lavishly ornate inside, this is the present location of St Ephrosinia's holy relics. The whole makes for an extremely pleasing excursion. Ladies should note that heads must be covered and that, if wearing trousers, you will be required to put on a skirt over the top of your trousers. Scarfs and skirts may be borrowed from the collection stored in the metal wardrobe on the right of the belfry.

GORODOK JEWISH CEMETERY Some 39km north of Vitebsk on the P115 road is the town of Gorodok, site of an important **Jewish cemetery** dating back to 1700. It is significant because it remains largely intact and is thus an uninterrupted physical record of the burials of a Jewish *shtetl* over a continuous period in excess of 300 years. This makes it an important site for archival research. Covering an area approximately 760m square, there are estimated to be 5,000–8,000 graves there. It remains in use for burials to this day. The Jewish community in the town is relatively small but is committed to securing the necessary funding for remedial work and improvements under the auspices of an international appeals committee, to ensure this site of major historical record is protected for the future. Two important Holocaust sites are also to be found in the vicinity. Elsewhere in the country, Jewish cemeteries have, largely been destroyed as a result of the neglect, vandalism and destruction that have followed wholesale victimisation of communities, resettlement and mass murder across the centuries. This makes securing the future of the Gorodok cemetery all the more important. For further information and to arrange a visit, contact the UK sustainable development charity **The Together Plan** (see page 107 for contact details) or Belarusian NGO **Dialog** (\ +375 (29) 627 34 00; e *dialogorganisation@gmail.com*).

OTHER TOWNS AND VILLAGES IN VITEBSK *OBLAST* Nestling in various locations throughout the Vitebsk *oblast* are many small towns and villages that are worthy of your time. The **church architecture** of this region (both Orthodox and Catholic) is particularly impressive, with stunning examples to be discovered all over the area. You will also find a number of romantic ruins of castles, palaces and fortified manor houses. Sadly, access by public transport is not easy unless you can speak the language and have lots of time to sit on a rattling bus, so unless you have your own transport the best advice is to arrange a tour or excursion through one of the state agencies. Those following are but a tiny selection of the many things you might want to visit and see. Some 50km due west of Vitebsk on the A245 road is the town of **Beshenkovichi,** an administrative centre that was first mentioned in 1460. Located on the Dvina River, noteworthy sites include the 18th-century palace and extensive parkland, together with the beautiful Orthodox Church of St Elias, built in 1870. Some 85km southwest of Polotsk on the A235 is the 16th-century town of **Glubokoye**. Numerous buildings in the Baroque style are to be found here, together with the stunning 17th-century Orthodox Church of the Nativity and the 18th-century Holy Trinity Roman Catholic Church. Established towards the end of the 11th century and located 70km due south of Vitebsk, at the crossroads of two major intercontinental routes east–west (the M1) and north–south (the M8), the town of **Orsha** is one of the oldest in the country. And as well as being a key port on the Dnieper River, it is also a major junction on the Minsk–Moscow railway line. The station is a glorious building, housing shops and an excellent restaurant. Also here is the beautiful Holy Epiphany Kuteinsky Monastery, originally home to a renowned 17th-century printing house, and, in a lovely riverside location, the beautiful walled Orthodox Church of St Ilia is a 'must see'.

BRASLAV LAKES NATIONAL PARK (НАЦЫЯНАЛЬНЫ ПАРК БРАСЛАЎСКІЯ АЗЁРЫ / НАЦИОНАЛЬНЫЙ ПАРК БРАСЛАВСКИЕ ОЗЕРА) (*1 Dachnaya St, Braslav;* \ *21 532 92 61;* e *braslavpark@gmail.com; www.braslav.com*) With the sprawling town of Braslav within its boundaries, this beautiful park of 70,000ha is located close to the border with Latvia, about 250km north of Minsk and the same distance northwest from Vitebsk, through Polotsk along the A215. Established in 1995 and famed for the unique nature of its aquatic ecosystems, the southern part of the park is mostly lowland marsh and forest, while the central and northern parts consist of beautiful blue lakes interconnected by a labyrinth of hundreds of rivers and streams, set in picturesque rolling hills. No fewer than 189 species of bird live here, including black stork, osprey, tern, bittern and ptarmigan. It is also possible to spot elk, wild boar, roe deer, beaver, fox, racoon, badger and wolf roaming free in their natural environment, although all are of course shy and evasive. There are also complexes consisting of large pens for closer study, although do bear in mind that these are enclosed spaces. Animals are not free to wander without boundaries and, as a matter of principle, the difficulties of this concept speak for themselves. Inhabiting the lakes are 28 species of fish, such as eel, whitefish, whitebait, zander, pike, catfish, carp, bream, chub, turbot, tench, perch, gudgeon, loach, ruff and stickleback. The park is rich in flora of more than 800 species. The areas of forestry include birch, pine, fir, black elder and aspen. All in all, the march of time has largely bypassed this delightful area and, as a sanctuary to step off the world in search of some inner peace and calm, there are many worse places to choose.

Visitors can dip into various organised tours on horseback or by car, as well as on the water or by foot, lasting from one to several days. The pastimes of hunting and fishing are particularly well served. One of the most delightful trips is by launch across the limpid lakeland waters.

Where to stay and eat In terms of facilities, there are four separate complexes. Stays, tours and excursions can be arranged via most of the state and privately owned tourism companies, all of which will offer a range of options to suit all tastes.

Drivyaty tourist centre (Sleeps 50; 2 4-storey buildings each contain 8 dbls & 4 suites) On the outskirts of the town of Braslav, on the shore of Lake Drivyaty itself. Facilities on site include secure parking, children's area, summerhouses, campfire, bathhouse & lakeside beach. **$$**

Leoshky tourist centre (Sleeps 14 across 6 cottages) 25km from Braslav on the shore of Lake Severny Volos. Facilities include 2 summerhouses, barbecue area & piers, with a bathhouse nearby. The waters are particularly clear here. **$$**

🏠 **Slobodka tourist centre** (3 cottages sleep 10 each) 12km from Braslav on the shore of Lake Potyekh, near the village of Slobodka. Facilities include secure parking, 3 summerhouses, bathhouse, barbecue area & lakeside beach. A designated path 2.5km long runs from here along the Sloboda ridge, with excellent views over the surrounding area. **$$**

🏠 **Zolovo tourist centre** (Sleeps 14–18 across 3 cottages) 25km from Braslav in a forest location near Lake Zolovo. Secure parking, 3 summerhouses on the lakeside, picnic area & bathhouse. **$$**

BEREZINSKY BIOSPHERE RESERVE (БЯРЭЗІНСКІ БІЯСФЕРНЫ ЗАПАВЕДНІК / БЕРЕЗИНСКИЙ БИОСФЕРНЫЙ ЗАПОВЕДНИК) (*Domzheritsy Building, Tsentralnaya St;* 📞 *21 322 63 18;* e *tourism@berezinsky.by; www.berezinsky.by*)

Now part of UNESCO's World Network of Biosphere Reserves, this special place was originally opened in January 1925 to preserve and nurture another splendid natural environment, as well as to conserve and protect the valuable wildlife living there, notably beaver. Covering around 85,000ha and attracting around 20,000 visitors per year from within Belarus and abroad, this substantial area of wilderness is situated 130km northeast of Minsk and the same distance southwest of Vitebsk, the M3 motorway between the two passing directly through it. There are several daily buses from Minsk and Vitebsk. Here is a land of virginal primeval forests (mostly pine and spruce), marshland (one of the largest in Europe) and lakes, rich in diverse flora and fauna, sitting right in the middle of the watershed of the Baltic and Black seas. The areas of marshland are particularly beautiful. Small wooded islands rise above marsh plains as far as the eye can see. Thousands of years ago they were proper islands, washed by the waves of the vast glacial lake that is buried now under a thick and impenetrable layer of rich peat. The largest and longest river, the Berazhina, is an integral link in the system that connects the Baltic Sea to the Black Sea. In times gone by it was a very important trade route. Today, trade has been replaced by leisure and the river is populated with visitors retracing the routes taken by Vikings and Greeks in history.

Around 52 species of mammal live here, including brown bear, elk, wolf, otter, wild boar, lynx, the once rare (but now flourishing) beaver and even the extremely rare European bison, along with 217 species of bird (including the golden eagle and the seldom-seen black stork), ten of amphibian, five of reptile and 34 of fish. And mosquitoes. Clouds of them. The vegetation is also richly diverse, with more than 780 herbaceous varieties being found in the reserve, as well as over 200 varieties of moss and lichen.

🏠 **Where to stay** Facilities for enjoying this special place at leisure are reasonably good – a few **hotels** are listed opposite. For people who prefer to spend time much closer to nature, there are also a few small but snug **wooden huts** located in the most picturesque areas of the park. These are situated at **Nivki** (accommodating ten people in five double rooms, with kitchen, bathhouse and picnic site; **$$**), **Domzheritskoye and Olshitsa Lakes** (accommodating six people each at lakeside locations, with kitchen, bathhouse, picnic site and piers; **$$**) and at **Plavno** (also accommodating six people in three double rooms, with kitchen, bathhouse, lounge and open fire, picnic site, pier, sports area and access to the beach; **$$**). This one is situated not far from the hotel of the same name.

Long accessible only by prearrangement with a state agency, it is now possible to make bookings direct via the informative website for accommodation, tours and the museum (details above). For the less independently minded, most state and private tourist agencies will still offer various tours, ranging from weekends that include a visit to the nature museum and the open-air pens along prescribed ecological routes, to specialised longer-term environmentalist tours to observe between 120 and 150 species of wild animals in their natural habitat. The emphasis here is on providing enjoyment through education and the raising of awareness of important ecological issues. Visitors have the opportunity to take a close look at local ways of life and traditions, be entertained by ethnic folk troupes, sample local and national cuisine, experience traditional trades, visit sites of important historical and cultural heritage and learn more about the scientific study undertaken here, as well as watching films on an ecological theme, observing nature and taking part in environmental discussions. And to hunt, for those so minded.

🏠 **Hotel Plavno** (10 dbl rooms) Formerly a presidential residence much favoured by Alexander Lukashenko, incorporating a restaurant, billiard room, hall with cosy fireplace, picnic areas & bathhouse. The best of the rooms are in the attic, all with views over the lake & the woods. There is a beach nearby. If you picture a large wooden ski chalet, with wall-to-wall pine panelling, then you won't be far wrong. Because it's a former presidential residence, you can land your helicopter here! It's located lakeside within a forested area, so the setting is picturesque. **$$$**

🏠 **Hotel Serguch** (36 rooms) This is part of a complex that inc. a recently renovated nature museum & the House of Ecological Studies with assembly hall seating 200 (for seminars & meetings), computer room, small cinema, café-bar, exhibition space & library. Facilities at the hotel inc. restaurant, bar, banqueting hall, billiard room & bathhouse. There is also a 4km nature trail here & open-air pens, but do bear in mind my earlier caveat concerning enclosed spaces for wild animals. **$$$**

6

Mogilev City and *Oblast*
Магілёў / Могилёв

Telephone code 222

Mogilev is a city of 360,000 inhabitants on the hilly western bank of the Dnieper River in eastern Belarus, close to the border with the Russian Federation. It is the capital of a region that has excellent transport links, with main connections to Russia, Ukraine and the Baltic states crossing the territory by road and by rail. Mogilev itself is a major rail junction, and the three large rivers that criss-cross the *oblast*, the Dnieper, the Berazhina and the Sozh, are still used for navigation and transport purposes. The city itself is one of the main economic and industrial centres of Belarus. At the end of the Great Patriotic War, an enormous metallurgy complex incorporating a number of steel mills was established here as part of Stalin's programme of mass rebuilding and reindustrialisation. There are also many other significant industrial complexes for the manufacture of cranes, tractors and cars, along with a vast plant for chemical production and many other light industries. Yet the economy of the region and its social infrastructure has been significantly prejudiced by the consequences of the Chernobyl catastrophe: 35% of the territory was contaminated by radioactive particles in the immediate aftermath of the explosion and there are still many areas forming hotspots of radiation that will remain out of bounds for a very long time. No fewer than 13 out of the 21 districts are officially recognised as being in need of specialist measures. Agricultural land makes up over 50% of the territory and, between 1986 and 1991, some 47,000ha of previously arable but now contaminated lands were taken out of use.

This is all the more tragic because the region is known for its picturesque scenery, with forest covering over 30% of the area. Another 18% is occupied by predominantly low-lying meadows and marshland (not dissimilar to the region of the Polyesye in the south of the country, but less extensive), while the growing of crops (predominantly rye, barley, buckwheat, oats and potatoes) plays a key role in the agricultural sector. Cattle breeding (both for meat and milk production) is also a feature, while in a number of districts there are fur, poultry and fish farms. At present, reorganisation of the agricultural sector is under way. Production co-operatives, joint-stock companies and private farms are being established, while for now and for the foreseeable future, collective farms (*kolkhoz*), state farms (*sovkhoz*) and supporting enterprises also continue to operate.

The region has a long and interesting history. These lands have been ravaged many times by fierce battles, with only monuments remaining to tell the tale. For example, near the village of Lesnaya, 55km southeast of Mogilev on the P71 road, stands the memorial complex commemorating the 200th anniversary of the Russian army's victory over the Swedes, consisting of a chapel and a museum dedicated to the history of the region. And the memorial of Buynichskoye Field keeps alive the memory of heroes of the Soviet Union from the Great Patriotic

War. Then in the context of contemporary history and current affairs, the village of Alexandria, just to the north of the town of Shklov (35km due north of Mogilev on the P76 road), is famed for being the birthplace of the first (indeed, only) president of Belarus, Alexander Lukashenko. You can visit the local museum in the village school, with its special section devoted to the president, see the location of his family home (2km away) and drink from the spring that can be found nearby at young Alexander's favourite childhood place. The Sports and Tourism Department of the Mogilev Regional Administration is currently marketing this as 'an unusual waterway route for canoe enthusiasts' under the strap line 'Paddle Your Way to President Lukashenko's Home Town'.

Today, Mogilev is a sprawling, noisy city of business and industry, the face of which presents a mixture of the old and the new, the traditional and the avant-garde. Nowhere is this better represented than Leninskaya Street. Now renovated and restored, with the enigmatic stargazer street sculpture on display in Star Square, it is regarded with affection by residents and visitors alike. And as Mogilev has less for the visitor to see than any of the other five cities, a walk along Leninskaya is a must.

Each year, Mogilev is home to two very different festivals: Zolotoy Shlyager (the 'Golden Hit Parade'), featuring retro-pop, in November and Magutny Bozha ('Almighty God'), dedicated to sacred music, in July and August. There is also an annual film animation festival.

HISTORY

Mogilev can boast many connections with famous visitors who have spent time here. The people of the city turned out en masse when Russian Tsar Peter the Great arrived by boat on the Dnieper in 1706; Catherine the Great famously met with the Austrian Emperor Joseph II here in May 1780; Russian poet Pushkin spent time in the city, as did writer Gogol; and, from 1915 to 1917, Emperor Nikolai II and his family were in residence for significant periods of time, right up to the point of his abdication. The headquarters of the vast Russian imperial army were located in Mogilev (due to its favourable geographical position) and he was of course supreme commander-in-chief. In every respect, therefore, the city can be said to have been the final residence of the last emperor of Holy Mother Russia. There are references to the royal family all over the city and *oblast*.

This and other towns in the area such as Mstislavl and Krichev were founded in the 12th and 13th centuries, although Slavic tribes of the Krivichi and Radzimichy had established settlements in the region in the 10th century. The city itself was founded in 1267 by around 200 settlers, although local archaeological excavations have suggested that there were early Iron Age settlements on the site of the current town, specifically where Gorky Park now stands. From the early 14th century, it was a constituent part of the Grand Duchy of Lithuania. After the Union of Lublin and the creation of the Polish-Lithuanian Commonwealth, it was transferred to new royal owners. There followed a period of strong growth in the local economy, owing to the advantageous geographical location of the city right at the centre of major trade routes from north to south and from east to west. Crafts such as weaving, metalwork, woodwork, leather processing, gun-making and the art of jewellery manufacture were all developing intensively here. In the 15th century, the city also became a pottery centre. Trading in many different crafts was so significant that it acquired a customs office of its own. Then in 1577, it was invested with new rights of self-government and granted city status by King Stefan Batory under Magdeburg Law. This was a golden age for the city. It was a large river port, more prosperous than Minsk, and many trade ships were to be seen moored here. By the end of the 17th century, there were 15,000 residents of the city living in 3,000 houses. At the same time, Mogilev became a very significant centre for Eastern Orthodoxy, the largest in all Belarus. There were many substantial congregations and a theological seminary was established to protect the faith. Meanwhile, congregation schools promoted the 'development of education', while printing houses published literature in the Belarusian, Greek and Latin languages. Around this time, the Orthodox Church of St Nikolai, the Epiphany Orthodox Cloister and the Jesuit Roman Catholic Church were built.

During the Northern Wars between 1700 and 1721, the Swedes sacked and destroyed more than half of the city's houses, while Peter the Great himself ordered that it be razed to the ground in 1708. After the First Partition of Poland it inevitably fell into the hands of imperial Russia, but continued to flourish as the administrative centre of the region. Then, during the war against France in 1812, French forces under Marshal Davoilt captured and plundered the city.

When serfdom was abolished in 1861, the social and economic development of Mogilev accelerated exponentially. The city's museum was founded in 1867. July 1883 saw the first issue of the *Mogilev Eparchy News*. In 1885, there were only 124 business enterprises employing 270 workers, but just 15 years later there were 220 businesses employing 790 workers. The first theatre was built in 1888 (it is still standing and worthy of your attention if in town – see pages 264–5) and by 1897 the population had swollen to over 43,000, nearly half of whom were literate. In the early part of the 20th century, there were three types of credit institutions, relating to commerce, land and small debtors, together with three printing houses and a number of mechanical workshops. Indeed, the city was widely regarded at this time as being the most developed and affluent of all the European cities of the Russian Empire.

However, internal economic crisis, the global depression of the early 20th century and emerging revolutionary ideas widened the gulf between the classes, and Mogilev's economic prosperity and social cohesion soon began to unravel. The year 1901 saw the first significant strike by workers at the dairy plant, followed by workers in the rag trade in 1903. Political rallies took place on 1 May from 1901 to 1904, and in late May 1905 there was a strike in the bakery, followed by a walkout of railway workers in December 1905. Demands for improved working conditions continued and in May 1906 hairdressers, shoemakers and tailors downed tools to demand that the working day be reduced to nine hours. At the beginning of World War I, martial law was imposed throughout the region. On 22 March 1917, in the aftermath of the February Revolution, the City Deputy-Council of Workers and Soldiers was formed. And the power of the collective ensured that, in the first half of 1917, Mogilev workers held a number of strikes, seeking various political and economic objectives.

After the ensuing October Revolution, the city remained under anti-Soviet forces for a whole month until, on 18 November 1917, the Deputy-Council of Workers and Soldiers passed a resolution that accepted Soviet rule and took over the administration of Mogilev. There followed the start of a short period of intense instability, when on 18 February 1918 German forces occupied the city, followed by Polish troops on 12 March and then the German army again on 26 May. Finally, in 1919, it was overrun and captured by Red Army forces.

It is thought that up to 25,000 people from the *oblast* volunteered for the Red Army in the early days of the Great Patriotic War and, from 24 June to 3 July 1941, its Western Front headquarters were located in the city. By that time, a significant proportion of the major industrial plant and machinery had already been evacuated east. But despite the frenzied construction of two encircling defensive lines in just seven days under the protection of the 172nd Division, Mogilev fell to the Nazis

7

on 26 July 1941, after 23 days of intense and savage fighting. A cruelly oppressive regime was immediately put into place by the invaders. Five concentration camps were created in the region and, during the period of the war, over 70,000 citizens of the city died and a further 30,000 were taken to Germany as slave labour. Most of them were Jews. Then on 6 April 1943, the Mogilev partisan army was formed. It very quickly grew to comprise 34,000 active volunteers.

In June 1944, the Red Army launched its Belarusian offensive operation and on 28 June the city was finally liberated by troops of the 2nd Belarusian Front. On 25 April 1980, Mogilev was awarded the Order of the Great Patriotic War (First Class) for the bravery and resilience displayed by its citizens during the oppression of the war years.

After the war, the city was reconstructed at an astonishing pace and by 1959 the population had spiralled to 122,000 people. New housing estates and 'micro-districts' were springing up all over town and new bridges were built over the Dnieper to cope with the increasing demands on the city's infrastructure. Today, Mogilev's place as a major (and modern) industrial city making a huge contribution to the economy of the country is assured.

GETTING THERE AND AWAY

Mogilev is well appointed in terms of transport links, with major rail and road routes passing through the city.

BY TRAIN Built in 1902, the main railway station is a most attractive building, adorned in pastel stucco. It is located 2km north of the city centre, at the western end of Grishina Street. There are plenty of local trains serving towns in this and adjoining regions. Mogilev is also a stop on several main-line routes serving Minsk (several trains a day), Gomel, Brest, Grodno and Vitebsk within Belarus, and international destinations such as Moscow, St Petersburg, Vilnius and Kiev. The journey time from Minsk is around four hours and the cost of a one-way ticket starts at US$3.

BY BUS There is also a bus station close by, with varied and alternative routes throughout the *oblast*. Several services also arrive from and depart to Minsk every day. As with the train, journey times are around four hours and the price of a one-way ticket starts at US$10. The town is located midway between the cities of Vitebsk and Gomel on one of the country's major routes north–south (the M8). Journey times and ticket prices are broadly the same. Minsk lies 203km to the west along the M4.

GETTING AROUND

The usual mixture of **bus**, **tram**, **trolleybus** and **taxi** is on offer, all cheap and all reliable, but you are unlikely to need to go far in this city as most of the sights are located on the western bank of the river, in a fairly small and compact area around Leninskaya Street. Walking is thus the best option.

Nonetheless, the integrated infrastructure for public transport is particularly impressive in this city. For up-to-the-minute timetables (sadly in Russian only), visit the excellent website maintained by the city's executive committee (*www. city.mogilev.by/content/category/3/22/105/lang/ru*). As an aside, this site does have a number of English pages providing all sorts of civic, cultural, tourist and administrative information for visitors and residents of the city alike. You can also download a very informative 56-page city guide in English.

MOGILEV
City Centre

Railway station

Cathedral of the
Three Saints †

Puppet
Theatre

Modern
restaurant

RC Cathedral of
St Stanislaw

Drama
Theatre

Regional Museum
of Local History
& Culture

Castle Site
(Gorky Park)

Sovyetskaya
Square

Orthodox Convent
of St Nikolai †

0 ———— 500m
0 ———— 500yds

N

Bradt

Dnieper

Memorial Complex at
Buynichskoye Field

Joker bar ↓

Streets labelled: KOSMONAVTOV STREET, LAZARENKO STREET, MIR AVENUE, PYERVOMAISKAYA ST, TIMIRYAZEVSKAYA ST, LEPESHINSKAYA ST, BUDENOVA STREET, LENINSKAYA STREET, PIONERSKAYA STREET, KARLA MARKSA STREET, KOMSOMOLSKAYA ST, CHELYOSKINSEV STREET, PUSHKINA AVENUE

For listings, see pages 260–2

⊖ **Where to stay**
1 Gubernskaya
2 Kim
3 Lira
4 Metropol
5 Mogilev
6 Turist

⊗ **Where to eat and drink**
7 Bellagio
8 Chalet
9 Da Vinci Coffee Bar
10 Gabrovo
11 Georges Simone Café
12 Imperia
13 Irish Pub Ale House
14 Izba Bar & Café
15 Karchma na Shklovskom Bazaari
   Latuk (see 1)
16 Modern Café

17 Parmezan
18 Pizzeria Bravo
19 Pizzeria Prima
20 Retro Café
21 Stary Gorod
22 Unosika Sushi
23 Zvezdnaya Ploschad Café

Off map
   Joker bar
   Modern

TOURIST INFORMATION

Although it does contain some architectural features of interest to the visitor, Mogilev is not yet geared up for the tourist trade. In this context, it is the least developed of the country's six major cities. Given that it's an industrial centre, most of the focus is on facilities for businessmen. Indeed, sites of interest to the traveller or leisure visitor are not well promoted at all. There are some tourist agencies in town offering excursions, but overall there are few options. The best of them is the state **Intourist agency**, handily located on the first floor of Hotel Mogilev (*6 Mir Av;* ✆ *70 70 28;* ⏱ *09.00–14.00 & 15.00–18.00 Mon–Fri;* e *mog-intourist@mail.ru; www.intourist.by*). It is thus easy to find, but by no means easy to gain access to its services. When enquiring as to its whereabouts on my last visit, staff at the hotel reception desk directed me to a door in the corner of the lobby, where a jobsworth told me I wasn't allowed in. Another jobsworth arrived after I pressed the issue, but he directed me to offices along the street, before the hotel receptionist marched over to crossly order them to let me in! Once I'd got upstairs and into the office, the staff there couldn't have been more helpful. English is spoken and some printed material in English is available, though not much, but a wide range of tours and excursions can be booked. I was given a categorical assurance with a broad smile that the office is open seven days a week from 09.00 until 19.00, but my advice is to expect no more than the official opening hours (see above). Otherwise, far and away the best option is to fix a stay as part of an organised tour arranged before you arrive in the country or from the capital Minsk, with one of the accredited state agencies or international operators (see pages 47–9). In truth, there's not enough to keep you here for more than a day and a night at most.

WHERE TO STAY *Map, page 259.*

UPMARKET

🏠 **Gubernskaya** (37 rooms) 56/6 Leninskaya St; ✆ 22 26 19; e gubernsky@gubernsky.by; www. gubernsky.by. Located centrally in one of the city's refurbished late 19th-century buildings & open since 2007, this is another hotel aimed at the business market. The bedrooms are spacious but the décor will not be to everyone's taste. Staff are friendly & eager to please. Facilities inc. free parking, café-bar, casino, business & travel services, swimming pool, spa, fitness centre, currency exchange & ATM. **$$$$**

🏠 **Kim** (7 rooms, 1 suite) 27 Lazarenka St; ✆ 22 91 11/13; e hotel_kim@tut.by; www.kim-hotel. org. Located just off the city centre, this small hotel offers the best value & comfort in town. Only built in 2002 & upgraded in 2005, the specification is of European standard, with all rooms being extremely well appointed. The staff are attentive & keen to please, while the modest size of the establishment gives it a homely & cosy feel. There is a small swimming pool, sauna & café, together with a travel booking service. The railway station is 4km away & the bus station 3km. Recommended. **$$$$**

🏠 **Lira** (8 rooms) 45 Leninskaya St; ✆ 25 25 43; www.lirastar.by. This is another small hotel that comes highly recommended. Only 6 years old & located in the heart of the city just yards from Star Square, all of the rooms are comfortable &

the service is good. There is a small swimming pool, sauna & billiard room, together with a travel booking service. **$$$$**

🏠 **Metropol** (53 rooms) 6 Komsomolskaya St; ✆ 70 70 51; e reception@metropol.by; www. metropol.by. Only open since Dec 2013, it's a decent attempt at creating the sort of hotel visitors from elsewhere in Europe will recognise, & its reputation is already high. Expect the staff to go the extra mile. Located centrally between the Drama Theatre & St Stanislaw Cathedral, facilities inc. restaurant, free parking, business & travel services, pool, spa, sauna & steam room. Recommended. **$$$$**

MID-RANGE

🏠 **Mogilev** (329 rooms) 6 Mir Av; ✆ 46 81 38; e hotel_mogilev@mail.ru; www.mogilev.amaks-hotels.ru. Another example of the omnipresent concrete monolith so favoured by the Soviet Union in the 1970s. Located downtown & 3km from the railway station (3.5km from the bus station), the rooms, ranging from sgls to suites, are exactly what you would expect: functional but without charm. It was built in 1972, so the concrete is past its best, especially on the balconies. Notwithstanding regular refurbishment, it always looks tired & drab. Last time I chanced a non-refurbished room to save on cost. Don't do it. These rooms may be cheap, but they are hideous. Facilities inc. self-service café & separate bar (both extremely avg), swimming pool, beauty parlour & currency exchange. Despite its modest charms this is my hotel of preference here, largely because of the delightful walk into town along the bank of the Dubrovenka River. You emerge at the bottom of Sovyetskaya Sq, one of the key sites of the city & the start of your promenade along Leninskaya St. **$$$**

🏠 **Turist** (141 rooms) 6 Pushkin Av; 📞 48 56 55; e mogilevtourist3@mail.ru; www.

mogilevtourist.by. Built in 1986 & situated downtown in a park on the banks of the Dnieper, the rooms of this concrete block are on 7 floors, ranging from sgls to suites. All are adequately appointed. Services available inc. parking for 40 cars, exchange bureau, travel & excursion office, business facilities, hairdresser, newspaper kiosk, pharmacy, souvenir shop, restaurant, bar & snack bar. **$$$**

✖ WHERE TO EAT AND DRINK *Map, page 259.*

I've spent less time in Mogilev than in any of the other five cities in Belarus, such that my personal experience of the charms of its restaurants, bars and cafés is limited. That said, I've asked local people about the establishments I've listed here, which means that a degree of local intelligence from corroborating sources has been garnered to assist in the presentation of information. This should give you enough base data to undertake your own road test with a degree of confidence. My advice is that your best option will be to reconnoitre along Leninskaya Street and within its vicinity, where locals and visitors alike are wont to spend leisure time in surroundings that are known to be safe, pleasing and easy on the eye. It's where you are going to be spending most of your time anyway. Do please let me know how you get on. To assist with your research in advance, visit the very informative listings site www.nightmogilev.com, though sadly it's in Russian only.

RESTAURANTS

✖ **Bellagio** 21 Leninskaya St; 📞 23 08 08; ⏰ noon–02.00 daily. Everyone tells me this is probably the best restaurant in town. Ideally located towards the bottom of Leninskaya St, expect Italian fine dining in a relaxed setting. Standards are consistently high & it's always busy, with award-winning chef Luigi Pomata running a tight ship. The listings website www.bellagio. relax.by gives a good indication of what to expect. Definitely recommended, but not cheap. **$$$$**

✖ **Chalet** 4 Darvina St; 📞 70 71 11; www. shale.by; ⏰ 11.00–23.00 daily. I stumbled across this restaurant while trying to find the Convent of St Nikolai on foot. It's out of the town centre in a plush residential location &, judging by the size of the SUVs in the car park, it's a haunt of the well-to-do. Shorts & T-shirt rendered me way too underdressed to sample its delights, but the décor is sumptuous, the menu imaginative, & when I asked elsewhere I was told that everything about this place is impressive. Extensive grounds provide ample opportunity for comfortable alfresco dining. Whenever you go, expect to pay for the experience. **$$$$**

✖ **Imperia** 23/2 Pervomayskaya St; 📞 22 57 94; ⏰ noon–01.00 daily. The cuisine here is primarily Belarusian & Serb. It's luxurious, with prices to match. **$$$$**

✖ **Gabrovo** 31 Pervomayskaya St; 📞 22 28 54; ⏰ 11.00–02.00 daily. Reasonably centrally located, this stock 1970s Russian-style eatery & nightclub specialises in Belarusian & Bulgarian cuisine. There's also live music every night except Mon. **$$$**

✖ **Karchma na Shklovskom Bazaari** 11 Budenova St; 📞 22 23 46; ⏰ 11.00–23.00 daily. Just off Star Square, the décor is clichéd medieval & the food is standard European. There are probably better choices in the immediate vicinity, but if you're feeling adventurous, give it a go. **$$$**

✖ **Latuk** 56/6 Leninskaya St; 📞 25 28 16; ⏰ 07.00–midnight. Located at the Gubernskaya Hotel, you'll find standard European fayre here. **$$$**

✖ **Modern** 12 Korolyeva St; 📞 46 79 96; ⏰ 11.00–midnight daily. Cosy & relaxed with good service, but it's off the main drag & probably not worth the detour unless you're close by. **$$$**

✕ Parmezan 34/1 Pervomayskaya St; ☎ 25 86 96; www.parmezan.by; ⏱ 09.00–23.00 daily. Long established & one of the most pleasing of the city's café-restaurants. It's another Italian, but it's done to a decent standard & there is also a take-away & delivery service. It's strollable from the centrally located hotels & the website is informative for a browse before you try. Recommended. $$$

✕ Pizzeria Bravo 2 Sovyetskaya Sq; ☎ 22 00 77; ⏱ 11.00–23.00 daily. Located in the corner of the square next to the Regional Museum of Local History & Culture, it's standard pizza fare, but it's a handy option for the start or finish of your amble along Leninskaya. $$$

✕ Pizzeria Prima 63 Leninskaya St; ☎ 22 56 29; ⏱ 11.00–23.00 daily. Formerly Pizzeria Avenyu & now refurbished, but it's still standard pizza fare. Nothing special, but it's functional if you're at the top end of Leninskaya. However, there are better Italian restaurants in town. $$$

✕ Unosika Sushi 23A Leninskaya St; ☎ 21 88 88; www.unosika.by; ⏱ 10.00–22.00 daily. For good-value sustenance on the hoof, this sushi bar & take-away is a decent option. The menu on the website tells you all you need to know, inc. prices. $$

CAFES

☕ Da Vinci Coffee Bar 68 Leninskaya St; ☎ 25 83 44; www.cdv.by; ⏱ 10.00–23.00 daily. Right at the top of Leninskaya & thus a little off your likely beaten track, but the coffee is good & the desserts are decent.

☕ Georges Simone Café 44 Leninskaya St; ☎ 31 15 18; www.simone.by; ⏱ 10.00–23.00 daily. Unsurprisingly Parisian in theme & décor given the name, it's directly opposite Zvezdnaya Ploschad Café & seems to suffer by comparison. It's never as busy as its rival.

☕ Modern Café 15 Leninskaya St; ☎ 31 13 39; ⏱ 09.00–23.00 daily (08.00–11.00 first Mon of the month). A pleasant bistro at the bottom of Leninskaya, with good coffee & decent ice cream.

☕ Retro Café 16 Lepeshinskava Street; ☎ 22 21 30; ⏱ 11.00–23.00 daily. Tucked away just off Star Square, it's unpretentious & easy to overlook, so less busy than others. It's worth a try.

☕ Zvezdnaya Ploschad Café 45 Leninskaya St; ⏱ 08.00–23.00 daily. Splendidly located right on Star Square, it's bustling & very popular.

BARS

♀ Irish Pub Ale House 61 Leninskaya St; ☎ 72 27 62; e info@ale-house.by; ⏱ noon–midnight daily. I have Irish antecedents, so this may be a less than objective view, but there's Guinness, football & loud music here; so what's not to like?

♀ Izba Bar & Café 29 Leninskaya St; ☎ 25 78 36; e valebana@tut.by; ⏱ 09.00–23.00 Sun–Thu, 09.00–05.00 Fri & Sat. Very centrally located, the décor is clichéd rural Middle Ages, & there was a wide variance in opinion when I asked around about this place. Some really like it, others hate it, but most shrugged their shoulders. Try for yourselves.

♀ Joker 1 Ostrovskovo St; ☎ 41 69 93; ⏱ 18.00–05.00 daily. The bar at a nightclub. There's little else to say.

♀ Stary Gorod 16 Pervomayskaya St; ☎ 22 46 21; ⏱ 19.00–05.00 daily. I'm told the food here is delicious & the service is excellent. Given that it's well located & ideally placed for you to be able to see & do other things in the vicinity, this should be a great place to recharge before continuing with your explorations. Give it a try.

SHOPPING

There are no specialist facilities here that cannot be found elsewhere, although the shop at the Regional Museum has some interesting souvenirs. The best place to browse and to purchase, not surprisingly, is along Leninskaya and other streets in the vicinity. Beware tacky souvenirs, though.

OTHER PRACTICALITIES

There are plenty of banks, currency exchanges and ATMs in town.

In all probability, your first visit to Mogilev is likely to be on a tour or excursion from Minsk, perhaps with an overnight stay. The area simply is not geared up for independent leisure travel, but the infrastructure for tours via the state agencies is excellent. This will not be to everyone's taste of course, but until such time as the tourism *industry* develops to match the breadth and quality of the tourism *product* in this country, a guided excursion is going to be the only way for visitors to gain their first sight of the riches on offer in the more remote areas. When you return next time, armed with the knowledge you will have acquired first time around (and preferably, some of the language), it will be a different story. For now, just relax and let someone else do the work while you soak up some local knowledge and climb on to that learning curve.

Here are the best of the sights that you are sure to see:

CASTLE SITE (GORKY PARK) The original castle was built of wood in 1267 when the city itself was established by around 200 settlers. It was then enlarged and considerably modernised between the 16th and 18th centuries. Today all that remains of the castle itself is an archaeological dig, but it is still possible to appreciate the strategic importance of the location, high above the confluence of the Dnieper and Dubrovenka rivers. Now Gorky Park, an Orthodox church was built here on the site of the old castle at the end of the 20th century, and it's only a very short walk along the top of the escarpment to Sovyetskaya Square, through the pleasant grounds of the park.

SOVYETSKAYA SQUARE Another Belarusian city, another square on the grandest of scales; and it's usually empty. When I was last there (in the height of summer) I had it all to myself, apart from a handful of Belarusian tourists. Associated with trade and government since the founding of the city, the lofty perch affords fine views from the edge of the escarpment across the Dnieper into the lower town and beyond. I like to sit on the balustrade with my back to the square. Below is a major road junction and bridge across the Dnieper, the noisy traffic and constant movement of humanity a sharp contrast to the quiet solemnity of the square behind me. Wherever your point of entry, your eye is immediately drawn to the magnificent **memorial** entitled 'the Fighters for Soviet Power'. Dedicated to the glory of the 23-day defence of the city in 1941, the statue itself is an impressive Motherland metaphor. Murals and displays abound, with images of heroism and of residents and soldiers individually honoured for their contribution to the cause. Also here is the splendid **town hall**. Sadly it's a reconstruction. The original 17th-century building was considered one of the finest examples of civil architecture, but it was significantly damaged during the Great Patriotic War and later demolished in 1957. Rebuilt and finally opened in 2008, it's a fine commemoration of the civic prosperity of the city and an interesting visual counterpoint to the image of Soviet might on the other side of the square. An observation platform halfway up the tower affords excellent views, and it's also possible to climb higher, into the clocktower, for an even better view. The building houses a small **museum** dedicated to the history of the city (*1A Leninskaya St;* ✆ *22 99 46;* e *ratusha.mogilev@gmail.com; www.ratusha-mogilev. com;* ⊕ *10.00–18.00 Wed–Sun, last entry 17.30*). The website is particularly informative on the history of the town hall and the city in general.

THE REGIONAL MUSEUM OF LOCAL HISTORY AND CULTURE (*1 Sovyetskaya Sq;* ✆ *22 01 20;* e *kraimog@list.ru; www.mogilewmuseum.iatp.by;* ⊕ *09.30–17.30 Wed–Sun, last entry 17.00; admission BYR6,000*) The first history museum was founded in the city in 1867. It survived a number of privations, revolution not the least of them, and was reincarnated more than once. Then at the outset of war in 1941, the treasures were hidden in an apparently secure facility. At some point during the Nazi occupation they disappeared and the search for them still goes on. After the war, it took many years for new collections to be amassed. Happily the museum is now open for business once more in a fine stucco building located between the war memorial and the town hall, on the left-hand side of Sovyetskaya Square. On display are over 300,000 artefacts, consisting of archaeological finds from the region, coins and treasures, icons and other holy relics, paintings, ethnographic displays, historical documents, war memorabilia and articles of everyday life from the 19th and 20th centuries, all collected since the liberation of the city in 1944. The reassembled historical collection from 1917 to 1945 is particularly interesting. Consisting of four exhibitions in 18 rooms, great historic events and significant periods of time are covered in considerable detail, including the 1917 Revolution, mass industrialisation, Stalin's purges, the Nazi occupation and subsequent partisan insurrection. Walking excursions of 45 minutes' duration, lectures on the move about history and the environment, can be booked for groups of up to 25 people, but only in Russian, although with advance notice an English speaker of sorts might be available. The museum's website is a treasure trove of information, though sadly only in Russian. Well worth a visit.

LENINSKAYA STREET Running from Sovyetskaya Square, on the left of the town hall, this street is worthy of a leisurely promenade, if you can shut out the noise of the city, that is. The architecture has been substantially renovated and the thoroughfare pedestrianised, with imaginative street furniture to complement the whole effect. The **drama theatre** and **Cathedral of St Stanislaw** are both close by. The buildings have attractive pastel-coloured stucco fronts in pale yellow, orange and lime green. But although the restoration work is very professionally done and the intention to recreate Mogilev of old is to be commended, it's all just a little twee, and somehow lacking the charm of similar projects in other cities, notably Brest and Vitebsk. It's probably because everywhere else in this city you'll find the noise and constant movement of business, industry and commerce, such that even though Leninskaya is made for promenading, it doesn't feel like a relaxed or relaxing environment, which is something of a disappointment. There's even a vague whiff of Disneyland about it all, down to the land train that chugs back and forth along the street, with the few tourists that come here on board. Still, there are some fine pavement cafés and a few shops that are worth a browse. And in the central **Star Square**, directly outside the Radzima cinema, stands the enigmatic **bronze sculpture of a stargazer**, pointing to the heavens, in the middle of 12 bronze high-backed chairs representing the signs of the zodiac, arranged around him in a semicircle. All around, sculpted into the pavement, are stars and symbols. It is the work of a modest and unassuming artist, the sculptor Vladimir Zhbanov. A veteran of the Afghan conflict, his work is to be found all over Minsk. It's urban art at its best. Do check out the stargazer, but take the time to look elsewhere in the square too. The sculpture is the obvious highlight, but there's also an interesting array of buildings. Look for the USSR mural from 1953 on the wall above Colin's store, as well as fine examples of 19th-century red brick among the pale stucco. If the rest of Leninskaya is a tad noisy and brash, all is generally calm and classy here.

DRAMA THEATRE (*7 Pervomayskaya St;* \ *31 00 45; www.mogdt.ru*) Built in May 1888, this charming red-brick building is worth a visit in architectural terms alone.

It now specialises in contemporary drama, but works of masters such as Gorky, Chekhov and Kupala are also performed here. When I was last in this city during the summer of 2013, a revival of the French farce *Boeing Boeing* was on offer! A night at this theatre was a favourite pastime of the last tsar Nikolai II and his family. Look for the charming bronze sculpture of an 18th-century lady and her dog at the bottom of the front steps. It's another work of Vladimir Zhbanov. Further along the street and not far from the Cathedral of the Three Saints is the popular and famed children's **Puppet Theatre** (*73 Pervomayskaya;* \ *32 66 90*).

THE ROMAN CATHOLIC CATHEDRAL OF ST STANISLAW Built between 1738 and 1752 in the Baroque style and fronted by four majestic colonnades, this cathedral is beautifully decorated with many exquisite murals depicting the entire cycle of the Scriptures. Magnificent though it is, the exterior of the building is a tad shabby and in need of some tender loving care. Organ recitals are regularly held here and it is also the location of the annual Magutny Bozha ('Almighty God') festival of sacred music in July and August.

THE ORTHODOX CONVENT OF ST NIKOLAI This walled monastic complex has preserved the structure of its magnificent Baroque cathedral, which was constructed in 1668, including the belltower, walls and gates, together with the original (and quite stunning) four-tiered iconostasis and some magnificent frescoes in dazzling colours from the 17th and 18th centuries on the exterior of the elevations. Much frequented by Nikolai II, including after his abdication, an icon portrait of the tsar is on display. It's a little way out of the city (I once set off to walk here but was defeated by the heat and topography of the land, which makes it difficult to find and keep one's bearings), but don't be put off; try very hard to organise transport for a visit to this beautiful place.

THE CATHEDRAL OF THE THREE SAINTS Located at the junction of Pervomayskaya and Timiryazevskaya streets, this splendid cathedral was constructed between 1903 and 1914 to honour three saints (Basil the Great, Gregory the Theologian and John Chrysostom). It is a fine example of retro Russian design. The most significant place of Orthodox worship in the city (and often frequented by Tsar Nikolai II), this is one of its architectural gems.

THE MEMORIAL COMPLEX AT BUYNICHSKOYE FIELD Located 5km south of the city centre on the P93 road, just to the west of the small village of Buynichi, it is here that a hugely significant military engagement took place in the early weeks of the Great Patriotic War. For 23 long days and nights, shortly after Operation Barbarossa began, this place was the scene of a heroic defence action on the part of Red Army soldiers of the 388th Infantry Division, who delayed the capture of the city (and thus slowed up the advance on Moscow) long enough to buy Stalin time and for the Soviet Union to gather its strength and resources for the defence of the greater part of the Motherland. The heroism displayed by regular Red Army soldiers and partisans here has passed into legend and the Regional Museum of Local History and Culture in Mogilev's Sovyetskaya Square has an excellent feature on the engagement. The complex is open to the public between 1 April and 31 October, though on many days of the year hero veterans of the Red Army can be found here, taking part in official ceremonies of remembrance or else visiting in small numbers to honour the memory of their fallen comrades. It is a sad, solemn, but ultimately uplifting place. After passing through a triple archway of simple but affecting design, the visitor comes to the chapel of remembrance and, adjacent to it, the memorial Lake of Tears. There are also displays of tanks and military equipment, together with a memorial stone upon which are inscribed verses of the renowned war correspondent, writer and poet Konstantin Simonov, a veteran of the battle who documented its events. Upon his death, his ashes were scattered over the field in accordance with his last wishes. There is an excellent English-language website (*www.simonov.co.uk*) devoted to the life and work of this esteemed writer and some research before you visit will help to set the scene for you. Also close by in the village of Buynichi is an interesting **open-air ethnographical museum and centre for handicrafts** recreating life in a 19th-century Belarusian village. It houses a reconstructed mill and a number of traditional workshops and buildings showcasing rural trades, plus a café and play area for children. Adjoining it is the **Zoological Garden** established in 2004, incorporating enclosures for a variety of wild animals. There's even a Siberian tiger. My own view on the morality of animals in cages is well documented in the pages of this book, but you must judge for yourselves.

OUTSIDE MOGILEV

Even though the surrounding countryside is attractive, particularly on and around the rivers that cross the region, access by public transport is difficult for two reasons: first, you're going to need to be able to speak the language and second, the infrastructure is not geared up for visitors who want to explore, but for local people who need to get from their homes to work, to market and to school or university. But some of the excursions arranged by the state agencies will include a tour of the rural areas, particularly if you arrange an overnight tour from Minsk. Noteworthy architectural monuments of the district include the attractive 18th-century **town hall** in the town of **Shklov**, 35km north of Mogilev on the P76 road; the 19th-century **Church of the Protection of the Virgin** in the village of **Veino**, 5km east of Mogilev on the P122; the early 20th-century **Assumption Church** in the village of **Golinyets**, 10km southwest of the city on minor roads; the 19th-century **outhouse** of the Zhukovsky estate, used as a military hospital for the Russian army during the 1812 campaign in the village of **Dashkovka**, 15km due south of the city on the E95 road; a **Dominican church** built in 1681 in the village of **Knyazhitsy**; and the early 20th-century **Assumption Church** in the village of **Sukhari**, 20km northeast of the city on the P96 road. Finally, there is a small but interesting **military history museum** in the village of **Polykovichi**, just to the northeast of Mogilev on the P123 road. There is also a **well and thermal spring** here, much revered in folklore since the 16th century for its supposed powers of healing. Tsar Nikolai II visited many times with his family so that the young tsarevich Alexei, a haemophiliac, could take the waters. Tourist agencies market it thus to this very day. This is a good reflection of the sites to be seen on an organised tour through the *oblast*, but there are many others further afield that are worthy of your attention. Come back with your own transport and explore one day.

8

Gomel City and *Oblast*
Гомель / Гомель

Telephone code 232

Gomel is the second-largest city of Belarus and the main administrative centre and capital of Gomel *oblast*. With a population of close on half a million people, it is located high above the western bank of the Sozh River, in the southeastern part of the country, 300km from Minsk and close to the borders with Russia and Ukraine. It is also only 120km or so from the deserted Ukrainian city of Pripyat, where the ill-fated nuclear plant at Chernobyl was situated. In the whole of Belarus, this region suffered the worst contamination of all and subsisting levels of radiation are still very high in some areas of its countryside. It will be so for a very long time. There are a number of 'no go' areas in the region to which access is available only by means of official pass. Additionally, strict rules remain in force about the production and distribution of foodstuffs, together with strong government advice about what to eat and drink in terms of natural products. To assist with the mitigation of the consequences of Chernobyl, the Polyesye Radiation and Ecology Reserve was set up in the *oblast* to study the effects of exposure to radioactive material and to undertake some strategic thinking to assist with the development of long-term contingency planning for the affected areas.

The city is a large and significant transport junction at the centre of a rail and road crossroads that connects the rest of the country to the west (and thence to the countries of western Europe beyond), the Baltic states to the north, Russia to the east and Ukraine to the south. There is also an airport (to and from which the state airline Belavia now operates services to destinations within a number of countries of the former Soviet Union, including Minsk) and a river port. Historically, the Sozh was a major trading route. Today, modern Gomel shares with Mogilev the accolade of being one of the largest industrial centres of Belarus. The region's southern position and mild climate also mean that conditions for the development of agriculture are most advantageous.

Away from the city, the countryside is particularly attractive. It is a land of forests and picturesque riverbanks, with low marshland in-between. Here is the eastern end of the Polyesye, the unique land of 'fogs and bogs'. In the days of the Soviet Union, the fragile balance of nature here was disturbed, as marshes, peat bogs and lakes were artificially dried up with the aim of increasing the proportion of land available for cultivation. Happily, the topography and ecology survived (while the USSR itself did not) and much of the area was preserved in its natural state and condition. Today, the Pripyatsky National Park affords visitors the opportunity to admire this rare environment in circumstances where the ecological balance, the animals that live here and the plants that thrive are nurtured and protected.

In addition to the natural delights to be enjoyed, there are also many manmade creations of great interest. Architectural delights in the region include the Bernadino Roman Catholic Church and Cistercian Monastery in Mozyr, the 18th-century church

Wherever they occur in the world, one consequence of disasters, manmade or natural, is that history thereafter is divided into 'pre' and 'post' periods. The catastrophic explosion at Chernobyl was one such event, and nowhere is the 'before and after' factor more acutely articulated than in Gomel region.

The damage to the republic as a whole is almost beyond measure. Analysts believe that the cost has totalled in the vicinity of US$235 billion; put another way, this equates to 32 annual state budgets of the pre-tragedy period. Practically all spheres of human activity have been affected in the regions, particularly those in the southeast. Farmland and pastures have been excluded from agricultural use, while the use of forest, mineral, organic, fuel and other resources is subject to restrictions. Among other losses suffered in the regions are the closure of enterprises and companies, output reduction, significant expenditure for the resettlement of whole communities, and the cost of ensuring safe living conditions and social security for residents of the contaminated regions, including their medical care and recuperation. In particular, the cost to the social and community infrastructure is incalculable. And the effect of the 'Chernobyl factor' on the lives of individuals and families continues to manifest itself in all sorts of unexpected ways. The existence of real and readily diagnosable medical problems and conditions is an irrefutable fact, with evidence and data to back up the claims. More difficult to analyse and articulate are the consequences of the despair and lack of hope that follow in the aftermath of such cataclysmic events.

Gomel *oblast* took the biggest hit and bore the brunt of the disaster. In the country as a whole, more than 135,000 people from 470 townships and villages, two-thirds of which were in Gomel *oblast*, had to leave the worst affected territories and resettle to safer regions of the republic and beyond, into the wider area of the Soviet Union. My own adoptive family in Vetka were forced to move many hundreds of miles east into the Urals, almost without notice. It was years before they were permitted to return.

In the aftermath of the disaster, the *oblast* developed a system of radiation monitoring and control, as well as a series of protective measures in agro-industrial production, which is financed from the state budget. The region is

and Jesuit college in Kalinkovichy, the early 18th-century Church of St Nicholas in Petrikov and the beautifully restored church at Zhelizniki (in Vetka district), believed to be the oldest in the entire region (and one of the oldest, if not the oldest, in the country). In the school at Nyeglubka (also in Vetka district), students are taught the art of weaving on wooden machines constructed exactly as they were many hundreds of years ago, to preserve the old and traditional ways. Many bitter engagements were fought on these territories in the Great Patriotic War; for example at Khalch, on the road from Gomel to the town of Vetka, there was great loss of life as the Red Army fought to cross the Sozh, with Gomel itself almost completely flattened under fierce bombardment. Monuments to heroism and sacrifice are everywhere to be found in this *oblast*.

HISTORY

First mentioned in chronicles in 1142, the original settlement here was established at the place where the Gomeyuk Stream flows into the Sozh River. Today, this point is marked by the ornamental swan lake at the bottom of a ravine in the Rumyantsev-carrying out a set of measures aimed at improving medical services to the victims of the catastrophe. There is also a system of social protection of all categories of the affected population.

Various foreign charitable organisations from Germany, Great Britain, Ireland, Japan, Italy, Austria, Belgium, the USA and other countries render significant support to Gomel in mitigating Chernobyl's consequences. They supply drugs and medical equipment, organise learning and development opportunities for Belarusian doctors in Western clinics and arrange recuperation visits to foreign countries for children from the most contaminated regions. More recently, on the initiative of the United Nations and the World Bank, the *oblast* launched projects aiming to promote the rehabilitation of the contaminated territories, insofar as that can be safely achieved. These projects seek the support of the international community in two ways. First, in securing loans for developing the industrial infrastructure and creating new jobs in the affected regions, thus providing an opportunity for local people to raise their level of social security themselves; and secondly, in the transference of skills to local people to enable the country itself to rebuild its infrastructure according to its own perception of where the need really lies.

The trouble with radiation pollution is that you can't see it, smell it or taste it. For the most part, everything looks exactly the same. The consequences are there to be seen, in terms of abandoned villages, derelict homesteads and signs by the side of the road displaying the familiar radiation logo barring access down some of the woodland tracks and old roads, but not the radiation itself. It is for this very reason that many people, particularly the elderly, have gradually moved back to their former homes in areas where it is still unwise to live, eat the fruits of the forest and drink water from the local streams.

In this region of great natural beauty, radiation is all around: in the water, in the food, in the ground and in the air that people breathe. It is part of the way of life and it won't be going away for a very long time. The challenge is to combat its consequences while making the safest and best use of natural resources, without compromising the health and well-being of all who live here.

Paskevich Park, as well as a relatively new sculpture depicting one of the first settlers. A number of different Slavic tribes seem to have coexisted peacefully in the area and, as with so many other communities in these lands, Gomel's geographic location was extremely favourable when it came to developing trade, because of the river routes connecting northwest and southeast Europe.

Originally included in the estate of Prince Rostislav Mstislavich, it subsequently shared the fate of most Belarusian towns, passing through the hands of one conquering warlord after another, from princes of Kievan Rus to Ivan the Terrible. In 1335, it was ceded to the Grand Duchy of Lithuania and in the 16th century its castle held a strongly fortified position high above the Sozh River in major engagements against invading Tatars from the Black Sea. Then in 1670, a significant step in the development of the region came with the grant of rights of self-determination and governance under Magdeburg Law. As in earlier times, tradesmen and merchants were encouraged to return once again as the commercial prosperity of the city and its satellite villages grew. Yet for the next hundred years or so, short periods of economic stability were followed by debilitating conflict as the strength and power of Gomel's warring neighbours waxed and waned.

It passed to Russia after Poland was partitioned in 1772, and then in 1775 Catherine the Great gifted the town to one Count Rumyantsev. A brave soldier as well as a tactically astute militarist, he was not only a hero of the people, but also a personal favourite of the empress herself. His loyalty to her was rewarded with many lavish gifts that included (among other things) extravagant jewels, military decorations, ornate silver trinkets and works of art. Emancipation of the serfs was still almost a century away and so the gift of the town also included 5,000 peasants living in the area. Finally (and most significant of all), she gave him 100,000 roubles to build a palace. It took him five years (between 1777 and 1782) to replace the old wooden castle with a magnificent mansion of stone. It was designed by Rastrelli, the architect responsible for the Winter Palace in St Petersburg.

Gomel quickly began to take on the architectural characteristics of a major European city. In 1834, Rumyantsev's younger son Sergei sold the palace and grounds to Count Paskevich, who added further features, built the nearby tower and designed the ornamental gardens that are still there today. In 1850, the first telegraphic communication line in all Russia was established between St Petersburg and Simferopol on the Black Sea, passing through Gomel. At the same time, the city found itself on the new highway between St Petersburg and Kiev. By 1888 it had become a major rail junction. This was a time of great prosperity, with trade, industry

INTO THE ZONE

I remember my first visit to the region in 2001 for two particular reasons. First, while visiting a large school, I asked the headmaster to explain the purpose of a digital display in the entrance hall, the numbers on the readout constantly changing, apparently in random fashion. He told me that it was a monitor showing the level of radiation pollution in and around the school (this monitor has now been removed). Then later that day, I visited a kindergarten. I passed from room to room, smiling fondly at the accoutrements of the toddlers and small children that were all around: toys, books, clothes and, in one room, a series of cupboards, the drawers of which were tiny beds for the littlest tots to take an afternoon nap. It made me miss my own children very much. And in this place of youthful innocence and apparent safety and security, my gaze fell on an object resting on the window ledge. When I went over to take a closer look, I saw that it was an old-fashioned Geiger counter.

On a later visit to the *oblast*, I was given the opportunity to spend a day in the restricted zone with two senior local officials, one an elected deputy and the other an ecological expert. On a warm spring day, we took the road from Vetka that leads towards Svetilovichy and then onward to the Russian border. It is a long, straight and flat road, with extensive silver birch forests on either side, just beyond the tarmac. Not far out of Vetka was the permanent militia post that was then manned 24 hours a day to monitor those who passed through this area. Unsurprisingly, we encountered no difficulty here. It is now manned no more. Some 5km further on is a road to the left and just before you reach it, you notice the first half-derelict property of the now lost village of Bartolomeyevka. As you turn in, there stands the telltale sign warning of dire consequences if you enter, the sinister international radiation logo leaving you in no doubt as to the violation of the natural order that lies beyond. We got out of the car to walk for a while. The sun was shining, birds were singing and everywhere we looked were the signs of new life, of growth and regeneration in the hedgerows and trees. Except that all around us, the insidious, and culture developing rapidly. Another major road route was completed by the construction in 1857 of a bridge erected over the Sozh. By 1913, the town's population had soared to over 104,500, including a large and influential Jewish community.

The early part of the 20th century saw much revolutionary activity in Russia, and in 1917 the empire fell at last. The first Soviet was established in Gomel in December 1917, and then in April 1919 the administrative area was incorporated into the newly independent but short-lived republic, which then became part of the Soviet Union. By 1926, it had become one of the most significant regions in the Belarusian SSR. Indeed, the 1920s and 1930s saw massive and rapid economic growth in terms of the industrial and infrastructural development of the town. Huge industrial enterprises were established. By 1941, the town was able to boast 264 of them, along with 144,200 inhabitants. Indeed, Gomel ranked third at this time in the whole of the republic in terms of industrial output.

By the time of the Nazi invasion in July 1941, the Jewish community had increased to around 50,000, approximately one-third of the city's total population. Some managed to flee in the early days of Operation Barbarossa but, after the city fell on 19 August 1941, those who could not or would not leave were confined to conditions of unspeakable barbarity. In the final analysis, over 100,000 people from the *oblast* were to die in five concentration camps and four ghettos, or after

creeping and degenerative radiation permeated the very ground on which we walked. The most obvious sign of incongruity was in the form of the buildings that we passed, all with the windows and roofs bulldozed by the authorities to prevent people from living there. The remains of the large village school were particularly poignant. We were assured that it was perfectly safe for us to be here on a short-term basis and indeed, the advice of medical experts sought prior to the visit had confirmed that this would be so. We drove further into the contaminated zone, passing another manned checkpoint as we crossed a small stream. Every time we stopped, I got out of the car to scan our surroundings. The countryside here is stunningly beautiful. Rivers, streams, woodland, marsh and meadow lie between small villages of delightful wooden houses. All empty, or at least, most of them. Very occasionally, we would pass individual dwellings with smoke spiralling from the chimney and a *babooshka* tending the crops in the garden outside. The state turns a blind eye to these people. On the face of it, produce from the land here cannot be sold. Regular checks on the radioactivity of fruit and vegetables are supposed to ensure that this is so. I couldn't help wondering, though.

On another occasion, I got to understand the extent to which limitations on access into the zone are rigidly enforced. I was in the second of two cars *en route* back to Vetka from a visit to a farm in Vyeliki Nyemki, a small hamlet north of Svetilovichy where I and others had been working on sustainable development projects. The state officials accompanying us on the visit were in the first car and I was travelling with colleagues who had never before seen the abandoned village described above. We slowed and turned in, the first car pulling away into the distance. We had only just got out of the car when it returned at high speed, one of the officials leaping out to shepherd us back into our vehicle. I was later told by a colleague who was travelling in the first car that as soon as the officials realised we had turned off, the driver performed a high-speed U-turn to fetch us back. Genuine regulation for all the right reasons, or just bureaucracy? I still can't decide.

having been transported to Germany as slave labour. The city itself was virtually flattened, with 80% of buildings being destroyed. The Nazis stripped the town of all industrial equipment, food reserves and stocks of raw materials for transportation back to Germany.

The region was a major centre for resistance activities of the partisan movement and, on 26 November 1943, the town was liberated by forces of the Belarusian Front of the Red Army. In 1946, the process of restoration and reconstruction of Gomel began, based on the preservation of original features in strategic planning terms. By 1959, the population had climbed to 168,000 and in 1962 the first trolleybuses appeared on the streets. Bit by bit in the four decades that followed, Gomel developed once more into a major European city, full of hustle and bustle, as significant new projects were completed, including newly established residential areas and the construction of a pedestrian bridge over the Sozh from the Rumyantsev Park. At the end of the 1990s, the works of construction for the new suburban railway station, another new river crossing and the impressive 'Ice Palace of Sports' (a huge facility for public sports use) were finished, as befitted the country's second city. And today, ambitious programmes of residential development are in the course of being realised, bringing whole new micro-districts into existence. Gomel's future looks to be a bright one.

GETTING THERE AND AWAY

BY AIR The Belarusian state airline Belavia operates services out of Gomel airport to a number of cities in the former Soviet republics. This includes a twice-weekly service to and from Minsk, on Wednesdays and Saturdays. Situated 8km from the city (a cab ride from the centre should cost no more than BYR30,000), the airport opened in 1968 and is the second largest in the country.

BY TRAIN The main railway station is located on Privakhsalnaya Square at one end of Lenina Avenue and only 15 minutes' walk from the city centre. It has the facilities that match its role as a major rail terminal. There are frequent trains each day to Minsk (the fastest journey time is just under five hours) and there is also a sleeper service. The price of a one-way ticket starts at US$4.

BY BUS The bus station is situated just a few hundred metres away (turn left out of the railway station's main exit). There are several daily services to Minsk (journey time around six hours, a one-way ticket starting at US$12.50) and regular routes also operate north and west to the major centres of population within the country and south and east into Russia and Ukraine. Local bus services also depart from here and the coverage is excellent, both in terms of frequency and also the number of destinations served.

BY CAR The M5 motorway heads northwest from here to Minsk and, all along the route, major works of upgrading are in the course of being implemented. This means the journey is currently not without delay or adventure, but when complete the new dualling will render it much less arduous than ever it was on single carriageway. The ring road around the city of Babrusk (almost halfway between Gomel and Minsk) has already made a big difference, though at the time of writing it was closed for an upgrade, leaving a challenging detour right through the city centre where signage for drivers is poor. Journey times are generally around five hours at present, but should fall to around three-and-a-half when the works are complete. Other major roads will take you west via Mozyr to Brest and then into western Europe, north via Mogilev to Vitebsk and then into the Baltic states and finally, east and south into Russia and Ukraine.

GETTING AROUND

The main thoroughfare heading north to south within the city is Sovyetskaya Street. The gradient rises as you head south and at the very top is Lenin Square, where you-know-who still presides over the city from his lofty perch on a granite plinth. Behind is the park where the palace and cathedral are to be found, then beyond and some way below the park is the Sozh River. Lenina Avenue leaves the square

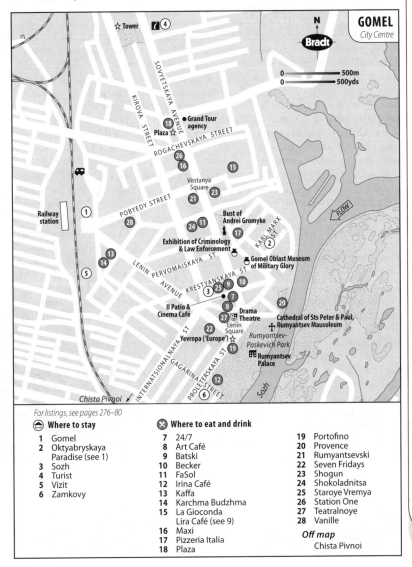

GOMEL
City Centre

For listings, see pages 276–80

Gomel City and *Oblast*   GETTING AROUND

8

275

from the same side as Sovyetskaya, but in a northwesterly direction and at an angle of around 45 degrees. It's then a straight 15-minute walk to the railway station. To access the bus station, turn left out of the main entrance/exit of the railway station and walk straight ahead for 200m. There are plenty of taxis to be found around here, particularly right outside the main entrance to the railway station.

The **bus, tram** and **trolleybus** services are plentiful and cheap, if overcrowded. Directly in front of you out of the railway station is Pobyedy Avenue and a straight ten-minute walk along here will bring you back to Sovyetskaya. Turn right to complete the triangle back up to the park. All in all, the centre is compact and everything you will want to see can be easily accessed on foot.

TOURIST INFORMATION

As with previous chapters, please bear in mind that in spite of continuing checks, regular corroboration with trusted sources and repeated personal visits, the still-developing nature of tourism in this country and the sometimes random (and inexplicable) divergence between readily available data and reality means that the information provided in these pages on opening hours, telephone numbers and prices for restaurants, bars, clubs, museums and the like occasionally will be different from what you find when you hit the ground. Actually, I reckon this adds to the charm of travelling here!

The city of Gomel has a number of tourist agencies, most of them on Sovyetskaya. The national state agency (under the guise of the agency 'GrandTour') has a **tourist information centre** at 61 Sovyetskaya Street (◯ *77 40 50/60 04 00/60 01 70;* e *grandtour.gomel@gmail.com; www.grandtour.by, www.belarustourism.by;* ⊕ *09.00–19.00 Mon–Sat).* Located on a major road junction and right opposite the Spartak chocolate factory (see below), English is spoken here and some of the information materials are available in English, although there are not many. It is also possible to book tours and make all the usual tourist arrangements. Otherwise, the reception desks at the larger hotels will have limited amounts of information. The agency **Gomeltourist** operates from a base in the Hotel Turist on Sovyetskaya, offering a full range of visitor facilities, including tours around the city and out-of-town excursions. The *oblast* executive committee's website (*www.gomel-region.by/en*) is packed with information, although primarily aimed at members of the community, but you can pick up some very useful intelligence about facilities and infrastructure. The city executive committee's website (*www.gomel.gov.by*) is also a very good source of practical information, particularly relating to hotels, restaurants, clubs, cafés and bars, as is the listings site www.hi-gomel.by. For notes on history and the towns of the area, the best resource is www.goldring.gomel-region.by. Incidentally, if you visit the state tourist agency at 61 Sovyetskaya, cross the road and drop in to the Spartak chocolate factory (*63 Sovyetskaya St;* ◯ *56 27 45;* e *spartakoao@mail.ru; www.spartak. by).* The chocolate produced here enjoys a particularly impressive reputation both within Belarus and outside its borders. Do visit the shop and sample its wares, as well as treating yourself to a drink of hot chocolate at the adjoining cafeteria. It's rich, viscous, full of sugar and utterly irresistible. Just around the corner is the Spartak restaurant serving passable European food (**$$**).

 WHERE TO STAY *Map, page 275.*

UPMARKET

Zamkovy (42 rooms) 6 Gagarina St; ◯75 04 60; e zamkovyj@yandex.ru; www.

zamkovyi.com. Only a few years old, this is the best hotel in town, though you will pay for the privilege. The difference here is that it's really good value for money. Ideally located at the top of the town next to Lunacharsky Park, mere yards from Café Irina, everything about it oozes quality & high-end service. Everyone I know in Gomel, from friends to staff at the tourist information centre, say so without hesitation. It's difficult to disagree. The theme is faux medieval (even the billiard room!), but here it is done well. Good English is spoken & the staff always go the extra mile. Services (some of them at additional cost) inc. free parking, business facilities, restaurant, bar, beauty salon, pleasing gardens, billiards room, car hire, travel services & sauna. Definitely recommended. **$$$$**

MID-RANGE

🏠 **Gomel** (184 rooms) 1 Privakhsalnaya Sq; 🔧71 67 25; e gost_gomel@gomel-hotel.by; www.gomel-hotel.by. Formerly in the same ownership as the Hotel Sozh, there has been significant refurbishment here, but it's still a sterile, soulless place. Services inc. restaurant, café, business facilities, hairdresser, gym, ATM & currency exchange. Its big advantage is in terms of location: it's the first high-rise you see on your left as you exit the railway station. B/fast extra. **$$$**

🏠 **Paradise** (34 rooms) 1 Privakhsalnaya Sq; 🔧71 25 26/77 41 11; e info@gomelparadise. com; www.gomelparadise.com. A small but significantly refurbished hotel, situated in the same building as the Hotel Gomel. The reception area is wall-to-wall pseudo-marble & it's tacky. There's also a small buffet restaurant & café here of acceptable standard, serving European, Russian & Belarusian cuisine, plus secure parking, a currency exchange, ATM, laundry, hairdresser & shop. Rooms range from sgls to apts & all are functional, but no more. Decent value though & with more foreigner-friendly service than Gomel Hotel. B/fast inc. **$$$**

🏠 **Sozh** (126 rooms) 16 Krestyanskaya St; 🔧74 81 73; e info@hotelsozh.by; www.hotelsozh. by. This passable 4-storey hotel was built in 1960 & has been refurbished a number of times. Centrally located just off Sovyetskaya (close to the top end) in the heart of the city, facilities inc. restaurant (it used to be highly rated by the locals but standards have slipped significantly), 2 24hr bars, currency exchange, beauty parlour, secure parking, business services & travel bureau. Beware the economy rooms – they are cheap, but to describe them as

basic is something of an overstatement. All in all, the location is probably the best thing going for this place. **$$$**

🏠 **Turist** (177 rooms) 87 Sovyetskaya St; 🔧57 49 51; e info@gomeltourist.com; www. gomeltourist.com. Built in 1986 & substantially refurbished in 2004, there's no escaping that this is an archetypical Soviet concrete block, situated 2km from the railway station & 2.5km from the bus station. With rooms spread over 7 floors, you pretty much get what you might expect: drab décor, little warmth in terms of atmosphere, but adequate & functional facilities. Services inc. currency exchange, Gomeltourist travel & excursion bureau (🔧 57 49 49), post facilities, restaurant spread over a number of rooms (all of which offer live music or evening cabaret), café, bar (🕐 24hrs) serving excellent coffee, newspaper stand, jewellery shop, pharmacy, souvenir shop, hairdresser, sauna & massage room. Rooms range from sgls to 3-room suites. All in all, it does the job, but at a price. My very first night in Belarus was spent here in 2001. Conference attendees & businessmen (national & international) use this hotel, so be wary of the unofficial 'services' that will be on offer, ie: the knock on the door & the late-night phone call after you turn in. **$$$**

🏠 **Vizit** (117 rooms) 6 Kisilyeva St; 🔧77 37 75; e spir_ros_aspekt@mail.ru; www.gomel.amaks-hotels.ru. A very shiny hotel in the Amaks chain, it's only a few hundred metres from the railway station. Services inc. free parking, limited travel facilities, bar, café, ATM & car rental. The subject of a full refurbishment in 2013, the standard of materials & workmanship is not great, but the staff are very helpful (most speak English) & if you don't expect too much, it's decent value for money. **$$$**

BUDGET

🏠 **Oktyabrskaya** (145 rooms) 1 Karl Marx St; 🔧77 68 91. Not far from the river & at the right end of town for most of the sights, there are sgls, dbls & suites on 6 floors. There's a bar & a café, plus a few other basic facilities, but b/fast is not inc. in the price of the room. This hotel is more or less constantly in a process of refurbishment, so only a proportion of the 145 rooms will be available at any given time (in spring 2014, the number was 38). It's cheap, but not very cheerful; a last-resort option. **$$**

RESTAURANTS

✘ **Provence** 1 Bilyetski St Lower; ☏ 44 773 03 03;
e provencegomel@gmail.com; www.provanc.by;
🕐 noon–midnight daily. 'There's a new restaurant
in town that I want to show you. I think it's the
best'. Thus spoke Olya on my last visit to Gomel. All
of my other Gomel friends say it's one of the best
restaurants in town too. Recently opened, it's a
2-storey establishment, right on the bank of the Sozh
River, with excellent views from the terrace up &
down the river. To find it, walk down to the riverbank
from the rear of the Rumyantsev palace, locate the
sculpture of the first settlers, & keep going riverside
under the footbridge that crosses to the other bank.
You soon come to the restaurant. Serving French &
Italian cuisine to a high standard, the décor is tasteful
& everything about this place is a cut above the rest.
There's also a bar on the 1st floor that is very popular
with Gomel's student population. $$$$

✘ **FaSol** 36 Sovyetskaya St; ☏ 44 790 33 33;
🕐 noon–23.00 daily. 'FaSol' as in 'doh, reh, me',
etc, so guess the theme! The interior is pleasing
Victoriana & the service is particularly good here. The
menu is varied & it's available in English. Quality is
good & the prices are reasonable. The ambience is
tarnished somewhat by the ubiquitous music screens
& by night it's a very popular karaoke bar, when you
should expect to queue to get in. My preference
is to go for lunch or an afternoon snack, when it's
relaxed & you'll probably have it all to yourself.
Olya likes it here, as do her friends, & I can see why.
Recommended, though not if you have a smoking
phobia, as the non-smoking section is just one half of
the area where everyone else is lighting up. $$$

✘ **Il Patio** 6 Kommunarov St; ☏ 70 14 30;
🕐 10.00–00.30 daily. Situated within the
'Continent' entertainment complex & next door
to a cinema towards the top end of town, this is a
chain restaurant, but the décor, quality of food &
service are all acceptable. It's nothing special, but
there's a wide variety of Italian classics, 20 or more
pizzas & a salad bar. $$$

✘ **Irina Café** Lunacharsky Park, off Gagarina St;
☏ 70 36 44; 🕐 noon–midnight daily. Very close to
the impressive Zamkovy Hotel, the park location is
near to perfect. The dining area inside is small & quite
ordinary, but outside is an attractive terraced eating
area under cover of a huge awning. There are patio
heaters for chilly evenings too, plus a large barbecue.

The cuisine is Belarusian & European from a varied
menu. Service is excellent & the food is of a very high
quality. It's my personal favourite in town. $$$

✘ **Karchma Budzhma** 3 Privakhsalnaya St;
☏ 77 71 81; 🕐 11.30–23.00 daily. Located near to the
railway station, this is a worthy attempt at creating
something traditional. The interior is modelled on
a village dwelling of old, with all the attendant
trappings & adornments that you might expect.
Classic Belarusian dishes (inc. *draniki* & *machanka* of
course) are served with unusual & extravagant drinks,
inc. *kvas* flavoured with mint & a very tasty honey
liqueur infused with herbs. The menu is extensive &
is available in English. My only word of warning is not
to over-order, as the portions are huge. I once came
here in a group of 5, & 3 meals between us would
have been more than adequate in terms of volume.
Good value & an entertaining night out. Locals like this
place, & I like it too. $$$

✘ **La Gioconda** 1 Vostanya Sq; ☏ 71 95 54;
🕐 08.00–04.00 daily. Located within the central
football stadium at the rear of the square, this
functional Italian used to serve the best ice cream
in town, but Olya tells me this is no longer the
case. The food is decent, but nothing to write home
about, which is a great pity; the pizza here used to
be excellent. $$$

✘ **Pizzeria Italia** 14 Pushkina St; ☏ 77 67 55;
🕐 noon–midnight daily. Handily located towards
the top end of town, decent Italian cuisine is
served in 2 dining areas – the veranda is the nicest.
Very good value for money. $$$

✘ **Plaza** 66A Sovyetskaya St; ☏ 71 32 00;
🕐 noon–05.00 daily. Standard pizza & sushi fayre
are on offer at this restaurant at the Plaza Club. In
fact, Olya reckons it's the best sushi in town. They
advertise hot food until 05.00, but it's perhaps best
not to rely on this. $$$

✘ **Portofino** 2 Lenin Sq; ☏ 55 77 77;
🕐 noon–midnight daily. Located within the
Europe Entertainment Centre, European &
Japanese cuisine is served here. A business lunch
menu is available noon–16.00, & there's even a
kids menu! Actually, it's all done rather well, from
the décor to the food to the service. $$$

✘ **Shogun** 29A Sovyetskaya St; ☏ 20 50 50;
e info@shogun.by; www.shogun.by;
🕐 noon–midnight (01.00 Fri & Sat). This relatively
new teppan-yaki grill & sushi bar is a big hit with

the locals. Situated next to the circus & incorporating Kelly's Bar (🕐 *noon–02.00, 04.00 Fri & Sat*), it's bright, shiny & the food is good. Worth a try. $$$

🍴 **Staroye Vremya ('Old Times')** 14 Krestyanskaya St; 📞 74 19 57; 🕐 noon–01.00 daily. Located next to the Sozh Hotel, it's very popular with out-of-town visitors, especially from abroad, but don't let that put you off. My Gomel friends like it too. As you might guess, it's an attempt to recreate days of yore, primarily the Soviet era. Spread over 4 rooms, each has its own theme entirely unconnected with the others (inc. the East, football & a bucolic idyll). There's even a full-size trolleybus! It's gimmicky, but the décor is never less than interesting & the food is decent value. $$$

🍴 **Turist** 87 Sovyetskaya St; 📞 57 49 51; 🕐 11.00–midnight daily. Situated at the Hotel Turist, there are 3 restaurants in this complex, all serving Belarusian & European cuisine to a decent standard, although the service is not the fastest & it's a little frosty too. The rooms are cavernous & it's all very shiny & rather noisy. Live floor shows while you eat will take you back to the days of 1970s-style cabaret. $$$

🍴 **24/7 Café** 12 Sovyetskaya St; 📞 29 395 95 35; 🕐 10.00–23.00 daily. Fast food. $$

🍴 **Batski** 12 Sovyetskaya St; 📞 44 595 95 95; www.batki.by; 🕐 11.00–23.00 daily. This one is a little out of left-field, but as a budget option & something different it can't be beaten. It's a self-service café, where you choose from the range of hot & cold dishes laid out before you. The décor, dark & medieval, is better than you might expect, the quality of the food is good & the prices are very reasonable. There's a pleasant outside terrace on Sovyetskaya for you to watch the world go by. If time is tight, it does the job. $$

🍴 **Station One** 2 Rogachevskaya St; 📞 77 17 16; 🕐 noon–01.00 daily. My good friends Oxana & Oleg live close by & they eat here all the time. Nothing is too much trouble for the hospitable Palestinian owner, who consistently serves up good, tasty food at a very good price. There's an on-street terrace for the summer. It's another one of my favourites, not least because the music is so good here! $$

CAFES

☕ **Art** 2 Sovyetskaya St; 📞 74 12 58; 🕐 noon–23.00 daily. Not bad, but nothing special, says Olya.

☕ **Cinema** 4 Kommunarov St; 📞 74 08 88; 🕐 noon–02.00 daily. This decent café, not surprisingly, is located at a cinema, the one next door to the 'Continent' entertainment complex where Il Patio pizzeria is to be found. The location is good & it's a functional venue for a coffee stop.

☕ **Kaffa** 34 Lenina Av; 📞 71 80 60; 🕐 08.00–midnight daily. The coffee is good here & the staff are always eager to please.

☕ **Lira** 12 Sovyetskaya St; 📞 74 88 02; 🕐 11.00–23.00 daily. Nothing exceptional, but it's always busy when I walk past.

☕ **Maxi** 46 Sovyetskaya St; 📞 71 72 13; 🕐 08.00–23.00 daily. Olya says that the cakes, ice cream & coffee here are among the best in town, although not the cheapest. I like it too. Pavement seating is available & there's another Maxi that looks & offers the same further up Sovyetskaya on the opposite side of the road, just after the mural depicting the history of the city, but it's not as good as this one.

☕ **Paradise** 1 Privakhsalnaya Sq; 📞 71 97 06; 🕐 noon–midnight daily. The café at the refurbished hotel of the same name – it's a decent option.

☕ **Rumyantsevski** 38 Sovyetskaya St; 📞 71 76 34; 🕐 11.00–23.00 daily. Gomel friends have little to say about this place, other than that it's OK.

☕ **Shokoladnitsa ('Chocolate Girl')** 30 Sovyetskaya St; 📞 77 37 45; 🕐 09.00–23.00 daily. One of my favourites: the location is excellent & the desserts here are scrumptious. A number of my Gomel friends rate it highly too.

☕ **Teatralnoye** 3 Lenina Av; 📞 74 77 95; 🕐 noon–midnight daily. Tucked away just off Lenin Sq, I rather like it here. Just up from Seven Fridays American cocktail bar & grill (see page 280) on the opposite side of the road, it's a decent alternative if you're looking for something a little quieter!

☕ **Vanille** 16 Pobyedy St; 📞 77 65 59; 🕐 11.00–23.00 daily. Located on a classy street, everything about this place matches its surroundings. Worth a visit.

BARS

🍷 **Becker** Il Sovyetskaya St; 📞 74 92 23; 🕐 noon–midnight daily. Handily placed, the beer & ambience are good. Always popular, my Gomel friends don't rave about it, but it's a decent option for a good night out.

🍷 **Chista Pivnoi** 4A Bratyev Lizyukovikh St; 📞 93 93 93; 🕐 noon–01.00 Sun–Thu, noon–03.00 Fri

& Sat. Located away to the west of the city centre, there's live music nightly.

♀ **Seven Fridays** 6 Lenina Av; ✆74 61 01; e 7evenfridays@mail.ru; www.7fridays.by; ⏰ noon–02.00 daily. An American cocktail bar & grill, my good friend Alicia raves about this place. Don't come for a quiet night out, but if Americana is your style & you're in the mood for a long night of eating & drinking in a lively atmosphere, then you're in luck. Alicia tells me the reputation of the place brings young people from far & wide, & that it's heaving on Fri & Sat nights. The party nights are legendary. The cocktails are excellent & the bartenders love to put on a show, so recline on one of the plush Chesterfields & take it all in. The food is also standard Americana & the quality is decent. Beware the loo, however. It has a challenging mirrored floor & ceiling, so only venture in when sober.

ENTERTAINMENT AND NIGHTLIFE

Gomel is home to a larger than average number of excellent universities and higher-education facilities, as befits its status as the country's second city. In fact, the State University, with over 10,000 students alone, is actually located on Sovyetskaya Street. With so many students in residence, the bar and club scene is thriving (see pages 279–80 for bars). And as you might expect, there is a wide choice of establishments. As in the other major cities, the coffee-bar culture that was lost in the West decades ago continues to thrive here.

The establishments on Sovyetskaya, the main hub of activity, tend to be lively. There are lots and lots of cheap and cheerful Soviet-style bars and cafés on both sides of the road, all the way up to Lenin Square at the top. Be adventurous and walk in any that take your fancy. The most chic street is Pobyedy, so bars here like to think of themselves as being sophisticated.

☆ **Plaza** 66 Sovyetskaya St; ✆71 35 40; ⏰ noon–05.00 daily. This club is especially popular with the city's student population.

☆ **Yevropa ('Europe')** 2 Lenin Sq; ✆77 88 00; e club@europaclub.by; www.europaclub.by; ⏰ noon–05.00 daily. Brash & loud, there's enough at this entertainment complex to keep you amused.

SHOPPING

A gentle amble up Sovyetskaya Street towards the park will take you past a variety of shops in increasing numbers, including two very good bookshops, one on each side of the road, and a number of small department stores that are worth a browse. The classiest shops are to be found in Pobyedy Avenue, off Sovyetskaya Street. An alternative place for purchases is the cathedral, which has two stalls at the rear selling posters, cards, beeswax candles and very cheap artefacts (such as images of icons for your wallet, desk or car) that make excellent souvenirs.

OTHER PRACTICALITIES

As befitting the country's second city, **banks** and **currency exchanges** are to be found all over the town centre, with **ATMs** in increasing numbers.

WHAT TO SEE AND DO

One of my favourite pastimes in the whole of Belarus is to take a stroll along **Sovyetskaya Street,** with its fine 19th- and 20th-century architecture, and into the park. If you begin on the eastern side of the street at **Vostanya Square**, opposite

Pobyedy Street, take a look first at the **tank** mounted on a granite plinth on your left. It's a monument to the Red Army heroes who liberated the city in 1943. Also here, incorporating the Top Tour travel agency (⏱ *09.00–19.00 Mon–Sat*) is the **pale orange stucco building** that was a hospital in the Great Patriotic War, and later a Nazi prison where up to 100,000 were interred. On the wall heading up to the football stadium are two plaques; the first commemorates those who lost their lives here and the second marks events in this square during the October Revolution. Head up Sovyetskaya past the circus and its fountains, where at the weekend families bring their children to promenade and to ride in the battery-operated cars. In the pretty park that you now reach, close to the pavement, look for the **bust of Andrei Gromyko.** He was the Soviet Union's foreign minister in successive governments for an incredible 28-year period that spanned four decades, notably under Leonid Brezhnev. Gromyko first entered government under Stalin and he was unquestionably one of the giants of Cold War diplomacy. He was born in a small village near here.

Further along, you will pass a series of **murals** depicting key events in the history of the city, beginning with its foundation in 1142. You very soon emerge into **Lenin Square**, a vast area of tarmac with the **drama theatre** to your right and, in front of you, the **statue of Lenin**, high on its plinth, gazing magisterially over the entire city. If you enter the **Rumyantsev-Paskevich Park** to the left of the statue, you will find that you are standing directly in front of the early 19th-century **Cathedral of Sts Peter and Paul**. Built to Classicist design, it is an imposing building, but its real delights are to be found inside, for the iconostasis and walls display a wonderful collection of icons. Daily services are held at 08.00 and 17.00 from Monday to Saturday. On Sundays, they take place at 06.30, 09.00 and 17.00.

Turn right out of the cathedral, then right again towards its rear aspect and you find yourself standing in front of an oddity: the pseudo-Classical **Rumyantsev mausoleum**. It's classically Russian and an excellent photo opportunity. Carry on past the mausoleum towards the railings and pause to take in the view over the Sozh. The countryside to the east stretches away in front of you beyond the river. On the far bank are wide groves of trees that come almost to the water's edge, leaving a strip of sandy, light-coloured soil that could almost be a beach. This is exactly the purpose that it serves for local people in the months of summer, though Olya never comes here: 'much too busy', she says. Now turn your back on the Sozh, lean on the railings and take in the panoramic view across the park. It was designed at the end of the 18th century by Count Rumyantsev around the **palace** that was built to his orders. Among others, the renowned British architect John Clark worked extensively on the project. Here is an exquisite example of Classical park design. Covering 25ha high above the Sozh, various species of tree have been deliberately arranged into groups that enhance their features. There is Belarusian maple, ash and chestnut, together with eastern white pine, northern white oak and Manchurian walnut. Standing away to your left, in the middle of the park, beautifully complemented by the woodland all around it, is the palace itself. This isn't the best perspective from which to view its charms; a better one soon awaits you. Head diagonally back towards Lenin Square and make for the ornamental fountain, with benches all around it. Beyond the fountain, along a path, is another seating area. From here, the view of the palace is at its best and by now you will have noticed the light classical music that is constantly relayed over speakers situated all over the park. Further extensive information relating to all of the sites that can be visited within the park, including opening hours and prices, is available from the excellent English-language website www.palacegomel.by. It's packed with a whole

8

For Part I see pages 108–9; for Part II see pages 110–11.

I love the contradiction and ambiguity that are utterly ubiquitous in this country, but sometimes, only sometimes, there will be an event or an experience that irritates beyond measure. It is usually connected with bureaucracy and paperwork and process: mindless, pointless, monolithic, impenetrable and duplicatory bureaucracy, utterly without worth and with no intrinsic value (see box, *The platinum emigration service*, pages 52–3).

David and I had one such experience during our first full week at the Children's Correction Centre in Vetka, when we had to take time out from being with Zhenya and Nina and the others to register our documents with the local militia.

It didn't look good from the moment we stepped into the office, and that old familiar uneasy feeling soon settled over the room. First into our line of vision appeared a young militia officer, clad in uniform and sporting a mug of coffee, presumably the minder for the stern and only fleetingly polite official on the other side of the room, who we concluded from our very first glance had little difficulty in accommodating the importance and significance of her position in officialdom. We feared the worst and our trepidation was not to be disappointed; after a cursory glance through our papers, we were sent away, unregistered, unstamped and unsigned (I still don't really understand why), with a suggestion that we 'come back tomorrow'. And guess what? Our visit that afternoon to the militia offices was within the 72-hour tolerance period for registration that applied in those days, but 'tomorrow' wouldn't be.

We returned the next morning for round two. She was waiting for us. She looked down her nose at our papers, she shook her head, her tight-lipped visage hardened still further, and she proclaimed that we didn't have the right papers. She couldn't possibly register, or stamp, or sign.

Now, David is a delightfully accommodating man and I love him dearly. But he also used to be a motorcycle cop. And when I saw him standing over our tormentor, arms folded across his chest, face set in granite, first tossing a document across the desk at her, then jabbing his finger into another piece of paper beneath her gaze, I knew that I could sell tickets for this one. For her part, the official didn't get flustered, although the pitch of her voice did rise slightly, and the volume of her

range of fascinating background information, so do spend some time browsing before your visit.

This is such a romantic location! I recall walking here one winter's day in watery sunshine, with snow on the ground, wrapped in scarf, gloves, heavy overcoat and hat, listening to the music playing over the tannoy, watching the sunbeams slanting down through the bare trees and deep in thought. I looked up to see an elderly couple. They were clasped in a tender embrace, dancing to the music, gazing deeply into each other's eyes as they twirled around and around, smiling and laughing gaily. I've walked these paths in each of the four seasons and there's always something to admire. It's one of my favourite places in all the world for reflective perambulation and deep thought. If you head across the front of the palace and follow the gradient of the path downwards, you find yourself entering a ravine. If you look up to the left, you will see the imposing 39m **tower** added by Count Paskevich after the original palace was constructed, while below you and to your right is Swan Lake, an ornamental pond with its resident swans. You have two choices now: you can delivery increased; she also said to our associates, in Russian of course, that he should back off. Happily this wasn't relayed to David, and the stand-off played on, as first she jabbered to someone, goodness knows who, via the desk phone, then, to show how incredibly important she was, to someone else on her mobile at the same time. Two ears, two conversations and a third conversation with her audience in the room. We were impressed.

For my part, I was leaning against the door in a rather slovenly and disrespectful manner, unshaven, scruffily clad, arms folded, detached, tossing in the odd phrase of Russian to suggest to the official that I could understand all she was saying, which I hadn't a hope of doing, such was the speed of her delivery, and vaguely amused by the *tableau* that was unfolding; except that even I was starting to get more than a tad irritated. I wanted to get out of there and back to the centre; I just wanted to be with the children.

I'm afraid I couldn't help myself. Let's call it a degree of impish mischievousness then, and nothing more, or 'alternative dispute resolution'. I was bored now and didn't want to indulge, massage or stroke the official's ego any more. I strolled over to a spare desk, sat on it, and took out my mobile phone. I scrolled through my contacts, found what I was looking for, and held up the screen to our translator. 'These are the phone numbers of *blah blah*, in the *blah blah* ministry in Minsk. Perhaps I should call him to get this sorted?'

'Shall I translate?'

'Yes please, translate to *blah blah* (one of our Belarusian colleagues), but loudly enough for the official to hear…'

Scrolling through my numbers, legs swinging lazily from the desk, I repeated this little charade, this pantomime, three times, with the details of three different contacts in London and Minsk. Whether it was David's show of fortitude, my less direct performance slightly off-stage, or just boredom on her part, the process of registration, stamping and signing was suddenly completed and our passports and migration cards were returned with a smile, of sorts. We wished her a cheery goodbye, swept out of the office, into the sunshine and back to the centre; back to our children, and back to what really mattered.

either climb out of the other side of the ravine and head through the woods until you reach a rickety tower, pay the attendant BYR1,200 and then climb the even more rickety spiral staircase until you emerge on a wobbly platform high above the treeline. The view over the city is simply fantastic, but your perch is a lofty one and it really does wobble quite dramatically. Or, if heights don't suit you, take a turn around the pond and head for the railings by the river, then stroll at your leisure by the side of its fast-flowing waters. At regular points along the riverbank and throughout the park are small café-bars serving soft drinks, alcoholic beverages and light snacks. You can also take a 40-minute cruise along the river from here, with some lovely views across the lower town.

There are several points at which you can turn away from the river and climb back into the park. When you do so, you have two things left to do. First, take a stroll across the high pedestrian bridge to the other side of the river and back, with splendid views on either side; then secondly, visit the palace. Opening hours are rather erratic, but if you strike it lucky it's well worth a visit (*admission for locals*

BYR3,500 and for foreign visitors BYR20,000). The entrance hall in particular is just stunning, and room after room is packed with artefacts and relics from the period.

When you have experienced all there is to see and do in this lovely park, head back down Sovyetskaya, window shopping as you go, to where your voyage of exploration began. Resolve to do it all over again on your next visit, preferably in a different season, when the experience will be very different.

And to understand more about the impact of warfare on the lands and people of the region, particularly the privations of the Great Patriotic War, visit the **Gomel Oblast Museum of Military Glory** (*5 Pushkina St;* \ *77 57 41;* e *gommilmus@tut. by;* ⊕ *May–Sep 11.00–19.00 Mon–Fri, Oct–Apr 10.00–18.00 Mon–Fri; admission BYR15,000).* I've been several times, and on each visit it was virtually empty of visitors. Several rooms tell the story of the region in military engagements across the centuries, through the medium of exhibits, models, uniforms and military hardware. The exhibits concerning the terrible events that occurred here from 1941 to 1944 are deeply affecting. Outside is a display of vehicles, guns, planes, helicopters and a huge steam locomotive proudly displaying that iconic red star (it's a brilliant photo opportunity). Try to find the time to visit – you won't regret it. For an unusual experience that is no less interesting, visit the linked **Exhibition of Criminology and Law Enforcement** (*1 Pushkina St;* \ *71 23 79;* e *gommilmus@ tut.by).* Two rooms house exhibits relating to the fight against crime and the work

THE METROPOLITAN FILARET COMES TO TOWN

When I first visited Vetka in 2001, the focus for the Orthodox congregation was a small wooden church on one of the roads out of town. It was badly in need of repair. The priest told me that work had started on a new construction in the middle of town, but that the project had come to a halt when the source of funds dried up. Each time that I returned, the half-built shell and surrounding building site felt like a metaphor for all of the infrastructural problems that beset the people of this country. And then, out of the blue, I arrived in town after an absence of 12 months to find the church complete, its golden domes glinting in the sunshine. It was to be consecrated during my visit by the head of the Orthodox Church in Belarus, none other than the Metropolitan Filaret of All Belarus himself, and when I went to see the Chief Executive of Vetka Executive Committee, Viktor Burakov, to update him on developments with our joint sustainability programmes, I was humbled to receive an invitation to attend.

The day of the ceremony dawned bright, with a cloudless blue sky. We made our way to the church and were greeted by a mass of local people. As we were led through, our eyes fell upon two trails of wild flowers, freshly picked, that lay along the sides of the path from the entrance gates, up the steps and into the church itself, leading all the way to the iconostasis. The riot of colour and the heady aroma presented a glorious living display. Inside, people were crammed shoulder to shoulder, and together we waited over an hour for the filaret's entourage to arrive. Then, without any warning other than a series of urgent whispers that reached us in a wave from the gates, the invisible choir in the gallery above burst into life with a soaring, a cappella Divine Liturgy that sent a tingle all the way up my spine and made my heart want to burst with joy.

There was a huge surge as the procession came into view, with priests in ascending order of seniority and bedecked in astonishingly ornate robes to match their status, all of them with huge spade beards, extravagantly swinging incense of various law enforcement agencies from 1917 to the present day, including with regard to 'post revolutionary terrorism'. There is also a corner devoted to the work of investigators preventing the removal of antiquities without the necessary papers. I kid you not!

OUTSIDE GOMEL

VETKA (BETKA / BETKA) This small town, 22km northeast of Gomel and founded in 1685 by 'Old Believers' who had fled from Russia, has been my Belarusian home since my very first visit in 2001. It has also made a huge contribution to my own personal development and, in spiritual terms, it has a very special place in my heart. It's a mix of provincial Mother Russia and the revolutionary CCCP at their finest, where the golden cupolas of the Orthodox church dazzle in the sunlight, the concrete of the 1960s Soviet apartment blocks continues to crumble and Lenin gazes with majesty and fortitude across Red Square. But there is also new build on a significant scale, largely residential, and a huge new supermarket on the edge of town. The street where I live when I'm here, and my home in Belarus for the last 13 years and more, is Karl Marx Street. Part tarmac, part sand and rutted with pot-holes, it is to be found in the old part of town. Number 42 is halfway down on the right, with the small shop that Valeri built with his own hands to one side. Between

holders as if their lives depended upon it, responding to the liturgy with chants of their own. Constantly and urgently, people all around me were muttering, bowing their heads, eyes to the ground and crossing themselves incessantly, almost obsessively. It was impossible not to be caught up and swept away by the tide of mysticism and ancient, holy ritual that was washing over us all. Then the filaret himself appeared, head high, exuding sacred power and influence, his gaze slowly passing over every corner of the congregation. Wherever his gaze rested, if only for an instant, people crossed themselves even more frantically than they had before (if that were possible), while His Holiness periodically responded with the slightest of inclinations of his head.

The entire process of consecration took almost two hours. At one point, the filaret blessed each of the walls with holy water flung from the bristles of an enormous brush, like something a decorator would use. At least twice, he changed his robes. To do so, he stood in the middle of the congregation, on a slight dais, while junior priests solemnly and reverently removed each layer of robe for him and replaced it with another. Once, he reached inside and produced a magnificent comb with a flourish, before proceeding to preen his flowing beard, deliberately, slowly and with more than a slight air of superiority.

When it was all over, we accompanied him to the local restaurant, where the tables were creaking under the weight of food and vodka. The priests came too. At various points throughout the meal, they broke into spontaneous, soaring a cappella harmonies, delivered ever louder and with more gusto as each empty vodka bottle was replaced by another full one. The celebration lasted long into the afternoon, until the filaret decided it was time to go. In an instant he was out of his seat and, after blessing all those assembled before him, he swept out of the room like a ship in full sail, his entourage trailing behind. An extraordinary day.

them, members of the family staff it from 08.00 until 19.00, every day of the week. If I'm in town, I wander in around 18.00 to share a beer and some dried fish with Valeri and his mates. Dexter the dog lounges on his old sofa on the front porch next door. Valeri and I took him out for a walk one night and inevitably ended up in a bar. We forgot to bring him home, much to Tanya's outrage, but he wandered back several days later, none the worse for the experience. Valeri says he's a street dog, and that the whole town is his home. We're good mates, Dexter and me. And Richard the cat, now 14 years old, has finally accepted me as part of the household. For ten years he barely gave me a glance, but each night now, we share the divan in the parlour. He has more room than me. Like Dexter, I wander the streets of this town in all seasons and all weather, by day and by night. There's something about it that keeps drawing me back and that I can't articulate. We just fit, I guess.

Located on the banks of the Sozh River, Vetka is surrounded by forest and marsh. The name is assumed to have been derived from an island of the same name in the river. It was twice burned to the ground by the tsar's troops, in 1735 and 1764, with its residents being forced to resettle to the outer provinces of eastern Russia. At the time, it was widely known for the unique style of icon painting that was practised here. There was also a specialist school for woodcarving. In 1772, the town was annexed to the Russian Empire and in 1852 it became part of the Gomel administrative region.

In 1880, Vetka is known to have counted around 6,000 inhabitants, 994 wooden and 11 stone buildings, six windmills, a rope factory and a tannery. Anchors were produced at local forges and ships were constructed at the shipyard on the Sozh from 1840. There is still a wharf there today. In the middle of the 19th century, the richest of the town's merchants had their own steamships. During the war years from August 1941 to September 1943, Vetka was under the occupation of the Nazis, who murdered 656 of its residents, the majority of them Jews. Behind the locked gates of a farm enterprise on the edge of town stands the recently and privately commissioned memorial to the Jewish dead of the district, 200 of whom were murdered in this very location. The atrocity was long rumoured to have taken place, but a mass grave was only discovered when building work was being undertaken at the farm. It is believed that some bodies are yet to be discovered. In recent times, the local newspaper has published the names of the collaborators who it alleges were involved in the murders. Even now, old wounds are being reopened in this community. On the other side of town, unseen behind a petrol station, is the site of the old Jewish cemetery. Once there were over a thousand graves here, but all that remains today are a few broken stones and some rusted railings. Valeri took me to see it once and told me how, 45 years ago, he and his friends used to play hide and seek between the gravestones as children. Over time all fell into disrepair and the cemetery was gradually taken apart by the Communists, who used the stones to build roads. School No 1 in Vetka has a display of materials and documents concerning the Jewish community of the town. I'm told that one of the teachers there is a particular fount of knowledge. During the war years, engagements took place all over the district, and remains of the fallen are still being found. Only recently, building work at School No 1 uncovered the bodies of a number of German soldiers. Valeri tells me this is happening all over Belarus.

A London-based foundation, the Belarus Holocaust Memorials Project (*www.belarusmemorials.com*), has a mission to place memorials at the location of each of the 400 known sites of Nazi massacres of the Belarusian Jewish Community. As the Vetka experience shows, there are likely to be further sites yet to be identified. By the summer of 2014, over 50 memorials had been erected through the good offices of this worthy cause.

Prior to the Chernobyl catastrophe the population of the district exceeded 40,000, but after a massive resettlement programme to take people away from the areas of radiation pollution, this number had shrunk to only 7,200 by the first anniversary of the disaster. On 1 November 1987, a splendid **Folk Arts Museum** (*5 Red Sq;* ☏ *02 26 70/02 14 49;* e *vetkamuszejj@rambler.ru; www.vetka.museum.by;* ⏰ *09.00–18.00 Tue–Sun; admission BYR7,500*) was opened here. Its exhibits are of the highest quality and display the unique historical and cultural features of the region. Located in a former merchant's house, its ceremonial entrance doors have beautiful wooden carvings worked by the founder and his assistants. The items on display, including ancient artefacts, icons, books, manuscripts, traditional costumes and woven *rushniki* (many from the unique weaving school in the nearby village of Nyeglubka) are simply stunning. This is particularly true of the icons. Most of the ones exhibited here were crafted by Old Believers in the 17th century in the style of those on display in Moscow's cathedrals. The founder of the museum was Fyodor Grigorievich Shkliarov, a native of Vetka and a fervent promoter of local culture. He began to assemble artefacts in the 1960s and continued to enlarge his collection into the 1980s. Public interest began to be engaged over the years and these items laid the foundation for the museum. Sadly, Shkliarov died the year after it opened. His portrait hangs there still, showing him surrounded by many of the items in his own collection. Today, the museum has a national reputation as an artistic educational centre, where research is undertaken into the study of traditional Belarusian culture. A visit here is highly recommended. I have encouraged quite a number of foreign visitors to come to experience the charms of this museum, and none have been disappointed. Just across the square is the **Sozh Restaurant** (⏰ *11.30–23.30 daily; $$*) serving traditional Belarusian fare. It's a vast, cavernous room that is almost always empty and always cold, but the food is nourishing and good value. On two separate occasions, I have seen it alive with colour and noise. On my first visit, I was honoured to be invited to the wedding of the daughter of a senior local official here. The second time was the lavish lunch given on the occasion of the consecration of the recently completed **church** (see box, *The metropolitan filaret comes to town*, pages 284–5). Located just off the square, it is well worth a visit. Inside, it is bright and airy. Painted on the iconostasis is a fresco depicting the fate of the victims of Chernobyl.

Directly outside is the **memorial stone and church bell** dedicated to the memory of those who died in the immediate aftermath of the Chernobyl explosion, along with the lost villages in the uninhabitable zone whose residents were required to leave their homes for good.

There is a small hotel here, a decent pizzeria, a number of bars, a bank with an ATM and shops serving everyday needs. Vetka is also home to the Children's Correction Centre, which has been the focus of WOVA's charitable works for some time. See boxes, *So who is correcting whom here? Parts I, II and III*, on pages 108–9, 110–11 and 282–3 respectively, and also www.wova.org.uk.

KHALCH (ХАЛЬЧ / ХАЛЬЧ) This small village in Vetka district, located high on the western bank of the Sozh, is notable for its **19th-century manor house** that is occasionally open to visitors on an ad hoc basis (major works of renovation have been on the go for years) and its small wooden **church.** As you cross the Sozh on the road from Gomel to Vetka and just before you enter the town, look up to your left. The brightly coloured blue church is situated high atop a bluff, looking down over the river towards Vetka. A heroic and bloody engagement took place here in 1943 as the Red Army, supported by groups of partisans, fought to cross the river to liberate Gomel.

Historically, Vetka was renowned as a centre for Старовери ('Old Believers'), the religious group that eschewed the reforms of Patriarch Nikon in the 17th century and suffered disenfranchisement and persecution as a result. Most fled or were forced to resettle, notably under Catherine the Great, who banished significant numbers to Siberia. Indeed, the group was still suffering prejudice and oppression into the 20th century, to the extent that members were forced to hide from the police and pass themselves off as mainstream Orthodox believers. As a result, Old Believer communities exist today in far-flung locations around the world and estimates as to the number of followers vary from one to ten million worldwide. Many Old Believer churches still exist throughout Gomel region, including in the city itself.

The most visible difference is that Old Believers will make the sign of the cross with two fingers only instead of three, as officially recognised by Orthodoxy. They continue to use the older Church Slavonic translation of the sacred texts. The performance of Baptism is only accepted through three full immersions; anything else, for example the pouring of water over the forehead, is wholly rejected. There are also many essential differences in church services. There is an Old Believers cemetery in Vetka, where the crosses on the graves are markedly different from those found in other Orthodox cemeteries. I have a number of very good friends in Vetka who are descended from Old Believer families, including Natasha and her Mum, fourth and fifth generation believers. They practise the old ways still. They tell me they have interesting stories to tell, but I'm still waiting…

There is a regular bus service to Khalch and Vetka from Gomel. If you are driving, the road there runs directly from the bottom end of Sovyetskaya. It's a straight road, heading in a northeasterly direction. Khalch is situated 18km along it, just before you cross the Sozh. Vetka is on the opposite bank.

NYEGLUBKA (НЕГЛЮБКА / НЕГЛЮБКА) Located on back roads 45km northeast of Vetka, this is another small village that is pretty but unremarkable, other than in respect of the **village school** there. For it is here that the descendants of traditional weavers are taught the skills and crafts of their forebears on intricate wooden looms crafted in exactly the same way as the originals. The headteacher is pleased to welcome visitors and always eager to showcase the skills of her students. It's difficult to find, but the tourist route devised by the local executive committee includes a visit here and tourist agencies in Gomel will be more than pleased to book you a place on the tour.

Only a few kilometres to the west of here is the tiny hamlet of **Zhelizniki,** where the restoration of one of the oldest Orthodox churches in all Belarus has now been completed. I have visited it several times at various stages of the works and it is a joy to be able to report that all is now complete. A visit here is also included on the locally devised tour.

PRIPYATSKY NATIONAL PARK (НАЦЫЯНАЛЬНЫ ПАРК ПРЫПЯЦКІ / НАЦИОНАЛЬНЫЙ ПАРК ПРИПЯТСКИЙ) On the western fringes of the *oblast* is the Pripyatsky National Park. Deep within the mystical Polyesye region and covering 82,529ha, it was established in the marshy lowland area between the Pripyat, Stivha and Ubort rivers to protect and preserve the unusual ecological systems that are to be found in this area, along with its landscape and biological diversity. The tract of oak forestation here is one of the largest in Europe, and the park is of particular interest to ornithologists: around 265 species are registered, including the greater and lesser heron, common crane, eagle owl, serpent eagle and marsh owl. Since 1987, the European bison has been reintroduced here and there are now believed to be 67 individual animals within its boundaries. The park's main town and spiritual heart of the Polyesye is **Turov,** where there is a fine **nature museum** (⊕ *May–Oct 10.00– 18.00 Tue–Sun, Nov–Apr 10.00–17.00 Tue–Sun; admission BYR3,000*), explaining all the visitor needs to know about the history and ecology of the area. Located on the Pripyat River, Turov itself is worthy of your attention in its own right, perhaps as a destination in a tour of the area. First mentioned in chronicles in AD980, it was the capital of a province that included the historic towns of Slutsk, Njasvizh and Pinsk. There is a particularly impressive monument erected to celebrate its one-thousandth birthday. Some historians believe that Turov was second in importance only to Kiev in Old Russia. Back in the National Park, there is a **visitor complex** at Lyaskovichy on the banks of the Pripyat River, where the accommodation includes three well-appointed lodges of wood construction. Another tourist centre is found deep in the forest at Khlupinskaya Buda, consisting of four smaller lodges, and there is camping elsewhere at the Kabachok and Cheretyanka centres, on the banks of the river and by Cheretyanka Lake respectively. There are even motorboats moored on quays at various locations with accommodation in a small number of cabins, and others that are used for day trips. Tours from one to ten days in the park can be arranged through the state tourist agencies.

Appendix 1

LANGUAGE

Editorial discipline dictates that the scope and ambit of this small appendix on language can be no more than the briefest of introductions, though it will be enough to get you started. To move beyond the basics, I strongly advise readers to pursue further study via the many media that exist today (see pages 77–9). **Russian** and **Belarusian** have equal status in Belarus as national languages. Both of them are of eastern Slavonic origin, and as such they share a great deal in terms of grammar and vocabulary. Further, both alphabets are based on the Cyrillic script. Today, the untutored ear and eye would discern very little difference between Belarusian and Russian. Everyone speaks Russian, although Belarusian is becoming more widely used, particularly on public signage. I have replicated the Russian alphabet below in its entirety and added the Belarusian equivalent for the few letters that are written differently. It will be enough for you to be able to recognise these letters to assist with your pronunciation. I have then included some words and phrases in Russian that should help you along the way. Wherever you travel in the world, faltering but earnest attempts at communicating in the language of your hosts are generally well received. This is certainly the case in Belarus. The people here think they are the forgotten country of Europe; and the rest of Europe (and indeed the world) might be on a different planet, given the paucity of interaction between Belarusians and Europeans. So, take a very deep breath and give it a go. You will always be greeted with a smile. Don't forget, though, that English is widely taught in schools and young people especially will be keen to try out their own language skills on you.

Most people are utterly daunted by the Cyrillic alphabet, and in a sense this is perfectly understandable, as you're going back to school to learn how to read all over again. But a little perseverance pays huge dividends. When you master the basics of being able to pronounce a few words, you will be surprised by how much you can begin to understand in a very short time.

If you are embarking on learning the language for the first time, it will probably be overly ambitious to attempt a full language course before you go, or to take grammatical texts and a dictionary with you. But I do strongly recommend that you take a phrasebook. The best two on the market are those published by Lonely Planet and Rough Guides. There is nothing to choose between the two in terms of quality and both balance just the right amount of academic detail with practical expediency. For details of language courses, see pages 78–9.

THE CYRILLIC RUSSIAN ALPHABET

Russian		Phonetic pronunciation
А	а	a, as in far
Б	б	b, as in bill
В	в	v, as in violin

Г	г	g, as in go
Д	д	d, as in do
Е	е	ye, as in yellow
Ё	ё	yo, as in your
Ж	ж	zh, as in pleasure
З	з	z, as in zebra
И	и	ee, as in eaten
Й	й	y, as in coy
К	к	k, as in kitchen
Л	л	l, as in lantern
М	м	m, as in my
Н	н	n, as in never
О	о	o, as in open
П	п	p, as in pillow
Р	р	r, as in growl (but roll your tongue extravagantly!)
С	с	s, as in suspense
Т	т	t, as in tea
У	у	oo, as in moose
Ф	ф	f, as in face
Х	х	pronounce loch like a Scot!
Ц	ц	ts, as in fits
Ч	ч	ch, as in cello
Ш	ш	sh, as in shampoo
Щ	щ	shsh, as in fresh shampoo
Ъ	ъ	hard sign, to keep a consonant hard
Ы	ы	i, as in mill
Ь	ь	soft sign, to soften a consonant
Э	э	e, as in envelop
Ю	ю	u, as in usurp
Я	я	ya, as in yam

For the purpose of rudimentary learning to enable you to read signage, all you will need to know is that in the Belarusian language, the letter И и is replaced by I i and that there is an additional letter Ў ў pronounced like a 'w', as in 'how'.

The main problem with English is that the frighteningly large number of rules is only exceeded by an even larger number of exceptions to those rules. This problem doesn't exist with Russian. It's much more phonetic, so when you've cracked the Cyrillic alphabet, the only thing left to worry about is locating which syllable in a word carries the emphasis. In the following pages, underlining shows which syllable to stress. For your first visit, though, none of this should be a problem; if you set your level of expectation appropriately, you won't have too much difficulty in being able to read the odd word, understand a few, have the confidence to utter a word or phrase and have them understood by the recipient. Try these for starters:

FIRST MEETINGS AND NICETIES

Hello (formal)	Здравствуйте	_Zdravst_voitye
Hi (casual)	Привет	_Preevyet_
Good day	Добрий День	_Dobri Dyehn_
Good morning	Доброе Утро	_Dobroye Ootra_
Good evening	Добрий Вечер	_Dobri Vyei_cha
Yes	Да	_Da_

No	Нет	*Nyet*
Thank you	Спасибо	*Spaseeba*
You're welcome	Пожалуйста	*Pazhalsta*
Please	Пожалуйста	*Pazhalsta*
Excuse me	Извините	*Eezvenitye*
What is your name?	Как вас зовут?	*Kak vas zavoot?*
My name is…	Меня зовут…	*Minya zavoot…*
Pleased to meet you	Очень приятно	*Orchin preeyatna*
How are you?	Как дела?	*Kak dyela?*
Good	Хорошо	*Hurashor*
Excellent!	Отлично!	*Atleechna!*
Bad	Плохо	*Plorkha*
Very	Очень	*Orchin*
Do you speak English?	Вы говорите по-английски?	*Vy guvareetyeh pa angleeski?*
Do you understand?	Понимаете?	*Punimahyetye?*
I don't speak Russian	Я плохо говорю по-русски	*Ya plorkha guvareyoo pa rooski*
I don't understand	Не понимаю	*Knee puneemaiyoo*
Repeat, please	Повторите, пожалуйста	*Puvhtareetye, pazhalsta*
I like…	Мне нрявиться…	*Minye nrahvitsa…*
I don't like…	Мне не нрявиться…	*Minye ni nrahvitsa…*
I love…	Я люблю…	*Ya lyooblyoo…*
See you again	До встречи	*Da fstryechi*
Goodbye	До свидания	*Dos sveedanya*
Bye	Пока	*Paka*
Good night	Спокойной Ночи	*Spakoinoi Norchi*
Bon voyage!	Счастливого пути!	*Shistleevava puti!*
All the best!	Всего хорошего!	*Fsevor harrorshiva!*

KEY WORDS

What?	Что?	*Shtor?*
Who?	Кто?	*K-tor?*
Where?	Где?	*Gdyeh?*
How?	Как?	*Kak?*
Why?	Почему?	*Puchyemoo?*
On the left	На лева	*Na lyeva*
On the right	На права	*Na pravha*
Straight ahead	Прямо	*Preeyarma*
near	Не далеко	*Knee dalyekor*
far	Далеко	*Dalyekor*

SHOPPING

How much does this cost?	Сколько это стоит?	*Skorlka ehta styeet?*
What is it?	Что это?	*Shtor ehta?*
A lot	Много	*M-norga*
A little	Чутьчуть	*Chootchoot*

FOOD AND DRINK

| bread | Хлеб | *Khlyeb* |

cheese	Сир	*Syrr*
meat	Мясо	*Myasa*
fish	Риба	*Reeba*
fruit	Фрукти	*Frookti*
vegetables	Овощи	*Orvashee*
mushrooms	Гриби	*Greebi*
potatoes	Картошки	*Kartoshki*
water	Вода	*Vada*
milk	Молоко	*Malakor*
juice	Сок	*Sok*
sugar	Сахар	*Sakhar*
tea	Чай	*Chai*
coffee	Кофе	*Korfye*
beer	Пиво	*Peeva*
vodka	Водка	*Vordka*
breakfast	Завтрак	*Zavhtrak*
lunch	Обед	*Abyed*
dinner	Ужин	*Oozhen*

ADJECTIVES

big	Большой	*Balshoi*
small	Маленкий	*Marlenki*
hot	Горячий	*Grryachi*
cold	Холодный	*Khorladni*
new	Новй	*Norvee*
old	Старй	*Staree*
beautiful	Красивый	*Krasseevi*
delicious	Вкусный	*Ffkoosni*

NUMBERS

0	Нуль	*Nool*
1	Один	*Ahdjeen*
2	Два	*Dva*
3	Три	*Tree*
4	Четыре	*Chyetearye*
5	Пят,	*Pyats*
6	Шесть	*Shhehst*
7	Семь	*Ssyem*
8	Восемь	*Vorsyem*
9	Девят,	*Dyevyats*
10	Десять	*Dyesyats*
20	Двадцать	*Dvahdsahts*
50	Пятьдесят	*Pyatdyesyat*
100	Сто	*Stor*
500	Пятьсот	*Pyatsort*
1,000	Тысяча	*Teesyatchsa*

DAYS, SEASONS AND TIME

yesterday	Вчера	*Vcherra*
today	Сегодня	*Sivordnya*
tomorrow	Завтра	*Zavhtra*

Monday	Понедельник	*Ponye**dyel**nik*
Tuesday	Вторник	*Vtornik*
Wednesday	Среда	*Ssre**da***
Thursday	Четверг	*Chet**vyerg***
Friday	Пятница	*Pyatnitsa*
Saturday	Суббота	*Soo**bor**ta*
Sunday	Воскресенье	*Voskres**yen**ye*
What time is it?	Который час?	*Ka**tory** chass?*
now	Сейчас	*Say**chass***
hour	Час	*Chass*
minute	Минута	*Min**oo**ta*
spring	Весна	*Vyes**na***
summer	Лето	*Lyeta*
autumn	Осень	*Or**syen*
winter	Зима	*Zee**ma***
day	День	*Dyenn*
morning	Утро	*Ootra*
afternoon	После обеда	*Porslye ab**yeda***
evening	Вечер	*Vye**acha*
night	Ночь	*Norch*

Wanderlust travel magazine

Wanderlust offers a unique mix of inspiration and practical advice, making it the ultimate magazine for independent-minded, curious travellers.

For more about *Wanderlust* and for travel inspiration visit www.wanderlust.co.uk

Appendix 2

FURTHER INFORMATION

Unsurprisingly for a relatively new country that is so little known in the West, not much has been written in English about Belarus. But if you search hard enough, there are some gems to be found, and those that I list are but a selection. I do urge you to read as widely as you can before you go, because any insight that you can gain into the history of this country and its people will only be of benefit to you as you travel around and forge relationships along the way. Just bear in mind that it's really difficult to find works of balance, proportion and moderation that are written with objectivity by those with detailed personal knowledge of what actually goes on in this fascinating country! I have also added reference to a few of the best books on the Chernobyl catastrophe; although it occurred outside the national borders of Belarus, no traveller and student of the issues facing Belarusian society today can hope to be prepared for the deeply affecting experiences to be gained from a visit here without at least a rudimentary knowledge of what occurred on that fateful spring night in 1986.

BOOKS
Travelogues and Memoirs

Applebaum, Anne *Between East and West: Across the Borderlands of Europe* Papermac, 1995. An account of a journey from the Baltic to the Black Sea made in 1991, in which the author describes her encounters not just in Belarus, but also Lithuania, Russia and Ukraine. That it is a subjective work adds significantly to the fascination of the tales that are recounted in these pages, and anyone who has travelled in this part of Europe will recognise much from their own experiences with great fondness.

Duffy, Peter *The Bielski Brothers* Harper Collins, paperback, 2004. This tells the courageous story of the brothers who saved the lives of countless hundreds of Jews in the forests of Belarus from the early days of the Great Patriotic War all through the Nazi occupation, at the same time creating, shaping and leading a ruthlessly efficient partisan fighting force whose contribution to repelling the invaders and delivering the ultimate liberation of the occupied territories is impossible to overstate.

Guterman, Norbert (introduction), Chagall, Bella (author) and Chagall, Marc (illustrator) *Burning Lights* Random House USA Inc, 1989. An affectionate remembrance of Jewish life in pre-Revolutionary Vitebsk. Beautiful drawings by the famous Belarusian artist delightfully illustrate the memoirs of his wife.

Hobson, Charlotte *Black Earth City: A Year in the Heart of Russia* Granta Books, 2002. This book contains only passing references to Minsk but, like Thubron (see page 296), Hobson has a deeply perceptive eye for humanity. The characters she describes paint a rich tableau of life for ordinary people in a provincial Russian town against a backdrop of major political upheaval as the Soviet Union broke apart. The beautiful cameo illustrations of the warm relationships within the author's circle of friends in Russia are charming vignettes that might very easily describe those that I have been fortunate to be able to experience over the course of my time in Belarus.

Kagan, Jack *We Stood Shoulder to Shoulder* Arima Publishing, 2010. Based on extensive Belarusian archives, this is another first-hand account of life as a partisan with the Bielski brothers in the forests of Belarus. Kagan has a particularly understated style that only adds to the potency of the incredible stories he relates. When I met him in the spring of 2014 he recounted some of the tales of extraordinary courage against a background of savagery and privation, including his escape from the ghetto, in the same matter-of-fact way. To hear them face-to-face had a profound affect on me.

Kagan, Jack and Cohen, Dov *Surviving the Holocaust with the Russian Jewish Partisans* Vallentine Mitchell & Co Ltd, 2001. More deeply moving stories of heroism and tragedy from the Nazi occupation of Jewish territories in Belarus, with detailed factual information taken from Belarusian archives.

Marsden, Philip *The Bronski House* Harper Perennial, 2005. This unusual and moving blend of history, tragedy, romance and travel writing is a real delight. Based on a journey shared with exiled poet Zofia Hinska returning to the Belarusian village of her birth, it recounts an ensuing 'rites of passage' experience that was to link the history of this troubled region to a poignant family tale. It's a fine illustration of the effect of momentous events in shaping the national psyche that endures to this day. Highly recommended.

Tec, Nechama *Defiance* Oxford University Press, 2008. This recounts the same incredible story as *The Bielski Brothers* (see page 295), and is the better known of the two. It also spawned the highly successful film of the same name and if you ignore the worst excesses of 'the Hollywood treatment', including some of the actors' accents, the latter is a very powerful dramatisation of a truly inspiring story of resilience against the odds. I suggest you read the book first and then see the film.

Thubron, Colin *Among the Russians* Vintage, 2004. A splendid memoir of the journey taken by the author across the Soviet Union in the 1980s, when he drove 10,000 miles from the Baltic to the Caucasus and then to the far east of the Soviet Empire in an old Morris Marina. Only the first chapter is about Belarus, his point of entry into the USSR, but the poignant tales that follow about the people he met along the way could easily have been written about Belarusians.

Yaffe Radin, Ruth *Escape to the Forest* Harper Collins, 2000. A children's book that tells the story of a young Jewish girl living with her family in the town of Lida at the start of the Great Patriotic War. Based on a true story (so it's also fiction in part), she describes life under the Nazis before she and her family fled into the forest to join the band of partisans resisting the occupation and saving Jewish lives.

Politics, History, Economy and Society

Bennett, Brian *The Last Dictatorship in Europe: Belarus Under Lukashenko* C Hurst & Co Publishers Ltd, 2012. Written by the UK's ambassador to Belarus from 2003 to 2007, this is an intriguing assessment of the man responsible for shaping this post-Soviet nation state. Not everyone who knows the country will agree with the conclusions drawn, but it is an interesting read for observers.

Beorn, Waitman Wade *Marching into Darkness: The Wehrmacht and the Holocaust in Belarus* Harvard University Press, 2014. An important contribution to the shameful story of Nazi oppression and brutality in this part of Europe that has long waited to be told. Essential reading for an understanding of the events that significantly contributed to the national psyche of this country and its people.

Coombes, Anne *Culture Smart! Belarus* Kuperard, 2008. This series of guides to countries all over the world, from Afghanistan to Vietnam, sets out to cover the basics of custom, belief, culture, history, politics, home life, business, society and sensitive issues in a standard format. Practical, sensible, easy to read and accurate, this slender tome slips easily into a pocket and will be a helpful companion on your travels.

Gross, Jan T *Revolution from Abroad: The Soviet Conquest of Poland's Western Ukraine and Western Belorussia* Princeton University Press, 2002. A scholarly tale of life in this part of Europe under the yoke of Soviet oppression in the period between the end of World War I hostilities and events prior to the Great Patriotic War, leading to the tragic consequences of the resultant clash of opposing totalitarian ideology from the West and the East.

Ioffe, Grigory *Understanding Belarus and How Western Foreign Policy Misses the Mark* Rowman & Littlefield Publishers Inc, 2014. A perceptive and timely assessment of the many challenges faced by this country in the complexities of its relationships with the West and with Russia.

Marples, David *Belarus: A Denationalized Nation* Routledge, 1999. Now somewhat dated, but as a commentary on the Soviet-style politics that developed in the country at independence and throughout the 1990s, it retains its legitimacy.

Parker, Stewart *The Last Soviet Republic: Alexander Lukashenko's Belarus* Trafford Publishing, 2007. Much of what is written and broadcast in Western media about this country is characterised at best by ignorance and at worst by the furtherance of an overtly anti-Belarus propagandist agenda. This knowledgeable and approachable book will help to counterpoint that misinformation with a sense of proportion and balance.

Silitski, Vitali and Zaprudnik, Jan *Historical Dictionary of Belarus* The Scarecrow Press Inc, 2007. Accessible and brimming with facts, there is much here to inform the reader intent on discovering all there is to know about this country. This is a welcome update of the edition published in 1998.

Snyder, Timothy *The Reconstruction of Nations: Poland, Ukraine, Lithuania, Belarus, 1569–1999* Yale University Press, 2004. A scholarly work of analysis into the turbulent history of these eastern European countries, whose past and present are inextricably interwoven.

Wilson, Andrew *Belarus: The Last European Dictatorship* Yale University Press, 2011. An approachable tome that attempts to place the reality of life in modern Belarus in a historical context. As with the Bennett work (see opposite), there will be those with personal experience of life in this fascinating country who will beg to differ with the conclusions drawn, but this should not detract from the worth of its contribution to the debate.

Zaprudnik, Jan *Belarus: At a Crossroads in History* Westview Press Inc, 1993. Also a little dated, but it remains a powerful commentary on the complexities of the country's history and its impact on political and social life in the immediate aftermath of independence. The fact that the author has Belarusian antecedents lends gravitas to his observations.

Chernobyl

Alexyevich, Svetlana *Voices from Chernobyl: The Oral History of a Nuclear Disaster* Picador USA, 2006. A collection of intensely moving remembrances from those who lived through the nightmare. These heart-breaking reminiscences are not easy to read, but their story is one that richly deserves to be told.

Dowswell, Paul *The Chernobyl Disaster (Days That Shook the World)* Hodder Wayland, 2003. A short (64 pages) but informative, no-nonsense resumé of the 24-hour period in which the explosion occurred. Aimed at the teenage market, it's a simple (but not simplistic) introduction to the key issues. If your time is limited, this is the one to read.

Mycio, Mary *Wormwood Forest: A Natural History of Chernobyl* Henry (Joseph) Press, 2005. This splendid book addresses the issues of the disaster from a different angle; that of the sanctuary for the natural world and its wildlife that appears to have evolved in the radioactivity of the exclusion zone.

Petrucci, Mario *Heavy Water: A Poem for Chernobyl* Enitharmon Press, 2004. Based on first-hand accounts from people who were there, this is a work of great dignity and impact displaying powerful humanity and insight.

Roche, Adi *Chernobyl Heart* New Island Books, 2006. This book is an excellent contribution to the story of the fine work undertaken by children's charities to help alleviate the plight of those whose lives have been so affected by the insidious radioactive fallout. Adi's selfless commitment is already well documented elsewhere and the stories recounted here are both tragic and uplifting all at once.

Health

Wilson-Howarth, Dr Jane, *Bugs, Bites & Bowels* Cadogan, 2009

Wilson-Howarth, Dr Jane, and Ellis, Dr Matthew *Your Child Abroad: A Travel Health Guide* eBook, Bradt Travel Guides, 2014

Magazine

hidden europe Available by subscription via the website of the editorial bureau based in Berlin run by Nicky Gardner and Susanne Kries (*www.hiddeneurope. co.uk*), this periodical is an absolute gem. Showcasing travel writing of the highest quality, it focuses on those cultures and communities of Europe that seem to evade other writers and observers, as well as the means of slow travel that connect them. Several pieces on Belarus have found their way on to the pages of various editions.

Index

INDEX OF ADVERTISERS